THE MODERN HISTORY OF
MONGOLIA

THE MODERN HISTORY OF
MONGOLIA

C. R. Bawden

Afterword by Alan Sanders

Kegan Paul International
London and New York

First published in 1968
Second revised edition published in 1989 by Kegan Paul International Limited
PO Box 256, London WC1B 3SW

Distributed by
International Thomson Publishing Services Ltd
North Way, Andover, Hants SP10 5BE
England

Routledge, Chapman and Hall Inc
29 West 35th Street
New York, NY 10001
USA

The Canterbury Press Pty Ltd
Unit 2, 71 Rushdale Street
Scoresby, Victoria 3179
Australia

Printed in Great Britain by
T. J. Press (Padstow) Ltd,
Padstow, Cornwall

© C. R. Bawden 1989
© Afterword, Kegan Paul International 1989

No part of this book may be reproduced in any form
without permission from the publisher, except for the
quotation of brief passages in criticism.

ISBN 0 7103 0326 2

For my wife

CONTENTS

Preface to the Second Edition   xiii

Preface   xv

1. An Introduction to Mongolia   1
2. The Loss of Mongol Independence   39
3. Khalkha in the Eighteenth Century   81
4. Social and Economic Developments in the Nineteenth Century   135
5. From Autonomy to Revolution, 1911–21   187
6. First Steps in Revolution, 1921–8   238
7. The Socialist Fiasco, 1929–32   290
8. The Destruction of the Old Order, 1932–40   328
9. Post-War Mongolia: Achievements and Prospects   381

Afterword by Alan Sanders   425

Notes   439

Maps   448

Bibliographical Note   451

Supplementary Bibliography   455

Index   459

ILLUSTRATIONS

1. The first Jebtsundamba Khutuktu
2. The eighth Jebtsundamba Khutuktu
3. The Consort of the eighth Khutuktu
4. Damdinsuren, Mongol commander at Khobdo, 1912
5. Dambijantsan
6. Tserendorji, first premier of the Mongolian People's Republic
7. Prince Khandadorji
8. The Dilowa Khutuktu and the Jalkhantsa Khutuktu
9. Baron Ungern-Sternberg
10. Jamtsarano
11. Sukebator
12. Marshal Choibalsang
13. Marshal Demid
14. Academician Damdinsuren
15. Statue of Amursana at Khobdo
16. Academician Rintchen
17. Commemorative stamps of Genghis Khan
18. Monument to Genghis Khan
19. A page from a handbook of divination
20. Pages from an illustrated almanac
21. Illuminated title page from a Buddhist Sutra
22. Cover of the 'Jungle Book'
23. The petition against *zasag* Tudeng
24. The Academy of Sciences and State Library
25. Street scene in old Ulan Bator
26. Street scene in modern Ulan Bator
27. State Theatre, Ulan Bator
28. Statue of Sukebator, Ulan Bator
29. Water delivery cart, Ulan Bator, 1967
30. Felt tents in Ulan Bator, 1959

ILLUSTRATIONS

31 A West Mongolian cooperative member demonstrates his Lasso
32 Part of a collectively-owned horse herd
33 Slogan extolling Mongol-Soviet friendship, Ulan Bator, 1967
34 The State University, 1967
35 Shop doorway, Ulan Bator, 1959
36 New department store, Ulan Bator, 1961
37 Itinerant bookseller, 1959
38 Wall painting promoting traffic control, 1967
39 The lamasery of Erdeni Juu
40 The Gandang lamasery, Ulan Bator, 1958
41 The late lama Gombodoo
42 Military band, 1959
43 Mongol soldiers of the autonomous régime
44 Kazakh musicians from West Mongolia, 1959
45 Mongol herdsman or *arat*, 1958
46 Noblewomen in national dress, around 1900
47 Traditional painting from Inner Mongolia, about 1938

MAPS
1 Mongolia in the Manchu Dynasty *page* 448
2 The Mongolian People's Republic 1966   449

ACKNOWLEDGEMENTS

For their kindness in permitting the reproduction of certain illustrations I would like to express my grateful thanks to the following:

For Plate 1: Dr F. Herrmann and the Völkerkunde Museum der J. und E. von Portheim-Stiftung für Wissenschaft und Kunst, Heidelberg.

For Plate 10: Professor R. A. Rupen.

For Plates 19 and 20: The Royal Library, Copenhagen.

For Plate 21: Dr R. J. Hayes and the Chester Beatty Library, Dublin.

For Plate 36: Professor Owen Lattimore.

For Plates 43 and 47: Mrs Martha Boyer and the National Museum Copenhagen.

PREFACE TO THE SECOND EDITION

The text of the first edition has been reprinted without alteration, except for the correction of some errors and misprints, and the elimination of some anachronisms. Hence all statements, particularly those in the last chapter, should be read as applicable to the situation and the state of knowledge as they were in the mid-sixties. The main lines of development in Mongolia over the last twenty years are presented in the Afterword by Mr Alan Sanders, to whom the author wishes to express his thanks.

C. R. BAWDEN

Iver 1988

PREFACE

The Mongols are one of the great peoples in the history of High Asia. Their name has been familiar over the whole of the old world for close on eight hundred years. Yet at the most generous estimate it would be anachronistic to speak of a Mongol state, in the modern sense of the word, as existing before the end of 1911. The imperial adventure under Genghis Khan and his successors left the Mongols exhausted and disunited politically, and in the seventeenth century they fell, piecemeal, under Manchu domination which continued for over two hundred years.

Yet a feeling of belonging together, a sense of identity as the subjects and posterity of Genghis Khan, seems never to have deserted the Mongols, and this was one of two internal factors which helped to give them the vision and strength to recover their independence from the Manchus when the last imperial dynasty in China was swept away. The other factor was the spiritual unity conferred by the universal acceptance of the Buddhist faith in its lamaist form, and by the reverence accorded to the Jebtsundamba Khutuktu, or Living Buddha of Urga, the head of the lamaist hierarchy in Mongolia. Undoubtedly this continuing sense of community would have been nugatory had not the international interests of Russia demanded the survival, if possible, of an independent or autonomous Mongolia, to act as a buffer along part of the frontier with China. Mongolia's inability to assure her own independent existence was clearly demonstrated, for instance, in 1919, when an aggressive China took advantage of the temporary impotence of revolutionary Russia to re-annex Mongolia. Nevertheless, had the Mongols not had the capacity for self-assertion, preserved under long years of subjection to an alien power, it would no doubt have proved impossible for the Russians to create and shore up for very long an artificial Mongol state.

PREFACE

Mongolia's situation between two great world powers forces her to a greater degree of adaptation and acquiescence than might be the case if her geography were different. An indication of this is that her frontiers are arbitrarily drawn, especially on the south, and exclude more Mongols, especially within China, than they embrace. But it is of great historical interest that the Mongols were able to keep alive, first some sense of group solidarity and, later, their newly gained but precarious independence, until it became possible to stabilize their frontiers, to create from the rump of the nation a viable state, and to profit by the exaltation of nationalism in the middle of the twentieth century to achieve international recognition of this new Mongol state within frontiers agreed with their two neighbours. No other central Asian people has been able to do as much, and Mongolia's present status compares very favourably with that of Tibet, whose historical development over the past two centuries is in many ways analagous to her own.

In the first half of this book I hope to have given a picture of Mongol society as it was during the comparatively static two centuries between the final submission to the Manchus in 1691 and the national revolution of 1911. The second part of the book describes the dynamic course of events since that revolution and more especially since the second, Soviet-inspired, revolution which began in 1921. For the past forty-five years Mongolia has been developing as the second socialist country in the world. Any attempt to study such a subject and such a period of history is fated to arouse controversy. Whatever opinions an author puts forward on a variety of topics, he will encounter dissent from one side or the other. The main point at issue will no doubt be the extent to which the Mongol revolution was a native growth and the extent to which it was a reflection of the interests of a foreign power, the USSR. It is impossible that at the outset the Mongol revolutionaries, whose purpose it was to enlist Russian support in expelling the Chinese and who enjoyed the confidence of the Living Buddha, can have envisaged the sort of control the Russians were to exert over their party only a few years later. This party included men of a wide range of opinion. As things turned out, the moderates were soon removed, but theoretical Bolshevism played only a negligible part in the first stirrings of the revolution in Mongolia. Nothing in Mongolia's history presaged the rapid movement towards communism which took place after 1921 and more especially after 1929. There was no Mongol revolutionary movement until after the October revolution had taken place, and for the first eight years or so the most influential figures in Mongol affairs were Buriats of Soviet nationality. The Mongol revolution in general followed the pattern of events in Russia. In the form which it took it was determined more by events in the USSR and by direct Soviet intervention than by Mongol needs, and though of course it dealt with Mongol problems these were often tackled in a way imposed by Russia. This analysis will not be acceptable in all quarters, especially as it points up the extent to which Soviet actions abroad under Stalin belied the conviction of Marx and Engels that revolution and socialism should not be imposed from without. Understandably, the relaxation of Soviet monolithic control since the victory of Tito, the death of Stalin, and the emergence of communist China, has made an enormous difference to Mongolia's situation, and in recent years she has been able to give effective expression, both at home and abroad, to her independence.

The source material for a study of recent Mongol history is fragmentary and not always reliable, and the remoteness of the country and her political isolation between 1929 and about 1956 were such that it was impossible for any westerner to acquire that personal background knowledge which comes from sympathetic, first-hand acquaintance with a foreign country. Where facts are few it is difficult to assess their relative importance and significance, and almost impossible to achieve a proper perspective. Hence to write a history of modern Mongolia in 1966 means inevitably to risk a charge of superficiality and prematureness. Yet there are good reasons for making the attempt. In the last ten years enough has been published from the Mongol side to afford us an insight, however limited, into the problems facing the early revolutionaries and the way these were tackled. That is to say, a provisional account of revolutionary Mongolia is no longer unrealizable. Secondly, Mongolia has ceased to be a secret land: she has emerged on to the international scene and there is a curiosity about her waiting to be satisfied. Thirdly, Mongolia has now reached a plateau of relative stability. The storm and stress of the early revolution are behind her, and the problems of the future – economic growth, modes of agricultural and industrial development, educational consolidation, and so on – are of a different order from those which exercised her during the first three or four decades after the revolution began. Those classes and individuals thought to be hostile to the revolution, in particular the lamas, have been eliminated, religion has been more or less extirpated, certainly as an institution if not as a residual attitude of mind. The economy is now differentiated, and no longer limited to a relatively primitive, extensive form of herding. Mongolia has now reached a stage where it is reasonable to take stock of the past and suggest the general lines the future will take. Given the continuance of the present determining factors, international peace, an effective administration, the continuity of financial and technical aid from abroad and the will to technical development, Mongolia will move in the direction forecast in the Party's fourth programme, promulgated in 1966. This programme concentrates on matters of economic and technical development in a Marxist framework, rather than on social change, and its appearance provides a convenient and realistic term for the study of Mongolia's early revolutionary history.

A note on the writing of Mongol words

The author has not tried to work out a unified scheme for the writing of Mongol words and names. For one thing, the Mongols have in recent years discarded their ancient alphabet in favour of the Cyrillic script and carried out a fundamental spelling reform. Strict adherence to either of these systems of orthography would produce spellings unacceptable to the English reader. Secondly, many names such as Genghis Khan, Ulan Bator, Sukebator and so on have accepted English spellings which differ from both the traditional and the modernized spellings. Thirdly, even in the modernized orthography, there is often no accepted standard form for a name. For example, the name of a well-known member of the Academy of Sciences appears, in European transcription, variously as Damdinsürüng and Damdinsuren on the title pages of his own books. The author has therefore aimed at presenting names in a simple and memorable form which varies as little as possible from the most usual contemporary spelling. Naturally this has involved some arbitrary decisions and apparent inconsistencies. For example, the final -i has been retained in names from pre-

PREFACE

revolutionary times such as Tserendorji so as not to dissociate these too much from contemporary Europeanized versions, but it has been dropped from names of modern personalities such as Natsagdorj so as to accord with Mongol usage today. The digraph *kh* has been retained, though its Mongol original could have been represented by *h* alone, because it occurs in so many familiar names such as Khobdo, Khiakta, Khalkha and so on. The two Mongolian vowels usually transcribed as *u* and *ü* have both been written as *u*, but it would have done too much violence to the sound of Mongol words to eliminate *ö* in the same way. A very rough equivalent of its pronunciation is the vowel sound of English *girl*.

C. R. BAWDEN

Iver 1966

CHAPTER 1

AN INTRODUCTION TO MONGOLIA

What is Mongolia?

What are we to understand by the expression 'Modern Mongolia'? Where are we to begin our story, and what lands and peoples are we to include? The solution to this problem is not at all obvious, either geographically or historically. Until the present century there has never been a 'Mongolia' whose boundaries were fixed and accepted. Even the great Mongol empire of Genghis Khan and his successors was an unstable, indeterminate grouping of tribes which flowed out in all directions as far as it could, engulfing lands and peoples which were never to be assimilated. We should cast our bounds far too wide if we tried to include all those parts of Asia where Mongols live or a form of the Mongol language is spoken, for even after the empire had disintegrated the Mongols maintained their nomadic pattern of life, and terrible civil wars and forced migrations again and again scattered them over the face of central Asia, so that today more Mongols live beyond the frontiers of the Mongolian People's Republic, the only independent Mongol state, than within them. Kalmuck Mongols have dwelt around the lower Volga for the last three hundred years, though many of this group migrated back to China in 1771, under their name of Torguts, and were settled in Jungaria, recently depopulated by the armies of the Manchu empire. The Kalmucks experienced a temporary break in the continuity of their life in south Russia in 1943 when their republic was abolished and they were deported to Siberia: in 1957 the Kalmuck Autonomous Republic was once again restored. Considerable numbers of Kalmucks also live outside Eurasia altogether, in settlements in the USA. Buriat Mongols live round the shores of Lake Baikal and farther eastwards inside the Soviet Union, and have been at home there at least since the time of

Genghis Khan. A mixed people known as Monguors live in Kansu in China, near the city of Hsi-ning, and Mongols nomadize in the wastes of Tsaidam and Kukunor. Remnants of Mongol-speaking people are still to be found in Afghanistan. The largest group of Mongols is formed by the one and a half million or so now living within the borders of China, where they form a small minority of the population of the Inner Mongolian Autonomous Region.

But it is only in the People's Republic, which is approximately coterminous with what always used to be known as Outer Mongolia, that Mongols govern themselves, use exclusively their own language, and form an overwhelming majority of the national population. Only here do we find a Mongol state as distinct from a Mongol people. It may seem an arbitrary solution to the problem facing us to limit ourselves mainly to the history of this part of Mongolia, but there seems to be no tenable alternative. If we strike out much farther we shall find ourselves adrift in a boundless ocean, whose shores are most often out of sight, and whose navigational fixes are deceptive. Fortunately there has always been, in the period we shall cover, a rough distinction between Outer Mongolia and other areas, even when no frontiers were drawn. We shall have to look fairly often at the history of Inner Mongolia, but to try even to survey the course of events there systematically would break the unity of our story and involve us too deeply in the history of China and, latterly, of Japan also.

There is another very practical limitation to the situation. For the greater part of its modern history, Mongolia has been a colonial territory of one sort or another. It is only in very recent years that Mongolian scholars have themselves begun to take an interest in their history and to publish at all extensively. Otherwise our sources have to be sought in travellers' records and in studies in the languages of those countries which were most closely involved with Mongolian affairs, and there is a limit to the range of source material which one person can manage to handle. To go too closely into Inner Mongolian affairs would mean too much dependence on Chinese and Japanese material, while for Outer Mongolian affairs one can rely far more on materials in European languages and in Mongol.

The historian enjoys the immense advantage of hindsight. Looking back from his privileged position after the event, he can systematize and rationalize the course of history, and at least try to pick out the direction it was taking, and the culmination it was approaching, both of which will have been hidden from contemporaries, supposing even that they had thought about the matter. The theme of a history of modern Mongolia written in the middle of the twentieth century is bound to be the achievement by some Mongols at least of their national independence. From what we know of the intense patriotism of present-day Mongols, and of the spirit in which modern literature and historical studies are developing, we can be reasonably sure that Mongols themselves look upon the establishment of autonomy from China in 1911 and, even more of independence in 1921, as the turning-point in Mongolia's destiny, a new beginning in the evolution of Mongolia from its political stagnation as a feudal component of the decaying Manchu empire into the self-assured republic it has already become. The picture is somewhat complicated by the Marxist background to current Mongol thinking, but is in general accurate.

Now this historical process will not have been at all self-evident to earlier generations of Mongols. If we may take as typical the chronicle known as the *History of the Mongol-Borjigid Clan* written between 1732 and 1735 by a Kharchin Mongol named Lomi, we can judge that the intelligentsia of the eighteenth century, owing its rank and authority to the established order of the Manchu empire, looked on Mongolia's history and position in the world in quite another spirit. Whereas modern writers tend to criticize the spiritual and temporal leaders of Mongolia, who in 1688-91 submitted to the emperor K'ang Hsi in return for his help against the invasion of the Oirat Galdan, as traitors or at best weaklings who should have made common cause with the related Oirats to establish an independent Mongolia, matters looked very different to Lomi. He was a descendant of Dayan Khan, the last emperor of a united Mongolia, who had died at some time after the turn of the sixteenth century: the sources are too much at variance to be reconciled as to the exact date. Hence Lomi was also a member of the Borjigid clan, the imperial family of Genghis Khan. Yet at the same time he was a loyal subject of the Manchus. In 1628 in order to escape from the pressure exerted on them by Ligdan Khan of the Chahar, who was attempting to emulate his ancestor Dayan and reunite Mongolia by force, the Kharchin of Inner

Mongolia had asked the Manchus for an alliance, and in a solemn ceremony, accompanied by the slaughter of a white horse and a black bull as a sacrifice to heaven and earth, the representatives of the two rulers swore alliance. It is significant, by the way, for the future impure Buddhism of Mongolia, mixed with all sorts of traits from popular cults, that the Kharchin representatives who took part in this bloody ceremony were actually four lamas. The Kharchin were not in fact the first Mongols to have gone over to the rising power of the Manchus. The Khorchin, who had long maintained diplomatic relations with them, had formed an alliance four years before, directed against the Chahar and the Khalkha. The ceremony was similar to that of 1628. A white horse and a black ox were slaughtered, and wine, bones, blood and earth set out in bowls. Then, with incense burning, the following oath was taken:

The two nations of the Manchu and the Khorchin are offended in righteous indignation over the insults and outrages of the Chahar. Therefore they enter into an alliance of friendship and announce this clearly to heaven and earth. If henceforth either of them allows himself to be seduced by the Chahar and makes individual peace with them, may heaven and earth send disaster and punishment upon him. As this is blood, as these are bones, as this is earth, may his mandate collapse. If after the conclusion of the alliance, neither of them ever reneges, may heaven and earth help him, grant him eternal years, and let his sons and grandsons flourish and prosper.[1]

Yet it was the Kharchin who got a reputation for treachery, and who were looked on, and slandered in popular and indecent rhymes, for not being real Mongols. However, the oath of loyalty which they swore, and the subsequent submission of all the eastern Mongols to the Manchu emperor in person, were the decisive factors in binding the Mongol nobility to the dynasty. There were rebellions of individual nobles over the course of the next century, but the majority of the Mongol nobility remained faithful to their oath. Lomi himself was such a loyal subject, looking on the Manchu emperor of China as the rightful monarch of Mongolia, blessed by heaven, the restorer of peace and order to a shattered Mongolia, and hence deserving of obedience. This is how he briefly summarizes the history of his people since the collapse of the Mongol dynasty in China in 1368 up to his own century:

When the succession came to the emperor Togon Temur, he lost China and went out beyond the frontier and dwelt in the old lands of the Mongols. As generation succeeded generation, the succession came to Ligdan Khan (d. 1634), and the chain of the nation was broken and all the tribes were scattered and dispersed and were hard put to it to find peace. Then, as it happened that the lofty emperor T'ai-tsu (Nurhachi) arose in the eastern lands, the imperial house and the regent and nobles of the Mongol nation severally submitted with sincere intentions, and were granted high and generous favours and enjoyed friendly treatment. Those who wished to dwell beyond the borders were entitled *wang, beile* or *beise*, and were settled as a shield on the northern frontier, each ruling his own subject appanage. Those who wished to stay within were allotted the hereditary titles of *kung, hou* and *po*, and were given imperial princesses or ladies, and their descendants were honoured from generation to generation. So when the three khans of the Khalkha, the Zasagtu Khan, the Tushetu Khan and the Setsen Khan were defeated by Galdan the Oirat, and their subject appanages were pushed back in confusion, the three khans and their officers came to submit, and the gracious emperor K'ang Hsi granted them the favour of restoring what had collapsed and continuing what had been interrupted, and cherished and protected them ... He restored the titles of the three khans and bestowed the ranks of *wang, beile, beise, gung, zasag* and *taiji* on the other nobility, and set up banners and *sumuns*. The emperor led his army to the defeat of Galdan, returned the Khalkha to their old territories, and let them dwell in happiness as before ... Can we say that it is not a great good fortune for us Borjigid that we have had the grace of the Holy Lord constantly bestowed on us? ... In my opinion, the fact that our Mongol nation, when about to collapse, was restored again, and when on the point of falling apart was reborn, is in truth entirely due to the amazing mercy of the Holy Emperor.[2]

This may have been a typical attitude among the pro-Manchu nobility and clergy, who were the authors of most of the surviving chronicles, though it was not an entirely universal one, and became rarer as time passed and the dynasty became less Manchu and more Chinese, and began to treat Mongolia rather as a colony to be exploited then as an equal ally. In the nineteenth century some articulate Mongols began to express their discontent and to satirize abuses in both religious and secular life. But though at that time a writer like the eccentric Inner Mongolian Injanashi might deplore the sinicization which was strangling the Mongol spirit among the nobility, he did not see political independence as the solution, but contented himself with calling for a cultural, nationalistic revival. In the lower ranges of society discontent expressed itself through round robins of complaint against the local nobility, addressed to the local administration, through banditry and through occasional riots or attacks on Chinese property. Popular sentiment kept alive in song and story the memory of the prince Chingunjav who in 1756 raised the banner of revolt and Mongol independence against the Manchus, but was defeated and executed in Peking. But the idea of real political independence for Mongolia was a child of the early twentieth century. Not till then did the impending collapse of the Manchu imperial house appear to offer the nobility of Outer Mongolia, who represented the only alternative political leadership, a release from the oaths of allegiance their forebears had taken in the late seventeenth century to the emperor K'ang Hsi.

Since the history of Mongolia has evolved in the way it has, and since it is our task to provide a history of modern Mongolia and not a survey of the Mongols in modern times, it seems reasonable to devote our attention mainly to the one Mongol territory whose people have achieved complete national independence, and to those centuries which saw the extinction of the old independence and its subsequent recovery.

The land and the people

Mongolia's territory is vast and her population sparse. This, and her severe continental climate, are the two factors which have most influenced her development. An area of 600,000 square miles contains a little over a million inhabitants, and of these nearly a quarter dwell in the capital, Ulan Bator. It is as if the population of Birmingham were spread out over an area equivalent to Germany, Holland, Belgium, France, Spain and Portugal combined, with one large city in the area of Paris. Lying roughly in the latitude of southern central Europe, Mongolia stretches from east to west as far as from Moscow to Paris, and from north to south as far as from London to Madrid. The whole country lies relatively high. The highest point, in the Altai mountains of the west, is more than 15,000 feet above sea level, while the lowest, the small lake Kukunor in the north-east (not to be confused with the much better known Kukunor in north-west China), has an elevation of as much as 1,800 feet. Few travellers can have gained an overall impression of the Mongol landscape. In the main it is a mountainous area: even in the steppe country of central Mongolia high ground is never far away in any direction, and the view is seldom lost in the far distance. The horizon is hilly and obvious.

The greatest mountain peaks are in the west, in the thousand-mile-long Altai range. This is a land of eternal snow on the summits, of glaciers, waterfalls and torrents, and of mountain lakes. North-east of the Mongol Altai, and bounded by the Siberian Tannu Ula range, lies a vast basin dotted with lakes, some salt water, some fresh. Central Mongolia is dominated by the huge mass of the Khangai mountains, a land of rich pastures and forests, rising to peaks also covered by eternal snow. North-eastwards, the foothills of the Khangai, marked by grotesquely worn granite tors, run out into the fertile pastures and agricultural land of the Tula-Orkhon basin, the heartland of Mongolia. Here have arisen one after another national groups and states of Turks, Mongols and other peoples, and here above all nomads have turned to settled life. Ruins of ancient cities, long deserted, dot the landscape, the most celebrated of them being the remains of Karakorum, the imperial capital of the successors of Genghis Khan. Karakorum was not the first city to be built on its site, and in its turn it provided building materials in 1586 and after for the construction of the huge lamasery of Erdeni Juu close by. Nowadays the wheel of history has left Erdeni Juu deserted also, and Karakorum is the site of one of Mongolia's thirty state farms. Its fields are irrigated through channels built a few years ago by Chinese labourers across the traces in the ground of medieval fields. Excavations carried out here after the Second World War unearthed agricultural implements and the workshops where they were manufactured, dating from the thirteenth and fourteenth centuries.

At the eastern edge of this basin lies Ulan Bator, set in the wide valley of the Tula river amongst hills which form the southern extension of the Kentei mountains, a range of medium height, still largely covered with virgin forest. From Ulan Bator southwards and eastwards stretches a grassy plateau, which sinks gradually into the semi-desert Gobi area and the volcanic plateau of the Dariganga region. There is little true desert in the Gobi. Sand and gravel make up only about 3 per cent of its area inside the

Mongolian People's Republic, and the four Gobi aimaks or provinces of south and south-east Mongolia are as rich in the five domestic animals, the camel, horse, cow, sheep and goat, as any of the other provinces, though life is more demanding for the herdsman. Indeed, Mongolia's land is potentially very productive. The worst deserts lie southwards outside her borders, and over 83 per cent of her land surface can be devoted to pasture, while only 5 per cent is not included in the categories of pasture, meadowland, arable land or forest.

Mongolia is happy in having a fairly homogeneous population. In spite of the movements of population caused by the great wars and invasions which swept over the country in the past, Khalkha Mongols form three-quarters of the population, and related Mongol peoples – west Mongols, Buriats and Darigangas – make up another 12 per cent. The only big compact non-Mongol group is the Kazakh Turkish minority in the far west in Bayan Ölgii aimak, who make up only some 4 per cent of the total population. There are small numbers of Russians and Chinese too, but these make no real difference to the homogeneity of the country's inhabitants. Khalkha Mongol is the national language and is understood everywhere. The republic's good fortune contrasts very sharply with the situation in Inner Mongolia, over the Chinese border. Here for nearly a century Chinese have been encroaching on the old Mongol pastures in ever-increasing numbers, reducing the Mongols to an impotent minority in their own autonomous region, where they are outnumbered by ten to one.

Most western Europeans who travelled to Mongolia in the past would set out from China and travel by horse, camel cart or motor-car up on to the Gobi plateau and across the grassy steppes north-westwards. Nowadays this route is difficult to follow, for China's political isolation almost entirely forbids its use, and in any case the European interests in north China and Inner Mongolia – interests which brought traders, missionaries, journalists, hunters and wanderers of all sorts there up till the war – no longer exist. Today travellers from the west take the direct approach across the Eurasian land mass rather than the imperial route by sea around the south of Asia to Peking and beyond. In 1954 Mongolia was tentatively opened to a few western travellers for the first time since the political swing to the left in 1929 cut off the promising contacts between the new republic and the outside world. In the last ten years or so traffic has grown in size and regularity, until by 1964 small parties of tourists were being admitted to travel a small circuit around Ulan Bator.

All travel begins and ends with the capital. Ulan Bator, "Red Hero", stands on the site of old Urga, the centre of Buddhism in Mongolia, which has now almost completely disappeared. In less than two hours a small plane can cover the flight from Irkutsk to Ulan Bator. By train the same journey takes a day and a night, but whichever route the traveller takes, the experience is grandiose and amazing. From Irkutsk the railway cuts through the mountains to make a steep descent to the southern tip of Lake Baikal, and for hours skirts the shore of this enormous mountain-fringed sea before following the Selenga river up to Ulan Ude, the capital of the Buriat Autonomous Republic. Then it curves south again to follow the Selenga through the forested mountains of the frontier zone, before breaking through into the true Mongol steppe country, rolling green plateau fringed with hills and speckled with the low, round tents of white felt which still house most of the population and make up so much of the charm of the Mongol landscape.

Ulan Bator is hardly typical of Mongolia as a whole. It is the only really large city, the greatest industrial centre, the seat of government and of diplomatic activity, and the focus of intellectual life. Concentrating in itself such a large share of what the country has to offer in the way of career prospects and sophistication, it acts like a magnet, drawing in more and more people from the provinces. No other town, and there is at least one in each of the eighteen provinces, has anything approaching a tenth of Ulan Bator's population, which is a third as numerous again as the total remaining urban population of the country. Yet if not typical of Mongolia's present, it is a significant portent for the future. Ulan Bator is symbolic of the complete renewal which has swept away the old Mongolia and is forming the future on quite different lines. In the official view Mongolia is to evolve, following the precepts of Marx–Leninism, from the agricultural–industrial country it is considered to have become, to a country where industry predominates over agriculture, 'by-passing the capitalist stage of development in accordance with the teachings of Lenin'. Ulan Bator is somehow indicative of this purpose. It is not the typical far-eastern city, with narrow lanes, ancient temples, market smells, beggars and plutocrats, but an extension into central Asia of provincial Soviet-style town planning. It is, if one turns a blind eye to the many felt tents which are still pitched almost up to the centre, an absolutely new town. That is, its monumental public buildings and its concrete blocks of apartment houses, their white monotony somewhat relieved by public gardens, bear no relation, architecturally or functionally, to the country's past. It is possible that the earliest buildings, planned and erected by technicians from western Europe, mainly Swedes and Swiss, some forty years ago, no longer exist. Since that time, Japanese prisoners of war, Chinese workers sent in as part of Mao Tse-t'ung's foreign aid programme and, most recently, Soviet troops, have supplemented the efforts of the inadequate Mongol labour force.

The city is built around the huge Sukebator Square, named after the celebrated hero of the revolutionary partisan war of 1921, and big enough, it seems, to take in the entire population of the capital, if need be. The northern side of the square is closed by the building where the Great Khural, or Mongolia's equivalent of the Supreme Soviet, sits. In front of this stands the mausoleum of Choibalsang and Sukebator, in conscious imitation of the more familiar erection in Red Square: Sukebator who died in 1923, lay buried at a place called Altan Ölgii, near Ulan Bator, for thirty years, and was exhumed and reinterred with Choibalsang in the newly-built mausoleum in 1954, two years after the latter's death. Isolated in the middle of the square is an equestrian statue of Sukebator. The constitution of the country states that: 'In the Mongolian People's Republic, the guiding and directing force of society and the state is the Mongolian People's Revolutionary Party, which is guided in its activities by the all-conquering theory of Marx–Leninism' and the appearance of the hub of the capital is an architectural confirmation of this declaration of political attachment. Traditional ornamentation, the colourful dress of both men and women, the occasional horseman in the street, or the red and yellow robes of one of the few surviving lamas flapping through the courtyard of the Gandang lamasery or up the steps of the building of the Academy of Sciences combine to assure the foreigner that he is no longer in Europe. Yet it is appropriate nowadays to approach Mongolia from the west through Soviet Russia rather than from the east through China, and to realize that here is a society which is central Asian rather than Far

Eastern in its roots, but which has been moulded in the recent past by influences from Russia rather than from its nearer neighbour China.

Old Urga was a city of monks. The only big permanent buildings until the Russians built a consulate late in the last century were temples, some in Chinese style, with swooping tiled roofs, others in Tibetan style, with a squatter, more massive outline. Some were mixed in style, part Chinese and part Tibetan, while others, like the early nineteenth-century Maidari temple, incorporated an imitation of the low dome of the felt tent as a specifically Mongol motif, but without much aesthetic success. The Mongol tent can be imitated life-size in brick and still appear symmetrical, but when translated into a grander scale it lacks the swelling dignity of the Mohammedan mosque. The destruction of most of the temple buildings in Urga during the troubled 'thirties, after the revolution, is an irreparable loss. Now little survives except part of the Gandang lamasery, the university of lamaism, together with the new Maidari temple behind it, both on the Gandang escarpment, the temple of the State Oracle near the city centre, and the palace of the last Living Buddha on the bank of the Tula river. And even these are all of late construction, with the exception of nineteenth-century Gandang dating only from the early years of this century. Mongolia has always lived by its flocks and herds, and nomadism, widely ranging or limited in scope, has been the underlying principle of economic survival. Until 1778 Urga itself was a nomadic city, following the general tradition. After imperial sanction had been obtained from Peking its site shifted every few years as the surrounding pastures and woods became exhausted. Thus Ulan Bator's architectural losses, though sad, are not losses of treasures preserved over centuries. They represent rather the disappearance of unique native or mixed styles of structure.

Indeed, not even all the religious buildings were of brick or wood. In 1883 the Russian traveller Przhevalskii described Urga as follows:

The Mongol city lies along the little river Selba, not far from the point where this joins the Tula. In the eastern part of the city, that inhabited exclusively by lamas, lives the highest saint of Mongolia, the Khutuktu, who occupies the third position in the Buddhist hierarchy after the Dalai Lama and the Panchen Lama. Here there is a school for the training of lamas. There have also been erected here important temples, of which the greatest is the Maidari temple. The enormous idol of this divinity, made out of gold-covered copper, and showing him in a seated posture, is sixteen metres high and weighs, so people say, almost 160,000 kilograms. ... In this eastern part of Urga are situated the following temples: Tsogchen, similar to our cathedrals, Duchingalabyn, with a gilded cupola and four gilded towers at the roof corners, Barun örgöö, consisting of a felt tent in which, according to tradition, there once lived Abdai Khan, the disseminator of Buddhism in Mongolia, ... and finally the small aimak temples [the aimaks of Urga were ecclesiastical districts, C.R.B.], twenty-eight in number. These latter are accommodated in simple felt tents with a wooden extension in the form of an altar. With the exception of the Khutuktu's palace and the main temples, the other living quarters in the lamas' district of Urga consist of little mud huts or felt tents. Both sorts are surrounded by high fences. The streets and alley ways between these erections are particularly dirty and narrow.[3]

No one will regret the clearing away of the wood and mud huts which clustered round the old temple centres. But even today many people still live in tent districts within the capital. Wooden palisades still enclose groups of these tents or yurts, called by the Mongols *ger*, a collapsible house built up of sections of lattice work disposed to make a circle, surmounted by a low conical roof of rafters meeting in a central wooden ring, and covered over with layers of felt and canvas. Nowadays the roof flap will possibly admit an electric cable, as well as the chimney of the cooking-stove, and a motor-scooter may perhaps stand outside the tent as well as a horse. The children of the family will go to school, dressed in neat uniforms and wearing Young Pioneers' scarves, and the tent seems doomed, though very slowly, to die out as a city dwelling as blocks of flats spread outwards from the centre.

A great city of a quarter of a million inhabitants set in the midst of a nomadic population might seem a terrible anomaly, but the explanation is that the population of Mongolia is no longer truly nomadic, and has not been for a long time. Even before the present régime succeeded to power in 1924, the subdivision of the land for purposes of administration into an ever-increasing number of hereditary princedoms or 'banners', and the growth of ecclesiastical estates attached to the ubiquitous lamaseries and to individual high clerics, meant that the population was limited in its possibilities of movement. As early as 1634 regulations promulgated for Inner Mongolia by the Manchus had established strict limits for the different Mongol tribes. Crossing of these limits was a punishable offence, and even movement over the pastures was to be carried out in a disciplined and co-ordinated manner. The result of the Manchu policy of dividing Mongolia progressively into more and more small units, from the aimaks down through the banners to the *sumuns*, was to enforce insularity and even encourage distrust towards members of a different unit. Movements over large distances were practically at an end. Permanent centres of population began to grow up around the monasteries, especially Urga, and administrative centres such as Uliasutai, Khobdo and Khiakta, and from the eighteenth century onwards markets and farms made their appearance there. The present régime has rationalized the tendency, which existed earlier, towards a more settled mode of life, but for which the economic and technical basis was lacking. It aims at transforming animal herding in Mongolia from the extensive nomadic type to a more intensive ranch type, and in order to carry through this plan it has grouped all cattle herders with their beasts into about three hundred herding collectives with fixed centres which are planned to house schools, shops, offices and other amenities. Small-scale movement known as *otor*, when a herdsman takes a temporary shelter with him, and pastures his animals at a distance from the central point is still regularly practised, but this is no full-scale nomadism, and the great wholesale shifts of population are a thing of the past. The last must have been the return of the Torguts from Russia in 1771.

But even in this century small but relatively important group movements, politically motivated, have not been unknown. For example, when the Manchus suppressed and scattered the Chahar of Inner Mongolia in the early seventeenth century, some were moved into what is now Sinkiang. The declaration of Outer Mongolian independence from China in 1911 encouraged some of these to desert China entirely. They moved by way of Russia and Khiakta into Outer Mongolia, where the autonomous government detached some pastures from other territories for them, and established them as a new banner under their leader Sumiya Beise. Other families moved from Inner Mongolia, especially Jerim League, into Outer Mongolia at the same time. But these were shifts of allegiance by malcontents, not true nomadism, though perhaps in some way they represent a throwback to the times when a local chieftain would attach himself to a new lord more or less at will. Whole communities were to desert the People's Republic to escape persecution in the 'twenties and 'thirties, and in the 'sixties refugees have been fleeing from Chinese Inner Mongolia into the People's Republic.

It is significant for the changing state of Mongol society that during the years of autonomy (1911 to 1919) the economic advantages of being subject to the jurisdiction of the Great *Shabi*, as the estate of the Jebtsundamba Khutuktu, at that time the King of Mongolia, was known, rather than the secular administration, were such that whole groups of people transferred from one to the other. The number of *shabi*, whom one might loosely term church serfs, increased from 55,500 in 1909 to over 89,000 in 1921. This change of status brought a welcome relief from civil taxation, and so appealed principally to the richer classes, both lay and clerical. An extreme example of such a voluntary transfer is that of the high lama known as the Mergen Bandida Khutuktu, who in 1914 took fifty families of his own *shabi* with him to become *shabi* of the Jebtsundamba Khutuktu's estate. In the same year a whole banner of the Soyote Uriangkhai entered the same estate. Shifts of allegiance such as this involved, however, no physical change of residence, since with small exceptions the Khutuktu's estates consisted of persons and herds rather than territories, and the new *shabi* continued to live on the same pastures as they had occupied before.

Around the turn of the century economic pressure on the poorer classes did produce actual changes in location, though here again no nomadic movement was involved. Poor and destitute persons, often possessing no animals at all, would move to the bigger centres of population and try to scape a living. They were always liable to be deported to their original homes, for their flight meant a loss to the local prince in taxes and corvées. Thus Damdin, the father of the revolutionary leader Sukebator, moved his family to Urga, where he helped around someone else's house while his wife took in sewing. Only the wire-pulling of influential friends prevented them from being returned to their home area, and Damdin was able to regularize his position by getting the job of stoker in the Urga office of the representative of his *aimak*, the very official who should have deported him.

Animal herding is the traditional occupation and still the basis of the country's economy. The sheep provides meat and wool for tent-felts and clothing. The horse can be ridden, and the mare milked and its milk fermented to make *airag* or koumis, and distilled into *arkhi*. Possession of large horse herds is, or was, also a sign of material prosperity. The camel is a beast of burden. With nearly twenty-five domestic animals to each inhabitant, Mongolia is basically a rich country. She can provide for her own staple needs and have enough left over to export meat, butter, sheep-skins and wool. The Mongol loves his horse. In 1594 a Chinese author, Hsiao Ta-heng, wrote:

The possessions of the barbarians consist solely of cows, sheep, dogs, horses and camels, but they cling to them more closely than the southerners cling to their fields and harvests. They love good horses much more than they love other animals. If they see a good horse they will gladly give three or four other horses for it. If they can obtain it they will caress it. . . .[4]

At that time the Mongols engaged in hunting also, as they still do, and Hsiao accurately noted that they were agriculturists also, even if not very good ones, in those areas near China with which he was familiar. They cultivated various sorts of grain and vegetables and Hsiao exploded yet another popular misconception about the Mongol nomads when he wrote:

Everybody claims that the barbarians eat only meat and do not eat vegetable products. They say also that they do not cook their food. This may have been so in the distant past, but when one sees how nowadays they cultivate and sow, one realizes that their methods do not differ greatly from those made use of by the frontier Chinese. They plough with plough and oxen. They grow wheat, millet, beans and glutinous millet. These cereals they have cultivated for several generations – it is not something which has started recently.

Many of the old occupations of the Mongols have disappeared. The collapse of lamaism in this century, when it came into conflict with a communism with which it was incompatible, meant the disappearance of a complete way of life. In its heyday the lamaist church embraced up to half the male population. Not only were there regular lamas in the lamaseries, and lamas who had tacitly left the religious life and taken wives, and so hardly counted, but in addition the shabi estates contributed their thousands of servants, herdsmen and so on for the upkeep of the church. There were lamas skilled in making religious images and sacrificial cakes, those who could paint *tankas* or temple banners, copy manuscripts or cut printing blocks, illuminate books, or model masks for temple dances. All this has disappeared, along with the families whose duty it was to serve the relay stations or to man the watch-posts along the frontier with Russia. The outward appearance of life in Mongolia has changed beyond recognition in the last half century, and the spirit moving it is a new one also. There is little room for comparison between the pictures in books such as Bulstrode's *A Tour in Mongolia* or Consten's *Weideplätze der Mongolen* published in 1920 and 1919 respectively, and those which any tourist may bring back today. Where similarities do exist, they are in the trappings, the detail, the ornamentation. For example, Mongols today are fond of utilizing traditional decorative motifs to adorn their buildings. Men, and to a greater extent, women, keep very much to their national costume, the wide-skirted robe or *deel*. Sports meetings are a compromise between internationally accepted types of contest, and the so-called three manly games of the Mongols, archery, wrestling and horse-racing. A few lamas still chant the daily services and keep up a small religious house in Ulan Bator.

But while these are delightful accompaniments to life, adding an exotic flavour to everyday existence, they are not the very stuff of life, as they would have seemed a mere fifty years ago. They are self-conscious survivals of a tradition, decorative but inessential. Mongolia is adapting herself to the modern undifferentiated world around her. Her future lies in the same direction which the rest of the world is taking, a future conditioned by industrialization, international contacts and co-operation, scientific research, modern techniques of social control and manipulation, education in a pattern of subjects copied from the USSR but familiar all over the world, commercial integration within an ever-widening framework. The outward signs of all this are many – lorries, trains and jet aircraft are replacing the camel caravan and the ox-cart train, children attend state schools, diplomats from numerous countries, including the United Kingdom, maintain offices in a capital which until less than two decades ago was recognized only by the Soviet Union. Ulan Bator has one residual lamasery and no church, but it has a university, a party high school, secondary and primary schools, shops, cinemas, a radio station, theatres, hospitals, prisons, traffic police and so on, and Mongol staffs to service all these. English, the international language of politics and trade, is now spoken by a number of Mongols, though it is still far less familiar than Russian. Tibetan, the language of religion and Buddhist philosophy, is unknown to any but a few aged and learned lamas and some university specialists. Mongolia's break with the past is symbolized most strikingly by her abandonment, twenty years ago, of her seven-centuries-old script and orthography in favour of a semi-phonetic spelling expressed in the Russian alphabet.

The physical changes in Mongolia are of course self-evident. No one can mistake the significance of airports, radios, newspapers and telephones, even if at the same time he must be very naïve and impressionable to take much notice of the Mongol version of developments similar to those taking shape in most other undeveloped countries. What is less obvious, however, is the sensation which the Danish traveller Henning Haslund, experienced in Inner Mongolia over thirty years ago – the consciousness of being in the presence of a young generation whose energy and purposefulness give promise of a new future for the Mongols. At that time western travellers in Mongolia already foresaw the break-up of the old Mongol society, and anticipated it with regret and nostalgia, all the more since the type of man who reached distant Mongolia in those days and was articulate enough to write of his inner experiences, was inclined to be a tough romantic, a man spiritually capable of appreciating the lost horizons and physically capable of making his way there. But for the Mongols of that generation the problem was less one of nostalgia than of their own survival, how they were to continue as Mongols with their society breaking up under Russian influence from the north and Japanese influence from the east. Modernization was bound to come, one way or the other, for between 1921 and 1945 Mongolia's isolation from the world was irrevocably breached, just as Tibet's has been in the last decade or so. In the event, it is Russian communism which has proved dominant in the People's Republic, and all development is taking place under the general slogan of ultimate progression by way of socialism to communism. But regardless of the political form which its revival has taken, Mongolia nowadays, with all its obvious shortcomings, such as a chronic lack of technical skill, is displaying a vigour and self-assurance which were repressed during its centuries of colonial dependence on China, a situation which led many foreign observers into the understandable error that the Mongols were essentially and incurably a lazy, shiftless and unenterprising race. The Russian explorer Przhevalskii recognized the roots of this error eighty years ago. He wrote then:

> Next to laziness and apathy, cowardice and religiosity are the most characteristic qualities of the Mongols. Apart from the fact that cowardice plays a dominant part in the character of all Asiatics, it is particularly strongly developed among the Mongols *because they are not active politically, because the influence of the Chinese has a stultifying effect,* and finally because the desert itself has its own influence, never affording man an opportunity for active work.[5]

The release of energies resulting from the achievement of national independence has not been a miraculous one; indeed achievements up to now have been quite modest. The Mongols have suffered terribly, too, from their association with Stalin's Russia, and have made their own sad errors and miscalculations. Even today there is, in many Mongols, an apathy and fecklessness which is a regular target for official disapproval. Nevertheless, the enjoyment of independent statehood has been one of the essential factors in Mongolia's material and intellectual development over the past decades.

The climate

Far from the moderating influence of the sea, surrounded by mountains, and itself at a relatively high altitude, Mongolia has a severe, extreme and unpredictable continental climate. The most that one can say with assurance is that the winter will be long and hard, though generally dry, and that there will be hot days and some heavy rain in the short summer. The passage from season to season is abrupt, and the weather can change equally abruptly in the course of a single day. The Russian geographer Murzaev describes as follows a day in Ulan Bator in June 1942: at 6 p.m. it was warm, sunny and still. Two hours later there arose a strong south wind. By 9 p.m. there was a wind of up to sixty m.p.h. with dust, fog and nine-tenths cloud cover. At 10 p.m. it was still again and warm – a cloudless night with stars visible. Between 1 and

2 a.m. came heavy showers. At 9 next morning there was full cloud cover, poor visibility, fog and driving snow, with a temperature of 1° C. As another example of instability he describes a summer's day in August 1943 in the extreme east, in the then Choibalsang aimak, where a sharp storm occurred lasting forty minutes. The storm, accompanied by hail-stones the size of pigeons' eggs, covered a strip of land fifteen to twenty-five kilometres wide, on both sides of which reigned complete calm with sunshine. The hail killed some smaller domestic animals and injured people. After the storm the sun shone again, only the ice-covered earth recalling the catastrophe. Mongolia is subject to earthquakes of the maximum severity, but fortunately her sparse population, with its few permanent buildings, does not suffer from them to anything like the degree that the people of Japan may do. Sudden and extremely heavy summer rainfall can cause disastrous floods with little warning, as in the summer of 1966 when continuous torrential rainfall from about 8 July onwards broke the banks of the Tula and Selbe rivers and poured through Ulan Bator flooding houses and factories, sweeping away tents and buses, and drowning dozens of people.

Between winter and summer there may be a temperature difference of as much as 90° C., while within a single day a variation of 20° to 30° C. may occur. The winter cold is terrible, and so are the storms which may set in from December onwards. Przhevalskii describes them as follows:

Only if you have seen with your own eyes the full might of a wind raging in the desert can you fully appreciate its destructive effect. At this time the atmosphere is not only thick with dust and sand, but sometimes even small pebbles are whirled up into the air and biggish stones rolled along the ground. We could even see how stones the size of a fist had fallen into hollows of large rocks lying around. The wind had set them rotating, so that they had produced deep hollows, rubbing through a layer of stone as much as two feet thick.[6]

Snowfall is generally light, but if snow falls and freezes it may prevent the sheep from reaching the grass, and if hay has not been laid in, or if it is not possible to get the hay to the animals, these may die off in enormous numbers. In 1938 nearly two million beasts died as a result of such a *dzud* or natural calamity, and even in the early spring of 1964, when there should have been more cattle shelters available, sudden snowfalls brought a catastrophe to the southern provinces which was relieved only by rapid help from outside the country. A sudden snowstorm can have a disastrous effect upon a herd of horses, which, perhaps several hundred strong, may panic, turn downwind, and gallop till exhausted and lost or buried in snowdrifts and hidden hollows. There is a graphic description of how this happens by a Mongol author, Nawaangnamjil, a government official who served in various posts before and during the present régime:

I was thirteen years old, and that spring I was doing night-watch over some horses somewhere or other. One evening, going to tend the horses, I saddled my gentle chestnut, put on a warm sheep-skin coat, took my cap of warm fox-belly fur, tied my overcoat to the saddle, grasped my horse-pole, and drove the horses off. We went up the valley to the south side of the mountain, and there I was keeping the horses, humming to myself the various tunes I knew, when all of a sudden the sky became overcast and it began to snow all around. In a few minutes the ground was white, and as the snow fell thicker, the earth became shrouded in a white pall, and it was just like the depth of night. I groped around as if I were blind, unable to see the head of my mount, let alone the horses I was guarding. I tried to keep near the horses by the noise they were making, but what with their whinnying here and the sound of their hooves there I had to give up.

Frozen ice tinkled on the body of my mount. He couldn't keep from shivering, and made off neighing in some direction. Snow and ice were clinging to my outer clothing, and I couldn't even manage to knock it off. My mouth and nose were stiff with cold, and my hands and feet were nearly dropping off. Though I had on my furry goatskin overcoat I couldn't keep warm. It was all I could do to think of surviving, and I settled down in a sheltered hollow wondering if I would ever outlive this blizzard and see my dear mother again. I shivered and shook, and wherever I looked there was nothing but snow flurries and white mist, and I could not even see my own body nor my mount. The sides of the hollow where I was surrounded me like cliffs, and pressed closer and closer on me. I cocked my ears and could hear the horses I had been guarding, and though I could make out the noise of the hooves of some of them on the side of the hill behind, it seemed that most of them had gone away down wind. I was so cold I didn't know if I could keep alive myself, let alone find the horses who had run with the storm. And then it seemed as if dawn was breaking. The blizzard died down, the sky seemed to clear, and it looked as if I could see my mount and the nearest mountain.

I was alive and glad to see the dawn. I got on my horse and went to look for the horses along the south side of the hill, and found about a hundred of them grazing in a hollow. Of the others there was no trace. I just managed to round these up, and set off for home, but with all the snow the ditches and hollows were filled in, and the horses were scared to move forward, and would fall through the snow up to their bellies in the ditches, and rear up struggling to get out. My own mount was worn out and frozen from the blizzard, and stopped, panting, by an old grave and would not go forward. Seeking where the snow was thinnest I drove my herd along, and just managed to get them home and hurried into the tent to thaw my frozen body. My mother had heard the dreadful storm and was worried, wondering whether I had frozen to death or lost my way, and she had passed a sleepless night and was just offering a sprinkling of milk to heaven. She put a dry coat on me, gave me some warm tea to drink and something to eat, but I was so frozen and worn out that my whole body was shivering and shaking, and my hands and feet paining so much that I just could not eat. The cold had got into me, and I had taken a fever from it, and my poor worried mother could only cover me up and tell me to go to sleep.[7]

It is no wonder that the Mongol pastures are strewn with the bones of beasts which have died where they stood.

In this enormous land, with its extreme and unfriendly climate, the Mongol people, tough and resilient, have managed to maintain their national identity as the only independent people north of Afghanistan and west of Korea, and to carve out for themselves a livelihood which, while anything but luxurious, has at least on the material side given them a standard of nutrition and accommodation whose minimum must be as high as any in Asia. Their standard of living is nothing extraordinary, measured in the enjoyment of consumer goods, but they are fed well, as they need to be, though the diet is not always balanced in accordance with modern standards, and many people, including children, suffer from vitamin and other deficiencies. But they are a food-exporting country, and even send meat to East Germany. Agriculture proper has never greatly attracted them. This is not so much for the reasons of religious prejudice which have been alleged, but to a great extent because climate and soil conditions are unfavourable, and also, of course, because agriculture is the antithesis to the nomadic way of life. Where farming did develop, it was in fact the church which was the main owner of farmland, especially at the beginning of the present century. M. V. Pevtsov, writing of the late

1870s, found only a few fields amongst the Khalkhas, but a much more developed agriculture amongst the Mongols of north-west Mongolia, especially among the Derbets, who supplied Khobdo and Uliasutai with grain. Around Urga he found vegetable gardens, and Chinese farms and gardens between the capital and Khiakta on the northern frontier, which supplied both towns with grain and vegetables. As an auxiliary activity only, agriculture must always have been of some importance to the Mongols in certain areas. A litany for the averting of disasters, composed in the eighteenth century, and forming part of the ceremony of the worship of the *obo*, the shrine or cairn of heaped-up stones which was, and still is, to be found erected in prominent places throughout the Mongol countryside, asks particularly for the crops to be spared, which it would not have done if agriculture was negligible. The particular text which the following quotation comes from was composed in Inner Mongolia, but its sentiments can hardly have been unique:

> Banish all plague and epidemic illnesses: avert evils like wolves attacking the flocks, thieves and brigands stirring abroad, hail, drought or cattle-pest occurring: and bring it about that rain and water come when needed, that the crops and seeds flourish, and living beings multiply their felicity and devote themselves to the White Virtues.[8]

Culture

The Mongols are one of the civilized peoples of High Asia. They have a tradition of literacy dating back at least to the first years of the thirteenth century, when Genghis Khan is supposed to have had the Uighur script adapted for the Mongol language. But the sophisticated state of the written Mongol language as it appears in the first extensive piece of literature, the epic-chronicle of the middle of the thirteenth century known as the *Secret History of the Mongols*, argues for a rather longer period of culture. Mongolia does not seem to have produced great artists. During the past three centuries her craftsmen have spent their skill mainly on the repetitive work of producing religious banners and icons and on book illumination, treating secular subjects, when they turned to them, in a very formalistic, literal manner. More recently, under Soviet influence, they have been crippled by the primitive demands of socialist realism. Mongol music, too, seems never to have developed, in its native state, beyond a more or less ornamented melodic line. Modern composers, often basing themselves on folk tunes, work as their Soviet training directs them and so far have produced only a few rather pleasing compositions, but nothing of importance. But in imaginative literature, in theology, history and philology, Mongolia is one of the important secondary cultures of Asia, after the great creative civilizations of India and China from which it has drawn heavily. This cultural development presupposes something more than a primitive nomadism as its background. Epics, tales and lyrics may be the product of a nomad society, but Mongolia shows also such enormous scholarly achievements as the translation between about 1580 and 1629 of the 108 volumes of the Tibetan Kanjur, with preliminary work for a translation of the Tanjur, a collection of scriptures twice the size, which was actually accomplished in the eighteenth century. Book printing was concentrated mainly in Peking, a Chinese city, and was in the hands of the Chinese book trade, but there were important temple printing houses in Mongolia also, notably in Urga, and later in Buriat Mongolia as well. Mongol theologians wrote in Tibetan, the language of the church, and to them we owe the existence of bilingual dictionaries of encyclopedic compass. Historical writing flourished from the early seventeenth century onwards, practised partly by lamas, partly by noblemen. Their careful attention to family records has preserved a mass of incidental information about Mongol life over the centuries.

The political situation at the beginning of the seventeenth century

When the Mongol dynasty was overthrown in 1368 and expelled from China, many Mongols remained behind, but the fleeing emperor managed to gather several *tumen* or ten thousands together and lead them back towards his new headquarters on the Kerülen river. Usually the chronicles put the number of *tumen* who escaped at six, and indeed the Mongols are often referred to as the Six *Tumen* throughout the following centuries. The imperial Mongol dynasty did not die out then, but was continued under the name of the Northern Yüan until the death of the last emperor, Ligdan Khan, in 1634. But for most of this period the actual emperors failed to exercise supreme authority. The years were filled with internecine quarrels and later with wars with the Oirats or western Mongols whose power was not broken till Altan Khan of the Tumet (1507-82), himself not emperor but a powerful feudal prince, recaptured Karakorum, the former imperial capital, from them. These civil wars were destructive to society. Lomi, writing in the early eighteenth century, complains specifically of the loss of family registers, which would have been important historical source material during the Oirat wars. They were also damaging to the prestige of the imperial family, and at one time its power sank so low that an Oirat, Esen, was able to proclaim himself emperor though he was not a member of the line of Genghis Khan.

The idea of Mongol unity under a lawful member of the imperial clan experienced a brief revival during the reign of Dayan Khan. He assumed control himself over the three *tumen* which had come to form the Left Wing of the Mongols, and sent his son to govern the three *tumen* of the Right Wing as *jinong* or regent. But certain leaders of the Right Wing revolted, discontented at having a ruler appointed over them from, as they saw it, outside, when they felt that they could quite well rule themselves. They killed the *jinong* and civil war broke out. After early defeats, Dayan Khan subdued the Right Wing, and with due ceremony declared himself emperor before the eight white tents which formed the sanctuary of Genghis Khan and the great holy place of the Mongols. His reign apparently ended peacefully, but a fatal disunity was at work amongst the Mongols, who could appreciate loyalty to an immediate overlord, but who, looking back only to Genghis Khan, the common ancestor of the whole Mongol nobility, as the one possible bond between them, lacked all sense of nationhood. Dayan Khan was succeeded by a grandson, and trouble-makers were at once at work, proposing the complete destruction of the Right Wing and the distribution of its people among the *tumen* of the Left Wing. The suggestion was rejected by the Emperor, but it is none the less indicative of the centrifugal tendencies which were going to bring about the collapse of the fragile unity of the eastern Mongols.

Though the empire itself was passed on, overlordship over its constituent parts passed to the nine surviving sons of Dayan Khan. The course of the sixteenth century is marked by the rise in Mongolia of chieftains, members of the imperial family, who profited by this division of authority amongst themselves to set themselves up as the *de facto* equals of the Emperor, though the latter's position was not really challenged till the very end. With the reality of independent power the newly-arrived petty monarchs began to make use of the title of Khan. The Emperor himself began to be known less as the Emperor of the Mongols than as the Emperor of the Chahar, his own appanage. Each new khan would allot fiefs to his relatives, who in their turn did the same, so that by the end of the sixteenth century Mongolia had ceased in all but name to be an empire, and was a mere collection of more or less independent petty princedoms. The most important of these was for a long time the realm of Altan Khan of the Tumet, the ruler of the Right Wing, whose personality dominated the middle of the century. He devoted his early years to piratical raids into China, with the intention of forcing the establishment of frontier markets where the Mongols could unload their surplus horses. His military campaigns led him far into north Mongolia and Jungaria too, to the Kukunor region, to Tibet and to Turfan. His power was so great that there was no longer any possibility of the Emperor's annexing the Right Wing. Instead, the Emperor Daraisun was even compelled to lead the Chahar, who made up the main part of his people, away from contact with Altan Khan, eastwards over the Khingan mountains to pastures in Liao-tung. In later life Altan Khan turned to Buddhism and was responsible for the effective penetration into Mongolia of the Yellow Sect of Lamaism, welcoming the future Third Dalai Lama into his dominions. His city at Köke qota, built with the help of Chinese refugees, is the first permanent Mongol city of modern times.

Yet Altan Khan's power seems to have been a personal one, dependent on his own initiative and enterprise. After his death in 1582 the influence of the Tumet declined, while the power of the Chahar seems to have revived in their new pastures in Liao-tung, so that the idea of Mongol unity could enjoy a brief revival. But other khanates were arising within the once united empire, none strong enough or keen to replace the dying Chinese Ming dynasty which was in fact to be overthrown by the Manchu, a Tungus people from Manchuria. Within Khalkha there arose three khanates. Abdai Khan, the propagator of Buddhism, and grandson of that one of Dayan Khan's sons who ruled the seven tribes of the Khalkha in Outer Mongolia, had the royal title bestowed on him by the Dalai Lama, and from him descended the line of the Tushetu Khan. The first Setsen Khan, Sholoi, assumed the title himself, as did the father of the first Zasagtu Khan. This proliferation of the use of the royal title was a sign of the disintegration of the empire. Against the aggressive power of the Manchus the various Mongol princedoms acted independently and in disharmony, and forfeited their independence for three centuries to come.

The conversion to Buddhism

The disintegration of the empire as a political unit, and the rise of independent feudal princedoms was one of the two formative, or deformative, influences acting upon Mongolia around 1600. The other, and by contrast a positive one, determining the course of Mongol intellectual life, the development of the language, and the shape of society almost to our own day, was the spread of Tibetan Buddhism, or Lamaism, in the second half of the sixteenth century. Buddhism was no stranger in the land. Even today, monuments of much earlier Buddhist civilizations loom up from the rolling steppes of north Mongolia. A hundred miles or so west of Ulan Bator, just off the road to Tsetserlig, lie the stark, deserted ruins of Khara Baishing, the 'Black Building', a walled city of Khitan times. Outside the grassy mound which marks the circumvallation rise two stupas, one half fallen into ruins, the other more or less intact, vestiges of Buddhist life in Mongolia two centuries or more before the rise of Genghis Khan. Buddhism flourished again under the Mongol emperors. Fragments of wall paintings from the thirteenth-century palace of Ogedei at Karakorum, recently explored and described, show representations of Buddhas, and we know of some printing of Buddhist scriptures in the Mongol language: the most famous is the commentary to the Bodhicaryāvatāra of 1312, recovered from Turfan.

Even after the collapse of the empire, the printing of religious texts in Mongol did not cease entirely. We know for instance of a polyglot edition of dhāranis or magic formulae dating from 1432, but long before that the centre of public and religious life had moved away from Mongolia itself to Peking, with the transformation of Khubilai into a Chinese, rather than a Mongol, emperor. The fate of Buddhism in the Mongol homeland is far from clear. Generally it is thought to have died out completely, the people reverting during the following centuries of confusion and civil war to more primitive forms of folk religion and shamanism. The records for this time are scanty and muddled, much material having been destroyed in the wars. Besides, until Altan Khan built his city of Köke qota in the middle of the sixteenth century, there can have been no permanent lamasery buildings in Inner or Outer Mongolia, for his was an enterprise of a new type. Nor did the Mongols pay much attention to the composition of chronicles till the seventeenth century, by which time they were devoted followers of the victorious Yellow Faith, whose accounts of the state of Mongolia before the conversion, when Buddhism of the rival Red Sect might have persisted, are not entirely unbiased.

One piece of negative evidence is that personal names, which had a Buddhist flavour under the later emperors, revert to non-Buddhist forms during the intervening years, and only after the middle of the sixteenth century do we again find records of people with Buddhist names in the chronicles. But there are indications that some traces of an older Buddhism may have survived among the Mongols. Lamaseries are recorded as having existed in the Hsi-ning area of west China, peopled partly by Mongols, throughout the Ming dynasty, and there are scattered references in some old documents to the presence of lamas of the unreformed Red Sect in various parts of Mongolia. Whether these were new arrivals, contemporary with the Third Dalai Lama and other representatives of the Yellow Sect, or whether they were remnants of an older tradition, it is difficult to decide. Legend tells that Altan Khan was converted to Buddhism through a dream in which lamas of both the Yellow and Red Sects appeared to him simultaneously, and we know also that his political rival, the Emperor Jasagtu, was converted by an unreformed lama in 1576. But whatever may be the truth, it was in the end to be the newly-arrived Yellow Sect which predominated in the conversion of Mongolia, leaving only small pockets of influence and activity to the unreformed sects.

How enthusiastically the Mongols took to Lamaism can be seen from the account of Hsiao Ta-heng, written in 1594, only a generation after the first conversations had taken place.

The customs of the barbarians [he remarks] used to be savage and cruel, and for a long time it was impossible to civilize them. But since they submitted and began to pay tribute, they have conceived a great regard for the Buddhist faith. Within their tents they constantly adore an image of the Buddha, and they make him an offering whenever they eat or drink. The rich . . . invite the lamas to recite prayers, offer incense, and bow reverently. All the money they can get goes for casting statuettes of the Buddha or stupas. Men and women, old and young, always have a rosary in their hands. Some of them make a little box of silver or gold, about two or three inches in height, into which they put amulets. They carry this box beneath the left arm, and are never without it, either sitting or lying, sleeping or eating.

Altan Khan's first contacts with Buddhism occurred in 1573 when he undertook a campaign against the Shira Uighur and took prisoner three of their chieftains and two lamas. One of the latter preached the doctrines of the Buddha to him and converted him, so that a side result of this military campaign was that Buddhism achieved its first foothold in Mongolia in the court of a powerful prince. From there it was to expand rapidly and confidently, reaching far into Manchuria, into Outer Mongolia, to the west Mongols who were converted before their departure from Mongolia, and took the Yellow Faith with them to Russia, and ultimately to the Buriats. This first enterprise of Altan Khan's came at a time, as we have seen, when small but ambitious princes were emerging in opposition to the Mongol emperor, and when they were acquiring greater wealth and sophistication. Altan Khan himself had just brought the Chinese, through repeated campaigns and raids, to the point where they were willing to flatter him with an honorific title as *Shun-i wang* or 'Rightful Prince' and a golden seal, and, more important, open the profitable markets on the frontier which he had demanded. Growing dissatisfaction was making itself felt with the barbaric notions of shamanism, its bloody sacrifices, its primitive cosmology, its unattractive revelations of the world beyond, and its complete lack of organization which made it useless as an instrument of political power and did not provide the careers and dignities offered by a hierarchical church. This dissatisfaction coincided with, and doubtless fed on, the discovery of the existence in Tibet of a superior and more attractive culture. An incident recorded from the time of Altan Khan shows how this discontent manifested itself, and illustrates the contradictory tendencies existing side by side as the new society was evolving. Altan Khan himself had, according to pagan custom, inherited one of his father's three wives at the former's death, and had had a son by her. When the boy died, the mother arranged for the children of a hundred families and the foals of a hundred camels to be slaughtered to provide him with a death escort on his last journey. Though this must have been a familiar custom, uproar broke out amongst the families of the victims, and a *taiji*, or member of the imperial family, stopped the whole affair by threatening to get himself killed to go and plague the dead child. Even after this rebuff the queen did not abandon her evil ways, and at her death her body became a *vetala*, or 'living corpse', and had to be exorcized by the Dalai Lama, who was in Tumet at the time (1585). The superior rituals of which he was master got the better of the *vetala*, which turned into a lizard and was consumed by holy fire.

The great turning-point in the religious history of Mongolia came three years after Altan Khan's conversion, when his nephew, Khutuktu Setsen Khungtaiji, persuaded him to invite to Mongolia the lama who was to become the third Dalai Lama of Tibet. His arguments are interesting, for they show that with the establishment of relations of equality with China, for that is what in fact existed in spite of Hsiao Ta-heng's euphemistic mention of 'submission', and the neutralization of the Oirats, Altan Khan's political destiny had fulfilled itself, and that he was in a mood to turn his attention to higher things. The Khungtaiji said:

You have taken your revenge on the Chinese who once conquered our city [i.e. Peking] and have established relations with them. You have avenged yourself on the Oirats, who seized Karakorum, and have overcome them and brought them into subjection. But now your years have increased, and you are approaching old age. The wise say that what is necessary for this and the future destiny is the Faith. Now it appears that in the western land of snows [i.e. Tibet] there dwells, in corporeal form, the Mighty Seer and Pitiful One, the Bodhisattva Avalokiteshvara. Would it not be wonderful if we were to invite him, and re-establish the relations between Church and State as they once existed between the Emperor Khubilai and the lama Pagspa?[9]

Two important points emerge from behind this pious verbiage. Firstly, it is clear that Altan Khan enjoyed enough power and prestige to propose to the high Lama of Tibet the long and arduous journey into Mongolia. Secondly we see the Khungtaiji making a conscious appeal to an unforgotten Mongol tradition of the alliance of the Buddhist Church with the secular power, which ran like a thread through Mongol political thought at the time of the Yüan dynasty. He was seeking the sanction of the imperial past for the political innovations he had in view. This tradition of the 'Two Principles' had been formally laid down in Khubilai's time, in a book of statecraft known as *The Tenfold Virtuous White Chronicle of the Faith*, and was revived by the Khungtaiji, who re-edited the text from two manuscripts which had survived the troubled centuries between. The principles contained in this book were applied to the settlement between Altan Khan and the head of the Yellow Faith when their meeting took place. Altan Khan conferred upon the lama the title of Dalai Lama, which was applied retrospectively to his two predecessors, so that this powerful line of Tibetan clerics owes its existence, with its mixed Mongol-Tibetan designation, to a Mongol prince. At the same time, the Dalai Lama was conscious of the psychological value of the appeal to antiquity and precedent, and proclaimed himself to be a reincarnation of Pagspa Lama, the great spiritual adviser of Khubilai Khan, and Altan Khan to be the reincarnation of Khubilai himself. Suitable pre-incarnations were discovered also for the Khungtaiji, who had engineered the meeting, for his younger brother, and for the Tibetan interpreter.

Mongol chronicles, and especially the *Erdeni-yin Tobchi* (or 'Precious Summary'), composed in 1662 by Sagang Setsen, a descendant of the Khungtaiji, present this meeting and the subsequent agreement on religious practices and the relative ranking of nobles and clerics, as an act of great piety on all sides, but it is evident that political considerations were fundamental to it, and that Altan Khan was making use of a superior culture, which was expanding in central Asia and enjoyed great respect and prestige, in order to strengthen his position *vis-à-vis* the nominal Emperor Tumen Jasagtu Khan. To have himself publicly proclaimed as the incarnation of Khubilai Khan can have had only one meaning, namely that he considered himself the rightful heir to the Mongol empire. His example led the way for other emerging princes also to establish relations with the new vital intellectual and spiritual force represented by the Buddhist church. In the same year the Emperor established relations with a lama of the Red Sect, countering Altan Khan's preference for the reformed Yellow Sect, and entered the Buddhist faith under his supervision. But soon after this, in 1582, Altan Khan died, and the

Emperor himself, recognizing the pre-eminence of the Yellow over the Red form of Buddhism, issued an invitation to the Dalai Lama to visit him. In the event, the Dalai Lama died on his way to Mongolia in 1588, whereupon the nobles of Tumet seized the opportunity to have a member of the family of Altan Khan, and hence, as is stressed by the nineteenth-century chronicle *Erdeni-yin Erike* ('The Precious Rosary'), a descendant of Genghis Khan, declared to be the next re-incarnation.

In 1577 Altan Khan's example of conversion was followed by Abdai Khan of the Khalkhas, who came from his territories near Karakorum to Köke qota to meet the Dalai Lama and receive from him the title of Khan. In 1586 he built the great temple of Erdeni Juu alongside the site of Karakorum, ensuring that the centre of religious might in north Mongolia would be in his own khanate, and that, as in Inner Mongolia, the Yellow Sect was to dominate over the Red. Unreformed lamaism was, however, never extirpated from Mongolia. Abdai Khan's younger brother Tumenkin earned from the Dalai Lama the title of Sain Noyon Khan for his devotion in combating the Red Sect. This seems to have been an honorific title only: his subjects venerated him as the equal of the three territorial khans of Khalkha, but it was not till 1725 that the religious title of Sain Noyon Khan was turned into a secular and effective one by the Manchu emperor, and was bestowed on a descendant of Tumenkin's, with a suitable number of subjects, as a reward for pro-Manchu military service. Red lamas have continued to exist up to the present day, sometimes even in the same lamaseries alongside devotees of the Yellow Faith. That two monasteries of the Ordos region supported at least until 1945 rival incarnations of Padma Sambhava, founder of the red Nyingmapa sect, though themselves Yellow Sect houses, points to some sort of reconciliation. At the very least, it is evidence of indifference. Moreover, the presence till recently in some lamaseries in Khalkha of female lamas or *Khandma* (a word derived from the Tibetan *mkha-hgro-ma*, meaning a goddess or sorceress) must be another survival of pre-reformed Buddhism. But the organizational capacities of the Dalai Lamas, and the greater appeal of the reformed faith ensured that this was to be the dominant form of Buddhism in Mongolia.

The new class of missionary lamas addressed themselves in various ways to the task of remoulding Mongol society, and at the same time of consolidating their own position. Already at the time of the meeting between Altan Khan and the Dalai Lama, the question of the recognition of the clergy as equals, rank for rank, of the nobility, had been settled, and offences against their persons were henceforth to be punished as if the corresponding member of the nobility had been aggrieved. The lamas addressed their missionary work principally towards the rulers and nobility of Mongolia, so that something like the principle of *cujus regio ejus religio* was in operation. The Torgut missionary Neichi Toyin (1557–1653), who preached in eastern Mongolia, achieved, for instance, a great success by curing the grave sickness of a princess of the Ongnigut, defeating with his superior magic powers the efforts of a great shaman. In consequence there took place a mass conversion of the ordinary people of the Ongnigut. Later, by curing a sick shamaness, he was able to gain such influence over Aoba, the Tushetu Khan of the Khorchin, that the latter declared himself for the faith, encouraged his people to do likewise, and took steps to suppress shamanism. Everywhere the process seems to have been the same. The lamas showed themselves superior to the primitive shamans in their theology and their practical abilities, and gained the confidence of the rulers who were not committed to any rival faith likely to be able to challenge Buddhism in its attractiveness. The princes had their people come over to the new faith, even permitting the missionary lamas to use fairly forceful methods. The lama known as the Jaya Pandita, who preached among the Oirats in the first half of the seventeenth century and who is known as the elaborator of the Oirat or 'clear' script and as the translator of numerous religious works, gave very definite instructions to his co-workers. They were to burn the *ongons* or family idols of anyone found worshipping them, and to confiscate the horses and sheep of the offenders. The horses of anyone found inciting male or female shamans to shamanize were likewise to be confiscated, and the shamans and shamanesses themselves to be fumigated with dog-filth. In this uncompromising manner the people were to be turned to the 'White Direction' and the religion of the Buddha was to be exalted. Violence against the shamans and their idols was exercised generally. The newly-converted Altan Khan allowed the Dalai Lama to burn up all his *ongons* in a ritual fire, and he also published decrees ordering his people to refrain from slaughtering their beasts, to reverence the lamas, to burn their *ongons* and in their place to make meatless sacrifices to the Buddhist deity Mahakala. If they did not give up their old customs they would be executed or have their property confiscated or be banished from their pastures. Neichi Toyin too, who gained much of his prestige from his superior medical skill, had the *ongons* of the people destroyed. Shamanistic practices of course survived, even in high places, as they do in residual form to this day. When, for example, an envoy sent from the Manchus to Ligdan Khan in 1618 failed to return on time, it was rumoured that he had been killed as a sacrifice to the Mongol war standard. This practice was revived in the present century by the Mongol commanders who captured Khobdo from the Chinese in 1912, while the living hearts were ritually torn from the bodies of prisoners as late as the civil disturbances of 1932.

While missionizing against the shamans the lamas took care to identify themselves with the ruling class, with the result that while Buddhism thoroughly penetrated all levels of Mongol society in the coming centuries, organizationally it developed almost as a state within the state. It was a body distributing high titles, owning enormous wealth in flocks and herds and in serfs, and enjoying such political prestige that the Manchu emperors tacitly recognized the supreme head of the Faith, the Jebtsundamba Khutuktu or 'Living Buddha' of Urga, as quasi-ruler over the people. When the Khalkhas submitted to the Manchus at the end of the seventeenth century, and when sixty years later a general rebellion had to be pacified, the Jebtsundamba Khutuktu was treated with as a temporal authority. From very early on the nobility and the higher clergy saw in mutual identification of interests the way to continuing power. That the Tumet should have got a member of their own ruling family accepted as the fourth Dalai Lama is a striking instance of this process, and it is paralleled in Khalkha by the elevation in 1650, at the age of fifteen, of the son of the Tushetu Khan Gombodorji to the position of first Jebtsundamba Khutuktu. Seven reincarnations succeeded to the first, though only one more was 'revealed' in Mongolia, the Manchu emperor Ch'ien Lung decreeing, for reasons of state, that the third and later re-incarnations were to be found in Tibet, and thus outside the imperial family of Genghis Khan and the Mongol nobility. We know that much earlier Neichi Toyin was born as the descendent of a powerful noble of the Torgut, and that the Jaya Pandita was born in 1599 into a well-known Khoshut family.

Relations between ecclesiastical and secular authorities were such that representatives of each conferred titles upon the other. The titles borne by Mongol princes and the Emperor often had a religious connotation, and far from being empty epithets must have served to demonstrate the solidarity existing between Church and State, and to suggest the identity of interests of the Yellow Faith of the Dalai Lamas and the posterity of Genghis Khan. As we have seen, the Dalai Lama received his title from Altan Khan, and while one tradition says that Altan demanded the title of khan himself from the Mongol emperor Daraisun Kudeng and was accorded it, it is also recorded that the Dalai Lama conferred upon him grandiose titles with a religious flavour. Many epithets are recorded in chronicles and in the colophons of religious texts for Ligdan Khan of the Chahar, stressing equally his imperial descent and his patronage of the Church. His legitimacy as monarch is maintained not only by the use of the title of Genghis Khan, first borne by his great ancestor, but by the deliberate association of his person with other Chinese imperial families. Ligdan was known as 'The Chakravarti Saint, Emperor T'ang T'ai-tsung' or as 'The blessed Ligdan, Wise Emperor of the Great Yuan', epithets linking him with the great second emperor of the T'ang dynasty and with Khubilai Khan respectively. More explicitly expressive of the alliance between Church and State was his title 'Blessed Ligdan, Marvellous Genghis Daiming Setsen, Conqueror of the Directions, Powerful Chakravarti, T'ang T'ai-tsung, God of Gods, Khormusda of all within the world, Turner of the Golden Wheel, King of the Law'. Lamas accepted their honorific titles from both religious superiors and from laymen. Thus the Jaya Pandita of the Khalkha had his epithet conferred by the Dalai Lama, while the better-known Jaya Pandita of the Oirat received his from Zasagtu Khan of the Khalkha. It was also not unusual for laymen of noble birth to receive consecrations in the Buddhist church, and to have the empowerment to perform certain rituals conferred upon them. Abdai Khan was so distinguished in 1577, and in the next century, in 1663, his descendant Chakhundorji, the successor as Tushetu Khan to the father of the Jebtsundamba Khutuktu, received certain consecrations from the Dalai Lama of the day in Lhasa, where he was studying. Ligdan Khan received secret initiations from his court priest, and in his turn bestowed a new title on the latter.

At first this mutual granting of titles seems to have been a reciprocal process, but as Manchu power grew the subordinate position of the Church was made clear. When the son of the Tushetu Khan was born in 1635, it was Setsen Khan, another of the three khans of the Khalkha, who had him examined by his own soothsayer, and pronounced worthy to be called a Buddha. He was educated in Mongolia and placed upon a religious throne at a general meeting of the Khalkha tribes in 1639, before receiving a Tibetan education in Lhasa and obtaining further ordinations from the Dalai Lama. Thus originally he was a leader raised up by the Mongols themselves. But, as an inscription in the Amarbayasgalangt Lamasery in north Mongolia records, after he had sought refuge with the Manchu emperor in 1688 from the Oirat invasions, it was the Emperor who restored him and appointed him Grand Lama, and accorded him power over the Yellow Church in Mongolia. As the system of re-incarnated lamas became institutionalized, it was decreed that the newly-discovered Jebtsundamba Khutuktu should be sanctioned by the Emperor, and that other incarnations should be sanctioned by the local authorities in Mongolia.

A third way in which the Buddhist Church strengthened its position was by the translation and circulation of the Buddhist scriptures, both canonical texts from the Kanjur and Tanjur, and other, non-canonical texts. Only later was a native liturgy to arise, called forth by the need to accommodate the tenets of Buddhism to the still powerful substratum of popular cults. The translation programme fulfilled two needs. On the one hand it made available, to the upper classes at least, an unending stream of literature which appealed to their new sophistication. A knowledge of reading and writing spread, summoned up and nourished by the new wave of literature. We know from Hsiao Ta-heng how much the Mongols respected those who were literate:

> When a barbarian knows how to write ... he enjoys a situation above that of the ordinary barbarians. That is why the barbarians respect the *bagshi* [clerics] very much. Originally there were only a few *bagshi* in each tribe, but now that they have embraced Buddhism, they are very numerous.

Young men, both laymen and clerics, were trained as translators, and from the last decades of the sixteenth century onwards, were producing for their lay patrons Mongol versions of Tibetan books. There can have been little literary competition, for the folk literature of the time was an oral literature, and all the skill of scribes and miniature painters was concentrated on the religious books. At first books were circulated in manuscript only, though some book production must have been magnificent, for example, the Tibetan version of the Kanjur which a Mongol noble promised to have prepared in letters of gold and silver when the Dalai Lama visited Altan Khan. Printing was an innovation of the mid-seventeenth century, and was concentrated mainly in Peking. But here too it was, with a few rare exceptions, books of religion which were in demand for printing and circulation.

The second need which the translation programme satisfied was the desire of rich princes and others to shine as patrons of the Faith and of learning. An early Maecenas was Altan Khan of the Tumet who sent to China to ask for a Tibetan lama to be sent to him with copies of the scriptures. In his turn, Abdai Khan of the Khalkha sent to Altan Khan for religious books. From 1579 onwards, when Altan Khan conceived the idea of having the book known as *Altan Gerel* translated, a regular stream of such translations began to appear, either from Köke qota or, later, from Ligdan Khan's residence at Chagan Suburga, the 'White Pagoda', in Baarin. Whether all the translations which emerged from Ligdan Khan's residence, culminating in 1629 in a complete version of the Mongolian Kanjur, and often incorporating colophons eulogizing the khan as a patron of the Faith, were genuinely done there, is another question. The German scholar Walther Heissig has shown convincingly that Ligdan simply lifted the work of earlier translators who had been active among the Tumet, and had them supplied with new and false colophons on purpose to increase his own prestige, such was the value attaching to the reputation of being an *öglige-yin ejen*, or Lord of Gifts.

There is little evidence for the popular belief that the Manchu emperors encouraged the circulation of Buddhist books in order to weaken the martial spirit of the Mongols. The colophons of surviving books show that the impulse to make translations came from within the Mongolian nobility itself. In any case, mere conversion to Buddhism would not have assured a peaceful population. It is a fact of history that it took the Manchus close on a century to quell the turbulent, but devout west Mongols or Jungars, who more than once seriously challenged their power.

With its close relations with the nobility, its active and clever proselytizing, and its publicity work, the Church quickly achieved a position of power in Mongolia, and began also to amass the temporal wealth which was to make it a formidable economic power until the 'thirties of the present century, when it was finally dispossessed and destroyed. Tribal conditions had long since broken down amongst the Mongols owing to the rapid displacements and regroupments of people from imperial times onwards. Tribes and clans were broken up, though their names survived in the chronicles of the noble families, and as feudalism grew, so ordinary people became attached to overlords, and the situation arose in which they could be given away to other lords along with their animals, without distinction between man and beast. The Manchus used such donations to assure themselves of the support of their subject peoples. Contacts between Khalkha Mongols and Nurhachi, the Manchu conqueror, began as early as 1594 and a Khalkha chieftain named Enggeder is found visiting Nurhachi in 1605. In 1624 he finally went over to the Manchus, moved to Liao-tung, and was settled in the city of Liao-yang, where he was granted land, agricultural implements and some Chinese as serfs. So it is not surprising to find the new Church in Mongolia being supplied with subjects in much the same way to tend its flocks and act as general servants. Several such donations are noted in the biography of the Jaya Pandita of the Oirat, and it is interesting that not all the novice-servants thus conscripted were Mongols, some being Chinese and Korean prisoners of war. The possessions of the Jebtsundamba Khutuktu, at first acquired in this way, ultimately formed the largest estate among the clergy of Khalkha, and were of such size and importance that they were considered as a fifth division of Khalkha, alongside the four khanates.

Thus at the beginning of the seventeenth century Mongolia bears the signs of what it was to become. It was a semi-theocracy, and, in its dependence upon China – a foreign power which itself was, after the great continental conquests of the seventeenth and eighteenth centuries, to turn in on itself and ignore changes occurring elsewhere – it was to become more and more isolated from the outside world. The promise of a new cultural revival under the influence of Tibetan Buddhism was to wither and fail, and Mongolia's colonial status and feudal organization were to condemn the country to political and economic stagnation.

CHAPTER 2

THE LOSS OF MONGOL INDEPENDENCE

Inner Mongolia

The fate of Mongolia today, in particular the lasting division of the eastern Mongols into Outer Mongolia, which has evolved into the People's Republic, and Inner Mongolia, now apparently inextricably incorporated within China, was determined by the succession of events in the seventeenth century, beginning with the rise of the Manchus from obscurity to imperial rule in China. The tribes of Inner Mongolia which lay astride and alongside the road into north China lost their independence during the course of the Manchu conquest through alliance with, or defeat by, the Manchus. As the newly-established Manchu state began to reach out to those 'natural' frontiers which it had to dominate unless it was to be permanently insecure, Khalkha, or Outer Mongolia, was squeezed into submission between it and the empire of the west Mongols, Oirats and Jungars, which was not finally destroyed till the late 1750s. In eliminating the independent existence of the Chahar empire and the princedoms of Inner Mongolia, and subsequently of the khanates of Khalkha, the Manchus were not so much ridding themselves of direct or potential rivals as clearing the field for final settlement with the only two serious opponents they faced: on the one hand the Chinese Ming dynasty, on the other hand the massive central Asian realm of the west Mongols. The disunity of the eastern Mongols, their fatal tendency to allow what remained of the imperial power to be challenged and contested by any powerful chieftain with the organizing ability to attract followers and wealth in the form of animals, meant that the Manchus, in the course of their gradual expansion and consolidation southwards towards China, were able to subdue, or acquire as allies, piecemeal, incoherent groups of Mongols. Even as early as 1594, when the Manchus represented a comparatively insignificant force fighting to establish themselves among their immediate neighbours, we hear of minor Mongol chieftains, Khorchin and Khalkha, sending ambassadors to propose the establishment of friendly relations. Between the two main antagonists, the rising Manchus and the declining Ming dynasty, who in 1616 ceased to receive tribute from the former, who had been till then their nominal vassals, stood only one relatively powerful third force. This was Ligdan Khan, the last emperor of the Mongols, or rather, by this time, effectively of the Chahar only, who had ascended the throne in 1604.

For the Mongols the Manchu conquest was to mean, in modern terms, the extinction of their independence, but it is reasonable to ask what sort of independence this was, and whether, in the conditions of the seventeenth century, the loss was a true one. It is only in relatively recent years that national independence for all has come to be considered the political *summum bonum*, and it may well be that we, together with present-day Mongol historians, are reading too much significance into the Manchu conquest of the Mongols and applying modern values to a situation to which they are not wholly applicable, by looking on the loss of independence as an evil in itself. There was at the time no cohesive sense of Mongol nationality expressing itself in a will to political identity. Loyalties were limited and personal. Political life had degenerated into a centrifugal free-for-all in which each leader tried to get as much freedom of action as he could, at the expense of his fellow nobles. Respect for the personality of the Emperor had lapsed, and loyalty to him and the tradition he represented, which alone would have given the Mongols a feeling of belonging together, was sadly lacking. Except in a backward-looking devotion to the now deified figure of the great ancestor Genghis Khan, there was no other common interest among the Mongol nobility. Ranging more or less at will over the steppes and looking back over a couple of centuries of petty and almost continuous war amongst themselves, they had no sense of community, of belonging together as Mongols.

Here and there a vigorous leader would emerge at the head of a petty princedom which for a time would prosper economically and perhaps reach a considerable standard of cultural refinement, but which would disappear without leaving any effective mark on Mongol history. Such a principality must have been that of the Khalkha leader Tsogtu Taiji (d. 1637) near the Tula river west of present-day Ulan Bator. The ruins of his palace still stand, together with a stone inscription commemorating the fact that he had erected Buddhist temples there. Another small administrative, religious and cultural centre was at Olon sume, north-west of Köke qota, where an inscription on stone in Mongol, dating from 1594, and the discovery of some hundreds of fragments of manuscripts roughly contemporary with it, witness to an intense religious activity only some twenty years after the revival of Buddhism in Mongolia. The most powerful of such khanates was, for the time being, that of Ligdan, yet even he lacked the political genius which might have enabled him to carry through effectively his policy of restoring the unity of the Mongol empire. His efforts to do so resulted finally in the opposite of what he had intended, namely in greater disunity among those petty leaders who felt their spheres of power threatened and themselves offended by the forward imperial policies of Ligdan. From 1616 onwards many of these turned for escape either to flight to the more independent khans of Khalkha, and especially to the nearest, Sholoi the Setsen Khan, or, as their prestige grew, to the Manchu Nurhachi and his successor Abahai. That the existing Chinese dynasty was about to collapse and be replaced by a new and vigorous régime meant that Ligdan's failure to restore the imperial power came at a critical time for the Mongols. Internal squabbles which in the fifteenth and sixteenth centuries had meant only the transfer of dominant power from one chieftain to another, at most the temporary loss of the imperial throne to the Oirats, now exposed an enfeebled Mongolia, in the seventeenth century, to a decisive take-over by a non-Mongol power.

What we know of Ligdan Khan, apart from the hostile accounts in Manchu sources, is to be pieced together from the laudatory colophons in the religious works he caused to be published in translation from the Tibetan, from the remains of inscriptions erected at his residence at the White Pagoda, a Liao dynasty monument in the Baarin district of Inner Mongolia, and from the interrelated accounts of his reign in various Mongol chronicles. The inscriptions disappeared completely at some time in the thirty years following their discovery and incomplete decipherment by the Russian scholar Pozdneev in 1893. They and the colophons bear witness to Ligdan's remarkable religious activities. He built temples, and carried through a programme of translation which embraced the whole of the Kanjur. The chronicles generally adopt a rather pro-Manchu viewpoint, understandably, since they all date from after the establishment of the Manchu power. They limit themselves to a brief review of Ligdan's reign and to a regretful description, in more or less metaphorical terms, of his last disastrous years.

Our sources, then, are scanty and inexplicit. They appear to show that at some period of his life Ligdan lost sight of his twin purposes of civilizing the eastern Mongols and reuniting them, and began to indulge in useless violence. Yet they are perhaps to be interpreted as showing him as a tragic failure, a man who appreciated the necessity for all Mongols to unite in face of the growing menace from the Manchus, and who yet, by the very measures he took to realize his vision, alienated those whom he should have attracted. Contemporary sources illustrate his dilemma in contemporary terms. From the Manchu-Chinese side comes the judgement, allegedly from the mouths of Mongols who had deserted his cause, that Ligdan Khan had destroyed the basic principles of morality. Other Mongols are said to have submitted to the Manchus because 'the Chahar Khan has no moral authority (Tao)', because he had injured and destroyed his nearest relatives, deceiving and ill-treating them, and robbing them of families and herds. On the Mongol side a similar feeling emerges from the lamaistic phraseology. The chronicle *Shira Tuguji*, 'The Yellow Record', a mid-seventeenth-century work, writes:

> He exercised the two principles of government to a high degree, but through the force of karma, acts of insubordination multiplied among the khans and commoners of the Six Tumen, and, unable to keep them peaceably, he dominated the six great peoples by brutality, occupying the throne for thirty-one years.[1]

Almost at the same time another chronicler wrote, in similar words, that Ligdan, with his mind affected by anger, was unable to control his people peaceably and had to rely on military measures. The reason for this lay outside his own personality: it was because a cylical period of decline had set in, as is inevitable according to Buddhist teaching. Another, much later, chronicle, presents an incredible narrative that Ligdan's mind became possessed of evil spirits after he had drunk some poisonous wine which he had found beneath the ground. All these accounts seem to be rationalizations of the failure of Ligdan Khan to consolidate the civil and military reorganization of his people which we know from the chronicles he did try to effect, and to get himself willingly accepted as emperor. In the absence of explicit accounts of his policies one can only surmise that his opposition to the Manchus compelled him more and more to use military rather than diplomatic means to rally other Mongol chieftains to him, and that, as is hinted by his willingness to insert forged colophons into translations of scriptural works, he was motivated more by an opportunist and short-term regard for his reputation and his personal power as emperor than by any more far-sighted concept of a united Mongol empire.

At a time when Ligdan's actual military strength still exceeded that of the Manchu khan, the latter was able to pierce the essential arrogance which buoyed up his opponent. In a letter sent to Nurhachi in 1619, Ligdan had boasted of his title of Genghis Khan, the lord of forty *tumens* of Mongols, and had scorned Nurhachi as the petty prince of a mere three *tumens*, dwelling on the river banks. Nurhachi's reply pointed out that Ligdan Khan did not really control all the Mongols he claimed to, and sharply questioned his military capacity.

> What strong places have you conquered, what mighty forces have you defeated, what fear do the Ming have of you? And as for the gifts which the Ming make you, and which have not been so generous up to now, they are only tempting you with a wretched reward out of fear of my campaigns.[2]

Political arrogance in Ligdan Khan's dealings with other princes was matched by personal arrogance within his family. In 1623 Nurhachi addressed Mongol chieftains who had submitted to him and warned them not to put up with any insubordinate behaviour on the part of the Manchu princesses who he had given them as wives. The princesses of Chahar were accustomed to insult their husbands and ill-treat their followers, but any Manchu princess who tried to do the same would be punished by divorce, if the case were not serious enough to merit death.

More important, as we have seen, Ligdan Khan abused his vassals and allies by robbing them of men and beasts. For a nomadic chieftain without a firm agricultural or urban base, such wholesale reinforcements in personnel and movable capital were the quickest and surest way of recruiting lost strength, but throughout Mongol history forced transfers of wealth have been a cause of quarrels or litigation. Moreover, in a nomadic society, discontented followers could desert their lord and take with them all their possessions, to an extent that would be impossible within a settled, agricultural society. In 1628, then, the disgruntled Kharchin allied themselves with tribes of the Ordos, Tumet and others and defeated Ligdan Khan with the loss to him of forty thousand men. Immediately afterwards, a further three thousand Chahars, sent to Kalgan to get presents from the Ming, were intercepted as they returned empty-handed, and killed.

The Kharchin reported this matter to the Manchus, and proposed that the time was ripe, while the Chahar were in disorder, to unite and smash them. The proposal was acceptable to the Manchus, and a Kharchin embassy, headed by four lamas, came to the Manchus and an alliance was sworn. This falling away of Mongols to the Manchus was no new process. Some of the earliest to make terms with the Manchus had been the Khorchin, who had presented the daughter of their prince Manggus as concubine to Abahai, Nurhachi's son and successor as emperor, in 1614. The alliance thus initiated was reaffirmed ten years later when Aoba, prince of the Khorchin, brought his people under Manchu rule. During the 1620s, when the Manchu assault on China grew in intensity, the process of Mongol fragmentation was also accelerated. Meanwhile Ligdan Khan showed himself incapable of committing himself to a consistent line of action. Had he been determined to resist the Manchu advance at all costs, logic would have demanded an alliance with the Ming dynasty. Such an alliance was in fact concluded in 1618, and under it Ligdan undertook to protect the northern frontier of the Ming in exchange for subsidies. This proved an effective though only temporary hindrance to Manchu expansion, though Ligdan was probably doing no more than let himself be bought off for a while. He lived at peace with the Chinese for the next few years, but in 1628 made an excuse to attack and plunder them again, presumably, as was reported by the Chinese official appointed to investigate the situation, because for a couple of years he had not received the subsidies he relied on, and was destitute. The Chahar were reported to be poor and hungry. They had eaten everything up and their land was covered with corpses like grass. It is no wonder that even Ligdan's own Chahars began to desert him and go over to the Manchus. In December 1627 for example, a nobleman took his family and followers over. Ligdan seems to have lacked all sense of the necessity of persuading allies rather than bullying them when one's own position is precarious, and to have envisaged Mongol reunification as identical with his own hegemony. Not only amongst the Mongols of Inner Mongolia who were near at hand did his clumsy activities provoke hostility, but even in the far north-west of Khalkha and in Tannu Tuva, the Altan Khan, Ombo Erdene, asked the Tsar of Russia for guns to defend himself, should Ligdan Khan move into Khalkha. The possibility of acceding to Russia in view of the troubled state of affairs was even mooted.

Only one other prince, Tsogtu Taiji of Khalkha, seems possibly to have perceived some merit in Ligdan's efforts towards imperial restoration, but his association with the Chahar Khan led to his expulsion from Mongolia by his more cautious, if perhaps less far-sighted fellows, who had no wish to see Ligdan enter Khalkha: they kept in mind the old Mongol saying that:

When a king gets angry he destroys his realm: when an elephant gets angry he destroys his pen.[3]

In 1632 the Manchus organized a final blow against Ligdan, who, caught unprepared and without the will to resist, fled westwards with some 100,000 persons. This was a complete shift of population rather than a mere raid or military campaign on the part of the Chahar, for the chronicles tell us that Ligdan 'nomadized' westwards. It is evident that, in spite of his activity as a builder of temples and at least one city, his realm was essentially a nomadic khanate, not bound to any particular pastures. Even on this last flight, which turned out to be a rout with seven out of ten persons falling by the wayside, Ligdan managed to squander the support of any local Tumet and Ordos Mongols who might have been prepared to help him, by robbing and plundering. That he intended to re-establish himself as Mongol emperor is indicated by the fact that he announced his accession, according to old custom, before the relics of Genghis Khan which were, and still are, preserved in the Ordos region. He also took the relics with him, no doubt to use the possession of them to substantiate the legitimacy of his reign, and as a device to rally support in the Kukunor area for which he was making. This was no meaningless gesture: three hundred years later the Japanese were to try to capture the relics and use them in exactly the same way as a cynosure for Mongol loyalties.

What happened in the short span of life which remained to Ligdan is obscure. He died of smallpox in 1634, prevented by death from allying himself with Tsogtu Taiji and two other princes who had set themselves up in Kukunor. Surviving accounts of these last months depict him as an enemy of the Buddhist faith, intent, together with his allies, on destroying it. If true, this would suggest a strange alteration in his character, for both he and Tsogtu Taiji are well known as having been, in earlier years, great patrons of Buddhist learning, builders of lamaseries and schools. The explanation of the riddle may lie in the fact that Tsogtu Taiji survived till 1637, supporting the King of Tibet in his unsuccessful struggle with the Dalai and Panchen Lamas, the heads of the Yellow Sect of Buddhism. His activities inevitably involved him in the struggle of the Red against the Yellow Lamas, and the fact that he was on the losing side in this religious quarrel in Tibet may account both for the brief and slanderous references to himself in chronicles composed by adherents of the Yellow Sect, and to the enigmatic references to Ligdan Khan's sudden apostacy from Buddhism. That Tsogtu Taiji and Ligdan Khan were in some sort of alliance is evidently true, but the theory favoured by one modern Mongolian historian, that they were united in opposition to the Manchu incursion into Mongolia, would seem to go beyond the available facts. It seems more likely that Ligdan was hoping to turn his flight westwards into the beginning of a venture to profit by internal dissensions in Tibet so as to carve out for himself a new kingdom based on Kukunor. In any case, the alliance came to nothing, for Ligdan Khan died before the two could meet, and Tsogtu Taiji came to an obscure end fighting in Tibet. The patriotism for which they are now celebrated was quite nugatory, and disunited Mongolia continued on its path to full subjection to the Manchus. Those Chahars who had stayed behind, refusing to accompany Ligdan Khan westwards, were summoned to submit to the Manchus, and after the death of the Chahar khan, his people began to move back from Kukunor, led by his son, who surrendered in 1635 and who was married in the following year to the princess Makata, daughter of Abahai and his Khorchin empress. With the surrender of Ligdan's son, the imperial seal is also said to have come into the possession of Abahai[3a]: this is a Manchu tradition legitimizing, as it were, his succession to the inheritance of Genghis Khan. Mongol popular tradition denies that the seal ever came into the possession of the Manchus at all. The relics of Genghis Khan, which Ligdan had carried off, were returned to Ordos.

The disappearance of the independence of the princes of Inner Mongolia may be dated at 1636, when Abahai proclaimed himself emperor and adopted the name of Ch'ing for the new Manchu dynasty at a grand celebration attended by forty-nine princes of sixteen Inner Mongolian banners.

Khalkha Mongolia

With the personal submission of the majority of the princes of Inner Mongolia to Abahai, it was only in Khalkha, that part of Mongolia lying north of the Gobi desert, that eastern Mongolian independence survived, though even there it was only a qualified independence. The position of the khans was equivocal. For the rest of the century, until their definitive absorption into the Manchu state in 1691, they offered periodic tribute to the Manchu emperor, who enjoyed a position of quasi-suzerainty over them. But in comparison with the princes of Inner Mongolia the khans of Khalkha still enjoyed considerable freedom of action. The practice of intermarriage with princesses of the Manchu house, which was intended to seal the loyalty of the Mongol aristocracy, and was typified by the gift of an imperial princess to the son of Ligdan Khan the year after his father's death, did not spread to Khalkha till later. It was only in 1697 that a grandson of the Tushetu Khan Chakhundorji (1634–98) married a daughter of the emperor K'ang Hsi. During the next few years a number of similar political marriage alliances were effected. In 1702 the Zasagtu Khan was given the daughter of a Manchu prince, and in 1706 Tsereng, a descendant of Tumenkin, the first holder of the title of Sain Noyon Khan, was married to the Emperor's tenth daughter. Tsereng is in fact an outstanding example of the 'loyal' Khalkha noble. He had a long and honourable career as a military commander against the Jungars, and was rewarded by successive promotions in the Manchu aristocratic hierarchy. His final distinction was to have a commemorative tablet installed to him in the Imperial Ancestral Temple. The connections of Tsereng's family with the imperial line were reinforced late in the eighteenth century by the marriage of his grandson to another princess, a daughter of Ch'ien Lung. But all this was characteristic of the period after Khalkha had submitted to the Manchus in 1691, when the latter monopolized Mongolia's foreign relations. Up till then contacts at diplomatic level with various foreign powers was commonplace. The Tushetu Khan and his brother, the Jebtsundamba Khutuktu, frequently sent envoys to Peking and received imperial ambassadors in exchange, and, until the late 1680s they were in touch both with Moscow and with other Russian authorities nearer at hand. The Tushetu Khan still felt himself free to wage war, coming to blows at various times with Jungars and Russians, though he also felt obliged, it is true, to report his intentions to Peking and to accept some guidance from there.

At this time central Asia was on the move. The Manchus were expanding southwards, consolidating their conquest of China. Russia was reaching out farther and farther across Siberia, extending her sovereignty eastwards, and making diplomatic contact with Jungars and Mongols on the way. Ultimately she came into sharp conflict both with the Khalkha Mongols in Transbaikalia, and with the Manchus on the Amur river. A branch of the west Mongols or Oirats, known as the Jungars, were busily establishing their realm in west Mongolia and Turkestan, while other tribes of the Oirat federation under pressure from the rising Jungar power, were migrating east and west far from their original homes. Frontiers were fluid. Even between what developed into the Manchu dependencies of Inner and Outer Mongolia there was at first no fixed line, till the emperor K'ang Hsi first stationed guard posts between the two areas, so hindering the free movement which had still been possible even after 1636.

Khalkha itself was at this time roughly divided between three independent khans, all descendants of Geresenje, that one of the sons of Dayan Khan who had taken the majority of the Khalkha tribes as his inheritance, and had nomadized with them north of the Gobi. After his death, which took place at an uncertain date in the sixteenth century, his inheritance was divided up between his seven sons, and Khalkha was organized, after the common pattern of central Asian states, into a left and right wing. The left wing was ruled by Geresenje's third son Noonokh and was based around the Tula river, while the right wing, under Laikhur, the nephew of his eldest son Ashikhai, was centred somewhat westwards, on the Khangai Mountains. Members of Geresenje's family did not at first enjoy the use of the royal title of khan, but individuals acquired it later by different means. We have seen how Abdai, son of Noonokh, obtained it from the Dalai Lama, and founded the line of the Tushetu Khanate. Another descendant of Geresenje, Sholoi, took the title for himself, and became known as the Setsen Khan, nomadizing in the basin of the Kerulen river. Laikhur also called himself khan, and his son Suvagadai became the first Zasagtu Khan. These three hereditary khanates were added to in 1725 by the formation of the Sain Noyon Khanate out of some banners of the Tushetu Khan's domain. In the eighteenth century they took on a new character. From being groups of nomads, associated only vaguely with particular pastures, the khanates developed into territorial units with fixed boundaries. The khanates were no longer primarily the totality of the followers of the individual khan, but the area where those followers lived. The four khanates survived as the basis of the administration of Mongolia until even after the setting up of the People's Government in 1924, but the authority of the khans themselves declined sharply with the fragmentation of Khalkha into more and more banners of equal status within the khanates.

A fourth important khanate of the seventeenth century, but one which did not long survive, was that carved out for himself by yet another descendant of Geresenje, Sholoi ubashi, known to history as the Altan Khan – but quite unconnected with the Altan Khan of the Tumet – in north-west Mongolia. His pastures touched in the east on the Selenga and Tula rivers, and reached westwards as far as Krasnoyarsk. Sholoi ubashi was the first of the Mongol khans to entertain diplomatic relations with Russia, partly in order to develop trade and so offset the difficulties and uncertainties of trade with distant and troubled China, and partly in the hope of finding a source of military assistance against the threatening west Mongols. In particular we know that the Altan Khan requested expert powder-makers and gunsmiths from the

Russians in a mission sent to Moscow in 1616. But the Russians, who wanted to cultivate relations with the west Mongols, refused military help, and Altan Khan indulged in local reprisals. Relations were strained till his death in 1620, but talks were resumed sporadically by each of his successors. The second Altan Khan, Ombo Erdene, even swore an oath of allegiance to the Tsar in 1634 or 1635 and offered tribute, but no lasting relationship developed from what appears to have been a piece of political opportunism.

West and south of Khalkha and the Altan Khan lay the realm of the west Mongols. The early years of the seventeenth century saw the rapid expansion and consolidation of the power of the Jungar tribe of the Oirats under Kharakhula (d. probably 1665). This was based on the Tarbagatai region of western Mongolia and extended into Turkestan. Kharakhula subdued other Oirat tribes, notably the Derbets, while his expansionist policies forced yet another, the Torguts, to migrate farther and farther westwards until they acquired new pastures in south Russia, astride the lower Volga. Yet another Oirat tribe, the Khoshuts, moved into Tibet to take part under their leader Gushri Khan in the wars between the last king of Tibet, who was supported by the Khalkha Tsogtu Taiji, and the Yellow Sect of Lamaism. They established a unified Tibet, nominally under the Dalai Lama, but in fact a Khoshut protectorate under the son of Gushri Khan. Gushri and his successors actually spent most of their time not in Lhasa, but to the north by the lake Tengri Nor. Kharakhula took part in the war on the winning side, obtaining as a reward the title of Erdene Batur Khungtaiji and a patent from the Dalai Lama in 1635. Meanwhile he was encouraging the diffusion of Buddhism in his realm, building monasteries and towns, and attempting to persuade his people to adopt a more civilized way of life – on the one hand to abandon their old shamanistic practices in favour of the superior religion of Buddhism, on the other hand to settle down, in part, to sedentary pursuits. He built himself a capital city on the banks of the Emil river, and along with carpenters, masons, blacksmiths and armourers, requested from the Russians the gift of pigs and chickens, both of them forms of livestock absolutely unsuited to the nomadic way of life.

In building up for the Jungars a power capable of challenging the Manchu empire for the control of central Asia, Kharakhula, followed in this by his descendants, saw quite clearly that it was necessary for a secure and stable state to be based on a more permanent economic foundation than could be provided by nomadic herding. Trade with the more advanced cultures of Russia and China was systematically encouraged, but the Jungars realized too that home agriculture and manufactures were an essential condition of power. Galdan, the son of Kharakhula, had some of his subjects cultivate the land along the Orkhon river, well inside Khalkha, and also round Khobdo, where he maintained his base, and where, incidentally the Manchus established state farms to supply their troops against the Jungars in the next century. In 1724, when the Jungar power had risen to its height, a Russian envoy returning to Tobolsk could report that the Jungars were by then growing wheat, barley, millet, rice and fruits, as well as raising cattle, while as far as crafts were concerned they were manufacturing leather and cloth and working iron. They had trade relations with India, Tibet, Russia and China. The tragic instability of the Jungar empire, which led to its total disappearance in the mid-eighteenth century, may be traced to the perennial family feuds which time and again frustrated common action, rather than to insufficient economic and military preparation. Galdan's downfall in 1696 in his war with the Manchus was due, as much as anything, to the fact that his nephew Tsewangrabdan had picked that time to attack him in the rear, robbing him of his home base, so that Galdan, only a few years before powerful enough to annex all Khalkha in the course of a summer campaign, was reduced to hunting and to plundering raids on his former subjects to get enough provisions to carry on. Some sense of west Mongol unity was created by the missionary and cultural activities of the Lamaist church, and in particular by the immense labours of the Jaya Pandita (1599–1662). He not only translated, with the help of his disciples, over two hundred religious books from Tibetan into Mongol and at the same time carried on a vigorous missionary campaign, but also elaborated an improved form of the Mongol script for Oirat use, a script which has only in the last few decades ceased to be used among the Russian Kalmucks and which is probably still employed by the Torguts of China.

To the north the expanding power of Russia began to impinge upon Khalkha with the settlement of Transbaikalia, followed by gradual movement up the valley of the Selenga river. Relations between the Russians and the leading princes of Khalkha, and in particular the Tushetu Khan and the Jebtsundamba Khutuktu, were bedevilled from the very start by such chronic disputes as those over the construction in what the Mongols thought of as their territory of the fortress of Selenginsk, and the escape from Mongol authority of certain of their subjects. Yet Russo-Mongol relations were pitched at a relatively low key from 1672 when the first embassy from the Tushetu Khan and the Khutuktu reached Moscow, to just before 1688 when the Khalkha khans sought refuge in submission to the Manchus. There was a lively exchange of envoys between the two sides especially after the arrival in Irkutsk in 1687 of the Russian ambassador Golovin, who had been sent with a diplomatic and military force of some two thousand men to conduct negotiations with the Manchus at Selenginsk, negotiations which were finally transferred to Nerchinsk in 1689. Inability to settle the minor questions which were at issue led to fighting in Transbaikalia between the Russians and the Mongols under Shidishiri, the brother of the Tushetu Khan, who was very possibly acting at the instigation of the Manchus. Yet it was not this clash with Russia which was in any way responsible for the sudden collapse of the Mongols, but aggression on the part of Galdan. Whether he was acting entirely on his own behalf, or partly as the agent of the regent of Tibet who was pursuing his own policies in the name of the deceased fifth Dalai Lama, is not entirely clear, but the latter explanation of events is probably the truer one. Galdan certainly worked in alliance with the ruling circles of Lhasa and enjoyed their support. He possibly owed his easy succession to the throne in Jungaria to the influential backing of the Yellow Church, and in the summer of 1688, when he was on the point of invading Khalkha in reply to provocative action by the Tushetu Khan, it was to the Dalai Lama that K'ang Hsi appealed to restrain him from making war. All in all, there is much to support the attitude taken by the *Iledkel Shastir*, the Manchu-Mongol official register of the nobility of Mongolia, that the regent of Tibet was the vital force directing Galdan's activities and which led both to his own collapse and to the subjugation of Khalkha by the Manchus.

The history of Khalkha during the seventeenth century is complicated by the rapid emergence of the Lamaist church as a formal institution: it was not merely a religious entity but also, and perhaps primarily, an economic and political entity of supreme importance in the land. The Buddhist revival had, it is true, begun in Khalkha in 1586 when Abdai Khan began the construction of the lamasery of Erdeni Juu, and in Inner Mongolia the conversion had set in somewhat earlier. But institutionalization and the establishment of a hierarchy and an internal organization on a national scale, came later in Inner Mongolia than in Khalkha. Ligdan's megalomania had apparently scattered the nucleus of cultivated lamas he had assembled at the White Pagoda, and soon afterwards Inner Mongolia submitted to the Manchus, who throughout the century engaged in a diplomatic fencing match designed to attract the Dalai Lama to themselves, not seriously paying attention to the founding of a national church for the Mongols till the 1690s. In Khalkha the political role of the Church took shape earlier, about 1640. The decisive step was taken in 1639 by the Tushetu Khan Gombodorji (1594-1655) who had his younger son, born in 1635, accepted by an assembly of the Seven Banners of Khalkha as head of the faith in the land. The child continued his education in Mongolia until 1649, when he went to Tibet and studied under both the Dalai Lama and the Panchen Lama, receiving from the former the title of Jebtsundamba under which he and his seven successors were subsequently known. The motivation of Gombodorji can only be deduced from the circumstances of the time, since contemporary and later Mongol accounts are all cast in the devotional and hagiographical mould characteristic of chronicles of the period, and ignore realistic political considerations. The child's birth had been accompanied by holy portents, and from his earliest years he would recite the scriptures without having had any instruction. Yet it is quite obvious that these miraculous happenings are only clichés, adduced retrospectively to enhance the splendour of the saintly infant and to account for his recognition. They were repeated in one form or another at the birth of his successors.

What really moved the Tushetu Khan to make a radical departure in the organization of Khalkha, what led him to visualize and initiate a novel institution, that of the 'Living Buddha' or Khutuktu of Urga, hereditary by re-incarnation and not by actual lineal descent, which, though it could not have been foreseen at the time, was to be of decisive importance in guiding his people's spiritual, and to a very large degree worldly, development also?

It seems most likely that what Gombodorji had in view was the creation of some centrally attractive force around which the remaining independent Mongols could unite themselves. The fate of Ligdan Khan must have shown decisively that a secular hegemon would be unacceptable to his contemporaries. Gombodorji's political acumen resided in his realization of the possibilities inherent in an alliance with the Church, at that time the only home of learning, and, in Tibet, a disciplined hierarchical organism. How better to exploit such an alliance than by creating a pontificate, after the manner of the Dalai Lama in Tibet – himself in the third generation owing his title to a Mongol patron, Altan Khan of the Tumet, in the fourth a Mongol by birth, and in the fifth owing his pre-eminence to the military support of the Khoshut Mongol Gushri Khan – and to install as the pontiff his own son? In any case, the intellectual predominance of Tibet meant that the culture of a Buddhist Mongolia was bound to be Tibetanized to some degree in the future. Tibetan would be the learned language in church circles, and from the very first Tibetan teachers, church officials and craftsmen were welcomed in Khalkha to build up the church spiritually and materially. It may then well be that Gombodorji was also hoping, by the installation of his son, to forestall a possible attempt on the part of Lhasa to establish a pan-lamaist theocracy in central Asia, directed from Tibet: the outlines of such a policy did become clearer later in the century. Equally he may have wanted to detach his own Buddhists from too much dependence on Lhasa in view of the possibility of an alliance between the Tibetan Church and the Manchus. Certainly in 1637 the Dalai Lama had sent a high lama, the Ilagugsan Khutuktu, to Mukden, bearing a letter whose purpose it was to sow the seed of the Buddhist faith in Abahai's mind. The latter was highly pleased and proclaimed the lama the object of his personal veneration, and sent back presents to both the Dalai Lama and the Panchen Lama. Later, too, the Manchus seem to have tried to exploit the prestige of the Dalai Lama to attract the allegiance of the Khalkhas. In 1652 the Dalai Lama accepted an invitation to visit Peking and the question arose as to whether the Emperor should go to the frontiers to meet him. The advice given by his Manchu ministers was that he should, for this would help persuade the still independent Khalkhas to submission, whereas a rebuff to the Dalai Lama would affront them.

Whatever the actual motivation of Gombodorji's action, from the outset he enjoyed the support of his colleague the Setsen Khan Sholoi (1577–1652), and the Jebtsundamba Khutuktu did prove to be a magnet attracting the allegiance of Khalkha Mongols everywhere. Setsen Khan had already prophesied, when Gombodorji's queen, Khandajamtso, was pregnant, that the boy who would be born, in the golden family of Genghis Khan, would be the leader of the Khalkhas, and he occupied himself very much with the young child, and was on one miraculous occasion actually rocking him when three Indian sages suddenly appeared from nowhere and the baby tried to talk to them. He conferred on the child his own name of Gegen, or 'Brilliant' and the boy was henceforth known as the 'Brilliant Child'. Finally he sent his own soothsayer, who discovered all the marks of a true Buddha upon the child's body.

The unanimous acceptance of the boy as the head of the Church by the Khalkhas was most significant for the future. It occurred a year before a great meeting of all the independent Mongols – the Jungars, the Khalkhas, the princes of Kukunor, and the Volga Torguts – at which a common legal code was adopted, regulating internal affairs, the status of the Church, and common defence, in an attempt to establish some sort of Mongol unity. But no lasting agreement between the various parts of Mongolia resulted from this political manœuvre: the ambitions of Galdan, the future ruler of Jungaria, and the succession squabbles of the Khalkha khans destroyed any hope of Mongol solidarity. In contrast to this is the remarkable durability of the line of the Jebtsundamba Khutuktu, undoubtedly a powerful factor in maintaining the identity of the Khalkha Mongols over the next three centuries. His religious headquarters, known in Mongol as *Örgöö*, 'The Palace', a name which was corrupted by Russian travellers into Urga, became the focal point of Mongol loyalties. No single secular ruler was ever able, under the Manchu policy of dividing and ruling, to extend his influence and authority beyond his individual banner. Even the khans, at first the nominal heads of the khanates or aimaks of which their own banners formed constituent parts, soon lost even this minor preponderance as the hereditary aimaks became transformed into 'leagues' which were placed under the control of league chiefs, who were appointed in rotation and were not necessarily identical with the khans.

It was the Khutuktu, a spiritual lord almost without territory, but with enormous religious prestige, to whom the Mongols looked as the symbol of their national individuality. Urga, originally a nomadic city of tent-temples, began to attract Chinese merchants very soon after the Manchu conquest. From the beginning of the eighteenth century these traders penetrated Mongolia, heading especially for the towns and army camps, for Urga and, rather later, for Khiakta, in such rapidly increasing numbers that by 1720 it was necessary to license them and to set up a special office in Urga to supervise them and to check the licences which had been issued in Peking. At the same time as Urga was becoming the most important trading centre in Mongolia, it was also acquiring considerable administrative functions as a subsidiary to the main Manchu apparatus which was located in Uliasutai. It was the continual fighting against the Jungars in the first half of the eighteenth century, necessitating a base in western Khalkha, which led to the emergence of Uliasutai. With the Jungar collapse on the one hand, and on the other the growing importance of communications with Russia through Khiakta and the almost incredible efflorescence of the prestige of the Jebtsundamba Khutuktu, Urga demanded more and more attention from the Manchu administration, so that in 1758 Manchu and Mongol ambans (residents) were appointed there. Though Urga never replaced Uliasutai as the actual Manchu capital of Mongolia, it became the real centre of the country, and when in 1911 the Manchus were expelled, and the Mongols declared themselves independent, Mongol Urga was a natural choice for the capital against the smaller Manchu Uliasutai, while the Khutuktu, whose residence it was, was himself the only possible choice as king.

The first Khutuktu became an almost mythical figure. Magical stories were woven about him, and old tales were refurbished and attached to his name. He and his successors were adored by the people, whose piety was not offended by the Khutuktu's disregard of the Buddhist obligation to chastity. Like the eighth incarnation, who died in 1924, the first maintained a wife. A legend tells how some of the Khalkha nobles, who at first took exception to this, were put to silence by the lady's evident miraculous nature. The Khutuktu was an excellent sculptor and founder of bronze images as well as being a prince of the church. One day, while he was exercising his craft, some nobles came to remonstrate with

him for keeping a woman. His consort, who was known as the
'Girl Prince', came out of the tent, and the Khutuktu sent her back
to fetch what was inside. She came out again, kneading in her
hands a lump of molten bronze as if it were dough, and formed a
Buddha from it in front of the visitors' eyes. In view of such
evident holiness the nobles abandoned their objections and left
without another word. When the Girl Prince died, her body was
cremated, but her right hand survived the burning, and the
ashes from it were incorporated in the materials used for the printing of a religious book which was subsequently kept in the
Amarbayasgalangt lamasery, one of the Khutuktu's personal
monasteries. One of the aimaks of Urga was named after her.
Miraculous stories about famous lamas, whether real or legendary
persons, are quite common in Mongol folklore. It was only within
aristocratic and clerical circles that a feeling for historical chronology and fact was cherished, and found expression in the many
chronicles of the seventeenth century and afterwards. Amongst
the ordinary people there prevailed a naïve and undisciplined
imagination which loved to combine the famous lamas of the day
with all sorts of Buddhas and heroes from the fabulous past of
India and Tibet and great names from actual Mongol history in a
timeless kaleidoscope of fact, legend and hope. Stranger even
than the tales told of the Jebtsundamba Khutuktu are those
attached to the so-called 'Girl Khutuktu'. The 'Girl Khutuktu'
was said to be the re-incarnation of the Mongol prince Chingunjav, who in 1756 raised the standard of revolt against the Manchus,
who were just then occupied with their final struggle with the
Jungars, but who was defeated, taken to Peking, and executed.
The story of his revolt is factual enough, but Mongol fantasy
spun a tale that the emperor Ch'ien Lung tried three times to
kill him, but each time he was reborn. On the first two occasions
he was re-incarnated as a son of the Emperor himself, and these
two children were done away with. On the third occasion the child
had the foresight to be reborn in Mongolia as a girl, and so
escaped death. Since then the 'Girl Khutuktu' lived an ambiguous
existence, manifesting herself now as a man, now as a woman.
Strange tales such as this served to keep alive among the Mongols
their longing for independence from foreign domination. But the
fame and prestige of the Jebtsundamba Khutuktu rested on an
even firmer basis than mere popular superstition. At some time

during the eighteenth century he was provided with an artificial pedigree of fifteen pre-existences, as was indeed the practice with all important 'Living Buddhas', and the names of these are recorded in official documents. His immediate predecessor was the Tibetan historian Taranata, and the initiator of the line was a disciple of the Buddha Shakyamuni. Thus the Khutuktu enjoyed a double prestige among the lay and clerical aristocracy, in addition to his miraculous reputation among the ordinary people. He was the spiritual descendant of one of the companions of the Buddha and, at the same time, as the son of the Tushetu Khan, he was the lineal descendant of Genghis Khan. When he died, in 1723, the discovery of the whereabouts of his successor was manipulated so that he was reborn once again in the imperial line of Genghis Khan, as the son of Dondubdorji, the great grandson of Gombodorji, the father of the first Khutuktu. Dondubdorji had been married in 1697 to a daughter of the emperor K'ang Hsi, though the future Khutuktu was the son of a secondary, Mongol, wife, a girl of the Oirat Khotogoit tribe. This combination of clerical prestige and aristocratic relationship proved in the long run politically unacceptable to the Manchus. The second Khutuktu died in 1759 at the suspiciously early age of thirty-six, murdered, so it is thought, by the Manchus, and the Emperor ordered that future incarnations were no longer to be discovered in Mongolia, but only in Tibet. Until the eighth and last of the line, no Jebtsundamba Khutuktu enjoyed the prestige of the first. He was known popularly as Öndör Gegen, the 'Lofty Brilliance', as much on account of his great stature as of his spiritual pre-eminence. His features are comparatively well known, from a statue in Ulan Bator thought to be a self-portrait, and from smaller statuettes and paintings on cloth belonging to at least one European museum. Such likenesses must have existed in even greater numbers before the destruction of lamaism and the dispersal of religious objects organized in the early years of the People's Government.

There was, in 1636, no visible limit to Manchu expansion, though the assumption by Abahai of a new reign title, and the change of the name of the dynasty to Ch'ing intimated that the throne of China was the immediate ambition. For the khans of Khalkha, who had watched the disintegration of Inner Mongolia during the last years of Ligdan Khan, receiving and sheltering many of his disaffected subordinates, and then the submission to the Manchus of the remaining princes, there were, theoretically two courses open. They could ally themselves with the Jungar state, or they could follow their fellow princes, into adherence to the Manchus. The great meeting in Tarbagatai in 1640 may perhaps be considered to have been a tentative step in the direction of the former policy, but it was quite an ineffective one, as no real will to Mongol unity existed. But before even this assembly took place the khans of Khalkha had to seek some sort of accommodation with the Manchus, now their immediate neighbours. In 1636 therefore, they expressed their desire to remain on friendly terms with the Manchu Emperor, and in the following year they sent him a mission with gifts of camels, horses, sables, eagles' feathers and Russian guns. The nineteenth-century chronicle *Erdeni-yin erike* or 'Jewelled rosary', the fullest source for this period, but one based to a great extent on Chinese and Manchu sources, and expressing the official point of view, says that 'from this time, by imperial command, the Khalkha khans offered every year one white camel and eight white horses each, and so was established the permanent regulation of the "tax of the Nine Whites" '.[4] This seems to anticipate by some years the reduction of Khalkha to true vassaldom, for the tribute was not regularly presented until after the death of the old Tushetu Khan in 1655. But the atmosphere of the time can be appreciated from the tone of a letter of admonition sent from Abahai to the Setsen Khan, who was still trading with the China of the Ming Dynasty:

> The Ming are my detested enemies. Formerly the Chahar Khan, Ligdan, tempted by presents which were given each year by the Ming, obstructed me, preventing me from fighting the Ming, and even helped them, sending them his own troops. For that reason I set my army in motion and beat the Chahars. Heaven disapproved of the Chahar and so gave their state to me ... Lately you have actually been helping and exchanging horses with them. You should learn the lesson of the Chahars![5]

The Khan apparently respected these instructions, for in the same year, wishing to trade with the Ming, he formally requested the Manchus for permission.

Opportunist and unconcerted action on the part of the Khalkha khans against the Manchus still continued to break out sporadically over the next twenty years, however. In 1638 Tumet Mongols reported to the Emperor that the Zasagtu Khan was massing troops and threatening Köke qota. An army of Mongol troops supplied by loyal princes joined the Manchus on this campaign, but reports came in that the Zasagtu Khan had already withdrawn in some confusion. Abahai's words to an envoy from him on this occasion are characteristic of a condescending superior:

> Heaven has been gracious and given me all the Mongol state. Now I have taken into my care all the sons of the Chahar Khan. By rights, seeing your lord is in my hands, you Khalkha should live in peaceful submission to me. It is against your interests to turn against me and move on Köke qota.[6]

The next recorded contact with the Manchus is the occasion of a tribute embassy sent by the Tushetu Khan in 1644, the year when the Manchus officially succeeded the Ming as the reigning dynasty in China. Yet only two years later we find both the Setsen Khan and the Tushetu Khan in alliance with the rebellious Inner Mongol prince Tengis of the Sunit. Tengis belonged to those Sunits who had earlier fled from the oppression of Ligdan Khan and taken refuge, as had many other chieftains, with the Setsen Khan. In 1637 he had declared his allegiance to Abahai, and in 1639 had personally offered the Emperor tribute of camels and horses, and had been received in audience. In 1646, together with the *taiji* Tenggidei and others, he renounced his allegiance, and fled back to Khalkha with his men, presumably with the connivance of the Setsen Khan. The Manchus pursued them with a strong force. At the Setsen Khan's request, the Tushetu Khan furnished 20,000 troops for the protection of Tengis, now in flight, but these were heavily defeated by the Manchus at a place called Jajibulag. The Tushetu Khan retreated in disorder with the loss of over a thousand horses and camels. Tengis fled to the Selenga river, but later saw the pointlessness of his position, and submitted once again to the Manchus. He seems to have escaped punishment. The chronicle *Bolur Toli* or 'Crystal Mirror', describing this incident, says that he fell ill and died: his comrade Tenggidei was pardoned and promoted to the princely rank of *wang*. The two Khalkha khans evidently saw no further reason why they should continue in dispute with the Manchus after this, and offered their apologies, but the Tushetu Khan was at the same time in trouble over another incident. His relative Erkhe Chökhur had plundered the Baarin tribe of Inner Mongolia, now subjects of the Manchus, and made away with a number of men and beasts. Abahai sent a message of reproof to the Tushetu Khan at the time, refusing to receive the Khalkha envoy Erdene Toyin, who from his name was probably a noble lama. Instead, he dismissed him with orders that Tengis, then still a fugitive, should be surrendered, and the plundered Baarin men and animals restored. The Tushetu Khan asked for pardon, whereupon the Manchus demanded that he send his own son and younger brother to Peking as hostages. This he refused to do, and the quarrel was never patched up in his lifetime. The lack of solidarity in Khalkha is once again revealed by the fact that at this very time the Zasagtu Khan, who seems not to have been involved in the Tengis affair, found it appropriate to pay a state visit to Peking, where he was ceremoniously entertained by the Emperor.

By 1651 the Tushetu Khan had still not surrendered the plunder from the Baarin, but contented himself with sending an unacceptable embassy with ten camels and a hundred horses to Peking. Two years later the Manchus dispatched a special official charged with the task of investigating the matter, but Gombodorji just hid the disputed men and beasts, declining to hand over anything. That same year yet another crack occurred in the fragile Khalkha façade. One of Gombodorji's kinsmen, a certain Buntar, son of Rakhuli, the Khan's fellow commander in the campaign in support of Tengis, took all his followers and possessions and went over to the Manchus, who accorded him the rank of *Zasag chin wang* and granted him pastures near Kalgan. Gombodorji and Sholoi, both now at the end of their lives, were members of an older and tougher generation. Buntar's secession characterized the less vigorously independent Khalkha nobility of the second half of the century, who were to let the last traces of independence slip from their hands. Gombodorji tried to turn Buntar's flight to account, claiming that he had taken off the Baarin plunder with him, and that Abahai could recover it from him: at the same time he demanded Buntar's return. The Manchus refused to entertain this request, even if the Baarin plunder were returned, and when Gombodorji sent them the traditional tribute of the Nine Whites they refused to accept it, turning it back at Kalgan.

Relations with Peking changed with the accession of Gombodorji's son Chakhundorji in 1655. He recognized the inevitability of some concessions to Manchu power. After the defeat at Jajibulag the Setsen Khan had indeed tried to establish relations with Russia as a possible counterweight to the Manchus. The Russians, in their advance towards Lake Baikal, had in the 1640s made contact with a prince Turkhai, who was nomadizing along the middle Selenga. Turkhai was the son-in-law of Sholoi, whom he put in touch with the Russians. The first Russian envoy, Ivan Pokhabov, reached the Setsen Khan in 1647, and broached to him the prospect of becoming a subject of the Tsar. In 1648 Sholoi sent his own envoy to Moscow in company with Pokhabov. A further embassy under a certain Yerofei Zabolotskii set out from Tobolsk in 1649 to present gifts from the Tsar to Sholoi and to continue the discussions, but on the way it fell foul of a local Buriat chieftain, and the ambassador, his son, and some others, were killed. By the time the embassy finally arrived in Mongolia, Sholoi was already dead, and his widow Taikha and Turkhai refused to go on with the talks about assuming allegiance to the Tsar or to send another embassy back to Russia. Chakhundorji, however, seems to have had no leanings towards Russia, and in the same year as he succeeded he decided to send members of his family to Peking as hostages. To what extent Khalkha had by now fallen under Manchu influence is clear from the fact that in the same year the Emperor reorganized the country into eight banners, adding one to the existing seven, and dividing them into a left and right wing. He nominated eight *zasags*, or governors, for the new divisions, and though the names of the original khanates were retained, the process of dividing Khalkha into an ever-increasing number of small hereditary units, each of equal rank, seems now to have begun. The annual custom of presenting the tribute of the Nine Whites was confirmed, and in exchange each *zasag* was to get from the Emperor a subsidy of thirty ounces of silver, a tea-pot and dish, thirty pieces of silk and seventy pieces of cloth. New *zasags* had to offer tribute and report their accession to the Emperor, so that the rulers of Mongolia had already become vassals of the Manchus, though no taxes were collected and there was no interference in internal administration.

The process of disintegration and enfeeblement of Khalkha

took a new turn with the death in 1661 of the Zasagtu Khan. A dispute broke out between his elder son Tso mergen and his second son Wangchig as to which should succeed to the khanate. For some reason which is not clear it was in fact the younger son who succeeded, contrary to custom, but in 1662 the Altan Khan, Lobsang taiji, who had succeeded his father Ombo Erdene in 1657, chose to take a hand in the dispute, again for obscure reasons, and attacked and killed the new Zasagtu Khan. Tso mergen took his dead brother's place, but many of the nobles of the right wing, to which the Zasagtu khanate belonged, angry and upset by this usurpation, deserted with their followers to the Tushetu Khan, the most powerful ruler of the left wing. At the same time, Wangchig's uncle, Gumbe Ildeng, also fearing violence on the part of Lobsang taiji, took refuge with the Manchus, who duly allotted him new pastures and granted him a title in the hierarchy of Manchu nobility. He was the first important Khalkha chieftain to submit entirely to the Manchus since the flight of Buntar. Chakhundorji took the part of the murdered Zasagtu Khan, and made war on Lobsang taiji, who withdrew to the Kemchik river in present-day Tannu Tuva. Mongol sources, often inclined to telescope events, say that after destroying the Zasagtu khanate, he fled and joined Galdan, the ruler of the Jungars, but Galdan did not in fact appear in Jungaria until 1671 and we know from Russian archives that Lobsang taiji continued to maintain himself as Altan Khan for several more years, and was engaging in diplomatic exchanges with Russia until 1667 when the Jungars, under Sengge, Galdan's brother and predecessor, suddenly fell on him, took him prisoner and mutilated him. Little more is heard of Lobsang taiji, though Galdan is said to have handed him over later on to the Zasagtu Khan as a pawn in the political game he was playing. Certainly he never again influenced the course of events in Mongolia, and with him the realm of the Altan Khans, founded by his grandfather, disappears from history. However, the troubles which he unleashed with the murder of Wangchig continued to plague Khalkha to the very end. A relative of Wangchig's, either his son or his brother, succeeded as Zasagtu Khan in 1669 or 1670. The sources are at variance, and are not even agreed as to whether he owed his elevation to the Manchu emperor or to the Dalai Lama. Wishing to reassemble his scattered subjects he made several demands on the Tushetu Khan to return the fugitives who had gone over to him. Such demands were fully justified by Mongol traditional custom, and specifically so by the legal code of 1640 to which the predecessors of both parties had agreed. The Tushetu Khan made no haste to comply, and presumably the Zasagtu Khan was not in a position to insist. Not very much is known about the state of affairs in Khalkha over the next few years, and it is possible that the strained situation might eventually have resolved itself unobtrusively, had matters not been complicated by the rapid expansion of the Jungars under Galdan, and his determination to exploit a ready cause.

In late 1670 Sengge, the son of Kharakhula, the *kontaisha* or ruler of the Jungars, was murdered in the course of what appears to have been a palace revolution resulting from a conspiracy of two of his elder brothers with some others. At this time Galdan was studying in Lhasa as a disciple of the Panchen Lama at Tashilhumpo. That he returned to Jungaria and deposed the rebels is certain, but the circumstances of his return are not so easy to discern. The chronicle *Bolur toli* simply says that his mother told him in a letter what had happened, whereupon he renounced his monkish status and, taking with him three blessed amulets, one of which was made up with the nose-blood of the Panchen Lama himself, 'returned home and defeated his two elder brothers, taking his revenge upon them'. For a young man of twenty-six or twenty-seven, as he then was, apparently without a domain or forces of his own, it was a considerable achievement to secure his position so rapidly. We know that in the autumn of 1671, the year he returned from Tibet, he was able to receive 'in a proper manner' the Russian envoy Seitkul Ablin, who was returning from China, and who reported the changes in Jungaria on his arrival in Tobolsk in October.[7] Galdan was also able to send his own envoys on to Russia in company with Ablin. Galdan must have enjoyed more tangible support than his amulets alone provided, but perhaps his possession of them is symbolic of the prestige with which the authorities in Lhasa may have clothed him. There are plenty of indications that he did not return to Jungaria entirely on his own initiative, but was obeying the instructions of the Dalai Lama. The *Ildekel Shastir* says so definitely, and so does the official Chinese history of the Jungar campaigns, the *Shuo-mo fang-lüeh*, which remarks that the murder of Sengge caused such unrest that the Dalai Lama was compelled to send Galdan back to pacify his subjects. It may well be that the Tibetan authorities did not want to see the Jungar khanate fall apart in civil war as a result of a mere family intrigue, since the Jungar alliance was a valuable counterpoise to the influence of Peking, and already, as a Russian observer noted, some Jungars were beginning to desert the troubled khanate and seek more peaceful conditions elsewhere. From now on Galdan can be seen to be working closely with Lhasa, more especially after the death of the Dalai Lama in 1682, when his natural son, the regent Sangs-rgyas-rgya-mts'o, who had been appointed in 1679, took full power into his hands. Further evidence of this collaboration is provided by the episode of Galdan's intervention in the affairs of east Turkestan in 1678 at the request of the Dalai Lama. A chieftain, expelled from Kashgar by Ismail Khan, had appealed for help to the Dalai Lama, who passed him on to Galdan with a letter of recommendation. Galdan was glad to use the opportunity both to oblige the Dalai Lama and at the same time to establish the dispossessed chieftain as his own viceroy in Yarkand, where Jungar authority lasted for the next half century.

Galdan's first efforts were directed towards the elimination of possible rivals among his own people. Having disposed of Sengge's assassins he next fell on the *ulus* or appanage of his uncle Chökhur of the Choros while the latter was on a pilgrimage to Tibet, 'ravaging both fields and people', as Chökhur complained in an embassy sent to Moscow in 1674. The immediate cause of the dispute is not known, but as Chökhur's envoy was accompanied by others from Ochirtu Setsen Khan of the Khoshut, son of Gushri Khan and the father-in-law of Galdan, and from relatives of both chieftains, it seems fair to deduce that Galdan's ambitions were already generally recognized among the west Mongols at this early date. Galdan dealt with Ochirtu in 1678, forcing him to flee towards Kukunor, and so providing himself with a pretext for intervention in this area. It was this campaign, too, that provoked the first armed clash with the Tushetu Khan, who was related by marriage with Ochirtu, and who attacked a tribute mission of Galdan's in revenge. The matter is reported to have been terminated by the diplomatic intervention of the Manchu emperor, an indication of his contemporary prestige.

In the spring of 1678, the year after the Jungars sent their first diplomatic mission to China for two centuries, it was suspected in Peking that Galdan was ready for an offensive in the Kukunor region. For some reason, however, he refrained from action there. Why, is not clear. It may have been, as has been suggested, that this was at the request of the regent of Tibet. Another possibility is that he was concerned not to provoke direct reaction at this time on the part of the Manchus: many of Ochirtu Khan's former subjects had fled towards China and were negotiating for the allotment of pastures to them by the Emperor. Such, for instance, was Batur jinong, the son of Ochirtu, who was reported in October 1677 on the borders of Kansu province. Another was Erdene khoshuuch, a descendant of Chökhur, who applied later, in 1684, for Manchu protection. Whatever the motivation, Galdan did not move into Kukunor, but in the following year he received from the Dalai Lama the title of Boshugtu Khan, that is, Khan by Divine Grace.

This was a significant moment in the development of Galdan's career, for it was a public declaration that the powerful Tibetan Church was backing him. No previous ruler of his line had held this title, not even the great Kharakhula, and his successors, down to Amursana, were to be satisfied with the lower dignity of *taisha*. By implication Galdan was now the equal of the line of Genghis, to which he did not in fact belong, and the potential rival of the Manchu emperor for Mongol loyalties. The latter, after the enforced submission of the princes of Inner Mongolia, and his appropriation of what was given out to be the Mongol imperial seal, had been considered the legitimate successor to the previous Mongol imperial family. Galdan sent an embassy to the Manchu court, bearing gifts of armour, guns, horses, camels and sable-skins, to report the new title which he had acquired. The Manchus were reluctant to accept the precedent of recognizing a Jungar khan, but it was impossible to ignore the existence of the new state, especially as the Manchus themselves were still involved with the San-fan rebellion of Wu San-kuei (d. 1678) and his followers, and had not long before been faced by a Chahar revolt. The Chahar prince Burni (1650–75), son of Abunai, who was himself the younger son of Ligdan Khan, had marched on Mukden in an attempt to free his father, who had been imprisoned on a charge of disrespect shown to the Emperor. The revolt had a limited objective, and was defeated before Burni could capture Mukden: but the Manchus, who had denuded their old capital of troops because of the San-fan troubles, only managed to avert disaster by mobilizing an army of cooks and camp-followers and other military odds and ends. The Manchu court agreed, then, to receive Galdan's embassy and its gifts, and the Emperor furnished the Jungar khan with a seal, similar to those issued to the Khalkha princes, attesting nominally to his relationship as a vassal of K'ang Hsi. This can hardly have been viewed by either side as more than a diplomatic fiction to cover the exigencies of the moment, and the Manchus were never in fact able to manipulate Galdan as they did the Tushetu Khan. The real feeling of distrust which they cherished for him is reflected in the chronicle *Erdeni-yin erike* which resumes Galdan's actions in these years in the following words:

> Galdan, a man of the Oirat, was separated from his family at an early age, and went as a hanger-on to the Dalai Lama. Later he returned to the Jungar Oirats and deceitfully got a false reputation for himself of having received from the Dalai Lama the title of Boshugtu Khan.[8]

During the next few years several embassies were exchanged between Galdan and K'ang Hsi. The principal matter at issue was that of trade between the two powers, Galdan insisting on far greater facilities than the Manchus were prepared to grant. Galdan attempted to procure the admission of trade missions of several thousand men at a time, while the Manchus refused to permit more than two hundred to cross the frontier at a time, alleging the demands they made for supplies and the troubles they caused with the local population. This was actually a perennial pretext put forward by the Manchu and Chinese authorities for not admitting too many foreigners: thus when the Dalai Lama took up his invitation to visit the emperor Shun Chih in 1652, the 'bad harvest' was put forward as a reason why his entourage of some three thousand men should not be admitted to China. The Jungars were not, in fact, being singled out for exceptional discrimination. The Manchu position was clearly explained to Galdan by an envoy of theirs in 1683, but in 1684 he was still trying to get a trade mission numbering three thousand men admitted. Manchu attitudes towards Galdan, at first conciliatory, were beginning to harden, and although Galdan let K'ang Hsi know that he had informed the Dalai Lama of the restriction placed on the strength of the Jungar trade missions, this restriction was not relaxed.

In the 1650s Manchu policy towards Khalkha seems to have had the double aim of weakening the Mongols by encouraging the growth of a number of petty princedoms each theoretically of equal standing, and of exerting as much control over the course of events as possible without actually assuming responsibility for Mongol affairs. As the aggressive intentions of the Jungars became more and more apparent, Manchu policy in the 1680s was directed rather to settling the internal disputes which were weakening Khalkha, the next obvious field for Galdan's expansionist ambitions. The old Tushetu Khan Gombodorji had been succeeded by his son Chakhundorji who was much more disposed towards friendship with the Manchus, and as the dispute between him and the Zasagtu Khan continued to simmer, the lines of foreign partisanship began to take shape. Galdan chose to take the part of the Zasagtu Khan, while the Manchu emperor, ostensibly, and at first perhaps in reality, impartial and concerned to resolve the differences, verged more and more to the side of the Tushetu Khan and his influential brother the Jebtsundamba Khutuktu. If Khalkha alone had been concerned, it is reasonable to suppose that the weight of Manchu authority allied to the stronger protagonists might have resolved this dispute between princes, which did not involve the interests of the folk at large, but Jungar intervention made a peaceful settlement unobtainable. Galdan appears to have been determined to exploit the situation in Khalkha to provoke a showdown with the Manchus, and to do so he was prepared to take the part of the enfeebled Zasagtu Khan, who not only lacked the prestige universally enjoyed by the Khutuktu and hence by his brother, but whose effective military strength too was very deficient.

The Jebtsundamba Khutuktu was by now a key figure in Mongol affairs, Gombodorji's far-sighted act of 1639 having borne fruit. He was the only influential religious leader amongst the Mongols. The great Jaya Pandita of the Oirats, who was as much responsible as anyone for the Jungar-Tibetan entente, had died in 1662. Though he was re-incarnated in 1664 his successor was of course a young child who at first played no immediate part in public affairs, and who was in any case overshadowed by the immense abilities of the originator of the line. In Inner

Mongolia the Manchus had not yet approached the problem of setting up a supreme pontiff to offset the influence of the Dalai Lama.

On the one hand the Jebtsundamba Khutuktu enjoyed the adoration of the ordinary pious people of Mongolia: on the other he was related to the most powerful ruling house of the time. In addition he was a temporal as well as a spiritual lord. The nucleus of his wealth consisted in donations of serfs, or *shabi*, made to him in 1639 by various Khalkha *taijis*, or aristocrats, on the occasion of his elevation to the religious throne. Subsequent additions to this clerical feudal estate increased the Khutuktu's wealth to the extent that Khalkha was, in the eighteenth century, usually referred to as 'the four aimaks and the *shabi*' or even, somewhat later, as 'the five aimaks', although the Khutuktu's administrative office, the *Shabi yamen*, did not control actual territory, apart from the pastures of the Darkhat in the far north-west of Mongolia. Economically he became the equal, then, of the four khanates. But for Gombodorji's initiative in realizing the coming significance of clerical prestige, related to, but not identical with, the secular power, it might well have been the Dalai Lama who would have attracted the loyalties of the Buddhists of Mongolia, rather than a native grand lama. The Jebtsundamba Khutuktu was never a rival to the Dalai Lama in the sense of challenging his power in Tibet, but as the focus of piety and loyalty amongst his own people he provided an acceptable alternative to a Lhasa-directed pan-lamaist theocracy. So, in the long run, even after the Emperor Ch'ien Lung forbade Mongols to be 'discovered' as re-incarnations of the Jebtsundamba Khutuktu, it was the Khutuktu who turned out to be the only magnet holding Mongolia together throughout its colonial centuries. But in the short run his very position was to lead him into bitter conflict with the policies of the regent of Tibet as expressed through his ally Galdan. The personal antipathy of the Khutuktu for the Dalai Lama and the regent was in fact the pretext for Galdan's invasion of Khalkha.

The Jebtsundamba Khutuktu emerges comparatively early, as a figure of international political significance. Mongol accounts of his life, even the biographies devoted to him, are to a large extent mere hagiography, paying attention most of all to the miracles he performed, and the religious foundations for which he was responsible. But from other sources, particularly Russian diplomatic archives and Chinese historical works, we receive the impression of a busy statesman, a personage whom both neighbouring great powers had to take into regard. The Khutuktu was equally conscious of his position, at times even inclined to overplay his hand which, as can be seen after the fact, was not too strong a one. The first embassy from the Tushetu Khan to Moscow was sent in 1672, but when the next arrived, in December 1675, it contained a separate ambassador from the Khutuktu as well, in the person of the Manjita Lama. While on its way, this embassy had encountered the big Russian mission under Spafarii going to Peking. Whether it was from Spafarii that the Manjita Lama got a hint about the existence of a great pontiff in Rome, or whether the Khutuktu already knew about the Pope from the Jesuits in China or from Russians in Mongolia, cannot be decided, but at any rate, the Manjita Lama asked the Russians for help in continuing his mission as far as Rome. One wonders what the substance and outcome of such a mission might have been, but the Lama was tactfully dissuaded from pursuing the project, and does not seem to have pressed it. A certain political *naïveté* may have motivated this request, for the Manjita Lama, in spite of his rank and position, was so impressed by the Russian church that he also asked to be baptized, and had to be politely talked out of that project too. But in spite of these little whims, both Russia and China found it advisable to take the Khutuktu seriously and to keep in regular diplomatic touch with him.

The Zasagtu Khan was sure of Galdan's support. At some time the latter returned to him Lobsang taiji, the murderer of Wangchig, who had been captured by Sengge. Moreover, to some extent family relationships bound the two khans. The wife of Galdan's nephew Tsewangrabdan was the daughter of Tsenggun, the Zasagtu Khan. With this backing the Zasagtu Khan continued to demand the return of the fugitives from his khanate. In 1684 the Manchu emperor appealed to the Dalai Lama to intervene in the quarrel in Khalkha. As ambassador he sent, as was usual at the time, a lama, the Achitu gelung, with a letter recalling a previous unsuccessful attempt on the part of the Dalai Lama to effect a reconciliation. An envoy named Jarbunai had been sent to Khalkha to persuade everyone concerned to respect the Zasagtu Khan and to return the fugitives, but the

Tushetu Khan had failed to attend the assembly called by Jarbunai. Now in 1684 K'ang Hsi reminded the Dalai Lama – in effect of course the regent, who was concealing the Dalai Lama's death – that on the one hand all the nobility of Khalkha were believers in the Yellow Faith and devoted to the teaching and the personality of the Dalai Lama, while on the other hand the Dalai Lama himself was accustomed to send tribute to the Court at Peking. The return of the fugitives had been requested over and over again, but without success, and now the Dalai Lama should send a mediator once again to Khalkha to obviate the threatened outbreak of war. K'ang Hsi promised to send his own representative to take part in the discussions. The Achitu gelung duly delivered the imperial letter, and in response the Dalai Lama dispatched a high lama, the Semba Chembo Khutuktu as he is called in Mongol sources. But by ill-fortune he died on the way at Köke qota and the weary diplomatic round had to be resumed while the Dalai Lama was informed of this and requested to send yet another mediator.

This he did in 1686, appointing the Galdan Shiretu, 'than whom none was more highly honoured in Tibet'. That year the long-planned reconciliation between the two Khalkha khans took place at a general assembly held at Khuren Bilchir. The Manchu delegates included the amban Arani and the lama Achitu gelung, who had in the meanwhile been promoted to the higher dignity of *chorji* or 'King of the Law' by K'ang Hsi. On the Dalai Lama's side there came the Galdan Shiretu, while the Jebtsundamba Khutuktu took part personally on the Khalkha side. Arani read a letter from K'ang Hsi advising a reconciliation, and this was accepted with approval by the representatives of both the khans. The khans themselves pledged their friendship, and all embraced in an atmosphere of apparent sweetness and light. It was agreed that the fugitives should be returned to their lord, and Arani was able to report the complete success of his mission to the Emperor. However, this reconciliation within the Mongol world was illusory and short-lived.

Meanwhile the Tushetu Khan was having to turn his attention to another problem in the north, that of Russian penetration into what was traditionally Mongol territory. Though the Manchus maintained an attitude of ostensible neutrality in the internal dispute in Khalkha, they were clearly affording the Tushetu

Khan moral and material help and encouragement over the question of Russian encroachment along the Selenga river. K'ang Hsi was himself exercised by similar Russian penetration in the Amur basin, and viewing the occupation of Transbaikalia as a related part of the same process, quite actively encouraged Chakhundorji's resistance. Conversations between Russians and Manchus had been planned to take place at Selenginsk in 1688, and on the Russian side a large embassy under Fedor Alekseevich Golovin (1650–1706) left Moscow in January 1686. He wintered on the Angara river where in spring 1687 a Russian envoy, Venyukov, returning from Peking, reported to him that K'ang Hsi was trying to involve the Mongols in the Russo-Manchu dispute, apparently not without some willingness on the part of the Tushetu Khan, who was still trying to recover some subjects of his who had sought Russian protection. The Jebtsundamba Khutuktu was reported to be less willing to involve himself in military adventures, and indeed, throughout the next year or two he seems to have adopted a wait-and-see attitude, not committing himself definitely to either Russia or China. Golovin took this report seriously enough to suggest to Moscow that the point at issue with the Tushetu Khan might be reconsidered, but he got no support, and in any case the swift collapse of Khalkha in 1688 made any compromise unnecessary. After Galdan's invasion and the flight of the Mongols to Inner Mongolia, the Russians never again had to consider the Tushetu Khan as a diplomatic principal.

In the summer and autumn of 1687 Golovin moved first to Irkutsk and then to Udinsk in Transbaikalia. He was at this time still on friendly terms with the Tushetu Khan and the Khutuktu. His envoy Perfiryev had, it is true, not been received personally by the Khutuktu, as he refused to go through the required ceremonial and receive a blessing, but the head of the Khutuktu's administration, the Shangjodba, had received him, and the Khutuktu had promised to send back his own ambassador with a letter and gifts. In fact in the autumn Golovin received a joint embassy from the khan and the Khutuktu and their brother Shidishiri. The usual formal remarks were exchanged about friendly relations, and the by now traditional issues of the fugitive subjects of the Tushetu Khan and the Mongol raids on Russian establishments in Transbaikalia were given another airing. Golovin, however, had discerned how matters really stood in Khalkha.

THE LOSS OF MONGOL INDEPENDENCE

Realizing the close relations between K'ang Hsi and the Khalkha aristocracy, he did not hand over, or send to Urga, the letters which he had with him from the Tsar, putting forward the excuse that he had had to leave Moscow in too much of a hurry to bring them with him. The fact of the matter was that the letters proposed that the Mongols might make a move against the Manchus, and Golovin correctly judged that it would be wholly inopportune to present them at that time.

After about a month the Mongol envoys left for home, and at the very moment of their departure Mongol horse-thieves stole a number of Golovin's horses. The envoys were informed of this, and promised to settle the affair, but the horse-stealing did not cease, and after Golovin moved to Selenginsk in October 1687 he was subject to such repeated raids that he was practically beleaguered. Yet at the same time yet another embassy arrived from Urga, indicative either of a double front on the Mongol part, or, more probably, of lack of co-ordination of action between different princes. At the end of 1687 Golovin sent off two envoys, one, Korovin, to Peking to announce his arrival in Selenginsk, and the other, Kachanov, to the Khutuktu, with instructions to assure him of Russia's friendly intentions and to collect intelligence about the local situation. Kachanov, like Perfiryev, refused to perform the ceremonial obeisance, and was kept hanging around the Khutuktu's headquarters for about two months, trying to negotiate his reception and the initiation of talks. The Khutuktu's detention of the two ambassadors, coupled with his refusal to see Kachanov, was very likely motivated by his desire to see which way the wind was blowing in Peking first. The two Russians were kept in Urga until an envoy from K'ang Hsi had reached the Khutuktu. At the same time Golovin, in Selenginsk, began to get news from friendly Buriats that hostile Mongol forces were massing in Transbaikalia. Various circumstances, the fact that the Mongols had Chinese weapons, and that there had been considerable diplomatic activity between Peking and Urga during the detention of the Russian ambassadors, point to the probability that the Manchus were putting the Tushetu Khan up to resistance to the Russians, or at least not discouraging him. Yet all this time Golovin continued to receive Mongol missions, and in January 1688 was able to send back one Mongol envoy with a demand for the release of his two ambassadors. But as soon as their forces were ready, the Mongols, under Shidishiri, Chakhundorji's brother, laid siege to Selenginsk. They beleaguered it for two months, before withdrawing to prepare to face the greater menace impending from Jungaria.

Galdan was furnished with a pretext for military intervention in Khalkha by an insult supposed to have been offered by the Jebtsundamba Khutuktu to the Galdan Shiretu at the assembly at Khuren Bilchir. He claimed that the fact that the Khutuktu had been seated on a throne similar to that of the Dalai Lama's representative and had maintained an unfriendly disposition towards him was an expression of disrespect towards the Dalai Lama himself. He drew the attention of Arani to this in a letter in April 1687, and also reproached the Tushetu Khan not only with this alleged misdeed of his brother's, but also with his own anti-Jungar intervention on behalf of Ochirtu Khan, and with the marriage of his daughter to the latter's nephew, Lobsanggomborabdan. The Tushetu Khan reported the receipt of this challenge to K'ang Hsi in June 1687, and asked to be allowed to go to war against the Jungars, but the Manchus advised him to keep to his promises and not attack Galdan. They were understandably anxious not to become involved in a war whose dimensions promised to be very uncertain, for Galdan had for years past been on friendly terms with Russia, and was letting false, but nevertheless disturbing rumours get around to the effect that he enjoyed Russian military support. In the autumn of 1687 Chakhundorji got news that Galdan's younger brother Dorjijab had moved into the pastures of the new Zasagtu Khan, Shara, the son of Tsenggun, and that Shara and other princes of the right wing were on the move to join forces with him. Without waiting this time to report to K'ang Hsi, the Tushetu Khan moved to the attack. As soon as K'ang Hsi had news of the outbreak of hostilities in Khalkha he hurried an ambassador to the Dalai Lama to warn him not to let Galdan stir up trouble among the Mongols, and sent another, Bayar, to the Tushetu Khan to order him to halt his attack. These two missions clearly show the alignment of power and interests at the time. The Manchu emperor considered himself authoritative enough to deal with the Tushetu Khan directly, but sought the aid of the Dalai Lama to bring pressure to bear on Galdan. In fact, the damage was done before Bayar could reach Chakhundorji's headquarters. Shara had been killed, and Chakhundorji, with his son-in-law Lobsanggombo, had pursued Dorjijab and killed him too, together with his detachment of Jungar troops.

K'ang Hsi made a final effort for peace, summoning both Galdan and Chakhundorji to meet him at a place called Tsogdos nor. Chakhundorji apparently obeyed the injunction, but Galdan, having found a convenient *casus belli* in the death of Dorjijab, invaded Khalkha through the pastures of the Zasagtu Khan in early 1688, and advanced along the north side of the Khangai mountains, capturing a number of Khalkha chieftains. Occupied by these events, Chakhundorji had been unable to support his brother Shidishiri in the siege of Selenginsk, and on 25 March this was finally lifted. Galdan had allied himself with some of the Oirat princes of Kukunor, and after a three-day battle at a place called Tömör he thoroughly routed Chakhundorji's son Galdandorji, who fled with only one hundred survivors from his force of ten thousand. In April another Jungar army, led by the allied Oirat princes, captured the great lamasery of Erdeni Juu, the centre of Buddhism in Khalkha and, Urga still being a tent city, the largest permanent settlement at the time. While Chakhundorji retreated to the Ongin river, the Khutuktu managed to rescue his brother's wife and children and flee to Ögöömör in the pastures of Setsen Khan, hoping to reform there and help the khan. But just about then the Setsen Khan had died, and his people were in some confusion, so that the Khutuktu was constrained to flee still farther from the pursuing Jungars and, moving southwards from the Kerulen river he made for the pastures of the Sunit in Inner Mongolia.

The rout of the Khalkhas after the capture of Erdeni Juu was described in a report to Peking by Arani, the Manchu amban who was just then on his way to confer with Golovin at Selenginsk:

Galdan's army has thoroughly plundered all the people surrounding Erdeni Juu and has reached the place called Black Orkhon. It is only one day's journey from where the Jebtsundamba Khutuktu was. The Khutuktu, with the khan's son, wife, people, lamas and disciples, in all more than three hundred persons, fled away by night. The Khalkhas abandoned all their yurts, their vessels and tools, their horses, camels and sheep, and fled, night and day alike, in all directions. I do not know where the Tushetu Khan is. Some say that Galdan himself is with the army, and that nearly ten thousand soldiers are advancing by various ways. Others say that Galdan had not come himself, but that Dugar and Rabdan have advanced along the north side of the Khangai Mountains with six thousand to seven thousand men. It is quite true that they have killed Khalkhas, forced nobles to surrender, set fire to temples, and destroyed scriptures and images.[9]

Galdan continued to pursue the Khutuktu, marching up the Tula river to the Kerulen, where he received the news that his quarry had succeeded in reaching the borders of China. Meanwhile Chakhundorji had organized another army and moved towards the Kerulen too. Galdan abandoned the chase, turned and moved back in the direction of the Tula river, and again beat the Tushetu Khan in a three-days' battle at Olgoi nor. He scattered the Khalkha forces and very nearly captured the khan himself. But Chakhundorji managed to escape and to rejoin the Khutuktu.

Thus by the late summer of 1688 the Khalkha forces had been decisively defeated and were camping on the borders of Inner Mongolia, where they are said to have debated what to do next, whether to seek help from the Russians or apply to the Manchus. Submission to the Jungars seems not to have been considered, the experiences of the bitter campaign and the plundering and destruction it had entailed perhaps arguing against this. The traditional reason why the Khalkhas decided in 1688 to seek refuge within the Manchu empire, rather than submit to Russia, is said to have been the Khutuktu's insistence that the Manchus were of the same faith, that is, they were lamaists, and wore similar dress to the Mongols, whereas the Russians had a different faith and manner of clothing. This may look like a rather superficial argument, but taken metaphorically it does in fact make good sense. The differences of tradition, custom, language and religion between Russians and Mongols were enormous. On the other hand the Manchus spoke a language not dissimilar to Mongol, while at least in Nurhachi's time Mongol had been the language of diplomatic intercourse between the two peoples. The Manchu alphabet was an adaptation from the Mongol one. The Manchus certainly looked with favour on the development of the lamaist Church. Whether they favoured lamaism out of conviction or merely as a device to win friends in Mongolia and Tibet is another, and irrelevant, matter: as a matter of interest, however, we know from the memoirs of P'u Yi, late Emperor both of China and of Manchukuo, that right up to the end of the Ch'ing dynasty in 1911 it was the custom for shamans to perform their ceremonies daily at court. But then, Mongol princes, good Buddhists, also often kept court shamans to perform divination and other magic arts for them, without diminishing in any way the respect enjoyed by the state religion.

But of course, by late 1688 the Mongols had little room left for manœuvre anyway. The recently arrived Russians in their blockhouses in Transbaikalia, cut off from the Khalkhas by Galdan's forces, were insignificant in comparison with the known Manchu power, on whose borders the Mongols were now encamped. Besides, the continual friction with the Russians, culminating in the unsuccessful siege of Selenginsk, would in any case have made it difficult for the Khalkhas, in their present position of weakness, to have extracted any very favourable terms from the Russians. Nor was Golovin, now about to begin important frontier negotiations with the Manchus, likely to spoil his chances by a doubtful Mongolian adventure. Again, and this was an important consideration, though in the past some Mongol chieftains had submitted to Russia, and even at this time, after the Jungar victory, some had moved northwards instead of towards China, the Khalkha khans had before their eyes the attractive example of the Inner Mongolian nobility. The latter, partly through intermarriage with the imperial family which was encouraged for them but forbidden to the Chinese, were becoming integrated into the ruling caste of the time and were coming to occupy a privileged position in what was developing into a Manchu–Mongol ruling aristocracy at the summit of a great empire.

In the late summer of 1688 both the Tushetu Khan and the Khutuktu addressed letters to K'ang Hsi asking to be received as subjects of the Manchus. The latter's request ran in part:

> Suddenly the Oirats have come and burned my temples and destroyed my scriptures.... My serfs are many. If I could live in the protection of the Holy Emperor, my desires would be satisfied. I beg the Holy Emperor to allot me an area with good water and pasture, so as to show mercy on me. I also ask for the restoration of my temples.[10]

During the troubled summer K'ang Hsi had not shown any eagerness to give military help to the hard-pressed Khalkhas, even when the Tushetu Khan had asked specifically for this, referring to the long-standing tribute relations between the two of them. K'ang Hsi's advisers maintained that Chakhundorji was not a subject in the sense that the forty-nine Inner Mongolian princes were, and that only if he submitted with all his people would it be possible for the Manchus to confirm his title of khan and extend help. Manchu reluctance to intervene in what was apparently still a Khalkha–Jungar dispute led to the complete rout of the Khalkhas. At this point K'ang Hsi probably realized that he would have to provide them with lands and the possibility of recuperation, since otherwise they might well attach themselves to Galdan in desperation. His acceptance of their submission, on the other hand, brought the inevitable Jungar–Manchu conflict nearer, but at least ensured that the Khalkhas would not be hostile.

The Manchus were therefore constrained to offer the fleeing Khalkhas asylum within their frontier posts. The numbers involved were considerable. The Tushetu Khan and the Khutuktu were accompanied by thirty nobles, some six hundred lamas, and over two thousand households, in all some twenty thousand people, and later another twenty thousand joined them. Galdan had invaded the pastures of the Setsen Khan too, where disorder was increased by the successive deaths of two khans, and the minority of the third. The regent also chose to flee to China, bringing with him a hundred thousand followers. The Zasagtu Khan's remaining people had been dispersed. Some fled to Kukunor, his son was captured by Galdan and settled south of the Altai Mountains, while a third group fled to the Tushetu Khan's pastures. Following this general submission other Khalkha chieftains gradually brought their subjects in to join the Manchus. The economic burden they imposed was a severe one. They had been reduced to such destitution that the imperial granaries at Köke qota and Kalgan had to be opened for them, both to relieve their destitution and to forestall the possibility of their turning to banditry. In fact for the next hundred years the Mongol economy never recovered from the ravages of this and other wars with the Jungars, and between 1688 and 1772 the Manchus had to make over forty periodic distributions of supplies to them.

What subsequently happened to Galdan, Khalkha's evil genius, is not in all its detail relevant to the history of Mongolia. He managed to provoke the Manchus to war, and, losing his home territories which were annexed by his nephew Tsewangrabdan, he suffered a decisive defeat in 1696 and died, possibly by poison, the next year. What seems to have concerned him at first, after the victory of 1688, was not so much the question of Khalkha's political allegiance as the personal fate of the Tushetu Khan and the Khutuktu. He continued to demand that they be surrendered to him, accusing them of having offended against the religion of the Dalai Lama. Galdan must have realized the unreality of his claim, but perhaps he was using up the time consumed by diplomatic moves to strengthen his forces for the coming war. The Tibetan authorities publicly involved themselves in the matter: the regent sent a high lama to Peking to ask K'ang Hsi to accede to Galdan's demands, and hand over the two offenders to him, and so put an end to the whole matter. K'ang Hsi brusquely rejected this intervention. As time went on, Galdan gradually moderated his demands, later asking only that the khan and the Khutuktu be executed in the presence of his representative, and finally requiring only that the Khutuktu be surrendered to the Dalai Lama, but each demand was rejected by the Manchus.

Hostilities began in the spring of 1690 when Galdan moved out from his winter quarters on the Selenga, in north Khalkha, eastwards towards the Khalkha river, and plundered the Mongols camping there. Thence he moved into Ujumchin, and came into collision with a defensive force led by Arani. Arani was defeated and had to withdraw. The Manchus, unprepared for war, punished Arani for allegedly exceeding his orders by fighting, and sent a mission to Galdan disowning him and stating that the conflict had not occurred at the wish of K'ang Hsi. Meanwhile they mobilized a large force which they sent deep into Mongolia. Galdan was defeated at the battle of Ulanbudang and fled, and in his temporary absence from Khalkha K'ang Hsi proceeded to regulate the position of the Khalkha khans.

In the spring of 1691 he assembled a great convention at Dolonnor in Inner Mongolia. Some 550 Khalkha nobles, headed by the three great khans and the Khutuktu, attended, as did the princes of the forty-nine banners of Inner Mongolia. Soon after their arrival the Emperor too arrived from Peking, and officially received the Khalkha nobility in a specially-erected pavilion in front of one of the city gates. The whole affair was conducted with impressive pomp, and the official reception was followed by several days of feasting, games and military exercises, during which K'ang Hsi showed off his artillery. The Tushetu Khan confessed that he had been wrong to kill the Zasagtu Khan, and a formal reconciliation was effected between the nobility of the two wings. The incorporation of Khalkha within the Manchu state on the same basis as the banners of Inner Mongolia was solemnly proposed, not as might have been expected by Chakhundorji or the Khutuktu, but by the protector of the young Setsen Khan. Mongol historians nowadays talk of the 'treacherous nobles' who handed Khalkha over to the Manchus, but in fact there was no alternative for them but to act as they did. They could not be expected to look into the future and foresee the stagnation which was to overtake Mongolia a century or two later. And had they been able to look forward, they might still have preferred the prospect of a Mongolia subject to the Manchus, but at least in existence, to that of utter annihilation, which was the fate of the more recalcitrant Jungars in 1759.

From the Convention of Dolonnor dates the formal disappearance of Mongolia as a political entity. The khans were formally confirmed in their positions by K'ang Hsi, who distributed Manchu titles to their relatives, and the Khutuktu, originally elevated to the religious throne by the free choice of the Khalkhas, was now appointed Grand Lama by specific imperial command. Under Manchu control, Khalkha became during the next half century a military base. Economically she suffered greatly throughout those years, first on account of the complete disruption brought about by Galdan's invasion, and later through the requisitioning of troops and supplies for the continual operations against the Jungars, fought out to a considerable extent on Khalkha territory.

In 1695 Galdan was to overrun parts of Khalkha once more, but by now he had shot his bolt. He left his base at Khobdo and moved once more to the Tula and Kerulen rivers, and assumed authority over the Khalkhas, claiming the country as his and even issuing patents to the nobility to govern in his name. This was an empty gesture. Galdan was defeated by the Manchus, and Khalkha began to settle down under the new administrative organization being imposed on it. For the next two centuries it played no independent part in international affairs.

CHAPTER 3

KHALKHA IN THE EIGHTEENTH CENTURY

The Social situation

From 1691, the year of the Convention of Dolonnor, Mongolia's world position underwent a radical change. Up till then the various khans, though not entirely independent in action, had played some sort of international role. They had negotiated on more or less equal terms with Russia and Jungaria, as well as on terms of less than equality with the Manchus, whose nominal vassals they were. They had been able to trade with Russia and to send down their trade missions to China as they had done through the previous century or two. Nomadizing with their followers they were not restricted to particular areas, though the biggest movements did admittedly take place only under the stress of compulsion. But now Mongolia was to become a frontier province of the Manchu empire, cut off as far as was practicable from contact with Russia. She was to be organized on feudal-military lines, so as to constitute a reserve of mobile soldiery ruled by hereditary princes who were to be bound to the Manchu royal house by a system of hierarchical ranks and titles, by salaries and rewards, and by marriage alliances. Their allotted role was to be the protection of the Manchu dynasty in China. To use the words of K'ang Hsi himself:

> Of old, the Ch'in dynasty heaped up earth and stones and erected the Great Wall. Our dynasty has extended its mercies to the Khalkha and set them to guard the northern territories. They will be even stronger and firmer than the Great Wall.[1]

The Manchus pursued a double policy towards the Khalkha nobility. On the one hand they broke the power of the khans by reducing them in practice to the level of authority and influence of the other banner princes when in 1691 they reorganized the three aimaks of Khalkha into thirty-four banners: over the next century or so these were further subdivided till their number was almost tripled. But on the other hand they tried to preserve the pure nomadic character of the Mongols. They made little change in the structure of society, except to elaborate the feudal system with a proliferation of previously unknown noble titles. The basic division of society into nobles and commoners remained as before. But administratively they imposed far-reaching innovations, trying to forestall the contamination of the Mongols by contact with Chinese immigrants or by the penetration of Chinese trade and agriculture. They policed the frontier with Russia by means of a continuous chain of watch-posts manned by Mongol soldiers, which formed at the same time a frontier zone where the Chinese were even more strictly forbidden to resort. Late in the eighteenth century internal watch-posts were set up, too, to check the movement of Chinese inside the country. They mobilized and equipped the Mongols as soldiers, and even after the Jungar menace was eliminated and most Manchu troops were withdrawn in 1761, they maintained a regular Mongol army which was trained by such age-old methods as the execution of regular large-scale battue-hunts.

Manchu policy was essentially a conservative and reactionary one: in theory it was the antithesis of a colonial policy in the currently accepted meaning of the term, since it aimed to prevent the economic penetration and exploitation of Mongolia from the homeland. But in practice it turned out to be quite unviable. It came into direct collision with powerful commercial interests within China which it was not resolute or capable enough to curb. Superficially the Manchu policy achieved a certain success in the political and military fields. There were serious exceptions, but by and large the nobility of Khalkha loyally supported the imperial house. This was not a case of loyalty to China, but of personal loyalty to the ruling dynasty, a family solidarity which collapsed with the fall of the Manchus in 1911 and 1912. Noble families became inextricably entangled with the Manchus through marriage ties, and some of them provided minor dynasties of generals and *ambans*, or ministers, administering for the Manchus in Khalkha. This situation did not always make for harmonious relationships, for imperial relatives sometimes acted with an independence which would have been unthinkable coming from a mere subordinate official. An extreme example will be described below – the case of the second Jebtsundamba Khutuktu and his brother Erinchindorji. On the other hand, however, there were men like the general of Tushetu Khan aimak, Sanjaidorji, who played a big part in the suppression of the rebellion of 1756 and spent many years afterwards as Mongol *amban* of Urga. His mother had been an imperial princess, and he himself was brought up in the imperial palace. His wife too was a Manchu princess, and he was succeeded as *amban* by his son Yundendorji who held the post till his death in 1827. For over forty years of blameless service he was raised to the posthumous princely rank of *Ch'in wang*. And if at the same time the ordinary people of Khalkha were bled white in the wars with the Jungars, the Manchus did succeed in keeping them as a loyal military reserve throughout the dynasty, using them to suppress troubles in China and even against the English during the Opium Wars.

The reverse side of the Manchu policy was its permissive, if grudging, attitude towards the penetration of Chinese trade, with its associated usury, from the early eighteenth century on. Operating at high interest rates, and enjoying the connivance and even occasionally the active partnership of local officials and lamaseries, the Chinese merchant houses were able, in spite of the restrictions imposed from Peking, to overrun defenceless Mongolia to the extent that the entire country was in effect mortgaged to them during the two centuries of Manchu domination. When popular resentment against the occupiers overflowed into nationwide revolts in 1756 and 1757, its fury was directed partly against the burdensome military services of the relay-stations and the watch-posts, but even more against the Chinese shops, which were attacked and plundered. The nobility may have conceived the rebellion as a struggle for the expulsion of the Manchus and the reassertion of their former rights, but the ordinary people, laymen and lamas, and many of the minor nobility, were simply trying to get their revenge by ruining a class of foreign merchants.

The Manchus were quite uninterested in the economic or social development of Mongolia. To them she was primarily a reserve of mobile military strength, and what changes in her economy were officially encouraged were directed towards her evolution in this sense. Agriculture was an innovation pushed by the Manchus for the purpose of supplying the armies and avoiding the long haul out of China, while a huge area in Dariganga in the south-east was set aside and specially organized as a herding ground for the imperial horse herds. There is a theory that the Manchus encouraged the spread of Lamaism in order to weaken the military might of the Mongols and soften their warlike spirit. This is not a purely modern idea. It turns up in China in the nineteenth century, but there seems to be little actual evidence for its validity. It would have been in blatant contradiction to the military reorganization of Mongolia which the Manchus carried out, and from very early years it can be seen that the Manchus were aware of the danger of overmuch concentration on religious activities. In 1633 Abahai had realized what a divisive effect the Mongols' great reliance on the words of their lamas had, and their devotion to such practices as displaying streamers, building *obos*, and so on, so as to get their sins remitted, and he suggested that this should be restricted. The Manchus in Khalkha took steps to limit very strictly the number of new lamas, and also to discourage the concentration of religious power in a single authority. The Jebtsundamba Khutuktu was never the head of the Church in the sense of being a pope, in spite of his enormous prestige, but local temples were allowed a great measure of autonomy under Manchu supervision. Besides, it is quite clear from a study of the colophons of lamaist books printed in Peking, the great centre of the Mongol book-trade, during the Manchu period, that this printing programme, which was responsible for the issue of several hundreds of volumes, was in no way planned or encouraged by the Emperors. It was rich men and nobles from among the Mongols themselves who patronized printing, and who endowed temples and paid for the erection of stupas and of *obos*. For instance, between 1779 and 1783 a number of noblemen, mostly Khorchins, subscribed 140 taels of silver to pay for the cutting on wood blocks of the 130 texts of the collected works of the celebrated eighteenth century cleric Mergen Gegen, while a certain *taiji* Sherab, as is recorded in the inventory of the Inner Mongolian temple of Mergen Sume, having heard an exhortation to erect *obos* for the greater glory of the clergy, built one at that lamasery and presented it to the community. The names, too, of those patrons who had the hundred and eight stupas which surmount the huge wall of Erdeni Juu to this day erected, have been recorded. Such pious donations did not, of course, always of necessity come out of the pockets of the patrons themselves, but might be a charge on the local people. An interesting case is known from 1866 when a levy of sheep was made by the office of the Shanzav of Urga on the *shabi*, to make up a fund for the immediate restoration and subsequent upkeep of the tombs of the deceased Jebtsundamba Khutuktus. The three thousand two-year rams so collected were to be sold to pay for the initial work, and the ewes to be constituted into a fund for later running expenses. The local officials were to select good fat animals from the *shabi* under their control and send them to the lamaseries concerned without delay.

Comparatively few lamaseries in Khalkha were built with direct financial help from the Manchu authorities. Amarbayasgalangt and Dambadarjaa, founded respectively in 1736 and 1737, were two which were. The former was built with an imperial subsidy of 100,000 taels of silver, but it was thought unwise to let the Khutuktu live in it as it was rather near the Russian frontier, and Dambadarjaa was built for him farther into the interior of the country. A third imperial lamasery was the Tugeemel Amarjuulagch lamasery, popularly known as the Yellow Temple, in Khobdo, which was to have been built at the same time, but which was not actually constructed till the 1760s, after the Jungar wars. And even here, though the state subsidized the actual building costs, the *jas*, or capital fund, was set up privately in a typically Mongol way. A loan of beasts collected from within Khalkha was made to the lamasery, and the animals were to be returned to their owners after breeding for three years and so furnishing the *jas* with a nucleus of animals. The capital funds of lamaseries were established in various ways. The pious might present contributions, or the lamas collect alms from the people of the banner. A rich lama might give cattle and money from his own resources, as the *chorji* Dagvadorji did at Erdeni Juu in 1770. In later years, particularly, a banner prince might even extract compulsory contributions from his people as a special tax. Old people might present part or all of their wealth to a *jas* to ensure the safe conduct of their departing souls. There were even cases of rich lamas who had made their money from usury founding or supplementing a *jas*. Imperial contributions were a great rarity. The Khobdo temple maintained itself subsequently by its own efforts, living on alms received and on the income from its business enterprises such as trading and caravanning, as well as from payments for the performance of special religious ceremonies. Naturally, the state tried to exploit the influence of the Church as much as it could to further its own policies. In particular it manipulated the rediscovery of subsequent re-incarnations of the Jebtsundamba Khutuktu. But it took no part in the actual task of missionizing and converting the people or of distributing the scriptures for which there was plenty of enthusiasm without its intervention.

The conversion to Buddhism in the late sixteenth century meant at first a cultural renaissance in Mongolia, but under the Manchus this promise was not maintained, partly because the policy of isolating Mongolia economically and politically inevitably involved her in cultural isolation too. But if there was no great flowering of literature, neither was there the complete sterility and mass illiteracy that some modern Mongol apologists, from their one-sided Marxist viewpoint, have tried to present as the lot of Mongolia throughout the century. The bureaucracy needed recruits, and schools were founded to supply these. One of the earliest was the school founded at Khobdo in 1761 for twenty pupils, who studied Mongol, Manchu and law at the expense of their own banners. Official correspondence was transacted in Mongol within the country and in Manchu with Peking, the use of Chinese being specifically prohibited. This meant that direct access to the classical culture of China might have been a little more difficult to come by than would have been the case if Chinese were the official language. But the difference was only marginal and cultured Mongols were soon at home in the Chinese language. Indeed, the nineteenth century Inner Mongol writer and historian Injanashi takes his countrymen bitterly to task for being far more familiar with Chinese history and lore than with the great past of their own people.

The Manchu period was not only the time when the scriptures were translated and printed, incredible as this enormous intellectual effort was. The currents of two popular cultures flowed strongly into Mongolia, bringing in from one direction stories and tales from India as a by-product of the religious revival, and from the other translations and adaptations of the great Chinese romances which soon became some of the favourite reading of ordinary Mongols. The scriptures were reproduced in the form of splendid illuminated manuscripts, encased in decorated boards or leather wrappers, and also as blockprints cut in Peking. On the other hand the libraries of Europe alone contain enough examples of cheap copies of stories and poems, both native and translated, written out on brown Chinese paper of poor quality well thumbed, greasy and torn, to prove that the Mongols were lovers of books, not ignorant savages, and that there was material for them to feed their curiosity on. It is a strange but unhappily true fact that officials of the Mongol People's Revolutionary Party, which at least till 1956 lost no opportunity to spread the slander that Mongolia never had any culture before the revolution of 1921, were at the same time organizing search parties, as late as 1955, to go round the countryside confiscating and destroying the old books which people still kept and cherished from the old days.

The learned language of the Church was Tibetan, which was studied by all lamas who had any pretensions to learning, and much of the religious literature of the Manchu period – biographies of high lamas, church chronicles and philosophical dissertations – was composed in Tibetan, a language which would carry a lama through his world as Latin carries the Catholic priest today. At the lowest level a lama who perhaps never mastered the Mongol script and at the same time was not a real scholar of Tibetan, might still be able to read and write the peculiar type of Mongol spelled out in Tibetan letters, with which some well-known popular poets used to record their compositions, and which was generally familiar enough for Chinese shops, which catered for the religious trade, to find it worth while to use it for their advertisements.

The implication of all this is that Mongolia did not remain a static, stagnant society during the whole of the Manchu period. Important changes in the economic and social structure began to occur in spite of the official policy of conserving the system as it was. If we accept the useful, though protean, term 'feudalism' to describe the condition of Mongolia at the beginning of the period of Manchu rule, then we can observe certain expected developments taking place during the following centuries as feudalism began to break up – the decline of the petty nobility, the growth of towns, for example. Other developments, and in particular the emergence of a native mercantile class, did not materialize, mainly because the economic scene was overwhelmingly dominated by external interests, mostly Chinese, which took out of the country an enormous amount of capital wealth. As in Europe, the Church occupied a position of extreme wealth and power, broken only in the course of a long campaign by the People's government after 1924, whose aims were far more radical than, for example, those of Henry VIII in this country.

The minor nobility, the *taijis*, were originally the descendants of the family of Genghis Khan, but their numbers were increased at first by the Manchus. They had, however, no specific function to exercise during the dynasty. They were no longer natural military commanders, and as it grew the bureaucracy was staffed to a large extent by commoners as well as by the hereditary nobles. So the *taijis* gradually degenerated to the point where many of them became denuded of their personal retainers, and might even be taken on as wage-earners by those who were nominally subject to them. In the early nineteenth century their special status was also eroded by their being made liable to pay state taxes, like any commoner.

In the European context land is generally considered one basic factor of the feudal system. In theory, land in Mongolia was the property of the Emperor, who enfeoffed the banner-princes. In turn these allotted pastures to their subjects for their use. Direct rent was not taken from the herdsmen of a banner for the use of pastures within that banner, though if, by agreement, members of a neighbouring banner crossed over with their herds, rent might well be charged. However, the recognized *corvées* due to the banner, in fact to the banner-prince, from its members, were considered as related to the use of the pastures of that banner, as appears from a document of 1846. At that time banner boundaries were being regulated, and the office of a certain banner in Tushetu Khan aimak tried to reclaim herdsmen of its own who had been accustomed to nomadize in the next banner. The people did not wish to forsake their familiar pastures and return, and they submitted to the offices of both their own and the other banner that they would be agreeable to performing *corvées* within both banners if they were permitted to remain where they were.

The banner-prince had no right to sell or otherwise alienate land, though of course with time this prohibition was evaded.

In particular, much land passed to the Church: a prince might cede the use of land free to a lamasery, which would then rent it out to others, perhaps to Chinese farmers. But this was a later development. The theory of land control is expressed concisely in a letter from a banner office in Sain Noyon Khan aimak to the League Chief of the aimak in 1877: 'Only the lord of the land, and the *zasag* [that is, the banner-prince] subject to him, may control the grass and water within the pasture area. No one else has any authority.'[2] The basis of Mongol feudalism was thus apparently conceived of as control of land use, which in the circumstances of the country meant allotment of pasturing rights, not as actual possession of the land or ownership of cattle. Cattle – a term which in the Mongol context must be extended to include all the 'five domestic animals', the horse, camel, cow, sheep and goat – had from time immemorial been owned by both nobles and commoners, and there is no evidence that the latter got theirs in the form of a feudal allotment. Where allotments of cattle are known, they are of quite different nature, being gifts or loans of beasts to enable people to build up their herds again after a natural disaster or for some other reason. Some of the declining class of *taijis*, for instance, were given a returnable loan by the Emperor in 1701 for this very purpose of rehabilitating themselves, but this has nothing to do with feudal organization. There are also clear instances of a banner-prince preserving his authority and wielding it successfully in an autocratic manner, even to the point of driving his subjects to law in protest, though in actual wealth measured in head of cattle he was no better off than his average subject.

But the picture of all pasturing rights being in the control of the nobility is an ideal, and, consequently to a great extent, a false one. There were certain areas, notably the pastures of the watch-posts and the relay-stations, and the imperial pastures in Dariganga, which were removed from common use and reserved, under penalty, for the specific use of those to whom they were assigned. But apart from these special exceptions there were strong traditions alive governing the enjoyment of pastures which conflict with the tidy concept of feudal tenure. The idea that land was there for common use prevailed although the tribal system in which it had been normal had long since broken down and the Manchu territorial divisions were made on quite a different basis. The principle of 'first come first served' as applied to pasture rights was recognized, for instance in the legal code of 1709 known as the *Khalkha Jirum* or 'Khalkha Code'. This was generally observed during the eighteenth century and continued in force within the clerical estate up to the end of the dynasty long after the four aimaks had been subjected to a new code elaborated by the Manchus. The Khalkha Code says: 'If two men have come looking for pastures together and quarrel over a pasture, let the first comer take it. If they arrive at the same time, the first to shoot at it or strike it with his whip shall take it.'[3] This, of course, is mere legal theory, but actual cases arising during the dynasty show how the rights of the nobility were limited by custom and by the sheer economic fact that the richest man would be in a position to take the best pastures for himself, no matter who he was. This was largely because he would have enough transport animals to enable him to move about to better pastures more easily than his poor neighbour, who might not be able to muster the beasts to shift his household away from worn pastures. In such cases it was quite usual for a poor man to attach himself to a richer one, and get taken along 'under his wing', in the Mongol expression, in exchange for work. Our documentation for disputes over pasture rights is unfortunately rather late, dating mostly from the nineteenth century, but nevertheless it serves to illustrate the complications involved and to show that the idea of 'feudal' pasture-tenure is susceptible of considerable qualification. Late in the century a lawsuit arose between a banner-prince in Setsen Khan aimak and a rich man of his banner, one Wangchig. The terms in which the prince complained to the League Chief show the conflict between the real situation and the ideal 'feudal' relationship:

> The subject Wangchig farms out his cattle to others to herd for him as a duty, and lets them pasture on the broad, luscious pastures just like the prince's herds. He monopolizes the winter quarters for the beasts belonging to me myself, the banner *taijis* and the commoners and causes them loss. . . .

Even though banner boundaries were not strictly delimited till the nineteenth century, unlike the aimaks which had long been clearly defined, there was a strong feeling among the people of a particular banner that they were the common owners of the grazing rights within their own territories. Thus in 1902 a certain *taiji* of Tushetu Khan aimak got permission from the amban of Urga to nomadize into the neighbouring banner. The ordinary people of that banner took this badly, and smashed up the *taiji's* tents on the grounds that the amban had no power to allot pastures to others, the inference here being that they regarded them as their common property with which the Emperor's representative had no right to interfere.

The prince of a banner might well reserve good pastures for his own use at all times throughout the dynasty, and establish his right to them by sticking up notices, or having them guarded by police. But the reservation of sites by notice, or merely by common consent, was not limited to the nobility alone. Winter pastures especially tended to become the traditional preserve of those families who normally used them, and would be recognized as such, though the temporary use of them might pass to someone else if the 'owner' neglected them, or let it get around that he was not intending to use a particular site one winter. Custom seems to have acted against the rights of the nobility, though it did not of course extinguish them. There are many instances recorded of herdsmen being expelled from illegally occupied sites by their princes, even in the depths of winter. In 1878 a lama appealed successfully to his banner authority to have two commoners expelled from the pastures and waters he considered his: this was not a dispute between banner-prince and subject, but between persons of similar status. More and more, personal rights in land came to be recognized, so that winter sites especially came to be rented, or even bought and sold. Meadows too passed into private ownership. How far matters had changed in this direction appears from a lawsuit of 1903. A certain *taiji* named Sonom had built an enclosure, inside which he had grown and cut hay for many years. One year a commoner, Yondon, cut the grass inside this enclosure and the question of the ownership of the cut hay came before the banner administration. It was decided that hay cut on the open steppes was anyone's property, but that individual rights of ownership were vested in grass grown for hay inside an enclosure and cut there, and so the hay, although cut by Yondon, reverted to the 'land-owner' Sonom.[5] A few years later, during the period of theocratic autonomy, there were much more frequent cases of meadow land being rented and sold to ordinary people, an indication of the extent to which the feudal system had broken down in the years just before it was to be replaced by state socialism.

A further development away from feudalism is the growth of a bureaucratic system, hierarchical in its nature, supported by taxation, and responsible ultimately to the Li Fan Yüan or Colonial Ministry in Peking. Before the Manchu conquest the khans had of course had subordinate officials to assist them, but during the eighteenth century the Manchus built up an administrative apparatus of considerable complexity which lasted till after 1911, and which very severely limited the scope of action of the *zasags*. It was an all-purpose bureaucracy, in which no separate judiciary existed apart from the administrative and executive organization. What the *zasag* did in his banner was supervised from above, and lawsuits frequently went as far as the Li Fan Yüan for decision. Hence, even if the penal code was a harsh one, there were successive opportunities for the revision of cases and for the fresh interrogation of witnesses, and incorrect decisions or illegal actions on the part of a *zasag* were likely to land him in trouble, and he could by no means act like a feudal despot and hope to get away with it every time.

To take one example, what must at first have looked like a straightforward case of a simple-minded girl indulging in mere vandalism started its weary course in 1784 when a girl called Ombokh was discovered at night slashing the back of the tent belonging to the *zasag* of her banner and smearing the door with sooty fingers. She maintained that she was tired of life and was trying out an old folk belief that she had learned from her parents, according to which anyone who behaved as she had done would die. The matter went up to the League Chief and beyond, and before it had run its course in 1791 a whole series of people had been convicted of associated crimes, and officials from the League Chief downwards were found guilty of dereliction of duty, and different improper acts. In particular the banner-prince Urjinjav, a *zasag* who was more than once in trouble at that time for his bad administration, was found to have indulged in some very underhand dealings. The girl's father had earlier been implicated in the theft of some horses, and as he could not refund them, the girl had been handed over to the owner of the horses in part restitution. The owner had passed her on to Urjinjav as the equivalent of three horses he was owed, and the *zasag* had been keeping her as a household servant for five years when the main case came up. By the time the matter was finally settled, several of those involved were already dead and no action was recorded against them, but Urjinjav was dismissed from his post, and his superior, the League Chief, lost a year's salary, and the case was held up as a warning to the officials of the four aimaks to behave themselves in future.[6] Nevertheless, what legal documents that have been published show that justice, while thorough, was one-sided. A case, in its progression through the various instances, was likely to bring retribution on both the accused and the banner-prince or the League Chief who had allowed the situation to develop. But whereas punishments for commoners included execution, banishment to distant provinces of China, and beatings, the nobility usually suffered nothing worse than a temporary loss of salary or a reduction in rank.

The exigencies of the Jungar wars during the first half of the century led to the emergence of a multiplicity of taxes and *corvées* due to the state, principally in the form of work at the watch-posts and relay-stations, and at the State farms and State herds. The private enterprise trade system which the Manchus allowed to grow up led to increasing impoverishment in the countryside, which manifested itself in such extremes as beggary, the selling of children, and actual starvation. At the same time there emerged a class of vagrants who could no longer support themselves in their banner territories because heavy taxation and indebtedness had swallowed up all their cattle. They migrated to the growing towns, particularly to Urga, where the *jasaa*, or offices, representing the two western aimaks became known towards the end of the century as Vagrancy Offices, and devoted themselves mainly to checking and supervising pilgrims and immigrants from their respective aimaks. These vagrants formed a rudimentary proletariat, working for wages wherever they could scrape a living. However, they were relatively few in number and unorganized, and did not form the nucleus from which the present working class in Mongolia has developed. This latter is a conscious creation of the twentieth century when, after the revolution, the State gradually became the main industrial employer and the promoter of new industries.

Urbanization was not a new phenomenon in Mongolia. It had occurred in the past whenever nomad societies had reached a size and complexity which demanded a fixed administrative centre, agriculture and handicrafts. The most familiar example of the settled city, with food supplied from the outlying fields, workshops making tools and weapons, and with palaces, temples and dwelling houses, had been Karakorum, the imperial capital. In the eighteenth century towns grew up in Mongolia for a variety of reasons. Urga, long a nomadic tent city, was at first the headquarters of the Khutuktu, and only in the latter half of the century did the expense of shifting it every few years, after imperial sanction had been obtained, outweigh the difficulty of finding pasturage and fuel supplies, and the city settled where Ulan Bator now is. Uliasutai and Khobdo were at first military camps, and they developed into centres of administration later. Other Manchu camps did not survive the period of their utility in the Jungar wars, failed to change their character, and disappeared. Khiakta fattened on the trade with Russia as regulated in the treaty signed there in 1727. But whatever their origin, all Mongol towns soon acquired attendant trade villages, where the Chinese merchants congregated and carried on their business.

Commerce

The economy of Mongolia had always been concentrated on animal-herding: breeding is too refined a term for the comparatively low standard of skill and care involved, though methods were not totally primitive. The more enlightened princes, such as the nineteenth century To wang, who will be discussed more fully in the next chapter, possessed, and passed on in written form, a lot of lore about weather recognition, the need to isolate sick beasts, artificial feeding (mixed butter and brandy for the beasts on a cold morning) and so on. For that reason, foreign trade, in effect trade with China, was quite indispensable as a source for flour, tobacco and tea, and other necessities of life. During the Ming dynasty, and for some time after its fall, the initiative came from the Mongol side, and Mongol trade missions would seek permission to come down into China and sell their surplus horses there. Trade was closely connected with politics, and from the Chinese side there was never too great an eagerness to accede to the demands which the Mongols made for markets. At the end of the Ming dynasty the Manchus cut off trade between

Mongolia and China as far as they could, only relaxing their prohibition when, after 1644, their position in north China was assured. At the same time they needed to buy horses for their wars, and also to gratify the desires of the Khalkha khans and edge them away from commercial alignment with the Russians. Sporadic trading with Russia did continue until the late 1680s, but at the same time the Mongols continued to drive their herds of horses, camels and oxen down into China. By this time the Manchus were incomparably stronger than the sixteenth-century Ming had been, and so the Mongol trade missions had to behave themselves, and not act as piratical raiders, as they used to. Trade was allowed only at certain definite places, and the Manchus exacted customs dues, though these might sometimes be waived. Inner Mongols were forbidden to go to Khalkha to trade under threat of severe penalties.

These trading relations collapsed during the wars with Galdan, and when trade was resumed it was on quite a different basis. The Mongols no longer brought their animals down into China, but traded with Chinese merchants who came to Mongolia. It was no longer a matter of Mongol khans sending down their surplus beasts to exchange them for what they needed, or of tribute envoys doing some business on the side, but of the thorough exploitation of Mongolia by a foreign mercantile class for its own profit. Exactly when this change took place cannot be determined beyond doubt, but the extreme dates suggested, the early seventeenth century on the one hand, and the middle of the eighteenth century on the other, are both wide of the mark. There is no evidence of Chinese traders in Mongolia before the Manchu conquest, while by the middle of the eighteenth century loan-trading was so well established that its abuses were a main cause of the rebellion of 1756. Trade seems to have followed the flag. Chinese traders probably first entered Mongolia in the wake of the Manchu forces sent in in 1696 to bring about the final defeat of Galdan. There had been some illicit trading in relief supplies issued to the Khalkhas when they took refuge along the Chinese frontier in 1688, but this, though characteristic of such a situation, was without historical significance. The Shansi men who circulated among the Khalkhas in the last few years of the century were the forerunners of the many Chinese firms, big and small, and mostly from Peking or from Shansi, who set up shop in Mongolia during the eighteenth century. By 1720 they had made themselves conspicuous enough to attract official attention and the Manchus made the first of their many attempts to limit the number of traders going to Mongolia, the amount of trade they might do, and the length of time they might stay there.

About 1720 the Manchus took two steps to control the growing numbers of Chinese traders in Mongolia, most of whom were seasonal, and who in the early years traded round the bigger centres of population, the lamaseries at Urga and Erdeni Juu, and the Manchu camps, before returning to China. The licensing system, in force in Inner Mongolia since before the turn of the century, was extended to Khalkha. The regulations were severe and explicit, but there were so many opportunities for evasion that they had no lasting effect on the development of Chinese trade. Too many interests would have been harmed by their rigid enforcement, not least those of the officials in Peking, and later in Dolonnor, Köke qota and Kalgan, whose job it was to allot the licences, and who were quite open to bribery. In theory a licence, or *piao*, issued by the Li Fan Yüan, permitted the licensee to trade, with a maximum of ten men and twenty cart-loads of goods, at specified points. Before a year was up, the traders had to leave Mongolia and return their licences. The limitation on time was aimed at preventing the Chinese from establishing dangerous relationships inside Mongolia. The goods to be imported were specified on the licence, and the import of certain items, especially those which the Mongols might convert into weapons, was forbidden. Once inside Mongolia, the Chinese were still nominally under strict control. They were not allowed to marry Mongol women, to spend the night in Mongol tents, or even to spend too long in them by day, and they were forbidden to erect permanent buildings outside the special trade town at Urga. When in the country they were allowed to use only a cloth tent or *maikhan*, not a proper felt tent or *ger*. Such regulations, if rigidly enforced, would have stopped trade from ever developing beyond an elementary level, and there are several indications of how ineffectual they were in practice. As early as 1725 the first permanent Chinese shop was set up in Urga, while periodic checks throughout the country disclosed large numbers of unlicensed traders in the country. In 1792 there were, for instance, 214 licences due at Dolonnor which had not been returned. Licences were specially checked in the years from 1775 to 1781 and many Chinese expelled, but by 1800 a register of Chinese trading in Mongolia not only showed that they were there in large numbers – as many as two hundred in one banner – but that a high percentage had never bothered to get a licence at all. Ten out of twenty-seven in one banner were unlicensed, and so were thirty-three out of sixty-six shops. An expulsion of unlicensed traders took place in 1805, but as traders with debts owing to them were allowed to stay behind to collect these, and the Mongols were never in a position to pay off their old debts before contracting new ones, the expulsions remained a dead letter.

The other step taken was the appointment of a trade supervisor or 'judge' in Urga, followed by another in Khiakta in 1727. It is not by any means an accident that the first proper officials to be appointed by the Manchus in addition to the banner-princes were those charged with regulating the activities of the Chinese traders. Both posts were highly profitable ones, open to bribery and corruption, which was recognized to the extent that their incumbency was bought and sold in Peking. The Urga superintendency fetched as much as five thousand taels of silver at the end of the nineteenth century.

The economic strength of the Chinese shops in Mongolia, protected against Russian competition and never worried by the few Mongol merchant houses which grew up in the nineteenth century, rested on a double foundation, and was well able to survive the half-hearted restrictions imposed from Peking. They were backed by the great wealth and experience of the parent shops in China and at the same time, being organized on a semi co-operative basis, could extract from the managers, and from the apprentices who would one day have a tiny share in the capital, hard work and devoted loyalty. The partners, known as *ts'ai-tzu*, or capitalists, were the main suppliers of capital, and usually remained in China. The managers, or *danjaad*, a Mongol corruption of the Chinese term *tang-chia-ti*, were working shareholders, who took a small proportion of the profits and also received a regular wage for their work. It was rare for a manager to move into the capitalist class. The ordinary workers were wage-labourers, and the majority of these were young apprentices who would work for their mere keep for some years, and then begin to receive a small wage which would usually be carried on the books of the firm for them. Their ultimate goal was to join the manager class. The Chinese would come year after year to one place, or would settle down there permanently, contrary to regulations. They knew their customers through and through, and often took Mongol wives, becoming Mongolized themselves. That the regulations forbidding mixed marriages were evaded was common knowledge. In 1805 the general of Uliasutai decreed that those of the traders who were to be expelled as unlicensed who were married might take their families with them if they wished. Otherwise the families were to return to their original banners. From this it is perfectly clear that Mongol wives and mixed children were involved, and that usually a blind eye was turned to the situation. The traders would try to enlist the help and sympathy of local officials or lamaseries in one way or another. A *jas* might go into partnership with a Chinese firm in money-lending, an activity particularly prevalent in the nineteenth century, but known in the eighteenth as well. As time went on, and the shops got a firmer economic hold over the banner authorities, the latter would even provide all the expenses for the Chinese debt-collectors to roam their banner.

The other pillar of the prosperity of the Chinese traders was the actual commercial procedure. The Mongols were producers of primary goods, meat, wool and furs, and the supply of these was strictly seasonal. Besides, the Mongols were usually keen to unload their goods as quickly as possible, but on the other hand their own needs were regular and immediate. Apart from semi-luxury foods, tea and tobacco, they came to rely on the Chinese more and more for manufactured goods, saddles, needles, cooking-pots, and so on, including things they had previously made for themselves. But it was the obligation to pay heavy taxes in kind, and later in silver, at a definite and perhaps inconvenient time, or to find money to commute their personal *corvées* which involved them most heavily in debt. The Chinese shops, which provided an elementary banking system in Mongolia, were able to grow rich simply by usury, knowing their clients and their periodic needs, and profiting by the improvidence of many Mongols. Rates of interest were high, and there were many ways of avoiding the legal restrictions attached to them. Nominally a debt, charged at 3 per cent per month, was not allowed to run beyond three years, by which time the interest would have equalled the capital.

But it was beyond the capacity of most debtors to pay even this amount of interest, let alone the capital sum, and the practice soon developed of calculating interest and capital together at the end of the period, and issuing a new loan contract for the total sum. Or if a Mongol incurred a debt of the value of a lamb, this would not only attract the regular interest, so that after three years he owed two lambs, but the natural growth of the animal would be reckoned in as well, and the Mongol found that he owed two three-year-old sheep. Or a Chinese, accepting payment in the form of an animal, would leave it with the customer while he completed his rounds, thus squeezing a season's grazing and care out for his beast. Methods of trading were sometimes thoroughly dishonest, different weights and measures being used for buying and for selling.

It was the aim of a Chinese shop so to monopolize a particular banner's trade and finances that it came to be considered its banker or *tunsh* (a word derived from the Chinese *t'ung-shih*, an interpreter or guide). In practice this would mean that the banner would be carried financially by the firm concerned, to which it was permanently in debt. It is not known exactly when this arrangement first originated, but by the middle of the eighteenth century it was in existence all over Khalkha, and it seems to have been connected with the growing tax demands made for the support of the watch-posts and the relay-stations. The *tunsh* relationship was a legal one, preceded by negotiations, and its conclusion had to be reported to the League authorities, who also received the shop's accounts.

Obviously it was to the advantage of the Chinese to keep their customers in debt, and this general indebtedness of the Mongols to foreign mercantile interests which annually took enormous quantities of wealth out of Mongolia in exchange for consumer goods of much smaller value or simply in the service of usurious debts, was the fundamental factor producing economic and social decay during the eighteenth and nineteenth centuries. The burden of the debts fell ultimately on the people, whether it was their own personal debts which were involved, the personal debts of the banner princes, or official debts incurred on behalf of the banner as a whole. In theory only the debtor himself, or his guarantor, if there was one, was liable for repayment, but in the course of time there grew up the custom of apportioning out the prince's debts over the whole population of the banner, while banner debts also were of course so shared out. A private person might have his debt paid off by the community, but he was liable to get into serious trouble with the banner authorities if things came to this. In later years the fear of punishment on this score was one of the causes of vagrancy. There is a case recorded for 1746 when a certain Ölziit owed a Chinese shop at the military camp on the Orkhon river the sum of fifty taels and eighty cents, which he was unable to pay. The creditor demanded it from the banner to which Ölziit belonged, arbitrarily seizing five horses from the banner's herds. A lawsuit grew out of the affair, and it was decided that it was illegal for the property of third parties to be attached in this way. Nevertheless the system prevailed, partly because the Chinese creditors would blackmail the Mongols by threatening suicide. Under the existing law the person who drove another to suicide could be made accountable for the death. This seems an extreme step to threaten, but a case actually arose in 1752 in a banner of Tushetu Khan aimak when some traders threatened to kill themselves if a banner debt were not repaid, and the banner officials were constrained to share the debt out among the people and pay it off.[7]

Manchu taxation and administration

There were other factors besides the growth of Chinese trade and usury which made for the impoverishment of the individual, both commoner and noble, during the eighteenth century and for the progressive concentration of wealth in the hands of large undertakings, principally the Chinese shops, but also the lamasery treasuries which were beginning to lend money and to venture into commerce. The wars with the Jungars were not only fought out largely over Mongol territory, with the enemy penetrating as far westwards as Erdeni Juu in Tushetu Khan aimak in 1732, but tens of thousands of Mongols were mobilized as soldiers, and animals in colossal numbers were requisitioned for mounts, transport and provisioning. These were paid for, though at a low valuation, and one which decreased in terms of silver between 1730 and the 1750s, but of course their withdrawal from use, and especially from breeding, meant a heavy capital loss to the Mongol economy which drew its income almost entirely from the natural increase of its herds. The Emperor Ch'ien Lung missed this point when, in reply to the grievances enumerated by the rebel leader Chingunjav in 1756 he said that all requisitions had been paid for, so how could the people have been inconvenienced? Records are not complete, but what figures there are show for instance that between 1715 and 1735 the Manchu army took over 4,000,000 beasts from Khalkha. In 1728 over 3,000,000 taels of silver were devoted to buying up hundreds of thousands of beasts at low prices. In 1733 the general of the Tushetu Khan aimak reported to Uliasutai that there were not enough sheep available to make up the half million needed for the army, and asked permission to substitute horses at the rate of one fat horse for five sheep or six goats. In 1730 some ten thousand men were mobilized for military service from one aimak, Zasagtu Khan, alone, and their expenses fell on the population of the aimak. At the same time the Manchu administrative apparatus in Khalkha was increasing in size and complexity, so that taxation to support it fell more and more heavily as the century went on upon the tax-payers, ultimately the ordinary herdspeople. And as we have already seen, the people had to resort to the Chinese money-lenders to pay off their taxes and fell into debts they could never free themselves from. Even before the great rebellion of 1756 a number of leading nobles deserted the Manchus and went over to the Jungars in 1732, and at the same time the common people took the desperate step of plundering military stores and herds of animals destined for the Manchu armies.

Strictly speaking the Manchus did not demand heavy direct taxes from the Mongols in the sense of requiring contributions for the general expenses of China. Most of what was extracted by officialdom was theoretically destined for expenses incurred inside Mongolia. But this was only the face of the situation. Douglas Carruthers, writing in 1913, gives an idealized picture when he writes that the Mongols were never subject to great oppression on the part of their rulers, the Manchus, who preserved intact their rights, and whose yoke, up to recent times, had been a light one. In fact heavy, tiresome *corvées*, which, if commuted, cost far more than their true rate, were a continuing drag on Mongolia's development, especially as the most burdensome ones, the relay and watch-post services, were almost entirely military duties, at least as first conceived, and played no productive role at all.

There were some direct taxes due to the Emperor, deriving from the original tribute of the Nine Whites. The Nine Whites were presented annually by the four khans and the Khutuktu, and there were other tributary and congratulatory embassies dispatched to the Emperor on special occasions. Although the return gifts from the Emperor were often of considerable value, the Nine Whites consisted of much more than the notional nine animals. Groups of animals would be offered, together with all sorts of other precious and elaborate gifts and rarities – silver Buddhas and sacred utensils, scriptures written in gold, camels with silver nose pegs, and so on. But what was more burdensome than the gifts themselves was the expense of getting the tribute missions to Peking, maintaining them while they were there, and bribing a way through the metropolitan officialdom. There were other useless ceremonials to be performed too – reporting the succession of a new khan, maintaining the regular ceremonial attendance on the Emperor as aides, a service known as 'going to the Ch'ien-ch'ing gate' – and others. The incidental expenses of these excursions have been put by one Mongol historian as anything up to half a million taels of silver a year, and the services of one thousand five hundred men. When the *zasag* Dugartsembel of Setsen Khan aimak went to Peking for the 1832 new year ceremonies, his costs amounted to the equivalent of five thousand taels, including the expenses of six camels to carry ice for his personal use from the Kerulen river. A spendthrift or lecherous noble could run through a considerable amount of money in the shops and other delights of Peking too. There were also innumerable other minor extravagances. To mention only a few, there was the annual or twice yearly worship of various designated mountains, which had their personal herds attached to them for the upkeep of these services, and even enjoyed the possession of noble rank and the corresponding salary. There was the dispatch and provisioning of lamas sent in rotation to Peking and to Dolonnor to hold the regular services for the well-being of the Emperor, and the support of the lamas sent to study in the Tibetan school in Peking. Occasionally, but more frequently than might be expected because of the high mortality rate in the office, there was the escort of a newly re-incarnated Jebtsundamba Khutuktu from Tibet to Urga to be paid for. All these *corvées* not only cost money and labour but provided opportunities for bribery and speculation. One of the more imaginative episodes concerns a certain Manchu amban of Urga who went out to celebrate the spring worship of the Bogdo Uul mountain near Urga and was caught in a heavy storm. He reproved the mountain as follows: 'I came here to worship you as a duty, not because I wanted to. What do you think you are up to?' Then he condemned the mountain to a whipping and to wear fetters, which were deposited on its *obo*. Later in the year he came back and fined the mountain all its horses, confiscated them and drove them away, presumably to his own benefit.[8]

These taxes bore more heavily on the people than might have been expected. For instance, households liable to supply camels for the transport of their banner-prince might not possess any themselves, and would have to hire them from others, at a cost sometimes equalling the value of the beast itself, and over and above this they would be liable to replace any camels which died on the way. But the main exactions were those concerned with the Manchu administration, and especially with the military establishment – the maintenance of the watch-posts and the manning of the relay-stations, the herding of the imperial and army herds, the tilling of the army fields, and the manning and supply of armies in the field and, after about 1760, in training. Here too, developments led to unproductive increases in the cost of taxation. Irksome *corvées*, which fell due at places far removed from the home of the households concerned, came to be farmed out to substitutes, but of course for a money payment much higher than the valuation of the *corvée* itself. And not only did the number of *corvées* increase with time, but their scope was extended, often illegally, so that for example Chinese merchants were often allowed to travel by the state relay-stations. The relay services made very heavy demands on the country's resources. The main imperial relays and the services within each individual banner accounted for probably as many as three million head of animals in a year, according to one estimate.

A consideration of the watch-post system serves to show the type of *corvée* demanded from the Mongols. Between 1727 and 1765 a chain of eighty-two frontier posts was established along the Manchu–Russian frontier, seventy of them being a Mongol responsibility. They were of two types. The twenty-three Altai posts, under the control of Khobdo and Uliasutai were known as *sumun* or 'arrow' posts and were manned by soldiers serving in rotation. The forty-seven Khalkha posts, set up east and west of Khiakta were known as *ger-* or tent-posts, and were manned by families specially detached from their own banners and settled there more or less permanently. The general purpose was to prevent communication between Russians and Mongols. Each of the twenty-three Altai posts had a complement of from thirty to forty soldiers, at first under Manchu officers, later commanded by Mongol *tajis*, who served for a year at a time. Each soldier had to be equipped with armour, bedding, and four horses, and every five soldiers had to have a cloth tent. These supplies together with the mounts and provisions for getting the soldiers to and from their posts were a charge on their banners. The soldier's pay, eighteen taels a year, came from the treasury of the amban of Khobdo. The Khiakta posts were also organized on military lines, under officers appointed for a term of years, but the families detailed for duty there tended to stay, not least because they were freed from other *corvées* due to their banners and were also in a favourable position for engaging in the Russian trade they were theoretically preventing. In 1760 there were some nine hundred troops stationed in these posts, and in 1777, 1,230, together with their families. The banners where the posts were situated had to set aside land for them, amounting to about eleven thousand square kilometres in all. The Altai posts took annually a considerable quantity of animals and supplies for their upkeep – four thousand horses and twenty-five thousand sheep, to name some items. In one year, a single banner, that of Urjinjav mentioned above, sent seventy-two men to eight posts, their transport demanding 263 horses, three camels, and over two hundred and ten sheep and goats as provisions. The Khiakta posts, with their pastures, were presumably not such a charge on the home banners, but of course their pastures could not be levied equally over the country but were cut out of those banners which lay along the frontier and meant quite a serious loss to them, and there were continual squabbles between local herdsmen and watch-post soldiers over grazing rights. Apart from the main watch-posts there were a considerable number of internal ones set up to regulate the movement of Chinese, or to prevent the exploitation of mineral resources. The latter, the so-called Gold Watch-posts, are a particularly glaring example of the negative character of Manchu policy which tried to prevent the normal economic development of Mongolia lest this conflict with its character as a military reserve. The expenses were not particularly heavy. In 1904 the wages reached a total of only 9,630 taels of silver, but the implications of such a police service, which by then had existed for a century and a half and was systematic of a general reactionary, conservative outlook, were most grave for Mongolia.

Except in that it put the majority of the population in feudal dependence on the Manchu Emperor rather than on their previous lords, the khans, the organization imposed on Khalkha by the Manchus in and after 1691 hardly affected the existing social order. Even the military system was not a new one, but, as the Mongol historian Natsagdorj shows, an adaptation of the old Mongol decimal system. Some new terms were introduced, replacing those Mongol terms which had fallen into disuse. The *sumun* for instance, a subdivision of the banner, was an imitation of the Manchu *niru*, both words meaning 'arrow'. But banners themselves had existed before the Manchus, and some of the old terminology survived much longer, especially in the ecclesiastical estates, which continued to be organized in units called *otog*, a word which dropped out of the vocabulary of the Khalkha state administration.

Apart from the *sumun*-people (*sumyn ard*), as the imperial subjects were called, and who formed units of a nominal male population of 150 soldiers, there was the class of so-called *khamjilga* or personal retainers of the *zasags* and *taijis*, left to them for their economic support by the Manchus. At first, and in theory throughout the dynasty, the *zasags' khamjilgas* were exempt from state *corvées* and were liable to serve only their overlords, while the *taijis' khamjilgas* were liable to some state *corvées*. This is how a *khamjilga* could describe his life at the beginning of the present century:

I used to be a *khamjilga* of Naidan taiji. Originally, the *khamilgas* of a *taiji* did not go for soldiers. But they used to perform quasi-military duties, such as army transport and so on. We used to do unpaid work like herding the *taiji's* horses, collecting dried dung (for fuel), shifting pastures, breaking horses, and so on. We were a poor family with ten-odd sheep and goats and two horses, and with no other beasts or property.[9]

Nobles often tried to get the richer members of the commonalty transferred to them as *khamjilgas*. But the distinction between imperial subjects and *khamjilgas* was always somewhat blurred, at least as far as the performance of duties was concerned, and became less clear as time went on. Nobles would extract personal *alba* or *corvée* from imperial subjects, while the progressive impoverishment of Mongolia meant that imperial subjects could no longer support the tax burden on their own, and the *khamjilgas* began to be made liable for state *corvées*.

A peculiar feature of the Mongol social order was the emergence of ecclesiastical estates, of which by far the most important was the estate of the Jebtsundamba Khutuktu, the so-called 'Great Shabi'. *Shabi* is a word originally meaning 'disciple', but later designating those persons who belonged to the estate of a Khutuktu and having a status similar to that of a serf, and then coming to embrace the estate made up by such serfs, and more loosely, the administration in charge of it. The foundations of the Great Shabi were laid in 1639 when the first donations of subjects were made to the child Khutuktu, but although soon afterwards he acquired experienced lamas from Tibet to make up an administrative establishment, it was only in 1723 that the Great Shabi was formally removed from the control of the Tushetu Khan and put under an independent official. This was the Shanzav or Shanzodba, an administrator whose title appears rather earlier than this in Mongol history, but who from 1723 onwards received his appointment from the Manchu emperor. A century later he was to be granted authority equal to that of a League Chief.

Church serfs were exempted from most state taxes and *corvées* and their relationship to the high lama whose subjects they were was similar to that of the *khamjilga* to his overlord. The few state taxes which the *shabi* did have to contribute to, for instance part of the upkeep of the office of the Urga ambans, were negligible besides the services they more normally rendered the Church. But as time went on there were small invasions even of their rights, as in 1870 when troops were levied from the *shabi* as well as the ordinary people to make up an army of some twenty thousand men at the time of the Moslem insurrection. But whereas the *khamjilga* tended to fuse with the imperial subjects as time went on, though their legal status was still distinct, the Great Shabi flourished on a level of political prestige and economic wealth equal to, and distinct from, that of any of the four aimaks, and after 1911, when the Khutuktu became king, it enjoyed an even more favoured and cosseted position. Its peculiar status was recognized under the People's Government when, for a short time, the Great *Shabi*, abolished as a religious unit, was constituted a separate aimak, but one which, unlike the existing four aimaks of Khalkha, lacked territory and consisted of people only – an interesting confirmation of the fact that in nomadic society what is really relevant is not land but men and animals.

For the first quarter of the eighteenth century Mongolia had no central aimak organization. Each banner had its office, but the khans had been reduced to the level of the other banner-princes and did not control them. It was in 1728, after the creation of the fourth aimak, Sain Noyon Khan, that the aimaks were, for administrative purposes, re-designated leagues, and given new names with topographical rather than personal associations, and were put under the control of League Chiefs who were appointed by the Emperor through the Li Fan Yüan. The League was the supreme authority in the aimak territory, which was coterminous with it, and the nobility of each league was supposed to gather every three years to discuss the apportionment of taxes, the settlement of boundary disputes, and the disposal of outstanding legal cases. Soon after the setting up of the leagues, the generalship of Uliasutai emerged as a permanent appointment, first as ancillary to the Manchu commander-in-chief in Mongolia, then as the office of an administrative official supervising, to begin with, the whole of Khalkha. The first three generals were Mongols, but from the 1780s onwards a Manchu was always appointed, with the assistance of two advisory ambans, one a Mongol and one a Manchu. Uliasutai soon became overburdened with work, and in 1758 the two eastern aimaks, Tushetu Khan and Setsen Khan, and the Great *Shabi*, were put under a new yamen set up in Urga under a Mongol and a Manchu amban serving concurrently, the Mongol at first being the senior, but in the middle of the nineteenth century yielding place to the Manchu. After the suppression of the Jungars and the final incorporation of Khobdo in Mongolia, a similar office was set up in the town of Khobdo to govern the predominantly non-Khalkha population of the west. These various officials, with the trade supervisors at Urga and Khiakta, were at the apex of the Manchu administration. Below them was a pyramid of league, banner and *sumun* officials, all Mongols, the lower levels of which maintained contact upwards by means of the *jasaa* or system of permanent representation with a staff serving for a fixed period of time.

As an example, the four generals of the Khalkha aimaks would in turn take their seals to Uliasutai and form the *jasaa* there for three months at a time, working under the permanent general. They might of course send a substitute rather than go personally. At the same time, each of the four aimaks would maintain its own *jasaa* at Uliasutai too, the officials serving for a fixed number of months at a time. This complex apparatus cost a considerable amount, for all the *jasaa* officials had to be supported by their local administrative unit, and transport expenses for the regular comings and goings had to be found too. While the banner office might be staffed on a very modest scale, at the other extreme the establishment of the ambans at Urga was not a negligible one, reaching in the early twentieth century a total of some 170 men, from the two ambans with their secretaries, interpreters and guards, down to door-keepers, powder-house guards, and police. This proliferation of bureaucrats accompanied a slow change in the social composition of Mongolia. The Manchus aimed, broadly speaking, as we have mentioned, at conserving the nomadic organization of the Mongols in isolation from her neighbours, and tried to achieve this by hindering the development of those factors which made for settlement, urbanization and specialization of labour. Yet these processes were nevertheless going on all the time, in spite of the Manchus who never exercised anything like totalitarian control over Mongolia. The phenomenon of a hierarchical civil service, based on territorial divisions, and initiating a mass of correspondence which travelled up and down the official ladder and might also be copied to interested offices on the same level as the initiator, was itself one of these undesirable factors. The growth of the church was another. Though many lamas returned to secular life, even taking wives and bringing up families, a large proportion continued to live in their lamaseries, which gradually formed the nucleus of towns, markets and agricultural areas. The towns themselves slowly expanded, attracting craftsmen, farmers, petty traders, day labourers and rogues. The need to staff the numerous watch-posts and relay stations alone meant that many hundreds of households were tied down, either for a period of time, or indefinitely, to certain designated areas and jobs. The relay-stations were organized as independent bases, each with an area of pasture land around it, and were staffed by a fixed number of 'households', the household in this sense being a notional unit which might require the services of more than one actual household to keep it up to strength. Many of the relay services were actually manned by Kharchins who had been transferred from Inner Mongolia, but others were manned by Khalkhas, and as the eighteenth century wore on, the Kharchins stopped receiving reinforcements and supplies from their home areas, and these had to be furnished by the local Khalkha population. One Mongol historian lists a total of around 120 bases in the eighteenth century, manned by 1,326 households, apart from the local relay services within individual aimaks. The frontier watch-posts, too, had their allotted pastures with households more or less permanently settled on them.

The workers in the army fields and in the official herds at Khobdo formed yet another settled element of the population, for the difficulties inherent in keeping up, over the huge distances of Mongolia, the theoretical system of rotating labour, meant that the farmers tended in practice to stay at their fields. The first farmers had been Tumets, imported in 1716 from Inner Mongolia, but the official fields which were set up at Khobdo in 1762 were worked by four hundred households specially detailed from inside Khalkha.

Finally, movement inside Khalkha was inhibited by the division of the country into banners and a number of temple areas, whose boundaries the herdsmen were normally forbidden to cross. Prominent points along the boundaries were marked out on the ground by means of *obos*, and each banner had to submit maps of its territory to the Li Fan Yuan at intervals of ten years. The size and population of a banner varied so greatly that no realistic average size can be given. Temple territories were generally small: the territory of the Narabanchen lamasery, south of Uliasutai, was a mere fifty by twenty-five miles in extent, and some of this relatively tiny area was given over to agriculture, which was an occupation both of the temple itself and, from at least the end of the eighteenth century, of some poorer families who had the tacit permission of the lamasery authorities to get their living in this way.

Thus in the eighteenth century the population of Mongolia was far from being a society of wide-ranging nomads, moving almost at will over the steppes of central Asia. The reality was much less romantic. The very demands of the Manchus for a closely organized Mongolia from which it could recruit and maintain troops, meant that the Mongols were confined more and more within definite territorial limits, and got attached to particular localities and to the performance of particular services. Fortunately for the modern historian, if not for the contemporary Mongols who had to finance it, the state control of so much of the activities of the population entailed an elaborate official correspondence, something unknown in pre-Manchu days in Mongolia. Much of this has survived and some of it is gradually being published and studied in Mongolia, so that as time goes on we may hope to be more and more in a position to see in detail how a basically nomad society evolved under the impact of foreign bureaucratic control.

The great rebellion of 1756–7

The drama of the decisive struggle for power in central Asia between Manchus and Jungars has always tended to draw attention away from political events in Khalkha in the eighteenth century, especially as this century has usually been treated by historians from the point of view of the growth and consolidation of the Manchu empire as a whole, not from that of the fate of the minor peoples who were caught up in the process. Historians have been very much inclined to regard the political history of Khalkha as having come to an abrupt end in 1691 when the princes swore allegiance at Dolonnor, and to look on the following two centuries as a sort of limbo during which nothing happened. Particularly to be blamed for this ignorance is the neglect of Russian writings. The principle of 'Russica non leguntur' is a dangerous one, and especially when the subject to be considered is one in which for centuries Russians have played such a big part, both politically and academically. The writings of some Russian travellers and scholars, particularly Przhevalskii, were translated in the late nineteenth century, not long after their appearance in Russia, but others, those even of such voluminous and expert writers such as Pozdneev and Potanin, have been almost totally neglected. Both of these scholars gave accounts, at the end of the last century, of the great rebellion of 1756, which was led by Chingunjav, the prince of the Khotogoit, and, what is of especial interest, of the deep and lasting impression which this rebellion had left in the minds of ordinary Mongols more than a hundred years later.

Pozdneev, writing in 1880, was a pioneer who seems to have been the first to realize that the legendary personage known as *Shadar chiang-chün*, the 'General aide-de-campe', about whom he had collected tales and poems in north-west Mongolia, was in fact identical with the prince of the Khotogoit whose rebellion is briefly recorded in the chronicle *Erdeni-yin erike*. He found and edited a great deal more relevant information in the *Iledkel shastir*. Shishmarev, the first Russian consul in Urga, writing a little earlier, and subsequently quoted by Potanin, referred to Chingunjav in terms almost better suited to the atmosphere of our own days, speaking of the prince's 'plan to liberate Mongolia from the Manchu yoke'.[10]

Next to ignorance of Russian scholarship stands the inaccessibility of the relevant Chinese sources, notably the *Ch'ing Shih-lu* of 'Annals of the Ch'ing Dynasty', which were first published in 1937 and have still not been fully exploited. Attention was first drawn to what they contain on the subject of the Khalkha rebellion against the Manchus by Michel Pavlovsky, who in 1949 was able to supplement the meagre hints published more than thirty years before by Courant, working from inferior sources.

Finally, and in the western scholar most pardonable of all, is the fact that the first selections from the rich documentation in the Ulan Bator archives were not published till 1963, while the study of the episode in Mongolia has resulted in only a few articles, culminating in a fairly detailed monograph published in 1962, which have appeared from 1955 onwards, all from the pen of a single scholar. All of this has appeared in the obscurity of the Mongol language. The subject of the rebellion was on the whole played down by subsequent Mongol chronicles as a discreditable episode, but even so we can still pick up hints from these and other sources about the equivocal role adopted by the Church, and especially by the second Jebtsundamba Khutuktu, and about the co-operation of some Mongol nobles with the Jungars from 1732 onwards, so that we can discern a quite novel picture of

Khalkha in the eighteenth century, and one which does not accord altogether with the accepted view that, once having sworn fealty, the Mongol nobles kept unbroken faith with the Manchus. To be sure, the Manchus could rely on the majority of the Mongol nobility, and drew some of their most successful generals and administrators from this source. The names of Tsereng, the first general of Uliasutai, and of Bandi, the commander in the field against Amursana, are two which spring to mind. Moreover, after the pacification which followed the defeat of Chingunjav there was never again any armed opposition to be feared from the Mongol aristocracy. But it is the events of the first half of the century which deserve closer attention than they have had paid to them up to now.

As far as can be judged at present there were two main causes of the rebellion of 1756; the irritation of the nobility at their high-handed treatment by the Manchu Emperor, and the war-weariness of the people and their exasperation at high taxation and commercial exploitation by the Chinese trading community, and if the causes were distinct, so were the manifestations of their effect. The rebellion itself was a ragged affair, with the nobility fighting apparently to expel the Manchus at a time when they were being harassed in Jungaria, and to re-establish their own lost authority. Even the highest in the land, and the most well-disposed towards the Manchus, had to put up with an irksome discipline. Tsereng was fined three months' salary for firing an unauthorized salute at the time of the signing of the Treaty of Khiakta in 1727. The Khutuktu was not allowed to move, even the relatively short distance from Urga to Erdeni Juu, without imperial permission. He did do so in 1743 and received the following reprimand from the Emperor: 'If the Khutuktu wishes to go to Erdeni Juu he should await my command. For him to have hurried there without reporting it, and in disregard of the remonstrances of his attachés, is very wrong.'[11] On the popular side the rebellion took the form of sporadic outbursts of violence, at first mutinies in the relay-stations and watch-posts which hampered communications for a time, and then the isolated plundering of Chinese merchants, activities which were locally spectacular and needing firm handling on the part of the authorities but which, being totally uncoordinated, had no lasting result.

The complex story of the relations between the Manchus and

Jungars in the eighteenth century, which involved incidentally the destiny of Tibet, and which led up to the defeat and physical annihilation of the Jungars in the late 1750s, does not, in its entirety, form part of the history of Khalkha Mongolia. However, at two points in these years the stories of Jungaria and Khalkha merge. In 1727 Galdantseren succeeded Tsewangrabdan as *taisha* of the Jungars. He was not disposed to peace towards the Manchus, but whereas his father's policy had been directed towards Tibet and Kukunor, he set himself to stir up trouble in Khalkha, to expel the Manchus, and to organize a unified Khalkha-Jungar state. Both sides, at one time or another, made propaganda appeals to the Khalkhas for their support. That the Manchus were unsure of the adherence of the princes of Mongolia may be deduced from the fact that the Emperor felt it wise to address exhortatory messages to the nobility of both Inner and Outer Mongolia in 1731. He chided the Khalkhas for having neglected the arts of war and spent too much energy in the worship of the Buddha, so that they had fallen an easy prey to Galdan. He approached the Inner Mongols on another tack, stressing the fact that they, like the Khalkhas, were the descendants of Genghis Khan, while the Jungars had always been traitors to the imperial house. Khalkha was as a shield to Inner Mongolia, and what happened in Khalkha could not be a matter of indifference to the Inner Mongols.

Matters were complicated at this time for the Manchus by war-weariness on the part of all Mongols, and by the current defeat of their general Furdeng, which the imperial exhortation rather glossed over. In the summer of 1731 the Jungars invaded Mongolia but were defeated by pro-Manchu forces under Mongol generals. These were generously rewarded with money and titles for their loyal services, yet in spite of that one of them, the Zasagtu Khan Tsevegjav, who had received a reward of five thousand taels for his staff work, chose to desert the Manchu army for the Jungars in the following year.

A letter from Galdantseren to the Khalkha prince Lhamjav, who was afterwards punished by the Manchus with the loss of his rank and with house arrest in Peking for trafficking with the Jungars, is of great interest in that it appeals, as did the Emperor, to the prestige of Genghis Khan as a factor to sway Khalkha allegiance.

We are [he wrote] of one religion, and dwell in one place, and have lived very well alongside each other. . . . Considering that you are the heirs of Genghis Khan, and not wanting you to be the subjects of anyone else, I have spoken with the emperor of China about restoring Khalkha and Kukunor as they were before. But now the emperor of China wants to organize us, too, like Khalkha and Kukunor, into banners and *sumuns*, and grant us titles, wherefore I am going to oppose him by force of arms. If all goes well, I shall restore Khalkha and Kukunor. May it soon succeed! Move over to the Altai, and dwell together with us in friendship as before. If war comes, we can face it together, and not be defeated by any man.[12]

The Manchus got wind of this appeal. They realized that the Mongol nobility as a whole resented the Manchu titles conferred on them, and deliberately let it be known that these titles were conferred, not as upon subjects, but as on the friends and allies of the Emperor. The war continued, with a big invasion of Khalkha in 1732. The Manchus feared that the Jungars might try to capture the Khutuktu and use him as a political figurehead, and so they removed him from Erdeni Juu to Dolonnor before the Jungars could catch up with him. Both 1732 and 1733 saw heavy Jungar defeats and the advance of Manchu forces deep into their territory as far as the Irtysh river, but the great distances involved and the manœuvring room still left to Galdantseren prevented the Manchus from finally settling the problem on this occasion. They were deterred too by the situation in Mongolia. It was clear from the defection of Lhamjav and others that there was considerable disaffection among the nobility, and clear too that the people were in a desperate state after so many years of campaigning, of which they had borne the brunt. Any continuation of the war might well have driven Mongolia into revolt. Indeed, although the records are not explicit, it seems as though an uprising may have taken place in 1732 in Setsen Khan aimak. The Chinese records say that in that year the young Setsen Khan was unable to put an end to the troubles in the administration of his aimak and that the prince Choijav, a Manchu loyalist and the first Khalkha *zasag* to solicit a Manchu salary, was appointed to rule for him. The next year Choijav became khan, and soon after that a Manchu amban was sent to the aimak to settle 'various affairs' which, though unspecified, were of enough importance to earn him a reward of five thousand taels of silver. Whatever the facts are, and whether or not these are covert hints of a rebellion, we know also that at this time, out of three thousand soldiers sent from the aimak to Erdeni Juu, only one thousand two hundred arrived, the rest having deserted on the way.[13]

A patched-up peace lasted until the early 1750s, when renewed family squabbles and civil war inside Jungaria gave the Manchus, under the vigorous and aggressively minded emperor Ch'ien Lung who had ascended the throne in 1736, the opportunity for decisive intervention. The factors making for rebellion, which we have noticed, and the interests of those concerned, were not contradictory or mutually incompatible, but neither were they mutually complementary or interdependent except in the sense that only a tightly united Mongolia, or Jungaria, or both together, could hope to stand any chance at all against the Manchus. A divided movement would be doomed from the outset. The brief survey we have given of Mongol history in the preceding two centuries shows that it was precisely this element of solidarity which was always lacking, and that there is nothing to be wondered at in the continuing chronic disunity which dislocated Mongol resistance to the Manchus right up to the time of the extirpation of the Jungars. Mongols and Jungars, and Mongols amongst themselves, would time and again make parade of national sentiments, would appeal to the name of the glorious ancestor Genghis Khan as a symbol of unity, and would talk of expelling the Manchus and uniting in a great Mongol state. But when it came to the point of action there was always a fatal individualism, at worst a selfish ambition, which proved stronger than the fine ideals, and predictably and inevitably inhibited the Mongols from doing anything but bring about their own ruin in the face of a determined enemy. Perhaps more than anything else, it was this tragic flaw which for centuries frustrated any hope of a national renaissance. The Jungars in particular seem to have been obsessively determined to allow their own internal jealousies and ambitions priority over their resistance to the common enemy, the Manchus, and right up to the very end they persistently and perversely turned aside from the struggle for their national survival to indulge in palace revolutions and civil war. How intent they were, so it seems, to effect their own ruin, is shown by the eagerness of Amursana, the last pretender to the position of *taisha*, to involve the Manchus once more in the internal affairs of Jungaria.

In 1754 Amursana submitted to the Manchus and brought some twenty thousand of his followers into Khalkha territory where the Manchus allotted him pastures, well inside Mongolia, and granted him a princely title. Then early the next year he marched out from Uliasutai, ostensibly a Manchu general leading a mixed army of some ten thousand Khalkhas, Chahars, Oirats and Chinese, making for Jungaria, with the task of restoring order there. The ruling *taisha* Dawachi, was easily defeated, and a settlement was proposed by the Manchus which would have left Amursana with far less than he was disposed to accept, namely the position of ruler over one of the four tribes of Jungaria, not supreme control. Amursana made no secret of his ambitions, and the Emperor, as a precaution, summoned him to court. On the way he escaped, and turned against his allies of yesterday, whom he had introduced into Jungaria, in open war. From late 1755 till his death in the autumn of 1757, Amursana, though still dogged by dissensions within the ranks of the nobility of his own people, who even then refused to see where the real danger lay, led a desperate struggle against the Manchus, a struggle whose epic proportions have quite obscured the concurrent uprisings in Khalkha.

Many factors contributed to the Manchu victory: they were better armed, they were at one with themselves, and they could profit from the utter failure of communication between the Jungars and the Khalkhas. But although during these years there was no effective common action by Jungars and Mongols, there had been, from the very beginning, a conspiracy between Amursana and certain Mongol nobles. The most important of these was Chingunjav, a Khalkha nobleman and a member of the family of Genghis Khan who had, in the fourth generation, inherited the control over the Khotogoits, an Oirat or west Mongol tribe who lived in the north-west, near the lake Ubsa nor. However, the advantage of this initial collusion was recklessly thrown away. Both princes did rebel, but at different times, and with no co-ordination of plans. In early 1755 Chingunjav had been with the Northern Route army of which Amursana was the deputy commander, at the time of the invasion of Jungaria and the defeat of Dawachi. They had conspired together, and had planned an anti-Manchu uprising which was to take place in Jungaria and Khalkha in the autumn of the same year. They had tried to recruit other Mongol nobles, particularly Sevdenbaljir, a prince of the Khorchin, and Tsevdenjav, son of Tsereng, the General of Uliasutai, but Tsevdenjav betrayed them to Bandi, Amursana's senior commander, and the conspirators were separated. Chingunjav was sent to take part in action against the Uriangkhai of the Khan khatan river far away on the upper reaches of the Ob. It seems that he meanwhile warned Amursana that Bandi suspected their intentions of rebelling, and that it was for this reason that Amursana slipped his escort on the way to court.

But the threads of complicity led wider than this among the Khalkha nobility. The commander of Amursana's escort was Erinchindorji, who was the younger brother of the Khutuktu. He was also the son of Dondubdorji, most probably not by the latter's second, Khotogoit wife Bayart, who was the Khutuktu's mother, but by Ginggun elhe, the senior wife, who was a daughter of the emperor K'ang Hsi. Erinchindorji was accused of permitting, if not actually engineering, the escape. Even if he did not actively assist Amursana, he quite certainly disregarded more than one warning that he was likely to try to get away from his escort. As the Emperor himself said later: 'Though everyone warned him that the bandit Amursana was going to escape, he thought to himself – well suppose he does. At the worst he himself would get punished, but it would not involve his life. So he just let the bandit Amursana go.'[14] Two other nobles in the escort made him aware of their suspicions, but Erinchindorji declined to take any action, trusting in the fact that Amursana was a *Shuang ch'in wang*, a prince of the first rank enjoying double salary. Amursana handed Erinchindorji his seal, saying that he wanted to make a detour to visit his wife and family who were in Khalkha at the time, and promising to rejoin the escort later. Erinchindorji raised no objection, but allowed his prisoner to ride off with some three hundred Jungar soldiers. When it was realized that he had taken a different road altogether there was an ineffectual attempt at pursuit, but it was not pressed. Erinchindorji was certainly guilty of dereliction of duty, if not of actual treason, and in the event he was arrested, taken to Peking, interrogated by the Emperor, and executed in the spring of 1756. Traditions vary as to whether the Khutuktu, who was in Peking at the time, was compelled to watch his brother's execution, or whether he was summoned to see the corpse displayed. Whatever happened, this execution, which the Khalkha nobility viewed as a grave infraction of their rights, was a powerful factor in the outbreak of the Khalkha rebellion two months later, and it undoubtedly affected the somewhat ambiguous activities of the Khutuktu himself.

From his distant post among the Uriangkhai, where he was in any case under supervision, Chingunjav had been unable to support Amursana with a Mongol rising when the autumn revolt in Jungaria took place. He was better placed in the summer of 1756 when, in command of some eight hundred Uriangkhai, Khotogoit and Khalkha troops, he formed part of the army of the Manchu general Hadaha, charged with the pursuit of Amursana. At this time the disaffection of the nobility had been brought to a head by the execution of Erinchindorji, and there was unrest throughout Khalkha as rumours spread that the Khutuktu and the Tushetu Khan were being detained in Peking by the Emperor against their will. Unfortunately, by the time Chingunjav was ready to profit by this situation, Amursana was a refugee among the Kazakhs and unable to take any sort of active part in the campaign: he had been defeated at the end of March 1756 and had no more than a hundred Jungars under his command. That Amursana intended to unite with Chingunjav again in 1757 is clear from Russian archival material, which shows that he was in touch with leaders of the Uriangkhai during the winter of 1756–7, and got supplies from them on various occasions. He told them of his intentions, and one Uriangkhai leader acted as go-between between the two princes, but by the time Amursana was ready to move, though only with a small force, it was already spring 1757, and by then Chingunjav had been captured by the Manchus, taken to Peking, and executed. To complete the sorry tale of disunity which delivered both Mongols and Jungars up piecemeal to the Manchus, Amursana then found himself forced to deal with subversion among his own people: two rivals of his had defeated the Manchus in his absence, but then fell out with each other. One killed the other, but was in his turn eliminated by Amursana in March 1757. Amursana's envoy to Chingunjav, sent to propose a joint expedition against the Manchus, was of course unable to deliver his message, and in the summer Amursana suffered his last defeat amid civil war and invasion, and died soon after of smallpox.

Chingunjav's previous history shows him to have been an

erratic and unreliable subject. He had been confirmed as prince of the Khotogoit in 1738 and at the same time was made an assistant general in Zasagtu Khan aimak. In 1744 he was reproved for slackness in the command of his troops and in 1752 he was cashiered and lost his noble rank of *beile* for failing to surrender a fugitive. In 1754 he performed meritorious service against the Uriangkhai, and got his rank back, and in 1755 was to be found in personal attendance upon the Emperor, a signal honour especially for someone with his record. His generalship had also been restored. He was supposed to take part in the campaign against Amursana in the autumn of 1755 but delayed till it was too late, and was then sent again against the Uriangkhai: it was from this expedition that he deserted and raised the standard of revolt against the Emperor. What lay behind these repeated lapses from loyalty is hard to tell, but they may well have been simply the expression of an irritable and ambitious character, excited by personal rancour against the overlord, and finally erupting, out of control, in open rebellion.

In the summer of 1756 Chingunjav deserted his post and addressed an insubordinate letter to the Emperor, listing the various grievances he was harbouring. The tone of the letter was so abrupt that his Manchu secretary refused to have anything to do with it, and Chingunjav wrote the letter himself in the Mongol language, an exceptional procedure. In particular he complained about the execution of Erinchindorji, and of another Mongol leader, Dambajav, who had been similarly punished for not pursuing a rebellious Jungar leader with sufficient dispatch. The Emperor sent him a reasoned reply, defending the legality of Erinchindorji's punishment. But Chingunjav, planning action all along, deserted the Manchu army, and brought his troops back to Mongolia, to his own pastures in Khotogoit, and began to recruit other nobles to his support. The tone of his remarks to the *beile* Tsevden are of particular interest, since they hint at the support Chingunjav was expecting to get from the Khutuktu:

Our general the *Ch'in wang*·Erinchindorji, and the *taiji* Dambajav have been executed because of the escape of the fugitives Amursana and Baran. Our Khalkha people are destitute, so that I have been compelled to come back. The Jebtsundamba Khutuktu said: 'Whatever happens, I shall head the seven banners of the Khalkha' and so I have returned. What do you think about this, Beile?[15]

Tsevden agreed to co-operate, as did various other nobles, many of whom were to be executed later for their part in the rebellion.

The Khalkha insurrection was, however, doomed from the start by its complete lack of any clearly stated aim and of coordinated action. The majority of the nobility remained loyal to the Manchus, even to the extent that the work of suppression could be, to a large extent, entrusted to Mongol generals, while the conspirators themselves showed an amazing indifference to the urgency of co-operation. The Khutuktu played an equivocal part throughout. On the one hand, together with the Tushetu Khan, he engaged in secret conversations in 1756 with the Russian commandant of Selenginsk, Yakobi, on the subject of secession from Manchu sovereignty to allegiance to the Tsar. Yakobi, in his earlier reports, expressed the opinion that only the lower classes were interested in secession, and was not too enthusiastic about the project, but when he became aware that the highest nobility of Khalkha were involved, he recommended the matter more positively.[16] The Russian Government itself was not at all averse to the project, and at the end of October 1756 gave the local authorities permission to discuss the matter further, and to find out under what conditions the Khutuktu would come over to the Russian side and where he would want to pasture his herds. But by then it was too late. Dilatoriness, and fear of the Manchus, caused the Khalkha nobles to let the matter drag on indecisively.

Chingunjav was in fact not the key figure in the crisis, although it was he who had taken the initiative and for the moment assumed the role of national leader. Everything depended on the way the Khutuktu would move, and very probably Chingunjav's apparent dilatoriness was forced upon him by the need to wait on the Khutuktu's decision. All factions were aware of the Khutuktu's vital position. The Emperor in Peking knew it, and was advised in this sense by loyal Mongol leaders. For example, in the middle of September 1756 Sanjaidorji, general of Tushetu Khan aimak, wrote to him:

Now if your slave follows orders and takes troops to suppress Chingunjav, it may have the unwelcome result that the Khalkhas as a whole will rally to his support, and it is my humble opinion that this is a matter of grave importance for your Majesty's polity and that it will be a setback if by fear the Khalkhas are moved to disturbance. My stupid opinion is the following: The only person whom the Khalkhas trust implicitly is the Khutuktu, and the most advantageous step would be to extend favour towards him and get him to pacify the Khalkhas.[17]

This was an absolutely correct analysis of the situation. In fact, Mongolia as a whole was waiting to see what direction the Khutuktu would take before committing itself. But the Khutuktu delayed, and allowed the initiative to escape him till he was manœuvred into a position of impotence and the rebellion collapsed under the weight of Manchu repression.

The Khutuktu, who was known in Peking to have been agitating against the Manchus after his return from China in the summer had already, by October, been got at by Manchu agents. The Emperor Ch'ien Lung had moved swiftly in the late summer to overawe him. He sent the Khutuktu a letter, ordering him to do his best to persuade the nobility of Mongolia to restrain their subjects and bring them back to their duty. Lamas were sent round the countryside preaching loyalty to the Manchus. The Emperor also summoned a general assembly of the Khalkha leagues at which he was represented by the metropolitan of Peking, the Jangjia Khutuktu. The presence of this dignitary, and the appointment of a new Mongol commander in the person of Tsengunjav, so impressed the Khutuktu and the nobles that they were prepared to swear an oath of loyalty to the Emperor. In face of this the messengers whom Chingunjav sent one after another to the Khutuktu to try to persuade him to come out on the side of the rebellion achieved nothing. Chingunjav also hoped to hold a meeting in Urga in early October to organize a coherent campaign for Mongol independence under the leadership of the nobility, but the reluctance of the Khutuktu to collaborate, the hesitation of many nobles, and the realization that the Manchus were not going to stand any nonsense, all told against him, and the meeting never took place. It is probably a true measure of Chingunjav's fatal impetuosity, and perhaps also of excessive egoism, that he did not try to discuss matters with the leading nobles of Mongolia at large, and win them over to his views, until a good two months after he had disclosed his hand to the Manchus by deserting his post.

The sorry tale of vacillation does not end here. Long after Chingunjav had himself been eliminated, the feeling was still abroad that when the next worship of the Khutuktu took place in Urga in summer 1757, the pontiff would lead the people over to allegiance to Russia. Everything depended on him. 'Whither the Khutuktu, thither the Mongols. Whither the Mongols, thither the Khutuktu',[18] Limbeldorji, general of Tushetu Khan aimak, was reported to have said to the Russian courier Sharin, but the Khutuktu could not make up his mind to move in any direction at all. Yakobi had further talks with Khalkha envoys in May 1757, and they confirmed to him that all Khalkha wanted to be under Russian rule, and in the following winter Yakobi could judge for himself, when crossing Mongolia on his way to and from Peking, what a general desire there was for this move. Absolute strangers told him that the whole of Mongolia down to the last man, with the exception of the Chahars, firmly intended to take Russian citizenship, and were kept from this only by the disunity of their chiefs. Meanwhile the great meeting in the summer of 1757 had come and gone, the nobles had dispersed, and the decision which everyone was waiting for had not been taken. The Khutuktu kept his own counsel, and at the end of the year Limbeldorji is said to have remarked that the transfer to Russian allegiance could not be accomplished because some of the powerful khans and princes would not consent, while many great and distinguished Mongols had been executed. The vacillations of the Khutuktu were partly responsible for the failure of this last effort to rid Khalkha of Manchu domination, but there must have seemed to him good reason for not encouraging a very doubtful uprising and for not wanting to exchange the suzerainty of the Manchus for that of the Tsars when it came to the point. Nevertheless, it is fairly certain that the Khutuktu was assassinated by order of Ch'ien Lung early in 1758, and that the speedy deaths of the Tushetu Khan and of Limbeldorji which occurred soon after were no accidents either. The Emperor had a fulsome eulogy of the Khutuktu published, enumerating all that he had done to defeat the traitor Chingunjav, evidently with the intention of concealing the details of his fate and his real role – a role which has to be pieced together mainly from the Russian archives.

Without support from the Khutuktu, Chingunjav's movement was bound to fail. His lack of enterprise is astounding. He had been plotting with Amursana in 1755, and knew that the Emperor was aware of this fact. Yet by the summer of 1756 he had done practically nothing to prepare for his revolt. He did not recruit an army: all he had was the small force of about eight hundred which he brought back with him from the Uriangkhai campaign, and the most generous estimates never allow him more than two thousand soldiers at any time. From the first he was having to spend his personal fortunes to win recruits. Only after he had deserted his post did he try to win over other members of the nobility by sending out to them, belatedly, a summons to action in which he reminded them of how the Manchus had for long been appropriating the wealth of the Mongols for their chronic Jungar wars, and how they had now unjustly put to death Erinchindorji, who was of the line of Genghis Khan. For that reason, he wrote, the Khalkhas should join forces and desert the Manchu emperor. Here again we note the appeal to the name of the common ancestor Genghis Khan, and yet again it proved an empty form of words. A few, but not many, nobles, joined the rebellion. Once having declared himself, Chingunjav should, if he were to achieve any military success, have struck at once while the Manchus were unprepared. As it was he seems to have frittered the next two months away while the Manchus called up much-needed reinforcements from Köke qota. In fact, Chingunjav seems never to have made a positive military move against the Manchus at all. From what one can piece together of the story, he and his forces never moved away from their base among the Khotogoit, and finally, in January 1757, Chingunjav was captured with a few remaining faithful followers and sent to Peking for execution.

The actual course of Chingunjav's movement was short, confused and disastrous. He tried to subvert the troops at Uliasutai, and called on the soldiers manning the watch-posts and relay-stations to desert their duty. A general desertion did occur. In his same report to the throne, Sanjaidorji wrote in some alarm of the extent of the rebellion, pointing out that nobles of all four aimaks were withdrawing their troops and deserting, and that the deserters were all of one party with Chingunjav. But the Manchus acted with vigour, and restored these essential posts to service by supplying them with Inner Mongol troops from their army. Moreover, widespread though it was, this mutiny was not a coherent national uprising. There was little direct confrontation of the Manchu army by rebel forces. Chingunjav apparently made an effort to arrest the general Tsengunjav, and his own former comrade Wangbudorji who had deserted him in order to replace him as prince of the Khotogoit, but both moves were a failure. There were a few minor clashes, but for the most part Chingunjav was never in a position to strike a blow against the enemy forces. From his base in the north-west he tried to recruit troops from the neighbouring Uriangkhai. He did persuade some to join him, but many of the Uriangkhai princelings and even his own Khotogoits refused to join him. One of his recruiting officers was arrested by loyal Uriangkhai and handed over to the Manchus. Besides this, the refusal of the most important Khalkha aristocrats to join him meant the failure from the very beginning of his vision, if it really was a vision and not just a day-dream, of uniting all Mongolia in a struggle for independence, and the scope of his activity was limited to his own immediate surroundings. His efforts to stir up the rest of the nobility, which continued right through to the end of 1756 when he even sent two of his sons to Urga in a last vain attempt to recruit the Khutuktu, never had much positive result. He could not even hold his own men together. As he was hunted farther and farther towards Russia, they fell away. When he had only two hundred men left, he had to suppress a mutiny in his own ranks. His forces dropped to one hundred. By the middle of January he was on the Russian frontier with fifty men, amongst the Black Darkhats, who sided with the Manchus. After a fierce final battle he was captured. But, as the Manchu commanders afterwards reported to the Emperor, in the end it had been the desertions of his own men which had told against him. 'We your slaves did not await the arrival of the army to catch the bandit, but his own subjects, even to his own kin, themselves abandoned him.'[19]

Simultaneously, the Manchus were exercised by outbreaks of violence all over the country directed against the Chinese merchants and their shops. But these, though undoubtedly stimulated by Chingunjav's call to revolt, were, like the army mutinies, unplanned, unco-ordinated, and not directed towards any particular objective, except immediate destruction and plundering. For example, Khiakta was taken and plundered by a force of three hundred Mongols, but the victors seem not to have known what to do next. They held the town for a couple of months on their own and were then, for the most part, taken prisoner by the imperial forces. Urga too was attacked, and the

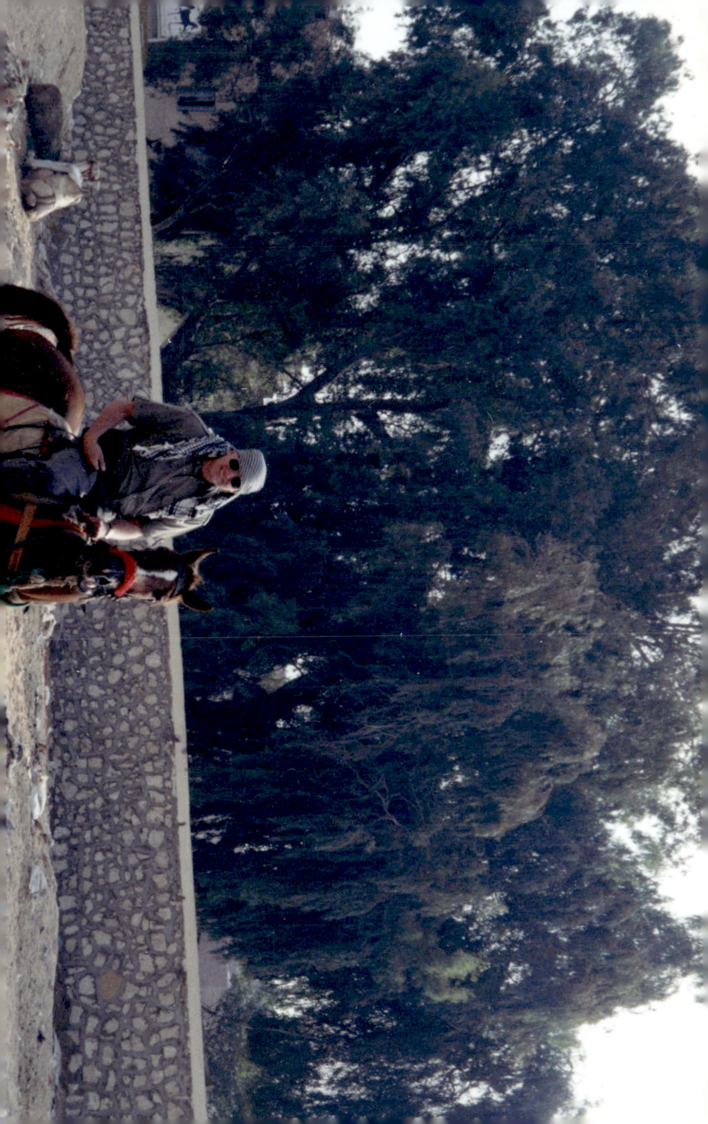

Chinese shops plundered, but an official report of the incident shows what an insignificant and ephemeral affair it really was.

In the matter of the attack on the goods and cattle of eight Chinese shops at Urga, the office of the Shanzav of Urga sent out twenty Chinese and Mongols, headed by the gate-keeper lamas Norovjantsan and Sharav, and had them pursue the bandits. Some forty men, armed with bows and arrows and guns, were going towards the river. Thereupon two of our men went on in advance and announced the Khutuktu's proclamation of restraint to them, but two of those bandits got out their bows and arrows and were about to shoot our men, who became afraid and withdrew and rejoined their comrades. They talked the matter over and all withdrew. Because we could not really get near the bandits we had no chance of recognizing them.[20]

From all over the country reports came in of isolated Chinese being attacked and robbed by bands of armed men. These bands were often small, consisting of no more than half a dozen herdsmen, and the official archives refer to them slightingly as bandits and robbers. But it is clear that this was something more than ordinary banditry, in particular since these outbursts of violence were occurring all over the country just at a time when life would be hard for robber bands – when there was a large and determined Manchu army in Mongolia. Several bands, moreover, were of considerable size, sometimes, as at Khiakta, running into hundreds of men, and reports put in by the general Limbeldorji show that these large bands were often led by members of the nobility or by officials of the Great *Shabi*. But all too often the troubles merely afforded individuals a chance to pay off old scores, and had no more generous aim. For instance, a number of Mongols were arrested for killing a Chinese named Sangaa and his associates, among them six Mongols. One of the accused had had a debt with Sangaa, and when the latter came to collect it, he tried to put off repayment by saying he was just going to shift pastures and would pay later. It came to a quarrel, but Sangaa escaped with the help of some bystanders. Then the accused talked the matter over with some of his relatives, and they simply decided to join a band of marauders who had come to plunder the local Chinese. This may have been a temporarily satisfying excursion, but it smells more of mob-violence than a war of liberation, and can only have attracted reprisals from the much superior imperial forces.

The Manchus took this uprising seriously, partly for its own sake, partly because it threatened their communications in the struggle against the Jungars. They withdrew all Khalkha troops from the Jungar front, suspecting their loyalty, and once they had stabilized the situation they set about crushing the dissidents with a savagery exceeded only by the viciousness with which they were to depopulate Jungaria. Special punitive units were organized to scour Mongolia and deal with the rebels on the spot. How they set about their work can be seen, to take only one example, form a report submitted to the throne by Huturinga and Dorji, two special commissioners who carried out much of the work of repression. Of one affair they wrote:

> Eleven bandits, including the ringleaders Nuvsh and Gombo, were beheaded, and their heads displayed as a warning at the place where they had made their raid. Nineteen secondary bandits such as Damchaa and Ravdan were also summarily executed to set an example to others. We propose to confiscate their tents and cattle and allot their wives and children as slaves to deserving nobles in the aimak. Of 183 men who made raids in various places in the districts of Khui and elsewhere, thirty have now been executed, and as for the 153 who remain and have not yet been caught, we are ordering the authorities concerned to arrest them and convey them here for execution as a public example, without distinction of whether they are ringleaders or secondary offenders.[21]

The captors of Khiakta were similarly dealt with, most of them executed, and their heads displayed on poles, while their families were dispersed into slavery. Chingunjav and his family were of course executed, as were several of the nobles who had supported him. The Manchus seem to have been reluctant to take direct action against the greatest princes and to have dealt with them by secret assassination, but others were openly done to death. The *taiji* Banjur, for example, defended himself on the grounds of ignorance and of loyalty. He said: 'The prince never gave me any explicit commands, but as he was the general and prince of our aimak I could not but follow him. In particular, I never understood that he was proposing to rebel.'[22] But Banjur was none the less publicly executed, his son lost his rank of *taiji*, and the whole family was enslaved to the local banner-prince. Damiran, one of the first noble conspirators, who had later withdrawn from the affair, and stayed quietly at home was nevertheless captured and taken to Peking, where he was put to death with his whole family.

Chingunjav's immediate followers were also dealt with severely, though some of them were mere children and they and others denied knowledge of what had been going on. We may quote parts of the surviving confessions:

Confessions of Tögs:

I am fourteen years old, a subject of Chingunjav. We had nothing much at home, so as Chingunjav was my lord I worked for him and stayed with him gathering dried dung for fuel to get my living. I don't know anything else about the matter.

Confession of Lasran:

I am thirteen years old, the grandson of Togd (one of Chingunjav's men). It is true that I followed my grandfather Togd, but I don't know anything else about it.

The judgement runs:

We have publicly executed Togd, Aravdan, Doolin and Dampil on the fourteenth of the month, and we propose that, as Tögs and Lasran are small children under fifteen who do not understand the matter, but were forced into following the bandits, they be pardoned from execution, and allotted as slaves to deserving nobles in other aimaks.[23]

Such harsh treatment was meted out all over Mongolia. Some rebels were let off, on the pretext that they were only 'stupid Mongols', but many were beheaded and had their heads displayed, while others, especially lamas, were banished on foot to the distant provinces of south China, a most unhealthy area for Mongols used to the clear cold climate of the steppes. Wives and children were enslaved to loyal nobles, or were handed over as reparations to Chinese traders whose stocks had been plundered. To judge by reports from Russian travellers in Mongolia at the time, the whole nation was reduced to beggary. Again and again they encountered beggars kneeling by the side of the road asking for charity, and with their own eyes saw women and little girls being loaded on to carts to be sent off as compensation to Chinese merchants for the losses they had suffered.

The Manchus had little difficulty in quelling the rebellion, wide-spread though it was. On the purely material side the Manchus were a well-armed, unified force, engaged in a fight to the death with the Jungars who had been troubling them for the past half century, and the Mongols were quixotic enough to get in the way. The latter were, by any standards, pitifully badly armed. Those soldiers who had deserted may have had their weapons with them, but for the most part the Mongols had only clubs with which to face the artillery and hand-guns of the well-disciplined Manchu forces. Their psychological handicaps were equally great. The Mongol movement, such as it was, was undermined from the start by the same fatal disunity and reckless individualism which seemed destined to frustrate any large-scale enterprise, Mongol or Jungar, in those years. At every turn the rebellion betrays irresponsible haste, rash opportunism, lack of planning and co-ordination, and absence of common purpose. In general the Mongol aristocracy did not join Chingunjav. Reports submitted to the throne by loyal Mongol nobles overflow with expressions of gratitude for the imperial favours they had long been receiving, and even if much of this is discounted as formal sycophancy, there is no doubt that the Mongol nobles did enjoy a privileged position in the empire, and knew where their advantage lay. Most of them can hardly have been disposed to jeopardize this position by rising in a rebellion against a powerful overlord at the command of a minor prince, who did not even control subjects of the ethnic majority, the Khalkhas, and who had no clear policy beyond issuing a vague appeal to the dream of independence. In those days of non-existent nationalism, such independence, even if achieved, would have meant only the exchange of one overlord for another. In any case, the whole trend of Mongol history had been for a couple of centuries away from independence under a Mongol Emperor, and towards fragmentation and a client relationship with the stronger neighbouring powers, and with the Manchus now at the height of their powers the time had not yet come to reverse this trend. Even the Khutuktu, as we have seen, did not apparently envisage a separate Mongol state, but was thinking along the lines of transferring his allegiance from the Manchu Emperor to the Tsar, and was probably considering actually leaving his old pastures and trekking into Russian territory, as the Torguts had done a century or more before. Besides, there had never been any real co-operation between Mongols and Jungars, but only mutual quarrels and dissensions for decades on end, and it is no wonder that they failed to work together at this late hour. Those Mongolian scholars who take the Khalkha nobles to task for missing their opportunity to collaborate with the Jungars in 1688 and again in 1756, and set up a unified anti-Manchu state, are reading into history ideas of nationalism and racial solidarity which are simply illusory and would not have occurred to those concerned at the time.

Chingunjav's personality was also a factor of importance in determining his failure. Not much is known directly of him, but a revealing remark made about him by one of the minor nobles of his own suite when testifying to his own behaviour, has survived. This man describes Chingunjav as fierce, hasty and rash, a man so harsh that many who at first followed him were later alienated and driven to desertion. Impetuosity and over-confidence may have caused him to rebel at the wrong time: his insurrection in the summer of 1756 cannot even be called premature, since he had missed his chance of timing the Khalkha rebellion to coincide with that in Jungaria, so catching the Manchus on two fronts, by months. His action looks more like the expression of an irresponsible and opportunist impulse to profit by the temporary discontent of the nobility at the autocratic mistreatment of one or two of their number by the Emperor on the one hand, and by the desperate impoverishment of the people at large on the other, two very different forces which Chingunjav never succeeded in harnessing and exploiting together.

Contemporary Mongolian historians, working within the framework of Marx–Leninist dogma, have seized on this incident in their country's past as an illustration of the people rising up to demand independence and being frustrated by imperialists, the Manchus, abetted by weak and treacherous native nobles. The alleged class nature of the struggle has had to be modified somewhat, since the main leaders, Amursana and Chingunjav, were themselves aristocrats, but these men have been classified as progressive representatives of the feudal class, and the whole period of 1755 to 1758, that is, the separate Jungar and Mongol insurrections being taken together, is characterized as exhibiting an armed uprising of the Mongol people in a struggle for independence. This point of view is tacitly accepted as an article of faith by students of the period, who start out from the assumption that they are investigating a war of national liberation.

There is a certain amount to be said for this analysis, but on the whole it seems to be a mistaken one, dictated by the exigencies of Marxist theory rather than by evaluation of the facts as presented. On the positive side the following may be said. It is difficult to consider the insurrection of 1756 as a mere eruption of malcontents, however vaguely conceived, ill-planned and raggedly executed it was. In its extent and violence it probably exceeded the successful national movement of 1911, but the conditions of the time were vastly different. The noble conspirators of 1911 enjoyed the good-will of Russia and even some calculating help too, while they had to deal only with the demoralized remnants of a dying dynasty which was in the throes of a national revolution at home. The rebels of 1756 were up against a far more ruthless and ambitious opponent in the emperor Ch'ien Lung, and were unable to develop their movement to the point where coherence might have been visible. Certainly there was at the head of the rebellion a declared will towards independence from the Manchus, though with what confidence it was expressed is doubtful. Chingunjav not only appealed to ideas of Mongol solidarity by his reference to Genghis Khan, but he directly summoned the nobles of Khalkha to 'join forces and secede from the Manchu Emperor'.[24] It is as the figure of a liberator that Chingunjav survived in Mongol folk memory. Before words like 'liberation' became suspect, Shishmarev, writing a century ago, had the acumen to observe the widespread discontent of the Mongols and to realize that in remembering Chingunjav in story and song they were cherishing the memory of their lost independence. Chingunjav was popularly believed to have started, or intended, to build a new capital for his new Mongol state in his own territories, to be called by the allusive name of North Peking. Relics of his were kept in certain lamaseries in the area, waiting for the day when he would appear to free his people from the Manchus, for Chingunjav soon turned, in the popular imagination, into a revenant, as Genghis Khan had done long before. The Mingats of Khobdo, for instance, considering themselves his special subjects, used to put special signs of blue cloth on their felt tents so that they would be distinguished from other Mongols when Chingunjav returned to set them free. To be a revenant is especially easy in a society where reincarnation is an accepted idea, and we have seen in chapter 2 how the fertile imagination of the Mongols soon turned the figure of Chingunjav into that of the Girl Khutuktu.

But the fact that Chingunjav's name, like that of Amursana, passed into legend as a symbol of the longing for independence, and was the subject of folklore when Russian scholars were in Mongolia a century later, though indicative of how the Mongols were feeling then and perhaps earlier, too, is not the true stuff of history. The question to be answered is, what real evidence is there that at the time the Mongols thought they were fighting for their independence, and how did they conceive this independence. What little we have is unreliable. The confessions of captured rebels are tainted evidence: commoners and nobles alike, they were trying to save their lives by denying that they knew what was going on. Evaluation of this episode will probably be bound to rest on varying interpretations of what facts we possess, rather than what the actors said about themselves.

There would seem to be a palpable difference between the utterance of the slogan of independence, or, as Chingunjav put it in rather more negative terms, desertion of the Manchu Emperor, and the demonstration of an active will to independence. The disarrayed nobility of Mongolia on one side, and on the other the mutinous troops and marauding bands of herdsmen, robbing and plundering, but alike lacking a cohesive purpose and doomed to succumb to imperial repression before long, would appear to convey rather less than the impression of a nation in arms pursuing its own destiny. It looks more like a descent into anarchy. National independence presupposes first of all some coherence within the group, some willingness to co-operate, and its achievement requires foresight and preparation. But in 1756 there was in Mongolia, as in Jungaria, a ragged series of outbursts of violence, perhaps loosely triggered off by each other, and initially connected with the leader's summons, but thereafter independent of him. Not only did Jungaria and Mongolia fail to rise together, but even in Mongolia risings took place in series and not in conjunction. There was, for example, a big rising of some Tungus people in north-east Mongolia, but it did not take place till six months after Chingunjav's first defection, by which time his fate was already sealed. Also, quite independently of this there was a rising of the Khoits of the Tamir river, former subjects of Amursana's, who had been settled in central Mongolia. In the face of such irresponsibility and fractionalism it is hard to talk of the will towards national independence.

The immediate effect of this unsuccessful rebellion upon Khalkha was little short of disastrous, especially as it had come after the exceptionally heavy winter of 1755–6, when heavy frost and deep snow had caused great losses in cattle, and an epidemic of smallpox had cut down the people. However, the pacification policy of the Manchus was much less severe than the genocide they indulged in against the Jungars, and the threads of life were picked up again, the general pattern changing little. The Manchu administration was reinforced, especially with the development of Khobdo on a new site, as the centre of government in the far west. Chinese traders continued to enter Khalkha and to consolidate their position there. The Emperor tried to relieve destitution by cancelling part of the official debt which the Mongol banners owed to the merchants, and paying off the remainder himself with a special grant. But this was only a palliative, and by 1775 the official debt was a quarter as much again as it had been in 1756, and continued to grow. Even so, 1756 is a real turning-point. It exhausted the opposition to the Manchus, and another century and a half passed before the Khalkha nobility, taking advantage of the decrepitude of the imperial house, organized another and more successful *coup*.

The one fundamental change which the Manchus found it necessary to make was in the position of the Jebtsundamba Khutuktu. The close relationship of the Khutuktu with the leading aristocratic families had proved a dangerous combination, and the Emperor determined to remove the possibility of a recurrence of the serious situation of 1756–7, when the whole of Khalkha was only awaiting a sign from the head of the Church to desert the Manchus. It was decreed that future incarnations were to be revealed only in Tibet. Though the discovery of a re-incarnation, in Tibet and Mongolia alike, was accompanied by much pious mumbo-jumbo – elaborate searching for suitable children as candidates, the testing of their recollections of their previous lives and, in the case of the Khutuktu, the drawing out of the name of the predestined occupant of the throne from a golden vase in Lhasa, in reality the whole affair was a farce, manipulated by the authorities to ensure that a candidate acceptable to Peking was chosen. In 1793 much stricter regulations still were published, governing all the re-incarnations of Tibet and Mongolia, and specifically excluding all noble families from consideration when a child incarnation was to be sought.

It is this political aspect of the institution of the Jebtsundamba Khutuktu which is of real interest, far more so than his religious activities, even though the individuals concerned, apart from the first, the second and the eighth, who was also the last, do not appear to have played any notable part in affairs personally. Their lives are conspicuous mainly for their brevity, and for the reasons which underlay their short tenure of office. The fourth, who reached the age of thirty-eight, had the longest life of any of these intermediate Khutuktus, while the sixth, who died at the age of six, occupied the throne for only thirty-nine days.

The elevation of the third Khutuktu, who was the first to obey the imperial command and let himself be born in Tibet, was symbolic of the deep estrangement which still separated part of the aristocracy of Khalkha from the Emperor. After the death of the second incarnation, rumours circulated throughout Khalkha that the third had appeared in one or other of seven different noble Mongol families, but the Emperor intervened to prevent this from happening, and in a curious decree issued in 1761 announced that the Khutuktu had appeared in Litang in Tibet. The decree ran:

> To the khans, princes, dukes and nobles of Khalkha: Earlier I sent the following order to the Demo Khutuktu (at that time the regent for the eighth Dalai Lama) in Tibet: The Jebtsundamba Khutuktu is an important lama, and the saint revered by the Khalkhas. Several years have passed since he departed this life, and he has been searched for throughout Khalkha. So far there has been no sign of his rediscovery, and according to the words of old disciples of the Khutuktu it says in the biography of the Jebtsundamba that the re-incarnation of the Khutuktu will not dwell for more than a hundred years in Khalkha but will then return to his own land. Therefore I am in great anxiety on behalf of the Khalkhas. Please inquire carefully into this ... so as to have the re-incarnation of the Khutuktu discovered as soon as possible, and so cause the faith to flourish in the aimaks of Khalkha.

The decree continues by announcing that accordingly the incarnation had been rediscovered in Litang.[25] The Emperor's anxiety for the people of Khalkha and their faith is clearly a political fiction, and what is of considerable historical significance is that this seems to be the first known instance of the secular authority paying lip service to a supposed popular belief so as to justify its own irregular activities already decided upon. In later years too there were to be rumours circulated, and tales told, that the current Khutuktu was destined, according to an old saying, to be the last. It happened more than once in the nineteenth century, and most recently, after the death of the eighth Khutuktu in 1924, the People's government and the Revolutionary Party adduced just such a rumour to justify their discouragement of the search for the ninth incarnation.

The third Khutuktu was not easily accepted by the nobility of Khalkha. While he was on the way to Mongolia in 1763 he was beaten up by his escort, and his Mongol teacher also used to beat him. He died at the age of sixteen, and a covert remark in the biography of the fifth Khutuktu hints that his death was not natural, but that he had been murdered by other lamas. Recently published documents show too that at the very time when he was being installed in Urga, a rival incarnation was being groomed, and a temple built for him, at the lamasery of a famous incarnation, the Chin Sujigt Nomun Khan, who had his seat in present-day Bayan Khongor aimak, in the south-west part of the country. Another way in which opposition expressed itself was the presentation to the Emperor of a petition from the Mongol amban of Urga, Sanjaidorji, requesting that the Khutuktu be made to reside in Dolonnor in Inner Mongolia and not in Khalkha at all. This demand was rejected. Attempts were made to get both the fourth and the sixth Khutuktus discovered in Mongolia, but without success. It was rumoured, for instance, that the wife of the Tushetu Khan of the day was to be the mother of the fourth Khutuktu, but unfortunately her pregnancy resulted in the inconvenient birth of a girl, and meanwhile the new incarnation was in any case found in Tibet. If one may use the term irony at all in history, then it may well be used to qualify the fact that it was a Tibetan Khutuktu, the eighth, who was to a great extent responsible for the recovery of Mongol independence in 1911, and who sat on the throne of an autonomous, and in later years, independent, Mongolia, until his death in 1924.

CHAPTER 4

SOCIAL AND ECONOMIC DEVELOPMENTS IN THE NINETEENTH CENTURY

Society and law

There can be fewer blanker pages in the history of the civilized world than the story of Mongolia in the nineteenth century. A few travellers traversed parts of the country and reported on what they had seen, usually in Russian publications which remained as obscure and generally unknown abroad as the curiosities they described. For the study of the actual history of this remote, depopulated and apparently barbarous corner of the Chinese empire there has been, until quite recently, neither the enthusiasm nor the necessary documentation. It continued to remain quite outside the range of interest of the ordinary educated man and only in the last few years with the appearance of source material in Mongolia itself and the devotion to academic research of a handful of western scholars, has the curtain of ignorance been even slightly lifted for us, so that we can begin to observe Mongolia and her recent history as a phenomenon in itself, and not just as a reflex of what was happening to her great neighbours, Russia, China and Japan.

In the course of the nineteenth century nothing of international significance occurred in Mongolia. Indeed, until 1860 when the first Russian consulate was opened in Urga, she remained cut off from any normal contact with the world. But inside Mongolia the century was one of considerable social and economic change, and its interest lies in the picture it offers of the decline of a semi-feudal system in relatively modern times. By 1911, when the collapse of the Manchu dynasty gave the Mongol aristocracy the chance of recovering their country's independence, Mongolian society was in urgent need of reform, and of a new direction and sense of purpose. But at that time Mongolia failed to produce a native reform movement, such as had helped Japan into the modern world a generation earlier, and when the real revolution began, in the years from 1921 to 1924, it came as an imitation, or rather a by-product, of the Soviet revolution. It relied for its theoretical content absolutely upon Soviet communism, and for the experienced personnel to take charge of the new policies it relied almost exclusively on Soviet citizens, especially Buriats and Kalmucks who were linguistically equipped to act as go-betweens. This was when the real break with the past occurred and still today it is Lenin – Stalin having been dethroned – who is looked back to as the source of inspiration and political wisdom, not any native theorist.

The period of autonomy, from 1911 to 1919, was, as far as internal affairs were concerned, simply a continuation of Mongolia's previous course, so that the nineteenth century can quite conveniently be considered as having lasted till about 1920 in Mongolia. Except that it had expelled the Manchus, autonomy altered nothing fundamentally in society, and the pre-eminent position which the Church came to enjoy under the theocratic monarchy of the Khutuktu only accentuated the divisive forces which had been, and still were, operating. The complete renovation in Mongolian society visible today is the work of the last forty years only. The social framework nowadays bears no relation to what it had been earlier, while the material conditions of life – nourishment, education, medical services, career possibilities, and above all ideas of social justice – have all been transformed beyond recognition, but this has all happened within the conditions inherent in Marx–Leninism. Nothing significant in the field of social change occurred during the period of autonomy. It was only in 1923, for instance, that the *khamjilga* system, that is, the allotment to the nobility of personal retainers, was abolished.

We have little enough detail of what it was like to be a Mongol at the beginning of the period of Manchu domination. From the late eighteenth century onwards there is, however, a satisfying amount of official documentation which often, particularly where criminal investigations are involved, goes into minute personal detail, while in the present century we have a growing mass of personal reminiscence to explore. It is possible, today, to begin to analyse the process of social and economic break-up in Mongolia on the basis of evidence presented by Mongols themselves, rather than that of travellers' tales alone, and to see what a formidable task of renewal faced the People's Government of 1924. Whether an appreciation of the dimensions of this task will lead us to view that government's blunders and excesses with a more tolerant eye is however doubtful, for it brought most of its worst trouble on itself solely through its inability to break free of Soviet tutelage. Nevertheless, not only had the country's economy to be entirely restored, and specific, tangible tasks such as the creation of a medical service and of a proper educational system faced up to, but the more difficult problem of nurturing a feeling of mutual responsibility in a society previously divided by extremes of wealth and poverty, privilege and subjection, had to be solved. The fact that the revolutionary government artificially exaggerated difference of class for its own purposes does not mean that such differences were of no account in themselves.

Society in Manchu times was a stratified one, as we have seen. The lay people fell into two main classes, the nobility above, and the subjects, or *albatu*, those liable to render *alba*, or *corvée*, below. That the nobility were liable to *alba* vis-à-vis the Manchu Emperor, the supreme overlord, in the form of personal attendance at court hardly affects this schematic division, since the financial burden of these periodic visits fell not on the nobility themselves, but on their subjects, from whom they levied it as taxation. The *albatu* themselves consisted of imperial subjects or *sumun* people, that is, commoners belonging to the *sumuns* or Manchu semi-military administrative units below the banner level, and *kham-jilga* or personal retainers, whom the nobility were specifically allowed to retain for their own support. The church, as it developed, acquired a similar, parallel organization, in which the lamaseries and high clerics were supported economically by the *shabi* or ecclesiastical serfs. Even the lamas themselves tended to fall into two, and later into three, separate classes. At the top was a small group of high incarnations, who were equated with the lay nobility, and who, during the period of autonomy from 1911 to 1919, often actually held titles of lay nobility as well as their ecclesiastical distinction. At the bottom of the scale was a large mass of poor lamas, many of them in effect labourers in the lamaseries or servants of their superiors. In between there grew up a class of learned lamas and clerical administrators, recruited from the lower class but distinct from it in interests, aspirations and functions. There were other minor classes of commoner too, of which the most numerous was that of the slaves. The slave-class was of varied origin, consisting of prisoners of war, bride companions of noble ladies, persons bought as slaves or given as a reward of merit by the Manchu authorities, and persons reduced to slavery as a punishment for crimes. But this was always a relatively small category of persons, and became smaller in the nineteenth century, as slaves became assimilated to the larger groups of imperial subjects, *khamjilga* and *shabi*.

In theory, then, society was tidy and stable at the outset of the Manchu period, with every family, except for the slaves, owning its own beasts for its upkeep, and occupying a fixed and definite position in society with a defined range of feudal responsibilities. It seems unlikely, however, that this is a true picture, though actual details for the very early years are not easy to come by. Indeed, documentation is altogether scanty and haphazard, and in trying to illustrate certain social phenomena we are sometimes forced to make use of material drawn from years somewhat earlier or later than those we are actually scrutinizing and trust that the picture they give is still generally a valid one. Even in the eighteenth century the personal fate of the individual might be none too secure, even within the established framework of society. The families of condemned criminals, if not executed as well, might be allotted as slaves to loyal nobles, as happened to many of the dependants of rebels executed after the failure of Chingunjav's rebellion, even to noble families. The defeated Jungars were in an even less favourable position, and those enslaved were so numerous that they formed a new class known as 'new slaves' or 'Oirat slaves'. There are many cases known of free persons being sold off as slaves by their overlords, and at least one curious one of a lama presenting one of his slaves, together with his family and animals, to the local prince, as an ordinary subject, in recognition of the services of the slave's late father. Persons could also be awarded to a successful plaintiff as compensation in a case of theft, and could be bought and sold thereafter. Families could sell off their daughters in exchange for a bride-price.

A curious document of 1764 describes the buying up of a num-

SOCIAL AND ECONOMIC DEVELOPMENTS

ber of women and girls from Chahar to be sent to Ili in Turkestan to be resettled among the Oirats there. A total of 420 was dispatched, consisting of 174 slave girls of fifteen and upwards, and eighty-four slave-widows of forty and below, together with eighty girls and eighty-two women from the ordinary population who went voluntarily. The total cost of the transaction, apart from the actual transport, was 6,912 taels of silver. Of this, 2,412 taels represented the purchase price of the slaves as paid to their various owners, 4,200 an allotment of ten taels per female as a subsidy for her to equip herself with clothes and to serve as travel money, and three hundred an allotment of fifteen taels each to the twenty officials who were to be in charge of the detachments of women. The money was supplied by the Kalgan customs office.[1]

The position of slaves was especially unenviable, and a legal document from 1789 provides illuminating details about the life and conditions of contemporary society. In that year a slave-woman called Dashjid, belonging to the soldier Orjin of the banner of Urjinjav, whom we have already met in the previous chapter, was accused of having killed her bastard child by strangulation. In her first testimony Dashjid gave a short account of her life. She was aged thirty-two and was the daughter of one Nomon, who had been the dependant of the late *taiji* Garvi. When she was small, her father had been unable to keep her fed, and had sold her to another *taiji*, Wangjil by name. Soon after this Nomon died of starvation. Dashjid was unable to get along with Wangjil, and when she was ten her mother had bought her back for one ox and sold her to Bayar, himself a slave of the head of one of the *otogs*, or administrative divisions, of the Khutuktu's estate, for a bride-price of three oxen. (One of the features of Mongol slavery is that almost anyone could own a slave, down to an ordinary imperial subject, or a *khamjilga*.) Dashjid was not happy there either, and deserted Bayar and came back home. Her mother sold her a second time, receiving a bride-price of one horse and five goats. This arrangement lasted a bare month, and the girl ran home again, upon which there followed another marriage, this time involving no bride-price, which lasted also only one month. At this point Dashjid's mother, having nothing left to live on, went to live with a relative, while Dashjid herself, with her three bastard children, as she terms them, tried to scrape a living for herself. Her banner gave her some sheep for her support, but she could not make ends meet, and finally she stole a sheep belonging to a *taiji* named Tseveen, and was arrested. She confessed further that the *meiren* Amindoo, a subordinate banner official, who tried her case, allotted her one cow with its calf, together with one of her daughters, to Tseveen as compensation for the sheep alleged to have been stolen. She herself was returned to where she belonged. After a time, a petty official there told her he had arranged with Amindoo for her to be sold again to a rich man in the banner, together with her two remaining children. She was duly sold for a bride-price of one horse and one camel, to Orjin, who had her do domestic work for him. Suddenly, and while she was once again pregnant, she had been seized with despair at her terrible fate, sold so many times into marriage, and she decided to end it all by strangling herself and her children. In fact, only the boy died, but the mother and daughter were revived.

The affair was reinvestigated by the League authorities, and reviewed also by the Li Fan Yüan and these later and more thorough examinations revealed a lot of evidence that had not come to light at the first interrogations. The accusation that Dashjid had stolen the sheep was a completely false one, for making which Tseveen was punished, while Amindoo was degraded from his position of *meiren* for having accepted this story without checking it properly. Almost everyone connected with the case was punished in some way, though Dashjid's original infanticide seems to have been overlooked: at any rate, no decision about this part of the case is given in the documents we possess. It turned out that at the time of the crime she had been upset by a rumour that her lost daughter had been brutally treated by Tseveen, who was alleged to have branded her on the face, but this was untrue. What Tseveen had actually done was to sell the girl to a lama in another banner, which was a criminal offence, though sale within a banner was permitted. Both Urjinjav and the *zasag* of the other banner were punished for condoning the crime, while the lama who had bought the girl for a horse and 270 tea-units was sentenced to a flogging. The bride-price was recovered from Tseveen and awarded to deserving individuals, and the girl herself was restored to her mother Dashjid.[2]

This case has been described in some detail for two reasons.

It has its own intrinsic interest as one of the few legal documents of the sort which have been published. It also shows the Manchu administration as diligent, though authoritarian, in the investigation of such cases as came to its notice. A case would move up to the highest instances, not as a result of appeal, but through bureaucratic necessity. The banner and league authorities could administer justice only according to the limited 'Mongol Code' and affairs which fell outside the scope of this went to Uliasutai or Urga, and even perhaps to Peking. But on the other hand this case reveals the social set-up in Mongolia as an essentially arbitrary and irrational one. There was no distinction between the executive and the judiciary, so that in effect a *zasag* was often in the position of trying, in the first instance, a case in which he himself was involved, and the administration of justice tended more and more, as the dynasty wore on, to be biased in favour of the ruling class. Where the nobility were concerned, punishments were in any case much lighter, and of a different type, involving merely fines and demotions rather than executions, beatings and banishment. Pozdneev quotes a case from 1822 when a *taiji* punished the son of a *khamjilga* of his, who was showing little progress as a pupil of the lamas, by tying him up naked outside the tent on a winter's night. The boy of course died, and the case went as far as Peking for decision. The *taiji* was merely fined two 'nines', that is, eighteen head of cattle, for his offence.[3] On the other hand, in 1833 a lama was found guilty of stabbing his hired maidservant to death in the course of a sudden quarrel, and was sent off in fetters to the prison at Dolonnor, the usual prelude to execution or banishment.[4] Once the judicial processes had been set moving they could be painfully long-winded, and decisions did not invariably go against the commoner in favour of the nobility, but the very structure of the system gave the authorities every inducement to procrastinate, to do each other a good turn, and to be swayed by bribes.

In its executive capacity the Manchu administration showed itself unable to take any effective steps to hinder the destructive economic forces which were at work inside Mongolian society, and were making for the material and spiritual impoverishment of which Dashjid's case is an exemplar. These forces were, essentially, the increase in the burden of taxation, the supplementing or commuting of *corvées* by money payments, and the cost of paying substitutes to perform inconvenient *corvées*, all of which, together with the extravagance of the aristocracy, led to the virtual enslavement of the population to foreign usury-traders who bought cheap and sold dear, on credit, bleeding the country of capital. No new forms of economic activity were able to develop. Agriculture, hunting and fishing, the latter practised by the Darkhats of north-west Mongolia, remained auxiliary occupations to the extensive herding economy. Handicrafts declined. Mongol craftsmen could not compete with the products of modern industry, especially Russian hardware which was imported in increasing quantities towards the end of the century, while many items which the Mongols had been used to make for themselves, and which they still needed in their daily life, such as tent-frames, were supplied by more efficient and competitive immigrant Chinese craftsmen. Trade was almost entirely in the hands of foreigners. There were retail Mongol traders, petty middle-men who sold local produce – meat, hats, boots and the like. The lamaseries were the largest native trading houses: they tended to work in with the Chinese firms, buying up local produce for them and getting their own requisites from them, but they also traded quite far afield with their own goods. So did individual rich lamas. During the period of autonomy the rich lama Chagdarjav, who later turned revolutionary, formed a co-operative group with fifteen rich partners to trade in competition with the foreigners. But this was an exception: in general, trade, and banking too, were Chinese perquisites.

There were certainly commoners who for one reason or another prospered and were even able to employ hired labourers, but as more and more wealth came to be concentrated into a few hands, those of a number of individuals and of the lamaseries, widespread and desperate poverty occurred. By 1855, it was calculated, there were 32,000 paupers in Tushetu Khan aimak, with some five thousand people on the verge of death by starvation. At this time the total population of Mongolia cannot have been much over half a million. By 1884 or 1885 the number of paupers in Tushetu Khan aimak and Setsen Khan aimak together had risen to nearly 71,000. In 1896 the office of one banner in Setsen Khan aimak reported to the League that the people were so destitute, *taijis* and commoners alike, that they had nothing to live on, let alone anything with which to pay their taxes, debt-interest, and *corvée*-substitutes. In the previous year eight people had actually died of hunger, and others were reduced to eating the flesh of dogs and wolves. People took to vagrancy to escape their misery, but were always liable to be pursued and brought back. Whether imperial subjects or *khamjilga* they were not legally entitled to move about and dispose of their labour as they wished, since this deprived their feudal overlord of part of his subsistence. Thus a herdsman called Bayar is known to have left his banner in 1905 because he had been unable to cope with the debt with a Chinese shop, which was piling up against him, and the shop had applied to the banner office which had paid up on his behalf. When this happened the defaulter was liable to extreme punishment. A case is known, for instance, of sixty-nine defaulters whose debts had been settled by their banner, and who were then forced to wear a cangue round their necks and make the rounds of the whole banner. The cangues were too wide for them to get through a tent door, so that they had to spend their nights in the open. Their hands also were fettered. This torture was continued for two years. Bayar therefore had good reason to run away, but five years later he was brought back and kept in fetters for a whole summer. Someone helped him to escape, and he stayed on the run until after the revolution of 1921.

Yet there was no industry to absorb this new proletariat, which could do no more than scratch a precarious living where it could, as day-labour, collecting dung and firewood, washing wool, doing farm-work, herding cattle and so on. Beggary grew more common. Where popular leaders emerged people might band together to bring a complaint officially against an oppressive banner-prince. They might even withdraw from their banner in protest and live apart as long as they could. This was quite a different phenomenon from vagrancy, since it aimed at bringing direct pressure on the overlord by depriving him of taxes and services. Finally we have to note the growth of banditry. More and more, individuals would abandon society altogether and live by theft. The folk-literature of the nineteenth century tells of many so-called *sain er* or 'good fellows', Robin Hood-like figures who became idealized as the robbers of the rich and the benefactors of the poor. In the early part of the century unrest was directed mainly at the excessive and often illegal exactions of the banner-princes and the Chinese merchants with whom they were in collusion, but in later years we can detect a growing anti-Manchu feeling which manifested itself particularly in army mutinies and desertions and in street riots.

The legal case recounted above describes a slave, but during the nineteenth century it became increasingly common for ordinary imperial subjects and even *taijis* to submit complaints against the arbitrariness of their banner-princes, and by the beginning of the present century persons of all sorts of social origin were suffering from the unequal distribution of wealth. In the past few years a large group of ordinary Mongols, partisans who fought in the war against the Chinese in 1921, have been interviewed and their memoirs published to illustrate the history of the early days of the revolution. A fortunate by-product of this enterprise is the mass of evidence we now possess, scattered throughout these autobiographical souvenirs, to supplement what we can gather from legal documents about social conditions in Mongolia in the nineteenth and early twentieth centuries. From some accounts, of course, nothing significant can be extracted, but sufficient does emerge to show how much personal poverty there was in Khalkha at the time, and how it was affecting the social set-up. The partisan army was not made up exclusively of rootless, destitute elements. That is to say, it cannot be discounted as an unrepresentative rabble, a dump for the refuse of society. There were many richer men in its ranks, men like the *shabi* Jambal, who had 113 animals with which to support his family of six, and others who had upwards of two hundred head of cattle. But the poorer class, cut off from their traditional livelihood as cattle-owners and herders, or living only partly on their depleted and quite inadequate flocks, certainly predominated, and these may be taken as an indicator of the way in which society was moving at the time, towards extremes of wealth and poverty.

Many of the families from which the partisans sprang had no domestic animals at all left in their possession, in a land where the proportion of domestic cattle to human population is the highest in the world. Thus Kh. Ayush, born in 1900, says of himself:

My mother Khorloo was destitute, without any cattle, so it was impossible for us to go on living in our native banner, and we came to Urga, where she supported us by taking in sewing, and so on.

A. Purevdagva, born in 1896, says:

My family was a very poor one ... From sixteen to twenty I was employed by a man called Yondon of the same banner, herding cattle, relay-riding, and collecting dung and firewood ... In 1920, when I was twenty-four, I was to become a dung-collector for the new *zasag*, but I ran away and came to Urga and worked for a butcher, carrying meat or herding the sheep.[5]

J. Gendenjamts was left alone with his mother at the age of eleven, his father having died and his other relatives having left home to become lamas. The two of them tried to live by hunting and herding their few beasts, but when these gave out there was no alternative but to come to Urga, where the boy hired himself out as a lama's servant. Some new arrivals in Urga enjoyed a better fate. Z. Galsanjamts tells of himself:

Till 1911 I used to do herding work in the country. My mother died in 1911 so my father and I came to Urga, and by dint of asking at the Shanzav's office I got a vacant child's place there and was trained in Mongol writing. But I never did clerical work afterwards, living on odd jobs together with my father.

Another partisan, D. Dendev, got his living as a boy by herding sheep for the administrator of his banner office, and by doing manual labour. At the same time the administrator taught him to read and write, so that Dendev was able to accompany him as 'half-scribe', that is, one of two boys who jointly did the work of one clerk, to the office of the ecclesiastical estate of the Jalkhantsa Khutuktu, one of the great incarnations of western Khalkha. In payment for his services he got a lamb and half a brick of tea a month. But getting an education like this was always a chancy business. The present President of Mongolia, J. Sambuu, born a *khamjilga* in 1895, was summoned to his overlord's in order to better his education there, but found on arrival that he was really nothing but an extra herdsman. He was never taught anything by the *taiji* but picked up what he could by his own efforts and by chance help from the clerks at the banner office when he accompanied his master there on duty.[6]

There were poor *taijis* amongst the partisans, too, whose stories illustrate the decay of the social order. D. Jambaljav, born in 1894, gives the following account of his family:

When I was nine years old, my father's mother, the old nun Ania, used to tell me how my grandfather, though he was supposed to be a *taiji* with four retainers, was chronically poor, and used to feed his children by such ways as hunting gazelles with his flintlock, or by watching the road and taking in caravaners for the night and by looking after their worn-out camels and oxen for them and returning them when recovered, in exchange for a bit of grain. My father, the *taiji* Dashzeveg, was a poor man's son, and from the time when he was young he used to hire himself out to his own retainer, the relay-rider Sonom, and do relay work for him, or caravaning, or farm-labouring. When he was thirty-seven he married my mother Namsrai, and I was their only child. In the end we had three oxen of the age of ten or so, four cows, and forty-odd sheep and goats. But we had no riding horse. The autumn I reached twenty we bought a pregnant mare for twenty-five bushels of grain and used her foal for riding. We began to get a start then, but we never had more than six horses all told.

At the other end of the social scale there was enormous personal wealth and extravagance, which fed on ignorance and superstition. It is not true, as many propagandists say, that there were no doctors in pre-revolutionary Mongolia, but it is a fact that there was nothing in the least like a modern scientific medical service. The traditional practitioners employed the classical Tibetan methods of diagnosis and treatment, based on untenable philosophical theories. Many of these doctors were really skilled in the empirical recognition of conditions, and in the compounding of medicines, and have left their case-books behind them, but their services were beyond the reach of most people, and it was itinerant magicians and quacks, working from grubby handbooks of divination, who were the familiar resource. Besides, there was in any case no effective way of treating the venereal diseases which plagued Mongolia till well on into this century. Swedish nurses, operating a clinic in Urga in 1924, calculated, according to the records they had kept, that venereal diseases affected practically the whole population and even in recent years the problem has been a worrying, though not intractable one. Now the lamaistic church ascribed these scourges to the sins of the people – in a sense with ironical justification since the venereal diseases were to a large extent spread by the lamas themselves, who were only very nominally celibate. But it could find no more effective way of attacking this evil than by organizing vast propitiatory exercises to compensate for the sin, and these swallowed enormous amounts of money. There was, for example, the *khailang*-assembly, which gathered 10,000 lamas together for a forty-five day prayer-meeting in Urga every year. More than half of these came from the provinces, at great expense. This custom, which began in 1913, lasted till 1922. Though it was of course absolutely futile, it was at least supposed to have some mystic effect on the welfare of the people at large, but not even this could be said for the enormous sums which were spent on the personal health of the Khutuktu and his consort. The Khutuktu was a syphilitic and suffered from blindness, and the prince Khandadorji, one of the ambassadors to Russia at the time of the 1911 revolution and an architect of Mongol independence, made himself instrumental in collecting the sum of 100,000 taels of silver for the erection of a gigantic Buddha, and of a further 230,000 taels for a temple to house it in, in the hopes that this pious act might cure the Khutuktu's defective vision. Equally staggering in its enormity was the purchase of 10,000 statues of Ayushi, the Buddha of Long Life, in 1912, on the occasion of services for the assurance of the Khutuktu's longevity. Nine thousand of these came from Poland, at an individual cost of over twenty-three Russian roubles. There are many other indications of the extravagance and effeteness of the ruling circles of Mongolia and their total ineptitude in the face of modern reality at the beginning of this century. One of the most intriguing is the story of the Khutuktu's imprisonment by the Chinese in Urga in 1920 when the white general, Baron Ungern-Sternberg was threatening to occupy the city. In order to effect his release, he had loyal lamas carry out a special ceremony of exorcism by fire, in which puppets of the Chinese commander and some Chinese soldiers and of the then Mongol Prime Minister were constructed and placed in a pit, and were then ritually burned. The officiating lama took a considerable risk in order to obtain real hair from Chinese soldiers to put on the heads of the ritual puppets and so make the charade more effective.[7]

All these reminiscences and anecdotes, different though the details are, have a common underlying theme, the breakdown of a traditional pattern of living under the impact of economic stagnation, and the collapse of a feeling of responsibility for the public welfare on the part of authority. The investigation of this process is the proper study of the nineteenth century in Mongolia.

Taxation

Besides being liable to state *corvées* and taxes, the imperial subjects in Mongolia, as well as the *khamjilga* and *shabi*, could be called upon to pay taxes to their *zasag* and to perform *corvée* for them. Mongol historians distinguish three types of exaction, to wit taxes in the form of *corvée*, taxes on produce, and money taxes, the third being basically a development of the first and second. Personal *corvée* was of several sorts. The people had to herd the nobles' cattle, do seasonal work in connection with the animals, such as milking the mares, shearing sheep, making felt, breaking horses, and so on. They had to collect dung and firewood, do domestic service, and attend the noble on journeys. There were two modes of herding. Either the herdsman would go to the prince's quarters and work there, or he would bring the animals to where he was grazing his own, and look after them all together. Lamaseries, too, would farm out their animals in this way. Usually the better-off herdsmen were chosen for this work, since they would be in a better position to follow the good pastures and also to make up accidental losses, for which they were responsible. Conditions of service varied from place to place. Sometimes the herdsman might get direct compensation, perhaps a sheep every year, but mostly no direct payment was given. The herders would be expected to deliver fixed quantities of produce, related to the animals entrusted to them, and over and above this could make use of the animals for their own purposes. Actually this was not always an unprofitable *corvée* for the families undertaking it, and some relied on it, right up to the dissolution of the lamaseries in the 1930s, for their livelihood. To take one example of the type of arrangement entered into, the sheep belonging to the *sang*, or personal estate, of the Dilowa Khutuktu of Narabanchen lamasery, used to be farmed out to families owning three hundred or less sheep of their own. They were allowed to keep all the summer milk, seventy per cent of the wool, and the lambs. In winter they froze milk and gave some of it to the Khutuktu, and had to hand over also the skins of any sheep which died. The conditions were so favourable that there was competition even among the richer families, who were economically speaking able to get on without this chore, to take over the care of the *sang* sheep.

SOCIAL AND ECONOMIC DEVELOPMENTS

In many cases the produce to be delivered would not be exactly that of the particular animals concerned. For instance, a herdsman who worked in his youth for an Urga aimak, or division of the church, told an inquirer that he used to have to deliver fifteen pounds of cream and ten pounds of butter a year for each head of cattle, even if there were no milch cattle among them. Similarly, each draught-ox attracted the obligation to deliver five cartloads of firewood. So *corvée* service inevitably merged into the money-tax system: in this particular case, which dates from the early years of the present century, the firewood deliveries could be commuted by a payment of ten silver dollars. In fact, during the later nineteenth century, the economy of Mongolia as a whole was becoming more and more a money economy. Though right up to the time of the Republic costs and prices were not calculated in any fixed medium, but in such units as sheep, bricks of tea, smaller 'tea-units', and *khadags* or ceremonial scarves, foreign notes and coins began to circulate, and as early as the 1860s the Khutuktu's private estate, and some of the wealthier nobles, were issuing rudimentary banknotes, known as *tiiz*, which served as local currency within their own purlieus.

The *corvées* were irksome, but the real drag on the country's progress, as the present-day historian Natsagdorj points out, was the tax on produce. As good a general statement of what this involved as can be found is contained in a report to the Emperor submitted by the amban of Urga in 1783 on the subject of taxes levied by the aristocracy in the two aimaks of Tushetu Khan and Setsen Khan. This runs:

> The khans, princes, dukes and *zasag-taijis* of the two aimaks take from their commoners everything which they need for their taxes and their own affairs, for living at home or travelling, or for paying to others. They draw from the commoners of their banners all the cattle and provisions for the various watch-posts on the Russian frontier at Uliasutai, Khobdo and Urga, for the Khobdo farms and for the troops stationed at Uliasutai and Khiakta. Apart from this they take in taxes from their commoners everything, such as cattle, provisions, money, felt and cloth tents and tea for the daily use of their own households, for the provisioning of their servants, for going to Peking and on hunt duty, for taking their turn of duty at Uliasutai, for the League assemblies, and for pilgrimages and for travelling on their own business.[8]

In fact, the commoners supplied everything for the public obligations and private consumption of the nobility, and in practice the taxes so levied went far beyond what was permitted by the regulations of the Li Fan Yüan, namely an annual levy of one sheep in twenty. One *zasag* of Tushetu Khan aimak, Tsedendorji, for instance, took one sheep in ten, and levied taxes in tea on herds smaller than this. In three years at the beginning of the nineteenth century his exactions in kind could be calculated at over 6,700 taels of silver, this figure covering for example 412 oxen, 2,160 sheep, 6,000 pounds of butter, 1,320 bushels of barley and 9,200 pounds of flour, as well as other items, while he also extracted over 21,000 taels to pay his debts to the Chinese shops. Without knowing the size of his banner and what its total wealth was, it is difficult to interpret these figures satisfactorily, but the exactions were certainly excessive, and were recognized as such by the League authorities, who in 1815 ordered him to repay 11,200 illegally levied taels of silver. However, this type of situation was the norm throughout the century, to the extent, for instance, that by its end the total wealth of the Khobdo district was reckoned not to be as much as half the debt owed to the local Chinese shops.

Money payments, both as a state tax and as tax paid to the banner-princes, seem to have originated as a means of commuting *corvées* and produce-taxes. For state *corvées* this can be well illustrated from the history of the official farms at Khobdo. Originally, four hundred families were detached from the three western aimaks of Khalkha to man these farms, Setsen Khan aimak being excused this duty because of its distance from Khobdo, in spite of representations from the other aimaks. However, from the beginning of the nineteenth century new categories of worker are found mentioned in official documents, and in the 1830 tax assessments, Setsen Khan aimak was ordered to supply thirty-four workers, but was officially allowed to commute this duty by a payment of 467 taels. As the century wore on, banners nearer at hand began to commute their *corvées* also, hiring substitute workers. The cost seems to have been higher than the official exemption for Setsen Khan aimak. In the same year, 1830, one *zasag* reported to his League office that substitutes were costing him one hundred taels a family. In 1895 a banner of Sain Noyon Khan aimak managed to borrow money from the Chinese firm which was its banker for this purpose, though with a warning that 'as your banner has a big debt with us, we will not give you money again'. Individuals might commute their *corvées* too. Sukebator, the future revolutionary leader, earned his living as a youth by performing relay-riding service for richer families whose duty it really was. On the other hand, from the early nineteenth century onwards, *zasags* began to demand money taxes from their people in part payment of their produce taxes or as extra taxes. One who did so was the well-known Togtokhtör, or To-wang, of Setsen Khan aimak, a prince of grandiose ambitions, the cost of whose projects, as we shall see in more detail later, led to discontent and an armed uprising in his banner.

We have already seen how impoverishment, the inability to pay taxes or even to make a living in the banner territories, led people to vagrancy. The process was going on throughout the nineteenth century and affected the *shabi* as well as the lay commoners. Though freed from most state *corvées*, the *shabi* were in hardly a more enviable position than the imperial subjects and *khamjilga*, since they were subject to heavy church taxes which had increased just like the state and banner exactions. The computation of produce taxes in terms of silver permits an estimate of the rate at which taxes were actually increasing. The tax-unit of tea, which up to the end of the nineteenth century had been valued at from five to ten cents, had become inflated by 1908 to thirty cents, and by 1921, the year of the revolution, to as much as two taels or two hundred cents. Thus a sheep, nominally taxed at two tea-units, a horse at from six to eight and a camel at from eight to ten, would actually cost in terms of silver from three to four, from twelve to eighteen, and from sixteen to twenty-four taels a year respectively, or as much as the value of a good quality animal. The practical effect of this can be seen from the personal reminiscences of a former *shabi*, by name Eenden. In 1960 Eenden recalled:

> Around 1902 to 1905 we paid two thousand taels on our assessment of 150 tea units. To pay our taxes we sold 150 sheep with their lambs to the Chinese shops for fifty cents each. In the end, all fifty families in our *otog* were rendered destitute, and were scattered as vagrants in all directions. Only two families stayed on the old pastures. When the People's government was set up, we had a tax debt of seven thousand taels, from which we were excused.[9]

The figures given by Eenden are not easy to reconcile with the general valuation of a tea-unit given above, though all these figures have been extracted from the same source. However, the main point is that it was excessive taxation which ruined the people of this particular *otog*. This tale comes from the end of the Manchu dynasty, but as early as 1823 the amban of Urga was trying to get the aimaks and the *shabi-otogs* to register and take back to their original homes some two thousand five hundred vagrants, lay people and lamas, who were living in the city, having left their homes to try and get a living outside the banner jurisdiction. In the same year the general of Uliasutai was urging the aimak authorities to deal with the problem by preventing people from leaving home and by allotting cattle as relief to those who had none. In 1828 the head of Setsen Khan aimak reproved the aristocracy of his League for not relieving their own poor, but for aggravating the situation by taking on vagrants from other areas as paid labourers. Just the same complaint was made nearly a century later in the petition put in by the herdsman Ayushi and his comrades in Zasagtu Khan aimak: 'The *taijis* are supposed to prevent the people from taking to vagrancy and to look after those who are wandering about, but they pay no attention to this. . . .'[10] From very early on we find richer families turning the situation to account by engaging vagrants to work for them, instead of returning them to the banner they belonged to, as regulations required. In 1801 we read of a fugitive *shabi* being taken on by the head of a *sumun* for a wage of three taels a month.

Urbanization

Many vagrants preferred to congregate around the lamaseries and the few towns, where they began to form an urban proletariat. The Russian traveller Pevtsov, who visited Uliasutai in 1879, found it a squalid town, with dirty, muddy streets, containing at most a thousand inhabitants, most of them Chinese merchants and craftsmen. The latter were engaged in making tent-frames, wooden vessels and grates for the Mongols.

In the vicinity of the town [he reported], one comes across yurts and miserable tents of worn-through felt. In these there live, in the most poverty-stricken conditions, Mongols, who get their daily bread as labourers in the town, or who live by begging from the Chinese.[11]

SOCIAL AND ECONOMIC DEVELOPMENTS

Pozdneev, who was there fourteen years later, found the situation of the Mongols unimproved. They lived, he wrote, in yurts as if still on the steppes, but did not engage in herding. The women were prostitutes, the men labourers, petty traders or, occasionally, craftsmen of one sort or another. The Mongols were the most dangerous element in the town, constantly stealing horses, cattle and camels which they would drive off to their yurts a few miles away and kill at once for provisions for the next month or two. For this reason the general was for ever trying to get rid of them. The aimak representatives were supposed to round up the vagrants within a hundred Chinese miles of the city, and send them back to their native pastures, but, as Pozdneev remarked, 'naturally this is only a formality, and the number of tramps round Uliasutai continues to increase'.[12] Uliasutai was only a hundred and fifty years old then, and Khobdo a younger foundation, yet both places were materially dilapidated and their occupants demoralized. Pozdneev's 'naturally' is no accident. In 1872, when some four hundred Dungans attacked Khobdo, the garrison of a thousand withdrew to the fortress and let the rebels plunder the trade city at their will. A sortie with five hundred soldiers turned into a rout, in which the Chinese army suffered a hundred casualties. Both travellers were as contemptuous of Khobdo as of Uliasutai. The population was small, consisting of only about a thousand in 1878, according to Pevtsov, and the civilians were almost all Chinese traders. Around the town he found miserable yurts, several dozens of them, inhabited by impoverished Mongols who would hire themselves out as day-labourers in the town and live on the good-will of the wealthier Chinese for whom they did various tasks. They were dependent of the Chinese, 'or, to put it more neatly, enslaved to them'.[13] Pozdneev wrote that the pursuits of the Mongols were the same as in Uliasutai, only here the Mongols were even poorer as they had to compete with the poor soldiers of the Manchu 'Green Banner' army. There were fewer prostitutes too, partly because the town was smaller, but also partly because it was the only town in Mongolia where the Chinese had brought their wives to live with them.[13a]

Hence, if one talks of the emergence of a Mongol urban population in the nineteenth century, it must be realized that this was a very small-scale phenomenon, even in Urga, the largest settlement, and important not so much in itself but rather as an indication of the decline of the self-sufficient steppe-society. In any case, no town in Mongolia was a truly Mongol town. Both Uliasutai and Khobdo were, as we saw in the previous chapter, Chinese centres where an official fortress and a trade town existed side by side, with a rabble of Mongol hangers-on on the fringe. No native urban middle class developed here or elsewhere in Mongolia. The so-called *panzchin* or 'speculators' who are referred to at the beginning of this century were mere money-lenders and middlemen whose activities did not contribute to the evolution of the Mongol economy. The capital they accumulated either re-circulated as new loans, or was put by in the form of animals, or went in offerings to the Church, but was not used constructively. Even apart from the big Chinese merchant houses, what enterprise there was was mainly in the hands of Chinese. At Uliasutai, for instance, Pevtsov noted the existence of a Chinese peasant settlement, consisting of about ten plots, 'cultivated in an exemplary fashion' on ground irrigated with water channels, and manured with dung and waste from the town. These must have contrasted sharply with the army fields at Khobdo, cultivated by Mongols and garrison soldiers, whose yield did not even suffice for the garrison itself.

Khiakta was the only town which had grown up purely as a trade centre. In Uliasutai and Khobdo, as in Khiakta, the Church played but a minor role. Khobdo had its Yellow Temple, which was the central temple for the various Mongol tribes of the district, but at its most flourishing it never held more than about four hundred lamas, and this figure decreased in the nineteenth century, while after its destruction by the Dungans in the 1870s the lamas moved for a time to another site some twenty miles away. Uliasutai was known for its temple of Geser Khan, the Mongol god of war, and Khiakta too had a temple for the use of the hundred soldiers of its garrison, stationed there since 1764. Other townships, such as Ulaangom and above all, Urga, were basically temple-cities. Urga was divided into two main parts, Gandang and East Urga or Zuun Khuree, while some few miles to the east lay the Chinese trade city or Mai-mai-khota. Ordinary lay Mongols lived both in special districts of the temple-city and also scattered among the Chinese of the trade-city, while in the nineteenth century new Chinese quarters grew up in and around the temple-city. In Urga, as elsewhere, it was Mongols who formed the proletariat, though here it was mixed in character since so many of the poorer elements were lamas. Living far from their native pastures, where they could have drawn support from their families, these lamas had to take up such outside jobs as working for foreign firms, to supplement their inadequate dole from the temples, though this was against the rules. Some turned to robbery, others to beggary. There were many *dulduichin* or 'rattlers', lamas who patrolled Urga ringing their bells to attract an audience and picking up a living by reciting prayers and blessings. The conditions producing a lama-proletariat can be judged from the reminiscences of men still living who were lamas in their youth, even under the early Republic. Manibadar, who came to Urga in 1913 and worked as a servant to richer lamas till 1930, said:

> We never got any special wage for our work. If we were lucky we got a bowl of food, or a corner of meal-cake. If ever we got cotton for a gown it was a rare piece of luck. We never got much of the food issued by the temple. We were lucky if we got it five or ten times a month, nor did we poor monks ever get much of a share of the temple-alms – on an average three Chinese dollars a month.[14]

Amongst the lay people too, poverty was rife. There was a quarter in Urga known as Beggars' Hill where so many beggars starved to death that the Shanzav's office employed a poor lama specially to clear away the corpses. He was known as the Church Boneman, and there were several like him in Urga. Beggars, lurking on the rubbish heaps, were a sight which shocked the eyes of the boy Nawaangnamjil, who we met in chapter 1, when he arrived in Urga to do clerical duty there.

> In front of the high rubbish heaps in the markets and temples were poor wretches lying about, with no homes or relatives, poor and sick, without eyes or noses. Some kind people would give them a bite to eat, but most passed by on the other side disgusted, and the wretches suffered from hunger and thirst, burned by the hot sun in summer and frozen to the marrow in winter, while neither the authorities nor the people, lama or lay, did a thing to help them.[15]

Agriculture

Alongside this incipient and small-scale urbanization in Mongolia we should look at the beginnings of agriculture there. The Manchu army fields have already been mentioned briefly and the role played by the Church as landlord will be touched on below. Apart from this there were also Mongols who went over from herding to agriculture or who tilled fields as a sideline on their own account. Natural conditions, especially the hard climate and the scarcity of water in the right place worked against the development of farming, and so did the prejudices of the Mongols themselves, whose natural mode of life, mounted herding, stood in contradiction to settled farming. The Emperor K'ang Hsi, who also realized that ploughing removed land from pasture use for many years if not permanently, and therefore discouraged it in Mongolia, observed the bad farming habits of the Mongols of Inner Mongolia, who would plant a crop and then move off and leave it to the vagaries of the seasons, perhaps not returning till it was quite spoiled by frost.

In Khalkha Mongolia agriculture was often something which people would only take up if they had failed to keep themselves by herding. In 1816 a *zasag* of Tushetu Khan aimak reported: 'I am doing my best to deal with the starvation and dispersal of the poorer people in the banner, who have been sowing crops, reaping and selling them so as to scrape a living.'[16] But not all farmers took up this way of life in desperation. There were those who did well at it, and whose methods, preparatory irrigation of the ground, ploughing with wooden ploughs, and even manuring, all imitated from the Chinese, were far from primitive. Some quotations from the personal reminiscences of a farmer about what life was like when he was a boy at the beginning of this century are very informative about Mongol farming, and go far to refute the popular myth that there was no agriculture in Mongolia until very recently. The informant, who came from near Lake Khuvsugul in the north-west, says:

> The fields in our banner were private, or belonged to the various *jas*. There were about a hundred farming families. At that time we had been farming for three generations. We paid no taxes to the banner office or the prince from our produce, but the prince used to buy our produce.... We would harness two bullocks to a home-made wooden plough. As we did not have our own bullocks we used to hire them for ploughing. We would sow a bushel of the owner's grain for him, and give him twelve bushels in return, or we would rent a bullock for

five bushels. We sowed by hand. We did not water the crops or harrow them, but we weeded by hand. Sometimes we took on hired hands, and paid them grain according to what they sowed. So a man who sowed ten bushels of seed got ten bushels of grain. . . . The family of Ganbolod, a rich man, employed four labourers and used two ploughs. Originally he had been a poor man with only five goats, and had begged some grain. . . . Three families had their own mills and we used to give seed as payment for milling. . . . People came from a good way away to buy our produce. The local Chinese would not get grain from their original homes but used to buy flour to eat from us Mongols. At harvest time the Chinese shop-people used to come along with their tents and pots and pans and buy from us. Some rich people would export our grain into other banners and retail it there, but mostly people came from other banners themselves to buy. We sold coarse flour at fifty pounds for a ewe, and fine flour at thirty. . . . Some people who came from afar brought salt and exchanged it for grain. For a ladle of salt they took a ladle of grain.[17]

What we find presented here is something usually ignored in accounts of Mongolia – a well-off class of yeomen, owning their own fields and trading freely in their own produce. It is a refreshing contrast to the tales of misery more generally told, and which are adduced by communist apologists to justify the necessity for the Soviet-style revolution of 1921, and it would be of interest to know to what extent this picture of modest self-sufficiency could be duplicated amongst the other communities of Mongolia.

The condition and function of the Church

The most important factor in the history of Mongolia was, however, the development of the Church in the nineteenth century, and in particular that of Urga, by far the most important single unit. Urga rested on two pillars, on the *shabi*, mostly lay people, who were Church-serfs and who provided the economic base, and on the thousands of lamas who constituted the Church itself. Modern Mongolian historians naturally view the Church as exemplifying class-structure and the class-struggle. They differentiate a rich minority aristocracy of *khutuktus* or incarnations and other high lamas, and an impoverished mass of lowly lamas who could never hope to rise to be anything else, and who, to a great extent, were mere temple-servants. In between these there grew up a third class of learned lamas and administrators. Like all neat schemes of social stratification, this one represents a generalization and is valid only subject to comment. Indeed, it was not always recognized as a valid one by the communist People's government which had enunciated it and claimed to base its religious policy on the existence of a class-struggle within the Church which could be exploited. This was particularly true during the period of so-called 'leftist deviation' after 1929, when all lamas were lumped together as social enemies and misused accordingly. Indeed, although there were gaping differences between the conditions of the richest and the poorest lamas, the People's government had an uphill task to convince the lamas concerned of the significance of these differences in Marxist terms of class antagonism. When finally the lamaseries were closed in 1937 and after, many thousands of poor lamas who had not been persuaded that their interest lay in voluntary secularization had to be turned out into an unfamiliar world.

The Church was certainly hierarchical, but its very nature as a celibate society, at least in theory, differentiated it from the hereditary feudalism of the lay world, and meant that there had to be a certain measure of social mobility in order to keep the upper ranks filled. There were of course famous cases of nepotism and favouritism, especially in the periods of office of the last two Khutuktus. The seventh, who died in 1868, had been deliberately corrupted by the then Mongol amban of Urga, the Setsen Khan Artased. Having run through his own fortune, Artased had his eye on the Khutuktu's *sang*, and by flattery and pandering to the Khutuktu's vices he succeeded in getting his young son appointed Da Lama, or second in command to the Shanzav. The younger brother of the eighth Khutuktu was appointed State Oracle-Lama, with a lavish temple, now the Ulan Bator Religious Museum, built for him and his wife. In general, however, family succession was excluded, and higher positions in the Church were filled by recruits from ordinary families. The late Dilowa Khutuktu, for example, did not come from a noble family: the only privilege enjoyed by his family was that his parents, together with those of his predecessor and of the Narabanchen Khutuktu were classified in the temple register as exempt from taxation on their animals. In theory Manchu regulations forbade the discovery of reincarnations among the nobility, so as to curb as far as possible an alliance between the aristocracy and the Church, and in practice the Church did to some extent offer the possibility of careers open to talent.

Individual case histories are not too plentiful, but a few enlightening details are available. We know, for instance, that the Da Lama Tserenchimid, the Minister of Home Affairs in the first Mongol government of 1911, was born of common parentage, and had worked his way up in the ecclesiastical administration. Likewise the Shanzav Badmadorji, who was instrumental in surrendering Mongolia's autonomy to the Chinese in 1919, was a commoner who had become a lama as a boy and had then gained administrative experience in successive appointments in the *Shabi* office. Another lama, Losol, who was one of the seven famous revolutionaries, including Sukebator and Choibalsang, who went to the Soviet Union in 1920 to enlist communist support, had a very varied career. Born in 1890 as an imperial subject, he had been transferred to the *shabi* estate, and from 1899 onwards was a lama. As a young man he travelled extensively, visiting Peking, Moscow and St. Petersburg, and in 1913 became army lama with Damdinsuren, one of the commanders at the siege of Khobdo the year before. After 1921 he held a whole series of administrative jobs, none of them ecclesiastical, till he was liquidated in 1939 on trumped-up charges. Another interesting career was that of the famous impromptu poet Gelegbalsang who was born in 1846. His father was a *khamjilga* of modest means who put the ten-year-old boy in a lamasery because he was intelligent and could profit from an education. Gelegbalsang studied Tibetan, but found the life uncongenial and ran away home. At the age of twenty, having learned to read and write Mongol, he hired camels and became a carrier for Chinese merchants. On these journeys he gathered a good knowledge of Chinese. By the age of thirty his skill as an impromptu composer of poems of circumstance, known in Mongol as *irugel* or 'blessings', had become apparent, and he came to be in great demand at festive occasions where the recitation of such poems formed an essential part of the ceremonies. His literary skill was so impressive that he was invited to return to the lamasery from which he had fled as a boy to serve as intendant. His poetical gifts continued to be much in demand, even as far afield as Urga itself, but when he died in 1923 he was only moderately comfortably off, possessing three tents, one horse, one camel, two oxen and twenty sheep.

The picture becomes distorted with the extravagances of the period of autonomy, when control of the Church, previously in Manchu hands, was transferred to the Khutuktu in his capacity as King of Mongolia: the 'Two Principles' were now united in the hands of a single man. A general round of promotions of the higher lamas took place, the establishment being enlarged with a consequent inflation of titles. Apart from the Jebtsundamba there were now six true Khutuktus or high incarnations in Urga, together with forty other high lamas who were granted the title of Khutuktu. For example, both the *khamba* or abbot of Urga, and his assistant, were for the first time accorded the title of Khutuktu with salaries of five hundred and three hundred taels of silver and the privilege of using a yellow and a green sedan chair respectively. Civil titles of nobility were conferred on high lamas, and they were allotted the appropriate numbers of *khamjilga* just like the lay nobility.

Without exception, travellers to Mongolia at about the beginning of this century condemned the lamaist Church there as an incubus exploiting the people and stultifying every aspect of life. Some, like the rigid Scottish missionary James Gilmour, who termed Urga the seat of Satan, objected to lamaism on theological grounds, but there was also general agreement that morally and materially the lamaist Church was the curse of Mongolia. In this century the elimination of the economic stranglehold of the Church was one of the main tasks facing the People's government after 1924: this task was not accomplished till 1939. Yet at the same time the Church was immensely popular and valued by the ordinary Mongols, who were, in a way, the slaves of their own piety and superstition. Each family would try to put one of its sons into a lamasery, not only because material conditions were rather better for lamas than for laymen, but also out of pure piety. Estimates of the size of the Church vary, but it would probably not be too far off the mark to accept the figure of seven hundred big lamaseries and over one thousand small ones in 1921, with some 113,000 lamas in all. A majority of these were not in residence, but lived at home, hardly distinguishable in their way of life from the lay members of their families. Superstition and ignorance kept people a prey to those lamas who made their living by selling images, performing rituals, casting horoscopes, expelling the demons who were considered the cause of disease, locating the souls of the dead and pacifying them, telling fortunes and so on. But apart from that, the Khutuktu of Urga radiated an enormous attractive power over the whole Mongol Buddhist world, and pilgrims came offering him gifts from far beyond the bounds of Khalkha – from Inner Mongolia, from Barga in north Manchuria, from the Tanguts of Tibet, from the Buriats, and even from the Kalmucks of Astrakhan, who used to come annually to Urga, even if in small numbers, ever since one of their princesses made a pilgrimage there in 1880. What went wrong was that the Church lost sight of its mission, limited as this was, with little conception of pastoral care for the faithful, long before the Mongols lost faith in the Church. There was no lack in later years of lamas, especially those of the middle grade, who criticized the abuses within their own ranks and called for a return to a purer way of life, but their voices were lost in the degeneracy of the late nineteenth century, in the collapse of personal morality and responsibility, and the transformation of the Church into a commercial enterprise to the detriment of its spiritual vocation. When a strong reform movement emerged in the late 1920s stimulated by the challenge of communism it was already too late, for the revolutionaries had made up their minds to eradicate the Church altogether, and after 1929 disposed of the power to do so.

The *Shabi* provided, by way of labour and taxation, a considerable part of the income of Urga, working for and contributing to the various *jas* or treasuries belonging to the aimaks, that is the administrative divisions of the temple-city, and the *datsangs* or religious colleges, as well as to the Khutuktu's private purse, the running of the *Shabi*-office itself, and the expenses of the Khutuktu's temples outside Urga. It is estimated that some thousand *Shabi*-families alone were employed herding the Khutuktu's private herds. Though exempt from state taxation, the *Shabi* were little if any better off than the rest of the commoners, especially with the sharp rise in taxation towards the end of the century, and its inflated computation in terms of silver, which became the main medium of payment. Even as far back as 1785 there had been nearly four thousand *Shabi*-families without cattle of their own, amounting to almost twenty-two thousand individuals, and this tendency towards the proletarianization of the individual, while the wealth of the Church as a whole increased, continued throughout the years. By the early years of this century it was quite common for members of the *Shabi* to be completely unable to meet their tax obligations, which were grotesquely out of proportion to their means. A report from the headman of the Gobi *otog* of the *Shabi* to the *Shabi*-office made in 1914 runs in part:

This petty slave, in accordance with the stern directive dispatched with an official of the Office to have our *otog* pay up the whole of its old debt, for which it is liable, made direct demands upon the few impoverished people of the *otog*, but without effect. I just managed to extract fifty taels, and have dispatched them with the official Choivsuren, but apart from that our *otog* has at present a debt of thirty thousand taels unpaid. Our *otog* consists of ten or so households, one hundred or so persons whose whole wealth is eleven horses, eleven camels, six cattle and 154 sheep. Please instruct me how I am to care for the livelihood of such poor persons, let alone have them reduce and pay off such an enormous debt.

But such impossible circumstances did not excuse those assessed from payment, and the archives disclose that severe punishments were inflicted for the non-payment of taxes to the Church. A report submitted in 1914 from the supervisor of the *otogs* south of Urga runs:

Following the instructions received that anyone, of whatever *otog*, official, lama, novice or layman, who had defaulted on payments of silver and butter is to be punished by beating and the extent of the punishment reported in writing, we report the following punishments ...

There follows a list of sixty-four persons, including lamas and *otog*-headmen and their assistants, who received forty blows each for defaulting on their tax assessments.[18]

Apart from their regular obligations to finance religious services, the repair of temples, the upkeep of the Khutuktu's relatives, and so on, many periodic demands were made on the *Shabi*. They were responsible, for example, for the greater part of the cost of the obsequies of a deceased Khutuktu. When the fourth died, in 1813, these services cost seventy thousand taels, of which the *Shabi* were assessed to forty thousand. A similar sum was levied for the obsequies of the sixth, who died as a child of six years of age, only a few weeks after his expensive induction at

Urga. In 1850, 130 lamas were sent to Lhasa to perform his obsequies. The escort of a new Khutuktu to Urga from Tibet was likewise very expensive. Enormous escorts used to be sent out from Mongolia to bring back a new incarnation. Thus the escort for the third consisted of eight hundred men with horses and camels, and for the fifth, in 1820, of 539 men, with 1,600 horses, nearly 850 camels, and almost twenty thousand taels of silver. In addition to this huge party, other escorts were sent out to meet the Khutuktu part way and accompany him to Urga, and by imperial command fourteen special relay stations were set up temporarily to cope with the traffic.

The number of *jas*-treasuries in Urga consisting mainly of property in the form of animals, increased with the years to about two hundred, and were placed under the control of bursars with a staff of clerks. The bursars were engaged in all sorts of activities connected with the administration of their *jas* – buying and selling cattle, farming out cattle to others to pasture, trading, lending money, renting out farmland, and running caravans. Their task was greatly aided by the lamaseries' exemption from taxation, so that, although temple herds were subject to the same natural hazards and calamities as those of the ordinary people, they increased steadily up to the time of the revolution. Income from cattle formed the largest sector in the money-economy of the average Urga *jas*. For instance, the Zoogoo aimak had a total income in 1889 calculated at 376,407 tea-units. Of this, 26,715 units came from offerings, 127,000 from transport activities, 33,600 from trade, and 189,092, or more than half, from the *jas*-cattle. Similarly, in 1899 the Badmayoga college owed nearly two-thirds of its income to its herds. This income was not only enough for consumption, but provided a surplus for sale and for the capital backing for trade and money-lending.

We know from surviving accounts that Urga was engaging officially in usury, at any rate by the end of the eighteenth century, but with the transition to a money economy in the later nineteenth century this became a much more important feature of its financial activity. The earliest accounts show a comparatively modest rate of interest being charged: in 1799 for instance, a rate of one per cent per month on a loan of one thousand taels. But as silver became more sought after, usury figured more largely in temple accounts and the rates rose. At the beginning of this century the average Urga *jas* was charging as much as one hundred per cent per annum, and in some cases a rate of two hundred per cent, extortionate not only in itself, but in comparison, for instance, with the eight per cent charged by the American firm of Anderson Meyer on a loan made to the Mongol government in 1917.

The fourth Khutuktu, the only one apparently who had a real sense of clerical discipline, and who was known in consequence as the 'terrible incarnation', tried to curb this un-Buddhistic activity as early as 1797, when he issued an encyclical letter condemning excessive trading and money-lending along with brawling and rowdyism, singing and archery, chess-playing and smoking, but this had no effect at all. Whereas at first only the *jas* lent out money, rich lamas later took to operating on their own account, charging equally high rates of interest. There was even a system of compulsory public loans in force in Urga: lamas and richer *shabis* would be assessed and compelled to take out loans at an interest-rate of from 3 to 4 per cent a month for the benefit of a *jas*.

Trade and transport work for foreign firms brought in a considerable income, as did the management of agricultural land. The Khutuktu had had his own farmers at least from the late seventeenth century, but it was around the beginning of the present century that agriculture began to play an important part in the economy of Urga. In Manchu times it had been mostly the Khutuktu and the imperial temples which had owned farm land, but later many *jas* began to ask nobles for lands and to receive these as pious offerings. The situation here changed, as much else did, under autonomy. Fields would still be given as alms to the *jas*, but were, in addition, prized out of the possession of various banners by the direct order of the Khutuktu. Both land already given over to agriculture and virgin pasture land were transferred arbitrarily to Church ownership in this way. The *jas* would not necessarily cultivate these fields themselves, but would hire them out to Chinese farmers, or engage farmers to cultivate them on their behalf.

The picture of the Church which emerges at the beginning of this century is that of a series of rich corporate societies. Of these, Urga was far and away the richest and most influential, though it exercised no definite spiritual or temporal control over lamaseries not specifically under its jurisdiction. That the Khutuktu and his associates represented in 1911 the only group able to fill the power gap left by the expulsion of the Manchus was due merely to the enormous prestige and wealth of Urga and above all to the mystique of the Khutuktu himself, not to any pre-existing legal authority over the Church or state as a whole. But within these societies the wealth was distributed very unevenly. The aimaks and colleges of Urga enjoyed large incomes from alms which were supposed to be shared out, *pro rata*, among all lamas who attended the services. Temple regulations provided that the higher lamas should get a bigger share, but theirs was not, in theory, grossly out of proportion. In practice, however, the dole received by the lower lamas was often quite insufficient to live on. Manibadar's experience, mentioned above, was common. Lamas had to do outside work to make ends meet, but this often meant that they had to miss service and their share of rations. Another lama, who came to Urga in 1917, describes his life as follows:

> When I first came in from the countryside, I experienced not a few hardships. I tried living as a rich lama's servant. Also I used to split firewood, do cleaning, and copy out Tibetan books. But as I had little time to go to service, I got practically nothing from the temple rations and alms. So I lived entirely by my work. I used to copy out Tibetan books at eight to ten cents per eight sheets, and saw and split logs at twenty cents a log.[19]

Lamas such as this were often too poor to be able to afford any fuel in winter, or to eat more than once a day, drinking plain tea for breakfast and supper. During the years of autonomy and the early republic it was reported to the *Shabi*-office that poor lamas, unable to put up with this life any more, were deserting their lamaseries and going back to the countryside, 'to the great damage of the Yellow Faith', a reverse movement of vagrancy.

The general moral decline within the Church matched its social and economic irresponsibility. The last two Khutuktus, especially, gave no example of morality. The seventh very early on gave himself up to drinking, whoring and homosexuality, to the great scandal of many lamas of Urga who tried to enlist the help of the Manchu amban against him. The eighth, too, was a drunkard and syphilitic, of all-embracing sexual tastes. The lamaseries themselves were often haunts of vice, where older lamas commonly maintained catamites known by the euphemism of *bandi* or 'pupil'. There was an atmosphere of degeneration about the *fin-de-siècle* court of the eighth Khutuktu, the first and last King of Mongolia. After the death of his consort he decided to take another wife, and sent out emissaries to collect suitable names: his choice fell on the wife of a wrestler, who let her go to the Khutuktu with a shrug. The girl herself was of light morals: she got herself made an 'oracle' and used her special tent to carry on with various lamas, and also had a liaison with the young lama who was her hairdresser. On a certain occasion the Khutuktu called in the four precentors and the four proctors of the main temple of Urga to meet his new wife. The couple received them in bed, and we are told how the precentor Galsang put his hand under the covers and felt her and said: 'Ah now, that's a fine girl!' The Khutuktu himself maintained for some time a liaison with one of his attendants, a man called Legtseg: the two used to change clothes and reverse their roles and had a regular homosexual relationship. A lama was once heard wondering aloud how long this would last, and Legtseg, suspecting that the Khutuktu was about to throw him over, hit the Khutuktu in the face, smashing his front teeth. In the end Legtseg was arrested, apparently at the Khutuktu's instigation, imprisoned for a time in Urga, then banished to a distant spot where the local prince made away with him by burying him in the sand. The Khutuktu arranged elaborate obsequies for him in Urga.

The last Khutuktu's vices and excesses may not have affected his standing among the ordinary faithful, but did lower him in the estimation of the lamas of Urga, and there was a vocal, though ineffective, opposition both among the learned lamas and the lower orders, to his display of immorality. The clergy was losing faith in its leaders, not only in the Khutuktu, but also in other high lamas who were despised for their drunkenness and lasciviousness. It was not always safe, though, to show discontent. In 1913 a lama called Bujig was executed for having calumniated the Khutuktu. There are various versions of what he is supposed to have said. One is 'Is that miserable old blind Tibetan still alive? What do we call him our king for? I don't care a fig for his orders and admonitions.' Bujig was drunk at the time, but was nevertheless put to death as a warning to others. A similar case occurred in 1921 when a lama called Damdinsuren was executed for calling the Khutuktu 'a wretched Tibetan beggar who has wandered here'.[20] The Khutuktu's justice was arbitrary and violent. A rich doctor of divinity came one day to the *Shabi*-office to report a debt due to him from someone, and an official called Puntsag was dispatched by the office to warn the debtor to pay up. Puntsag, aiming only to accelerate the repayment, told him that this was by the Khutuktu's order, and as a result was executed for taking the Khutuktu's name in vain. The Khutuktu is also suspected of having arranged the assassination of inconvenient political leaders during his reign, though in fairness to him it has to be remembered that nothing he did approached in its deliberate inhumanity the organized brutalities and cynical treacheries of the terror of the 1930s under the People's government.

The lapse of the Church from the principles of Buddhism is seen also in the violent behaviour of its proctors and the savage way discipline was sometimes maintained. Law and order were upheld within the Church by reference to the 'Khalkha Code' which was elaborated early in the eighteenth century. Many cases, with their penalties, as adjudicated under this code, are known to us and show the judiciary to have been, in principle, a reasonably just one. Punishments, while severe, were mainly in the form of fines. Thus in 1821 the lama Sambuu was fined one *angju*, or unit, of nine animals for drawing a knife on the *shulengge* or *Shabi*-official Tseringjab of the same *otog*. A similar fine, plus an extra camel, was imposed in the same year on a lama of Urga who swore at a precentor. A commoner was fined one 'nine' plus one 'five', computed at a higher rate of valuation in terms of tea, for lewd behaviour with a girl called Delger, resulting in infection with disease. Smaller fines were imposed on petty officials for allowing unauthorized persons to store their belongings overnight in an official treasury. But the regulations were often infringed. At the end of the nineteenth century and beginning of the twentieth it was not rare for lamas to die from the beatings they had received, and more often than not the proctors escaped all liability for these abuses of their authority, or, if they were punished, got off very lightly. Thus the proctor Sonom of Amarbayasgalangt lamasery was accused in a general complaint submitted by the lamas of his lamasery of inflicting beatings of the utmost severity for all infractions, whether serious or trivial, fining the lamas excessive amounts, tearing their clothes off, breaking heads, and drawing blood. Complaints to the temple authorities had been disregarded, in consequence of which lamas were deserting the lamasery, while novices were deterred from coming in. In the end Sonom was merely demoted. This happened in 1920. In 1908 a proctor called Tserendorji had beaten a lama to death, but escaped all blame for it. The ordinary lamas had nicknames for the most notorious proctors of the Urga temples – butcher Gunggataya, hungry wolf Tsembel, mad yak Badmagarav, and so on. In 1895 there occurred a celebrated case of theft. A special dish, used in a twice-yearly service, disappeared after the summer service and could not be found when next wanted. A special tent was erected by the *Shabi*-office for interrogating the suspects, and here beatings and questionings went on for ten days and nights. Several victims died from their beatings, and another old lama, who was falsely implicated, was arrested and executed. The dish was never found – the rumour went around that the Buriats, who were terrible people, had beaten it into paper to steal it away. Similar cases of brutality continued to occur within the Church even after the revolution. They are indicative of a split between the upper and lower classes of lama which was of little importance as long as the Church maintained its spiritual and temporal authority, especially under the Khutuktu's theocratic monarchy, but which was turned to effect by the People's government as soon as it was realized how to recognize and exploit latent class differences in a revolutionary situation so as to divide and weaken the opposition.

Douglas Carruthers, writing in 1913 on the results of his own observation, considered the 'tyranny of the lamaseries' to be the primary cause of the decadence of the Mongol race. He pointed with justification to the poor showing the Mongols made in comparison with the nomads of the Moslem Kirei-Kirghis, who followed a similar pattern of life but a different religion. It is not a matter of dispute that the Buddhist Church did exercise a terrible drag on Mongol life, but it was not solely responsible for the degradation of the nineteenth century. It is commonly said that one of the demerits of lamaism was that it withdrew so large a proportion of the male population – estimates are as much as forty per cent – from productive labour, and accustomed them to idleness in the lamaseries. Carruthers even attributes the failure of the Mongol herds to increase to this factor, a failure which led in his opinion to the consequential over-population of Mongolia, in the sense that the population, minute though it was numerically, was still too great for the country's resources. This analysis ignores both the fact that enormous wealth was being regularly drained off into China, and that a large number of lamas lived at home just like ordinary herdsmen, and would resist attempts to concentrate them in temples far from their familiar pastures, where they could work to help their families and also draw support from them to eke out the meagre subsistence they would get from temple doles. This is no mere academic point. A former lama who came to Urga as a boy of twelve in 1901 recalled in 1960: 'As our family lived near by I could get food from them and so did not starve, but poor lamas who came from afar went hungry, and even stole from their teachers to eat.'[21] Carruthers's analysis also stands in direct contradiction to the argument of Professor Natsagdorj, that the Church offered, in the nineteenth century, the only alternative way of life for surplus manpower no longer needed in the cattle-rearing economy, where in any case much work was done by women. The Church absorbed this surplus manpower: it did not create it. But in the conditions of the time it was an unproductive, economically stagnant, and inward-looking alternative, able to absorb the manpower but not to employ it usefully. (It is interesting to note in this connection that there does not seem to have been a regular establishment of nuns in Mongolia, to complement the male lamas. There were a few cloistered women, but the word usually translated 'nun' means in the Mongol context nothing more than an elderly woman, beyond child-bearing age, who lived at home keeping a few elementary vows.) Thus this withdrawal of potential productive labour by the lamaseries was not so much the cause of economic contraction in Mongolia as a function of that situation. It accelerated towards the end of the dynasty as it became more and more urgent to avoid the heavier state and feudal taxes, so that fewer imperial subjects were left to share out the burden of these amongst them, and the situation made itself more acute. The basic factors responsible for Mongolia's decline seem to have been purely economic ones, involving an unmanageably high level of taxation wastefully spent inside and outside the country, the growth of indebtedness to foreign merchants who bought cheap and sold dear at extortionate rates of credit, and the inability of the inexperienced and unsophisticated Mongols, hampered by an inept and alien administration, to adapt themselves to a totally new concept of economic life. Their livelihood depended on their animals, and before the days of refrigeration there was a limit to the productive usefulness of herds of increasing size: horses, especially, were often no more than conspicuous evidence of wealth. Moreover, the time when the Mongols could live in semi-isolation from the world, bartering surplus animals for the products of the sedentary civilizations to the south, was disappearing as Mongolia was being drawn more and more into the world trade system, where the initiative lay in the hands of infinitely more skilled and organized foreign professionals, mostly Chinese and Russians.

Discontent within the Church

What critical writing there was in Mongolia in the nineteenth century had the limited purpose of exposing abuses in Church and society and advocating a return to a purer way of life. No Mongol thinker seems to have alighted on the theme of political independence. An eccentric genius in Inner Mongolia, the poet, novelist and historian Injanashi, (1837–91), made a plea for a heightened Mongol national pride in the preface to his historical prose saga *Köke sudur*, 'The Blue Chronicle', in which he castigated those of his contemporaries who were steeped in Chinese culture but knew little or nothing of their own past, in particular ignoring the mighty deeds of Genghis Khan. But Injanashi's work remained unprinted until some thirty years ago, and though manuscripts of it circulated, it is hard to imagine that it made much impact in its own time, while now it is really only of antiquarian interest. In Khalkha there were a number of learned lamas who tried to point out how far the Church had strayed from the true path, and warned it to mend its ways. An early representative of this current of reform was the Urga lama Nagwangkhaidav (1779–1839) whose parable 'Conversation between a sheep, a goat and an ox' contrasts the pious credulity of these three animals, who are lying bound in a temple courtyard waiting to be slaughtered for the lamas' dinner, with the smooth cynicism and brutal insensitivity of a lama to whom they pray for mercy. The three animals argue with an eloquent mastery of dogma and scriptural language, the lama rejecting their pleas each time with an appeal to necessity and inevitability. The satire is sharp, and stylistically witty, but hardly likely to have been of any practical effect. In other works Nagwangkhaidav censured extravagance and worldliness on the part of the high lamas, his purpose being solely to promote the good of the Faith and of humanity: in his own words:

> In directing this to you I have not written angrily, moved by malice, hatred or jealousy, but I have written with the intention of helping. Consider it for yourselves. My support and stay is the scriptures. . . . For aiding the Faith and humanity, high thrones, rich property, many serfs and great fame are all unnecessary.

A generation later another learned lama, Dandar, took up Nagwangkhaidav's work and commented upon it. In his book: 'The thunderbolt which crushes the thorns of the evil-doers', composed in 1860, he speaks scathingly of the sins of the time, that is, the period of the debaucheries of the seventh Khutuktu and his cronies.

> It is indeed pitiful how the incarnations and nobles go shamelessly after profit, lechery and drink, like dogs which have tasted blood. . . .
> These ostensible lamas sit on the heads of the people, torturing them with the spurs on their feet. . . . They pay no heed either to the scriptures or the law, pursuing their evil ways at their own sweet will. These men who bear the name of lamas, wearing the yellow dress of the Church, and boast to the skies of their empty fame, these deceitful robbers of other men's goods – in their dress and appearance they are like clerics, but can we call them clerics in fact? It is hard to rank them as clergy, and impossible to count them laymen.[22]

There has always been a strong moralistic strain in Mongol popular literature, from the earliest times, when many didactic sayings were attributed to Genghis Khan. But while the reforming lamas of the nineteenth century who were to be found not only in Urga but, like the dramatist and lyric poet Rabjai, in country lamaseries also, still stood in this tradition, a sharper and bitterer note begins to become apparent in their work. As well as enunciating the traditional principles of good behaviour they are disturbed at the moral decay around them. Towards the end of the nineteenth century, yet another lama, Shijee, was calling attention to the state of the Church, and went so far as to put his criticisms into the mouth of the fifth Jebtsundamba Khutuktu

(1815–40), whose biography he composed. The printing of his work and of Dandar's was forbidden during the period of autonomy, and are little known now, but the *surgaal* or 'Instruction' of the Inner Mongolian incarnation, Ishidanzangwangjil, which followed the same line in pointing out the sins of society at all levels, was familiar in Urga where the author lived for several years, and has been reprinted two or three times since its first appearance as a booklet published there in 1928.

Even the *lungdengs* or encyclical letters of the last Khutuktu, which were carried all over Mongolia by wandering lamas, and were recited to those who could not read for themselves, contained ironical, half-veiled anti-Chinese sentiments, alongside what were, by that time, merely conventional condemnations of the popular sins of the time – drinking, smoking and fornication. One such letter is quoted in the historical novel 'Ray of Dawn' by the Mongol scholar and poet Rintchen. Though fictional in form, this work, published in the 1950s, is a mine of factual information about life and society in the early years of this century and this letter, reputedly circulated in 1900 when China was being thrown into turmoil by the Boxer rebellion, can probably be accepted as authentic:

> The ten black sins which you have all committed are as clear upon the palms of my left and right hands as in the mirror of the King of Hades. For all these things, I, the Khutuktu, am in distress.
> I am in distress lest war be waged beneath the skies.
> I am in distress lest the white-hatted Chinese, one and all, be ruined.
> I am in distress lest there be fighting in towns and cities.
> I am in distress lest the Chinese be in travail beneath the skies.[23]

Thus within the Church there was both an awareness of internal weakness and a sensitivity to coming political change. But all these various types of expression of unease, anxiety or rebelliousness were sporadic and unsystematic, nor did they aim at any fundamental change in society. There was no spirit abroad in nineteenth-century Mongolia able to give form and purpose to the diverse and inchoate murmurings of dissatisfaction now rumbling in all ranks of society. No news of events in the outside world seems to have penetrated Mongolia to serve as even a remote inspiration for thought and action. Linguistic isolation, lack of education beyond certain narrow limits, poverty which prevented travel abroad, meant not only that no knowledge of such happenings as the French revolution seems ever to have reached the Mongols, but that, if we can credit Rintchen's novel, the very names of France, Germany and Japan were a novelty in Mongol ears at the end of the nineteenth century. The established order, with the Khutuktu at the head of a rich and splendid Church, and beyond him, in the mystic surroundings of Peking, the 'Holy Lord' or Manchu Emperor, must have appeared for ever immutable to the ordinary Mongol of the nineteenth century. This is the background against which to judge the phenomena we must look at in the rest of this chapter, that is, the increasing number of popular protests and uprisings that helped throughout the century to undermine the old order.

Social and national unrest

These manifestations of discontent took various forms. At the lowest level there were rabble riots in the course of which the mob, including lamas too from the very beginning of the century, would attack the Chinese trading community, beating up the merchants, plundering their warehouses, and destroying their account books. The earliest case of which there is published record took place in the summer of 1829 on the occasion of the great Tsam or temple-dance in Urga, when a number of lamas assaulted some Chinese who had come to watch the performance. The lamas were punished with unfrocking, beatings, and being fettered for a time. A similar fracas took place in 1887, also at a temple dance, when it was the turn of Chinese soldiers to be attacked: possibly the lamas and the Chinese, who never had much love lost between them, were particularly irritable at holiday-time, when the drink would be flowing a little more freely. A more serious affair both in its extent and its implications took place in 1881 when a mob of three to four hundred lamas and laymen smashed up a Chinese shop. It shows signs of premeditation: it began when a lama who had bought a lot of goods which he could not pay cash for was being escorted to his quarters in the Gandang monastery to fetch some money. As he and his two escorts neared Gandang, the lama shouted out something and a mob appeared from a ditch and freed him. The riot reached its climax the next day, and what is significant is that, in spite of a stern admonition from the office of the amban of Urga to the *Shabi*-office, the ringleaders of the riot were never caught. There was another large-scale riot in 1900 when a mob over seven hundred strong, led by a lama, and with some Russians armed with guns in its ranks, set upon forty or more Chinese shops in Setsen Khan aimak and thoroughly smashed them up. The ringleader was put to death by strangling, various others were beheaded, and of those who were punished in other ways, some 360 were lamas. Clashes like this continued, especially in Urga, right up till the final one in 1910 against the new Manchu amban Sando, which signalled the beginning of the end of foreign rule in Khalkha.

It is always difficult to see what lies behind any riot, and the Mongol author of the recently-published book *Urga before the Revolution* from which most of the above facts have been taken probably overstates his case by heading the relevant chapter of his work: 'On the participation of the lower class lamas in Urga in the movement for national liberation'. But nevertheless it is safe to conclude that there was a great deal of sympathy for the rioters among the Mongol authorities of Urga, and perhaps even connivance with them, since more than once after the affair of 1881 they failed to apprehend the culprits. In 1904, for instance, some Mongols, lamas and laymen, wrecked a shop and were arrested by the Chinese. A mob several hundred strong, again including lamas, released them and beat up the shopkeepers. Although the names of the original rioters were known they were never caught, in spite of repeated demands made by the amban on the *Shabi*-office and the aimak and banner authorities.

These riots were, however, affairs of the moment. Like the mutinies which broke out more than once during the final years of the Manchu dynasty, and the desertions and failures to report to the army for service, especially in the campaigns against the Dungan rebels, they were essentially destructive and negative in character. So was the banditry which began to figure more prominently in Mongolia. The individual rebels, the so-called *sain er*, we have mentioned before, but especially at the time of the Dungan rebellions big armed bands of Mongol bandits appeared, in imitation of the Moslems, so it was said, carrying black banners. Their actions were however mere raids, not an insurrection, and the Mongols, estranged by the indifference with which the

Moslems attacked all and sundry, Manchus, Chinese and Mongols alike, and destroyed their holy places such as the Yellow Temple in Khobdo and the Genghis Khan sanctuary in the Ordos, never made common cause with them, though a few individual Mongols were to be found in the Dungan ranks.

Much more information about the conditions of the time is to be gleaned from the archives of the local administration of Mongolia. On the one hand we have reports of criminal cases. In 1797, for instance, a man of a banner of Tushetu Khan aimak stabbed his *zasag* to death, for which he was executed. He was in desperation at the ruin of his life through years of forced labour, including the task of breaking in wild horses for which he had been wilfully denied the use of saddle and bridle. But in the nineteenth century we come across with increasing frequency a new type of protest, and a case which occurred in Tushetu Khan aimak in 1788 is perhaps a prototype. From this year we have a document, drawn up by the *zangi* or administrator of a *sumun*, accusing the *zasag* of the banner of various irregularities, including commandeering from lamas and imperial subjects sheep to which he was not entitled, and demanding from them personal services which they were not obliged by law to render. Unfortunately, in the form in which the document is quoted, it does not reveal to whom it was submitted, nor what the outcome of the affair was, but at least we can conclude that here a subordinate official was acting on behalf of the ordinary people in opposition to the *zasag*.

From the early nineteenth century onwards there are many instances of people of all classes within a banner joining together to list their grievances against the *zasag* in a composite petition which would then be presented to the League office. This in itself was a risky proceeding, as commoners making a complaint were forbidden by law to go over the head of their *zasag* and approach the next instance, that is the League, directly. But as the *zasag* was the person against whom the complaints would naturally be made, the people were caught in a dilemma, and the authorities, as is plain from published cases from the period of autonomy, made full use of their commanding position. Even when a complaint was recognized as just, as for instance in 1917 when a brutal *taiji* in Setsen Khan aimak was demoted and lost his retainers, the people who brought the complaint to the

League were punished more severely than the culprit with heavy fines and beatings, for going over the *zasag's* head.

The carefully-kept archives of the pre-revolutionary administration happily enable us to trace fairly clearly the course of some such actions, the social background of those involved, and the nature of their grievances. Certain significant features emerge from a comparison of some of these affairs. They were not, strictly speaking, of a class nature. Although the majority of those taking part were commoners, both lamas and the minor nobility added their names also to the petitions and subjoined their personal complaints, which might well, from a logical standpoint, harbour a latent conflict with the interests of the commoners, especially when the question of the illegal taxation of the *taijis* was a point at issue. Nevertheless, where tradition was offended against, such conflicting complaints went in side by side. That the petitions were cast in a very formal mould, with the names of the plaintiffs written out in the same practised hand, not as signatures, shows that those involved enjoyed the sympathetic help of minor officials in the banner administration, who gave them the benefit of their chancery experience. In any case, this participation of officials may be deduced from the affair of 1788 and from later petitions in which ranks and titles of the plaintiffs are listed against their names. There was, too, a certain democracy at work in the organization of these petitions. The malcontents would, in later years, form what was known as a *duguilang* or 'circle', a term first found about the middle of the century in the Ordos in Inner Mongolia, but which later spread farther afield. They would add their names to their petition in the well-known form of the round robin, *taijis* and commoners together, none taking the responsibility for leadership so as not to attract reprisals.

The aims of these petitions were limited to the specific points raised in them. Even when, as in the quarrel between To-wang and his subjects at the end of the 1830s the people took to arms, this was no more than a desperate action taken in a moment of despair. There was no intention to usurp authority, or to replace the feudal system of the time by some other, as yet unimagined, social order. The most that might be aimed at, or achieved, was the redress of grievances by the repayment of illegal exactions, with perhaps the fining or the removal of the noble concerned –

only to be replaced by another. The Setsen Khan Sanjaidorji was thus demoted from being League Chief in 1800 and lost the right to the title of Khan for himself and his successors, while in 1815 the *zasag* Tsedendorji lost some of his official salary as well as having to pay back illegally extorted taxes. Even as late as 1919 when a complaint was put in to the Ministry of Justice of the autonomous régime against the *zasag* Tudeng, it merely said that the people were unwilling to be governed by him and to form a banner under his rule any more, because of his brutality. This was a mere two years before the sovietization of Mongolia first began. Moreover, although such joint complaints are known of for more than a century, they were always separate events, inspired perhaps by one another, but not part of a nationwide movement. To a great extent geography and poor communications would have hindered the emergence of a co-ordinated movement of any sort. When an agitator did arise, as was the case around 1771 when a mendicant lama from the Ordos, Luvsanjamts, appeared in Khalkha and began to summon great meetings for the recital of prayers, to which people would come in their hundreds with offerings of animals, it was an easy matter to order his arrest and return to where he belonged. The sparse population, scattered over a huge area, would have found it impracticable to unite beyond the limits of a single banner, while the actual organization of Mongolia, fragmented as it was into something like a hundred banners of equal status, both kept the people compartmentalized and presented no single objective for a national protest to direct itself against. There was no connection, for instance, between the troubles within the two banners of Dugartsembel and To-wang, though these occurred simultaneously and inside the same league. Further, although some banner lawsuits and *duguilang* movements occasionally degenerated into mob violence or expressed themselves in a withdrawal from the banner, on the whole the process was kept within the due bounds of law.

This bears incidental witness to the remarkable persistence and tenacity of purpose on the part of the leaders, who, in spite of the often arbitrary and violent action taken against them, kept their lawsuits alive for as much, in one case, as eighteen years. This persistence, coupled with the bureaucratic diligence of the time, has preserved very full documentation of several cases, though only a little has actually been published. The events in To-wang's banner, for example, which reached their climax in 1842, are detailed in 170 surviving archival items.

The points at issue between a typical banner-prince and his subjects varied very little from the time of the first lawsuits we know of up to the outbreak of the revolution. Usually they referred to what the people considered to be illegal or excessive taxation and *corvées*. Between the terms of the complaint of 1788 and one of 1917 in which a group of commoners in Setsen Khan aimak, led by their *zangi*, put in a complaint against their *zasag* for excessive levies of animals, felts and money, and for exactions to cover expenses incurred in private travel for such purposes as making a pilgrimage, there is little difference.

Some very full documentation has been published for a few specific petitions and it is instructive to examine these and see how such an affair developed and was handled, and also how wide and varied the area of discontent was. The petitions sometimes reached considerable proportions: one of 1916, for example, contains 148 separate items of complaint. Analysis of such documents shows that economic grievances dominated. However, antipathy might go beyond exasperation at this or that piece of selfishness or financial skulduggery on the part of a greedy *zasag*. People's feelings might be outraged by shameless behaviour, and this found expression in their petitions. The petition put in against the *zasag* Tudeng, to judge from the archives a mere privileged ruffian and one of the first to be turned out of office after the revolution, is a mine of information on this point. He was accused of a lack of filial respect to his mother and elder sister, whom he had cursed and beaten. He insulted the lamas, seizing their sacred bells and drums, interrupting their assemblies, tearing off their robes, and forcing them to drink spirits against their will. He beat innocent Chinese merchants, and he slandered the Khutuktu for giving him too little authority in exchange for big subsidies. Behind the outraged feelings was an even deeper unease. Pious and superstitious people felt their security being undermined by impious actions on the *zasag's* part. Item twenty-five of the petition says: 'Rejecting the Yellow Faith, he adores the male and female shamans, and has drunk the blood of their tongues, and had the feathers of owls brought as holy idols', and the preceding item runs: 'In unlawful, heathenish fashion he has had cursing magic performed against people, threatening to kill them, and has terrified them unbearably'. Another item accuses him, apparently, of setting up his own heretical faith, known as the Blue Faith after the model of the Yellow and Black Faiths, Buddhism and shamanism, and forcing lamas to take part in its ceremonies.[24]

It is not sufficient, then, here as always, to look only for an economic explanation to the phenomenon of popular discontent against some of the nobility. Outraged piety, the undermining of spiritual security, was also a factor. This lesson was indeed not learned soon enough by the People's government after the revolution, and the indiscriminate attacks on the Faith and on cult objects which people held dear, which it encouraged and organized especially between 1929 and 1932, brought about serious clashes. Even nowadays the matter is still not resolved, and people can still argue seriously over whether the demolition of religious structures is necessary. In an account of an archaeological expedition made in 1959, for example, a Mongolian scholar, Damdinsuren, finds it appropriate to make the following remarks:

> Above these two passes was a big round *obo* (cairn). Wayfarers would add stones to it. Although some fanatics would raze *obos*, most people have been re-erecting them. Seeing that *obos* are not an obstacle to socialism, they say, why not let them be?[25]

Finally, the documentation serves to show how trouble which had long been seething under the surface would boil over on account of some isolated event, perhaps of apparently minor importance. The petitions retail item after item of grievances of individuals and the community, but the immediate cause of a flare-up might be, as in the case of To-wang's banner, the seemingly innocuous proposal to combine a number of country temples into one big lamasery.

To-wang, or, in Mongol, the *zasag* Togtokhtör, was a rare bird amongst his fellows at about the midpoint of the nineteenth century. He was an educated man, knowing Chinese, Manchu and Tibetan as well as his native Mongol. He had travelled several times in China and Tibet, and had taken an active part in the administration of Mongolia, where he had the reputation of opposing Manchu rule and hoping for Mongol independence. He was the grandson of Sanjaidorji, the deposed Setsen Khan.

Within his banner he was an innovator who tried to run the territory as an integrated and diversified economic and cultural unit. He developed all sorts of activities as alternatives to herding. Agriculture was made compulsory for some people, and he was able to supply his own banner with grain and have some over for sale elsewhere. He set up his own water mills. From his travels he brought back skilled workmen to instruct his people, and he set up handicraft shops for producing textiles and finished woollen goods. He mined gold, and had salt and soda gathered. He encouraged fishing and hunting and the gathering of mushrooms and fruits as supplementary foods, so as to cut down the demands made on the capital of the domestic herds. He had building materials prepared from local sources, bricks and tiles baked to be used in a palace for himself, and in temple building. He developed mineral springs as spas for the treatment of various ailments, and recorded the properties of the waters. At the same time he tried to provide for the cultural needs of his people. He organized small training schools for musicians and actors, and put on theatrical performances. He set up a primary school where children, including commoners, were entered for compulsory instruction, To-wang himself having worked out teaching material for them to learn to read from. He organized the translation of scriptures into Mongol and their circulation, and tried to set up a central lamasery for the scattered monks under his jurisdiction, where the services were to be recited in both Tibetan and Mongol.

To-wang embodied his principles in various 'Instructions' which he drew up, and which he circulated among the herdspeople of his banner. In these he provided practical advice based on traditional experience, which he had had the enterprise and ability to collect and codify, and he also tried to inculcate such basic virtues as frugality. Much of what he tried to instil was of a very elementary, but no doubt necessary, sort. For instance:

> If you just sit about at your ease, and go to sleep when you feel tired, so neglecting your livelihood, and then, as soon as you wake up, drink some more tea, and eat up whatever there is, this will surely mean that in one day you will eat up three days' food and drink, three months' requisites will go in one month, and three years' will be exhausted in one year, leading to poverty. For that reason, discipline yourselves to get up early.... Your wives ought to work continuously, educating

their children, doing sewing or other work, dealing with the cattle stalls and so on, and only eating and drinking when the husband comes home. . . . For yourselves, be sparing of how much animal produce and grain you consume. Collect mushrooms, onions, wild grain and nuts for food. . . .[26]

Judgement on To-wang has generally been rather negative. The Soviet historian Zlatkin, writing in 1950, pours scorn on his so-called 'science' which he says was nothing but a formulation of age-old folk practice. But Zlatkin, sneering at To-wang for not possessing scientific knowledge which was completely unimaginable to him at his time, misses the point.[27] To-wang had collected and written out in his instructions a great deal of helpful lore designed to help his people. He told them how to select horses, how to fix a saddle properly, how to choose draught-animals and feed them on the journey, how to pasture the different domestic beasts in the four seasons of the year, how to choose pastures, how to build shelters and make stalls, how to protect the beasts from blizzards, how to look after the young animals, and how to exploit the produce of the animals. What was progressive about him was that he saw the necessity of classifying what knowledge there was and applying it where it was needed. Observation and practice, care and economy, were virtues of great value in animal herding, as the life experience of the present President of Mongolia, J. Sambuu, shows. As a boy he had been taught very thoroughly by his father what made a good herdsman, and in his book of advice to herdsmen, published in 1945 and since reissued in both Mongol and Russian, many of the chapter headings recall the lore of To-wang's book. Sambuu's father gave him, too, the practical lesson that dropped wool, usually neglected by the Mongols, was of value. He encouraged him to collect it and then exchange it with a Chinese trader for writing materials, which were a great rarity on the steppe. Sambuu learned these lessons half a century after To-wang's time.

Professor Natsagdorj comes nearer to reality than Zlatkin, but even he dismisses To-wang curtly.

> To-wang's severe demands on the people in his Instructions to economize [he says], and his setting of strict limits, did not in the least spring from his consideration of the welfare of the people, but are to be explained as being aimed at reducing the people's consumption as

far as possible and increasing his own exploitation of them as much as he could.[28]

The basis for this judgement is a passage in To-wang's own book in which he tells the people why they should be frugal. They should not just aim at satisfying their own appetites when increasing their herds, but should realize that by taking proper care they could better pay their taxes and make offerings to the Buddha – in contemporary terms, be better citizens. It is possibly a little hard on this thoughtful and energetic prince to judge him out of hand on the strength of an exhortation cast in a form suited to the outlook and mode of expression of his own time, and meant to be intelligible to herdsmen whose low level of sophistication can be surmised from the elementary nature of much of the practical instruction offered them.

In any case, the people themselves did not think outside the framework of the feudal system. They hoped only to alleviate its pressure on them. But Natsagdorj's verdict has substance, for To-wang's enterprises did after all provoke his people to rebel against him. However, what caused him to fail must have been more than his own character: a man of his vision must have had more in mind than the brute satisfaction of his own greed. It seems rather the case that Mongolia was plunged into a hopelessly lethargy because of the general social and economic injustice of the time. There was no incentive to work and save, since the mass of the people were already totally mortgaged in any case and there was no way open to progress. The native aristocracy was demanding ever larger taxes, and whatever surplus wealth Mongolia produced was being ruthlessly drained off into China in exchange for trivial imports of consumer goods, or, too often, in exchange for nothing at all. It is no wonder that To-wang's people saw his reforms only as so much extra *corvée*, and kicked against them.

The immediate cause of the trouble was To-wang's plan to concentrate some one thousand lamas from eleven local temples into one new central temple in 1837. This proposal met with opposition from all concerned. The higher lamas saw the curtailment of their privileges and authority in the offing, while the lower lamas, only nominally clerics and living the same life as the ordinary herdsmen, saw their whole way of life and their subsistence threatened. The local people, too, did not want to have to say good-bye to their relatives, and were equally reluctant to lose the familiar Buddhas they had been accustomed to worship. From this simple beginning there grew a five-year-long quarrel. At first a petition was submitted to the banner office, and though at first To-wang appeared to yield, he bore a grudge against the complainants and treated them more harshly than before. The movement took a violent turn: there was a brawl between the people and To-wang's soldiers, and at the same time a riot at the new temple where the lamas stoned the proctor's tent with shouts of 'Let us go home!' To-wang put the matter to the League authorities, who sent an officer to speak to the rebels. They refused to obey the summons to go to the League headquarters. Thereupon To-wang informed Urga of the course of events, but Urga pushed it back on to the League as quickly as possible. Some of the rebels' enthusiasm had cooled off by now, and there was a readiness to talk. A forty-point accusation was presented to the League, but the bearers of it were arrested and soon after some of the plaintiffs withdrew their names. In the event the League sided with To-wang, disregarding the accusations against him, and when the matter was decided at Urga the amban, too, sided with him. He was, it is true, lightly punished, and the temple project was cancelled, but the rebellious commoners were condemned to severe punishments such as banishment, which To-wang executed with unnecessary brutality.

Though the immediate cause of this uprising was connected with religious matters, it was far from being a religious dispute: the lamas involved were concerned with their livelihood, while the leaders were ordinary commoners. A similar dispute, in which *taijis* and lamas were also involved, but which again was led by a determined commoner, is that between Ayushi and the *zasag* Manibazar of Zasagtu Khan aimak at the beginning of this century. This affair first flared up in 1903 with a lawsuit brought against the *zasag* on the grounds of illegal taxation, intended mainly to finance his personal debts. In money alone these debts called for an annual contribution of twenty taels of silver from each family. One man, who had defaulted on his own debt, had been beaten to death by a debt-collector, and the debt then assessed to the banner as a whole. There were other grievances too, particularly over the commandeering of camels. The *zasag* proposed to let the Chinese use these in part payment of his debts, and promised to pay the people a fee for their hire. Not only did he fail to pay the fee, but he did not return the camels either. The complaint was brought to the League for decision, and once again we find some of the plaintiffs losing their enthusiasm for the cause, and the trouble was easily put down.

Unrest went on simmering in the banner, and it broke out again in 1911 in connection with the national revolution against the Manchus. The expulsion of the Manchu amban and of the Chinese from Urga had been bloodless, but in the provinces, especially in the west at Khobdo, things were very different, and there was fighting and plundering with considerable loss of life. All over the country the Chinese merchants were being expelled, and the representative of the Chinese shop in Manibazar's banner, fearing for his life and property, ran away towards Ku-ch'eng in Sinkiang at midnight one night, taking with him twenty camel-loads of valuables, and leaving his shop to its fate. This was inevitably plundered by the people, and the debt-accounts destroyed. Manibazar sent out troops and arrested the ringleaders, including Ayushi. They were imprisoned, heavily chained, and the news got around that the *zasag* was intending to torture them by the well-known method of tying them up in a wet hide with only the head showing, and then leaving them exposed to the elements. This was a sure way of bringing about the death of the victim without actually executing him, which the law forbade a *zasag* to do. From now on the movement took on a more defiant character. A band of herdsmen freed the ringleaders, who could not walk, and carried them off on horseback to where they could conveniently be freed of their chains. Then, unable to return home, they formed a *duguilang* or rebel band some two hundred strong, in the hills. The League became involved, since Manibazar had to report that he could not control his banner, and the rebels, suffering considerable hardship in their isolation, agreed to negotiate. They drew up a complaint in forty-four articles for submission to the League. A first trial was to be held in 1913, but the people refused to attend, and in the autumn Ayushi and others were arrested and tortured. These proceedings disgusted even the guards, who began to demand his release. The authorities temporized, condemning the people to pay considerable fines and imposing a trivial fine on Manibazar for exceeding his competence. The people refused to pay, and Ayushi and some others withdrew from their banner again for the next two years. The *duguilang* was revived, but poverty and weariness once more undermined the unity of the rebels, and many of them agreed to take no further part in the protest. In 1915 Ayushi and his friends were again arrested and brought to Uliasutai where they were tortured to the point where Ayushi's health broke down and the trial had to be postponed for a year. The rumour spread abroad that the *zasag* was trying to murder him, and again he escaped his guards and came to Urga, bearing with him the original petition and pieces of flesh which had been torn off during the torture. Here again officialdom was obstructive and hostile, and the matter was finally referred back to Uliasutai. However, in the meantime Manibazar died, and the affair seems to have fizzled out.

The forty-four articles of Ayushi's petition have been published, together with some references to a memoir of him entitled 'The struggle of Ayushi against the aristocracy' written by members of his family. The articles of complaint fall into three categories. A few are evidently exclusive to the *taijis* and one probably stemmed from the lamas. The remainder concerned the common people. The *zasag* was accused of having, quite illegally, sold *jas* animals, on which the lamas and their hired herdsmen relied for a living, to some Chinese merchants. Most of the complaints, however, are concerned with the maltreatment of the common people, and disclose a situation of arbitrary and cynical disregard for custom, law and justice. He had extracted heavy taxes from the people, often on false pretences. For instance, on a visit to Köke qota he had bought fifty camels with pack-saddles from the Chinese shop whose representatives financed his banner. The cost of these, three thousand taels, had been paid out at home by his banner in silver. After these camels had brought their loads to Khobdo he kept them for himself. He had arbitrarily transferred poor retainers of his to the register of imperial subjects and taken on richer imperial subjects as his retainers. The vice of this proceeding lay in the fact that the now poorer community of imperial subjects still had to find the same amount of tax money. He had taken no steps to prevent people being forced to leave home through destitution, so that fifty-five persons, lamas and laymen alike, had had to move away from the banner. One of his subjects had been so tortured by two petty officials, on suspicion of having stolen from a Chinese merchant, that he had died. The two officials and their families had been barred from ever holding office again, and this fact entered in the registers, but nevertheless their sons had been given official appointments within the banner. There were allegations of bribery and extortion, and of misappropriation of money levied in taxes.

These are samples of the injustice prevalent in Mongolia at the time. Ayushi himself was a tough and determined character who survived the hardships he suffered and died only in 1931 at the age of seventy-two. His history is an outstanding one, which is probably why it has been the subject of considerable study in Mongolia in recent years. Yet it was not an isolated incident, and it has been mentioned here in some detail because it is a specific illustration of how far Mongol society had progressed along the way to disintegration by the early years of the present century.

CHAPTER 5

FROM AUTONOMY TO REVOLUTION, 1911–21

From independence to the treaty of Khiakta, 1911–15

At the end of 1911 Mongolia proclaimed her independence from China as a monarchy under the Jebtsundamba Khutuktu, and so for the first time for over two hundred years re-entered the main stream of history. She was one of the first nations in modern times, outside Europe, to escape successfully from subjection to an alien power. Tibet, in contrast, though her legal and factual status was very similar to Mongolia's, never managed to accomplish the same transition to nationhood, for want of a powerful protector. Mongolia's leaders were inexperienced, and to a very great extent naïve in their approach to international realities, and there was at the time no acceptable pattern of decolonization for them to imitate. It is therefore not surprising that the decade which followed, in any case one of the most unquiet of modern times, saw Mongolia tossed about like a shuttlecock at the mercy of foreign interests. Independent Mongolia's immediate ambitions were grandiose, and encompassed the incorporation within her boundaries of huge areas, hitherto subject to the Manchus, where Mongols happened to dwell. Barga, Dariganga, Alashan, and most of the banners of Inner Mongolia, were to form part of the new state.

But Mongolia's capacity to achieve her aims, and even to maintain her own independence within a territory limited to the aimaks of Khalkha and the Khobdo district, was strictly limited and, in the event, quite inadequate to the purpose. Both her great neighbours, Russia and China, had their own interests to pursue in Mongolia, and Russia's freedom of action was, in addition, circumscribed by secret treaties with Japan. Mongolia failed to achieve any effective international recognition for her new independence, and this was scaled down by the Sino-Russian Accord of 1913 and the three-power Treaty of Khiakta of 1915, to mere autonomy under Chinese suzerainty. However, even to have achieved so much was a positive gain, since it meant that two important and interested powers had publicly recognized Mongolia's existence as a separate entity. The turmoil of the Soviet revolution, which left Russia temporarily impotent, gave China the opportunity to re-assert her control for a while, and in 1919 autonomy was cancelled, ostensibly at the request of the Mongolian government, though not at that of the Khutuktu himself. For a time Mongolia was incorporated in the state structure of the Republic of China, an advance in Chinese imperialism over what had been claimed by the Manchu Emperors. In early 1921 there followed a brief restoration of the monarchy under the brutal, though historically irrelevant, régime of the white Russian leader Baron Ungern-Sternberg, while simultaneously with this a 'popular' revolution was being prepared by a few conspirators, for the most part inside Soviet territory, and a provisional government was being organized just inside Russia at Khiakta. This provisional government took upon itself to invite the Soviet army into Mongolia in April 1921. It occupied Urga and overthrew the existing government, taking over its seals of office, and establishing what on the surface was a constitutional monarchy which was presided over by the Khutuktu, once again restored to the throne thanks to the Red Army, until his death in 1924.

The story here given in the barest outlines has been told several times, though with the exception of Russian and Mongol scholars, historians have on the whole concentrated on the international aspects of the period, the interests and fate of Mongolia herself figuring almost as an irrelevancy. It has been left to Marxist writers to present and comment on internal developments in Mongolia, and in particular on the emergence of the first revolutionaries in Urga, their early contacts with the Comintern, the transfer of their activities to Russian soil, and their seizure of power in 1921. The trend of Mongolia's history over the past half century since the revolution has been, first, the transformation of what had been a backward, feudalistic dependency of China into a 'People's Republic' and, secondly, the search for international recognition, both by individual states and by the United Nations, of Mongolia's independent nationhood. There is no room for doubt that both these aspirations have been fully realized in fact, and it is an anachronism for journalists to write, or politicians to behave, as though Mongolia were an integral part of the Soviet Union on the one hand, or a chunk of Chinese territory torn more or less unwillingly from the motherland on the other, however much reason there may have been in the past for speculating along these lines. The involved diplomatic transactions which accompanied Mongolia's progress from independence, through autonomy, to dependence once again upon China, have their own interest, but they are less relevant for the study of Mongolia's future development than the initial stirrings of revolutionary thought and action inside the country during the years just before 1921, which have been rather neglected in the work of European writers. How Mongolia's revolution, which even in 1920 was still aiming, to judge from a revolutionary placard of the time, only at representative government in place of the hereditary authority exercised by the aristocracy, was transformed into a full-scale Soviet style revolution in the course of a few years, is the true theme of the study of that time.

Mongolia underwent two distinct revolutions in the decade between 1911 and 1921. The second was inspired by the Russian example, was carried out under Russian guidance and control, and was the prelude to a period of profound change which is not over yet. The first, which resulted in the declaration of independence, was essentially a nationalistic movement, aimed merely at the removal of Manchu authority. That the form of state adopted, a monarchy based on the Two Principles of church and state, provided, as tradition demanded, with a reign title after the Chinese manner, indicates how little fundamental change was intended. This revolution came as a reaction of the whole people to the rapid replacement, around 1900, of the traditional, conservative, isolating 'Manchu' policy, by a forward, colonizing, 'Chinese' policy on the part of Peking. It expressed itself through the leadership of the nobility, the only group cohesive and influential enough at that time to more than indulge in violent, but unproductive, acts such as army mutinies, plundering of Chinese shops, and street rioting. The new régime which replaced the Manchus was in many ways progressive. It initiated a number of necessary reforms. The beginnings of a modern army were laid at this time, under Russian instructors: some sort of order was brought into fiscal matters, again under Russian supervision: and a start was made with the introduction of a systematic modern education. Agriculture was promoted, and coal mining made its first appearance.

The decade began with high hopes. Jamtsarano, the Buriat director of the new secondary school, and an orientalist of international reputation, declared to the Finnish scholar and diplomat G. J. Ramstedt that a new and happy time was opening for Mongolia, and that popular education was going to be able to reach the same level as in other countries. But autonomy went sour. The new régime showed itself unable to break away from narrow class interests, particularly as power became more and more concentrated in the hands of the most conservative, though efficient, class, that of the high lamas. The church became more and more of a state within a state, supported not only by the contributions of the *Shabi*, but by a large slice of the state budget too. There was even a special minister appointed who could overrule the prime minister to protect church interests.

The 1911 revolution and the period of autonomy are well characterized by Professor Natsagdorj in his recent *History of Khalkha*, and a quotation from this book might form a fruitful point of departure for a consideration of the period. He writes:

> The movement of 1911 was the beginning of the awakening of the Mongol people, and an important step in the future struggle. But all the 1911 movement did was to remove the reactionary Manchu officials and troops. It left the Mongol people as before under the oppression of imperialism and feudalism. The experience of the eight or nine years of autonomy clearly showed the Mongol people the impossibility of going on in the old ways. It became clearer than ever that without fighting for and achieving real independence, without destroying the rotten feudalistic structure which had in fact reached its end, it would be impossible to achieve any progress in Mongolia. What was needed to jerk Mongolia out of her centuries' old backwardness was not just a half-hearted reform, but a social revolution.[1]

In the event, this revolution was carried out on Soviet lines. This was inevitable, though it was geographical proximity to the incomparably more dynamic Soviet Union rather than the demands of Mongolia's own internal situation which made it so.

Jamtsarano, who had at first been so hopeful about the possibilities under autonomy, and who was to come to a sad end as a counter-revolutionary in a Russian concentration camp, moved towards the left, and emerged in 1921 as the author of the programme of the newly established Mongol People's Party and as a Comintern adviser. The revolutionary leadership, which had at first included men of all backgrounds and points of view, subsequently eliminated from its ranks all those who disagreed with the pro-Soviet faction, and in the years after 1921 the history of Mongolia began to run uncomfortably parallel to the course of events in the socially and economically very different Soviet Union.

The early years of the twentieth century saw a decisive change in Chinese policy towards Mongolia. Indeed, by now it becomes unrealistic to talk any more of the foreign presence in Mongolia purely as Manchu, and it was against Chinese authoritarianism and economic aggression that the opposition of ordinary Mongols was directed. Pozdneev, travelling in Mongolia just before the end of the nineteenth century, had noticed this anti-Chinese feeling and spoke of the 'deep antipathy of the people towards their rulers, often even a real hatred of them'. The Mongols had an 'avid, if passive, desire to be liberated from the yoke which the Chinese imposed on their life'.[2] Chinese immigration, which had traditionally been forbidden, was now to be actively encouraged and assisted. A special office for this purpose was set up in Peking in 1906 and in 1911 a colonization bureau was established in Urga itself. Fortunately for Outer Mongolia this foreign colonization never achieved the same intensity that it did in Inner Mongolia and Manchuria, where the building of new railways facilitated the influx of Chinese peasants. Moreover, the process was soon halted by the declaration of Mongolian independence in 1911, and the Khalkha nobility never had the opportunity to sell off their banner lands to Chinese buyers at the rate their Inner Mongolian fellows did. But the danger was there, and so was the Chinese threat to enforce their presence by military means. The construction of army barracks in Urga was begun, and the Chinese planned to recruit a Mongol army under Japanese-trained instructors.

The sharpening popular discontent manifested itself in many ways. People were looking for a liberator to appear, and Pozdneev tells how they were expecting an army to be assembled in Siberia to invade Mongolia and expel the Chinese. This hope they had built up on rumours spread by a curious character called Dambijantsan, a Kalmuck lama from the Volga, who claimed successively to be a grandson of the last Jungar leader Amursana (who had died, it will be recalled, in 1757) and then the reincarnation of Amursana himself. Dambijantsan was to play a vital part in Mongolian affairs on two subsequent occasions, but at this time he is significant merely as a symptom of the vague and unorganized unrest troubling Mongolia. People sang the old songs and told the old stories about Amursana and Chingunjav, and were looking too for the return of Genghis Khan. Vagabond story tellers and singers, like the renegade Inner Mongolian lama 'Crazy Shagdar', would use their fool's licence to spit out bitter and pointed satire against all those, Chinese officials, Mongol nobles, and Japanese traders, who were battening on the misery of the people, and sometimes even made no attempt to hide their disillusionment at the failure of the Buddha to protect his people. The tales about Shagdar, a Baarin man from Inner Mongolia, are not strictly speaking relevant for Khalkha, but the spirit they show was common to all Mongols, and a sample story bears quotation:

The administrator of the west banner of Baarin, Hafungga, was not content with taking bribes, but also he sold the place called the Three Hollows of Buura in the western part of Baarin to General Tsui, an officer of the Chinese garrison army at Lin-hsi hsien. Shagdar heard about this and went for the second time to call on the administrator Hafungga. The administrator was standing gazing for a long time in his courtyard, and Shagdar said: 'Well, administrator, you've sold the Three Hollows of Buura and eaten them up and you're still not satisfied. Are you planning to sell the sky too? The sky's a nice blue so you'll get a better price for it, Sir!'[3]

More effective than these gnat-bites were the mutinies in their army which now faced the Chinese, though these, like the well-known mutiny of 1900 at Uliasutai, were, while popular in origin, unorganized and not directed towards any specific purpose. But the Uliasutai mutiny was far from insignificant. What happened was that the troops, exasperated by their poor conditions and lack of pay, surrounded their officers and demanded to be sent home. The amban and his officers ran away to the hills and their bodyguard and the local people joined the insurgents to plunder the Chinese shops and vegetable gardens. Neither the Manchu nor the Mongol officials were able to do anything to quell the mutiny, but the mutineers, having no other aim except to get out of the army, simply deserted and disappeared, whereupon the authorities returned to Uliasutai and made ineffective attempts to arrest them. They failed to accomplish this, and contented themselves with disbanding the disaffected troops. If the mutiny did nothing positive, it did effectively demonstrate the thorough demoralization of the existing administration in Mongolia. All that was needed to overturn it was a properly directed movement operating at the right time, which was soon to come.

The plundering of Chinese shops continued, especially in eastern Mongolia, where an Inner Mongolian freebooter, Togtokh taiji, a future revolutionary, and then a victim of the first purge in the ranks of the government in 1922, was active for some years. In Urga too there were sharp clashes between the lamas and the ordinary people on one hand, and the Chinese on the other. In one of these, in 1910, the newly-appointed amban Sando, whose forward policy made him especially hated, was actually stoned. However, it was not from any popular movement that the revolution of 1911 finally sprang. It was directed exclusively by the lay and clerical nobility acting in consort with the Jebtsundamba Khutuktu, although the ordinary people were willing enough to co-operate in throwing out the Chinese. The Mongol nobility had for some time past been uneasy at the purposeful encroachments of the Chinese, and although the Manchu dynasty collapsed just at the right time for them to be able to clothe their declaration of independence in a cloak of legality, the first active steps were taken some time before the outbreak of the decisive Wu-ch'ang uprising in China in October 1911. In July of that year, on the occasion of the annual offering of worship to the Khutuktu, which was attended by nobles and commoners from all over Mongolia, a mixed group of lay and clerical aristocrats discussed the current situation with the Khutuktu, and subsequently met for further deliberations in the wild mountains north of Urga. The Khutuktu accepted their proposal that a delegation should be sent to Russia to ask for help against the Chinese, and accordingly a small mission set out and reached St Petersburg by the middle of August.

The composition of this group of three is significant. It was made up of a lay noble, the prince Khandadorji, who was the general of Tushetu Khan aimak and was rumoured to have been assassinated later by order of the Khutuktu, a high clerical dignitary, the Grand Lama Tserenchimid, and an Inner Mongolian noble, the Kharchin duke Khaisan, whose presence foreshadowed the pan-Mongolist policies of the first few years of the autonomous régime. In the account of Korostovets, the Russian ambassador at Peking and later at Urga, the aims of the mission were somewhat contradictory: they wanted the Russians to help them assert their independence, and at the same time offered to accept a Russian protectorate. More specifically, they asked for a loan and the supply of weapons. The Russian attitude was very cautious, and the achievements of the Mongol delegation modest. They were warned not to make a rash break with China, but were promised a limited quantity of weapons for self-defence, and in fact the Irkutsk army district was ordered to place fifteen thousand rifles and seven and a half million rounds of ammunition at the disposal of the Mongols.

By the time the Mongol delegation reached home again the situation had changed decisively with the revolutionary uprising in China in the middle of October, and it was only a matter of time before the Mongols took the bit between their teeth and broke away from China in spite of Russian warnings to be moderate. In face of the new situation the nobility pressed the Khutuktu for a decision, and in a pastoral letter the latter stated that 'The time has now arrived for all the Mongol tribes to unite and establish themselves as a separate state, to let the Faith flourish, and to see an end to suffering under foreign oppression.'[4] A provisional government was set up in Urga, and an army mobilized under the pretext of offering loyal help to the Manchu dynasty. The Manchu amban was asked, at impossibly short notice, to arm these troops, and the Mongols used his hesitation as an excuse to cast doubt on his loyalty and force his departure from Urga under Russian protection. Manchu rule in Mongolia was at an end, and these protestations of loyalty to the empire were hardly to be taken seriously. After the actual collapse of the dynasty the line was changed. In the following year, when Yuan Shih-k'ai's government was trying, in an exchange of long-winded and futile telegrams, to persuade the Mongols to return to the

Chinese fold, the Mongols adopted a new interpretation of events, and claimed that although China and Mongolia had both for a time been administered by the Manchus, once the dynasty had disappeared both of them were entitled to set up their own governments and rule independently.

The immense prestige of the Khutuktu made it inevitable that only he would be acceptable as the head of the new Mongol state, and the provisional government addressed letters to the Mongols of Inner Mongolia, Barga and elsewhere, arguing that Mongolia's way to salvation lay in raising the Khutuktu to the throne. This had already been implicitly recognized by the revolutionary nobles who had judged the situation rightly in undertaking their mission to Russia only after getting the sanction of the Khutuktu, though at the time he had no actual temporal authority at all. He himself was a Tibetan, but had lived all his life in Mongolia, and was identified with Mongol interests and not with those of Tibet. He was the spiritual successor of an ancestor who had been a lineal descendent of Genghis Khan, and by virtue of his holy office he was regarded with the deepest veneration by all Mongols. He was the natural rallying-point for the sympathies of Mongols almost everywhere at this time, not only in Outer Mongolia. Moreover, central authority was rapidly disintegrating in China, and the status of the outlying territories such as Tibet and Mongolia was not at all definite. For the time being there was no visible limit to the extent to which the new Mongolia could extend her borders within Mongol-inhabited territory, and for a moment the dream of pan-Mongolism, the reunion of all the Mongol tribes who had been separated by the Manchu conquests, became a military and political possibility. The Khutuktu's pastoral letter quoted above more than hints at this, but it is probably more correct to assume that once the Khutuktu assumed power, the reawakened feelings of Mongol nationalism began to be concentrated on him, than to suppose that his elevation was consciously intended to exploit this temporary possibility.

At the end of 1911 the provisional government proclaimed actual independence and the end of Manchu authority in Mongolia. Five ministries were established, and the Khutuktu was raised to the throne, with control over all matters both secular and religious. He was accorded the reign-title 'Exalted by All'. This was not meant to show deference to any as yet unknown democratic principles, but was rather a conscious appeal to the legendary past of the Mongols as seen through Buddhist eyes. 'Exalted by All' had been the name of the mythical first king of India, from whom seventeenth-century lamaist chroniclers, intent on providing Genghis Khan with a lineage theologically more acceptable than the primitive zoomorphic legend that his ancestor had been born of the union of a wolf and a hind, had ingeniously traced his descent. The new reign title looks very much like a subtle claim to legitimacy by association, and its doctrinal and national overtones were bound to have some persuasive effect. The establishment of the monarchy was reported to the Mongol princes beyond the limits of Khalkha. And the Khutuktu, whose authority was for the time being limited to not much more than the two eastern aimaks, called upon the generals of the two western aimaks, where, at Khobdo and at Uliasutai, the greatest concentrations of Manchu officials and troops were, to expel these and accept the authority of Urga.

In the west the Manchus were dealt with comparatively easily. At Uliasutai there was no fighting, the cowardice of the Mongol amban and the Mongol general being exceeded only by the faintheartedness of the Manchu general. The latter had to be rescued by the Russian consul, not from any Mongol violence, but from the exasperated fury of his own colleague, the Manchu amban, who was disgusted at the compliancy with which the Manchu forces had been surrendered. At Khobdo events were more violent. The Manchus were not disposed to give in easily there. At the time, the alternate Mongol representative at the Manchu amban's office was the general Magsarjav, one of the great figures of the coming revolution. Magsarjav passed on to the amban at the end of 1911 Urga's orders to surrender his authority to the new régime, but the amban rejected this demand and began to reinforce his garrison and to fortify the official city. It seemed that the Manchus might well mount an offensive against Urga from Khobdo, and Magsarjav, taking his seal of office with him, slipped out of Khobdo to report on the state of affairs to the government. The Urga authorities, impressed by the seriousness of the situation, but misjudging the mood of the Manchu amban, sent two emissaries, the Torgut prince Tömörjin, and the lama Lhagva, to effect a settlement. These men were, in the words of a contemporary annalist, by nature superficial characters, and did not exercise any forethought, but just hoped to dislodge and expel the amban and other Manchu personnel from Khobdo by quick talk and empty bluff, and so acquire a reputation. They hurried openly into Khobdo, where the amban straightway seized and imprisoned them, and put them to death after all sorts of torture and ill-treatment.[5]

The Urga government thereupon appointed Magsarjav, and the Bargut leader Damdinsuren as 'dignitaries for pacifying the western region'. Damdinsuren, who had come to Urga in 1911 as a representative of those Barguts who wanted to join the Khutuktu's Mongolia, was actually a descendant of a group of Mongols who had migrated out of Setsen Khan aimak into Inner Mongolia in the 1730s. Magsarjav and Damdinsuren, together with their colleagues the Jalkhantsa Khutuktu and the duke Khaisan, were allotted five hundred soldiers. They picked up others on the way and approached Khobdo with an army of some three thousand. Some of these belonged to the private army of the freebooter Togtokh taiji, while others owed allegiance to the ambitious lama Dambijantsan. At the end of July 1912 this mixed force began to encircle Khobdo. Chinese reinforcements were sent up from Shara süme in Sinkiang to relieve the city, but the Mongols heard of this in time, it is said from information provided by the Torgut prince Palta. Though Palta was eventually to side with the Chinese and keep aloof from Mongolia, he apparently took this opportunity to get his own back on the Manchus for the murder of Tömörjin, who was his younger brother. The relief army was smashed by a force of Derbets and Uriangkhais, and in August Khobdo itself was stormed, to the spiritual accompaniment of prayers recited on the top of a neighbouring mountain by the Jalkhantsa Khutuktu and a company of lamas.

It was one thing to expel the foreigner from Khobdo, and another to hold it for Urga. The Chinese shops were thoroughly plundered, and the Mongol commanders – some say it was Dambijantsan, others say it was Magsarjav and Damdinsuren – performed a grisly ceremony of dedicating their war banners. The living hearts were torn out of the chests of Chinese prisoners of war, and the banners were daubed with their blood, while ancient ritual texts were recited. Then apparently the government forces were withdrawn and two commissioners, the Derbet prince Galsangnamjil and the Khalkha nobleman Nawangtseren, were left in nominal command. It is the custom nowadays for Mongol historical writing to tone down the part played by Dambijantsan in the liberation of Khobdo, since he later proved a danger to the revolutionary government and had to be assassinated. Indeed, some scholars go so far as to deny, in the face of all the evidence, that he took part in the battle at all. All the credit is given to Magsarjav and Damdinsuren, and the decisive contribution of Dambijantsan and Togtokh's comrade Genden, is minimized. However, it was Dambijantsan, with his comparatively large force of western Mongol troops, who profited most from the new situation, which suggests that all along it was he who enjoyed the initiative, not the Urga authorities. On the strength of his services the Jebtsundamba Khutuktu rewarded him with high clerical and feudal titles and he was the *de facto*, if not the legal, authority in the western region for the next two years, until he was arrested and removed from the scene, not by the Khutuktu's orders, but by Russian forces in 1914.

How Dambijantsan managed to maintain himself for two years as an autocrat in the west, if not by superior force of arms and prestige, it is difficult to fathom, though even the annalist quoted above in connection with the deaths of Tömörjin and Lhagva puts it all down to bluff. He writes:

> Now at the time when there was fighting and disorder in this area, a cunning fellow known as the fugitive lama Dambijantsan, a Russian subject, wormed his way in, and, spinning all sorts of fine and deceptive plans and words he took everyone in from top to bottom, and on the pretext of having acquired merit by helping in the affairs of that region, he got the most outstanding appointments, rank and authority, and on the strength of a legend that a man called Da in a land called Hou would reign as king, he perpetrated all sorts of unlawful, crooked acts, oppressive and cruel beyond all reason and measure, and he oppressed and enslaved the Mongols of the region most wrongly and severely, looking on the lives and property of the people as so much grass and earth, ruining, destroying and confusing them till he was arrested and disappeared in Russia, of which he was a subject.[6]

The old secretary Nawaangnamjil is at one with the annalist in deploring Dambijantsan's cruelties, but is equally indefinite in his account of how the Kalmuck lama maintained his authority there. He says that having got title and rank for his services at

FROM AUTONOMY TO REVOLUTION, 1911-21

Khobdo he presumed on this and set himself up as a little king there, oppressing and exploiting the people till he was arrested by the Russians. The local people, he continues, though so ill-treated by Dambijantsan, were estranged from Urga by the central government's failure to help them, and a special commissioner, the Grand Lama Tserenchimid, had to be sent to pacify them. What lies behind these hints is not certain, but it looks as if Urga, unable to oust Dambijantsan, was buying him off. His story is significant for the times he lived in. With, in absolute terms, a small number of troops, but flaunting the reputation of being the reincarnation of the hero Amursana, he was able to defy Urga's authority and rule his territory more or less independently. He appealed most immediately, because of his origin, to the Derbets, western Mongols like Amursana his spiritual forebear. There was in any case always a separatist feeling among the Derbets, and we know that even in 1913 there were Derbet lamas who violently opposed the recognition of Urga's authority, and had to be subdued by force. Dambijantsan's sectional appeal was such that, when he reappeared after the Russian revolution, the revolutionary government did not feel secure till, in 1922, it managed to liquidate him. Even then the commander of the execution squad turned back in the bitter depths of winter to cut off his head and bring it back with him, since otherwise no one would believe that the incarnation of Amursana was really and truly dead.

If the reduction of the west might be considered a domestic preoccupation, Mongolia's ambitions in the east were nullified by Russia's reluctance to complicate her own situation. Not only was Russia exercised by events in the Balkans and by the prospect of the coming conflict in Europe, but in the Far East her hands were tied, as far as pan-Mongolism was concerned, by secret treaties with Japan which divided the respective spheres of interest of the two countries at approximately the eastern frontier of Khalkha Mongolia. So in committing his new state to a programme of absorbing all Mongols to the south and east at a time when his own position was far from secure, the Khutuktu was treading a very dangerous path. In January 1912 a revolt took place in Barga. Hailar was captured and the rebels declared their allegiance to the Khutuktu. Before long, thirty-five of the forty-nine banners of Inner Mongolia too had offered their allegiance.

On the other hand, some Inner Mongol princes had become very sinicized and were unwilling to break with China, although ordinary people from certain banners actually migrated into Khalkha at this time.

In the autumn of 1912 fighting broke out in Inner Mongolia between the forces of Yuan Shih-k'ai, who was trying to re-establish China's position there, and those of autonomous Mongolia which was pursuing the dream of a pan-Mongol state. In the next two years the reality of the situation was borne in upon the Khutuktu. Russia, while willing to help and advise Mongolia, and incidentally strengthen her commercial position there, was not going to burn her fingers by championing more than a limited autonomy within the old boundaries of Outer Mongolia. This was all that was recognized in the protocol signed by Korostovets in Urga that October, and Khandadorji, making a second visit to St Petersburg at the end of the year, could not extract any greater concessions. Mongolia's international position was extremely weak. She had totally failed to get diplomatic recognition from any of the powers, and her only success, a treaty signed with Tibet early in 1913, was not taken seriously by anyone.

Fighting continued throughout 1913 on a considerable scale, though with no observable result except to confuse even further the financial situation of Mongolia, where a proper fiscal system was entirely lacking. At the end of 1913 Russia and China finally agreed on the autonomous status of Mongolia, in an accord which corresponded with the protocol of the year before, but even then the Mongols were still not convinced of the limited possibilities of their situation. The Sain Noyon Khan was sent to St Petersburg with a double mission, firstly to get recognition for the boundaries of a greater Mongolia, and secondly to negotiate for a new loan and the provision of enormous military help. The autonomous régime had been unable to bring up the strength of the brigade at Urga, which had been formed in early 1913 and was being trained by Russian instructors, to its nominal 1,900 men. Lack of recruits, desertions and sickness kept it around a figure of a mere six hundred, yet at the end of the year the Sain Noyon Khan was asking for the totally unrealistic amount of one hundred thousand rifles, and artillery and machine guns suitable for an army of one hundred thousand men. Russian ideas were more modest, and the ambassador was promised a loan of three million roubles and a quantity of armaments, though a Russian expert was to be appointed to supervise financial affairs in Mongolia.

More significantly, the Sain Noyon Khan managed to make a fool of himself and his government by admitting that the Mongols had been negotiating at official level with a totally unauthorized Japanese individual named Kodama and by asking the Russians to continue these negotiations on their behalf with the Japanese government itself. This false step gave the Russians the chance to put the Mongols firmly in their place, and the Sain Noyon Khan was finally convinced that Mongolia would have to join in a three-power conference with Russia and China to settle the matter of her status on a basis satisfactory to both her neighbours. This conference met at Khiakta in 1914 and 1915 and reaffirmed the autonomy of Mongolia under Chinese suzerainty. Mongolia and China ceased hostilities and withdrew their armies, and China was permitted to station five ambans, four in Mongolia at Urga, Uliasutai, Khiakta and Khobdo, and one in Tannu Tuva, with a small number of troops for their protection.

Autonomy and its loss, 1915-19

What Mongolia achieved at Khiakta in 1915 was less than she had hoped for in 1911, but nevertheless her situation was not unpromising. Her existence was now recognized by international treaty, without which recognition she might well have been swallowed up in later years, as Tibet has been, by a reinvigorated China. Though China exercised a nominal suzerainty, the real influence in the country was Russian, and for a time, progressive, if only the autonomous régime had been disposed to take full advantage of the opportunity. With Russian help many basic and essential reforms were initiated. The Russian military mission, working at the newly-established military school at Khujirbulang near Urga, introduced the Mongols for the first time to modern military methods, and, incidentally, to field medicine. It was only from the poorer class that soldiers were recruited into the Mongol army from 1912 onwards. Not only did the military training they received prove useful in the battles against China which continued throughout 1913 and flared up again in 1917 along the Manchurian border, but it had the wholly unexpected result of providing a nucleus of trained men, who knew one another from the old days, for the embryo revolutionary army mobilized in early 1921. Sukebator himself, the revolutionary general, was a professional soldier for seven years, and was demobilized as a sergeant-major of machine guns in 1920, and he was able to recruit many old comrades who had suffered along with him from overbearing Buriat and Mongol officers, bad food and irregular pay.

Mongolia's first acquaintance with modern medicine came through the doctors attached to the Russian consulates. The clinic at Urga treated six thousand to seven thousand local patients a year. Proper veterinary work was carried out for the first time, with animals being immunized against anthrax at a number of points throughout the country. The Russian financial adviser Kozin brought some order into Mongolia's fiscal affairs, and introduced for instance such novelties as a system of ground rent and forestry licences. The coal mines at Nalaikha, near Urga, still today the country's main source of supply, were opened in 1915. A printing press, a blacksmith's shop and a telegraph office were all opened, and a power station built. The Russians encouraged agriculture and imported some farm equipment, ploughs and harrows. A secondary school was opened in 1912, and in 1913 ten pupils were sent from it at government expense to continue their education at Khiakta and Irkutsk. So far from being, as is sometimes stated, a school for the sons of princes, it was boycotted by the nobility and was frequented by poorer boys who were supported by scholarships. The teachers were mainly Buriats, racially similar to the Mongols, but much russified and culturally more advanced. The revolutionary leader Choibalsang, later to achieve fame as Mongolia's Stalin, was a pupil here and at Irkutsk. The first Mongol newspaper, *Niislel Khureenii Medee* or 'Urga News', and a new magazine edited by Jamtsarano and entitled *Shine Toli* or 'New Mirror' were issued at this time and under Russian auspices.

Yet all these innovations were scratches on the surface. They were, in any case, doomed by the collapse of Russian power in 1917 and the reassertion of Chinese sovereignty, but apart from that they failed to affect Mongolia's ultimate problem, her hopelessly backward social order. Not only was the feudal system not dismantled, but it was even reinforced as high lamas were given titles of lay nobility and were allotted the corresponding number of *khamjilga*. The internal administrative system of the Manchu dynasty remained, with the superstructure of five ministries, those for home and foreign affairs, finance, justice and war. The aimak and banner system remained, and the *zasags* continued to hold hereditary office. The Khutuktu's *Shabi*-estate naturally continued to exist, and was added to by the transfer to it of thirty thousand commoners, who thereby ceased to contribute to state taxation. Not only were the *shabi* exempted from state taxation, but the church now became entitled to a share of the state's income for its own use.

Although some scholars have written to the contrary, the servicing of Chinese debts continued throughout the period of autonomy, except perhaps in the Khobdo district, where the debt registers had been destroyed in 1912. There is clear documentary evidence of repayment of debts incurred before 1911 being demanded by the Chinese creditors throughout the period, while new debts were still being run up. The grotesque nature of these debts can be judged from a look at the situation of one banner, that of Achitu beise, one of the poorest in Setsen Khan aimak. There were in this banner 2,780 commoners, of whom 1,548 were *khamjilga* and 1,232 ordinary tax paying commoners. On the other hand there were 346 *taijis* and 2,707 lamas. The livestock in the banner, calculated against the population (the source does not make clear whether all the population is meant, or only the taxpayers, but the figures are so small that it makes little difference) were: 0·1 of a horse, 0·8 of an ox, 0·7 of a sheep and 3·6 goats per head. The banner owed a capital sum of 12,704 taels of silver, plus interest of 6,987 taels, to the Bank of China in 1916. At the same time it had debts with various Chinese shops, incurred sometimes for the most frivolous reasons. For instance, in 1916 the wedding of the *zasag's* younger brother necessitated a further loan of over 2,000 taels of silver, only half of which fell to the *zasag* while the other half was assessed to this subjects. An even more impossible situation was that of the banner of Darkhan gung in Sain Noyon Khan aimak, which had a population of 238 households and owed a debt of 240,000 taels, or over one thousand taels each, which far exceeded the total capital value of the banner.

Destitution and actual starvation are reported from all over the country during this period. People had not only to cope with the severe climate which every year took a toll of their animals, with heavy debts and the extravagance of many nobles, but with a new drain on their livelihood which opened with the continuing military operations in the east. There was no proper army supply system, and the army was expected to support itself from the resources of the place where it happened to be. The standing army was quite small, but in times of emergency special detachments were raised which at first had to be equipped by their respective banners, and were then a charge on the local population. Thus in 1917 when the Manchu-loyalist Bavuujav, once a general in the Khutuktu's army, was threatening to raid eastern Mongolia, an army of three thousand men, half of them raised from the three western aimaks, was stationed in the easternmost, Setsen Khan aimak, to the distress of the local people.

Yet until the international situation changed, with the consolidation of Soviet power in Siberia, there was no earnest attempt made to deal with Mongolia's problems in a fundamental way. There were a few popular uprisings on a small scale, like Ayushi's movement, directed against individual *zasags*, and there were a number of mutinies and other disturbances in the army which the authorities were more or less powerless to deal with. But the trigger for purposeful action was undoubtedly not the gradually growing distress of the people, but the sudden shock of the abrogation of autonomy in the autumn of 1919. Chinese intervention in Mongolia had been increasing during 1918 and 1919, partly on the pretext of securing the country against Soviet aggression which was feared from the north, partly in face of the Japanese-sponsored pan-Mongolia movement in Dauria whose leaders were making overtures to the Khutuktu in 1919. Ch'en I, the Chinese resident in Urga, persuaded the autonomous government to allow him to bring in Chinese reinforcements, and the first of these arrived in Urga in September 1918. In the summer of 1919 Ch'en was engaged in discussions with the Mongol government on the question of the relinquishment of autonomy. A document in sixty-four points, guaranteeing the feudal rights of the nobility in exchange for their surrender of autonomy and acceptance of Chinese sovereignty, was drawn up and accepted by the Khutuktu, but met with opposition on the part of the two-chamber parliament. Before the question could be settled amicably, the Chinese general Hsü Shu-tseng, or Little Hsü, was appointed commander-in-chief and arrived in Urga with a large military force. Meanwhile the Khutuktu had sent the Jalkhantsa Khutuktu to Peking to continue negotiations over Mongolia's status, but Hsü precipitated a *coup d'état*, winning over some princes by bribes, and terrorizing others, and extorting from them a petition requesting the abrogation of autonomy. A show of force compelled the government to accept Hsü's demands. The 'petition' was signed by sixteen ministers and high lay and clerical nobles, though not by the Khutuktu himself. The circumstances by which it was obtained show quite clearly that it was only the superior military strength at Hsü's disposal which enabled him to extort it, but this is also recognizable from the list of signatures. Though this contained some pro-Chinese names, such as that of Nawangneren, the Setsen Khan and Minister of Justice, it also included the name of at least one pro-revolutionary figure, the Minister of Foreign affairs Tserendorji, who was in 1924 to be the first Prime Minister in the first government of the People's Republic, and whose reputation never suffered from his adherence to the enforced 'request' for the abrogation of autonomy.

In February 1920 the actual ceremony of the handing over of authority to the Chinese took place in Urga under humiliating circumstances. The twenty-two items of the ceremonial included the kowtowing of all officials to Hsü and the personal reverence of the Khutuktu to the Chinese flag. Immediately afterwards the five Mongol ministries were dismantled and their archives transferred to the Chinese authorities, and the Mongol army was demobilized, with a few minor exceptions such as the fifty soldiers retained at Khiakta. Weapons and equipment were confiscated by the Chinese.

3 Preparation for revolution

Such then was the situation in which the first rudimentary revolutionary clubs were founded at Urga. There was no history of a long-prepared revolutionary movement, and no working class to act as a revolutionary force. Nor was there much contact with foreign 'progressive' thought, except what help and advice could be got from those few Russian workers in Urga and instructors in the army who happened to be Bolsheviks. Few of the revolutionaries knew Russian. Choibalsang, who had studied in Irkutsk, was an exception, and he was able to keep in touch with Russian comrades, particularly with two workers whose names are given as Kucherenko and Gembarzhevskii, and who did not survive the white occupation of Urga. Choibalsang's *Concise History of the Mongol Revolution* betrays what sort of instruction the Mongol revolutionaries got from their Russian friends, and it was indeed of a very elementary and arbitrary character:

> Kucherenko was a typesetter in the Russian-Mongol Printing House, and in his leisure time he explained to the members of the revolutionary groups the great October revolution, and how the small nations which had been oppressed in the Tsarist era had obtained their entire freedom of government, and how the Russian proletariat wielded governmental power and had abrogated the unequal treaties established between Tsarist Russia and the various small and weak nations, and moreover how it was helping those nations in the struggle for gaining their freedom. After the explanations of Kucherenko and Gembarzhevskii the members of the groups understood the internal revolutionary situation in Russia.[7]

There can at that time have been little or no knowledge of communist theory at all in Mongolia, except what little was passed on by word of mouth. A catalogue of books printed in Mongolia since 1913 shows that the first classics of communism did not even begin to appear in book form till 1925, though Mongol revolutionaries must have been acquainted with them to some extent earlier through the revolutionary newspaper *Mongolyn Unen* or 'Mongol Truth', which was published in Irkutsk from November 1920 onwards, and printed the Communist Manifesto in its first number. But it was not till 1930, at the height of the anti-religious campaign, that a determined effort was made to popularize the theories of communism, and a special office for disseminating Marxist literature in the Mongol language was set up inside the propaganda department of the Central Committee of the Party.

There are other indications that the aims of the revolutionaries were at first quite modest. Two revolutionary clubs are known to have been founded in Urga at about the same time, towards the end of 1919. One of these is said to have been led by Sukebator, who had been working as a typesetter in Urga since 1918, specially detached by the War Ministry for this purpose, the other by Choibalsang. The membership of both groups was very mixed. There were men of humble origin like the two leaders, there were lamas such as Bodo, who was executed as a counter-revolutionary in 1922. Some men, such as Danzan, one of the seven heroes who undertook the secret, and now legendary, journey to Russia in 1920 to attract Soviet interest and get help, and who was liquidated without trial in 1924 by the Third Party Congress, might perhaps be classed as bourgeois. There were members of the official class, such as Jamyang, a civil servant in the Ministry of Finance and a scholar, who was later the first president of the Mongolian Committee of Sciences. The revolutionaries also enjoyed the good will of a number of nobles and other influential and prominent figures, especially the general Magsarjav, the high lama Damdinbazar the Jalkhantsa Khutuktu, and the Grand Lama Puntsagdorji who was to lose his life along with Bodo. The revolutionaries and their sympathizers were certainly not Bolsheviks: they represented a wide spectrum of origin and outlook, but the Bolshevik element ousted all others, and, as in Russia, the history of the revolution has always been based on the false assumption that only the faction which emerged victorious ever had the interests of the country at heart, the others being base traitors. Thus the association of men like Choibalsang with men like Puntsagdorji has been justified by Marxist apologists on the theoretical grounds that it was correct tactics to create this 'alliance' between the true revolutionaries and members of the aristocracy and so consolidate all those elements who might be of help, even temporarily, to the revolution. It is never admitted that the aristocrats too were exercised by the problem of Mongolia's future, and were honourable men and patriots. But dogma apart, it is rather doubtful if the choice of action, whether to make an alliance or not, lay so obviously in the hands of the extremists, who were members of a powerless conspiracy at the time, and if they themselves approached the matter in so self-conscious and theoretically correct a manner as it later became *de rigueur* to make out. They may never even have appreciated the theoretical basis of what they were doing when they tried to recruit a nucleus of patriots. Although divergencies of interest began to make themselves apparent very soon, it was not in fact till 1939 that the last 'counter-revolutionaries', men like Losol and Dovchin, who have since been rehabilitated, were unmasked as traitors and spies and executed by Choibalsang, and such contradictions between the orthodox revolutionaries and their opponents cannot possibly have been foreseen by the little groups of amateurs who were conspiring in Urga in 1919. Moreover, at the practical level it was only through the mediation of such highly placed individuals as the Jalkhantsa Khutuktu and Puntsagdorji that the revolutionaries would be in a position to make contact with the Khutuktu, and without his agreement it was unlikely that they would get very far in their negotiations with Russia. In fact they were advised by Borisov, a Comintern representative who came to Urga, that it would be in their best interests to obtain the Khutuktu's sanction.

Until the Urga revolutionary groups made contact with representatives from the Comintern, their activities were quite limited in scope, and their objectives ill-defined. Apart from an abortive attempt to assassinate Little Hsü, they seem mainly to have met to discuss the situation, and to have composed and posted up placards in the streets of Urga. Fortunately the text of one such placard had survived and has been published. The language in which it is formulated is the stiff and formal chancery style used in official documents at the end of the Manchu dynasty, indebted here and there even to Chinese idiom: it is dignified, ponderous and difficult to understand, hardly the language, one might think, of men who in a very short while were to show themselves as Soviet-inspired revolutionaries. In part the placard runs:

In particular, recently the *zasags* and nobles, far from devoting themselves to acquiring wisdom and governing their people, have been taking advantage of their descent and their high appointments wrongfully to oppress the honest, peaceful folk gaining their livelihood. They have taken excessive taxes, gone against custom and forgotten the rules, rejected the wise and attracted the flatterers, completely abandoned the three bonds and the five eternals, and done nothing but try to satisfy their own personal desires, all of which is quite out of tune with the times.[8]

The proposal was made to Hsü that the old principle of hereditary *zasags* should be abolished, and that 'as in all other countries of the world', an elective government should be set up. The placard was addressed in the most polite terms to 'His Excellency Hsü, who is endowed with all skill and wisdom, like the judge Hsi-mergen of ancient times'. It strikes one nowadays by its complete inapplicability to the contemporary situation: Hsü, who was a ruthless member of the Japanese-supported An-fu clique and had just annexed Mongolia for the purpose of exploiting her for the benefit of China, was not the man to be swayed by polite appeals of this sort. Nor did it have much relevance to the sort of revolution the Mongols were to experience: it was not the other countries of the world who were to be Mongolia's model, but simply and solely communist Russia which she was to imitate in every respect. The placard gives an impression of ideological woolliness, though this was soon to be replaced by the sharper dialectic of communism as the revolution passed from the idealistic, patriotic, to the realist stage, and came irrevocably under the influence and direction of the Comintern and the Soviet communist party.

Russia intervenes

The first fruitful contact with Soviet Russia came early in 1920 when a secret Comintern agent, I. A. Sorokovikov, came to Urga to spy out the land on the spot, and was put in touch with Sukebator and the others by Kucherenko. Sorokovikov advised them to make a *démarche* to the eastern section of the Comintern without delay, immediately after his departure, and he promised to instruct Makstinyak, the Soviet representative at Khiakta, to facilitate their crossing of the frontier. This advice was accepted, and soon afterwards, in June 1920, the two revolutionary groups in Urga amalgamated, and for the first time called themselves the Mongol People's Party. This was of course still a small and quite unrepresentative group, with as yet no contacts outside Urga in the countryside, a fact which must be remembered when we consider how in the course of the next few weeks it was to arrogate to itself the right to speak on behalf of the Mongol people as a whole, most of whom knew nothing of its existence. One of the first activities of the new party was to draw up a party oath in nine clauses, of which the first was a statement of the party's aims. Even as late as the middle of 1920 the defence of the Buddhist faith was one of the principal objectives of the new party. In full the clause runs:

> The aims of the People's Party of Outer Mongolia are to purge cruel enemies who are hostile to the Faith and the nation, to restore lost authority, loyally to protect and encourage state and church, to protect our nationality, loyally to reform the internal administration, to plan

fully for the well-being of the poor people, constantly to guard our own internal authority and to let people live free from suffering, neither oppressing nor being oppressed.[9]

The comrades who were to go to Russia to seek help were chosen by lot. This fell on Sukebator, Choibalsang, Danzan, Bodo, Losol, Dogsom and Chagdarjav: all of these, except for the first two, were to be liquidated on one pretext or another during the next twenty years. The first to set out were Choibalsang and Danzan, who made contact at Verkheneudinsk with Boris Shumyatskii, at that time President of the Council of Ministers of the Far Eastern Republic. The interpreters at the interview were Jamtsarano and another Buriat, Rinchino. Both of these were to play a considerable part in Mongolia's revolutionary development, and both were to fall victim to the Soviet purges of the 1930s. According to Choibalsang's own account, the delegates were received with some scepticism, and in a coded message sent back to Urga, Choibalsang urged his comrades to get a letter of authority from the Khutuktu, a matter which was simultaneously being suggested to them by Borisov, the Comintern agent there. Meanwhile, Bodo and Chagdarjav had set out for Khiakta with a letter for Makstinyak which designated them as representatives of the Mongol people, empowered to present requests to the Comintern, and spoke of their group of delegates as a

delegation from the whole Mongol people to the Soviet power, whose aim is the establishment of close relations between the revolutionary people of the Russian republic and of Mongolia, the clarification of relations between the Soviet power and Mongolia, and the holding of conversations with the central authority about the possibility of giving active help to Mongolia.[10]

The revolutionaries are seen in this unofficial document to be moving closer towards a full alliance with Soviet Russia, though as yet they did not constitute even a sizeable party inside Mongolia, let alone the beginnings of a government. At the same time it was clear to them that authority from the Khutuktu would be necessary if they were to get anywhere with the Russians, since in spite of the reoccupation of Mongolia by the Chinese the Khutuktu was still the legal head of state though owing allegiance to Peking.

The matter was channelled to the Khutuktu through the Grand Lama Puntsagdorji, and a letter composed by Jamyang received the Khutuktu's official seal. Similar letters were addressed simultaneously to the Japanese and American governments, though without any positive reaction from these quarters.

The request for aid was couched in carefully modest terms. It reviewed the circumstances in which Mongolia had lost her autonomy and went on to say that the Mongols of Khalkha and Derbet wished to restore their 'independent small state' as it existed under the ambans of Uliasutai, Urga and Khobdo, and to get rid of the clause in the Treaty of Khiakta which stated that Mongolia was part of Chinese territory. Nevertheless, lacking an army, the Mongols were powerless to do anything for themselves, and they requested the Soviet authorities to take account of the circumstances and to agree to help them. If such agreement were reached, the Soviets were asked to communicate their ideas as to how the restoration of Mongolian autonomy might best be effected by means of discussions and without recourse to violence.

It is apparent from this letter that the Khutuktu must have abandoned, if only temporarily, all ideas of pan-Mongolism, and hoped for nothing more than the restoration of Mongol autonomy within the boundaries sanctioned by the various agreements of 1912 to 1915, especially the Treaty of Khiakta to which Russia was a party. It is also clear that the letter empowered the bearers to negotiate only on the basis of obtaining advice about how to manage their affairs. The Mongols wanted to get rid of the occupying Chinese forces which had been terrorizing the population since Hsü's *coup d'état*, but the Khutuktu was not authorizing the conspirators to request immediate material help or military intervention, still less to hint at any possibility of internal change in Mongolia. It is probable too that this plan of action corresponded to the intentions of certain members of the party, though not to those of Sukebator and Choibalsang who were soon to be committed, if they were not already so, to the establishment of a government of their own making at Urga, and to full alliance with the Soviet government. Before the last three delegates left Urga there was discussion among them as to whether they should take with them an additional document of their own, sealed with the party's own seal which had already been prepared and cut out of wood, as well as the Khutuktu's letter. But on this occasion it was decided that the latter was all that was needed.

The story of Sukebator's journey to Khiakta has passed into legend in Mongolia, and the whip handle in which he hid the Khutuktu's letter during the first part of the journey is preserved as a relic of the revolution in an Ulan Bator museum. However, for many years during the period of the cult of personality which blighted life, thought and writing in Mongolia just as it did in the USSR, the part played by the other conspirators was suppressed, and the story of the epic journey was told as if only Sukebator and Choibalsang had undertaken it. Now that more, and more reliable information is available, Sukebator's role, though an important one, can be seen in better perspective, and he emerges as the military organizer of the partisan war which preceded the revolution, with most of the diplomatic and political work being undertaken by others who later fell from favour and became 'un-persons'.

Sukebator crossed the frontier after a thorough search by Chinese frontier guards, who did not find the Khutuktu's letter, now hidden in an amulet. He was accompanied by an old soldier named Puntsag, a future commander of the revolutionary army, and his two comrades followed soon after. They were met by Makstinyak, who passed them on to Sorokovikov in Verkhneudinsk, where they rejoined Choibalsang and the others. Jamtsarano and Rinchino again put them in touch with Shumyatskii who advised them to move on to Irkutsk.

Together with Buriat advisers and helpers, they reached Irkutsk in the middle of August, and engaged in conversations with Gapon (or Kupon), head of the section of the peoples of the east of the Siberian bureau of the Russian communist party. At the meeting on 19 August the Mongols explained the aims of their party and asked for military help, a loan, and the dispatch of military instructors and of advisers to help in revolutionary work, with the eventual purpose of freeing Mongolia from Chinese domination. If this main aim is that expressed in the Khutuktu's letter, the means by which it was to be achieved go well beyond what had originally been sanctioned, and it seems to be from the time of this meeting that an incipient break between the delegation and the Urga government is apparent. Gapon's interest extended beyond the mere expulsion of the Chinese from Mongolia, and he asked the delegation to draw up a document for him in which they would explain what sort of a government they would set up after their aims had been achieved, as well as how they proposed to go about the matter of actually getting rid of the Chinese. He said he realized that they had brought with them a letter from the Khutuktu, which might at some time or other come in handy as an authorization, but what was needed if the matter was to be passed on to higher authority was a statement from the People's Party itself.

This blunt demand produced a temporary but significant rift in the Mongol delegation. Some members were of the opinion that as the matter of a party letter had been discussed and rejected at Urga, it was unnecessary to bring it up again, and in any case they had the Khutuktu's letter, so that a second one was superfluous. It was Danzan and Dogsom, the latter of whom was liquidated in 1939, in particular who took this view, but they were overruled by Sukebator. Mongol historians today, looking back to these times, say that the events illustrated the sharpening struggle between the Sukebator faction and other members of the group, who displayed a 'limited point of view about the restoration of autonomy and of bourgeois-nationalist elements'. Choibalsang himself wrote later that on this question Sukebator 'stood firmly on the party's position. From this time on, comrade Sukebator really began to lead the activity of our party'.[11] In other words, Sukebator was now definitely no longer acting as the agent of the Khutuktu, but was working primarily for the Mongolian People's Party, and, as Choibalsang suggests with the advantage of hindsight and the elimination of all rivals, for an incipient fraction within the party. It would be a thankless task to discuss, half a century later, what were the legalities of the situation, especially as the Party and the Khutuktu reached a compromise agreement in late 1921 which was institutionalized in a formal oath, but the activities of the Mongol delegation from this time on aroused the distrust of the Khutuktu and amply explain his overt opposition to the revolutionaries over the ensuing months.

The Mongols overcame their disagreement and drew up a document which was handed over to Gapon and to Puzorin, the head of the soviet of the Fifth Army, on 28 August. In its preamble this document sets out in outline the programme of activities of the People's Party over the next few years. It was intended to recover autonomy, to appoint the Khutuktu a constitutional monarch and then destroy the hereditary power of the aristocracy. Then, when people had been prepared for it, the Party would renew the revolution and eliminate the oligarchy which held power. Several concrete proposals for action put forward in the document stressed the necessity of constant liaison with the Soviet government. At this moment the delegates split into three groups. Losol, Danzan and Chagdarjav were to travel to Moscow and discuss the question of Soviet help, Sukebator and Choibalsang were to remain in Irkutsk for liaison purposes, and Bodo and Dogsom were to go back to Urga to organize revolutionary activities inside Mongolia. As it happened, it proved impossible for them to do anything once they had returned. All sympathizers with the revolution, including Jamyang and the generals Magsarjav and Damdinsuren, were arrested by the Chinese, and so far from being able to reorganize and develop their activities, the Urga revolutionaries had to disperse and remain passively underground.

The demands of the cult of personality, which exalted Choibalsang, and, to a lesser extent, the dead Sukebator, over their former comrades, meant that for a long time all supposedly serious accounts of the events of these times were subjected to grotesque distortions, though these have now been corrected to a certain extent. The doings of the delegates who went from Irkutsk to Moscow have been almost ignored, and, as Shirendyv, the President of the Mongolian Academy of Sciences notes regretfully in a book published in 1963, there is practically no reliable information to be had about this embassy, although the members met the highest in the land, including Lenin himself. Moreover, in spite of official rehabilitations, the legend about the treachery of all the revolutionaries but Sukebator and Choibalsang lives on to this day. A case in point is a fictional account of the life of Sukebator by the Russian novelist Kolesnikov which was published in 1959, before the cult of personality was fully abandoned, but was not translated into Mongol till 1965, by which time it was, politically speaking, out of date. Though Losol and Dogsom, though not Danzan, have long since been restored to respectability, and have been referred to by the present head of state, J. Sambuu, in a speech in 1966, as 'chosen sons of our people', this novel still builds them up as congenital traitors, and maintains a prudish silence about exactly who it was who was chosen to go to Moscow and undertake the task of negotiating with Chicherin and Kamenev. It refers merely to 'a special representative'. Choibalsang's *Concise History of the Mongol Revolution* avoids mentioning these names too, but this is not surprising when it is realized that this book was published at the height of the personality cult surrounding its author, and that it is an abridgement of a longer history which was the joint work of Choibalsang, Losol and Demid. Demid, Marshal of the Mongol army, was another so-called traitor, eliminated by poison in 1937 apparently in connection with the Tukhashevskii affair. Because of illness, Losol did not actually reach Moscow, and it seems that at one point Chagdarjav turned back to Irkutsk as a result of a disagreement, but Danzan at least achieved his purpose, and subsequently met Lenin. What is significant is that it was not Sukebator or Choibalsang who was chosen for this critical and honourable task, but others of the group, and precisely those who, if we are to accept Choibalsang's account, had just shown themselves bitter opponents of the 'true' party line. Explanations can be only a matter of speculation, but it may be inferred that this so-called party line was one which was only elaborated in retrospect, and that neither Choibalsang nor Sukebator occupied a position of such overwhelming importance inside the revolutionary movement as was made out later.

Sukebator and Choibalsang waited at Irkutsk, where they underwent some military training which was interrupted by a serious illness which befell Sukebator, probably a precursor of the illness which carried him off prematurely less than three years later. Sukebator also maintained contacts with Comintern personnel, including members of its Mongol-Tibetan section. On 10 November news arrived from Moscow that the mission there had achieved its object. But by now the situation inside Mongolia had changed drastically. Ch'en I had come back to replace Hsü who had fallen with the An-fu clique's loss of power, but a new threat had arisen with the invasion of north Mongolia by a band of white Russian troops under Baron Ungern Sternberg at the beginning of October. Ungern moved towards Urga and laid siege to it. The Chinese had played into his hands by their murders, rapings and robberies, as well as by their attacks on lamaseries and the imprisonment of the Khutuktu. Mongols of all classes began to look to the white Russians to deliver them from the Chinese. Ordinary Mongols enlisted in great numbers in the Baron's army, and Magsarjav himself, on his release from prison, was even to serve as Minister of War in the new government and to hold active field command.

On 3 February 1921 Ungern occupied Urga and restored the Khutuktu to the throne. At this time he enjoyed general support and respect, and the Khutuktu conferred extravagant titles on him, extolling him as the 'invincible general, incarnation of the fierce divinity Jamsarang'. But his short reign of terror in Urga, during which he and his men slaughtered every Russian they could find who was not wholeheartedly for them, and tortured, killed and plundered indiscriminately among the population, lost him all regard as quickly as he had gained it.

Meanwhile, preparations for a revolutionary take-over were going ahead in the Russian part of Khiakta, also known as Troitskosavsk, where Sukebator arrived on 22 November 1920, leaving the returning delegation from Moscow temporarily in Irkutsk to keep up liaison with the Comintern. It now became the revolutionaries' purpose to recruit an army, to win over people in the accessible areas of north Mongolia to the party's ideals, and to lay a sound basis for the new régime they hoped to introduce. The enthusiasm with which the Khutuktu and the population in Urga and elsewhere had welcomed Ungern threatened for a moment to make the Soviet authorities withhold the help they had promised. In early January, 1921, Sukebator had an interview with Makstinyak in Khiakta, when the latter said to him, in reviewing the situation:

In view of the bitter state of the oppressed masses of Mongol herdsmen, and both following the declaration of your representatives and honouring the aspirations of the Mongol people, our Soviet government agreed to give help to the Mongol people's revolution. In view of the present situation in Mongolia, if the oppressed Mongol people wish to obtain their freedom by struggling against internal and external oppressors with revolutionary determination and strength, then I am sure they will not make friends with the enemies of their own revolution. Yet many of your Mongol people have invited in the White Baron, who is the enemy of our Soviet state, and are allying themselves with him and are restoring the old autonomous government, which is very doubtful from the political point of view, and is a source of much difficulty in the way of help being furnished as was previously promised by the Soviet state. This is not only my opinion but is the policy of my government.[12]

Sukebator thought this over for some time and then replied to the effect that the autonomous régime had been taken over by reactionary elements intent solely on their own private interests, and hoping also to achieve their aim of 'selling out the country to the Japanese'. Hence it would be incorrect to consider the Mongol People's Party as dishonest in their presentation of their cause. Makstinyak accepted this explanation but gave Sukebator a further warning:

What you say is quite right, comrade Sukebator. Politically a very dangerous policy is in train. There is no question of the Soviet state's completely breaking off relations with you Mongols and refraining from helping and safeguarding the Mongol revolution, but in the present situation we cannot say that we will immediately give help as previously arranged. We can however hold discussions on the basis of the experience of the work your party is doing.[13]

This was fair warning to the Mongols that the Soviets were going to take a very close interest in the type of régime to be set up in Mongolia after the expulsion of foreign forces, and that no Soviet help would be forthcoming unless the future plans of the Mongols corresponded with Soviet policy. The Mongols now made their first task the recruitment of an army to take action against the Chinese troops who were straggling northwards towards Altan Bulak, the Mongol part of Khiakta, plundering and murdering as they went, after their defeats by Ungern's force. The situation was too urgent to wait for the arrival of military aid from Russia, which in fact began to dribble in only at the end of February. What is so striking about the events of the next few weeks is the unwonted speed and energy displayed in the planning and recruitment of an army, the successful staging of the first Party Congress in Russian Khiakta, the establishment of a provisional government, and the decisive defeat of a numerically far superior, though demoralized, Chinese army and the occupation of Mongol Khiakta, the first piece of Mongol soil actually to be liberated by the revolutionary forces. Some propaganda work had been done in the frontier regions after the return of the revolutionaries from Irkutsk, but it was not till 10 February that a revolutionary council decided to speed up the work of enlisting an army, and appointed Sukebator to be its commander. Between then and 18 March, when Khiakta fell, all the events just enumerated had taken place, and it must also be remembered that but for the supply of some weapons and necessities such as bread, tobacco and matches which some of the partisans smuggled across the frontier from Russian Khiakta, it was Mongol soldiers who carried out this first campaign on their own, relying on their own resources though aided by Russian staff officers.

Partisan warfare

During the second half of February Sukebator himself, and a few lieutenants of his, began to recruit a force of partisans from the area near Khiakta. One nucleus was the banner of Sumiya beise, the Chahar leader from Sinkiang who had brought his people around into Mongolia through Russia at the time of the 1911 revolution. Another nucleus were the so-called fifty soldiers of Khiakta, under the command of Puntsag, a veteran of the Khujirbulang military school and the Chinese wars of 1912 to 1914, and an old comrade of Sukebator's. One of these men was Darijav, who rose to be Minister of War and perished in a framed-up treason trial in 1937. Recruits came in from all sides, many volunteers, some not so willingly, until by the end of February a force of some four hundred men, divided into four brigades, had been assembled. They were ill-armed. Some had guns which they had bought from white Russian stragglers, others got weapons from Chinese whom they surprised and killed. In the words of one soldier:

> At first there was one sword to ten men, and one gun to twenty men. The soldiers got sabre practice slicing willow trees. But though we had some guns, there was little ammunition, so that we could not fire. Food, clothing and mounts we supplied from our own resources, and those who had no horses or clothes or food were supplied by the people of their banner. We had no special quarters, and lived scattered among the population.

The first engagements were on a very small scale. The account of one, given by a soldier who took part in it, shows it to have been rather less than an epic battle. Zagd, a lama who was recruited rather against his will, recounts the story as follows:

... so I decided to go along, and I abandoned my old white horse there and then, and put the waistcoat on on top of my lama's robe, and forty or more of us set out from Khuder under the command of the lama Khasbator, and we marched night and day and came to the *zangi* Damdinsuren's place at Khyaraan watchpost. Then our chaps heard the men there say that there were some Chinese coming from the east with carts. They were doing transport for the Chinese revolutionaries. There was a hue and cry to kill them. I was not keen on it, and I was frightened too, but I had to go along with them. We saw six or seven Chinese drinking tea and resting their five or six cart-horses. Those of my comrades who were in front went straight up to them and knocked them down and killed them. I tagged along behind, pretty scared. We looked at what they had got, and it was only vegetables. There was nothing else. Some buns and so on that they had been eating were put into a sack and given to me. I didn't want to take part, but I had to, and I tied them on to my saddle and then we went back.

Later on, hunger got the better of Zagd, and he tells how the next day he ate up the buns he had been almost too scared to touch the day before.[14]

But this personal story is interesting as reflecting rather the small beginnings of the revolutionary war than the spirit in which it was going to be fought out. More significant engagements were fought towards the end of February, in the course of which small groups of Mongols, fighting with cunning and ruthlessness, were able to annihilate much larger Chinese forces. Typical of the partisan warfare of the time was Sukebator's encirclement and destruction of a force of between one and two hundred Chinese soldiers who were gathering hay. These troops had come to steal the grass which had been cut by the local people, and Sukebator, informed of it, rode to the spot, posted most of his few troops in ambush, and then with one or two comrades rode into the middle of the Chinese and began to parley with their commander, trying to persuade him to surrender. The Chinese would not give up their arms, but agreed to retire without the grass, and as Sukebator was shaking their officer's hand, firing broke out. The official biography of Sukebator says it was the Chinese who fired first, though an account published by Laasag, one of the Mongol officers on the spot, in the Mongol army paper 'Red

Star' in 1946, says it was Puntsag's troops who did so.[15] Yet other versions of the event suggest that the Chinese were lulled into a false sense of security by Sukebator, who opened the attack on them as soon as he had reached cover. This seems entirely in character. In another engagement fought a few days later across the Orkhon River, the Mongols used a similar plan. While Sukebator was parleying with enemy representatives, he had riflemen aiming at them from under cover, and had them shot down the moment the talks were over. At any rate, the Chinese foragers were taken by surprise. A few escaped to Khiakta, where they reported the existence of a large and brave Mongol army, but most of them were massacred. The battle was a fiercer one than Zagd's petty affray with the carters. Laasag describes how the Chinese were bowled over like ninepins by the Mongols, who had the advantage of firing downhill from under cover. Most important, the Mongols were able to capture the equipment of over one hundred Chinese soldiers. They had proved themselves in this engagement, but nevertheless, right up to the time of the capture of Urga in July, they remained a weak force, lacking proper equipment and practically all military training, as a Russian officer commanding in Mongolia at the time states, and in the final and fiercer stages of the war they served more or less only as a cover to the main forces of Soviet troops in action against the whites.

Interest now moves back for a while to Russian Khiakta, where at the beginning of March the first Party Congress was held, and a provisional government set up, thus presenting a direct challenge to the Khutuktu, who still headed the legitimate, if ramshackle, régime in Urga. Here, for the first time, a revolutionary party and government were prepared on Soviet soil, with the participation of Soviet citizens, and then moved into the country they were to take over, effecting the overthrow of the existing government under the cover of the Red Army. At this time the Mongol People's Party was still unrepresentative of anyone but its own members. Of the troops who had been recruited for the partisan army, few were, or became, members of the Party. Some who did, like Zagd, showed an initial lack of comprehension of what was involved. Zagd says:

One day in March Sukebator called me and said: 'You're a party-member, see? You must get someone to read you the party rules and our ten aims.' He gave me a white book. One day I went to his place and said: 'That book you gave me when you said I'd been made a party-member – what am I to do about it?' Sukebator looked very angry and said: 'What do you mean? There's the eleventh party cell at the party Central Committee. You enrol there! You mustn't miss the cell meetings. Look sharp now and get registered.' So I got myself registered.

The first Party Congress

The story of the first Party Congress at Khiakta is, like so much of the subsequent history of Mongolia, obscured and confused by the unsatisfactory nature of the documentation. The evaluation of what has been written about revolutionary Mongolia, and even of the original sources when they can be found, becomes, indeed, a major hazard from this time on. Several factors are responsible. Geographically. linguistically and psychologically, Mongolia is one of the most remote areas of the civilized world, where few Europeans have travelled, and fewer still have known Mongols as close friends or carried on a correspondence with them, least of all during the years of the revolution. We lack the human sympathy which enlivens, for example, the study of the Soviet revolution: we cannot check the official myth against what our friends and relatives tell from their own experiences, as we can with countries nearer at hand which have passed under totalitarian control. Neither was there any vocal emigration from Mongolia. Again, until recently no scholars outside Mongolia were interested in anything written in the Mongol language or able to read it, so that, even if it had been possible in the 'twenties and 'thirties of this century to collect Mongol books, magazines and newspapers, it would never have occurred to anyone to do so. For that reason there is, generally speaking, nothing in European libraries in the Mongol language dating from the first three and a half decades of the revolution, that is from 1921 till about 1955. But what makes the situation much more serious is that much of what we do have is formalistic, or suspect, or both. By the time we in Europe could obtain Mongol historical works, the official legend was already in being. Moreover, until the most recent years there has been almost nothing of what one might call personal documentation – letters, memoirs, diaries, autobiographies and so on. What biography there was took the form almost of hagiography: the life of Sukebator as published in 1943 presented him as an almost epic hero – indeed epics about Sukebator imitating the old forms have already sprung up amongst the people – and its exaggerations can be appreciated by comparing it with the revised version published in 1965. We must also remember that only the winning side has a voice in contemporary Mongolia, and that all accounts of the revolution present it as the necessary and right conclusion of a process whose outcome was never in doubt, and the justice of whose cause is not subject to argument. The original revolutionaries were by no means all committed to communism. Many of them would have been content to see autonomy restored, the Buddhist faith rehabilitated, and a national democratic constitution elaborated. However, it was the communist faction, supported by the Comintern, which triumphed, with the result that Mongol history has for ever been narrated as if this were not only the inevitable outcome, but also in some mystic way, the only 'right' one. Consequently, historical figures are evaluated according to the degree they were considered to have aided this progress, that is, as to whether, in the eyes of the winning faction, when it finally emerged, they were to be considered revolutionaries, and so good, or enemies of the people and so bad. Facile but definite judgments, which had to be revised when the political line changed, have been made on all the protagonists of the early revolution. One may well realize that most contemporary Mongol historical writing proceeds from an act of faith, but it is more difficult, in the absence of contrasting opinion and presentation of fact on the part of native scholars, to correct the bias they openly display.

Over and above this, however, we must consider the grave fact that not only is secondary material often slanted, but that source material itself has been corrupted and falsified, either by the suppression of facts or the deliberate alteration of texts: and once doubt has been thrown on source material it is difficult ever again to have confidence in whatever material comes from the same source. In the 'thirties and 'forties, Mongol life and scholarship suffered severely from the perversions which accompanied the cult of personality. Many old revolutionaries were done to death, and their part in the foundation of revolutionary Mongolia either ignored altogether or traduced to make them appear congenital traitors. Thus the book by I. J. Zlatkin on the

Mongolian People's Republic, published in 1950, completely ignores the part played by a man like Jamtsarano, and dismisses an old revolutionary like Danzan as 'a disreputable spy in the service of the Japanese imperialists, as whose agent he joined Sukebator in 1920–21, wormed his way into the confidence of the Party, and reached a leading position.'[16] No charge was too grotesque for Choibalsang to bring against his old friends of 1920 during the purges of the late 'thirties. From 1962 onwards, rehabilitations have gradually been taking place, and to some extent the record is being rectified. Hoary old articles of faith, such as that Sukebator, who died in 1923, was poisoned by 'enemies of the people', seem to have been quietly dropped. In its most extreme form this legend was expressed as follows in 1940 by Choibalsang: 'The enemies of the people, with Danzan at their head, separated Sukebator from his family and poisoned him, under the pretence of curing him.'[17] Strangely enough, this charge had not been laid against Danzan at the time of his summary condemnation in 1924, while nowadays most accounts of Sukebator's death suggest that he died of illness brought on by excessive devotion to duty when he was already ill.

It is a most chancy business to try to exploit the sources for the period now concerning us, the primary sources being open to question. That they are so is a self-evident fact, whose point is only laboured by a sentence such as the following, taken from the preface to a collection of memoirs about Sukebator by his contemporaries, published in 1965:

This collection differs from the *Memoirs and Conversations* printed in 1945 and from similar earlier collections in two respects, in that memoirs by people who knew Sukebator in his lifetime have been taken down afresh, and that memoirs by such men as D. Dogsom, D. Losol, L. Darijav and Ts. Dambadorj, which were suppressed during the period of the cult of personality, have been revived and brought to the attention of our readers.[18]

Care was taken to eliminate proscribed names even from published archives. To take but one example: an official report of the proceedings of the first Party Congress, which now concerns us, was printed in 1957. In this, three dots were inserted to replace the name of the comrade who acted as chairman of the first meeting. Only chance comparison with a similar account of the same events by L. Demberel (d. 1938), reprinted in 1965, shows that these dots do not cover an innocent editorial abbreviation, but serve to obscure the fact that it was the subsequently unmasked 'counter-revolutionary' Danzan who was the chairman of the meeting.[19]

The Party Congress was held on the first three days of March 1921. The number of participants, which included Comintern representatives, grew from day to day. There were seventeen on the first day, and nineteen and twenty-six at the later meetings. These included party members originating from, but in no way representative of, each of the four aimaks, and from three *otogs* of the *Shabi*-estate. As might be expected, of the ten banners (out of around a hundred in the whole country) from which party members came, five were in Tushetu Khan aimak, the aimak around Khiakta. Several of the members of the congress were soldiers of the partisan army who were elected to the Party on that occasion, a fact which shows that the Party at this time had no sort of mass appeal or membership in the country as a whole. This state of affairs is reflected in the Biography of Sukebator which writes:

> Because the white Russians had occupied Urga and the internal situation had much deteriorated, it had become impracticable to carry out properly the organizational preparations prior to the congress, and so it was decided to limit the composition of the congress to the revolutionaries who had gone to Russia and to representatives from the partisan army and a few banners.[20]

On the first day the Congress drew up its agenda. There were four points: to discuss the current situation and how to deal with it, to organize a supreme command for the army and to set up a general staff, and to popularize the party's ideals and aims. The first point was settled at the second session. It was decided that although the white Russians on their first incursion into Mongolia had been of some temporary assistance – a reference no doubt to the expulsion of the Chinese from Urga by Ungern – it was impossible to work with them since they were 'beckoning to Mongolia's enemy', by which is clearly meant here Japan. Danzan, the chairman, accepted the general opinion that Mongolia should seek Soviet help and make a clean break with the white Russians. It is hard to see in this more than a form of words. The Mongol

People's Party, enjoying the hospitality of a Soviet city, and assisted by Comintern delegates, could hardly have decided to join up with the whites. Perhaps this resolution is rather to be construed as a declaration of intent not to go along any longer with the Khutuktu's régime, which was a puppet of Ungern's. On the second and third points concerning the army it was agreed to set up a general staff with five members, three of them Mongols, including Sukebator and Danzan, and two of them Russians invited from the Red Army. At the third session it was agreed to send telegrams of greetings to 'all foreign parties', to confirm the Party's platform, and to set up a Central Committee of the Party.

The Party's ideals and aims were set forth in two separate documents whose composition owed much to the Buriat Jamtsarano. The 'Preamble to the Mongol People's Party's Proclamation to the Masses' shows an obvious indebtedness to Marxist theories and jargon, while the 'Platform' itself, drawn up in ten points, is in striking contrast. The Preamble is essentially a historico-political analysis of the rise and decline of feudalism and of the influence of capitalism, and an application of the lessons to be learned from this to Mongolia's situation. The style is perhaps a shade easier and more direct than the Party's earlier publications which still affected the old official language, but it bristles with technical neologisms such as 'koloni', 'kapital', 'proletari', 'imperialism', 'feodal' and so on, some of them annotated, others left unexplained, which cannot have contributed much to the comprehension of this remarkable document by the Mongol masses, still immersed in their lamaist superstitions and for the most part illiterate, for whom it was ostensibly intended. This was indeed realized by the Party later. At the second Congress in 1923 it was decided to omit 'foreign, unintelligible words' from the Preamble and substitute Mongol terms for them. The tenor of the Preamble is unmistakable. It extols the Third International as the one force able to effect world revolution, states that the transfer of power to the people is the only way of salvation, and declares that it is in training men to accomplish this transfer that the International can best help.[21]

The language of the Platform is not tinged with jargon in the same way, but is a sober application of the ideas of the Preamble to the Mongol situation. It is here that we are faced for the first time with a major distortion in a Mongol document. The Platform was undoubtedly drawn up under ten heads, yet for years the official text, as it appeared in Choibalsang's *Concise History* contained only nine items, one having been omitted and the remainder renumbered. Fortunately, more reliable publications now make it possible to restore the original text, and to see that the missing item was one expressing Mongolia's willingness to participate in a federal state of Chinese, Manchus, Tibetans, Muslims and Mongols. Since Choibalsang attended the meeting at which the Platform was agreed he must have made this falsification to a familiar text quite deliberately. No acceptable reason has ever been alleged for the omission. The likely inference is that later subservience to Stalin's Russia was difficult to reconcile with an expressed intention to join in a federal state which would not be communist and in which Russia would have no part, so that this clause had to be made an 'un-clause' to avoid offending Stalin's susceptibilities. Yet, surprisingly, another clause, which envisaged the incorporation of 'all the Mongol tribes' in one state, and thus implicitly raised the spectre of pan-Mongolism which had been laid by the Treaty of Khiakta in 1915 and even perhaps suggested the possibility of Buriat secession from Russia to adhere to the new state, seems never to have attracted any displeasure in later years, and remains, in summary form, in Choibalsang's book.

The Platform stresses the need to re-establish national sovereignty, if possible uniting all the tribes of Mongolia. The Party reserved to itself the right to review the whole national situation, and to take whatever steps might be necessary to effect reforms, 'taking account of the present situation of the countries of the world', and to eliminate what was useless or harmful, 'by gentle means if we can, but if not, then by severe methods'. Matters of detail, such as local self-government, justice, education, economics, medical services, supply of food and other necessities, and the equalization of the tax burden, would all be considered by the Party and decided on later: for the moment all such questions were left vague. The Party welcomed within its ranks all those of Mongol race, 'whether high or low, lama or lay, men or women' who, being persons of good will and in agreement with the Party's principles, were prepared to support the Platform, and it also promised to co-operate with any other parties which might be formed, as long as their objects seemed likely to agree with the People's Party's platform of national independence and regeneration. Only those 'cunning lickspittles' who had sold out to the Chinese were rejected from the outset. There was nothing in the programme therefore to alarm, but an open breach had been made with Urga, and from March onwards the two sides took up ever more irreconcilable attitudes.

The provisional government

A further decisive step was taken by the Party on 13 March when, under the leadership of the newly established Central Committee, a meeting was held to set up a People's Provisional Government, in direct defiance of the legal government at Urga. By this time the leaders must have been perfectly clear in their own minds that they were going to go along with the Soviets and the Comintern: all their actions of the last year had tended in this direction. Yet a member of the partisan army, who attended this meeting as a fresh party member, has written that on this occasion Sukebator asked for the general opinion again as to whether the Mongols should follow the red or the white Russians, and that Bilegsaikhan proposed that the firmly-based Reds, rather than the unstable Whites, were the proper choice.

The public announcements of the decision to set up the provisional government, as reported in different collections of archival material published since 1954, have been tampered with so as to omit the names of comrades later purged for deviations. A text of 1954 gives no indication at all that any omission has been made from the list of party delegates to the meeting, and speaks only of 'the party representative Choibalsang'. A version of the same document published in 1957 mentions 'party representatives' in the plural, and shows by three dots that some names have been omitted. Most recent studies, made after the rejection of the cult of personality, let it appear that these dots cover the omission of such important names as that of Dambadorj, secretary of the Central Committee at the time, and an army commissar who took an active part in the capture of Khiakta from the Chinese a few days later. Subsequently he was ordered to the west where he headed the Party organization, and took part in operations to liquidate the remaining white Russians in western Mongolia.

In 1928 he fell from grace, while chairman of the Central Committee, on a charge of 'rightist deviationism'. Other leading revolutionaries whose part in this decisive meeting was later hushed up were Losol, executed in 1939, and Chagdarjav, executed in 1922.[22] Similarly, the archives have been tampered with to convey a false impression about the composition of the government itself. The text of 1954 is illogical to a painfully obvious degree. It runs: '... we shall appoint seven men to the government. The government ministers shall be Sukebator, Bilegsaikhan and Choibalsang.' A text of 1956 does a bit better than this, eliminating the *non sequitur* of a seven-man government with only three members, but still does not name the missing ministers. It runs: '... we shall appoint seven men to the government, of whom one shall be from Tannu Tuva. The remaining six shall be chosen by the meeting and the heads of the government shall be Sukebator and Choibalsang.' In 1957 a further rectification was made, and the text then read: '... the remaining six shall be chosen by the meeting, and shall be ... as head of the government, and Sukebator, Bilegsaikhan and Choibalsang as member ministers.' Once again, only the most recent publications give what is presumably the full story and show that it was the 'traitor' Chagdarjav who was actually appointed chief minister of the provisional government, though soon afterwards he was detached for special party duty to north-west Mongolia and was replaced by Bodo. The remaining members of the government were Bodo, later premier of the 1921 People's Government at Urga, and executed in 1922, and Sumiya beise, the Chahar aristocrat from Sinkiang.[23]

These distortions and successive partial restorations of official documents cast a revealing light not only on the attitude towards historical accuracy taken by the Mongol authorities, but on the subsequent history of the revolution itself and on the various forms taken in later years by the legends which grew up round it. They show for one thing that in 1921 the Mongols still hoped to assert control over Tannu Tuva. There were strongly expressed wishes at the time that the two peoples might be united, but these were ignored by the Soviet Union which first engineered the setting up of a 'Tuvan People's Republic' in 1924 and then, during the Second World War, unostentatiously annexed Tannu Tuva. Only between 1954 and 1956 did it become possible once again to restore to the announcement about the provisional government any hint of its 1921 policy towards Tannu Tuva.

The corrections now being made to mutilated archives also put into proper perspective the parts played by all the leading revolutionaries of the time, and reveal that in 1921 the cracks in the façade of unity, which were, in retrospect, made to seem so crass and obvious, were at the time by no means so apparent. The right and left wings of the Party seem to have been working very much in harmony, and in fact it is men of the right wing, Danzan, Chagdarjav and Bodo, who at this time held the most important positions. The impression which the falsified archives were intended to convey was that the Leninist path to socialism in Mongolia was from the first the generally accepted one, obstructed only by the machinations of a few men who were, *ipso facto*, traitors. In reality however, even as late as 1921, the leading circles of the revolution included a considerable number of men whose outlook and whose vision of the future were not necessarily identified with those of the Soviet communist party. The proclamation concerning the provisional government and its future tasks, though no longer mentioning the restoration of the Khutuktu as one of its aims, is still a very moderate document, emphasizing the need to clear out of Mongolia the remnants of the Chinese and of the white Russians, whom it accuses of deceiving the Mongols with false promises of independence simply in order to buy their help in restoring the Tsarist régime in Russia. It reasserts the principle of Mongol independence, and promises, what it was able to fulfil in 1924, the calling of a National Khural or Assembly, to determine the future constitution of the country.

A collision with the Urga régime was now inevitable and intended, and the outcome could hardly be in doubt, since the Khutuktu had only the ephemeral military power of Ungern to rely on, while the provisional government, though disposing of only a smallish force itself, was backed by the Red Army. The coming Soviet campaign against the Whites in Mongolia must be considered to a great extent as nothing more than an extension of the civil war in Russia itself, since the white bands were no respecters of frontiers but moved from Russia to Mongolia and back as necessary, a situation which the Soviets could hardly be expected to tolerate. Their intervention, when it came in 1921, was legally covered by a request made by the provisional government, though not by the Khutuktu's régime in Urga, but it was in any case an inevitable outcome of the Russian civil war.

The expulsion of the Chinese and the occupation of Urga

On 14 March Sukebator proposed at a joint meeting of the Central Committee and the Provisional Government that Altan Bulak, or Mongol Khiakta, should be captured from the Chinese. This move had a double purpose, since it would deprive the Chinese troops, who were plundering and marauding in north Mongolia and earning a bad name which has still not been lived down, of their main base, and at the same time would furnish the Provisional Government with a first foothold of Mongol territory to establish itself on, and strengthen its claim to legitimacy. The proposal was criticized by Danzan, who maintained that there was too great a disparity in the number of troops on the two sides and that it would be better to try and get the co-operation of the Chinese commander, General Ko. Danzan's objections were overruled. It was thought that his tactics, if followed, would not only blunt the enthusiasm of the young partisan army, but would also give the enemy time to reinforce his position. The assault was planned to take place from three sides at once, with a small force of ninety men in reserve. No Soviet troops seem to have been involved, though Russian staff officers took part in the planning. On the 15 March Sukebator called on the Chinese in Khiakta to surrender, but received no reply. On the morning of the 18 March the assault began in miserable conditions: wet snow had been falling and the Mongol troops had been forbidden to light matches or smoke or talk to each other, or to go to sleep. The order to open fire was given at 10 a.m. and well before noon Altan Bulak had been practically occupied. A sudden Chinese counter-attack, coupled with a shortage of ammunition on the Mongol side, forced a temporary withdrawal. However, new supplies were brought up, two cannon, which could not be laid before because the horses pulling them were exhausted, were brought to bear on Khiakta, and by midnight the city was in the hands of the Mongol army and the Chinese were in full flight. The Mongol victory is all the more surprising when we consider the relative numbers involved. The Chinese had some ten thousand men against four hundred Mongols, but they were a demoralized rabble rather than a properly constituted garrison. Only a few days before, indeed, Ch'en I, the Chinese resident in Urga who had fled to Altan Bulak, in spite of having this large force nominally at his disposal, had applied, though in vain as matters turned out, to the Soviet authorities for military help against the white Russians in Mongolia.

Most of the Chinese fled into Russia by way of Khiakta, but others retreated southwards, to the west of Urga, and were dealt with either by partisan groups or by troops of the Khutuktu's army, including a force under Magsarjav. The almost incredible victory of Sukebator's little force at Altan Bulak thus eventually brought about the entire collapse of the Chinese position in Mongolia, which had appeared so impregnable eighteen months earlier.

The Provisional Government was immediately transferred to Altan Bulak. From March onwards it devoted itself to organizing revolutionary activities in areas so far untouched, and to recruiting more soldiers. Dambadorj and the Inner Mongolian lama Khasbator were sent to Uliasutai, Khobdo, and Ulaangom to recruit partisan bands there, and to establish local party organizations. Chagdarjav was sent to north-west Mongolia, while Choibalsang, Danzan and others busied themselves in the northern banners. At the same time various questions concerning local administration, collection of rents from foreigners, and tax reform, were mooted, but the new government was far too occupied with the war situation, and controlled far too little of Mongolia, to be able to do anything effective. In a moment of frankness a few years later, at the Third Party Congress of 1924, the Buriat delegate Rinchino admitted how feeble the revolutionary organization had been at the time. Criticizing another delegate's utopian views, he had this to say:

Comrade Gombojav scolds the Party for delaying the reorganization of local government elections. He also says that we should have reorganized the local administration the day after Baron Ungern had been destroyed. Let me ask comrade Gombojav on what force he would have relied to carry out so important a change. At that time the party was only thirty or forty strong. There was no Revolutionary Youth League yet in existence, and our army consisted of a few hundred exhausted partisans. We had only one party cell in the countryside. . . .[24]

Relations with Urga were now reaching a crisis. Both governments were issuing orders and proclamations intended to undermine each other's position. The Ministry of the Interior at Urga sent out instructions for Sukebator to be brought to Urga, and on 23 March the Provisional Government published a letter addressed to the nobles and lamas of Mongolia in which it expounded its *raison d'être* and gave them a warning not to go on supporting Ungern. If they opposed the Provisional Government and helped Ungern there would be a stern reckoning when the time came, and the revolutionaries were simply advising them of this in advance. At approximately the same time, the Khutuktu's Ministry of the Interior put out a strangely worded summons to Sukebator to come and surrender to Urga, in which, for the first and perhaps the only time in Mongolia's history, there is deliberate expression of anti-semitism. This was undoubtedly a reflection of the influence of Ungern, who was noted for his vicious persecution of the Jews, and who had massacred all those Russian Jews he could lay hands on in Urga, where most of the frontier trade with Russia was in their hands. If the revolutionary party's declarations understate their dependence on Marxist doctrines, the Khutuktu's order betrays a keen anti-Bolshevism, suggested to him no doubt by what his white Russian advisers and masters had told him of events in Russia:

> The proclamation to the Mongols by the People's Party is nonsense, written at the direction of the Red Party which is trying to deceive the Mongols as it has deceived its own Russians, and it is a dangerous thing. The Red Party, deceiving the people into believing that it will afford them happiness, has taken power into its own hands, and has in the end plundered the property of farmers, merchants and nobles, destroyed temples, monasteries and other shrines, and killed many tens of thousands of people. They have plundered what the Tsars and their subjects built up in the course of many years, and have brought the whole Russian people to experience poverty and starvation. The majority of the Red Party are Hebrews, also known as Jews, who, without distinction of Russian, Mongol, American, Japanese or Chinese, are intent merely on robbery, and therefore they are not to be trusted or aided. This Red Party is not trying to reinforce or help the Mongol state, but is weakening it, and trying to appropriate from the Mongols much of their cattle and horses. The Mongols are well aware of the doings of the Chinese revolutionaries who are the disciples of the Red Party. Now, at a time when the state should be established

in accordance with the mercy of the Khutuktu, the Red Party is deceiving the simple-minded people, and trying to set up a party without the permission of the King. . . .[25]

The Khutuktu's order ends with an appeal for all Mongols to unite to restore autonomy under Chinese suzerainty, that is, in accordance with the terms of the Treaty of Khiakta of 1915, and to form a strong state in which the Buddhist Faith would be protected. The clash of interests is apparent. The Khutuktu was looking simply for a return to the situation as it was before Little Hsü had forced the abrogation of autonomy and before his régime had lost credit by its reliance on Ungern, who turned out to be a more fearful menace than the Chinese. But the revolutionaries had gone beyond this. While they may conceivably have intended a simple restoration at the time they left Urga with the Khutuktu's letter in mid-1920, before Ungern's adventure had drawn Mongolia into the orbit of the Russian civil war, they were now committed for help and advice, and possibly their very existence, to the good will of the Soviet régime, which dreamed of world revolution, and to the armed might of the Red Fifth Army.

In April the Provisional Government which, as we have seen, had been organized on Soviet territory by a self-appointed group, requested Soviet armed intervention in Mongolia, and from early May onwards Russian forces began to move in. The white Russian forces in north Mongolia were soon routed, though at one point Sukebator was in serious danger of losing Altan Bulak and only defeated Ungern with the help of two Russian regiments sent quickly to his aid. The combined Soviet and Mongol armies now made for Urga, which they were to occupy at the beginning of July. The Provisional Government was doing its best to win people over to accept the intervention of the Red Army. In a proclamation issued on 28 June it extolled the Soviet Army as a friendly force which would never harm the Mongol people, and promised, somewhat optimistically, that it had entered Mongolia for the sole purpose of expelling such white bandits as Ungern Sternberg, and would withdraw to Russia as soon as this task was completed. In actual fact Soviet forces remained in Mongolia for much longer, not withdrawing until after the establishment of the People's Republic in 1924. In the early days it was Soviet troops, mainly Kalmucks, which carried out the work of policing Urga and organized intelligence for the Mongol army staff. The city commandant of Urga in 1921 was not a Mongol at all, but a Kalmuck officer from the Red Army.

The Khutuktu, once relieved of the presence of Ungern, who had left the capital and moved northwards to his ultimate defeat, was doing what he could on the political and magical planes to obstruct the entry of the communist forces into Urga. In early July he issued a declaration that the central government had been able to re-establish its authority, that the white troops had gone back to their own country, and that the People's Party could only be waging war in ignorance of the fact that the situation was now stabilized again. The revolutionaries were summoned to return to their allegiance, and this summons was reinforced by magic ceremonies of exorcism performed at Urga to keep the people's army from coming any nearer. A *dui* or magical structure for repelling demons and evil influences was conveyed out of Urga towards the north in the presence of the Khutuktu, and a crowd of Tibetans fired after it with guns, but to no practical purpose. The red forces continued their advance, and the small detachment of soldiers and police left in Urga by Ungern was quite incapable of offering any resistance, and fled on 5 July. Some leading lamas, including Jamyangdanzan, the Saji Lama, who was to be implicated in a plot and executed the next year, and the Grand Lama Puntsagdorji, Minister of Internal Affairs in the first revolutionary government and also to be purged in 1922, were said to have proposed armed resistance to the opposing army, but the Khutuktu recognized the futility of this and forbade it.

The first Mongol and Soviet forces moved unopposed into Urga on the afternoon of 6 July, and the occupation was completed on the morning of the 8th. On the 9 July a joint sitting of the Central Committee of the Party and the Provisional Government took place and agreed to establish a constitutional monarchy, in which the Khutuktu would wield only very severely limited authority. New Ministers were selected: Bodo became Prime Minister and Minister of Foreign Affairs, Sukebator Minister of War and Commander-in-Chief, the Grand Lama Puntsagdorji Minister of Internal Affairs, Danzan Minister of Finance, and Magsar, an elderly official who had served the Manchus and the autonomous régime, Minister of Justice.

Mongol historians writing today claim that from the very first it had been the intention of the People's Party to establish the dictatorship of the working class in Mongolia, but it is difficult to accept this thesis without considerable modification. For one thing, there was no working class as such in existence at the time, while for another, the composition of the Party and the Government of July 1921 does not lend itself to this interpretation of events: at most it can have been a few extremists who looked forward to ultimate communism. Certainly some important subsidiary posts in the government were held by men who were more radically inclined than the chief ministers. Jamtsarano was Puntsagdorji's deputy, and Choibalsang was deputy Commander-in-Chief. But the government as a whole was formed on a fairly broad basis, and acted with moderation for some years to come, before veering decisively to the left.

During the troubled months since the loss of autonomy it had been no easy task for Mongol patriots to know to what principles or what authorities to remain loyal, and in the event, with the exception of the few revolutionaries who had gone to Russia, loyalty was generally directed towards the Khutuktu, as the symbol of Mongolianness, in spite of the shortcomings of his policies and the disaster of his temporary alliance with Ungern Sternberg.

From what is known of the lives of some leading Mongols at this time we can see how the clash of loyalties presented by the appearance of a new type of régime sheltering under the wing of the Red Army was resolved. There were a number of men like Tserendorji and Magsar, both of them of humble extraction and career civil servants, who, though servants of the Khutuktu, retained the respect of the revolutionaries. Tserendorji had served as deputy executive head of the Ministry of Foreign Affairs in 1911, becoming later vice-minister and minister. In 1916 he had a short spell as premier during the absence on leave of the Setsen Khan, then holder of the post. He had been one of the most vehement opponents of the Chinese at the Khiakta negotiations, and was nicknamed by them the 'old wolf' of Mongolia. Yet in 1919 his name is found amongst those senior officials and nobles who 'requested' the Chinese to abrogate autonomy, and during Ungern's brief occupation of Urga he worked as vice-minister of the Interior. He was, however, simultaneously a sympathizer with the revolutionaries, and when the group in Khiakta wanted to send their Platform and the news of the setting up of the Provisional Government to their supporters in Urga, it was to Tserendorji that they addressed the message. Under the first revolutionary government he became executive head of the Foreign Ministry: in 1923 he became Premier, and in 1924 headed the first government of the New People's Republic, dying full of honours in 1928. A soldier like Magsarjav was able to pilot himself through these difficult years with similar success. He commanded the troops of the Khutuktu's government at Khobdo in 1912, and later against the Chinese, but in 1920, after the loss of autonomy, he was imprisoned along with his former colleague Damdinsuren, by the Chinese. Damdinsuren did not survive his imprisonment, but Magsarjav was released to serve as Ungern's Minister of War. At a critical moment in mid-1921 he was sent with a detachment of troops to camp near Uliasutai next to a force of Mongols and Buriats under the white commander Wangdanov. The accounts of what happened there, though given by men who took part in the events, are difficult to reconcile with each other, though all are agreed that on a certain day, at the time of evening prayers, the Mongols turned on the Buriats with clubs and slaughtered them to a man. Wangdanov himself escaped but was brought back and shot. Some say that Magsarjav had secret instructions from Sukebator to liquidate Wangdanov even at the time when he was detailed from Urga by Ungern. Others indicate that a messenger arrived from Urga with news of the *coup d'état* there, and that both Wangdanov and Magsarjav had to decide in a hurry how to adapt themselves to the new situation, and that Magsarjav got his blow in first. Whatever the truth of the matter, Magsarjav adhered then and afterwards loyally to the revolutionary régime, with which he had indeed sympathized in the early days in 1919 and 1920, and enjoyed his reputation till his death in 1927.

Among the high clergy too there were those who were more or less sympathetic to the revolution, and the Provisional Government soon set itself to woo likely supporters in the Urga government, notably the Jalkhantsa Khutuktu, then Premier, and Puntsagdorji. They, together with Tserendorji, were invited by letter to come and hold friendly discussions with the provisional authorities about the gravity of Mongolia's situation under white Russian occupation. A second letter was sent to the Jalkhantsa

1 The first Jebtsundamba Khutuktu

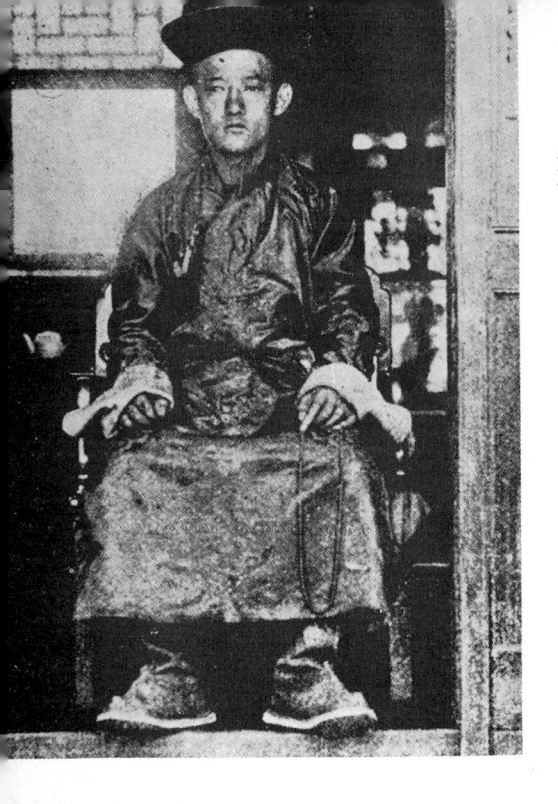

2 The eighth Jebtsundamba Khutuktu as a young man

3 The Consort of the eighth Khutuktu

4 Damdinsuren, Mongol commander at the storming of Khobdo in 1912

5 Dambijantsan

6 *below* Tserendorji, the first premier of the Mongolian People's Republic, 1924

7 Prince Khandadorji

8 *below* The Dilowa Khutuktu (left) and the Jalkhantsa Khutuktu, about 1912

9 Baron Ungern-Sternberg

10 Jamtsarano, aged about thirty-four

11 Sukebator

12 *above* Marshal Choibalsang

13 Marshal Demid

14 Academician Damdinsuren

15 Statue of Amursana at Khobdo

16 Academician Rintchen

17 Commemorative stamps issued for the 800th anniversary of the birth of Genghis Khan, 1962

18 Monument to Genghis Khan, erected at his birthplace at Deluun Boldog, 1962

Mongol book production.
19 A page from a handbook of divination from the scorched shoulder-blade of a sheep. From Inner Mongolia, early twentieth century

20 Pages from an old illustrated almanac. From Inner Mongolia

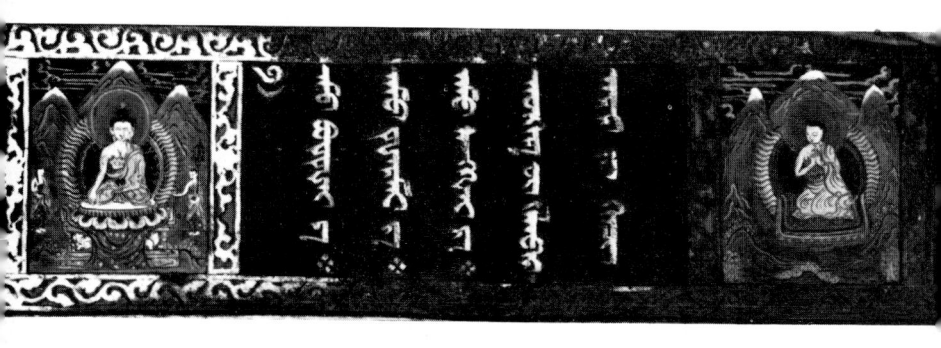

21 Illuminated title page from a Buddhist Sutra

22 Cover of a recent translation of tales from the 'Jungle Book'

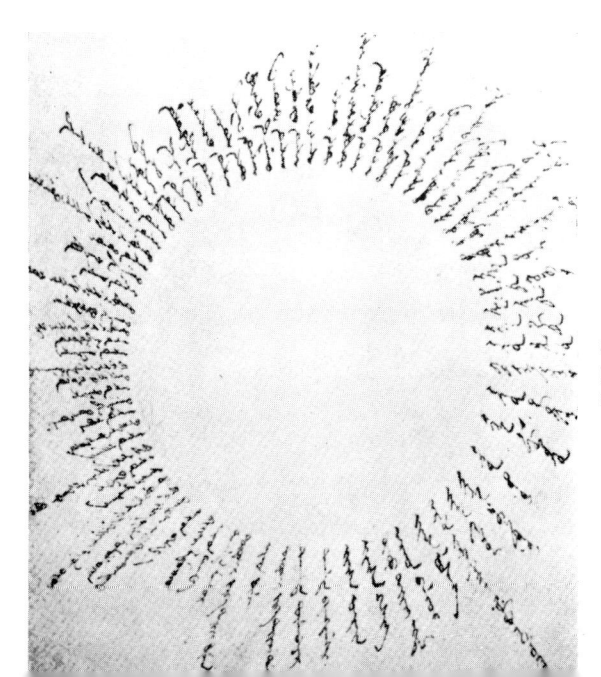

23 Names of the plaintiffs in the petition against the *zasag* Tudeng

24 The Academy of Sciences and State Library

25 Street scene in old Ulan Bator, 1959, since redeveloped

26 *above* Street scene in modern Ulan Bator

27 *below* The State Theatre, Ulan Bator

28 Statue of Sukebator, Ulan Bator

29 Water delivery cart, Ulan Bator, 1967

30 *above* Felt tents in Ulan Bator, 1959

31 A West Mongolian cooperative member demonstrates his Lasso

2 Part of a collectively-owned horse herd

33 Slogan extolling Mongol-Soviet friendship, Ulan Bator, 1967

34 The State University, 1967

35 A shop doorway, Ulan Bator, 1959

36 New department store in Ulan Bator, 1961

37 Itinerant bookseller, 1959
38 Wall painting promoting traffic control, 1967

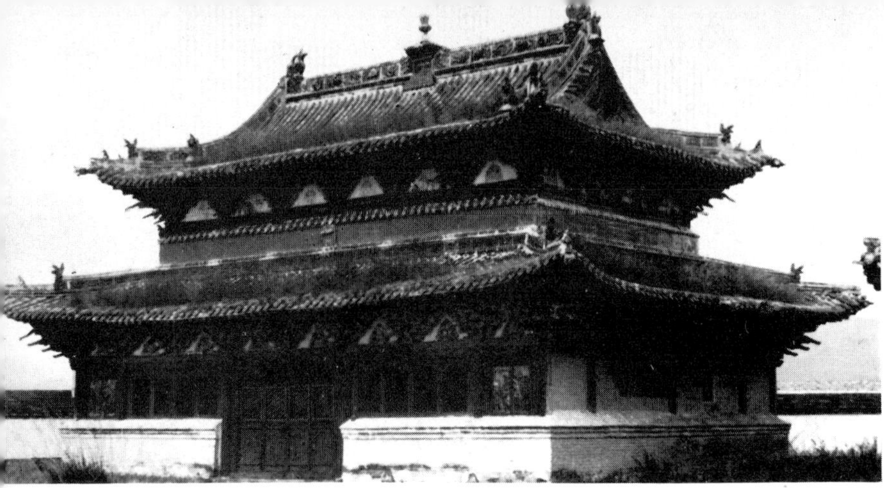
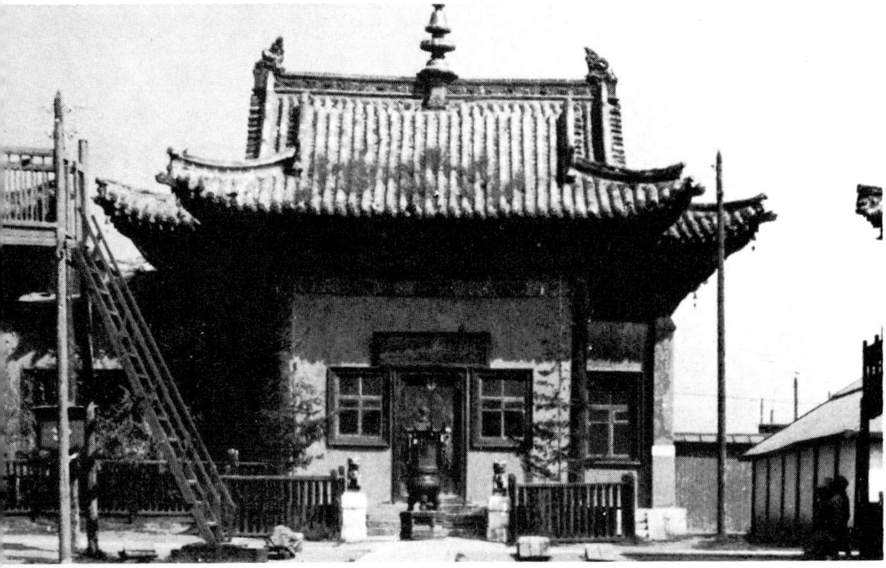
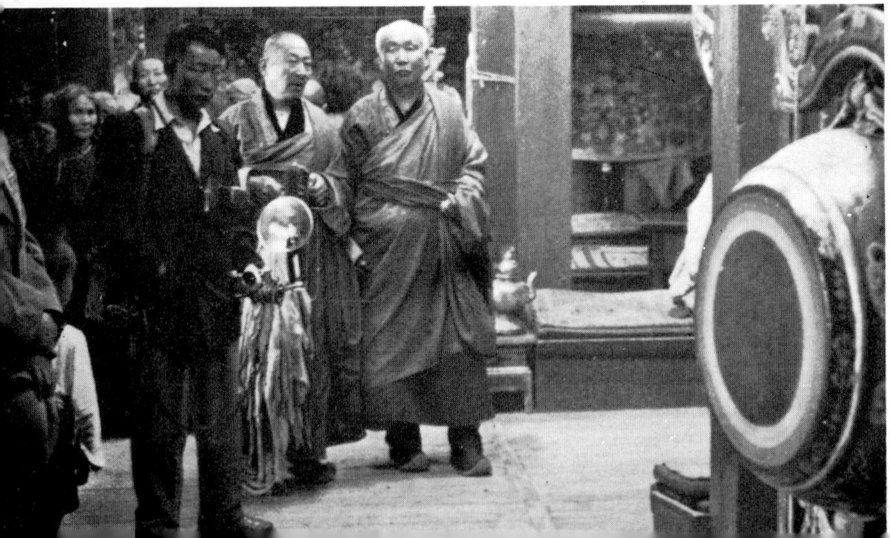

42 Military band, 1959

43 Mongol soldiers of the autonomous régime

39 *opposite* View inside the lamasery of Erdeni Juu

40 A solitary worshipper in the Gandang lamasery, Ulan Bator, 1958

41 The late lama Gombodoo, proctor of Gandang and founder of the lamas' craft cooperative there (centre)

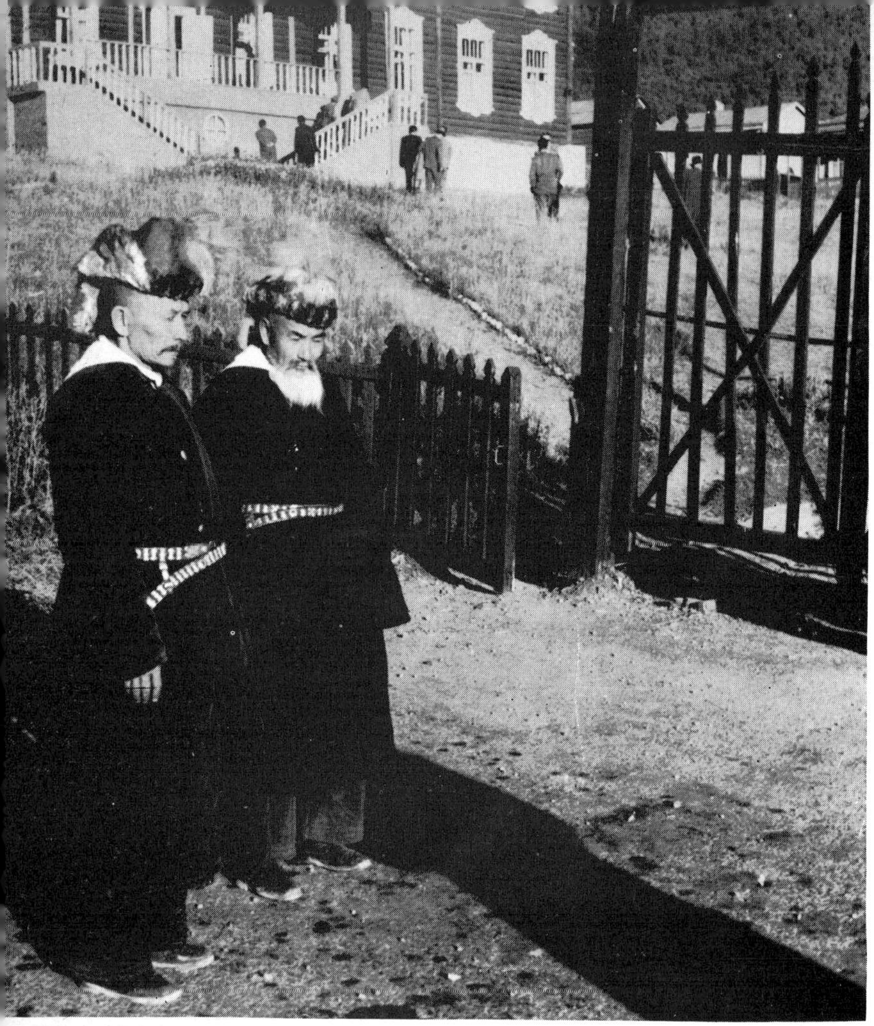

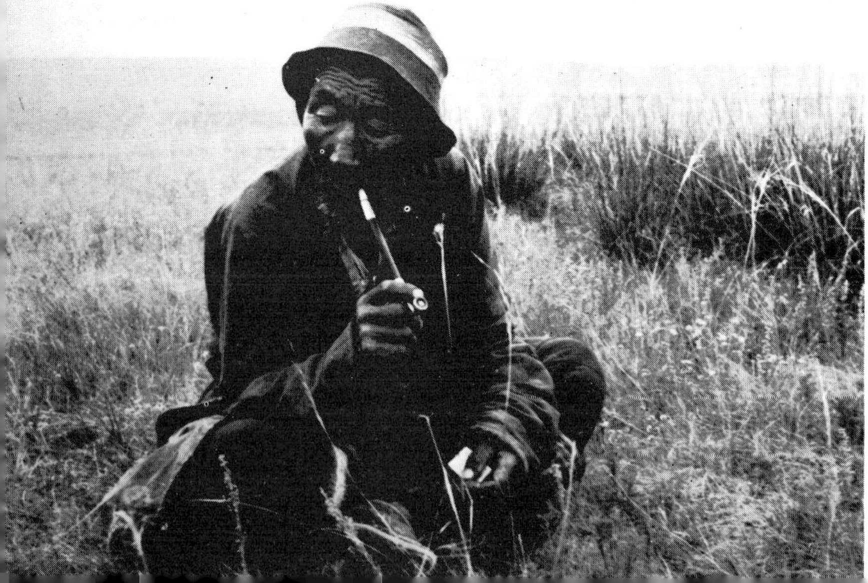

46 *above* Noblewomen in national dress, around 1900

44 *opposite* Kazakh musicians from West Mongolia at the First International Congress of Mongolists, Ulan Bator, 1959

45 A typical Mongol herdsman or *arat*, 1958

47 Painting of scenes from daily life in the traditional style. From Inner Mongolia, about 1938

Khutuktu alone, in which the Provisional Government reiterated its aims under five heads, of which the first proposed the restoration of the rights of the Khutuktu, and the second the restoration of the holy Buddhist Faith. The Jalkhantsa Khutuktu, presumably in view of his official position and the dangers of leaving occupied Urga, did not respond to these invitations, but his reputation as a thoughtful patriot and modernizer was apparently not stained. He played a part in negotiations for Soviet troops to enter western Mongolia to help Magsarjav in mid-1921, while in mid-1922, after the execution of Bodo, he was asked by Sukebator, who went in person to the lamasery of Erdeni Juu to discuss the matter, to head the government. This he did until his own death the following year, introducing a number of democratic reforms. It was the Jalkhantsa Khutuktu's public denunciation of Bodo and his followers, after their apprehension and execution, as traitors who had been planning to admit foreign forces into the country and destroy the revolutionary government, which, enhanced by the prestige he enjoyed amongst all pious Buddhists, did much to convince people that there really had been a plot, and raised the reputation of the People's Party at a critical moment.

Mongolia did not lack influential men of all classes who were gravely disturbed at the state of their country and honestly tried to rescue it from foreign occupation, restore its independence, and help its modernization. However, the fact that, as present-day Mongol historians are the first to recognize, it was to the guidance and help of the Comintern and the Soviet communist party that the revolutionaries owed their success, meant that in a country which moved directly from a medieval theocracy to a dictatorship of the proletariat, without any intervening democratic experience, those men who failed to conform to the pro-Soviet line as developed by Choibalsang and his faction, and reinforced from 1922 onwards by a department of internal security and a secret police force largely under Russian control, were to fall from power and most often be denigrated and liquidated as and when they ceased to serve the narrower purposes of the revolution and became an inconvenience to the 'general line' of the party.

CHAPTER 6

FIRST STEPS IN REVOLUTION, 1921–8

Revolutionary Mongolia and the USSR

The history of the first two decades after the revolution of 1921 is generally divided by Mongol historians into three periods. The years up to 1924 were a period of preparation for the proclamation of the republic, years of consolidation and preparation. Some radical reforms were planned, but for the time being it was impracticable to put them into effect. After the remnants of the invading white Russians had been mopped up, efforts were directed mainly towards the task of building up a rudimentary party organization in the countryside, and planning elective local government organs. The next period, from the death of the Khutuktu and the proclamation of the People's Republic in 1924 up to the year 1932, is usually described, somewhat euphemistically, as that of 'the struggle for the maintenance of the General Line of the Party'. From 1932 to 1940 Mongolia is said to have been engaged in 'resolutely following the path of non-capitalist development'. The actual form of words used to describe these two latter periods may vary somewhat, but in all cases the dividing point is the year 1932, by which time Mongolia is supposed to have laid the foundations of the struggle for the liquidation of the economic power of the feudal class, and to have detached itself from the economy of the capitalist world. There is some measure of truth in this periodization, but it needs a certain naïveté on the part of the inquirer to accept this picture with all its implications, and if one looks at Mongolia's recent history from outside the rigid scheme imposed by communist dogma, it seems far more rational to take 1928, the year of the decisive Seventh Party Congress, as marking the watershed.

There are good reasons for suggesting this. In the first place, it is futile to try to appreciate Mongol history without making up one's mind about the degree to which her administration was a puppet of the USSR. Naturally enough, the Mongols themselves are still very sensitive on this point, and the easy way out would be to avoid offending susceptibilities by skirting round this thorny subject, or by accepting current dogma, with its full share of mythology, as a substitute for one's own conception of factuality. But to do this would make nonsense of the study of the whole period after 1921, a period in Mongol history which, more than any other, calls for objective, non-partisan investigation, and one is obliged to offer one's own interpretation of events at the risk of offending Mongolian colleagues.

It would over-simplify matters to assert that everything which happened in Mongolia after 1921 was directed by Soviet interests and Soviet intervention, even though the most influential voices in the Mongol People's Party were those of Soviet citizens such as the Buriat Rinchino, and the left-wing League of Revolutionary Youth took its line from the Youth International in Moscow. For one thing, this would be to credit the Russians with an efficiency and consistency which they did not possess. Still, Soviet influence in Mongolia was continuous and paramount after 1921, Mongolia being the unique territory outside the USSR, with the insignificant exception of Tannu Tuva, in which a government in sympathy with the USSR had been successfully installed, supported by a party which was in correspondence with, and generally accepted the leading role of, the Comintern. But just as the extent to which totalitarianism prevailed in the USSR was not uniform over these two decades, so the extent to which Moscow could enforce its writ in Mongolia was not constant. At least until 1928 there was considerable freedom of manœuvre for Mongol statesmen, both internally and in their foreign relations, and it was not beyond the bounds of possibility that under the leadership of Dambadorj, the rightist leader who was purged in 1928, the Mongolian revolution might have rejected dependence on the USSR and gone its own way, as Chiang Kai-shek had chosen to do in China. There were plenty of influential men perturbed at what they saw even then as Red Imperialism and Soviet colonialism. Yet even Mongolia's ostensible freedom to establish commercial relations with capitalist countries during those first few years must not be mistaken for an absolute freedom of choice. In looking to Germany for help in developing her rudimentary industry and supplying some of her commercial and technical needs, she was merely copying the contemporary Soviet example, and when this phase of Soviet history ended in 1928, the corresponding period ended for Mongolia too.

It would however be quite absurd to take the opposing view and to imagine Mongolia cruising on her own tack, helpfully guided at moments of crisis by the friendly advice of the Comintern or the Soviet communist party, which is, in general terms, the impression which contemporary Mongol and Russian historians would like to convey, and which has been adopted by some western writers. It is precisely because the scope and effectiveness of Soviet interference in Mongolian affairs seem to alter so abruptly in late 1928 that this year stands out as a turning point. From then on, Mongolia's internal affairs, together with those of Tannu Tuva, show such a pointed similarity, both in the nature of events and their timing, with what was happening in the USSR, that it is embarrassing to try to explain them in any other way than that they were directed, in all three cases, from the same place, that is from Moscow. The clearest evidence for this, as far as Mongolia is concerned, in what is admittedly a very confused time, is the decisive way in which the Comintern and the Soviet communist party were able to intervene in 1932 to reverse the catastrophic policy of all-out assault on private enterprise and on religion which was ruining Mongolia. This episode will be discussed in more detail in the next chapter, but briefly we may note here that while a minority of Mongol party leaders had realized that the Party was on a fundamentally wrong course they had been afraid and unable to say so, let alone change the course, until a Russian directive was received, at which point a complete and utter reversal of all that the Party had stood for over the last three years was decided on and realized almost overnight.

The key to this period is undoubtedly Stalin's rout of the Trotskyist and Bukharinist opposition in Russia, and his adoption of the slogan of 'Socialism in one country'. Abandoning for the time the ideal of world revolution, Stalin began to concentrate on a process of ruthless extirpation of the kulaks, of agricultural collectivization and of industrialization, accompanied by a first purge of intellectuals. Mongolia seems to have been included in the scope of the Soviet experiment. Instead of being the vanguard of revolution in the east, which is what some of the more internationally minded party members of the 1920s hoped for, instead of being the liberators of their oppressed brothers in Inner Mongolia, and even, in more expansive moments, the nucleus from which the liberation of the Chinese masses would spring, Mongolia became, from early 1929, a landlocked appendage of the USSR, to whom she was henceforth attached, to the utter exclusion of all other contacts – political, commercial, educational and military. From being a cross-roads of revolution she was reduced to a cul-de-sac.

A second reason for rejecting 1932 as a turning point, in favour of 1928, is the illusory nature, at least to the uninvolved observer, of the concept of the struggle for the maintenance of the General Line. This line was supposed to have been laid down in 1924 at the Third Party Congress, and to have been enshrined in the constitution of the same year, which was closely modelled on the Soviet constitution. In the next seven years Mongol historians distinguish two periods of error and deviation, which taken together account for practically the whole of that period. First came a time of 'rightist opportunist capitulation' which lasted from 1925 till 1928. This was succeeded almost at once by an even more violent swing to the left which began in early 1929 and was not corrected until the so-called New Turn Policy of 1932 to 1934 was ushered in by the Comintern directive of June 1932. The General Line is then supposed to have been restored, and, in spite of a further incipient rightist deviation around 1934, which was followed by the now acknowledged and regretted excesses of the era of the cult of personality, to have led to the achievement, by 1940, of the take-off position for the march towards full socialism.

To a non-Marxist observer, this analysis, which allows very little time for normality between successive 'deviations', looks highly specious. It ignores the fact that the General Line can, in the years either side of 1928, have been little more than a vague abstraction which was not accepted by either of the groups successively in power. Mongol historians avoid this practical difficulty by suggesting that the two periods of deviation came as a result of enemies of the revolution worming their way into power, and somehow over-awing or outmanœuvring the true but anonymous supporters of the General Line: they ignore the necessity of explaining how the Party can have been such a labile organism that for years on end it could be penetrated by enemies of one sort or another, a situation which reached the heights of absurdity in the late 1930s when most of the leadership of government, party and army turned out to be Fascists or other counter-revolutionary elements.

Mongol historians are reluctant to admit that the Party as a whole can ever have been in error. Just as Stalin, in his pamphlet 'Dizzy with Success' put the responsibility for the excesses of the Soviet collectivization drive, which had to be temporarily slowed down in 1930, on to the shoulders of local officials who were supposed to have exceeded their brief, so the simultaneous Mongol excesses are nowadays blamed primarily on local party leaders who went too far, and to a lesser extent on some party bosses who followed their own heads. Nevertheless, at the time, a plenary meeting of the Central Committee of the Party and the Control Commission confessed that 'these deviations and distortions and the majority of the errors and mistakes, are to be ascribed to the Central Committee and to the Party as a whole'.[1] To shrug them off nowadays as the work of enemies within the Party is, then, mere sophistry, and it seems that the General Line can have had few, if any, friends, between 1929 and 1932. Besides this clear statement, there are other indications that the Party as a whole was backing the extreme leftist policy. The Soviet historian Zlatkin says that during these years the Central Committee of the Party had replaced the Council of Ministers, while the provincial People's Assemblies had had their functions usurped by the local party committees. 'The Party did not thus represent the vanguard, the organized spearhead of the masses, but was the administrative organ. This distortion led to massive offences against revolutionary legality and the constitution'.[2] And finally, 1932 was not the year when this struggle for power between Party and Government was to be decided. The feud went on for years, first with the Premier, Gendung, denying even that the Party should have a role at all as leader, then with Choibalsang uniting all authority in his own person for a decade and a half.

Zlatkin maintains that it was the party leadership which was responsible for the leftist mistakes and that with few exceptions the party membership in toto was in error. It is this admission that the Party as a whole could follow a mistaken policy which makes the General Line appear more than ever an illusion, not an ideal which was unfortunately temporarily mislaid and then recovered in 1932. Moreover, in the 1930s Mongolia fell ever more thoroughly under actual Soviet control. In 1932 and 1937 Soviet troops were in the country, both times operating to suppress disaffection, though certainly in 1937 they had the additional duty of keeping the Japanese at bay. The Mongol security services were penetrated by the Soviet police, and as Choibalsang stated in public and with approval, it was only with the help of 'experienced Soviet Chekists' and with the intervention of the 'broad masses of the Soviet people' that the various counter-revolutionary plots of the 1930s, most of them in fact only fabrications based on false charges and perjured evidence, could be crushed.[3] 1928 seems then to have been the critical year in which Mongolia slipped into positive dependence on Stalin's Russia, and may be taken as the real parting of the ways in her post-revolutionary history.

The situation in 1921

A less promising field for the development of a socialist society along Marxist lines than Mongolia in the year 1921 can hardly be imagined. It was the antithesis of the industrial society in which the proletariat would be the vanguard of revolution. Mongolia was poor, backward, feudalistic in structure, dominated spiritually and to a great extent materially also by a powerful, well-organized and self-assured church. Her economy was a primitive, undifferentiated one, based almost exclusively on extensive, nomadic, unscientific animal herding. For manufactures she relied on imports, and even internal trade was largely in foreign hands and financed by foreign capital. Primitive coal mines near Urga furnished a few hundred tons a year, but for the most part it was dried animal dung, patiently gathered and stored, which represented the main source of fuel. The tiny population was scattered over a huge area and was overwhelmingly rural. Even when it became possible to organize party cells in the countryside, the members of a cell sometimes lived dozens of miles from each other, on temporary sites, and had no easy means of communication, especially as most of them could neither read nor write.

There was no working class, and no native capitalist class either, for though there were recognizable groups within the population these did not coincide with social classes in the Marxist sense. Divisions were vertical rather than horizontal. It was the work of years to engineer class consciousness and a class struggle. Delegates to the important Third Party Congress held in 1924 to lay down the lines on which the new republic was to develop, were confused by talk of classes. As one of them put it: 'Whom are we to consider as capitalists, as middle herdsmen and as poor herdsmen? And how are we to distinguish them?'[4] Even a middle-class intelligentsia, where the nucleus of revolutionary leadership is usually to be found, was lacking, and initially it was a group of Buriats, Russian subjects long half-Europeanized, who directed the affairs of the Party and government.

Though there were harsh differences in Mongolia between rich and poor, social cleavages ran in other directions. The sense of local loyalty, of belonging to a group with different historical traditions from those of other Mongols, was far more important than the ill-understood concept of class solidarity. Western Mongols in particular felt themselves distinct, in language and in background, from the predominant Khalkha population, and local separatism was a matter of concern for at least a decade after the People's government was first established. The Derbets of the Khobdo district were especially restive in the late 1920s for example, and the problem of Derbet separatism was important enough to be considered by the Comintern, which condemned it as contrary to its own policies.

The most important sub-group within the population was the lamaist church. Perhaps one hundred thousand men and boys, a quarter of the male population or more, were lamas, living either in lamaseries or at home, or roaming the countryside performing religious ceremonies for people who needed them, telling fortunes, exorcising the demons which had brought sickness or death into a family, and spreading rumour and gossip. Some lamas were rich and influential, others poor and humble, but they were united in their membership of the church and in their devotion to the Yellow Faith, and all alike enjoyed the respect of the laity.

Such an enormous clerical class could exist only within a society where people at large identified themselves with it and with the faith it professed, took it as part of the natural order of things, and kept it going with regular contributions and with recruits, each family hoping to get at least one son accepted into a lamasery. The Party saw its task as a double one – to wean people away from belief in religion and awe of the clergy, and to create and exploit artificial class differences within the religious community itself. This involved it in a long and bitter struggle, which at times flared up into armed battles and civil war. During the period of leftist extremism after 1928, doctrinaire party leaders, aping Stalin's atheistic campaign, failed to appreciate the strength of the sense of self-identification with the church which permeated the Mongol people. They ignored the precepts they had themselves laid down that lower lamas were to be treated differently from the higher lamas in order to sow dissension and win over the former to the revolution, and they rejected, if indeed they had ever grasped it, Marx's teaching that it is no good declaring outright war on religion, since this will only strengthen it. They pushed through a policy of deliberate assault upon religion, characterized by expropriation of church property, desecration of holy places, and indiscriminate vilification of the clergy, with the result that they came near to wrecking everything the revolution had by then achieved.

An urban proletariat, the revolutionary class according to Marxist theory, was almost totally lacking, and was for years to come a quite negligible political factor. In fact, it was only with the dissolution of the lamaseries in the late 1930s that an industrial force of any significance at all could begin to be built up from the now redundant secularized lamas. Those Mongols who had drifted to the towns before 1921 were a depressed rabble, mostly vagrants who had failed to make a living in their home banner at the traditional occupation of animal herding. The towns, such as they were, offered no constructive alternative to poverty in the countryside, but only the opportunity to eke out a poor living as day labourers. The urban Mongols were few in number, economically far inferior to the Chinese who formed the bulk of the trading and craft community, and devoid of solidarity or political initiative. Even as a mob they seem never to have played any part in the early days of the revolution.

Even when, after 1921, factories began to appear in Mongolia, the native share of the labour force remained pitifully small.

The Nalaikha coalmines near Urga, which were operated by the most primitive methods, employed in 1922 only twelve workers, none of whom was a Mongol. By 1930 Nalaikha had seventy-eight workers, of whom eight were Mongols. The tannery at Altan Bulak, a Russian enterprise taken over by the Soviets and transferred to Mongol ownership in 1921, employed not more than one or two Mongols as late as 1926. The bulk of the labourers were Russians who came in daily from Khiakta. The Urga printing works employed in 1921 a staff of a mere seven, which slowly grew to thirty-five by 1925. A metal works, probably no more than a large smithy, was opened in Urga in 1927, and two years later employed thirty workers, but of these only ten were Mongols, working under Russian supervisors. The first trade unions in Mongolia had been organized in 1917, but none of the members had been Mongol. In any case, these unions had been destroyed by Ungern Sternberg who massacred the Russian unionists. As a final example of this slow growth of Mongol urban society into an industrial proletariat, of the 242 delegates to the Ninth Party Congress in 1934, only seventeen were drawn from among industrial workers.

In modern terms the Mongols were a backward, uneducated people. This is not to say that learning and culture were unknown to them, far from it. Marxist writers have over the last forty years been assiduous in spreading the most pitiful tales about the squalor of ignorance in which their forebears allegedly lived until the 1921 revolution opened the way of progress and enlightenment to them. These falsities and half truths have unfortunately been perpetuated by western writers who had no other basis to go upon. Literacy was said to be almost nil, schools non-existent except for Jamtsarano's middle school in Urga. But once the Stalinist era was over, something could be done to correct the distorted image its propaganda had imposed, and some Mongolian scholars, in particular Academician Damdinsuren, have done what they could to present the reverse of the coin. Some essays written by Damdinsuren in 1956 and 1957 give useful facts and arguments, but as they have been printed only in Mongol they have done nothing to rectify the opinion generally accepted abroad, and fostered by Marxist apologists, that pre-revolutionary Mongolia was a barbarous sub-civilization. Damdinsuren states quite openly that the purpose of the propaganda of the Stalinist era was to decry the traditional Mongol culture so as to make the achievements of the revolution stand out the more vividly in contrast. He shows that for twenty years since 1936 nothing was allowed to be taught about early Mongol literature in Mongol middle schools, so that a whole generation and more of Mongol children was allowed to grow up ignorant of the realities of their people's past. In the same period, only one book from the pre-revolutionary period was reprinted. While some scholars were doing their best to salvage what they could of the country's literary past, other 'responsible workers' were organizing searches for old books in order to destroy them by burning or by throwing them down ravines – this as late as 1955. Of schools in pre-revolutionary Mongolia, Damdinsuren wrote:

Some of our intelligentsia, instead of finding out the truth from the facts of past history and uttering it, distort it and falsify it in every possible way. They make the ignorance and backwardness of the past even more ignorant and backward than it was, and their writings show how they insult as savages their own parents and grandparents. For example, under the autonomous régime there were forty-nine primary schools. But some writers state that in that period there was only a single school, and others that there was not even one.[5]

From all the details he gives, Damdinsuren concludes:

Before the 1921 revolution there was a lot of literature of democratic character amongst the old writings. It is only a pity that as we have been unable to edit and collect these writings which form the cultural heritage of the Mongols, they have to a great extent got lost. For this regrettable and sorry state of affairs the destroyers of the Mongolian cultural heritage are greatly to blame. They have declared old literature feudal in its entirety and have inflicted no small damage on the work of editing and caring for our old literature. . . . Literary readers and histories of literature do not exist, and so the study of Mongol literature in all our higher and middle schools is in a deplorable state.[6]

Literacy statistics are quite unreliable, especially as the basis on which such figures as we have were compiled is unrealistic. In Manchu days only those who could write as well as read were marked down on the local registers as literate, and as the ability to write involved liability for clerical service in the administration, many men would disguise their capabilities or even fail to learn to write properly, though they were fluent readers. As Academician Rintchen recalls:

Following this age-old custom all persons who could not write were marked down as illiterate. I myself, as a 'half-scribe' in the administration of Altan Bulak, often used to register in 1921 as illiterates, following the directions of my chief and master of the tent-school Bilegsaikhan, persons who could not write, amongst them many an old booklover who would in the evenings tell me delightful stories from his ancient manuscripts, yellowed by time and the smoke of the tent.[7]

The enormous numbers of manuscripts collected in the Mongol countryside in recent years, dating from the late sixteenth century onwards, and now kept in libraries, are a sufficient witness of the devotion of ordinary people to their traditional literature. Even outside the schools there were always opportunities for a boy to learn to read and write. Tibetan could be studied in the lamasery schools, and this was not a negligible skill in a theocratic society where Tibetan was the learned language, and the mastery of it a key to advancement. Nor is it wholly true, as is often repeated, that children learned the Tibetan alphabet parrot fashion, so that they could do no more than reel off a few half-understood prayers. Some no doubt did, but to others the Tibetan script was a living vehicle for the Mongol language. In the middle of the 1930s, when a special magazine was published for a year or two directed at the lamas, to try and win them over to new ways of thought, this was printed in both the Mongol and the Tibetan script. Outside the lamaseries there were the so-called tent-schools, private teaching circles run in their own homes for local children by officials and others who could read and write. There was a sense of responsibility for seeing that the coming generation learned the traditions of the past, which must not be underestimated. It is a matter for reflection that no less a man than Jamyang Gung, future head of the Mongolian Committee of Sciences, and a correspondent of the famous French orientalist Paul Pelliot, did not feel himself above giving a poor boy like Sukebator an elementary education in his tent-school. Choibalsang was another poor boy who, with help, overcame the handicaps of the most unpromising childhood. He was born in 1895 to a poor herdswoman of Setsen Khan aimak named Khorloo. Who his father was is not known, and Choibalsang, like many another boy of uncertain parentage, adopted his mother's name as his 'patronymic'. (There seems to have been little stigma or disability attached to being a bastard in pre-revolutionary Mongolia. At the great treason trial in October 1937 when twenty-three high lamas were condemned, five of them, including the deputy to the abbot of Gandang, Damdin, were officially listed as bastards.) Life was hard for the little family, and young Choibalsang was put into a lamasery by his mother to ease the problem of getting a living. After two years he ran away from the lamasery and came to Urga where, after living the life of a waif for a while, he managed to get accepted into the newly founded middle school, and progressed so well that in 1914 he was one of a group selected to go to Irkutsk for further education. A really gifted boy could do well for himself in the days of autonomy and even before. An outstanding example is that of the telegraphist Badarchin who kept the seven revolutionaries in touch with Urga while they were in Russia in 1920. Born in 1893 he studied first at a Chinese elementary school in Urga, then in the Urga middle school and telegraphists' school, and knew Manchu, Chinese, Russian and English as well as Mongol. Nor was literacy the monopoly of the nobles as is sometimes made out. As Damdinsuren puts it:

If there were no literates among the common people, how could they read and understand the directives of the revolutionary party, the newspapers, and so on? Or did the literate feudal classes propagate these writings among the masses? We have to ask ourselves this. There must have been many literates among the masses.[8]

There is, however, another side to the matter, and in correcting one set of errors we have to take care not to swing too far the other way and suggest that all Mongols had chances and took them. There was for at least two decades after 1921 a crippling illiteracy amongst the ordinary people of the countryside, that sector of the population which the Party tried hardest to recruit from, and whence it drew most of its mass popular support. Successive purges of lamas and other educated party members, and their replacement by simple herdsmen meant that even in 1932 four out of every five party members were illiterate, and it was as much mass conscription into the army as the slow growth of elementary schools which finally solved the problem. At the same time, the Party could afford the luxury of using the privileges of education as a weapon of class warfare. At least during the period of leftist extremism the children of certain classes of the population were deliberately excluded from school as a matter of policy. This measure hit the children not only of the nobility and rich herdsmen, but of the so-called middle herdsmen too.

It comes, though, as a shock to realize, from chance revelations, just how uninformed many ordinary party members were, and at what a low level of intellectual achievement this so-called spearhead of social progress operated in Mongolia. When Choibalsang spoke in 1940 at the Tenth Party Congress, he invited questions from the floor. One party comrade, interested in the plan to adopt Arabic numerals, wanted to know who the Arabs were. Another, and this was nearly a decade after the initiation of a tentative adaptation of the Latin alphabet to the Mongol language, wanted to know where the Latin letters came from, and in what countries of the world they were used.

What made the task of the revolutionaries difficult was the fact that what education there was was unsystematic, free of any central control, and orientated to the traditional Buddhist way of life and thought, so that they had to operate *as if* there were no education. When children had learned to read, what had they to exercise their newly-acquired skill and their curiosity upon? There were translations of popular Buddhist scriptures, lives of famous lamas, collections of tales, many of them with a Tibetan or Indian, at any rate a religious, background, and didactic works teaching a mixture of traditional Mongol and Buddhist morality. The classics of Confucianism also circulated in Mongol translation. Thus the acquisition of literacy opened children's minds, not to the 'new' world of Marxism, or even of modern knowledge, but to the traditional, conservative culture of the past: from the few isolated copies of Mongol translations of encyclopedias of popular science which are to be found in Europe, it seems that such popularization got going only after about 1927. This situation, as much as any jealousy for the image of the revolution as the unique civilizing influence, helps to explain why the authorities, especially after 1936, tried to eradicate the memory of the old Mongol culture.

Moreover, piety and superstition were palpable obstacles to the new political theories. Magic, divination and the taking of omens still often governed important enterprises. When a group of security police was sent in 1922 to dispose of Dambijantsan, they first scorched a sheep's shoulder blade and examined the cracks in it to find out which of them should undertake which part of the action. In 1924 the Ministry of Education issued a decree about the severe drought which had been affecting the country for several years, and which was no doubt mainly responsible for the loss of five and a half million head of cattle that year – a loss later ascribed by Choibalsang, though without explanation of the causal connection, to the alleged conspiracies of the Saji Lama in 1921 and of Bodo in 1922, and to the poisoning, as he maintained, of Sukebator in 1923. The Ministry ascribed the onset of drought, equally arbitrarily, to lack of faith on the part of the people, who no longer believed in the rain-summoning powers of lama magicians, and to the inactivity of officials. The Khutuktu had been the only one to understand these matters and to concern himself with the organization of prayers to induce precipitation. The Ministry of Finance should provide the urgently needed funds and issue instructions for the performance of the relevant ceremonies, and any officials who showed hesitancy should be punished.

Superstition is of course largely a matter of generations. A fascinating instance of this is presented in the recent autobiography of J. Sambuu, the President of Mongolia. When Sambuu's father died in 1929, he was unable to get leave at once from his post in the Ministry of Finance. A few days after the death, a local lama who was a practitioner of semi-Buddhist, semi-magical ceremonies, came to the widow and informed her that the dead man's soul was imprisoned in his favourite animals. It would be necessary, before the critical forty-ninth day after the death came round, to liberate it by special rites so that it could pass on to the realm of the Buddha. Sambuu's mother was a simple woman and believed this, and gave the lama her husband's best horse and his white gelding camel as a fee to perform the liberation ceremony. Sambuu, young and educated, heard of this, and planned to prosecute the lama, but his mother persuaded him not to involve her in a lawsuit in her bereaved state, and Sambuu let the matter drop. In the 'sixties a family was persuaded by a soothsayer that a series of petty and unrelated disasters that they had suffered had come upon them because the well they had dug with the help of other members of their herding collective was haunted by a demon, and that they had better abandon it and move to other pastures.

Outside the few schools teaching was largely in the hands of lamas, who in 1927 were teaching five children for every one in a state school. In 1934 the proportion was still nearly four to one. Mass political consciousness was simply not a factor in the Mongol revolution. The revolution had not come in response to mass demand, but had spread outwards and downwards from a small group of zealots at the centre. People had to be jogged or driven along by carrot or stick. At first the Party was content to wait for a popular demand to make itself felt before proceeding with some controversial item of policy they had long since decided upon, and sometimes it took years for such a demand to be formulated. The Party had to be purged, moreover, not only of hostile class-elements, but also of mere passengers, on at least three main occasions between 1924 and 1932. The level of 'party-consciousness' of the members can perhaps be judged by the fact that in 1932 over thirteen thousand of them left the party on learning that membership of it was in fact voluntary. However, in fairness to their acumen it must be recalled that this purge took place after a period of vicious leftist extremism, during which it might have been expedient to affect ignorance of this knowledge.

Three years of constitutional monarchy

The years from 1921 to 1924 were a period of slow and piecemeal preparation for the promised first National Assembly which was to promulgate a constitution for Mongolia, and which in fact met some six months after the death of the Khutuktu. Internationally, Mongolia long enjoyed an ambiguous status, which was not finally regulated till 1946, but to all intents and purposes her existence was guaranteed by the first Soviet-Mongol Treaty, negotiated in Moscow at the end of 1921. *Vis-à vis*-China the USSR still accepted the fiction of that country's formal suzerainty over Mongolia, but for all practical purposes treated Mongolia as capable of acting independently of her overlord. Internally the new régime faced a series of troublesome problems. The country was not even pacified. The last remaining white Russian bands were not expelled till late 1921 after some hard fighting, and then in 1922 the lama Dambijantsan, thought to be leading a separatist movement from his stronghold in the Maajinshan mountains just inside Chinese Sinkiang, had to be dealt with by assassination.

Considerable mystery still surrounded Dambijantsan. Even in 1921 Magsarjav was having him spied on, yet in 1922 the security policeman Nanzad, who was later one of the execution squad sent out to kill him, was uncertain, when he first heard that Dambijantsan had been in communication with the amban of Uliasutai, whether the lama was a friend or enemy of the state, and he reported back to Urga for instructions. Dambijantsan was not an isolated adventurer. He enjoyed the respect and help of both lamas and nobles in the western regions. In 1921 and 1922 he was visiting certain lamaseries there to bestow blessings on the occupants, and had cultivated with the Zasagtu Khan the traditional relationship of teacher and disciple. The Khan had allotted him a complete banner in the south of his aimak as his personal *shabi*-domain. In 1922 Sukebator issued orders for Dambijantsan's removal. Several armed bands were sent out to execute these, for it was not certain exactly where he was, and more than one impostor who was exploiting the name and prestige of Dambijantsan for his own purposes was flushed out and captured. The authorities put out rumours to lull suspicions. The story was spread that Magsarjav himself, who had once been Dambijantsan's *protégé*, was planning to join him in a *coup d'état*. The successful ruse adopted by Nanzad and his companions to gain admittance to the lama's stronghold was to pass themselves off as travelling lamas sent to invite him to visit the Khutuktu. They shot him dead, dispersed his followers, and commandeered his herds and property. Then they set out for Urga: but such was the dread that Dambijantsan could inspire that people refused to believe that they had really got the better of him, and, as briefly mentioned above, Nanzad had to ride back from Uliasutai and fetch the severed head of the dead lama which he had tossed away as useless.

The new régime was not at one with itself, and did not enjoy the universal confidence of the people. Hardly a year passed when there were not plots discovered and others rumoured, and in 1922 it was necessary to enlist Soviet experience in organizing an Office of Internal Security and a secret police force. The first plot to have been uncovered seems to have been a real attempt in 1921 on the part of the Saji Lama Jamyangdanzan to overthrow the revolutionary government and to re-establish the full authority of the Khutuktu with the help of three hundred armed Tibetans who were in Urga. The Khutuktu himself was supposed to have been informed of the conspiracy but to have refused it his sanction. The following year latent cracks in the Party itself were painfully revealed by the affair of Bodo and his supporters. Bodo, as already mentioned, was a lama who had been one of the seven delegates to Russia in 1920 and the first premier of the revolutionary government the following summer. He had had to resign early in 1922 and was then supposed, partly out of pique, to have engaged in a plot to overthrow the revolution he had helped to bring about. Multiple charges were brought against him and his associates. They were supposed to have been in treasonable contact with the Chinese, particularly the war-lord Chang Tso-lin, with Dambijantsan, and with the American consul who at that time used to reside in Kalgan, not in Mongolia itself. Amongst the accused were revolutionaries, Bodo and Chagdarjav, high lamas such as Puntsagdorji who had been sympathetic to the revolution, the freebooter Togtokh taiji, soldiers like Altangerel, the amban for the eastern region, and others. What little is known of the confessions of the accused tends to show that they may well have been in contact of some sort with Dambijantsan. Bodo testified that he had sent him a partisan's cap and some hand grenades as a gift, and that he had suggested to Chagdarjav that they should go and ask him to join them in a direct revolt against the government. What can have possessed these men, experienced revolutionaries and politicians, to engage in such an ill-found plot, if indeed they did, is hard to fathom. They knew, for instance, that the Soviet army was in Mongolia in strength, and that Russians were running Mongol intelligence. None of these conspirators has been rehabilitated, so that it appears that there is no intention to revise the judgements against them. But the charges laid against them are so similar to those brought two years later against another delinquent revolutionary, the Commander-in-chief Danzan and against his associates, that the episode leads to the suspicion that what was concerned was not actually treason, but something much less ambitious, perhaps an unsuccessful attempt on Bodo's part to oust a hostile faction he disagreed with, or even a successful move on the part of others to forestall such a possibility. From the beginning, there was never room in Mongolia's revolutionary development for democratic compromise. Internal disputes inevitably took the acute form of a relentless duel between the ultimately victorious faction, which then personified revolutionary rectitude, and the defeated faction which accordingly appeared in the light of traitors. The inadmissibility of any opposition party only accentuated this tendency.

It was a long and slow task, sometimes executed in what seems quite a haphazard manner, to assure the authority of the new régime, and to map out the lines the renewal of Mongol society was to take. There was muddle, scarcity of talent, lack of material and of personnel everywhere. Some basic reforms, such as that of the administration of justice, took years to accomplish, and were not effective till long after the end of the monarchy. Naidansuren, a contemporary of Choibalsang's at school in Irkutsk, tells in his reminiscences of Sukebator how the cruel punishment of shutting a condemned man up in a wooden coffin with only one small hole in the side for him to be fed through, and leaving him there till he died, came to be done away with, and it may well be typical of those confused times.

After that [he says] I met Sukebator once again. Bakunaev, the city commandant, was going round the city, when he happened on a man in a chest on the rubbish heap in the Sain Noyon Khan district. As he was taking him out, Sukebator appeared. He got some water from the army kitchen, and cleaned the man up. He was so exhausted he could not move. Sukebator was very sorry for him, and asked him why he had been put into the chest. The man was a lama called Damba of the Amdonar district of Gandang, who had got drunk and abused the noble lamas, and that was why he had been so punished. Sukebator ordered all the chests to be destroyed that day, and therefore troops from the commandantura went round with ox and horse carts and confiscated all the chests in the city, and that cruel punishment was never used again.[9]

Chance brought about this one reform, though it would have happened sooner or later in any case. The first steps to modernise the administration of justice in all its aspects were however not taken till late 1925, when courts with elected judges were instituted.

The lack of men with knowledge of modern concepts and techniques of administration which crippled justice to the extent that more than four years after the revolution the old Manchu code of laws was still in use, because there were no officials with a knowledge of modern jurisprudence to draft a new one, affected all aspects of life. Most of the staff of local government offices, where it had been possible to set up such organs, were illiterate. They were unable to decipher the directives they received from the central government, and quite incapable of replying to queries submitted to them or of organizing and passing on information. If we couple with this incompetence the fact that people in the countryside distrusted the policies of the new régime, it is not surprising that it took so long to build up a network of local party cells and to establish any sort of local government. It was one thing to decree in August 1921 the abolition of feudal ranks and salaries, and in the following March to abolish the tax exemptions which the nobility enjoyed, but quite another to enforce these decisions in the countryside where the only effective authority was the nobility itself. For years the nobles continued to wear their proscribed buttons of rank and to act as they had before.

A beginning with the task of replacing the Manchu administrative apparatus was made in 1922 when a few unpopular *zasags*, including the vicious Tudeng wang, were dismissed and their successors were elected. In May 1922 a decree was issued permitting men of non-noble rank to be appointed as *tusalagchi*, the *zasag's* right hand man in a banner. Although the provisional government had, in its first revolutionary thrill of confidence, planned a rapid transition to a pyramidal system of elected local assemblies and officials, this was of course impossible to achieve at once, and such changes as were made were effected here and there as occasion served, not, as yet, as part of a national plan. In fact, at the outset, local administration had to be organized in exactly the opposite way, special commissioners being dispatched to the provinces to regulate affairs on an *ad hoc* basis. Many of these were incompetent, others were not real supporters of the revolution, and were either dismissed or arrested and dealt with as traitors by squads of security police sent out after them. In the two following years elected assemblies were set up in many parts of Mongolia, but it was the old nobility and their sympathizers who mostly got elected, being the only class with any administrative flair, and the central government had to declare many elections void and hold them again to ensure that candidates of the right social origin were elected. The further the outlying banners were from the centre, the longer it took to organize them and persuade them to accept the central authority, and some western Mongols were actually not incorporated into the new governmental structure till 1928 or 1929. What more than anything obstructed the designs of the new régime was the ease with which disaffected nomads could simply pack up and move away, at worst over the frontier into China. This manner of protest and escape reached its climax in the years 1929 to 1932, but as early as 1924 and 1925 some west Mongol peoples, Torguts and Khoshuts, were deserting to China in organized groups under their princes, in spite of inducements such as temporary exemption from taxation, and even financial subsidies, intended to attract their allegiance.

What was achieved during the few years before the Khutuktu's death was the promulgation of a number of essential reforms. These were, however, to a large extent nullified by the executive incompetence of the new régime and the inertia, ignorance and ill-will it had to overcome. Some of the leading men seem to have been possessed of limited understanding associated with keen ambition. Bodo, for example, wishing to get the reputation of a thorough-going revolutionary, which he was not, brought the party into temporary disrepute by issuing instructions that women were to discard the old style of elaborate head-dress, with the tresses swirled up into an imitation of the horns of the mountain goat, and secured by trinkets of traditional pattern. The women were so upset by this measure, and its violent enforcement, that Sukebator was impelled to disown Bodo in a public speech, and the order was rescinded. Bodo himself was dismissed from office, apparently over this incident. Yet at the same time when men could be diverted to look after women's hairstyles, the most elementary tasks remained to be done, and that some of them were undertaken at all was due only to the practical drive of Sukebator. It was he who had the medical services in the army reorganized, or rather, created. He had an army dispensary and hospital set up, though even so the conditions were appalling. There was no western medicine, no proper bedclothes for the patients, no isolation of infectious cases, no special diets. Sukebator arranged for a Russian doctor, P. N. Shastin, to come from Irkutsk with some nurses and set up a pharmacy. But Shastin was treated with such indifference after

Sukebator's death and met with so much obstruction, that, as was reported at the Third Party Congress, he was almost driven away again.

The reforms actually decreed fell far short of sovietization. Naturally they tended to affect the privileges of the nobility and the church, but not yet in such a way as to cause general alarm. The church was in any case too strong to be deliberately affronted, although it was not long before it would be putting out propaganda warning the faithful that ultimately the new régime would try to mount a deadly assault. The lay nobility presented a less difficult problem. As Sorokovikov, the Soviet military adviser at the time, recalls:

> The main blows had to be directed against the lay and clerical nobility. But by 1922 the lay nobility was still not actively opposing the People's Government, but even welcomed it as a help in its own struggle to overthrow clerical authority. There were even nobles who actively supported the revolution, hoping to win personal advantage from this. The revolution had not yet interfered with the feudal economy, and they hoped to become a local commercial capitalist class as soon as the economy in general had recovered. The clerics were in a different situation. They had a disciplined and powerful religious organization and were respected throughout the country. They were a real political force, relying on numerous lamas.[10]

It was not till 1929 that either class was really threatened. Only a few fringe benefits of the nobility and church were cancelled or limited up till then. In 1922 the *khamjilga* system was abolished and the nobility lost their right to exact *corvée* from the commoners. Lamaseries were forbidden the free use of the state relay stations, herdsmen were nominally exempted from the obligation to herd church cattle against their will and to make up accidental losses, steps were taken to regulate money lending and to reduce the rates of interest charged by the church, and state subsidies to the Church were discontinued. But none of these measures approached the fundamental problem as the revolutionaries saw it, and indeed as it really was, which was the existence of a powerful, essentially conservative body inside what was intended to be a progressive state. As long as the Khutuktu remained alive as a focus for pious sentiment, it would be a disastrous affront to the people to meddle with the position of the church. This was realized, even though at times revolutionary ardour got the better of discretion. For example, it was as early as 1922 that the Party had accepted, at a Comintern meeting, the policy of developing and exploiting latent class differences among the lamas so as to bring about dissension and the collapse of the church from within, but not till 1925 did they dare to do anything about it. But not only sentiment was involved. To undermine the church's economic position was a serious matter. The livelihood of thousands of ordinary people who depended on the church herds which were farmed out to them for their subsistence was at stake, and it would have been unreasonable to disrupt this system all at once. When the authorities forsook reality in the exuberance of 1929 and abolished the system, the resulting destitution did as much as anything to alienate people from the revolution.

What renders the history of revolutionary Mongolia unique in a century whose watchword is revolution is the fact that its main opponent, the main conservative force, was not a foreign colonial power or a class of native capitalists, but the church, and the most interesting aspect of her history is the study of how the church was first wooed, then weakened, and finally, to all intents and purposes, destroyed. The anti-religious campaign of the 'twenties and 'thirties in Mongolia has been compared to the Reformation of the English Church by Henry VIII. There are certain similarities, especially in that both churches were enormously wealthy, but had in their contemporary form outlived their usefulness, and presented a challenge to the temporal authority. But there was a fundamental difference. It had never been the intention of the English crown to destroy the Church and to replace Christianity by some other theology or philosophy. It was merely to be transferred from allegiance to Rome to a position of harmless dependence on the crown. The Mongol revolutionaries went further than this. They always paid lip service to the principle of freedom of belief, as a private matter, a freedom which is still guaranteed by the constitution, but to most of them Marxism and Buddhism were, and still are, irreconcilable enemies at all levels, even, at times, that of personal piety. The two could not co-exist and attempts which will be described below to reconcile them were especially anathema to the more extreme party leaders, and are still today spoken of with scorn as displaying the lamentable ignorance of Marxist theory of those men who did try to find common ground. The Church in

Mongolia was to be eliminated, not reformed, and by and large this is what happened over the next twenty years. The process was a gradual one. For the first three years after its installation, the revolutionary government even recognized the Khutuktu as monarch, though his authority was strictly limited, by the Oath-taking Treaty of 1921, to religious matters.

State and Church

Even the fact that the church was deprived of its head when the Khutuktu died did not immediately open the way to a direct attack upon it, mainly because power was still effectively in the hands of relatively moderate men within the Party who were conscious of the hold the Church still exercised over the ordinary people, and were realistic enough to act on their knowledge. As Dambadorj said to Anna Louise Strong in 1926: 'We could not possibly attack the Buddhist religion. For three hundred years the people have learned to reverence lamas. They will not unlearn in six years.'[11] Indeed, during the years up to 1928 a curious contradiction between theory and practice is seen to exist in the relations between Church and State. The two had been formally separated by the constitution, a separation reinforced by a special law promulgated in 1926. Officially the state was committed to an anti-church, anti-religious offensive, in which it was confessedly guided by the Comintern and the Soviet communist party, and a whole series of measures was decreed to undermine the Church's economic power and to aggravate the latent class differences among the lamas. At the same time, atheistic propaganda was disseminated as far as the primitive methods of publicity available permitted – by means of the press, pamphlets and crude theatrical sketches. On the side of the Church there was a steady stream of anti-communist propaganda flowing out from the lamasery chanceries and printing presses, carried through the countryside by wandering mendicant lamas. Plots and uprisings of one sort or another followed each other almost without interruption. Yet at the same time there was a tacit agreement to suffer one another's existence which frustrated the plans of the more extreme wing of the party. Many lamas were party members and were jealous of their party loyalty. As one lama-delegate to the Third Party Congress shouted: ' "Japan" Danzan (then chairman of the Central Committee) has claimed he is an honest upright working man. Well, what about us? Are we supposed to be reactionaries?'[12] Besides, many functionaries charged with carrying out the government's proposals were sincere believers themselves. Leading party theorists let it be known that they favoured the reformed Buddhism which was evolving under the guidance of some thoughtful and responsible high lamas. Thus, in spite of the abolition of the *Shabi*-estate in 1925, followed first by the organization of these former Church subjects into an aimak of their own with people but no territory, and then by their absorption into one or other of the old aimaks, in spite of measures decreed but not enforced to limit the number of children of school age to be accepted into lamaseries, to make lamas liable to military service, and to subject the *jas*-funds to state taxation, the church flourished in these years. Over twelve thousand lamas deserted the church for civil life between 1924 and 1927, but the total number of lamas increased all the same. The church grew wealthier. The *jas* were not actually taxed till 1926 and then at a low rate, nothing effective was done to interfere with the traditional arrangements whereby lamaseries farmed out their herds, and the Church continued to draw a large income from trade, money lending, transport and the collection of alms.

How the Party disposed of the problem of the succession of a ninth Khutuktu illustrates very well the gradualist nature of its approach to the church in the middle of the 'twenties. From the very moment of the decease of the old Khutuktu in 1924 the high lamas were agitating for the search for his successor to be set in train, and requested official sanction for the search. It will be remembered that even in Manchu times, the installation of a new incarnation was never a matter for the Church alone to decide. The Party felt itself too insecure to forbid the search outright, and so temporized. Within its own circle it was determined not to throw away the tactical advantage now gained, which enabled it to weaken the Church through keeping it without a spiritual head. So in public it spoke equivocally, delaying the moment when it would have to show its hand until it was strong enough to do so. A reincarnation was in fact found almost at once in north Mongolia, and some high lamas of the dead Khutuktu's suite went to interview the child's mother Tsendjav and instruct her in the details of the life of the former incarnation, so that she could familiarize the child-candidate with the tests which he would have to undergo. Faced with this situation, and the possibility that a new Khutuktu, born in Mongolia itself and no longer even a foreigner from Tibet, might be a rallying point for those who wished to restore the theocratic monarchy, the Party still temporized. It acted decisively enough in the case itself: in July 1925 the Central Committee decided that there were not sufficient grounds for accepting this particular child as an incarnation, and sent out a special commission to settle the affair. On the general question of searching for a ninth Khutuktu it made its first suggestion that the government should take it up with the Dalai Lama – a procedure which could be dragged out indefinitely. There was, however, continual agitation in the country for the new Khutuktu to be brought to light, and in 1926 the high lamas organized a regular political campaign and formalised the matter by submitting a request to the government to be allowed to proceed to a choice.

The Party Congress held in the autumn of that year discussed the matter and came to a surprising decision. Publicly it recognized the great merits of the Khutuktu and his predecessors, reaffirmed that there could be no question of allowing him to be reincarnated, since theological tradition was against this, but proposed to win over the lamaist opposition by submitting the question, as previously suggested, to the Dalai Lama. The whole resolution, with its curious reference to the popular belief in the apocalyptic realm of Shambala, which was sometimes a mystical kingdom somewhere in the north, sometimes identified with Russia, and sometimes, especially in the 1930s, with Japan, and its expressed deference to the superstitions which still ruled people's minds, is worth quoting as an indication of the gulf which separated the atheistic Marxism professed by the Party – at least in retrospect – and the conservative, mystical Buddhism which still informed the country as a whole:

> The Jebtsundamba Khutuktus have deserved extremely well of our Mongol religion and state, and when it came to the Eighth Incarnation, he freed Mongolia from Chinese oppression and laid the foundation for it to become a state, cherishing and protecting it, and finally demonstrated the impermanence of this transitory world and passed away. And as there is a tradition that after the Eighth Incarnation he will not be reincarnated again, but thereafter will be reborn as the

FIRST STEPS IN REVOLUTION, 1921-8

Great General Hanamand in the realm of Shambala, there is no question of installing the subsequent, Ninth Incarnation. Nevertheless, many of his unenlightened disciples, with their fleshy eyes and stupid understanding, are unwilling to grasp this, so it is decreed that the Central Committee to be newly elected shall take charge of reporting this and clearing it up with the Dalai Lama. Apart from this, all other incarnations are to be treated according to the Law separating Church and State.[13]

This law, which had been passed a few days earlier, did not directly envisage the prohibition of the discovery of lesser incarnations either. It simply required that all such activities be reported for approval to the government. The National Assembly which met in November 1926 to turn the Party's resolutions into executive decisions took approximately the same line about the Khutuktu. Omitting the mumbo-jumbo, it referred to the absence of a tradition that there would be any incarnations after the eighth as a reason for submitting the question to the Dalai Lama, and repeated that there was no question of inviting the ninth incumbent of the office.[14] The reference to a tradition about whether or not the line should come to an end with the eighth Khutuktu has no basis in Church documents. There is, for example, nothing about it in the official Lives of the Khutuktus. But it became almost a tradition in Mongolia that when a Khutuktu died, anxious rumours should circulate amongst the people that he would not be born again. A similar folk belief is known as early as 1848 when the sixth died, and it was popularly rumoured that the line was to fail with him. So Party and government were not applying to the authority of Church dogma but simply playing cleverly on doubts and anxieties which were already vaguely familiar to the public, in order to push through their intended policies without arousing too much resentment. By February 1929, after the decisive Seventh Party Congress had expelled all right wing party leaders, the authorities felt secure enough to issue a decree categorically forbidding the installation of the Jebtsundamba Khutuktu or of any lesser incarnation.

This was not the end of the story, as there were further attempts made to discover the ninth Khutuktu. But these were now strictly illegal, and as those responsible for them came to rely more and more on Japanese help and on the prestige of the Panchen Lama, who was in exile from Tibet in China, and who, curiously enough himself in the guise of a general of Shambala, was supposed to be sheltering the ninth Khutuktu and preparing an invasion of Mongolia, they naturally became tainted with treason to the state. In 1926 the lamas had been able to petition to be allowed to rediscover the Khutuktu, but in 1930 many lamas and nobles were condemned in a big treason trial for having undertaken the same search in collusion with the Japanese and the Panchen Lama. From then on the matter ceased to have much practical importance.

For several years after 1921 Mongolia was to all intents and purposes under Soviet military occupation. Young Kalmucks and Buriats, who alone were linguistically equipped to act as go-betweens between Russians and Mongols, who for the most part were ignorant of each other's languages, ran the police force and the army. Successive Soviet officers headed the Mongol army staff and ran the intelligence network. Much of the day to day work of pushing through the government's decisions fell to the soldiers of the Mongol army, who had been through the hands of Russian instructors. The Office of Internal Security and the secret police were also supervised by Russians, though nominally under Mongol control. On the civilian side there were Buriats of Soviet nationality in high position, and regular Comintern agents in Urga. Inevitably the administrative, financial and social reforms which the government was slowly bringing about, and which included such fundamental and politically neutral measures as the founding of a national bank, the replacement of the haphazard media of exchange by a national currency, the erection of a series of courts, the slow introduction of western medicine, the opening of secular schools, all tended in some way or other to circumscribe or threaten the power and privileges of the Church and the nobility. Thus Mongol susceptibilities were offended at their most tender, since lama and overlord were still to an overwhelming extent the focus of individual loyalties, rather than any larger concept such as the state, let alone such distant abstractions as the revolution or international communism. True, Sven Hedin, travelling in Mongolia in 1923 and 1924, detected signs of the decline of lamaism in Urga. He was in Urga for only five days, but got all the same a distinct impression of the decay of lamaism. It was no longer what it had been, and the lama was no more than an ordinary man. But Urga, as Hedin suspected, was not Mongolia, though it was the heart of Mongol lamaism, and piety and superstition, and reverence for the three jewels of the Faith, for the Buddha, the Law and the Clergy, took a long time to die. Reforms were identified in people's minds with Russian atheistic communism. The Reds were seen as only continuing the aggressions of Tsarist Russia, with the added vice that they were godless. The people were thus an easy target for the effective anti-Soviet propaganda which was circulated in written form or by word of mouth, throughout the 'twenties. The Party was at a disadvantage here. Printing was in its infancy, and the state printing works rather inefficient, whereas the Church disposed of trained scribes and blockcutters who could duplicate tracts in Mongol and in Tibetan script. At a time when radio was still unknown, the Church could reach all corners of the country through the itinerant mendicants or *badarchin*-lamas, and it kept up a respectable proganda counter-fire. Some of this was crude in the extreme. Those who supported the communists were called:

heretical creatures, who have licked the mouth of the gun and sworn that they would be willing to kill their lama, teacher, father or mother, who tread on the *Zungdui* and the *Jadamba* and other Buddhist scriptures, or pass them under the knickers of Russian women or under pictures of them giving birth, and who, once they have taken the oath and joined, immediately conceive evil thoughts and fail to respect the Buddhist Faith.[15]

Nevertheless, the Church's propaganda was cast in terms the people could understand and appreciate. It knew how to talk the language of Buddhism, and it appealed to legends and tales engrained in everyone's mind. People knew what the Church meant and what it stood for, whereas they were often at sea with the strange new concepts of the revolutionaries. A typical example of a church tract from the 'twenties is the following:

Hunger has struck the Red Russians, and they are robbing the Mongols of their cattle to relieve themselves. The virtue and destiny of the present incarnation of those men who have joined the Party and the Youth League is exhausted, and in their future incarnation they will experience the sufferings of hell. Red Russia and Lenin are the reincarnation of Langdarma [a ninth century apostate Tibetan king], the enemy of the Faith, and the People's Party is bringing in the Red Russians to harm the Faith and humanity. If you do not abandon the

Russian and Mongol Reds, you will be torn from the Faith and the Buddha. Do not be deceived by the wiles of the People's Party. The time is nigh when the People's Government will collapse. From the east the Panchen Lama and the Japanese army will come to annihilate the People's government and re-establish the old order.[16]

For several years the Panchen Lama was a bogy-man to the Mongol government. To what extent he was a real threat is hard to decide nowadays. He cannot have had the armies of apocalyptic Shambala under his command, but it is certain that messages were going to and from between him and various Mongol conspirators, and that he was interested in anti-communist disaffection. The Party could not fail to take all rumours of discontent seriously during the 1920s, for besides the crises inside the Party and government, there were endless plots, actual and rumoured, in all parts of the country throughout the decade, fanned by a real resentment of what was seen as the impact of foreign atheism, and nourished by constant clerical propaganda. Some of these conspiracies were organized and led by men in the highest places in lamaseries, and the suspicion was never absent during his lifetime that the Khutuktu was involved personally, as for example in the case of the Manjushri Khutuktu Tserendorji and his associates in 1923. On this occasion there had allegedly been an agreement to seek help from Japan and one of the conspirators had actually been sent from Urga to go to Tokyo with a letter sealed with a forged seal of the Ministry of the Interior. He had been apprehended in China before reaching his goal.

As well as political conspiracies originating in Urga there were actual uprisings in the provinces, mainly in the west. High lamas of a lamasery in present-day Gobi Altai aimak, irked at the loss of some of their privileges, planned to send a delegate to Peking to recruit Chinese help for a *coup d'état*. This was in 1924 and early 1925. Again in 1925 there was an actual insurrection in Ulaangom, where the high lamas tried to abolish the newly set up local administration. They succeeded in arresting the officials and in sabotaging the relay services so as to cut off communications with Khobdo, but ultimately they were put down by armed force. In 1926 there was an attempt in a big lamasery in Bulgan aimak to eject the civil administrator recently installed there and in other large lamaseries to supervise their internal functioning, and in the same year at Bayantumen in the east of the country there was a big affray between lamas and the civil authorities over the question of the assessment of Church cattle to taxation. Some two hundred lamas attacked the local *tamga* or office and wrecked it. A special commission was sent out from Urga to settle the affair, and it had the ringleaders executed. What makes this uprising particularly significant is the fact that not only the mob, but the riot-leaders also, were ordinary lamas. The high clerics of the lamasery were not implicated, or if they were, as some writers nowadays maintain they were, they managed to cover their tracks well enough to escape detection by the investigating commission, and it was ordinary lamas who were executed. In 1927 there was a big conspiracy of nobles and lamas at Khobdo, led by an official named Shaalov, which had as its object to detach the Khobdo district altogether from Mongolia and unite it with Chinese Sinkiang. At the same time other conspiracies were uncovered all over the country, at Yeguuzer lamasery in the extreme east which was to be one of the centres of a more widespread counter-revolutionary movement in 1929 and 1930, at Namnan Uul lamasery in the centre, and elsewhere.

These plots and riots were a reaction to the comparatively mild, though ominous, measures of reform which the People's government was trying to carry out, measures which alongside the brutalities and obscenities which disfigured the years between 1929 and 1932 must in retrospect have looked restrained and moderate to a degree. As an indication of how close the People's government was all the time to overstepping the limit and provoking counter-revolution they were serious enough, but they were doomed to remain ineffective since they were mere sporadic outbursts of fury, limited perhaps to a single monastery. People were not driven to despair, there was no nation-wide counter-revolutionary organization working against the régime, and neither China nor Japan was in a mood to burn its fingers in a conflict with the USSR over the fate of Mongolia just then. If not a phoney war, the struggle between Party and Church was, in the middle of the 1920s, largely a propaganda one. The Church's aim was to play on the *naïveté* and ignorance of the people at large. A well-known pamphlet of the time was that known as the 'Stone Text' which threatened imminent disaster to those who abandoned the Church and promised rewards to those who helped to circulate the pamphlet. The primitive force it must have held for its superstitious readers can be judged from a short extract:

> Now the time of disaster has come, and heaven is angry at lack of respect for the Buddha, and will punish the disaffected. There may be crops, but there will be none to eat them, there will be disaster from robbers, fire, water, knives, war, cattle-plague, enemies, thunderbolts, untimely death, earthquakes, those who fly in the sky, wild beasts, and devils. If you will adore the Buddhist Faith, and perform good works, and refrain from evil, sinful thoughts, you will escape these disasters.

Graded rewards were promised those who passed on religious tracts by word of mouth, or, better still, in written or printed form.[17]

On the other hand the basic aims of the Party's propaganda were two-fold. They hoped to educate people away from their adherence to the Church and to draw them out of their medieval backwardness by patient teaching, and they planned to sow dissension within the ranks of the lamas themselves by accentuating potential and exploitable class differences. Once the seeds of class consciousness had been sown, the lower lamas were to be attracted to the revolution by means of preferential treatment. A beginning with the work of instruction had been made by setting up some secular schools, but only a small minority of children attended these, and it was the press, aiming at adults, rather than the schools, which was the main vehicle of propaganda against religion. At the lowest level the lamas were satirized, and scandalous tales about their immoral lives spread. This type of propaganda was to become commoner when the Eighth Party Congress of 1930, realizing that the new reformed Buddhism coming into fashion represented a far greater danger to communism than the degenerate lamaism it was replacing, deliberately adopted vilification and disparagement of individual lamas as one aspect of its policy. But even in 1925 satirical articles and pamphlets were being put about, poking fun at lamas whose lives were less than ascetic. These lampoons followed a traditional pattern of ironical comment which had been familiar from long before the revolution, and were no more vitriolic than Ishi-danzangwangjil's *surgaal* had been. The party newspaper Unen ('Truth') brought out a series of little satirical pieces with such titles as 'Comic and Shameful', or 'How to tell a lama from a layman', whose tone is almost gentlemanly. In the latter the reader was told:

> Now I shall instruct you how to tell a lama from a layman nowadays. If you see what an increase there is in men who offend against the principles of Buddhism, men with shaven heads, dressed in red and yellow lop-sided robes, all smart and showy, carrying on with the girls, sullying their religious vows, amassing flocks of animals, well, that's what the old proverb means – A priest in every tent, a *jas*-fund in every ravine. With some of our incarnations and noble lamas accepting consecration and assuming titles and privileges and attending services, yet on the other hand taking mistresses, amassing wealth, engaging in trade – are they to be called lamas or laymen? Gentlemen, I ask you![18]

At a more sophisticated level the Party exploited the writings of such lamas as the theologian Darva Bandida, an important incarnation of Sain Noyon Khan aimak, who died in 1927, and who, while reverting to the early, comparatively puritanical principles of pure Buddhism, tried consciously to reconcile these with communism, and to this extent gave his support to the Party. At this time the Central Committee was not unsympathetic to the principles of Buddhism themselves, though with the shift to the left in 1929 this willingness to compromise and to adapt was jettisoned along with the rest of the policy of gradualism. Co-operation with a reformed Buddhism must have appeared an attractive alternative to a head-on collision with the Church, especially as the latter was so tightly integrated with the national economy that meddling with one would have meant a thorough overhaul of the other. The theoretical conflict between Marxism and Buddhism posed in these years has still not been solved even today when the social and economic preponderance of the Church has completely vanished. A historian like Natsagdorj may nowadays isolate the 'progressive' factors in Buddhism and set them off against its supposedly basically reactionary nature. As he put it

> How are we to view the dissemination of Buddhism in Mongolia? In my opinion, Buddhism played a civilizing role in some respects in Mongol life in the sixteenth century. As well as replacing the coarse and primitive shamanist cult, it cherished and spread in the steppes of Mongolia some of the achievements of Indian and Tibetan culture. But [he goes on to qualify] it became a weapon for reinforcing the power of the exploiting classes and the exploitation of the working

masses of the Mongol people, and in this respect caused enormous harm to the progress of Mongolia.[19]

This is a fairly moderate Marxist analysis of the role of Buddhism, with which not everyone would fully agree but which has the merit of being reasonable and arguable. It refers, however, to the conditions of the sixteenth century, and those, especially lamas, who still at the present day try to reconcile religion and 'scientific Marxism' and adapt themselves to socialist ideology while remaining faithful to Buddhism, are rejected as heretics by contemporary Marxist theorists. These deny the lamas' view that there are points of contact between Buddhist and socialist ideas, and that the Buddha was a precursor of Marx and Lenin. Such erroneous views are held to be especially dangerous since they would tend to slow up the process of the disappearance of religion, which according to Marxist theory is not something automatic, but a consummation to be struggled for.[20]

At present, though, a temporary alliance with the truncated church is of considerable practical utility to Mongolia, whatever theory may require, because of her growing contacts with other, and more genuinely Buddhist countries. The existence of even a vestige of what was once a flourishing religious society is exploited so as to gain sympathy and cement solidarity with these other states now that Mongolia has emerged from her isolation of the 'thirties and 'forties. Similarly, such a temporary alliance could have been of enormous importance in the middle of the 'twenties when the Church was still a factor to be reckoned with. In actual fact, the Central Committee did put out feelers towards the Church and show itself ready to make concessions, and some *modus vivendi* might have been reached if it were not for the whipping up of the Soviet anti-Church campaign of 1929 and after, which spilled over into Mongolia. In 1928, for example, the Central Committee issued a pamphlet entitled 'Declaration by the Central Committee of the Party on policy concerning the future improvement of the condition of religion' in which it spoke warmly of Darva Bandida, whom it described as 'one of not a few upright scholars who have approved of the People's Party'. It quoted a tract of his with the title 'Book known as the people's pure principle', in which he had sharply contrasted the autonomous period, during which the selfish nobles and lamas had, so he said, neglected the welfare of the people, rejecting the poor and succouring the rich, with the people's government, which he welcomed, comparing it to water coming to a fish or a frog in a dried-up lake. He looked forward to a time when the sufferings of the people would be brought to an end, and when they would all enjoy proper education and be decently cared for. It was the nobility alone, he declared, who were responsible for all the troubles in the world.[21]

If more of the thought of the Darva Bandida were available for study it might turn out to be less jejune and sanguine than this short extract promises, but be that as it may, it is certain that from the very beginning, from the time when the Jalkhantsa Khutuktu as premier was willing to issue statements condemning his predecessor Bodo and summoning the people to give their support to the revolutionary government, there existed a considerable fund of good-will towards the revolution, not only on the part of the lower lamas, but on that of many Church leaders as well. But the secular authority followed, as it was probably bound to, an equivocal policy towards the Church. It realized the necessity for change. The rich ecclesiastical estates could no longer escape taxation, nor could one third of the male population stand aside from productive work or from participation in normal social and family life. It was intolerable that there should still be, in 1926, some 84,000 Mongol women who could not find husbands because their contemporaries were celibate lamas. A party which, though it included many lamas in its membership and believers such as Jamtsarano among its leaders, confessed itself obliged to the atheistic Comintern and Soviet communist party for guidance, could not ultimately accept with any satisfaction the fact that the great majority of children who were receiving an education were getting it in lamaseries and not from the state schools, and that the new generation was being trained up in the same outlook as the old.

But the government was none too keen to push matters to extremes or to follow up everything the Party proposed. Its policy of gradualism, which permitted it to defer action on controversial or unpopular questions, such as the subjection of the church's cattle to taxation, until a positive demand for such a step made itself felt in the provinces, seems to have been only one aspect of a general dilatoriness, a disposition to let sleeping dogs lie, rather than stir up, for purely theoretical reasons, a conflict whose consequences could not be foreseen. So while on the one hand the Party's propaganda machine was doing its best to foment mutual antagonism between the different classes of lama, on the other the government was doing what it could to prevent dissension getting out of control and actually disrupting the lamaseries. Matters did reach the point of violence in Urga in 1925 and 1926 when some of the lower lamas got together to demand the limitation of the privileges of their superiors, as they had been encouraged to do. They formulated various specific proposals, such as that lower lamas should be taught to read and write in Mongol as well as in Tibetan, that they should be admitted to lamasery management, that the joint income of the lamaseries from alms should be shared out more equally amongst the community than was the custom, and so on. But when the crisis arose, the Party failed to back the dissenters it had encouraged, and the high lamas were able to reject the proposals out of hand and to expel some of the ringleaders from their lamasery. They even set fire to the tent of one of them, burning him to death inside it. This seems to have marked the end, for the time being, of the movement for the democratization of lamasery life.

What was happening in Mongolia was, in the inelegant jargon of the time, that the country was undergoing a period of 'rightist capitulationist deviation'. This expressed itself in all aspects of life, not only in a deliberate campaign to co-operate with the Church in practice and to justify this co-operation in theory, but also in the encouragement of private capitalism. Marxist historians explain the emergence of this phenomenon on the basis of 'objective and subjective causality conditioned by the internal and external state of the country'[22] but managing to omit mention of the most telling factor of all, which was that Mongolia's path was determined as much or more by her political and ideological association with the USSR as by factors peculiar to her own condition. One may admit the presence of all the factors adduced, the dominance of feudal relationships in society, the prevalence of petty capitalism, the excessive prestige of religion, the lack of a native working class, which are held to have obstructed Mongolia's revolutionary progress along the non-capitalist path and to have diverted it into wrong channels. But what is not taken into account by this analysis is that Mongolia's experience at this time was not a unique one. With a slight time lag separating them, developments in Mongolia were precisely those which were taking place in the USSR, and what was happening in the USSR was being paralleled in Tannu Tuva also. We are thus faced with the task of finding an explanation for the simultaneous appearance of a 'rightist deviation', followed by a sharp swing to the left, a party purge, a campaign of religious persecution, and a brutal collectivization drive, in three countries which were nominally independent of each other and in which social and economic conditions were quite different. Mongolia, with a few little workshops and not even the basis of an industry, was immeasurably far behind Russia, and Tannu Tuva was rather more primitive than Mongolia, though the contrast was not so glaring. The explanation can only be sought in the dependence of the Tuvan and Mongol parties on the Soviet communist party, their incapacity to think for themselves and show an independent initiative in moments of crisis.

What had happened in Russia, briefly, was that Lenin had proclaimed the New Economic Policy under which a limited amount of capitalism, private enterprise and speculation was tolerated as a way out of the disasters caused by the First World War, the Civil War, and the failures of his own war communism. Mongolia and Tuva followed in the wake of the NEP. There was no reason for them to show themselves more extreme than Moscow, and they took to heart Bukharin's slogan 'Get rich!', which began to be repeated in Mongolia. In both countries the economy boomed. The richer elements, that is the lamaseries, the large herd-owners and the emergent capitalists grew richer, though at the same time the proportion of poor households also rose. As capitalism began to develop in Mongolia, so there naturally arose a demand to widen the country's commercial contacts, in particular with China, but also with Europe. Men like Dambadorj began to speak of the dangers of red imperialism and Soviet colonization. Mongolia was evidently threatening to move out of the Soviet sphere and enter the wider sphere of world commerce.

The Third Party Congress

Such developments were already taking place before the decisive

Third Party Congress met in 1924. Danzan, the chairman of the congress till he was shot at the end of August, was himself known to be a speculator, and was not the only one. In May 1924 the Khutuktu had died. His demise had come opportunely, though there is no reason to suspect that it had been hastened, as had that of some of his predecessors, and as he had been wont to accelerate the departure of uncomfortable opponents. The only wonder was that, worn out with spirits and syphilis, sometimes lost in a drunken stupor for a week at a time and transacting state business in the lucid intervals, he had actually managed to last out to the age of fifty-four. A few weeks later the People's Republic was proclaimed, and then in August the Third Party Congress met to determine the future lines of policy and development. The official evaluation of the congress's work, as stated for example by the Soviet historian Zlatkin, is quite explicit. 'For the first time the General Line of the Party was clearly formulated by this congress, which expressed its determination to fight for the non-capitalist development of the country.'[23] This was a defeat for those men who like Buyannemekh, the leader of the Youth League, had shown themselves good Marxists but bad tacticians by expressing the view that Mongolia would have to pass through the stage of capitalism which prevailed throughout the world except in the USSR. This, it was urged, was not a bad thing, since capitalism would destroy feudalism and the workers could then in their turn destroy capitalism.[24]

If Zlatkin's assessment of the congress's work is correct, some explanation has to be sought for the failure of Mongolia to adopt the favoured path of non-capitalist progress. Partly this will have been due, as suggested above, to the confused conditions of the time, partly to Mongolia's reliance in practical affairs of commerce and finance on Soviet experience, techniques and finance. The Mongol State Bank, for example, which was founded in 1924 and was responsible for issuing the first national currency and capitalizing the Mongol Central Co-operative, was a joint-stock undertaking in which the Soviet government was a financial and managerial partner. The USSR cannot then have been ignorant of, or, more significantly, in disagreement with, the course Mongolia's economy was following – a course which was set by the existence of the NEP. But there is a third factor to be considered.

Even to the extent that can be judged from the incomplete records of the congress which are available, it was more than a mere policy-making meeting. To begin with, not all the delegates were native Mongols. The most active elements were Buriats, and there was at least one Russian observer, Vasiliev, who was elected an honorary member of the congress. There were also Inner Mongolian representatives, whose purpose it was to use the congress to press for the liberation of those Mongols whom they described as still suffering under the yoke of Chinese oppression. Nothing was of course done about this appeal, which was launched by the representative from Barga, Fumintai, and it was perhaps nothing more than a manifestation of revolutionary euphoria. What Fumintai said was: 'Our people in Inner Mongolia and Barga are like men still frantically struggling in the water, and we hope that our Outer Mongol brethren, who have managed to reach the bank, will do all they can to rescue their brothers of the same Mongol race.'[25] This much was only to be expected, since ever since its inception the Party had had the penetration of Inner Mongolia by revolutionary propaganda, and, if possible, its detachment from China, on its programme. The Second Party Congress of 1923 even declared that the unification of all people of Mongol race and the revivification of Mongol culture was one of the Party's main aims, and the Third Congress itself also issued a resolution calling for Mongol unity. In this it regretted that up till then it had proved impossible to incorporate Barga and Inner Mongolia, still under Chinese domination, and Tannu Tuva, effectively under Soviet control though nominally independent, in Mongolia, and it instructed the Central Committee to look around for new ways of attempting this task.

Though declarations like this gradually ceased to have any significance, and perhaps even in 1924 can have represented little more than lip-service to an illusory dream of greater Mongol unity, they are lively evidence of the persistence of ideals of Mongol pan-nationalism which were bound to conflict with Soviet interests. Buriat Mongolia is omitted from these resolutions, but Tuva is not. In 1924 Soviet penetration of Tuva, and its enforced separation from Mongolia was a very sore point, taken up at the congress by certain provincial delegates who, however, seem to have got no reply to their questions about Russian brutalities there.

What was, however, far more important than these signs of a preoccupation with issues which cut across the ideals of international revolution was the revelation that the congress was disastrously split into irreconcilable factions. Two cliques at least can be distinguished among the leaders, one associated with the name of Danzan, the other an opportunist alliance between the left wing Rinchino, and the right wing Dambadorj. Towards its final sessions the congress lost all cohesion and abruptly degenerated into an arbitrarily and illegally self-constituted court. On the spur of the moment it had the congress chairman Danzan and some others arrested, interrogated and condemned to death by a special commission of their erstwhile colleagues. That men of an outlook so different as Rinchino and Dambadorj could for the moment work together to bring about the downfall and death of their associates is a hint that what was involved in this little *coup* was not a vital clash of high political ideals but rather a struggle for individual survival and power: careers and not principles were at stake. With Danzan, a right wing revolutionary, a partisan of private enterprise who favoured trade with China in preference to the USSR, eliminated, one might have expected a swing to the left to ensue. But in fact there was no change in Mongolia's course: if anything it swung more than ever towards private capitalism, though under new management, that of Dambadorj. The assassination of Danzan had been only a flash in the pan. The introduction to a recent edition of documents about the Third Party Congress states baldly that this congress 'exposed and smashed the anti-party activities of Danzan and his associates and so protected and strengthened the Leninist General Line adopted by the Party'.[26] What is known of events at the time does little to bear out this flat assertion.

The Party itself was never effective as a mass organization. Its membership on occasions reached huge proportions – 42,000 by 1932, for example – but the lack of a working class in the country meant that most of the members were either lamas and minor nobility, who could not be relied on, or, when as in 1929 these had been purged, illiterate herdsmen who were mere passengers. The party leadership preferred to keep real power in its own hands. As Dambadorj put it in 1924:

It is quite wrong to say that there is no need to purge the Party because we are so few. Quality is far more important than quantity. When the Party first came into being it consisted of only seven men, but these were of one mind and purpose and so, as you know, they were able to accomplish great things.[27]

But it was not only hunger for power which produced what the congress recognized as a dictatorial attitude on the part of certain members of the Central Committee, who were said to be isolated from the public. There was such widespread apathy amongst the membership at large, and especially amongst country members of the Central Committee who never bothered to attend any meetings, that the 1923 congress had been a mere sham, perfunctory discussion being followed by the rubber-stamping of pre-arranged decisions. But for the energy of a few men, nothing at all would ever have got done. Quite apart from this we must bear in mind that the Party's attitude to the existence of other parties had changed radically since 1921. In that year these had been welcomed as long as they were not likely to obstruct the People's Party, but in 1924 attitudes had hardened to the point where Rinchino could declare: 'We will not permit the existence of any other party, either of the right or of the left.'[28] Hence, when cleavages and differences of opinion appeared, as they were bound to, they tended to crystallize in the shape of temporary opportunist factions, in which personal antipathies overshadowed political principle.

In political terms the basic disunity within the party leadership expressed itself as a disagreement between those who wanted Mongolia to follow the Soviet path straight away, and those who considered she was not ripe for an experiment in communism. In personal terms it was a duel between the Buriat Rinchino and the Khalkha Danzan. It was common knowledge that the two simply could not stand each other. The impetus for the extraordinary events which disfigured the last days of the congress and stunned the delegates seems to have come from the illegal action of some League of Revolutionary Youth leaders in arresting comrades of theirs, associates of Danzan's, who had deliberately failed to turn up for compulsory military training. The exuberant youth leaders seem also to have been hoping to take over the Party Congress whose chairman was far too conservative for their satisfaction. Tserendorji, then premier, warned them to moderation. He advised them not to meddle with what was beyond their competence, to consider above all things the welfare of the state, and not to follow blindly the dictates of Rinchino and the Buriats. Rinchino was a gifted man, but they should not obey his every word and trust him in every matter – surely they knew that there was a long-standing feud between him and Danzan? He accused Rinchino of deliberately stirring up trouble amongst the congress delegates, and he blamed both him and Danzan for allowing their personal quarrels to damage the national cause.

That Rinchino and Danzan held diametrically opposed views is clear from the records of the first sessions of the congress. Rinchino stated categorically:

> Now that we have got our independence, we have the power to build our life as we wish. There is no need to pass through all the stages of reactionary capitalism. There is no need for us to submit ourselves to the yoke of exploitation, is there?

This was the cue for cries from the floor of 'We won't submit! Never!' and though the more pragmatic Danzan, with an eye to the realities of Mongolia's backward and primitive economy, had a reasonable answer to this piece of demagogy, he could not put it over in the face of Rinchino's emotional appeal. What Danzan said was:

> Is it necessary to limit private capitalism in our country? Such a resolution may be issued and I would agree with it. But at present there is no individual capitalism in our country, and so this is not a matter for discussion today, but a subject for tomorrow. We may issue a resolution as Rinchino proposes, but to issue such a resolution is irrelevant from the point of view of our work.[29]

Rinchino saw things in wider perspective. To him, the professional revolutionary, Mongolia's story was only a small fragment of a vast process. Danzan was not prepared to insist, and he let the matter go by default, as later he was to let his whole position go by default.

If personal antipathies outweighed ideological differences, there were nevertheless some very cogent reasons why the USSR was less than popular in Mongolia in 1924. Rinchino must have been conscious of this coolness which was pointed up by Danzan, who opposed the reiteration of a formal expression of Mongol-Soviet friendship which had been carried at the

1923 congress. He had nothing against friendly relations with Russia, he said, but he had no intention of toadying to her.

The Russians had got themselves a bad name for their brutalities in Tannu Tuva, and in Mongolia did not always endear themselves to the people. The Chinese traders were, for example, far more efficient than the Soviet-sponsored Mongol Co-operative, and the trading ethics of the latter were often no improvement on those of the less scrupulous among the Chinese. A provincial delegate to the congress had this to say:

> There is a section of the co-operative at our place, but this section operates with different weights for buying and for selling. In a word, they are no different from the Chinese. The co-operative buys wool on fine sunny days, but as soon as it gets a bit overcast they stop buying for fear the wool will weigh heavier. But on the other hand the Chinese will buy whatever the weather. The officials are all Russians, and are rough and greedy, and ought as foreigners to be replaced. The Chinese buy a lot of wool, but the co-operative buys very little. And why is this? It is because the officials are men of bad character, and carry on in a rude and overbearing manner, so that the Mongols are put off and sooner or later stop trading with men from the co-operative.[30]

Matters came to an abrupt head on 26 August, when Danzan made the elementary but fatal error of boycotting the day's session, so that he was not in the chair at the crucial moment. He was apparently taking shelter with the army from what he claimed was an attempt to intimidate him by force. Whether Dambadorj and Rinchino were acting in collusion, or whether Rinchino simply exploited Dambadorj's outburst of fury is uncertain, but we do know that it was Dambadorj, who was almost hysterical, who was the first to get up and denounce Danzan. Rinchino lay low until the delegates had been worked up to the point where his intervention would have most effect. The frantic atmosphere which hung over the congress that day can still be sensed even through the turgid sentences of the official report, now nearly half a century old. Armed treason was Dambadorj's theme. He complained that Danzan had accused the congress of overawing him with armed men. 'What is the meaning of this?' he shouted, 'Where are these armed men? Danzan is slighting the congress. He wants to be a second king in Mongolia.' And a little later, 'Danzan is holding up the work of the congress and intimidating it. Who knows if we shall see the night out?

Who will guarantee the safety of our lives?' Meanwhile a delegation from the Youth League burst in to demand a share in the work of the session, and their presence, together with Danzan's voluntary absence at the critical moment, sealed his fate. Some delegates, including Choibalsang, wanted the session suspended since the chairman was not there, but with Dambadorj still ranting that Danzan was busy getting a mobile column together and arming the drivers for an attack on the congress, Rinchino judged the swing of feeling and the mood of the moment correctly and got his proposal that the congress should go on at once under a new presidium accepted without difficulty.[31]

The fact that Danzan was supposed to have taken refuge with the army probably served to lend credibility to the rumour that he was preparing an armed *coup d'état* against the congress. This will have told against him, but it was a most improbable accusation. We have it from Sorokovikov, Sukebator's old adviser and the Soviet organizer of Mongol army intelligence, that Danzan was no military man, and Gonjoon, one of those who followed Rinchino in pouncing on him, accused him of gross neglect of his military duties. Danzan never went near the soldiers except for ceremonial parades, unlike Sukebator who had been inseparable from them. Sorokovikov drew up his memoir at a less hectic time. Writing in 1958 he said:

> Danzan knew nothing about military matters. When I tried to inform him about the frontier situation, enemy concentrations, or the work of the espionage department, or spoke to him about the accommodation of Mongol army units and the espionage detachments, he not only never understood these matters but showed no interest in them either. He would change the subject and speak of other matters, such as the quarrels the drivers would pick with the loaders, customs, trading across the frontier, and so on. He had no interest in matters concerning state security. If he had worked as Minister of Finance he might have done all right, but he was absolutely unfitted to be chief of the army council or a general.[32]

From this analysis Danzan appears as the last man who could have whipped up military support for a putsch from soldiers he had never taken an interest in. He was rather a man of the entrepreneur type, and this was what convicted him in Rinchino's eyes. Rinchino worked up a recital of Danzan's commercial activities into a damning web of evidence of treachery. On the wave of hysteria prepared by Dambadorj he launched a comprehensive, reasoned, and yet emotionally persuasive assault upon the character, abilities and doings of the absent Danzan. Posthumously these were enlarged to a ludicrous extent. Danzan was later said to have been a Tsarist agent since 1914, then a Japanese agent, and to have wormed his way into the confidence of the Party so as to destroy it. The absurd calumny that he had helped to poison Sukebator, who in any case was most probably not poisoned at all, has at least been quietly dropped. Rinchino was less extravagant in his accusations, but very damning, though nothing in what he said really amounted, when one examines it more carefully, to a reflection on Danzan's loyalty as a Mongol. It was his alleged abandonment of the principles of the People's Party which convicted him. Detail after detail was piled up. Danzan had speculated in grain prices. He had sent Mongol soldiers to protect Chinese speculators, a matter which Rinchino said he had known about at the time, when he was in charge of the Office of Internal Security, but which he had not dealt with there and then out of feelings of delicacy about exposing the reputation of the Party to calumny. Danzan and Rinchino had agreed about setting up a system of motor transport between Mongolia and China, but nothing had been done about it on a state basis. However, a few months later Danzan went into private partnership with a Chinese firm to exploit this very project. Danzan had been against the Russians putting so many Buriats into positions of authority in Mongolia. In particular he had called the loyalty and revolutionary fervour of Rinchino himself into question, calling him a political agitator installed by the Russians, and an 'oppressive reactionary'. Accusation followed accusation. In the printed version of Rinchino's speech Danzan begins to be referred to as 'comrade' in inverted commas, he is a 'cunning element' who penetrated the Party by force. He had tried to revive old debts due to Chinese firms. He had put a secret agent of his own, a Chinese spy, at the head of the military training department. He was dangerous for the whole future, the incorporation of opposition. The delegates had a clear choice: they could move to the right and follow Danzan, and fall into a hell of misery for the people, national disgrace and disaster, or choose the left and march towards the bright sun of freedom and true democracy. 'Danzan is a thief, a traitor. As long as

Danzan is in power, our country will never have peace. We must destroy this thief!'[33] Other speakers jumped on Rinchino's bandwagon, and the Office of Internal Security was instructed by the congress to arrest Danzan and some others. Choibalsang replaced him as general, the first step on his intricate way to ultimate dictatorship.

A commission was set up to investigate Danzan's activities, to determine the penalty and carry it out within twenty-four hours. Rinchino, having engineered his rival's downfall, declined to join the commission, which consisted of Danzan's old comrade in Russia Losol and six other men, on the scrupulous grounds that he, like Dambadorj, was a well-known anti-Danzanist, and besides that a Buriat and not a Mongol at all. The commission's report, presented on 30 August, outlined the misdeeds of Danzan and Bavaasan of the League and recommended their execution. This was carried out. The other prisoners were jailed.

The report was heard in silence, broken by a few whispers and then a little applause. Then the Russian, Vasiliev, broke the embarrassment with some strange words of comfort. He confessed that he had not grasped all of what had been said, not knowing Mongol, but he fully approved what had been done.

Don't be afraid of what you have done [he said]. Such things happen not only in Mongolia but in Russia too. You have done absolutely right. None of us is keen on shedding blood, but every now and again it happens that you have to liquidate a few men so as not to sacrifice the majority. What you have done will, in my opinion, be of great help and advantage in strengthening the bonds between Mongolia and the USSR. Your decision is in every way a legal one. There is nothing to worry about. The only country which can save you is in the north – tell this to your masses. And now you must elect a new Central Committee.[34]

The Party Congress, thus reassured that it had done the right thing in the way such things were done in Russia, and not foreseeing that many of their own number, men like Rinchino and Jamtsarano, were themselves to form part of expendable minorities in the future, closed its session on 1 September.

The revolution veers to the right

Despite Danzan's elimination there was no change in the general direction of Mongolia's evolution. Private enterprise continued to flourish, together with co-operation between church and state. A conscious Mongol nationalism began to characterize the next two or three years. In commerce and politics the Mongols were doing their best to draw away from unilateral dependence on the USSR. In 1921 they had notified the USA of their new-found independence and had asked for recognition, but failed to get any response. In 1925 *ad hoc* relations, below the diplomatic level, were established with Germany and, to a lesser extent, with France. Taking advantage of the temporary rapprochement between Russia and Germany the Mongols sent a trade delegation to Berlin which stayed there till the middle of 1929. It had the duties of developing Mongolia's foreign trade and of recruiting technical experts to help build up her embryo industry. Then an educational mission also arrived, consisting of some forty children under the supervision of the Minister of Education Erdeni Batu Khan. These were to acquire a western education followed by a technical or commercial training. Great care was taken in the selection of schools, and a considerable number of the children were sent to the *Freie Schulgemeinde Wickersdorf*, an unconventional establishment where academic training was accompanied by encouragement of independence of thought and initiative. This unique group of forty children represented a considerable proportion of the available school children of the proper standard at the time. In 1925 there were only 1,550 children enrolled in seventy-five secondary schools, and the one middle school, from which the experimental group was drawn, held thirty-two boys and fourteen girls. Had the experiment been continued it might have furnished Mongolia with an educated class of a balanced and moderate outlook, men and women with experience of the world beyond the narrow confines of Stalinist dogma, but this was precisely what the leftists of 1929 feared. Both delegations were withdrawn. The leaders of the trade delegation, men like the Buriat Sampilon who by now knew their way around the world of international commerce, disappeared into obscurity, and some were murdered. The children suffered a variety of destinies. One or two were executed in the 'thirties on the strange charges in vogue then. Gombojav, for example, was condemned to death for sabotage of the wool factory of which he was sub-manager. Some were imprisoned for long years. Some died, but many survived the vicissitudes of the times and now hold positions of academic or executive responsibility. One is an artist and theatrical director, another a well-known veterinarian, a third a literary historian, a fourth a photographic expert, a fifth a library assistant, and so on. They are a curious vestige of the past, survivals of a short episode when it seemed that Mongolia might develop within the comity of nations instead of in complete reliance on the USSR and in total isolation from the rest of the world. If their technical skill has proved of value, the influence they have been able to exert as products of a broader culture than the Soviet one has been nil in face of the intervening period of totalitarianism and the complete ideological and educational subservience to Russia which ensued.

Up to 1928 there were certain positive signs that Mongolia might be able to evolve into a liberal democracy along lines which were a natural extension of her own unique past rather than, as actually happened, be squeezed into the same mould as Stalin was preparing for Russia. A remark of Dambadorj's at the Seventh Party Congress is significant for the atmosphere of those years:

The elimination of private capital [he said] and the confiscation of the capital of the old feudal nobility and the *jas* of the lamaseries, are absolutely incompatible with the government's policies. The power of our party does not stretch to confronting the old feudal nobility, the rich and the lamas by any other policies than those in force at present – nay more, if the Seventh Party Congress were to suggest the installation of the Khutuktu the delegates would clamour for his installation.[35]

The Central Committee became more and more keen to work actively with the Church and not to estrange it. Nowadays of course, this willingness to compromise is abused on the doctrinaire grounds that the Central Committee was 'following bourgeois-idealistic views' rather than Marxist ideology, and sold the pass by accepting that religion was no obstacle to the modernization of the country, all that was needed being a few reforms. How they would have succeeded had they had time to win the confidence of the Church is one of the profitless speculations of history: in the event they never had the chance. But it must have been plain that if even the mild restrictions of Church privilege which had so far been imposed were sufficient to arouse suspicious mistrust and lead to plots on the part of the high lamas and riots on the part of the rank and file, anything more radical might have a ruinous effect on the nation. This of course was what happened a few years later, and the whole force of the Mongol police and army was insufficient, without Soviet intervention, to put down the insurrection of the people against the People's government. Up to 1928 there were men like Jamtsarano who felt that religion was one of the essential characteristics of an independent state, and they wanted to cherish and preserve the 'precious jewel' of the Buddhist Faith, and so did their best to minimize the contradictions between it and Marxism. Their failure was simply that they took too academic a view of Marxism: on the level of ethics pure Marxism may be compatible with primitive Buddhism, but what Jamtsarano may not have appreciated was that in the jungle of practical politics temporary allies of communism are allies only so long as they serve a purpose. After that they revert to their role of enemies.

It was not an accident that one of the chief proponents of the policy of reform within the Church and of reconciliation between Church and state was the scholar-politician Jamtsarano. With other Buriat nationalists he had, twenty years earlier, been one of the moving spirits in a campaign to revitalize Buriat lamaism according to the principles of primitive Buddhism. A significant step they had taken then was to petition the Tsar to be allowed to change the name of the religion from that of 'Yellow Faith' to 'Buddhism'. Presumably they hoped that this change of name would symbolize both their rejection of the corrupt and superstitious accretions which characterized the now degenerate form of Tibetan lamaism prevalent in Buryatia as in Mongolia, and also their own return to the simple principles enunciated by the Buddha himself. In 1925, at the Fifth Party Congress, Jamtsarano explained himself unequivocally, appearing at the same time as a sincere Buddhist and as a Mongol nationalist. He could still express himself without fear then, but in 1930 he had to recant and deny his principles in an abject self-criticism, and a few years later was done to death in a Soviet concentration camp.

Jamtsarano's 1926 views are of great importance, for, like Dambadorj's in the commercial sphere, they were meant to show up Mongolia as a special case, with problems unique to herself.

In this they complemented aspirations on the part of Church leaders to identify Buddhism with Mongolia and especially with the figure of the Khutuktu, and to play down whatever connected it with Tibet. A well-known theologian of the time, the *chorji* or 'king of the law' Choinzon, had produced a number of pamphlets critical of communism, in which he had begun to refer to Lamaism not as the 'Yellow Faith' or the 'Religion of Tsongkhapa' (the fourteenth-century Tibetan reformer) but as the 'Faith of the Jebtsundamba Lama of the North'. The leftists of 1929 not only rejected Jamtsarano's theories, but maintained that Soviet experience had to be imitated in everything. They were in a position to turn this naïve illusion into practice, and within three years to ruin the country. What Jamtsarano had been saying is summarized in the following extract:

> Seeing that the basic aims of our Party and of Buddhism are both the welfare of the people, there is no conflict between the two of them. They are mutually compatible. It is sheer folly to put on a show of revolutionary bluff and misunderstand this, and to drivel about the Party's doctrine and the Government's policy being contrary to religion. Hence Party and Youth League members ought not to act in this way. *It is a special case that in Russia religion is the opium of the people.* What our lord Buddha taught cannot be equated with aggressive religions like Mohammedanism and Christianity, and though the communist party rejects religion and the priesthood, this has nothing to do with our Buddhist Faith. Our Party wants to see the Buddhist Faith flourishing in a pure form, and approves of lamas who stay in their lamaseries, reciting the scriptures and faithfully observing their vows.[36]

Jamtsarano maintained that it was the Buddha and the Bodhisattvas who would protect humanity, and cited as trustworthy authorities for his opinions not Marx and Lenin but the theologians Nagarjuna, Jobo Atisha and Tsongkhapa.

In a booklet published in 1927 under the title *The Mongol League of Revolutionary Youth and Religion* Jamtsarano came back to the same theme and declared:

> Our People's Party has always cherished the Buddhist Faith. And why? Because the Buddhist Faith and scriptures explore the most intricate subjects radically, they distinguish good and bad. What they teach is very profound, and however it is examined it corresponds

perfectly with science. That is why we truly revere and cherish it. When Buddhism expanded in Mongolia, the minds of our people, which were dull and backward, were for the first time awakened. They abandoned their savage customs, became gentle and peaceful, learned to distinguish black and white, virtue and vice, and acquired culture, and so appreciated the value of Buddhism. What a good thing it would be if the members of our Party and League were to acquire a proper understanding, to the best of their ability, of the qualities and teaching of the Buddhist Faith, and, in their criticism of matters of religion, were able to distinguish right and wrong, without groping about as if blind.[37]

Jamtsarano was not theorizing in vacuo. Many high lamas were anxious to reform and strip down Buddhism to its pure essentials, and political leaders like Dambadorj rationalized their support of this movement by saying that Buddhism was too deeply engrained in the people to be eradicated overnight. Rather the government should aim to weaken the influence of the lamas by supporting a return to the teachings of the Buddha, which rejected property and wealth, ceremonial and worldly power. Slogans such as 'Let us promote Religion and the State' were bandied about. From 1926 onwards the 'Pure Buddhism' or 'Renewal' movement began to gather impetus. Pamphlets were published calling on the Party and the League to become reconciled with the Church and to work with it, atheistic propaganda work amongst the public was relaxed or called off, and attempts were made to have Buddhism taught in the state schools. At the end of 1928 Jamtsarano and Dambadorj and other 'rightists' organized the first meeting of a special commission for the improvement of religious affairs, at which it was resolved to call for the teaching of the main principles of Buddhism and the history of the rise and diffusion of Buddhism in the schools, and for the suppression of propaganda aimed at vilifying the manner of life of Church leaders. All this was condemned by the Seventh Party Congress and the 'rightists' expelled from office. The Eighth Congress in 1930 turned its attention specifically to the renewal movement and to those high lamas who were directing it in collusion with 'nationalist, pan-Mongolist' elements such as Jamtsarano. It noted that the renewal movement was intended to clean up the lamaseries and adapt the lamas to the 'new state of social relationships'. While the movement tried to fit in with the policies of the People's government, its very enlightenment meant that it attracted the ordinary people and lamas to it, hindering the Party's work of exacerbating the class struggle within the Church. The congress declared: 'Hence this is an ideological force of greater, not less, influence than the old reactionary lamas'[38] and urged the authorities to step up the ideological struggle with its supporters. Between 1928 and 1930 the Party had swung to a position diametrically opposed to that expounded by Jamtsarano in 1926.

In all respects then, 1928 marks a definite watershed in the history of revolutionary Mongolia. By then certain irreversible changes had taken place which were essential for her development as a modern community. Theocratic monarchy had given way to a republican form of government based on the elective principle. The monopoly of the nobility in local affairs had been broken, though its economic power had not been noticeably reduced. Some schools had been set up, open in theory to all, though denial of education was soon to be used as a weapon of class warfare. First steps had been taken to introduce western medicine, though the badly needed Swedish missionaries were to be expelled soon along with all other foreigners. A Committee of Sciences supervised research in all fields. A national bank and a national currency had been instituted. Mongolia had a postal service and although she was not a member of the International Postal Union, letters were sent safely to, and received from, foreign countries. A few small factories were already in existence, including for example a much needed brick works built by a Swiss specialist. A German geologist was prospecting for mineral resources. But at the Seventh Party Congress the Comintern and the Soviet Communist Party, whose authority had till then been a doubtful quantity, demonstrated their ability to direct Mongol politics by engineering, in conjunction with the so-called 'country opposition', the left wing of the Party, the downfall and disgrace of Dambadorj, and the complete reversal of the gradualist policies followed up till then. This victory directed Mongolia along the Stalinist path to communism. All foreign contacts except with the USSR were ruptured and Mongolia's economy was linked exclusively with that of the USSR. She now entered a period of total isolation from the world which lasted till well after the Second World War. Though she maintained her identity as a separate state, the course which her history took during those years, especially during the 1930s, shows such crass similarities, both overall and in detail, with that of the USSR, that it is hard to credit that she was capable at that time of maintaining her independence of action.

CHAPTER 7

THE SOCIALIST FIASCO, 1929-32

The Seventh Party Congress

In late 1928 Mongolia did not present the picture of a country engaged in fundamental revolution. The confiscation of feudal property had been proclaimed as a matter of policy between 1921 and 1924, but nothing had been done to implement this declaration. The old cattle-owning nobility and the Church continued to flourish, and lent their support to the Party and the Government, in which they still played an influential part, in spite of the Party purge of 1924. By 1927 some six hundred members of the nobility, over two hundred entrepreneurs, and over one hundred lamas had found their way back into the ranks of the Party. The Fifth Party Congress of 1926 has piously repeated the slogans and resolution of the Third, re-affirming the Party's determination to overcome resistance on the part of the Church to its policies, but nothing effective was done. Mongolia was in fact making steady economic and social progress, not in the direction of communism, but along the divergent road of free enterprise. The State was not systematically interfering in normal commercial transactions, though Chinese merchants had been complaining continually since 1921 of chicanerie and discriminatory treatment. What figures we have for the year 1926 show that Mongolia's external trade was still to an overwhelming extent with countries other than the USSR. Only 15 per cent of her imports came from that country, and only 20 per cent of her exports were sent there. On the home market a similar situation prevailed. Of the 1,700 shops said to be active in Mongolia, over 1,450 were Chinese, while there were also eighty-one shops run by English, American, German and Russian companies. Nearly three-quarters of retail turnover was in the hands of foreign firms. The remainder was accounted for in almost equal proportions by the Mongolian Central Co-operative and by

Soviet state organs. Internal transport was still in private hands, and there were some seven hundred privately-run petty handicraft shops functioning. Foreign specialists from western Europe were setting up small factories and power stations. A German firm had developed the first Mongol typewriter, successfully solving the problem of a vertical script running in lines from left to right by having the carriage travel in the direction opposite to the normal one. The first Mongol atlas had been designed and printed in Germany. A German firm manufactured Mongolia's first military medals. Mongolia was still open to enterprising foreigners who wanted to come in and set up their own businesses. It was at this time, for instance, that a group of Scandinavians, including the well-known author Henning Haslund, was able to set up in north Mongolia what promised to be a profitable and up-to-date trading post and farm. For a short while the Swedish YMCA was able to run a school and hospital in Urga, before both were closed at Soviet instigation and the missionaries expelled.

All this represented a falling-off from the socialist principles expressed at the Third Party Congress and in the 1924 constitution, and though to a very considerable degree a private enterprise economy and integration in world trade rather than a one-sided reliance on the Soviet economy corresponded to the stage Mongolia's economy had reached and to her real interests at the time, it was inevitable that a left wing reaction should grow up amongst those with more extreme views. This opposition is generally known as the 'country' opposition, since its mass strength was derived from party members in the provinces, and it was responsible for the basic error, as communist apologists see it, of considering that Mongolia was ready to be a socialist country just like the USSR instead of, as it was to be dubbed in 1932, a 'bourgeois democracy of a new type'.

The country opposition remains an anonymous group, nor is it easy to define even who its leaders were at the source of power, that is, in the Central Committee of the Party. The suggestion has been made that even as early as this it was in Choibalsang's hands that the direction of the country opposition lay, but to accept this proposition would be to anticipate by several years his rise to political pre-eminence. The legend of Choibalsang as the father of the revolution and the counterpart in Mongolia to the omniscient genius of Stalin in the USSR, was the creation of later years, when the part he had played in the revolution was grossly exaggerated, and that played by others correspondingly played down, under the pernicious influence of the cult of personality. In later years, particularly after 1940, it became *de rigueur* to regard Choibalsang as Sukebator's sole heir, just as in Russia Stalin had to be adulated as the chosen one upon whom Lenin's mantle had fallen. However, what few Soviet and Mongol reports we have actually from the 'twenties and early 'thirties do not mention Choibalsang at all as a figure of exceptional contemporary importance. Now that the incense of the cult of personality has drifted away, the more up-to-date studies by Mongolian scholars once again lay no special stress on Choibalsang's share in events around the year 1930. The inflated reputation manufactured for him retrospectively has been cut down to size again, and he is shown not to have been, at that time, a front-rank man. Even Zlatkin's book, written at the height of the Stalin cult in 1950, does not cite Choibalsang specifically as the leader of the country opposition, and from what we know of Choibalsang's career from other sources it would seem wise to accept this omission at its face value, since any other interpretation of Zlatkin's account would involve us in more ingenious and less plausible reasoning. It would be necessary to suggest that he had perhaps deliberately disociated Choibalsang's name from the swing to the left of late 1928 and after because the results of that swing were to turn out so disastrously and were to be decisively condemned by the Central Committee itself a few years later.

The fact that Choibalsang's speeches and writings up to about 1934 form an insignificant proportion of his collected works, and that his intervention at the Seventh Party Congress is contained in less than two pages of text, is a further, if indirect, measure of his relative unimportance at the time. But though he was not the sole leader of the opposition, we know that Choibalsang did support the swing to the left, and that he favoured total alliance with the USSR. In his speech to the Seventh Party Congress he acknowledged that it was only thanks to the guidance of the Comintern and to the Soviet alliance that Mongolia had maintained her independence. 'We shall never be able to set up mutual relations with any other country as we have with the USSR,' he said, 'and in political matters we have no other close friend but the USSR.'[1] This was a stark contrast to Dambadorj's fears, which he expressed at the same time, about Soviet imperialism. Moreover, during the whole of the period of leftist deviation, Choibalsang was active as an executor of the Party's policies. He headed the commission which organized the expropriation of the property of the nobility in 1929, and the extermination of a good many of the nobles, and in early 1931 he was appointed Minister of Livestock and Agriculture so that for more than a year he had executive responsibility for the continuing policy of confiscation and collectivization laid down by the Eighth Party Congress of 1930, which he had also helped to formulate.

By the middle of 1932 Choibalsang begins to be presented in a new light, as a critic of extremism. He is supposed to have been one of those few members of the Central Committee who, even if belatedly, expressed doubts about the wisdom of blindly following 'Soviet experience' in every aspect of the Party's work, Mongolia not have progressed so far along the road to socialism as had been imagined. This may be part of his legend. So far there is no positive record available of his having declared himself in this sense, and as far as we can tell it was a later rival and victim of his, Dovchin (1895–1939), who first dared put into words, at a Party meeting in April 1932, what many had been thinking, though at that time he could not get his views accepted.

When in the middle of 1932 the New Turn Policy replaced the extremism of the preceding years, Choibalsang was one of those party leaders charged with the executive task of seeing that this policy was understood by the ordinary people in the provinces, and that it was put into effect. That a man who had been a prominent leftist should figure in a contrary role need not surprise us. Choibalsang's experience was not a unique one. Mongolia had too little talent at that time to be able to waste much of it in spectacular purges: it was not till the years of Choibalsang's own dictatorship that common sense in this respect was to go down in front of hysteria, and statesmen, soldiers and intellectuals were to be ruthlessly wiped out. But, once again, in 1932 Choibalsang's task was not quite a top one. He had the job of supervising the correction of blunders in South Gobi aimak. There had been a fair measure of disaffection and violence in this province. Apathy towards collectivization had turned into direct mass protest in the form of large-scale emigration and partisan warfare, but South Gobi, though sensitive as a frontier district, was well removed from the storm-centre of civil war which in the early summer of 1932 was raging in the north and west, especially in Khuvsugul, Uvs, Zavkhan and North Khangai aimaks.

If it was not Choibalsang, then who did lead the country opposition of 1928 and the subsequent left extremism? There is no satisfactory answer to this question, and this is only one aspect of the frustration one is continually conscious of in trying to re-create a psychologically acceptable pattern of events in Mongolia at the time. This frustration springs, to a great extent, from the failure of Mongolian and Russian historians to treat the history of the country in anything but impersonal terms – apart of course from the falsification of facts mentioned previously. They interpret history almost exclusively as the result of the dialectic interplay of abstract movements and tendencies, in which the personalities and ambitions of individual actors are suppressed as of little account. Historiography of this type displays the paradox that during a period of the cult of personality, personality is the most neglected of all historical factors. The figure of the leader is inflated to superhuman proportions. Conversely, others are presented, like Trotsky as the personification of all evil, or they are relegated to the neutral, supporting role of mere supernumeraries, or they are totally ignored, especially if the part they played cannot be easily adapted to the form the official mythology has taken. Men become stereotypes: in Mongolia, Choibalsang's enemies, men who like him had been revolutionaries from their early twenties, turn into agents of Japanese imperialism, Trotskyists and Fascists. Their real accomplishments are suppressed and false histories of treachery invented to substantiate the tags applied to their names. A barren and mechanical type of historical writing results from all this. Zlatkin's book, as we have noted, manages to suppress all reference to men of the calibre and importance of Jamtsarano, Rinchino or Losol, though an appreciation of Jamtsarano's complex personality, as a Buriat and a Mongol nationalist, as a scholar and collector of folklore, as a Buddhist reformer and purist, and only then a revolutionary, is essential to the understanding of one of the main currents of Mongol life in the early years of the revolution. Likewise, Zlatkin's chapter on the leftist deviation avoids revealing who the leaders of this movement were.

The result of this depersonalization of history is that Mongolia's story is made to appear simple and straightforward, but so deprived of vitality, variety and complexity as to defy credibility.

To some extent the most recent Mongol publications correct this tendency. It is possible once more to discern names as well as movements in history, but the personalities of the late 'twenties are still not put across in a convincing manner. It is impossible to visualize, in most cases, the men behind the names. They flit across the stage, like shadows in an eastern puppet play, distinct in two-dimensional outline, but lacking all substance. The inconsistencies and imperfections which constitute the normal being have been so fined down that men appear as little more than personification of single qualities or of the movement and factions to which they are supposed to have belonged. They tend to fall into two categories. There are positive figures, without a flaw in their revolutionary make-up, who contrast with the enemies of the revolution, unrelieved in their turpitude. Sometimes the inadequacies which led to a man's tragic downfall are suggested, as is the case with Bodo, who is said to have been attracted into the counter-revolutionary camp by resentment at losing his post as premier, but such recognition of human motivation is all too rare.

With minor figures the consequences of this formalization of history are not too grave. A typical instance occurs in the recent revival of interest in a young girl named Bor, who was a party propagandist in South Gobi at the time of the leftist deviation, and who, with six companions, was captured and done to death in the most brutal manner by some armed *émigrés* who had slipped back over the frontier on one of their periodic sabotage raids. Bor, who was only nineteen at the time of her death, has been, as it were, canonized as the embodiment of superhuman courage and the singleness of purpose of the ideal revolutionary. She is said to have died shouting: 'Long live the Party, the Government and the League of Revolutionary Youth!' Nothing daunted her, no flaw mars her memory. Whether she was a woman of sensitivity and courage, or a mere fanatic, is not known, and is really by now irrelevant. Her part is to be the centre of a legend. Her story is a tragedy and a real one, for the friends who set out to rescue her were infirm of purpose. They were deterred from the pursuit by rumours that the enemy was well armed, while they themselves had only one old rifle. Later it turned out that the raiders had had only a single flintlock. The stylization of this tragedy is a necessary part of Mongolia's mythology. Rationally unconvincing, it is comprehensible as the personalization of the epic of the revolution as seen by its contemporaries, and as they wish to hand on its memory to the new generation, who never knew the revolution itself, and have been born into a relatively comfortable and settled existence.

Much more serious is the neglect, or the facile manipulation, of the part played by individuals who were at one time or another in leading positions. We know, for example, that after the leftist deviation had come to an end, one of the chief exponents of the New Turn Policy which followed it was the newly-appointed premier Gendung, who later fell foul of Choibalsang and the Party for swerving once more too far to the right, for trying to reduce the Party to the position of adviser rather than guide, and for advocating a break away from Soviet tutelage. Gendung was later shot as a Japanese spy whose treasonable activities stretched back as far as 1932. But Gendung did not suddenly emerge from obscurity, nor was he the leader of some now successful opposition group, in 1932. He had in fact been one of the most active leftist leaders, and is mentioned as such in Sambuu's autobiography, along with other extremists, such as Shijee and Badrakh. Gendung had been a member of the secretariat of the Central Committee, and had been responsible for running the campaign for the expropriation of the property of the nobles, and the liquidation of the nobles themselves, in North Khangai aimak, soon to be one of the hottest beds of disaffection. Sambuu took his orders from Gendung when carrying out his share of the campaign. How did Gendung manage to change horses in mid-stream in June 1932, and not fall into the same obscurity as other leftists, among them Shijee and Badrakh? Sambuu offers us an explanation which is too jejune to merit serious consideration. He writes: 'At the end of June 1932 ... most of the men who had been in the Central Committee of the Party were removed, but Gendung, who had been responsible for the most serious deviations, *made use of a trick*, and remained.'[2]

There was certainly a purge of some leftists in 1932, but equally certainly many of those who had approved of and collaborated in, the policies of confiscation and forcible collectivization, not only Gendung, but also men like Choibalsang and Sambuu himself, survived politically, trimmed their sails, and adapted themselves to the new and contrary line determined for the Mongols by the Comintern and the Soviet communist party. That this should happen is not inherently improbable. That it has not been commented on before is due partly to the scarcity of information about individual revolutionaries, partly also to what one might term the 'hypnosis of terminology'. The modern history of Mongolia has been so rigidly systematized, and phrases like 'general line of the Party', 'rightist opportunist capitulation', 'leftist deviation' and so on have been bandied about so freely, that they have come to be accepted at their face value and Mongolian history interpreted as if these rationalizations offered a complete and honest analysis. Without asking who made up these various groups, or embodied the tendencies they betrayed, one has come to consider them as independent entities, each with a tidy personnel of protagonists. In actual fact the so-called leftist deviationists do not seem to have constituted a clearly defined bloc, faced by an opposition which defeated and replaced them, at all. The whole party leadership, as other evidence too indicates, was, with insignificant exceptions, behind this mistaken policy. The leftists were not a faction, but to all intents and purposes they were the whole of the Central Committee backing a course of action which had run away with them, and, as Vasiliev had advised in the case of Danzan in 1924, some men had to be ditched so as not to jeopardize the whole crew. What happened in 1932 was that a reshuffle of posts took place among those men who had been active throughout the period of leftist deviation, but who were too valuable, or too acute, to be dropped from public life. Thus Sambuu moved from being head of the administration of South Gobi to the post of Minister of Livestock and Agriculture, while Gendung now became Premier. Some comrades were eliminated.

What is, however, very remarkable about the success of the country opposition at the Seventh Party Congress is that the swing to the left was, if we may accept literally a statement by Sambuu in a book he published in 1961 on the question of religion, planned and directed from outside Mongolia, that is, by the Comintern. Sambuu writes: 'With the intention of correcting the erroneous policies of the rightists, and putting them on the correct path, the Executive Committee of the Comintern dispatched B. Shmeral and other representatives.'[3] Shmeral was a Czech. The others were Macdonald, an American communist, and the Buriat Amagaev. It was these men who, according to Sambuu, exposed the errors of the rightists in the Party, that is, of the then majority, at a plenary meeting of the Central Committee, after which the Seventh Party Congress confirmed the defeat of the rightists.

Sambuu's summary of Shmeral's intervention at the Congress itself, as given in his autobiography, does not add anything to his earlier account. Here he writes: 'Comrade Shmeral and the other representatives from the Executive Committee of the Comintern took part in the congress and assisted in exposing the errors of the rightists in the Party and in preserving the General Line of the Party.'[4] In other words, the swing to the left was not altogether decided on by the Mongols themselves. There is unfortunately as little documentation to trace the actual course of Shmeral's intervention as there is to illustrate the extent of the part played by the USSR in the succession of events in the collectivization campaign in the next few years. A few texts from among Shmeral's papers which have been published show him as superficially doing nothing more than patiently analyse the faults of the Central Committee in particular their neglect of advice offered them earlier on several occasions by the Comintern. But he made no secret of what the Mongols were going to have to do:

> You must discuss and analyse in a calm atmosphere the course taken by the Party during the past seven or eight years, make bold criticism of the errors committed by leading comrades, and honestly recognize your errors. . . . The coming congress is of enormous historical importance. Important and complex tasks concerning the activities of the Party and government face it, in particular the strengthening of the tight bonds with the Comintern, the elaboration of measures for the struggle against foreign imperialism, for the upsurge of the activity of the masses of herdsmen, and their participation in political life.[5]

Shmeral can be seen indicating to the Mongols, from a position of evident and confident authority, certain lines of action which were soon to be taken up, and which were simultaneously being introduced, by other Soviet agents, in Tannu Tuva. That Shmeral's intervention was so effective suggests that he was backed by Stalin to an extent which his predecessors had not been. The steps he suggested, in particular the mobilization of the herdsmen as the vanguard of political activity were, when exaggerated and distorted as they were, to endanger the whole political and economic stability of Mongolia. The leftist campaign, in its day-to-day management, will have been in Mongol hands, but the USSR must bear the responsibility of having sponsored and pushed it, and let it run for more than three disastrous years, during which a number of leading Mongols became aware of the mistakes being made, but were powerless to voice their concern for fear of being dealt with as rightist opportunists and counter-revolutionaries.

Though they recognize that it was the USSR's 'development of socialist construction and the reorganization of its rural economy in a socialist manner on the basis of heavy industry, thus demonstrating to the whole world the immeasurable superiority of the socialist world to the capitalist world which provided a suitable opportunity to deepen the anti-feudal, anti-imperialist revolution in Mongolia',[6] Mongolian historians are inclined to treat the events of 1929 to 1932 as if they had occurred in isolation from what was happening elsewhere, as a product of factors peculiar to Mongolia. Certain reasoning is put forward to account for the excesses and distortions of the 1924 Party Line which occurred and which characterize these years. Basically what was supposed to have happened was that the Party, especially at the Eighth Congress in 1930, had misjudged the position and its own capacities. It had considered that Mongolia had accomplished the destruction of feudalism and had reached the stage where it could begin building socialism. At the same time it ignored the Leninist principle, which should equally have commended itself to it as a matter of common sense, that the peculiar conditions of each country should be taken into account in evolving a policy. It failed to recognize that its situation differed radically from that of the USSR, which had a numerous working class, a strong communist party, and other theoretical requisites for effecting the transition to socialism, and it perpetrated, and continued to perpetrate in the face of experience, the error of trying to copy Soviet experience mechanically and totally. Thirdly, the personnel of the Party was inadequate for the problems it had set itself. Most of the leadership was leftist anyway, and the rank and file, especially after the purges of 1929 had excluded all those of slightly higher social origin, was ignorant of politics and of everything else except how to herd cattle. The Party was packed with what are described as 'non-class' elements who had no liking at all for their role. No attention was paid to the quality of new members. Quantity was the watchword, and as long as recruits satisfied the standards of social origin, measured in terms of the number of beasts they owned, they were simply drafted into the Party. They did no good as members, and when things went wrong they deserted just as easily as they had joined, and went over to the rebels. In two years thirty thousand members were enlisted, quadrupling the size of the Party. Most of them were compelled to join. One member, at his release from the Party in the 1932 purge, confessed of himself: 'I never wanted to be a party member, but they forced me into it. They said party members would get special perquisites over ordinary people, but now we don't get these any more so I want to get out of the Party.'[7] Finally, excessive enthusiasm on the part of inexperienced party members, who overrated the original successes of the collectivization, and raced ahead of the Party's directives on their own responsibility, is also blamed.

In some ways this analysis may appear formalistic, and may appear to obscure the truth with jargon, but there is undoubtedly a great deal to be said for it. Nevertheless, it does not go deeply enough into the matter, and leaves the impression of being more a rationalization than an explanation. The problem to be solved is not only why these excesses and idiocies occurred at all, but why they occurred just when they did, that is, when similar policies were being pursued in Stalin's Russia and when precisely the same extravagant developments, with the same ruinous results, are to be observed taking place in Tannu Tuva. The time has not yet come when it will be possible to answer this question without reserve, and meanwhile opinions continue to vary. A German scholar, Otto Maenchen-Helfen, who was director of the Sociological-Ethnological Section of the Marx-Engels Institute in Moscow, and who was in Tuva in 1929, describes the party purge and the confiscation of private property there as having been carried out by a commission of five Tuvan students who had been specially trained at the Communist University of the Toilers of the East. He states quite unequivocally that the swing to the left in Tuva was ordered by Moscow, and was carried out under threat of military intervention. According to him, it was Moscow which ran Tuva, through the Comintern representative there. The local Party was a nullity. Though he did not visit Mongolia, Maenchen-Helfen suggested, on the basis of his Tuvan experience, that the Russians forced through the party purge and the adoption of a leftist policy there by similar threats. There is no real documentation that would let us judge how far this might be true. But the course which the Mongol revolution now took – confiscation of property, collectivization, establishment of state farms, violent destruction of religious life, imprisonment of intellectuals, often without trial, herding of lamas into concentration camps, and so on, together with the unilateral association of the Mongolian economy with that of the USSR, which now monopolized Mongolia's foreign trade, indicates that Stalin's Russia was making its writ run in Mongolia to a far greater extent than before 1928. That things went so disastrously wrong, even more so than in the USSR so that a total retreat had to be beaten, is possibly due, as the Mongols admit, to local incompetence and the arrogant ineptitude of the Party. The convenient tag of 'leftist deviation' covers a period characterized by an almost unimaginable display of panic, obtuseness and incompetence. Events took charge to such an extent that the Comintern which had set the Mongols on their leftist course in 1928 had to rescue them from it, in collaboration with the Soviet communist party, in 1932. The mere fact that it was a foreign body which was the decisive factor at these two critical turning points of Mongol history – the abandonment of private enterprise and world contacts for a totalitarian economy and economic integration with the USSR, and the rejection by the Central Committee in 1932 of all it had stood for since its election in 1928 – is one of great significance for the assessment of Mongolia's actual status at the time.

The revolution turns left

After the Seventh Party Congress had been held, the Party first turned its attention to the task of the extermination, as a class, of the feudal nobility. The nobles were less coherent, and less numerous, than the Church, which still presented a formidable front. Less rich than the clergy, and less organized, they offered an easier target. In the autumn of 1929 a special commission was set up under Choibalsang to attend to the confiscation of property belonging to the nobles. Figures vary, according to the source from which they are taken, as to the number of estates which were taken over from their owners: some inconsistencies may be due to the fact that some estates were plundered twice over, the number of head of cattle which a noble might retain for his support having been drastically reduced in the meantime. The lowest estimate is that in the period from 1929 to 1932 the property of 1,136 households was confiscated, 555 of them in 1929 and 1930 and 581 in the following two years. Zlatkin gives a higher total: 669 estates dealt with in 1929, and 837 in 1930 and 1931. He does not mention 1932. The property of some noble lamas was taken over in these operations: according to the lower estimate, 114 estates, according to the higher 205. Again, according to Zlatkin, the campaign undertaken in 1930 and 1931 involved, in the suave language of the time, 711 estate owners being 'called to account, or removed from their original place of residence, for having offered resistance, by legal or administrative process'.[8] The discrepancies in the figures are not important. What was of importance was that not only did the Mongol Government provide itself in this way with an initial stock of beasts to distribute first of all to poor herdsmen, but very soon to hastily set up collective farms where most of them soon perished from lack of attention, but that it had finally annihilated, not only as a class but in the person of many of the individual members of that class, the old Mongol nobility. The leftist deviation was condemned in 1932 as erroneous, but it was only the excesses which were condemned, as being the result of the application of policies temporarily unsuitable. The policies themselves were not disowned, and it must be appreciated that the leftist deviation was responsible for certain irrevocable changes in the composition of Mongol society which were actually desired by the Party and which could not have been brought about by other means.

It would be unprofitable to speculate on what might have happened in Mongolia if it had been possible to keep the extreme left out of power, but had it been, the Seventh Congress's proposals for action might well have speeded up the collapse of the Church as a factor of economic importance without disrupting society and state, without estranging the people from the revolution and provoking them in their despair to rebel, to slaughter or abandon their herds, or, where they could, to migrate across the frontiers. The so-called *jas*-campaign, for example, had as its object to effect the transfer of lamasery herds to the common people, not by way of confiscation, but by forcing the lamaseries to farm out their animals to a much greater extent than before, under properly drawn-up contracts which would provide for the payment of cash wages to those herdsmen who took the animals over. In actual fact, over two million head were transferred while the campaign ran, out of a possible three million, and though the campaign collapsed in confusion and disorder, and thousands of beasts perished through lack of care, such transfers turned out to be to a considerable degree final and irreversible. Only rather less than 300,000 head of cattle were given back to the lamaseries in 1932 under the New Turn Policy. Other pertinent reforms were decreed. The Church was finally forbidden to engage in usury, and its private ownership of land was abolished, together with the practice of compelling the common people to till church farms as a feudal duty. Heavier taxes were imposed on the *jas*-funds, on a sliding scale. A big *jas* would pay more, *pro rata*, than a small one. This of course led to the lamaseries practising tax-evasion. A large *jas* would be split up into several small ones so as to come under the lowest tax rates, animals were converted into fixed assets, which were for the time being left untaxed, and in some cases animals were simply slaughtered to reduce their numbers. Nevertheless, the Church did at last begin to contribute something of consequence to the state budget. A special tax was imposed on lamas of military age who did not become secularized, while those who left the clerical life were allotted animals for their upkeep, which were taken from the *jas*-funds, were given the chance of some education, and were freed from liability for military service for three years so that they might set themselves up properly in their new life. Most lamas who abandoned their lamaseries in these years were in fact forced to do so, but there was a small number who left the religious life voluntarily and never returned. The regulations forbidding children under eighteen to become lamas were enforced rather more strictly, and evasions, which had been the rule, now became less common.

Collectivization and the leftist deviation

The extremism of 1929 to 1932 manifested itself in every aspect of life, but particularly in the collectivization of cattle-herding, the unplanned and unprepared nationalization of other forms of private enterprise, especially transport and retail distribution, and in the brutal and indiscriminate assault upon all lamas as a homogeneous class of enemies of the revolution. 'Leftism' began in 1929, soon after the Seventh Party Congress, and was confirmed as a correct course of action by the Eighth Congress which met in the spring of 1930 and which, packed with extremist delegates by the leftist leaders who were now in the saddle, failed to recognize that anything was going wrong in Mongolia, approved the current trend of developments, and elaborated a hopelessly ambitious five-year plan.

Ignoring Mongolia's lack of capital and of experienced managers, technicians, skilled workers and teachers, and of an organized labour force of any sort, the planners decided to push ahead with a comprehensive crash programme of education, medicine, industry and railway building, as well as the complete modernization and collectivization of animal herding. At the same time as they were elaborating schemes which were in themselves far beyond Mongolia's capacities, they were assiduously ruining the mainstay of her economy, herding, by upsetting traditional ways of life and production without substituting anything better. Their utopian plan relied for its implementation on massive Soviet help, which never materialized, which was perhaps never even promised and which Mongolia certainly could not have digested. The five-year plan airily expressed the 'deep hope' that the USSR would generously offer assistance in the form of technical advice, tools and machines, seeds, pedigree breeding stock, and instructors, to help Mongolia effect the transformation of its economy. It was hoped to send students to profit by Soviet instruction in schools, industries, state enterprises and collective farms, and all this at a time when the USSR was undergoing the colossal upheaval of Stalin's collectivization drive. The Mongol five-year plan was written off in total disorder, and when, after the Second World War, the Mongolian economy was once again considered ripe for planning in five-year units, the plan of 1931 was ignored altogether, and series-numbering began again, in 1948, from one.

A conference of the Central Committee held at the end of 1930 did not do anything to correct the disaster course Mongolia was now set on. Enthusiasm for collectivization and the extirpation of religion seems to have blinded the Party to such an extent that it could lay down principles of action which it was simultaneously and exuberantly failing to observe. Thus at the same time as party officials all over the country were taking power out of the hands of government officials, and indulging in a wild spree of desecration of lamaseries, putting out the eyes of Buddha statues, distributing sacred vessels and vestments to the ordinary herdsmen as private property, taxing lamas indiscriminately, rich and poor, in such an arbitrary fashion that many of the poorest were reduced to selling the clothes they wore to pay the exactions, the Eighth Congress could solemnly declare that it was its policy to split the clergy by favouring the poor lamas, to bring these over to the side of the revolution by distributing cattle to them, and to give them help to establish themselves in civil life after voluntary secularization.

The distinctions drawn by the Central Committee, such as that between rich and poor lamas, or that between poor, middle and rich herdsmen and the feudal nobility, were probably too fine for the party activists on the spot to appreciate. It was now declared policy to mobilize the poorest elements of the population as the basic support of the Party and the revolution, discarding even well-to-do herdsmen who had never belonged to the nobility. Sambuu, whose autobiography opens up one of the most original perspectives we have on the events of these years, which he describes from the point of view of one who took part in them, explains what happened. Most accounts of the period skirt glibly round the obtuseness of a party which could create such a situation, in such typically neutral phraseology as 'The fact that our new young Party was lacking in proletarian ideology and political hardening and experience contributed not a little to the occurrence of such errors' but Sambuu is more direct and down to earth. The party organizations, he says, were packed with the poorest herdsmen, who, newly promoted to organizational responsibility, were completely bewildered by the practical tasks which confronted them. They were uneducated and illiterate, so that try as they might they could make nothing of the special courses of instruction they were hastily put through, and they were scared to death that anything they did might get them into trouble later as 'rightist opportunism' or 'leftist deviation'. They lost their heads and made a thorough mess of their jobs.[9]

If the local party organizations demonstrated the ineptitude of the masses when charged with unwanted responsibility, the Central Committee must take the blame for permitting the disasters of the leftist deviation. There has been a tendency to try and shift this responsibility from the shoulders of the Central Committee on to those of local officials. This excuse seems to have been officially formulated for the first time at a joint meeting of Party, Control Commission and Youth League leaders which met to consider the shortcomings of party policy in May 1932, after the revolts in the west had broken out, but before the Comintern's directive was received. This meeting resolved that 'the work put in hand from the time of the Eighth Party Congress onwards was fundamentally correct, but that shortcomings had arisen in the work of leading men in local organizations and some leaders at the centre.'[10] The responsibility for continuing to insist, even at this late date, that the Party's line was the correct one, and that such errors and deviations as had occurred were merely due to shortcomings on the part of local organizations, is laid at the door of extremists such as Gendung and Badrakh, while Choibalsang and Eldevochir are credited with being among the first to realize that the Party was altogether off course. But only after Russian intervention the following month was it publicly admitted that it was the Central Committee and the Party as a whole which had been to blame, and the complete presidium and secretariat of the Central Committee were replaced as having been incapable of carrying out a policy 'suited to the life, culture and economy of Mongolia'.

The obstinacy of the Central Committee in refusing to recognize that it was itself the main exponent of the leftism it affected to reject, delayed national recovery. Even while promoting extreme action, the Eighth Congress declared that it must 'lay equal stress upon opposing the extremes of both right and left'. But at the same time the party leadership recognized the existence of only two lines within the Party in 1930: one was the line of the rightists, the other the correct line of the whole Party. It accepted in theory that there was a danger from the left, but left no scope for the identification of leftists. It fulminated against those party members who failed to use their brains in interpreting their instructions and who substituted a bullying authoritarianism for the appreciation and manipulation of public sentiment. But what the Central Committee refused to admit was that those party members who were behaving in this outrageous way were in fact the majority, and that they were acting in the full confidence that what they were doing represented the execution of the General Line of the Party and enjoyed the full support of the Central Committee. The central party authorities were certainly not out of touch with what was happening in the provinces, nor were they unable to control their servants. There is unmistakable evidence of this. For one thing, when the Comintern directive was received in June there was to be little difficulty in calling provincial extremists to heel. One must assume either that the Central Committee failed to recognize that what was happening all round it amounted in fact to what it was condemning in theory, or else, as is more likely, that its protestations were not meant too seriously, that it was quite content to watch the dictatorship of the proletariat in action, and that it was prepared to turn a blind eye to excess and illegality, even where material loss was caused, as long as what the extremists were doing seemed for the time being to be furthering the advance of the revolution in the wake of the USSR.

What happened in South Gobi aimak illustrates the untenability of the excuse that it was local extremists who betrayed the purpose of the Central Committee and the Party Congresses by going too far. South Gobi was a province with a sparse and scattered population, more than usually exposed to the vagaries of Mongolia's hard and unpredictable climate. The local administration had used this as a pretext to avoid whipping up a campaign for complete collectivization. They preferred instead to concentrate on getting the herdsmen to co-ordinate their labour at a low level of organization – to do in fact what the Seventh Party Congress had intended, and band together to carry out regular tasks such as tending the beasts, digging and repairing wells, cutting hay, and so on, and to rationalize the use of their draught animals. The collectivization of livestock was not enforced or encouraged. The provincial authorities were in continual trouble with the Central Committee for their alleged dilatoriness in enforcing collectivization, and finally the Party and the Youth League got together and took matters into their own hands. They usurped the functions of the local government and browbeat the herdsmen into joining collectives. Though many of these went through the motions of joining, under compulsion, they never took part in the word of the mushroom collectives, and many of them simply vanished over the frontier into China as and when they could.

The idea that Mongolia, like Russia, had reached the take-off point for the complete realization of socialism was a fundamental misreading of the situation. If the Mongols were acting freely and not under external pressure in making this assessment and acting upon it, then they condemn themselves as political incompetents, rigidly applying theory to a set of totally inappropriate circumstances. The real danger to Mongolia lay, not as was feared in the recrudescence of 'rightism' by which was meant the private enterprise economy of before 1928, but rather in the uninhibited imitation, in an underdeveloped society, of what was happening in Russia under Stalin's iron purpose. Mongolia lacked every prerequisite for the steps she was now to take. There was no material basis, no trained managers, technicians or teachers and the people as a whole did not want collectivization, they did not want to see their familiar and cherished lamaseries dismantled, the precious objects in them smashed or desecrated, the lamas they respected reviled and beggared. The Party was following a course dictated to it by developments in Russia. But, once they had committed themselves, even if not unwillingly, to alignment with the USSR as they did at the Seventh Party Congress, it is difficult to see how the Mongols could have done anything else but go along with the irresistible revolutionary wave which was sweeping through the communist world of which Mongolia formed a tiny, backward and insignificant part. From 1929 Mongolia was obliged to the USSR for all foreign trade, for military supplies and training, for higher education facilities, medical help and so on. It is no wonder that she accepted Soviet ideological tutelage too, and began to adapt her social organization as far as possible to suit the Soviet mould, or that in doing so without a competent leadership, a disciplined rank and file of officials, or a viable objective, she soon got hopelessly out of her depth.

From the beginning party policy in and after 1929 came up against the apathy and then the active antipathy of the people. The confiscation of the property of the nobility, for example, was not carried out on a wave of popular enthusiasm, but was planned and executed over the heads of the people. The Central Committee issued an order concerning the matter, and then sent out a number of special commissioners charged with enforcing the confiscation speedily and simultaneously throughout the whole of Mongolia. The people were kept in ignorance of what was afoot until after the lightning campaign was over, and only then were they, the designated beneficiaries of the action, presented with the *fait accompli* and for the first time informed of the Party's intentions.

Sambuu has given us his personal account of how the job was done in North Khangai. He was sent to Tsetserlig, the provincial capital, to arrange the confiscations in one banner. He was allowed twenty days for the whole operation, including setting up communes with the confiscated cattle as common property, and recruiting the poor and middle herdsmen into them. Sambuu got his final instructions from Gendung in Tsetserlig. Then he and two activists from the town rode to the banner office and immediately had a secret conference, by night, with the banner head and the secretary of the local party cell. They drew up a list of the lay and church nobles 'who had been cruelly oppressing the masses' and a tally of their cattle and fixed assets.

In all secrecy we divided these nobles up into three groups, and before dawn we went off in various directions on ready horses from the relay station, and before midday we had seized and sealed the fixed assets of those nobles, and then we registered their cattle, warning them that if they suppressed any, or got rid of them by surreptitiously passing them on to others, they would be committing a criminal offence. After that we arranged meetings of the local poor and middle herdsmen, and we explained the decrees of the Party and the government to them, elicited their criticisms about the way the nobles whose property had just been confiscated had oppressed the masses during the time of the despotic government, and then explained to them that people's communes would be established and the confiscated property transferred to them as common property.

The party members were met with a solid front of non-enthusiasm. The only people in the least in favour of the communes were a few crippled and blind beggars who used to haunt the lamaseries. These said: 'We'll join these communes of yours if we can get something to eat there.' Otherwise the people not only refused to join but left Sambuu and his colleagues in no doubt that they were disgusted with the whole affair. Undaunted, he organized the people into communes anyway, transferred the cattle and the registers to them as common property, put what gold and silver he had collected into the state bank, auctioned off a few other things, and then left the new communes to their own devices and returned to report the accomplishment of his task to the Central Committee.[11]

Sambuu attributes the appearance of the leftist deviation to the Eighth Party Congress's wrong assessment of the stage which Mongolia's progress had reached, but other writers offer an alternative analysis and consider that 'leftism' had appeared as early as 1929 and was only confirmed by the 1930 congress. This seems on the whole a more acceptable point of view. By 1930 the Party was jubilant over its apparent successes in eliminating the nobility and using their former property to establish communes, actions which already betrayed arrogance and excess. Its ill-founded elation led it to ignore the dangers it was creating. It was, however, this Congress that took the mistaken decision to copy mechanically what the USSR was doing and so confirmed and exaggerated the swerve to the left. Originally it had been intended merely to encourage rational forms of labour pooling, the herdsmen retaining ownership of their animals. But now it was decided to leap forward to the 'most advanced' forms of co-operation, namely to the organization of artels and communes. For such collectives there was, on Sambuu's own showing, little enthusiasm or understanding, and people had to be dragooned into them by intimidation or by economic discrimination. One herdsman who experienced this process wrote about it in the party newspaper *Unen* in 1932 soon after the New Turn Policy had been introduced.

A man called Luvsantseren came to our *sumun* from the city to start the collective. He forced the *sumun*-people to set up a tent and gather there, and he kept us there for six days without food, and got at us to join the collective. Some two hundred herds-people were collectivized, and as directors of that collective there were chosen comrades who did not know black from white, and who ran around like sheep with the staggers.[12]

Sambuu too recalls how most of the local people would fail to turn up when meetings were held about the new collectives. If any did come, it was mostly those who for one reason or another were incapable of work. They had no interest in collectivization and did not want to hear about it, and would even try to disrupt the meetings by pretending to be ill and falling down in a faint.

The collectives had no one competent to run them, no one felt any responsibility for the animals which had been confiscated from the nobles and put into them as common property, and the country's herds went to rack and ruin. As Sambuu had found, people were still uneducated enough in the ways of socialism not to want to have anything to do with what they regarded as stolen property. Very soon, too, the slightly better off amongst the common herdsmen were themselves picked on as class enemies, and found themselves being treated, and their possessions confiscated, as if they had belonged to the class of feudal nobles. Herdspeople were divided into three categories. Of these, the middle class consisted of those who owned from twenty to one hundred *khuv*. The *khuv*, a word meaning 'share', was a new accounting unit which was introduced at this time: it represented approximately the money value of the old cattle-accounting unit called the *bod*. A *khuv* had roughly the nominal money value of thirty tugrigs, and corresponded to the value of one horse, seven sheep or twelve goats, and so on. To own even one hundred *khuv* was not to be exceptionally well off. Just before the revolution of 1921 it had been estimated that the wealth of the average ordinary Mongol household was the equivalent of about forty or forty-five *khuv*, that is, only a little below the mean point of the scale for the new middle herdsmen. Yet these middle herdsmen were now falling victim to the anti-feudal campaign themselves. They were treated as outcasts just like those who had resisted collectivization. They were taxed at exorbitant rates, they were denied the use of pasture and watering, and allotments of consumer goods were refused them. Their alleged class-status was taken out on their children who were excluded from school and arbitrarily denied an education.

For the herding economy, the country's sole source of wealth, the results were catastrophic. The Eighth Congress could hail the founding in 1929 and 1930 of some four hundred collectives, including 152 communes, as a great achievement in the building of socialism, but it was an achievement which cost Mongolia seven million beasts, or roughly speaking one-third of the total stock as it was in 1929. The collectives were set up without any organization or concession to reality: it will be remembered that Sambuu had twenty days to finish his assignment completely and return to report to the Central Committee, and the other special commissioners sent out from the capital had an equally short time at their disposal. The collectives had no labour discipline, all members got the same rewards in kind whether they worked or not, capital was distributed for consumption regardless of whether there had been any joint income. One commune, founded in 1929, managed in these circumstances to get through its entire capital during the first year of its existence and to run up a debt of twelve thousand tugrigs for consumer goods with the local retail co-operative. Not only did the *jas* slaughter their beasts rather than see them confiscated, but individual herdsmen did the same, hoping at least to keep their herds within the lowest tax categories. Thousands of beasts were driven off into China as people emigrated to escape the commandeering of their property. This meant a definitive loss to Mongolia, because though some refugees were attracted back after 1932 by the promise of preferential treatment, many families never returned at all. The emigrations were massive. No complete figures are available, but it is known that in one month in 1933 over two thousand households returned to the Khobdo district alone, and another 195 to the Altai district. Taking an average of four persons per household, these returning refugees alone must have amounted to well over one per cent of the population of Mongolia at the time. The greatest loss of wealth, however, was in the animals which were allotted to collectives which existed only on paper, and which perished from simple lack of care once they had become everyone's and no one's responsibility. Even Marxist apologists are appalled at the damage Mongolia managed to inflict on herself at this time. Zlatkin, for example, can find no other explanation other than that sheer blindness or a deliberate will to sabotage had possessed the party leaders by 1931.[13]

Other sectors of the national economy suffered from the same irresponsible determination to exalt socialist theory over the facts of life. Millions of tugrigs were spent on schools, clubs and 'red yurts' (tents used as agitation and propaganda centres) for which there was neither equipment nor personnel, and often even no premises. Six huge state grain and cattle farms were set up without a hope of profitability, and were kept going only by massive loans. The socialist sector of the economy, which almost totally replaced private enterprise, needed such extravagant support that the tugrig lost its value as currency and was not restored to confidence until 1933. Private trade was declared illegal and replaced by a state monopoly in defiance of the fact that the State had no network of shops, or anyone competent to run them. In 1933 a prominent party leader, Eldev-ochir, was to confess, with hindsight, that the turnover of personnel, most of them inefficient and many of them dishonest, had been greater than the turnover of goods, and as most officials were replaced without a proper hand-over taking place, there was wide open opportunity for peculation. Private transport was forbidden, and responsibility for internal transport transferred to a joint Soviet–Mongol company known as Mongoltrans. This was totally unequipped to take over, at a moment's notice, from a closely integrated system of private transport which had evolved gradually over the centuries and depended on privately-owned draught animals, local knowledge and mutual trust for its efficiency, and the result was a complete breakdown, with a nation-wide famine of consumer goods.

Towards the Church the leftists displayed an equally intransigent and equally calamitous hostility. The Eighth Party Congress paid lip service to the by then traditional intention of splitting the Church by playing on and aggravating the class differences between the upper and lower lamas, but it prefaced its reiteration of this principle with the statement of its overriding view that 'the lamas are a class which sits on the neck of the people and exploits them', and hereby once again betrayed the fatal inconsistency and inflexibility which characterized the party leadership. True, as mentioned above, a little was done to curry favour with the lower lamas, and not all of the thirty thousand who abandoned the Church did so under compulsion, though most of them did. But nothing which was undertaken in this direction weighed at all heavily against the brutal and unimaginative treatment of the Church at large, which not only united the lamas in solid opposition to the revolution, but offended the ordinary people too, and turned indifference into a deep disgust and hatred for the Party. The Party had begun to exhibit what Lenin had long before condemned as empty revolutionism and to lose the allegiance of those who should have been its supporters, the ordinary herdsmen.

The central authorities knew that matters had been pushed to harmful extremes, but did nothing effective to curb the offenders. In September 1930 the Central Committee of the Youth League sent an official letter to its local members warning them to behave themselves, but it had little effect, nor could it have been expected to, since in the same year an Anti-Buddhist League had been founded on the lines of the League of Militant Godless in the USSR with the duty of organizing and carrying out atheistic propaganda. It translated and published tracts by Lenin on religion, and also produced original booklets with such titles as *Ways for the Anti-Buddhist League to carry out propaganda against religion* which were circulated in editions of several thousand from 1930 onwards. The Church and believers can have been left in little doubt about the Party's plans for them. The interest of the Youth League's ineffective letter lies in the details it gives of typical abuses.

The arbitrary expulsion of young lamas from their lamaseries has taken place in almost every aimak, and other actions contrary to policy have occurred, offending the piety of the people and the lamas. Such activities include: the destruction of stupas, the gouging out of the eyes of statues of the Buddha, stopping people giving free-will offerings to the lamaseries, and so on. Offensive actions of this sort have proved a great hindrance to the work of getting the poor lamas on the side of the People's government, and attracting the people away from the authority of the lamaseries. In Tsetserlig Mandal aimak, Chultem-ochir arbitrarily confiscated Buddha-pictures and burned them. . . .[14]

The Party's actions were organized in several 'campaigns'. Sambuu recalls six of these running concurrently, and of these the two most important were undoubtedly the *jas*-campaign and the collectivization campaign. The main purpose of the *jas*-campaign had been to get the temple herds into the hands of the ordinary people without necessarily confiscating them. But, as Sambuu saw it, the trouble was that the leftists got these two campaigns muddled up, and were very soon commandeering the *jas* cattle to form a fund for setting up collectives with. The actual *jas*-campaign did not arouse too much resentment among the people. It represented only a modification of a familiar and traditional arrangement which was profitable to both parties. But what did discourage them, and hit them economically, was seeing the temple herds put, not under their personal control, but into the hands of ill-found collectives where they perished. People who had relied on what they made from the temple herds found themselves destitute. Nor was the Church of course backward in claiming that the animals were being confiscated to feed the Russians, and that this was but one more step in the planned destruction of Buddhism

Chicanerie and sheer illegality accompanied the interpretation of the *jas*-campaign. Occasionally the central authorities were constrained to send out commissioners to correct specific abuses, as for example when they reversed a decision in one aimak to treat all fixed assets belonging to the *jas*-funds as 'feudal' property and confiscate it. But piecemeal intervention here and there did not affect the general picture, and the crudest infringements and evasions of the law took place. Zlatkin records, for example, that the 1930 regulations governing the drawing-up of contracts between lamaseries and herdsmen for the farming out of *jas* cattle were deliberately formulated in a way which made the arrangement unprofitable to the lamaseries. 'Those who issued the instructions knew very well [he writes] that the conditions prescribed for the pasturing of temple beasts could not be fulfilled. The instructions served as a mere pretext for confiscating the animals belonging to the lamaseries'.[15] Lamaseries would be charged tax at excessive rates, quite arbitrarily. In South Gobi, for instance, rates were put up by 300 per cent. If a *jas* could not pay up, the individual lamas would be assessed personally to a share of the communal tax-debt. In Khuvsugul aimak one lamasery was squeezed in this way and the lamas were called upon to pay from fifty to seven hundred tugrigs each. Amongst them were some thirty-three destitute lamas who had to sell their miserable tents and the clothes off their backs to pay their taxes. Elsewhere exorbitant taxes were demanded with an impossibly short period of grace, perhaps only three days, and when the amount could not be found the lamasery would be closed, the *jas* commandeered, and the tax re-assessed individually to the lamas. Sacred vessels, costumes and masks for the temple dances, were seized and distributed to the secularized lamas as private property, or used to pay the wages of people who had been herding the lamasery's animals, all to the extreme scandalization of the common people as well as the lamas.

Civil war

The direct loss to the Mongol economy of all this was enormous. But, and this was even more ominous, armed uprisings broke out, mostly in the west and centre of the country, though in other districts as well, which proved to be beyond the capacity of the Mongol authorities to deal with themselves. Units of the Soviet army had to be called upon to help put down the rebels. Mongol historians generally adopt the formalistic explanation that the errors and excesses of the leftists aroused discontent and distrust among the people, which the surviving nobles and high lamas, the inveterate enemies of the revolution, were then able cunningly to exploit to further their own counter-revolutionary plans. To the extent that there had always been a latent feud between the

Church and the Party, which at times broke out in the form of conspiracies, often involving the Panchen Lama and the Japanese, or of riots, there is a modicum of justice in this analysis. The Church was a natural rallying point for discontent, and some of its high lamas were turbulent partisans of the old way of life. But from 1930 to 1932 the risings against the Mongol government took on a different and more serious aspect, and the official analysis is quite inadequate. What threatened the country was no longer the sporadic recurrence of small scale riots, limited to one or other lamasery, nor ineffectual conspiracies of groups of high lamas looking to the Panchen Lama for sanction and to the Japanese for vague help which never came, but a general upheaval of the people at large, and this happened without reference to Japan or to any other foreign power. It was the misery and muddle into which Mongolia had been plunged by the obstinacy and insensibility of the Party, the wanton destruction of the people's livelihood and the sapping of their sense of security which were responsible for the scale of the uprisings, and these were entirely an internal matter, perhaps sanguine of support from abroad, but in no way reliant upon it.

Many of the rebel leaders, especially in the big uprisings in the western provinces in 1932, were lamas and nobles, but when a Mongolian scholar describes the rebellions of these years as 'the sharpest manifestation of the class-struggle in our country, reaching the scale of civil war' he is engaging in sophistries and an exercise in self deception. The situation offered the recognizable enemies of the revolution the most favourable opportunity they were ever likely to enjoy to overturn the People's Government, and they took advantage of it, but this is only part of the story. The Party itself was faced by a thoroughgoing crisis of confidence which affected all classes in the country, not least its own adherents. It was the belated recognition of this by the Comintern and the Soviet communist party which dictated Russian intervention to make the Mongol party see reason and beat a retreat. Hundreds of members of the Party and the Youth League came out against the revolution and were found fighting on the side of rebellion. When the Party was purged in 1932, nearly fourteen thousand persons had to be expelled in the four disaffected western aimaks alone, where the whole party organization was found wanting, dispersed, and then re-formed. There were massive organized desertions from the country. In spring 1932, for example, four hundred households left South Gobi aimak alone in a single emigration, in spite of the resistance offered them by officials and soldiers. South Gobi is the least populous of Mongol aimaks, with a population in 1960 of less than 22,000, so that this one exodus alone meant a loss of something approaching a tenth of the inhabitants. Some of the *émigrés* formed armed bands which infiltrated back across the frontier to raid and destroy where they could, but the majority were simply refugees who preferred to leave home rather than see their property confiscated and ruined.

Letters supposed to have been sent to the Panchen Lama in 1929 show that at that time what the leading lamas were aiming at was nothing less than the complete reversal of all that the revolution had achieved since 1921. They welcomed the news that hostilities had broken out between China and Russia in north Manchuria, and declared that they wanted to see the Russians expelled from Mongolia, and Mongolia reintegrated as a province of China. They asked the Panchen Lama for troops to secure the northern frontier against the return of the Russians, and promised that the Jebtsundamba Khutuktu would be re-installed and the whole church apparatus built up again to what it had been. Some of those allegedly involved in this particular conspiracy, notably the Dilowa Khutuktu, had once been in sympathy with the early revolution, and their estrangement is a measure of the disappointment and despair affecting Mongolia.

The actual value of the Panchen Lama as an ally at this time was probably not very great. His name occurs over and over again in connection with plot and conspiracies, but there is an element of unreality about his person and potentiality that leads to the suspicion that he was less a practical ally than a mystical patron. rumours flew about, for example, that he and the Japanese would come to liberate Mongolia after having overwhelmed Russia and captured Moscow. The retinue of the Panchen Lama, who was said to command eight ten-thousands of soldiers and eighty-eight paladins, smacks rather of the magical armies led by the heroes of alliterative Mongolian heroic epics than of flesh and blood cavalrymen, while the fact that the herdsmen of Mongolia also looked to the arrival of another high pontiff, the unmilitary Jangjia Khutuktu of Peking, with an army of Chinese, to free their country, strengthens the suspicion that these great churchmen were significant only as chimerical figureheads, as generals of the ghostly armies of Shambala rather than the real, but still distant, legions of the Japanese. At any rate, though the Panchen Lama entered into correspondence with the conspiring lamas in Mongolia, and in 1932 gave his specific approval to the revolt in the west and to the names of those selected to lead it, and promised to appear in Mongolia in person in the autumn and smash the people's revolution wherever it might be found, he never crossed the frontier and never supplied any troops – which in any case he did not dispose of.

In spite of the alleged links with the Japanese, who were in occupation of Manchuria in the east, but were by now only on the threshold of extending their aggression into Inner Mongolia and north China proper, it was far from here, in the north-west and west-centre of the country, where the People's Government had always had difficulty in making its writ run, that the main trouble-spots lay. There were several contributory causes for this. It was not that there was any special concentration of troops in the east which forestalled action there and shifted the outbreaks westwards. Mongolia did not, in fact, have sufficient troops at this time even to police her frontier with China thoroughly. Lack of a proper network of frontier guards had made it relatively easy for refugees to abandon the country in large groups, brushing aside what opposition they met, and there was little to prevent raiding bands coming back across the frontier on occasional missions. *Émigré* lamas, such as the Dilowa Khutuktu, are supposed also to have kept up communications from across the border with the centres of rebellion in North Khangai and elsewhere, by way of lamaseries in South Gobi. West Mongolia, dotted with several large lamaseries, was a more populous area than the open plateau and Gobi region along the eastern and southern frontiers. The lamaseries here were chronically disposed towards trouble making, and had been the scene of the most serious outbreaks of rioting since the revolution. Communal separatism added to the general feeling of aloofness from Ulan Bator. For instance, when the rebellious lamas of the Ulaangom lamasery drew up a list of their aspirations, they added specifically that these were the 'duty of all Derbet people'.

The most turbulent lamaseries were those of Tögsbuyant in Uvs aimak, Bandid Gegeen at Rashaant in Khuvsugul, Tariatyn in

North Khangai, and Ulaangom. In 1930 a mixed group of lay and clerical nobles had mobilized and armed seven hundred lamas from Tögsbuyant. They smashed the local Party and government apparatus, and set up an administration of their own, and a party known as the 'Party of equal rights for furthering religion and the race'. They were in touch not only with other Mongol lamaseries, but with the leaders of similar revolts which were occurring in Tuva, and with Chinese generals in Sinkiang from whom they hoped to acquire weapons. Their aims were straightforward and comprehensive. They included the scrapping of the programme of confiscation of cattle, the discontinuance of the campaign for forcing young lamas into the world, the restoration of the lamas' right to receive alms, the restoration of the old government headed by the nobility, the cancellation of the law separating Church and State, and, resuming all this, the destruction of the Mongolian People's Republic, the Party and the Youth League, and the 'protection of religion and the race'. The rebels recruited an army which they armed with hunting guns, and whose numbers soon reached two thousand. This sedition, which required armed force to quell it, was followed in 1932 by the most dangerous uprising of all, which was called forth, immediately, by the Party's arbitrary meddling in the affairs of the Bandid Gegeen lamasery. Here lamas by the hundred had been forcibly secularized, four hundred of them being expelled from the lamasery in a single day. The payment of impossibly high taxes had been demanded, followed by the confiscation of church effects. The local authorities had affronted the common people as well as the lamas by their desecration of sacred objects, tearing off the wrappers of volumes of the scriptures and burning the books themselves, digging out holy relics embedded in stupas, stripping the oracle lama of his special vestments and helmet in full view of the people, and so on. The nobility and the lamas of a number of lamaseries wove a comprehensive plot, under the patronage of the Panchen Lama, which was to culminate in an armed uprising in July 1932. Its threads reached as far as South Gobi aimak and allegedly abroad to where the Dilowa Khutuktu was in exile. Armed raiders came back over the frontier and on at least one occasion captured loyal party members, including the girl Bor, whom they hurled to their deaths over a cliff.

A central rebel government known as Ochirbat's Yamen was

set up in the Rashaant lamasery in Khuvsugul. The premier was a Buriat by name of Choijin and there were a number of ministries under renegade nobles, including a Ministry of War headed by the commander-in-chief of the rebel army, one Sambuu. Armed detachments were formed in various lamaseries. The course of the civil war which followed was marked by savagery and a reversion to barbaric practices of earlier times: we possess official accounts only, so that very little is said about the methods of repression adopted by the authorities and a lot about the excesses practised by some of the rebels. In North Khangai party members were hanged on trees, while others were flayed alive. Anyone suspected of sympathy with the People's Government was tortured or put to death in the most cruel manner. Pregnant women were raped, others had their feet cut off. Terror forced many people to join the rebel ranks, refusal to do so being more than life was worth. The old shamanist practice of ritually tearing out the living heart from a prisoner's chest, which formed part of the traditional cult of the black war banner of Ghenghis Kahn, and which had disfigured the capture of Khobdo in 1912, was revived once more by an especially brutal rebel by the name of Tugj, who is said to have disposed of some ten prisoners in this way with his own hands. The pacification of the rebellious area after the troubles had been put down by the Mongol and Soviet armies was also marked on occasions by ruthlessness. Though it was declared policy to pardon those who surrendered, we have it from Sambuu that when Shijee, a leftist member of the Central Committee, and others came to South Gobi to square accounts, their only method of dealing with those who had been arrested as counter-revolutionaries was to liquidate the old men of sixty or seventy and to sentence those who were still capable of work to long periods of forced labour. Some of these fierce sentences, which took no account of the degree of gravity of the crimes alleged against the accused, were later reviewed by the Ministry of Justice and quashed.

Correction of the leftist deviation

The Party had been guilty of a number of elementary but crucial errors. It had operated in arrogant isolation from the public, acting through emissaries sent out from the centre rather than through local organs. It had usurped the executive functions of the government and ruled in a dictatorial manner. It had shown itself insensitive to popular opinion, and finally, the central party authorities had overruled more restrained officials on the spot who had a first-hand knowledge of the particular problems and conditions of their areas. The wonder is, not how this could happen, but how it could continue so long, from early 1929 to the middle of 1932, in the face of rising discontent, galloping inflation, and the evident ruin of the country's flocks and herds. The fatal defect seems to have been the determination to prefer dogma to common sense, and to copy the USSR come what may. The Central Committee was not unanimously in favour of the leftist course, but the critics were too few, and too frightened, to be confident that they would do anything more than effect their own ruin if they opened their mouths too widely in a time of public hysteria. Arrest and imprisonment on suspicion of 'rightism' were a real danger. Even the young poet Natsagdorj, who has since been built up as the founder of revolutionary Mongolia's new literature and the embodiment of its revolutionary spirit, was himself hauled off to jail on the last day of 1931, and spent six months there until the defeat of the leftists brought his release with it.

Enormous damage was done by the rebellion in the west. At the time it was estimated, on the basis of incomplete information, at ten million tugrigs. Some forty-five co-operative stores and thirty-five government offices had been destroyed, together with collectives, post offices, telegraph offices and lines, as well as the private effects of ordinary people. It was probably only the scale and intensity of this civil war which finally persuaded those members of the Central Committee who had realized what was going wrong, but who up to then had been scared of exposing themselves, to speak out for the first time. The majority of the Central Committee still refused to admit that anything fundamental was amiss. In details, they allowed, such as the weakness of propaganda, or the temporary collapse of retail supply, there might be room for improvement, but even as late as a joint session of the Central Committee and the Control Commission in April 1932 they would not accept the view expressed by Dovchin that the Party was altogether on a wrong course. By then it was too late, for the uprising planned for July had been brought forward to April and trouble had already started. In the provinces too there was a continuing insensitivity to the realities and the demands of the situation. In South Gobi, as Sambuu tells us, party leaders continued to call for more and more compulsion, and for more forced labour for lamas in concentration camps as the cure for the crisis. Gradually, however, it was borne in upon the party leaders that they were responsible for the country's plight, and that they were going to have to change their tack, but even so the extremists held on as long as possible.

The eyes of the Central Committee were opened by the fact that poor lamas, ordinary herdsmen, and Party and Youth League members had all risen in revolt. They slowly realized that the revolt in the west was not to be explained away as simply another manifestation of the class struggle, but that it had come as a result of the complete estrangement of the people as a whole from the Party's policies, in particular from its attitude towards the Church. Having accepted this, in May the Party summoned a joint meeting of the activists of the Party and Youth League in Ulan Bator to present its discoveries to them and to suggest alternative lines of action. The meeting confessed that 'brainless and mindless' deviations had occurred in the Party's work, and it accepted that the reason why the lower lamas had joined the rebellion was that they resented the cruel and often illegal treatment meted out to them. On the basis of the meeting the Central Committee issued a resolution condemning its own leftist policy towards the Church and promising sweeping changes, whose nature and scope were defined. In spite of all this, the declaration remained largely a dead letter, since the majority of the Central Committee was still inclined to the left and was strong enough to resist the imputation that the Party itself was in error. It was lamely admitted that excesses and illegalities had occurred, but these were put down to undefined 'elements' who had brought the name of the Party into disrepute while claiming to be working under its aegis. It was at this point, when the Central Committee had demonstrated the full extent of its ineptitude, and its complete inability to recognize its own shortcomings, that the Comintern and the Soviet communist party stepped in with their now historic resolution and told the Mongols what they had to do.

The association of the Soviet communist party with the Comintern in this *démarche* signifies the decline of the role of the latter as the agent of the Soviet government in Mongolia. The Comintern's influence in Mongolia's affairs in the past had not always been too effective, and on occasions, as in the case of Dambadorj and the 'Petrov letter', Comintern instructions had even been kept secret from the Mongolian Central Committee by the particular comrade who had received them. Comintern representatives were to take part in one more Mongolian party congress, the ninth in 1934, but a new relationship between Mongolia and the USSR evolved as Stalin's personal will replaced the often clumsy and uncertain pressure exerted by the Comintern. Mongolia was left with less and less room for manoeuvre, and this is reflected by the increasing subordination of her policies to those of Russia, by the absorption of her internal security services by the Soviet police, by the purges of all ranks of society, from party leaders downwards which paralleled the Soviet purges, and by the ever more hectic adulation of Stalin as the sole benefactor of Mongolia.

There is no indication that the Mongols asked for Russian intervention in June 1932, though they may conceivably have done so. Far more likely is the inference that Stalin realized the potential dangers to Soviet security of a feeble Mongolia, riven by civil war, lying on her flank with Manchuria and Inner Mongolia precisely at a time when Japanese aggression was most to be feared. Japan's choice of south-east Asia as a field for expansion, rather than Siberia and Mongolia, had not yet been made. For a long time to come Mongolia was to have no foreign relations worthy of the name: her external policies were to be indistinguishable from those of the USSR. But her geo-political position, as a buffer against Japan, who for nearly a decade would be probing the Mongol frontier, testing for any weakness, was of supreme importance to the USSR. It was not until long after the Second World War that Russia was willing or able to devote any appreciable attention towards building up Mongolia's home industry or foreign trade. All her efforts went towards the training and equipment of the young Mongol army which proved itself in two short campaigns against the Japanese in 1939 at the battle of Khalkhyn Gol, and again in 1945, and towards building up her own military position. Hence it was most probably not out of any love for the task itself, but simply to secure her own flank that the USSR undertook in 1932 to analyse the reasons for Mongolia's frenzy of error, to force upon an allied government the odium of publicly eating its own words at the direction of a foreign political party, and to saddle herself with trouble beyond her own borders: she simply could not tolerate the collapse of society and administration in Mongolia.

The Comintern issued its resolution on 29 May: it is not clear when the Mongols got to hear of this. The resolution did not, as far as can be seen from the extracts available, put forward any new ideas, but simply warned the Mongols in direct language that they had to go back to the line they had abandoned, and concentrate on separating the high lamas from the rest of the population while seeking allies not only among the poor herdsmen but amongst the well-to-do also, and amongst the lower lamas. This advice was accepted in full at a meeting of Party and government delegates held in Ulan Bator on 23 June as the future guiding principle of the Party's policies. The Party expressed its loyalty to the USSR in somewhat fulsome terms:

The plenary meeting of the Central Committee, having attentively examined and discussed the advice and directives of the Comintern and the Central Committee of the Soviet Communist Party, declares: 'This advice and directive correspond fully to the Party's work in the country's actual situation, and moreover are aimed at the welfare of the people. The special plenary meeting of the Central Committee promises the Comintern and the Central Committee of the Soviet Communist Party that it will exert its every effort to carry out the directive most accurately and unswervingly. This directive shall become the essential programme of the work to be carried out at all times by the Party and government in the field of our country's economic affairs.' Long live the Comintern! Long live Lenin's Communist Bolshevik Party and its leader Stalin![16]

The excuses for, and the rationalizations of, the leftist deviation put forward at various times by Mongol and Russian apologists are, at their most jejune, breathtakingly reminiscent of Animal Farm. Just as the so-called rightist deviation had been engineered, as the History of the Mongolian People's Republic published in 1955 puts it, by 'enemies of the revolution who had wormed their way into the party leadership', so the leftist deviation was to be attributed to similar class enemies: indeed, in some cases these were identical. A Russian writer describes the leftist leaders as 'camouflaged enemies of the revolution and agents of foreign bourgeois espionage'[17] who tried to wreck the programme of the destruction of the nobility. A collection of Mongolian party documents published in 1956 offers a similar analysis: the leftist deviation was the result of the criminal activities of ex-rightists masquerading as leftist extremists, and of additional enemies of the Party who also succeeded, by undisclosed means, in worming their way into the Party leadership.

> The remnants of the rightists, the sworn enemies of the Party and the people, at this time changed their colours and intensified their destructive activities under the cover of revolutionary words and slogans. Revolutionary success produced haste and attempts to overvalue the course of the revolution amongst some sections of the party membership. Enemies of the Party, who had wormed their way into the leadership, cunningly exploited this error and deliberately exaggerated it.[18]

This legend of enemies of the Party being responsible for all disasters conflicts with the Central Committee's own confession of error at the time, but it must have been taken seriously on occasions, for it turns up again in the biography of Choibalsang by Tsedenbal, the present premier of Mongolia. However, it is difficult to accept that the Party was, during the 'twenties and 'thirties, so totally unobservant that until Shmeral pointed it out in 1928 it did not realize that its leadership was full of rightist enemies, and until the Soviet directive was received in June 1932 it did not notice that since 1929 its leadership had, conversely, been penetrated by leftist enemies of the revolution, who were moreover paid agents of the Japanese intelligence service. It is perhaps wisest to dismiss these pleas as so much camouflage designed to exculpate the incompetent leadership of the time, which dared show no initiative, to preserve the myth of the omniscience of the Party, and to flatter Stalin.

How could the Party persevere for over three years in policies which were subsequently recognized as completely erroneous and as having been foisted on it by enemies, without doing something about it? One must infer that the Party was not in ultimate control of its own destinies. This inference is strengthened by the knowledge that on various occasions between 1930 and 1932 the Party and government, or members of them, had realized that they were countenancing gross errors, and had tried, by putting out decrees, to correct the worst of the abuses, but that 'their repeated efforts had been unsuccessful'.[19] This bland admission of the impotence of Party and government, put forward in a recent monograph by two Mongolian historians calls for some elucidation, but such explanations as have been offered are not satisfactory. It is generally said that 'they were unwilling to understand fully the errors committed by the Party itself, and on the basis of this to expose and correct them',[20] which does not advance us very far. Yet in June 1932, the receipt of a Soviet directive at once banished all trace of this reluctance. The logical deduction is that the Mongol party was not so much unwilling to correct its own errors, as incapable of taking any policy decision without the express approval of the Russians. One of the main accusations brought against the rightists in 1928 had been that they failed to act upon, and had even suppressed, advice and guidance offered by the Comintern. The leftists swung to the opposite extreme and allowed their country to reach the verge of economic and social disintegration, until they were sharply brought up by Stalin. The success of the Soviet directive is, if this analysis is correct, not a matter for any surprise. If the Comintern and the Soviet communist party, as appears likely, had the Mongol Central Committee in their pocket, they did not have to manœuvre in mid-1932 to ally themselves with a moderate opposition group which had so far not been able to assert itself, and oust the leftist faction, as has been suggested. What they had to do was less delicate, simply to instruct the whole leadership to make a complete, if humiliating, about-turn, to drop the most offensive extremists like Shijee, and to enforce a completely new line of policy under a reshuffled management, consisting essentially of the same personnel as before.

The leftist deviation was succeeded by the New Turn Policy which ran, as such, for two years, and was reviewed and pronounced successful by the Ninth Party Congress in 1934. Between then and 1940, the year of the next Party Congress, the final destruction of the Church was ruthlessly carried through, all opposition to subordination to the USSR was stifled, and the ranks of Party, government, army and intelligentsia were brutally and thoroughly purged. The New Turn Policy was conceived as a return to the General Line of the Party. In fact it began to look more like a partial return to the permissive policies of the years before 1928, and the Party, now increasingly the creature of Choibalsang's personal ambitions, made use of it as a breathing space to let the country's ruined economy recuperate, to restore people's confidence in the régime, whose prestige had suffered a disastrous battering, and to allow itself a pause before reverting to what it had always had in mind, the total elimination not merely of the economic power of the Church, but of its very physical existence.

The leftist deviation was a deviation only in the sense that things got out of hand. The ideology which underlay it was basic to communism as understood in the USSR and Mongolia, and only the fact that collectivization and the suppression of religion ran away with themselves and plunged the country into ruin necessitated a temporary retreat. It was the tempo of leftism, not the policies themselves, which was the mistake. Those Church leaders who after 1932 put about anti-party propaganda to the effect that the New Turn Policy was a temporary alleviation only, and that the course of events would soon swing to the left again, knew what they were doing and were soon proved right. Much of what was done during the years 1929-32 was irreversible, in particular the destruction of the nobility. The Church, too, was deprived of much of its wealth in the form of livestock, and never recovered this, having in the future to rely for its income more and more on gifts and alms. Most of the projects scouted prematurely after the Eighth Party Congress have since been realized, even if only in part and a generation late. Cattle herding has once again been collectivized, successfully this time, though not without disturbance. A small national manufacturing industry has been set up, and extractive industries promoted. Secular education and western medicine have replaced the Tibetan lamaistic varieties completely. Russian has displaced Tibetan as the learned language. Railways have been built. All private enterprise has been eliminated. But all this has taken far longer to accomplish than the Eighth Congress was prepared to allow. The aims of the first five year plan are only now being achieved, after thirty-five years.

Contemporary Mongol writers are fond of stating that their history provides a lesson and a pattern for other emerging countries, particularly in the matter of dislodging a powerful church. If this is so, then the history of the leftist deviation offers itself rather as a cautionary tale, and a serious warning of the dangers of trying to run before one can walk.

CHAPTER 8

THE DESTRUCTION OF THE OLD ORDER, 1932-40

The emergence of Choibalsang as dictator

True national independence for Mongolia in the 'thirties was never a practical proposition. In theoretical terms the choice lay between alignment with the USSR, with whom she had thrown in her lot in 1921 and again in 1929, and penetration by Japan, whose sphere of imperial ambition was beginning by now to embrace Mongolia. China herself, the main objective of Japan's expansion, was becoming more and more a negligible quantity. But in practice Mongolia was never faced with a choice of this sort. The whole history of her revolution predisposed her towards the Russian connection. Her ruling party was a Soviet creation and many of her leaders had undergone training in Russia. There was no organized opposition to the People's Party in the country. The Japanese were certainly probing Mongolia, sending in agents and, at times from 1935 onwards, testing out Mongolian frontier defences with reconnaissance raids. But the extravagance of the wholesale accusations which were flung about in the late 'thirties, and which stuck to nearly all Mongolia's erstwhile leadership, make it impossible to assess whether the Japanese really did enjoy any support in Mongolia, or whether, as in the USSR, allegations of spying on behalf of foreign powers were not just another weapon of terror. All indications are that the latter is likely to be the true explanation. To judge by the reports of trials in the 1930s, Mongolia was penetrated from top to bottom by Japanese intelligence. Every ministry and public office was a hotbed of sedition, and the whole of the Presidium of the Central Committee of the Party, more or less, with the exception of Choibalsang, were Japanese agents. So was the Commander-in-Chief together with many other members of the High Command. At the top the Japanese were allegedly in a position to engineer the assassination of Choibalsang through the agency of the Mongolian surgeon-general, and to call forth a mutiny to coincide with their own invasion. They could persuade the Mongolian High Command to let their own soldiers die, of poison, malnutrition, and medical mistreatment, in the most despicable way. Farther down the scale, the Japanese could pay attention to such minutiae as organizing a roof fall to block two shafts at the Nalaikha coal mines, and floods to waterlog three shafts. Yet in spite of this comprehensive penetration of practically the whole of Mongolia's administration and economy, which should have brought the system down like a worm-eaten house, the Japanese were never able to bring off a single effective *coup*. It is now admitted that the alleged army plot was a fake, and that the treacherous commanders were really heroic defenders of Mongol-Soviet solidarity who were unfortunately framed and done to death. The same is doubtless true of most, if not all, the other evidence of Japanese penetration. At any rate, no uprising in the rear ever accompanied Japanese aggression on the frontiers between 1935 and 1939. On the other hand, Mongolia was in all practical matters reduced, after 1929, to unilateral dependence on Russia. Her economy was integrated with the Soviet economy, and her military organization and internal security apparatus were similarly co-ordinated. Not only did the USSR, for ideological reasons, need to uphold the existence of her first associate in revolution, but she needed Mongolia as a buffer and military deployment area against Japanese aggression, which from 1931 onwards, was increasingly threatening the security of the whole Far East, but whose southward direction, avoiding the bare steppes of Mongolia, was not assured till after the decisive victory of combined Soviet and Mongol forces at the battle of the Khalkha river in 1939. The definitive choice having been taken in 1921, all logic was on the side of Mongolia's continuing loyalty to Russia.

This much admitted, a second question has to be faced. Was the violence and treachery which characterized the political life of Mongolia in the second half of the decade a direct result of Mongolia's internal necessities, or was she the victim of her association with the USSR? There seems no doubt as to the likelihood that the second is the true explanation. Chronology alone, the coincidence of Mongolia's purges with the purges being carried out in the USSR, makes such a conclusion inescapable. Admittedly, the destruction of the Church, which had been prepared under the New Turn Policy and was the main feature of the late 'thirties was bound to result in the dislocation of society. Such dislocation was after all its purpose, and on this occasion the Mongol government disposed of sufficient force, as well as more careful preparation, to see its campaign through to the end. However, in the process, Mongolia became caught up to a fatal extent in contemporary events in Russia, that is, in the purges and show trials which followed the murder of Kirov in 1934. Not only was her Church eliminated – this had been intended all along – but her own army, Party and society at large were decimated by methods exactly parallel to those being employed in Russia, by trials, and by executions without trial, based on perjured evidence and groundless denunciation.

There can be no doubt that Choibalsang profited by the violent removal of all his opponents and of his powerful associates too, to further his own career. Between 1936 and 1939 he succeeded in taking over the posts of Minister of Internal Affairs, in which capacity he controlled the security services, Minister of War and Commander-in-Chief, Prime Minister, and Minister of Foreign Affairs. By 1939 he had also ousted from the Presidium of the Central Committee former comrades like Amor, Dogsom, Baasanjav, Luvsansharav and Dovchin, from the Control Commission its chairman Losol, from the Army its Commander-in-Chief Marshal Demid, his deputy Darijav, the Chief of Staff Malji, the commander of the armoured brigade, the surgeon-general and others, and from the government the former Premier Gendung, the deputy Premier Sambuu, the Minister of Education Battömör and many others. All these he did to death. Choibalsang gives the impression of having been an all-powerful dictator, and the tone of his speeches at this time is one of omniscience and of vicious self-confidence.

Nevertheless, the question has been raised as to how far he was responsible for these incredible acts of perfidy and brutality, of which he was the ostensible beneficiary, and how far things got out of hand through Choibalsang's own ignorance of the excesses being perpetrated by his security services and his inability to check them. Owen Lattimore, who met Choibalsang in 1944, and found him a bluff, straightforward character, the antithesis of the plotter and intriguer, has put forward this suggestion. As supporting evidence he has quoted the gist of a conversation he had in 1961 with a leading Mongolian intellectual who had himself suffered imprisonment in the late 'thirties on false charges of treason. This man told how, having been released from prison, he came back to Ulan Bator where he met his old comrade Choibalsang on the street one day. Choibalsang seemed genuinely surprised not to have seen his old friend about for some time and asked him where he had been. The explanation offered to Lattimore was that Choibalsang was a good man but his authority was limited by the heavy pressure he was working under and he did not know all that was going on.

This unique statement, made by a man who had himself been a victim, merits serious consideration. It was, after all, made in 1961, long after the event itself, and years after Khrushchev had exposed the cult of personality. But it is a disquieting exculpation. We are asked to infer from this particular incident the general conclusion that Choibalsang, at the head of Mongolia's security services, did not know what these were doing, and that though he had replaced Namsrai in charge when the old Office was enlarged into a Ministry, and had hence been at the head of things throughout the expansion of the service, he was incapable of controlling his subordinates. If this is literally true, the source of the pressure that was circumscribing his initiative remains to be identified, since a period of prolonged police terror is not something spontaneous or haphazard, but rather implies an organization managing and stimulating it. The most likely explanation will be that in and after 1936 effective power in Mongolia was in the hands of the NKVD, and so ultimately of Stalin, for some years. That is, Mongolia's purges were being directed from outside the country, and were dictated by the course of events in, and the interests of, the USSR.

There is nothing inherently unlikely in such a situation. Events in post-war Europe have clearly shown the extent and nature of Soviet police control of her satellites there. Direct evidence from Mongolia is, however, in the nature of things, regrettably scanty. Lattimore has suggested that as soon as Soviet troops were stationed in Mongolia, that is in 1937, Mongolia's security services became integrated with, and subordinated to, those of the USSR.

In itself this is sufficient comment on the nature of Mongolia's independence of action at the time, but the situation seems to be rooted rather further back in the past. Mongol police and security services had in fact been co-ordinated with Soviet organs ever since the beginning, when men like Sorokovikov had been organizing military intelligence for Sukebator. Soviet citizens, Kalmucks and Buriats, played an important role in the early years. Pre-revolutionary Mongolia, unlike Tsarist Russia, had no tradition of a centrally controlled police force which could be adapted by the revolutionaries for their own purpose. Her security services had to be created from the beginning and were built up on the Russian pattern. The swamping of the Mongolian security services in 1936 and later represents rather an exaggeration of the existing situation than the emergence of a new situation, and is directly linked with the increased use of terror as a weapon for the manipulation of society in the USSR. Neither Choibalsang nor the Central Committee made any secret of their dependence on the NKVD. Choibalsang has already been quoted, in chapter 6, as referring with gratitude and approval to the indispensable help of the Soviet 'Chekists' as he continued to call them, in exposing and smashing counter-revolutionary plots which are now publicly known never to have existed. Likewise the resolution of the Central Committee reporting the Gendung affair in 1937 stated that 'the fact that we have been able to preserve all that we have fought for and gained in our revolution is due to the alert attentiveness of the Ministry of Internal Affairs, and the help of the USSR, the only true and tested warm friend of Mongolia'.[1]

Further evidence of Russian control of Mongolia's security is offered by the strange case of Marshal Demid, which will be explored more fully below. Demid's death is a mystery which has never been satisfactorily cleared up. He lost his life by poisoning in a Russian restaurant car of the trans-Siberian express inside the Soviet Union only a few weeks after the condemnation and execution of the Soviet Marshal Tukhashevskii and his colleagues, with whom Demid had been closely collaborating in planning Far Eastern defence. Finally, there is the fact that, although Demid and others have been declared the victims of false accusations and fabricated evidence, no rehabilitation was pronounced in Mongolia until after Khrushchev had blazed the trail at the Twentieth Soviet

Party Congress, and thus intimated to the Mongols that it was permissible and desirable to expose injustices which had taken place during Stalin's day. The point hardly needs to be made that this implies that Mongolia's purges could not be righted independently of Russia's, and that there was a logical connection between the two.

The excesses of the 'thirties are now officially ascribed to the cult of personality. But it is important to realize, in trying to evaluate Mongolia's history, that in that country the cult of personality meant the cult of Stalin over and above that of Choibalsang. Though it was Khrushchev who dethroned Stalin, and Tsedenbal who subsequently deflated the reputation of Choibalsang, the man who had made his career, this does not mean that each leader was a deity in his own country only. Stalin was paramount as leader and oracle in Mongolia as well as in the USSR, and this must not be allowed to be obscured by the circumstance that the dismantlement of the cult of personality was carried out on national lines. The cult of Stalin reached as absurd proportions in Mongolia as it did in Russia, and was a function of the real pre-eminence he enjoyed there in the realm of actual power, which is what counted. First signs of the elevation of Choibalsang are to be noted perhaps in March 1936 when the resolution of the Little Khural appointing him Minister of Internal Affairs referred to him as 'honoured comrade Choibalsang . . . the first leader of the revolution'. Devotion to Stalin had already begun. For example, the Ninth Party Congress of 1934 addressed a message of thanks to Stalin for his 'openhearted and wise advice' offered in 1932, and assured him personally of the continued solidarity of Party, Government and people. At least one ode of praise was offered to him, in 1941, in terms of the sickliest adulation:

> Thanks to Stalin's concern, in the country where the Living Buddha was worshipped there appeared the industrial combinat; into an uncultured land there penetrated the light of culture; black-eyed children made friends with paper and pencil; rosy cheeked girls went to school. The high sky – our father; the vast world – our mother; the father of the people – Stalin; the mother – the native soil.[2]

Such panegyrics bear a superficial similarity to old Mongol poems of praise to the Dalai Lama whose blessing spread happiness over the people, but differ fundamentally in that they were the effect of totalitarian control, and that no one could escape participation in the cult. When the Central Committee addressed a flattering letter to Stalin on the eve of his seventieth birthday assuring him that his name was the 'banner of the working class for the triumph of the great ideas of Marx-Leninism, peace and democracy' and so forth, 641,223 Mongols appended their signatures, we are assured, showing that 'each adult inhabitant of the Mongolian People's Republic thus testified to his sense of love and deep gratitude to the USSR, the great Russian people, and the leader of progressive humanity throughout the world – J. V. Stalin'.[3]

Even if Choibalsang was not entirely his own master, the vindictive tone in which he denounced and vilified his former colleagues, and went on doing so for years after their death, and the skill with which he used his powers of rhetoric to work on the passions of his listeners, suggest that he was well in control of himself and knew what he was about. In July 1939 he spoke at a meeting of delegates from the countryside held to celebrate the eighteenth anniversary of the revolution, and he took the opportunity to refer to Amor, who had just been liquidated, to Dovchin and to others, men he had worked with for twenty years. Amor was an old revolutionary who had twice served as premier and had only been dismissed that same spring. He was the author of a history of Mongolia which was subsequently suppressed. Dovchin had had an exemplary origin and revolutionary career, and his case may stand as typical of countless others. He was born in 1895 in a poor family, and earned his living as a boy by hunting, herding the cattle of local owners, curing skins, slaughtering animals and so on. In the meantime he learned to read and write, ran away to Urga, and worked from 1914 to 1919 first as a relay rider and then as a clerk and draughter in the War Ministry, getting a rank button as a reward for good service, like Sukebator. Till 1921 he worked in his own banner and aimak administrations as an official, and in 1921 came back to Urga and took up a post in the new War Ministry. Thus, though not a member of either of the original groups of revolutionaries nor a veteran of the partisan wars, Dovchin early identified himself with the revolution. From 1921 onwards he was a party member, and from 1937 to 1939 a member of the Presidium of the Central Committee. He held a number of government posts, of which the most important was that of

Minister of Finance from 1926 to 1939, in the course of which he supervised the entire process of the elaboration of a Mongolian fiscal system. He is now said to have been an unswerving champion of Mongol-Soviet friendship, and of ever closer relations between the Mongol Party and the Comintern. This is what Choibalsang found to say of him and Amor in 1939:

> Damba, Naidan and Dovchin, remnants of the Gendung-Demid organization, and likewise other insidious enemies have meanwhile been exposed. And since then, Amor, who went under the name of premier of this country, and who in his whole person was a feudal noble, imbued with the reactionary doctrines of the old feudality, the Buddhists and the Manchus, has, together with other devils, been arrested. Even now we are utterly rooting out the enemies who have tried to obstruct the people's freedom and the warm friendship of the USSR and Mongolia (Thunderous applause: shouts of 'Hurrah').[4]

That Choibalsang could publicly denounce in terms like these, not only once but repeatedly, in practically every one of his recorded speeches between 1937 and at least 1940, men he had worked with since the first days of the revolution, suggests a sinister purpose, whether as principal or agent, and not the mere ignorance of the ill-informed.

The fact that men like Demid have been cleared of the charge of having been Japanese spies and agents does not mean that there was no danger at all from Japan in the 'thirties. Nevertheless, this danger was magnified and exploited by Choibalsang for his own purposes, to assure his own survival and pre-eminence. There is even room for doubt whether the high lamas who were condemned at the same time as the army leaders for plotting with the Japanese were themselves really ever guilty at all. When Amor was dismissed in spring 1939 one charge brought against him was that he had vigorously opposed the arrest by the security organizations of these lamas, which prompts the reflection that Amor may have suspected, or known, that the lamas too had been framed. In any case, the army itself was certainly loyal, and its commanders were not, as was said at the time, spies who had been in the pay of the Japanese since 1932.

Choibalsang's rise to dictatorship runs parallel with that of Stalin, but with an overall time-lag. The full story of events in the 'thirties in Mongolia has never been told, and no doubt never will be. Most of the written evidence is still unpublished, and all the men who could have spoken from personal knowledge are now dead. The truth will probably never be known, and indeed, after so much prevarication and falsification of facts has intervened would in any case not be recognizable as the definitive version. One is left to speculate, but may assume, as a working hypothesis, that Choibalsang modelled his career on Stalin's, and that for the sake of the enjoyment of power and personal survival, he was content to go along as Stalin's agent, protected by the Soviet security services.

The story of how Choibalsang rid himself of possible rivals is interesting in itself as an exemplification of the perversion and degradation inherent in a totalitarian society, and also as an illustration of the impossibility, when one is studying a period such as the one now under review, of ever feeling morally certain that that version of the onion of truth which approximates closest to what really happened has been reached, and that there are not still further, and contradictory, layers waiting to be peeled off. Moreover, history is, in such times, invented as a whole, but afterwards is corrected only piecemeal. The legend, once created, may be tampered with, thus indicating its fundamental unsoundness and untrustworthiness, without a new and fully coherent version of the whole series of events ever being offered. The story of the Gendung-Demid conspiracy is typical of this process: until about 1962 belief in the reality of this conspiracy was the keystone of every official presentation of the events of the 'thirties. We may best look at it now, at the risk of a slight anticipation of developments, since it brings us as close as we are likely to get to the character of the man running Mongolia and to the murky atmosphere of the time which it is so hard to penetrate.

The purges in Mongolia, apart from early treason trials like that in which Lhunbo, the secretary of the Central Committee, was condemned in 1934, the trial in 1935 of alleged saboteurs in the newly-built Choibalsang industrial combine and the trial of the groups of high lamas in April 1936 and January 1937, began in mid-1937. After the execution of Gendung and the death of Demid in the summer, two big show trials were held in October, in which the high lamas of Mongolia and the army command respectively were condemned on linked charges of treason. It was at this time that the Gendung-Demid clique, which had not been heard of before, was first exposed, and the unmasking was done, personally and in enormous detail, by Choibalsang. It was he who reported to the Central Committee all the infamy of the treachery of the High Command, treachery, of course, which had been framed on them from beginning to end. We know, as a result, all the minutest details of the conspiracy with the Japanese that never took place – the arrangements for the poisoning of Choibalsang, those for the unopposed Japanese invasion, and those for the mutiny of the Ulan Bator garrison. We know the dates on which the various key conversations were held, and, for example, the name of the hotel in Hailar where an emissary of the conspirators stayed, and the name of the hotel where he met a Japanese agent and handed him a letter from Gendung. We know that the alliance in treachery of Gendung and Demid was discovered to have stretched back at least to 1932, and that they were in league with the various high lamas who were shot at the same time, but who have not been rehabilitated. This last fact, together with the fact that Demid has been exculpated but not Gendung, leaves the massive plot in a very embarrassing condition. The 1955 History of the Mongolian People's Republic devotes several paragraphs to it, emphasizing that Gendung, Demid and the high lamas were all conspiring together. The 1966 edition of the same work avoids all direct mention of the army plot: it does indeed refer to the high lamas as having been guilty of a counter-revolutionary conspiracy, but does not link them with Gendung and Demid. Of course, it rehabilitates Demid, but passes over Gendung's fate in silence, simply saying of him that in 1936 the Central Committee discovered his crimes and smashed his rightist opportunist views. His supposed association with Demid is ignored, as is his execution. Here, in sharp and uncomfortable clarity, is the dilemma of contemporary Mongolian historiography. Until about 1962 everything written about the 'thirties depended on the central fact of the army plot. The pattern was laid down and all writers followed it. Now that the chief conspirators have been shown to have been innocent, some alternative version of the history of the 'thirties must be produced to account for the insistence on Japanese penetration of the Mongol army and the country at large, and the assassinations this entailed. So far only a negative revision has been undertaken, in that unacceptable 'facts' have been dropped from the official legend. Mongol historians do not seem yet to have made up their minds how to tackle in a positive manner this new lacuna in their history.

As a background to a consideration of the events of the 'thirties as a whole and the power struggle which overshadowed them, it may be instructive to follow through, as far as we may, the story of the downfall of Gendung and Demid.

In summer 1934 a big purge of 'traitors' took place, in the course of which five persons were shot and twenty-seven were sentenced to periods of imprisonment varying from five to ten years. The decree announcing their condemnation and the putting into effect of the sentences was signed by Namsrai, chief of the Office of Internal Security. There are certain significant things about this event. First of all, twenty of the accused were Buriats. Most of the leading Buriats in Mongolian affairs had long since been removed, and were back in the USSR, but Choibalsang was deeply suspicious of Buriats as 'whites' and Japanese agents, and was concerned to get them out of public life in Mongolia. With this purge the 'Buriat episode' in Mongolia's history came to an end. Secondly, the chief of the prisoners was Lhunbo, who had been secretary of the Central Committee of the Party and Chairman of the Central Committee of the Trade Unions, while several others were men of high military rank. The soldiers shot included for example the chief of staff of the Second Cavalry Corps and the commissar of the First Cavalry Division. The accusation was that the conspirators had made a secret agreement with the Japanese in which a Japanese protectorate over Mongolia was canvassed. The traitors were apparently not brought before the public courts but were condemned by a special commission of the security service. This conspiracy, if it ever took place, must have been evidence of grave disaffection, especially in the higher echelons of the army, and the events to which it related must have taken place some time previously, since one of the accused had been in jail since 1933 on other charges of counter-revolutionary activities. However, there is surprisingly little to be discovered about it nowadays in Mongol and Russian books. Zlatkin mentions it only in a footnote in the 1954 German edition of his book which was originally published in Russian in 1950. He records the names of a few of the accused, with a brief note of their alleged crime, and gives a source reference. In the 1957, post-Stalin revised Russian-language version of the book, all names have been dropped. The footnote survives, but has been abbreviated so as to give only the source-reference which now relates merely to a general, anonymous statement about Japanese espionage and its Mongolian agents. The 1955 History of the Mongolian People's Republic describes Lhunbo's group as 'one half of the Gendung-Demid conspiracy, which was later seen to stretch back as far as 1932' and this complicity of Lhunbo, Gendung and Demid is the basis of the charges brought against the accused in the military show trial of 1937 as detailed in a collection of documents published in 1956. But the revised, 1966, edition of the History casts quite a different light on the matter. It states that the Lhunbo affair was a put-up job and suggests that it was Gendung who had engineered it. Innocent persons, it says, were subjected to baseless accusations, and were condemned on perjured evidence.

What Demid's part, if any, was in this affair, is not known. Namsrai, who signed the announcement of the trial and the executions, was later accused by Choibalsang, in March 1936, of having been Gendung's man, and of following his instructions while neglecting those of the Central Committee and the government. Namsrai lost his post and was sent as representative to Tannu Tuva. When Gendung was killed in mid-1937, Namsrai lost his life too. Gendung himself was accused in a resolution of the second plenary meeting of the Central Committee in 1936, which brought about his downfall and removal from office as premier, of 'having tried to turn the Office of Internal Security into an instrument of his own interests, which are not compatible with the Party's political aims'.[5] This may be a general reproof, or it may refer directly to the Lhunbo affair. But at any rate, when Gendung fell from power in March 1936, there was no suggestion that he had been a spy of the Japanese or a co-traitor with Lhunbo. Only posthumously, in and after October 1937, was his name linked with other alleged Japanese spies and traitors such as Demid and Amor, who were all, after their death, vilified by Choibalsang as 'poisonous snakes'.

Gendung's relations with Demid are equally opaque. The two names have been linked together since 1937 with such assiduity that the impression has taken hold that the two men actually were associated. However, this association, let alone the actual conspiratorial group, seems to have been a retrospective invention on the part of Choibalsang, with no substance to it. Demid, like most of his colleagues, held, during the infancy of the new Mongol state, a variety of simultaneous posts. He was a young man of poor family, born in 1900. At first a carpenter and a caravan driver, he became a partisan of the 1921 war, though his rehabilitation did not come early enough for anything about him to be included in the volume of reminiscences of veterans of that war which appeared in 1961. He became a student and an instructor at the officers' academy in Ulan Bator, and from 1926 to 1929 was a student at the Tver cavalry school in Russia. In 1930 he became Chief of the Army Council, War Minister and General. He was a party member from 1921 onwards, and from 1930 was a member of the Central Committee and its Presidium. From 1932 he was a deputy premier. In 1935 he took part in diplomatic discussions in Moscow. He received the Soviet Order of the Red Banner once and the similar Mongolian order four times. He was promoted Marshal in 1936 at the same time as Choibalsang. According to the biography of him printed in the party newspaper Unen in June 1965, he 'struggled against both the rightist and the leftist deviations' and while fighting to maintain the unity of the Party, had done his best 'to expose the opportunist line of Gendung'. Now Gendung's opportunism developed between 1932 and 1936 and this duel with him will have fallen in these years, and thus will have coincided precisely with the period during which Gendung and Demid were allegedly plotting together in concert with the Japanese.

In March 1936 the Central Committee expelled Gendung from its presidium, recommended that he be dismissed from his post as premier, which of course ensued, and warned him that if he did not mend his ways it would expel him from the Party. Choibalsang had denounced him in a brutal speech, tearing to pieces a letter of self-exculpation which Gendung had apparently just sent to the Central Committee, but whose text is not accessible except as quoted in Choibalsang's denunciation. Gendung was found guilty of all sorts of offences against Mongol-Soviet solidarity. He had tried to slacken the bonds of friendship between the two countries. He had abused the Russians for using Mongolia as a captive dumping ground for their shoddy manufactures, and had suggested that Japanese goods be imported instead, via Russia. He had alleged that, in aligning herself totally with the USSR, Mongolia was defending, not her own interests, but those of the USSR. He had complained that various treaties recently drawn up with Moscow, and in which he himself had been concerned, had been forced on the Mongols who signed them under duress. He had also said: 'If the Japanese enter Mongolia, I shall not leave, but I shall stay where I am and work with the Japanese.' Gendung had also made it impossible for certain Soviet specialists to stay in Mongolia in 1935 and these had been forced to return home. He had accused the USSR of carrying on a real red imperialism, and had wondered if this did not mean the 'revolutionary colonization of Mongolia'. Altogether, what the Central Committee agreed on was a comprehensive denunciation of Gendung, but though he, Namsrai and Demid had just come back from a joint mission to Moscow, and Namsrai also lost his post, nothing was said against Demid, nor was any hint dropped of any connection with the Japanese intelligence services. Gendung certainly fell heavily from power, but mainly for reasons connected with the interpretation he had been placing on the New Turn Policy, and which excited the suspicions of Shmeral, once again involved in Mongolian affairs, that Mongolia was veering sharply towards the right and away from the General Line.

In fact, no accusation was ever levelled against Demid during his lifetime, certainly not openly. As late as 23 July 1937, some weeks after Tukhashavskii's death, Demid's report to the Central Committee on the state of the army was accepted, and he was still being referred to as 'Comrade'. In August, while travelling by train to Moscow, he died suddenly. At first his death was explained as having been due to food poisoning, and his corpse was received with honour in Moscow. By October Choibalsang was able to reveal to the third plenary meeting of the Central Committee that Demid and Gendung had been involved in a far reaching plot to betray Mongolia to the Japanese. In the meantime, a number of the highest staff officers and commanders of the Mongol army had been arrested, had made grotesque confessions of treachery, and had been shot.[6]

No definite statement was ever made as to exactly how Demid met his death, so that the newspaper biography mentioned above is able to say merely that he 'suffered an untimely death'. However, the Central Committee's statement that 'it is due purely to the alert devotion to duty of the Ministry of Internal Affairs and its subordinate organs that we have been able to expose repeated counter-revolutionary lama-organizations, and hangmen and traitors to their country such as Gendung and Demid'[7] suggests either that Demid committed suicide on realizing that his fate was linked with the executed Russian generals with whom he had been planning the defence of Mongolia against the Japanese, or, more likely, that the NKVD put him out of the way. The Ministry of Internal Affairs, which took the credit for exposing, though not for inventing, the Gendung-Demid plot, had been created in March 1936 out of the old Office of Internal Security, as we have seen, and given to Choibalsang. However, the resolution of the Central Committee suggests that the USSR had a hand in Demid's death, too, which is all the more likely since it took place on Russian soil. Speaking of the activities of those 'revolting hangmen' it paid specific tribute to the help rendered by the USSR. It is a fairly safe inference that Stalin was implicated in the framing of Gandung and Demid and the army staff as well as in revealing their one-existent conspiracy.

The confessions which the accused made in the army trial were so base and so comprehensive as, nowadays, to defy credibility. They disclosed that they had been recruited in 1932 by Lhunbo, Gendung and Demid, at the behest of the Japanese General Staff, since when they had been planning agitation, sabotage, arson and assassination, to prepare the way for a military take-over by their Japanese paymasters. They had maintained contact with the Japanese in three distinct ways: through Darijav, a partisan of 1921 who became deputy commander-in-chief and was at the material time ambassador in Moscow, and who passed on military information to the Japanese military attaché there, from whom he received instructions; directly via the army staff, 'which became to all intents and purposes an office of the Japanese intelligence';[8] and through agents who were in touch with Japanese staff officers in Manchuli. Thanks to their work the Japanese were able to plant their agents in the Central Committee of the Party, the National Little Khural (a caucus of the Great Khural or parliament for which it substituted between sessions), various ministries, the central councils for trade, transport and the trade unions, provincial offices, co-operatives and artels. After the military takeover the People's Government would be abolished and a pan-Mongolist monarchy set up under Japanese auspices. In preparation for this the Japanese were to be supplied with all the information they needed about the Mongolian army, and the army was to be deliberately weakened by the poisoning and maltreatment of the soldiers. The conspirators detailed what they had actually done to achieve this result. They had made the soldiers drink from poisoned wells, they had seen to it that they did not get the medicines they needed, they had denied them proper clothing and tents, kept them short of food so that they had to beg or scavenge on rubbish heaps and so on. Unless these details, like the general accusation that the High Command had deliberately organized military sabotage, are pure invention, they picture the Mongol army in 1937 in an appalling condition of chaos and disintegration. Soldiers were dying off by the hundred. In the first half of 1936, of five hundred soldiers who had died, three hundred had succumbed to pulmonary diseases and scurvy owing to the deliberate omission of essential medicines from the consignments dispatched. Another seventy died in the winter of 1936 to 1937 because they had been denied medicines and proper food. Soldiers had to live in damp tents with no floors in the hard winter, they had to collect frozen dung for fuel without gloves, and were sent out on night guard duty in sub-zero temperatures without gloves, fur coats or felt boots. In summer, on the other hand, they were made to wear padded clothes and felt boots. Hygiene regulations were not observed, sick soldiers were not given special diet, and infectious cases were purposely placed among the other sick so as to spread disease. The soldiers were made to eat carrion, or bread baked in the ashes of dried dung. Their food was cooked in dangerous copper pots from which they got stomach troubles and diarrhoea, some 20 per cent of deaths throughout the army being due to these unsafe pots. It may be that conditions were actually like this in the Mongol army in 1936 and 1937, but if so, it was doubtless due to general incompetence and muddle, not to organized sabotage.

The accused in the army trial were found guilty of other types of counter-revolutionary activity as well, designed to sabotage the Mongol economy, blacken the name of the USSR in people's eyes, and generally prepare for the Japanese takeover. Yadamsuren, the director of the State Theatre, was found to have composed 'counter-revolutionary literature'. With his contemporary Buyannemekh he had in fact been experimenting with themes and forms not always compatible with socialist realism. For a quarter of a century after his execution he became an un-person, and only recently have he and Buyannemekh come to be mentioned once again in histories of Mongol literature. Yandag, a member of the presidium of the Central Committee, and in charge of state transport, had organized traffic accidents with consequent loss to life and property. Jigjid, deputy chief of the co-operative union, had sabotaged retail distribution, organizing arson, cutting down the number of distribution organizations, and so on. The Minister of Education, Battömör, was convicted, among other things, of 'trying to destroy the Mongol national script'. There are no further details of what lies behind this extraordinary charge, but possibly it refers to the transitory experiment of writing Mongol in Roman letters. This romanization had a brief vogue in various parts of the communist world, including Mongolia, in the early 'thirties. The adaptation of the Roman alphabet 'which is used throughout the whole world' to the Mongol language, had been decided upon at the Sixth National People's Khural which followed the Eighth Party Congress in 1930. The reasoning behind the change was purely practical. The Mongol alphabet was recognized to be archaic, it no longer corresponded to the contemporary language, and was inadequate for expressing modern terminology, especially scientific vocabulary. Rather than tamper piecemeal with the old script, which was in any case used only by a million or two Mongols in Russia, Mongolia and North China, it was thought preferable to make a total break and adopt the universally used Roman alphabet. A special Romanization Bureau was set up, but was disbanded in the general dismantlement of extraordinary offices which accompanied the New Turn Policy, and romanization died a natural death. If Battömör's condemnation was linked with this experiment, only cynical opportunism can explain how it could be considered a capital offence. Four years later, in 1941, the Central Committee was to decree the replacement of the old script by the Russian alphabet, for reasons which were equally practical or equally specious. It declared: 'The further cultural development of the country can only succeed along the path of the strengthening of friendly relations with the peoples of the Soviet Union and the acquisition of the extraordinarily rich Russia culture'. Alphabet reform was thus one facet of political manœuvring, and whether or not the old Mongol script survived was never at any time more than a secondary consideration.

In 1962 the Central Committee of the Party reinforced the

condemnation of the cult of personality which it had first attacked in April 1956. It stated:

All this led to gross infringements of revolutionary legality and the baseless destruction of enormous numbers of people between 1937 and 1939. Amongst those who were wrongly done to death were many honest workers and officials of Party, State and Army. Further, the majority of the leaders of Party and State were condemned on framed charges. In this state of affairs, the whole merit of bringing to its climax our anti-feudal revolution and protecting our country's independence from the Japanese imperialists was associated with the name of Choibalsang alone, and his merits were exaggeratedly exalted. Thus the personality cult of Choibalsang developed and inevitably led to the depreciation of the role of the Party and the working masses.[9]

This appreciation of the effects of the personality cult, with its emphasis on the ill-effects on the Party's reputation rather than on the human degradation and material losses caused, is an astonishing argument. What these losses actually amounted to it is of course impossible to estimate, for the effects on the country's material and intellectual prosperity were to stretch far into the future. Nor can one judge the extent of the blow to the self confidence of the people of Mongolia on being told that most of their trusted leaders were the lowest of traitors. In purely statistical terms the following provisional balance may be drawn. Between 1935 and 1938, sample years for which figures have been published the female population of Mongolia rose by 12,500. The male population should have risen by a similar amount, but in fact fell by 3,200, indicating a total loss of about 15,700 men or some four to five per cent. Between 1938 and 1944 the female population rose by a further eight thousand: thus in these six years an increase of only two-thirds the amount of the previous three years was registered. At the same time, the male population increased by only half as much, by about 3,600. Between 1944 and 1947 the population as a whole increased by only three hundred. A separate statistical table indicates that between 1935 and 1940 the total population aged eight and over dropped by 9,300. Few of these losses can be attributed to the war with Japan: a note addressed by Mongolia in 1945 to the Far Eastern Commission detailing her contribution to the defeat of Japan mentions that the *total casualties* suffered between 1935 and 1945 were 2,039 men. Possibly wartime privations were responsible for some losses:

food rationing in Mongolia, which had to deliver great quantities of meat to the USSR during the war, was not lifted till 1950. But the effective cause of the population drop and the stagnating birth-rate in the late 'thirties and early 'forties must have been the great purges. Quality too was affected, since those killed and imprisoned comprised a good proportion of Mongolia's already inadequate reserve of educated and experienced men, statesmen, technicians, scholars and teachers. Quite apart from the sense of moral outrage one feels at the inhumanity of those years, from a practical point of view one is still baffled, even today, at the nature of the political mentality which can drive a poor and underdeveloped country to tear itself to pieces in this way in the alleged service of an imported ideology, and to substantiate its brutality with detailed but wholly false evidence, and persist in this attitude until the change of the political course in another country permits a partial rectification of the record.

In spite of the public rectification of the story of much of what happened in the 'thirties, no coherent account of the period which might command credibility has yet appeared. The army plot has been exposed as an empty myth, but we still do not know at what point, and for what reason, Demid's death, and the deaths of his subordinates, were decided upon. Doubt legitimately exists about the reliability of what has been written about Mongolia in the 'thirties, even about the reliability of the corrections which have been issued. Once it has been conceded that the official record is a sham and requires correction, confidence is forfeited. It is impossible to know at what point factuality has at last been attained, to be sure that today's revised version will not turn out tomorrow to be another invention. Until much more documentation is published from the Mongol side, any history of Mongolia in the 'thirties, including the present one, is bound to be, except in general outline, provisional.

The 'New Turn'

In June 1932 the Mongol authorities were faced with the urgent problem of suppressing the rebellions which were raging in the countryside, restoring the country's economy, and regaining the confidence of the people at large. The 'great leap forward' of the years 1929 to 1932 was followed by a temporary retreat, which was to allow a breathing space before the Party could once again begin its assault on the old order. Though at times it looked as if the pendulum was swinging decisively away from the dogma of the General Line of the Party, and towards a repetition of the comparative liberality of the middle of the 'twenties, the Party itself, more and more under the personal control of Choibalsang and hence of the Soviet communist party, never lost sight of its ultimate aim of destroying completely all that was left of the old 'feudal' order of society. The tempo of change slackened drastically. Some of the desiderata of socialism, particularly the collectivization of herding, were not to be attempted again for another quarter of a century. Railway building and the establishment of industry on a significant scale, were put off, as it happened, till after the Second World War. Private retail trade still existed, alongside state enterprise, till the end of the 'fifties.

But before 1940 the negative side of the programme, the destruction of the old social order, had been accomplished. The lay nobility having been disposed of in and after 1929, this meant that it was the Church alone which was the last bastion of resistance to communism in Mongolia, and during the 'thirties the struggle between Party and Church took on an increasingly-sharp and uncompromising character. The Party no longer made any secret of the fact that its intention was not only to destroy the political and economic power of the church, but to eradicate the last vestiges of religion itself in Mongolia – a much more difficult and elusive task than the physical destruction of the lamaseries and one which, as in the USSR, has still not been accomplished to official satisfaction. Though this was clearly realized at the time, Choibalsang publicly abused the lamas for making anti-government capital out of the Party's obvious intentions. The crude tone of his assault on them illustrates how far the Party had moved away from the Church since the early days when lamas had been welcomed to take part in the affairs of the revolution. Speaking in 1938, after the campaign for closing the lamaseries had reached its climax, he said:

> Now the lamas are deserting their lamaseries and fleeing in numbers to the countryside. Most of them are spies and agents of the Church. Having fled to the countryside they are spreading frenzied anti-revolutionary rumours. They are telling the ignorant and superstitious:

'This People's government and Party of yours are going to obliterate religion. They are going to arrest and annihilate the lamas. No one will be able to stay in the lamaseries. You realize this, don't you?'[10]

Choibalsang reiterated the Party's declared policy of helping the poor lamas, and of not even interfering with the religious activities of middle lamas, as long as they kept out of politics. In fact, the lamas were absolutely correct in their suspicions, and by 1939 practically all lamaseries had been closed and their occupants scattered, and organized religion had come to an end in Mongolia.

In the last few years, since Mongolia has once again entered the comity of nations, and begun to engage in diplomatic intercourse with other countries than those of the Soviet bloc, to receive foreign visitors and to send its own propaganda abroad, even if on a tiny scale, its leaders have become aware of the possibilities of holding up the experience of their country, as a poor and backward community engaged in struggling first of all against foreign domination and then against internal 'feudal' reaction, as a model for the emerging countries of the 'sixties. Books and articles on Mongol revolutionary history not infrequently refer to the relevance of methods employed in Mongolia to cope with definite problems, to other countries supposedly faced with situations which are superficially similar. This is especially so with regard to religion. For example, an article on the 'Struggle against feudalism' in a symposium published in 1961 to celebrate the fortieth anniversary of the Mongol revolution, ends with the words:

The experience gained in destroying the structure of the lamaseries and resolving the question of the lamas is not only instructive for our Party, but offers a lesson for all countries and their parties where, as in Mongolia, religion is strong.[11]

Similarly, a treatise published in 1965 on the way the religions question was decided in Mongolia, puts forward Mongolia's experience as a model for other countries:

The policies followed in the Mongolian People's Republic in resolving the problem of the lamas and the lamaseries, and some of the tactics employed, are without doubt an appropriate lesson for other countries in resolving the problem of religion, and in particular for those countries of Asia and Africa which are gaining their independence and are entering on the path of progress and development.[12]

THE DESTRUCTION OF THE OLD ORDER, 1932-40

The Mongols are evidently setting themselves up as the pattern of a semi-developed nation to be followed by countries which have achieved independence since she did, and which have a vigorous religious element in society. The applicability, if any, of the lesson, is, however, so strictly limited as to be negligible. In the first place it implies the intention not only to initiate a positive anti-church campaign, but to continue it to the point where religion is effectively exterminated and replaced by atheistic Marx-Leninism. It is thus, strictly speaking, of interest only to countries where a communist party is in control, and where there is a willingness to subordinate material prosperity to the dogmatic disruption of society. Mongolia's experience would be difficult to adapt to the conditions of most of the emerging nations of Asia and Africa, where neither the will nor the means to extirpate traditional beliefs and institutions exists and where the existence of a church is not recognized as a problem at all. Besides, the didactic impact of the lesson has been lost, since at the time Mongolia was engaged in solving her religious problem she was living in total isolation from the rest of the world. Thirty years have passed since lamaism was destroyed behind closed doors, and even today very little has been written about this episode, even in the Mongol language. On the whole, no one outside Mongolia knows anything at all about the details of her practical experience in uprooting an old-established church, and time has passed the matter by and eroded the urgency of the appeal of Mongolia's 'solution' to the point where the main interest is now an academic one.

At the time, only a few vague rumours trickled across the frontiers about how lamaism was being eradicated, the lamaseries destroyed, and the lamas dispersed into civil life. Rumours of battles between the Mongol and Soviet armies on the one hand, and armed lamas on the other, which were supposed to have occurred in 1937, have never been denied, though there is little positive corroboration for them nowadays, except in the ruined state of many lamaseries. Erdeni Juu, for example, which flourished till that year, was ruined and desecrated then, and has lain deserted ever since. Yet there is no reliable account of how Erdeni Juu came to be sacked: some recent statements from Mongolia even go so far as to suggest that the damage occurred during the struggles against the Manchus, and that the part of the People's Government was solely to carry out restoration work.[13]

Nor has the other side of the coin ever been fully exposed either. The policy of sowing discord amongst the lamas had some effect. Though many thousands of lamas abandoned their houses solely because these were made untenable and the cloistered life rendered impossible, and though Zlatkin says, for example, that in the late 'thirties most of the lamas, though they no longer possessed any organization, were hostile to the revolution and to the People's Government, on the whole the lama population was integrated, somehow or other, effectively if not willingly, into ordinary society. In particular, lamas formed the backbone of the new handicraft co-operatives which were being encouraged to develop in the 'thirties. Others were recruited into Mongolia's new industrial proletariat – still a minute fraction of the population, but a factor of slowly growing significance. The problem was a real one. If Mongolia was to modernize itself, it was essential to remove the drag imposed by a huge clerical society, celibate in status but often promiscuous in habit, economically unproductive in the eyes of the Party, though it provided a livelihood of the traditional sort for its own members and for many poor herdsmen as well, and in outlook mainly conservative (if the Party is considered progressive). The State, too, needed the lamas for military service at a time when there was a real threat of invasion by Japan. The idleness of many thousands of lamas meant the loss to Mongolia's economy – in theoretical terms only, since it was a long time before secularized lamas could be mobilized – of the work, in the mid-'thirties, of some eighty thousand men, a sizeable proportion of the total of 350,000 males of all ages in the country. Moreover, their upkeep was seen as a continuing drain on resources. The expenses for the maintenance of the lamas and their temples amounted to a yearly average of about thirty-one million tugrigs, or sixteen times as much as could be devoted to the educational budget. Thus, though the Church was doomed primarily for ideological reasons, there were practical considerations involved too.

The real interest of the anti-church campaign in Mongolia lies not so much in the extent of its applicability, or otherwise, to very different situations elsewhere, as in its exemplification of communism in action. Unfortunately an inquiry of this sort is vitiated from the very start because the campaign against the Church coincided with a period of general extremism and terror directed against all levels of society and all groups within society, and this terror was largely the outcome of a situation beyond Mongolia's own borders. It is thus very difficult to isolate the treatment accorded to lamaism, which is a unique feature of Mongolia's history, since the Church in Mongolia enjoyed a position of even greater economic and perhaps spiritual predominance than in Russia, and to consider it apart from the general reign of terror, the suspicion, denunciation, arbitrary arrest and liquidations which were affecting society as a whole. As we shall see, the disappearance of the Church was by no means a foregone conclusion, even in the mid-'thirties, as long as Gendung remained in power. It was his fall in early 1936 which opened the way to the final solution, a solution which was repeatedly being urged on the Mongols by the Soviet communist party. Nor did the Church collapse of itself in spite of the extent to which it had been undermined. In the end direct and forceful action was necessary.

The New Turn Policy represented an ideological retreat from socialism in that it was publicly admitted that only by fostering private enterprise could prosperity and confidence be restored. The new motto was 'Raise high private initiative, and bring the private cattle-herding economy to a high level'. Most of the policies of the Eighth Party Congress were cancelled. Loans were offered to all small cattle herders, including those previously classed as rich householders because they owned more than one hundred *khuv* and who had been savagely discriminated against. These loans were intended to enable the private herder to rehabilitate himself after the collapse of the ill-found collectives. State benefits were given to those who built shelters for their animals or who dug or repaired wells. Cattle and valuables confiscated from the rebels of 1932 were taken over by the State, and other items recouped in the same way were allotted to those who had suffered in the troubles and to poor herdsmen and poor lamas who had not taken part in the rebellion. Those collectives which had been formed under duress were disbanded by special commissions set up for the purpose. What capital remained to the collectives was devoted first to paying off outstanding communal debts, and what was left over was then distributed proportionately to the ex-members. Those collectives whose members wished it were in theory supposed to be left intact, but the commission, made up of men lacking experience in interpreting instructions, and scared of using their personal initiative too much, carried out a wholesale dismantlement of all collectives, and the most simple forms of labour-pooling were discouraged. Emigrants were persuaded to return from abroad. They were promised freedom from prosecution, the return of their cattle and property, except for weapons, freedom from all discriminatory treatment, and even priority in the allotment of good pastures and watering, the granting of loans, and exemption from taxation for a year. The freedom to practise religion was declared again. All measures tending to vilify religious ceremonies, or to terrorize people into refraining from worship or into worshipping in secret, were forbidden. Tibetan medicine, banned by the leftists, was once again permitted. This was not only a concession to a tradition, but a matter of sheer necessity, for the Party, having forbidden the lamas to pursue their medical calling, had found that they themselves had made totally inadequate alternative arrangements. Here, as elsewhere, the Party lost far more ground than it need have done. Tibetan medicine, and the conditions in which it was practised, were far inferior to western medicine. The trouble was that people were addicted to it, and distrustful of innovation. For the Party to have to call a halt in the replacement of lamaist medicine only enhanced its prestige and increased people's attachment to it for quite illogical reasons. It was not till 1938 that steps could once again be taken to get rid of this backward, and often harmful quackery. The religious commission and the Anti-Buddhist League were allowed to disappear. Lamas who had been forcibly secularized were allowed the choice of re-entering the religious life. Secularized lamas, and poor lamas who lived outside their lamaseries as ordinary herdsmen though still maintaining their clerical status, were accorded electoral rights, which the lamas as a whole had lost during the leftist deviation. These rights were now denied only to those lamas who lived the cloistered life, and to those few incarnations who had left the Church. The destruction and desecration of shrines was stopped, the compulsory farming out of *jas* animals (now much reduced in numbers) discontinued, and the *jas* restored to the full management of their own property.

The effects of this sudden and complete reversal of policy soon made themselves felt, demonstrating that ordinary people were much more sensitive to the day-to-day realities of the situation than to the theoretical background to the change of course, and that they were unable to visualize that the New Turn Policy was only a temporary halt in a long-term plan. In two years the country's stocks of cattle recovered miraculously. If statistics are to be credited, there was, in private hands and under state-encouraged private management, an increase of 3,500,000 head in one year alone, 1933 to 1934. At the same time some realistic work was being done in building shelters, cutting and storing winter fodder, digging wells, exterminating wolves, and providing much needed veterinary care. By 1934 Mongolia had thirty-four veterinary stations, with 104 personnel of varying standards of qualification – not an outstanding network for such a vast country, but evidence of a little solid progress in the right direction compared with the vapid futilities of the first five-year plan. Retail trade, now partly in private hands again, was able to satisfy demand to a greater extent than a few years earlier. Nevertheless, demand still exceeded supply, even for basic necessities like tea, tobacco and sugar, and prices tended to rise well above the level fixed by the State.

However, the New Turn Policy did not by any means have an easy passage. There were those who distrusted it because it seems to be a surrender to private capitalism, and those who undermined people's confidence by whispering that it was only a temporary retreat, and that leftism would soon appear again. Ordinary people and officials were too confused by the sudden change in policies to be able to evaluate properly what was expected of them, and would show as little initiative as possible, so as not to be compromised if the official line changed again. The way the Party was purged illustrates very well the difficulties inherent in getting inexperienced people to carry out somewhat complicated directives based on policies which must have seemed inconsequential. The very mistakes of authoritarianism and literal interpretation of instructions without the application of common sense, which had been observable before June 1932, emerged once more in the correction of the earlier errors. Just as sheer increase in numbers had been the watchword in the campaign for recruiting the poorest herdsmen into the Party, so the control commissions charged with purging the Party made the sharp decrease in numbers their sole aim, paying no regard to the quality and background of the members they were expelling or retaining. As an example we are told of one commissioner in Kentei aimak who, instead of explaining the significance of the purge to the party members simply said: 'Tomorrow I am going to put three questions to you. Anyone who cannot answer them will be expelled from the Party.'[14] Many members resigned voluntarily, rather than face the ordeal of answering the threatened questionnaire. In other areas loyal, but undoubtedly stupid, party members, who had been told that the Party wanted to reduce its numbers, thought they would be honouring this directive by leaving the Party, and resigned voluntarily *en masse*. Elsewhere the commissions merely looked at the answers to the questionnaires and did not interview individuals, with the result that honest members got expelled, while less scrupulous ones retained their membership.

Over and above this, the Party had to contend with the sheer immaturity of the populace, and their inadequacy in face of all the new ideas and institutions which were being forced upon them. Years before, Mrs Bulstrode, who travelled in Mongolia in 1913, had remarked that the Mongols had never worked and it was unlikely that they ever would. Their needs were simple and such as they were could be satisfied by the Chinese. Like all sweeping statements, this one needs modification and Mrs Bulstrode has not lacked for critics of her generalization. But there is a measure of truth in her observation. It is not that the Mongol is by nature lazy or idle: the care of his herds requires hard work in the fiercest of climates. But this willingness to devote himself to the care of his own animals is not the same as a willingness to work for a fixed number of hours at the factory bench or at the coal face and the Mongol's reluctance to give up his nomadic life for that of the proletarian has been remarked on again and again since Mrs Bulstrode's time. The conviction that machines and offices are to his advantage has not always been brought home to the Mongol. The attitude of Gendung towards the Choibalsang Combine is a case in point. Soon after the Combine was built it suffered some severe fires, probably through incompetence on the part of the personnel, though the affair was blown up into a show trial and certain officials were executed as saboteurs. Gendung showed no keenness to rebuild the destroyed sections. 'Our herdsmen can make their own felt,' he said, 'so why rebuild the sections? What use is a felt-making factory to our herdsmen?'[15] Amongst the people there was apathy, a widespread lack of enthusiasm for revolutionary change, and on the part of those who suddenly found themselves entrusted with public funds an absence of social responsibility which did not evolve as fast as the public sector of the economy grew. In 1934 the Central Committee had to consider a report by Gendung about slackness in party organizations and amongst trainees. The revolution was now thirteen years old, and needing to recruit cadres, and was running into difficulties. Party officials were neglecting their work, going off on long leave, or simply abandoning their jobs. Instead of training young specialists, they were taking the easy way out and employing Russians and Chinese, who could do what was asked of them, but meant in the long run no gain to Mongolia's trained labour force. Trainees were themselves failing to profit from their Soviet instructors: they were making little attempt to learn, but sat back without participation, and left everything to the foreign experts. The retail co-operatives were found to be fostering rackets, selling at inflated prices and pocketing the profits and otherwise embezzling funds and misappropriating goods. At the beginning of 1934 they were short by nearly two and a half million tugrigs for this reason.

Though the New Turn Policy was not intended to be a return to pre-1928 attitudes, in practice this is very much what resulted. After the rout of Gendung by Choibalsang in 1936 the mistakes in the implementation of the New Turn, which were adjudged mistakes not because they conflicted with Mongolia's immediate interests, but because they were not compatible with her eventual socialist transformation and had supposedly injured relations with the USSR, were put down to Gendung's anti-party character as a 'rightist deviationist' and to the embryo personality cult he was said to have been building up for himself. Gendung was said to have looked on the New Turn as his own creation: he allowed himself to be flattered as the one man who knew what was good for Mongolia, and his every word was accepted as dogma. Choibalsang accused him of having a swollen head, and of intimidating any comrade who dared to disagree with him. In particular, he said, Gendung had quite misunderstood the purpose of the New Turn and from the very beginning had trotted out the old Bukharinist slogan: 'Get rich!' It is difficult nowadays to form any idea of what sort of a man Gendung may have been, since he fell from favour early on and was for years abused as a traitor and Japanese spy. Even nowadays his reputation has not been restored though the accusation of pro-Japanese treason has been dropped, and anything written about him is written in a tone of disparagement. An opportunist he certainly seems to have been, no doubt unavoidably in the circumstances of the time. In any case, the borderline between being an opportunist and being a good Marx-Leninist exploiting temporary alliances is always a very tenuous one, and seems largely to depend on the success of the person concerned in surviving. Whether Gendung opposed the growing Soviet control of Mongolia in the 'thirties out of principle, or whether his opposition was part of his campaign of personal careerism, is, today, neither here nor there, but the fact is that he took this line and in doing so condemned himself. He was dissatisfied with the course Mongolia was steering, and wanted to slow up the forced disintegration of the old society and detach Mongolia from unilateral dependence on the USSR. But in doing so he was grossly overrating Mongolia's capacity for independence at a time when Russo-Japanese rivalry was what mattered. Superficially he gives the impression of having been a premature Tito, prepared to break with the USSR on the practical question of Soviet domination of his country's economy and domestic affairs. But such a display of independence in the pre-war communist world was ill-judged. Gendung spoke out against Soviet imperialism, and denounced the very commercial agreements he had negotiated with the USSR as unequal treaties, but the situation was against him and these were mere quixotic gestures. Mongolia was too deeply committed to the USSR, too essential to her neighbour's security to be able to play at independence. She had a common frontier with the USSR and no effective outlet to the non-communist world. There were certainly men like Choibalsang who were wholeheartedly for the Soviet alliance: to some extent they may have been making a virtue of necessity, but at least they realized that Mongolia had no choice in the matter. She could not stand aloof from sovietization on the one hand and from Japanese imperialism on the other, and once having cast in her lot with the USSR there was really no chance of changing horses in midstream. Gendung's aim seems to have been, as far as one can discern it, to dissociate Mongolia from Russia while not falling a prey to Japanese aggression. This can only have been based on a total misreading of Mongolia's geo-political situation, for ever since the seventeenth century Mongolia had been limited in her freedom of action by the necessity of taking one or other of her great neighbours as a protector.

What are nowadays described as Gendung's opportunist policies led to a general slackening off of revolutionary ardour during the first years after the relaxation of tension in 1932. Whereas during the years of leftist deviation the Party had usurped the functions of the Government, so that from top to bottom it was the Party organizations which both formulated policy and executed decisions, so as the New Turn progressed the roles of Party and Government were reversed. A plenary meeting of the Central Committee in 1933 accepted Gendung's definition of the role of the Party, which was to be one of complete subordination to the Government. Gendung asked plainly 'Is the Party to lead the Government, or is the Government to lead the Party?' and his reply was equally direct: 'The Party is not to have any say in leading the Government.'[16] This formulation found its way into the new party rules which were drawn up at the time. The Party's functions were reduced to informing the people at large of governmental decisions and seeing that they were implemented. This was one reason for the falling off in the enthusiasm of party members already mentioned. At the same time, religious sentiment, which was still far stronger in many party officials than the foreign and imperfectly understood theories of Marx and Lenin, was bolstered up by a further radical change in the Party's rules. The old provision that Marx-Leninism was the theoretical basis of the Party and that all members should strive at all times to master it was cancelled, and party members were specifically permitted the exercise of a free conscience in matters of belief, and were allowed, if they wished, to make voluntary offerings to the lamas out of their personal property.

Gendung maintained, now and later, that at a time when the country was facing extreme danger from the Japanese, it would be unwise to estrange an influential part of the population by making a deliberate assault upon the Church. With the experience of the civil war of 1932 behind him, which his own leftist excesses had helped to provoke, he had a good deal of reason on his side, and in fact it was only from 1937 onwards, when Soviet troops were in Mongolia in large numbers under the terms of a mutual defence pact signed in 1936, that the campaign against the Church was carried to its conclusion. Between 1932 and 1934 the

Church did manage to exploit the New Turn to recover much of what it had lost in the preceding years. On the one hand the high lamas again felt sure enough of themselves to evade the existing regulations. They compelled secularized lamas to return to the lamaseries, recruited children under eighteen, built new temples and shrines, and paid scant attention to the regulations governing the farming out of *jas* herds. Over three hundred lamaseries and temples were re-activated between 1933 and 1936, and the number of *jas* increased by about six hundred, though as *jas* were kept small for taxation purposes this does not indicate a startling rise in actual wealth. The number of lamas grew by ten thousand according to one estimate, by twenty-four thousand according to another, in any case very considerably. This showed convincingly that the ordinary people were still far more attached to their traditional way of life than to revolutionary innovations. On the other hand, government officials, confused by the about-turn in policies, often took the view that the aim of the New Turn really was to promote the Church, and they interpreted instructions in the way most favourable to the lamas. Some were honestly afraid to do anything which might offend the lamas, in case they should subsequently be found to have been perpetrating new 'deviations'. Others actively co-operated with the lamaseries, permitting Party and Youth League members to surrender their documents, and soldiers their registrations, and become lamas.

The way the regulations were framed actually encouraged young men of eighteen to enter the Church. The intention of the law that no children under the age of eighteen could become lamas was a simple one. By the age of eighteen, especially if he had been to a state school, a boy might be expected not to want to enter a lamasery where he would live a celibate life, cut off from the new world he had grown up in. Ultimately the supply of recruits would dry up of itself. But in practice things worked out differently. Deliberate pressure was brought to bear on young men to make a decision between the lay and the clerical life as soon as they reached the age of eighteen. If they opted for the lay state they were immediately enlisted into the army. As a result, many young men chose to be lamas, which they otherwise might not have done, simply to escape the even less attractive prospect of military duty: if the accusations of dereliction and sabotage brought against the High Command in 1937 were only half true, army service was anything but a passport to health. The Party achieved the opposite of its intentions. Between 1933 and 1936 the complement of lamas increased sharply. When it was realized what was happening, new regulations were suggested. All young men were to be placed on the military register at the age of eighteen without being asked, and only those who put in a special request to become lamas would be released. Gradually this new procedure seems to have had its effect, and fewer young men opted for the Church. The blame for this muddle has been put on to Gendung, but, like the absurdities of the 1932 purge, it seems more likely that inexperience, incompetence and timidity on the part of local functionaries, who were regularly out of their depth, was responsible.

The elimination of the Church

The increasing threat from Japan after 1935 when the first frontier probings took place, undoubtedly created or facilitated the creation of an atmosphere of tension inside Mongolia, in which it was easier to carry out the final work of liquidating the Church. Accusations of treachery and collusion with the Japanese brought against high lamas were more plausible in an ambience of uncertainty and expectancy in the face of attacks which did in fact materialize, sporadically, in the years up to 1939. From the time of the Ninth Party Congress in 1934 when the Czech Comintern agent Shmeral intervened for a second and last time to point out Gendung's sharpening swerve to the right and to demand its correction, Gendung's control over Mongolian affairs began to slacken, and by early 1936 Choibalsang was in a position to supplant him and, with the help of the security services, to initiate his personal dictatorship. At the same time the persecution of the Church sharpened, but this time it was more skilfully planned and prepared than during the leftist years. The same target was aimed at – the total destruction of the Church and the appropriation of its property, and the absorption of lamas into ordinary life, but the second attempt was successful. The presence of a large Soviet army in the country, and of a reinforced NKVD apparatus, alongside the parallel Mongol organs, was decisive. The enforced closure of the lamaseries could be accomplished now without the danger of uprisings threatening the stability of the State. There were other factors also. The Party had by now acquired the wisdom to try to educate the lower lamas in the advantages of abandoning their clerical life, and offering them a tangible economic inducement to do so. Many, but not most, lamas were won over by propaganda and grants. The State weakened the Church by a number of innovations. The arraignment of high lamas on charges of treason must have helped to alienate public opinion from the Church, while the spectacular confessions made in the full publicity of show trials held in the Ulan Bator theatre during which the state security apparatus showed itself tough enough to eliminate the high lamas and the army staff at the same time, must have impressed people with the futility of resistance. After 1936 many lamas began to drift away from the lamaseries, and either took up animal herding, or went into industry, trade, or craft co-operatives, and when the time was ripe the remaining lamaseries were closed by administrative and military action. There was resistance, but nowhere on a scale too great to cope with, and by 1939 the operation was at an end. The Church had to all intents and purposes ceased to exist.

How this was accomplished so completely, in the course of four or five years, when similar action a few years before had ended in civil war, is an interesting story. In the first place, as we have seen, military preparedness was far more adequate. Then too, Choibalsang took care not to repeat the error of setting the whole of the population against the régime by attacking on all fronts at once. There was no attempt to repeat the fiasco of collectivization. Also the Party had learned its lesson and refrained from assaulting the Church as a whole until it had sapped its resistance. For the first time it put into practice in a more or less intelligent way the tactics it had always held to in theory, that is, to split the Church by emphasizing and exploiting class differences. The whole campaign was assisted by a planned war of attrition against the Church's wealth, against the wealth of individual lamas, and against the Church's internal autonomy. Finally, a planned campaign of enlightenment was carried out amongst the poorer lamas. They were taught to read and write Mongol, were given the opportunity to learn and practise trades, and were introduced to the benefits of modern hygiene and medicine. As most of them suffered from something or other, most frequently venereal diseases, the availability of effective medical treatment, which some of them were even taught to practise at a low level, had a considerable effect on their loyalties to the Church, which also professed a systematic, but unscientific, form of medicine. Still, the effect of this campaign of enlightenment must not be overrated. Superstitions die hard, and are not, by their very nature, susceptible to the force of logic. There is an excellent illustration of this from the previous decade. One of the children sent to study in Germany fell ill and died, and the Mongol government was constrained to send a lama to Berlin to supervise the children's health, so as to allay the anxieties of the parents, though in fact medical treatment when necessary continued to be given by German doctors. Ex-lamas are still found today in Mongolia, holding services and attracting the faithful, though clandestinely, and people still believe them and support them with offerings. The authorities are still exercised by this problem, and propose such solutions, logical in theory, as reprinting the Buddhist scriptures with 'scientific commentaries' to point up their inadequacies. In the 'thirties it was too much to expect that a couple of years' elementary education would make much impact on the mass of the ignorant clergy.

The leftists had lumped all lamas together for discriminatory treatment. As far as the military tax was concerned this had meant that all were taxed alike, lamas of military age, young children and old men, rich and poor, even the *chavgants* or old women who were not cloistered but lived at home with shaven heads under vows, and the *ubashi* or laymen who had taken minor orders. From 1933 onwards lamas were divided into four classes according to their social origin and present function, and were taxed accordingly, the assessments varying from sixty tugrigs down to five. Those of military age paid double. With the years the rates went up steeply, so that a young high lama who was paying 120 tugrigs in 1933, was charged 1,000 in 1938. Taxation was looked on not only as a means of getting money but as a factor in inducing social change. The liability to pay tax discouraged men from taking vows to escape military service, but nevertheless the differential rate meant that a poor lama was never assessed to more than twenty tugrigs a year. Besides this, lamas who had made themselves literate in Mongol, and so were accessible to propaganda, and those who were doing socially useful work, were taxed at reduced rates or exempted altogether. While it ran, this military tax campaign brought in considerable sums. At its height, in 1938, over twenty-three thousand lamas paid more than twenty-six million tugrigs. From then on, as the Church collapsed, figures fell off sharply, and in 1940 there were only 251 lamas left to pay sixty-one thousand tugrigs between them.

Two further economic weapons were applied. The *jas* still survived, though the cattle then owned were far fewer in number than before 1929. After 1932 taxation rates were reviewed. All animals were valued in money terms and a money tax levied. As before, the *jas* tried to avoid taxation by converting their wealth into fixed property: as a result this too was made subject to taxation, as was the year's income from all sources. Only actual sacred objects escaped assessment. This fiscal action had the effect of impoverishing the *jas* to the point where they began to disappear, even before the lamaseries themselves were forced to close. By 1937 a number of *jas* had no cattle at all, and from then on more and more *jas* had to sell up in a vain attempt to pay their taxes. By 1939 the *jas* were in effect bankrupt throughout the country.

Secondly, the private property of well-off lamas was attacked. Since the cattle confiscations of 1929 the high lamas no longer possessed much wealth in the form of livestock, but tended more and more to rely on alms for their income. These could be very high. One lama of Gandang was reckoned to be making twelve thousand tugrigs a year in 1936. In that year a special tax was imposed on lamas' incomes. The high lamas were divided into four classes for this purpose, according to their rank, and their incomes were taxed at differential, but high, rates. The highest rank, for example, paid between five hundred and one thousand tugrigs on incomes of 1,500 tugrigs, and a percentage on anything in excess of that. This tax was, like others, conceived of partly as a fiscal measure, which brought in fifteen million tugrigs in three years, but primarily as an economic lever to prise the high lamas out of their lamaseries and make proletarians out of them. Some of them were reduced to going begging to raise the money to pay their taxes. Two lamas of a lamasery in Kentei aimak, for example, managed to collect forty-four oxen, two horses, some sheep and goats, flint boxes and knives, and three hundred tugrigs in cash from the local people before they were discovered and stopped. Equally, lamas took out loans, which in the nature of things, they would never be able to repay, of some hundreds of thousands of tugrigs altogether, from public offices and co-operative stores in the countryside, until this too was put a stop to. Inside the lamaseries the tax sometimes led to trouble within the community, since the higher lamas would try to deprive the others of their share of alms-incomes so as to be able to meet their personal obligations.

A further weapon used against the Church was direct intervention in the internal administration of the lamaseries. In August 1932, when the regulations for farming out cattle were revised, it was decreed that disputes between the herds-people and the lamaseries were no longer to be adjudicated by the lamasaries but were to come before the local courts. From then on the semi-autonomy of the Church was undermined in various ways. In 1934 special government representatives were sent to reside in a number of important lamaseries to check their internal working and see that this did not conflict with the law. They had no power to interfere in the conduct of services, but they had to see, for instance, that children were not admitted as novices, that the people were not compelled to give alms, that taxation was not evaded, that the ordinary lamas were not fined or beaten by their superiors, and so on. Violence, strangely enough in a religion which rejected violence, was still resorted to by the lamas of Mongolia, even now that their position was becoming so precarious. In the mid-'thirties the lamas of one lamasery in South Khangai, for example, had been detected judging the local people in illegal courts of their own, and executing them by the time-honoured method of tying them up and leaving them exposed on the open ground. Against this sort of brutality the action of high lamas elsewhere of fining secularized lamas sums up to ten tugrigs seems quite mild, though this too was illegal. All such actions as this came within the purview of the new government representatives.

The law of 1926 separating Church and State was revised in 1934. In some respects it represented a retreat from the earlier legislation, particularly in its assertion that 'the State will not promote religion, but neither will it hinder it'. This may have been, as is nowadays stated, one of the new provisions inserted into the law by Gendung in order to slow down the process of attrition of the Church. It may equally have been no more than a restatement of the accepted principle that the practice of religion was a matter for the individual conscience. At any rate, it provided those who wanted to protect the Church with a pretext for avoiding rigorous measures. But in other details the new law went beyond the old one and helped further to undermine the Church's position. The teaching of religion in schools, and the holding of services in public places, were forbidden. Those lamas who wished to leave the Church were not to be obstructed. No new building was to take place. The lamaseries were specifically ordered to submit themselves to the jurisdiction of the courts, and to register their domestic regulations with the local administration. Lamas were no longer obliged to accept punishments awarded by their superiors. Lower lamas were given the right to belong to craft co-operatives, to take work in factories or in public offices, and to engage in trade and transport work. The total effect of this was not only to give the State a considerable share in the management of the lamaseries, but to widen the horizons of the ordinary lamas, and give them a foretaste of the wider world beyond the lamasery walls. At the same time the new regulations were supported by stiff penalties. Lamas who built new buildings, or recruited minors, or who forced people to give alms, were liable to a year's imprisonment or a fine of six hundred tugrigs.

From 1935 onwards the campaign against the Church was directed by a religious commission of the Central Committee, under the party secretary Eldev-ochir, which had branches in provincial party headquarters, and by a control office for religious affairs attached to the Ministry of Internal Affairs. Thus religious policy came under the direct management of Choibalsang and Eldev-ochir, both of them enemies of Gendung. When they had brought about Gendung's fall in 1936, the last obstacle to the all-out assault on the Church had been overcome. The Comintern and the Soviet communist party had several times advised the Mongols to make a clean sweep of their lamaseries, and in the next three years this was done. The internal autonomy of the lamaseries was still further weakened. The provision of the 1934 law that there would be no joint administration of two or more houses, which had been interpreted liberally up till now, was strictly applied, with the result that each lamasery now stood entirely on its own. All disputes between lamas were in future to be brought before the public courts, instead of being settled domestically. The so-called 'religious administrations' which had been installed in some lamaseries since the 'twenties as an internal check on the authorities were reorganized and provided with new regulations. This happened first in Ulan Bator in 1936. The religious administrations, with direct access to the government, were in future to be composed entirely of middle and low lamas, with incarnations, bursars and others specifically excluded from participation. They were to supervise practically every aspect of lamasery life, from the exclusion of minors to the prevention of fraudulent divination. They had to check expenditure, to help in establishing craft cooperatives, and prevent encyclicals from the late Khutuktu being circulated. This was an over-ambitious programme of change, and when the system was hurriedly introduced in Bulgan aimak without preparation and collapsed ignominiously, the religious administrations lost their prestige.

Other irritants were applied. The State tried to alter the internal organization of the lamaseries by direct action, ordering new *jayig* or lamasery codes to be drawn up in Mongol and not in Tibetan, and to incorporate recent legislation. It was decreed that services were to be performed in Mongol rather than in Tibetan, a change-over that would have meant an intolerable labour of translation and adaptation. But when the final blow came in 1937 and 1938 it was dealt in quite another way. It was not a mere extension of the measures so far taken, though these had certainly had the cumulative effect of sapping the Church's resistance. Lamaseries were forcibly closed and their occupants scattered, or were squeezed into a position where 'voluntary' dissolution was the only escape from persecution. Exactly how this was done in all cases is not clear. Zlatkin describes the operation only in outline:

> The practice of the class struggle taught the Party that it is impossible to count on successful defence against the external enemy if the hostile organization of traitors, saboteurs and spies in one's own rear has not been liquidated. Led by these considerations, the Party brought the liquidation of the lamaist counter-revolutionary centre to its conclusion in 1937 and 1938, by shutting one after the other the lamaseries implicated in hostile activity, and severely punishing their heads. After this action the old feudal lamaist church in Mongolia, with its numerous lamaseries, its huge herding economy, its mighty riches, its army of thousands of lamas, ceased in effect to exist.

Speaking of the Mongol army he says:

In these years the Mongolian revolutionary people's army disposed of its own infantry, cavalry, artillery, intelligence, pioneers, armoured troops and fliers. It was not strong numerically, but was on a par with the leading armies of the world and was a mighty weapon of the people's power in the fight against external enemies and *against the forces of internal reaction*.[17]

From this we may conclude that the final struggle against the lamaseries was not a non-violent campaign, but involved the use of the army. Certain other evidence of this survives. It is impossible to find recorded in any book how the great lamasery of Erdeni Juu came to be ruined, but an album of photographs, kept in the lamasery, showing how it looked originally, and how it looked immediately after the closure of 1937, with stupas overthrown, walls breached and temple buildings shattered, suggests the use of high explosive. We do know how some lamaseries came to be closed. In April 1937 sixteen lamaseries were ordered to move themselves from the frontier areas where they were situated, on the pretext that they had been engaged in smuggling goods and Japanese agents in and out of the country. In November of the same year another fifty-nine lamaseries were similarly ordered to move not less than one hundred kilometres from their established sites towards the interior of the country. At the same time it was made known that if the lamaseries affected preferred to dissolve themselves rather than undertake the move, they would not be stopped from doing so. The property of all lamaseries which did voluntarily disband themselves would be nationalized. It was out of the question that long established lamaseries, consisting of fixed buildings as well as living-tents, should uproot themselves from the pastures they relied on, and from the community of the faithful who supported them, at a moment's notice. The move was made even more impracticable, and the real purpose of its requirement all the more obvious, since it was ordered in the depths of winter, which, as usual in Mongolia, was a time of bitter cold. The lamaseries had no alternative but to eject their occupants into the world in mid-winter and close their doors.

The Church was thus destroyed. All over the country lamaseries were shut down or ruined, precious objects smashed, gold and silver vessels seized as bullion. Thousands of buildings were taken over by the State to be used as offices of warehouses, but most of the great monuments of Mongol architecture, illustrating the rich fusion of Tibetan and Chinese tradition with Mongol innovation, disappeared. Practically nothing survives in Ulan Bator to suggest that it lies on the site of old Urga, the centre of Mongol lamaism and once a rival in artistic splendour to Lhasa. This phase of Mongolia's past, a phase which covers the last three hundred years, or almost half her known history, is recorded now only in a few museums: in the 'living' museum of Gandang where a few old lamas preserve the shadow of their former life, the 'religious museum' maintained in the former Oracle Temple, the surviving parts of Erdeni Juu, and some local museums, like that of Tsetserlig, where the remains of the great lamasery of the Jaya Pandita have been refurbished and house a small collection of religious objects. Fortunately a considerable amount of Buddhist literature, manuscripts, printed books, and elaborately produced books made of embroidery or of beaten metal, escaped damage and have found their way to libraries.

In destroying the Church the Mongol State faced a double problem. It had first of all to discredit an ideology, destroy the internal solidarity of the Church, and detach the people from it. In itself this was an enormous task, since every family either was, or would have liked to be, integrated with the Church by having one or more of its members a lama. As late as 1936 a new law had to be passed forbidding boys to become lamas if there were less than three sons in the family. Then the State had to cope with the problem of some ninety thousand former lamas being released upon society, a society still to all intents and purposes without factories to absorb what was probably a sudden growth of some 25 per cent in its labour force. One of the most interesting aspects of the anti-church campaign is how the authorities tried to prepare the lamas, especially the poorer ones who were ignorant of modern life, for integration in modern society, and what success they had. Unfortunately, only part of the story has so far been written up. We can follow the period of preparation up to about 1939, but know far less of how the ex-lamas who survived the closures fared during the next fifteen years. That they were somehow assimilated is clear, since they no longer exist as a separate social group, but how, and in what proportions, they found their niche in herding, craft co-operatives, the army and elsewhere, has still not been fully described.

The negative aspect of the Party's programme was the discriminatory nature of the treatment accorded to lamas of different social origin, culminating, as Zlatkin implies, in the liquidation of the higher lamas. The positive aspect was the effort to educate the lower lamas in the first essentials of modern living, to teach them to read and write in their own language, to give them basic notions of hygiene – the use of soap and water for example – to help those who wished to join co-operative workshops, and to provide others with a little capital to set themselves up as herdsmen, no longer celibate, but living an ordinary family life. This was no easy task. The inherent difficulties of retraining an enormous mass of adults with totally inadequate resources was complicated by the active and often cunning opposition of the lamas themselves, traditionally an unruly crowd as the Manchus had found, right up to the affair of the amban Sando in 1910.

Inside the lamaseries literacy circles were established: the first of these was set up in Gandang in Ulan Bator in 1934 and was taught by a lama. By 1936 some 160 literacy circles had been set up, and counted over eight thousand pupils. Results were modest. In 1937 there were over fifty thousand poor lamas, of whom less than five thousand had learned to read. In one aimak for which figures are given, we find that only ninety-three lamas had put in subscriptions for newspapers and magazines. Schools for young lamas were set up in each of the main ministries in Ulan Bator in 1937, and over seven hundred children were entered for instruction in arithmetic, Mongol, hygiene, gymnastics, games and some elementary trade schools. What this meant for the lucky few who got into schools run on modern lines, compared with the medieval curriculum of the lamaseries, can be seen from the account of one of the first pupils. P. Batsukh, now a doctor, recalls:

When I was a little chap, my people put me to school in a lamasery as a pupil of a lama called Lofty Gombojav. This man made me work hard, and used to beat me a lot. He taught me Tibetan letters, and if I couldn't remember them the first time he would beat me till I yelled, and then scratch the letters on my head with the sharp point of a bamboo stylus till it bled. But one day someone came and told us about the new schools, and I went off with him and came to town, and entered the so-called lamas' elementary school at the co-operative. There I was taught Mongol, sums, geography and book-keeping. Everything was provided by the state. We were lodged and had good teachers. It seemed a paradise after the cruel old lama teacher.[18]

The primitive methods of lamaistic discipline recalled by

Batsukh were no rarity. Children were in fact often badly treated in lamasery schools: cases are known of their being blinded by being jabbed in the eye with a stylus.

The new secular schools did not enjoy an easy time. The lamas tried to undermine their prestige by spreading tales that children were tortured there and would be taken away from their parents. New teachers were warned of the battles they would have to face. A teacher now in Ulan Bator, L. Baljir, still only in his fifties, recalls an episode in his early professional life. At the beginning of 1930 he had joined a school at Tariyat in North Khangai aimak, one of the trouble spots of the time. The school had a lama doctor. Baljir soon noticed that a lot of the little children were running away, and that those who remained were dirty and sickly and liable to fainting fits and delirium. It took a long time before he could find out from the older pupils what was happening, and then only by threatening them with expulsion. The lama doctor was working on the minds of the little children, by nightly bell-ringing and by displays of ritual fires, for which he recruited the older pupils, into believing that the school was haunted by demons. He hoped in the end to bring about its complete collapse when the children had all been frightened into running away. Baljir says: 'Truly things were difficult then. One day the head of the local red-yurt said to me: "Keep an eye open!" I used to carry a gun. At night I could hardly get to sleep for fear one of the hostile lamas might kill me.'[19]

Direct propaganda among the lamas was carried out in various ways. In Ulan Bator a special paper, the *Lamas' Journal*, appeared for a couple of years. Using the traditional language and turns of phrase of Buddhism it tried to put over the Party's policy. In Ulan Bator many lamas used to attend what was known as the 'Saturday Meeting' organized by the religious commission of the Central Committee of the Party, at which speeches were made and the lamas could ask questions. The proceedings were sometimes turbulent, sometimes ludicrous, but with some lamas effective. A lama who took part in them recalls the atmosphere of the time:

I used to go and watch the Saturday Meeting. It used to be very argumentative and interesting. Once when I was there, my old friend the lama Flap-ear Jambal made a speech. He stood in front of the theatre curtain and spoke very well and keenly. We were all impressed and surprised and said to each other: 'What a card old Flap-ear is, isn't he!

Full of knowledge and revolution!' But afterwards Jambal said to me: 'How do you think I could make a speech like that? The Party Secretary Eldev-ochir was standing behind the curtain prompting me. I listened to what he said and passed it on to you'. Sometimes there were big disturbances at these meetings and it would even come to scuffles. The former lama Namjil, who took part in the meetings, enjoyed criticizing the higher lamas. They used to call us the 'Saturday Precentors' and some of them would say: 'When the Japanese take over, Flap-ear Jambal and Kid Namjil will catch it!' Some meetings ran into real trouble. Once Eldev-ochir came and spoke sharply about some lamas who had spoken out of turn, and some of the lamas got up and hooted and clapped their hands and stamped to show their disapproval, and things began to get out of hand. Eldev-ochir said angrily: 'If you don't stop misbehaving we'll have to get the troops in' and he calmed the meeting down and closed it.[20]

Many lamas were in fact won over to the side of the revolution, including learned men like the *gabj* Gombojav, an expert Tibetan scholar who succeeded in the mid-'sixties to the post of abbot of the revived Gandang lamasery. But most were never reconciled to the assault on their traditional way of life. They used religious festivals as occasions to distribute anti-Soviet propaganda, and tracts praising Japan, as well as encyclicals emanating from the late Khutuktu, and there were riots in which lamas would wreck red-yurts, smash cinema projectors and beat up members of propaganda teams. When the lamaseries were finally closed, the great majority of the lamas were still unreconciled to the new ideas, but their disorganized dispersal throughout the countryside prevented them from raising any significant protest. What, then, became of the lamas? Some, especially those of high rank, were executed as a result of show trials, or after the closure of their houses. Many were killed in fighting, and others shared the common fate of imprisonment with other members of the population at large. But these probably formed a minority: the majority had to be resettled.

There were many lamas who would have been glad to abandon the religious life earlier, but who lacked the skill and capital, and the self-confidence to set up for themselves. They were forced to hold on to what they knew, eking out a living on temple doles and on what they could make from odd jobs. For these and others rehabilitation was necessary, and a certain amount of thought was devoted to this problem. Loans were given to lamas to enable them to buy tents and an initial stock of animals, and those who took up useful work, such as caravanning or trade, were exempted from taxes for a while. A few lamas found jobs in Mongolia's infant industry, or as road and bridge navvies, or as miners. But the state industry was too tiny to be able to absorb many fresh workers, the main factories employing, in 1938, only a little over eight thousand Mongol work-people all told. The answer did not lie in industry. Of the ten thousand odd lamas who went to work in 1936 the majority found employment in animal herding, transport or trading. The craft co-operatives which were rapidly increasing in numbers between 1936 and 1938 played their part too in absorbing lamas. There were considerable numbers of skilled craftsmen in the lamaseries, and the first lamas' co-operatives were formed by men still living the cloistered life. In their most elementary form these early co-operatives consisted merely of a few lamas who made an agreement with the Central Crafts Bureau to supply so many finished articles out of material advanced to them. It was in 1936 that the first real workshop was formed by a group of lamas in Gandang as a regular commercial enterprise. The success of this organization was publicized in the *Lamas' Journal*, and it served as a model for other co-operatives, but it seems to have been an outstanding, rather than a typical, example of co-operation and of readjustment to a new way of life. It was not formed entirely by the spontaneous enterprise of lower lamas: its genesis was a suggestion made by the government representative in Gandang to two lamas that they ought to take up useful work. These men went to the town administration to look for jobs but were laughed at as paupers and renegades and went home discouraged. On the way they decided to have a word with the proctors Gombodoo and Luvsanjambaa, men accustomed to wield authority, in the hopes that if they could enlist their interest other lamas might follow them. Gombodoo was an old revolutionary and a man of initiative and ability. He had been a subordinate official in the first days of the revolutionary government, and had taken part in the Second Party Congress of 1923 and the First National Khural of 1924. When he died in 1965 he was assistant to the Abbot of Gandang. With his support and participation the first Gandang co-operative got on its feet, and did so well that Choibalsang awarded it a special prize of five thousand tugrigs.

From small beginnings with five members this co-operative grew to employ three hundred lamas, and was properly organized with fifteen separate workshops for different crafts and with an accounting system. Other co-operatives followed, and in 1937 twenty-one were set up out of thirty planned, with a total membership of 510 lamas. In the first year their finished products were valued at half a million tugrigs, a small beginning but a significant new departure. By October 1938 there were ninety-nine craft shops in existence, employing some 5,200 workers of whom over four thousand were former lamas. The numbers continued to increase and the proportion of ex-lamas to other workers remained about the same.

However, craft co-operatives were not the answer to the problem of how to employ ex-lamas. For one thing, like the state-owned factories, their capacity to absorb new workers was limited. At the end of 1938 only five thousand lamas had joined co-operatives, where they formed about 80 per cent of the workers. What percentage these five thousand formed of the whole it is difficult to tell, as statistics are incomplete and at variance, but in any case they were a small fraction. Probably the most reliable estimate we have for the total number of lamas in 1937 is about ninety-four thousand: of these, more than fifty thousand were classed as lower lamas while somewhat over fifteen thousand were classed as 'exploiting elements'. How the remainder were considered is unclear, and such discrepancies as this make the exploitation of Mongol statistics a very chancy process. When we come to examine what happened to all these lamas there are big apparent discrepancies. One source tells us that after the closure campaign was over, 7·7 per cent of the lamas, or some seven thousand, remained in the surviving lamaseries, while 22 per cent, or over twenty thousand went into herding: these percentages, incidentally, confirm the total figure of ninety-four thousand as more or less accurate. Elsewhere we learn that between 1936 and 1938 about thirty-five thousand lamas left the lamaseries: adding to these the fifteen thousand of the 'exploiting' class, who may have been liquidated, we obtain a maximum of only fifty thousand lamas accounted for. Other must have left the lamaseries in 1939, but for these we have at present no figures.

Probably many more than are actually specified drifted back to their families, and there is no guarantee, in any case, that statistics relating to this violent period are accurate, but quite evidently the craft co-operatives represented only a minor easement of the problem of resettlement. In practice, too, they did not offer a satisfactory solution. The trouble was the perennial one in Mongolia, the gap between high level planning and the realization of the plans by low-level officials of limited capacities. Once the workshops had been set up, the competent Party and local authorities took no further interest in their organization or running, and since the lama-members were in a good many cases not interested in the success of the workshops either, the consequences were serious. Many of them simply fell apart, and those that survived were in constant trouble. Without experienced or interested management there was no accounting, no stocktaking, and no supervision of work. Some workshops had only two or three members, others were little more than old people's homes for the aged and ineffective. Co-operatives carrying on different trades tried to ruin each other. Most members sat around and did nothing. Production quality was abysmal, and pay too low to be any incentive. Co-operatives did not stick to their trades, but did a bit of everything, wood-working, sewing, even canteen work, on a seasonal basis or even haphazardly with no plan at all. Many co-operatives had been formed from lamas from the same lamaseries and so were little nests of disaffection, and as no one had bothered to check the recruits there were plenty of unenthusiastic ex-lamas who did not mind when things went wrong. All these defects were detailed in a resolution of the Central Committee of the Party in January 1939, and local organizations were instructed to carry through a check, with what effect is not known.

In fact, comparatively little is known of Mongolia during the war years, and what finally happened to the lamas is uncertain: it is probable that most of them became private, small-scale animal herders, petty traders and drivers, while a minority only went into factories and craft co-operatives.

Mongolia in 1940

In the officially accepted periodization of Mongolian history the year 1940 is a climacteric, and it was marked as such by the promulgation of a new constitution and the formulation by the Tenth Party Congress held that year of the Party's Third Programme, the first two having been those of 1921 and 1925. By 1940 'the first stage of the people's revolution had been completed, and the period of gradual progress from democratic revolution to socialist revolution entered upon'.[21] This programme is now, a quarter of a century later, considered to have been accomplished, with socialism a fact in Mongolia, and it was replaced by a fourth at the Fifteenth Party Congress held in June 1966.

If we examine what in fact had been achieved by 1940 it seems that the main progress up to then had been of a preparatory, even negative, nature in which the old substructure of society had been cleared away, and an assault made on the cultural superstructure. But little except the outlines of the new building was yet visible. Mongolia's main achievement had been to effect the total disappearance as an organized social group of the old secular nobility, and of the Church as an economic and cultural force. What opposition there remained was ineffectual, because it lacked any organization after the destruction of the Church. Few of the old nobility and high lamas survived the 'thirties, so that when in 1944 the Government decided that those elements who had previously constituted a danger to the State and had been disenfranchized, had become harmless and could be entrusted with the vote, they formed only a tiny minority, 0·08 per cent of the population, or about six hundred individuals.

Even allowing for the different meaning attached to the word democracy in communist societies, democracy in Mongolia was a very tender growth. Popular participation in revolutionary government had not sprung into being on its own, not even to the extent it had done in the USSR with local Soviets, before these were rendered harmless. Local administration had been imposed from the centre outwards. The new organs had taken a long time to establish themselves, especially in the West, and during the leftist deviation had forfeited what credit they had possessed by their complete surrender to the Party. Critical new departures in policy, for example the confiscation of cattle in 1929, the elimination of the nobility and the creation of collectives, were effected without the slightest reference to popular demand through the agency of special commissioners sent out by the Central Committee of the Party, and by local party zealots who explained what was happening only after it had been accomplished. The Party had, it was later recognized, been able to infringe the national law with impunity. During the 'thirties power became increasingly concentrated in the hands of Choibalsang and his security service. The Party itself, never in effect more than an agency of the Central Committee, lost even more of its prestige: only two Party Congresses were held in the decade after 1930 as compared with eight in the first decade of the revolution. The Great National Khural too met only twice, to confirm the decisions of the two Party Congresses. Government was more and more exercised by decrees issued in the name of the Little Khural, or caucus of the Great Khural. From 1940 onwards the chairman of the presidium of this organ was Bumtsend, a former officer of the partisan army, and a police chief during the 'twenties, but not an outstanding personality: he had spent the 'thirties in relatively minor posts supervising co-operatives in Selenga aimak, where he was head of a party cell. Against Choibalsang he was a nonentity, and by 1940 Choibalsang's personal dictatorship was secure. Not only had recognizable reactionary elements like the high lamas been annihilated, but all the old revolutionaries of sufficient calibre to challenge Choibalsang's pre-eminence had been executed too, on the most scurrilous charges of treason which the Central Committee has since admitted to be false. They were replaced by a new generation of managers, young men loyal to Choibalsang and owing their careers to him, men like Tsedenbal the present premier, who had for the most part been born not long before 1920 and had grown up entirely in the post-revolutionary era.

Culturally Mongolia moved along a new path. In the older days the Church had certainly influenced the evolution of literary forms and themes, but this was a general, unplanned influence. By 1940 the totalitarian pretensions of the Party meant that all creative and artistic life was directly subject to the overriding purpose of building socialism. Soon after the revolution little dramatic groups sprang up such as the one at Altan Bulak in which Academician Rintchen took part as a young man, and these composed and acted little plays based on old Mongol and Chinese themes. Such plays were condemned in 1928 by the Seventh Party Congress which criticized the dramatic groups for being guided by 'right deviationists' who foisted on them the idea of 'pure', non-political, art. The Congress demanded that in future all plays should have a political message. Art, literature and scholarship became tools of sectarian politics. The effects of this were seen most plainly in the field of creative writing, where Soviet literature was taken as the model, and old Mongol forms were rejected. Even experimental literature which was not compatible with the strict demands of 'socialist realism' was forbidden, and the works of men like Yadamsuren and Buyannemekh, who lost their lives in the political purges, were condemned and suppressed for their supposed ideological deviations. There was an ambivalent attitude towards the preservation and publication of old Mongol literature. Individual scholars, and the Committee of Sciences, did what they could to collect and write down Mongolia's rich oral folk literature, but were hampered by the attitude of the Central Committee which charged them in 1935 with disseminating literature among the masses in an easily assimilable form, but at the same time with suppressing 'useless, feudal compositions'. The result was that while folk literature continued to be collected, very little of it ever appeared in published form until the late 'fifties, by which time the original manuscripts made thirty years before had become dilapidated and were no longer complete. Scholarship being subject to the whim of the politicians, the latitude enjoyed by literary historians and folk-lorists varied according to the political climate. This led to the most curious contradictions. In the late 'twenties, for example, Rintchen, then a young literary scholar, collected considerable quantities of oral literature, epics, tales and proverbs, from folk singers, but was never able to publish them until, from 1960 onwards, an opening was found in western Europe. Between 1926 and 1929 he was fortunately able to record almost all the repertory of a well-known contemporary poet 'Fiddler' Luvsan, who had to emigrate to Verkheneudinsk when, at the end of 1929, the leftists in Mongolia forbade folk-singers to recite in public as an 'illicit continuation of feudal traditions'. Luvsan's epics and tales were not published in full till they appeared in Western Germany in 1960. Literary monuments such as the ancient Geser epic and the thirteenth century *Secret History of the Mongols* were found to be ideologically 'good' or 'bad' according to political necessity: in 1950 they were condemned as feudal and reactionary, and the Geser epic was dropped from the syllabus of Ulan Bator university, but at the end of the decade they were rehabilitated as being of a 'democratic' tendency and the Committee of Sciences was able to plan and execute an ambitious programme of publication of various texts of Geser. It must be observed, however, that the restoration of Mongolia's old literature to favour was not motivated, at least publicly, by purely literary or artistic considerations or by a demand for freedom of artistic or academic expression. The first shots in the campaign were fired by Academician Damdinsuren, who argued from a political viewpoint, from within the compass of communist *idées reçues*. Mongolia's old literature was to be cherished not because the preservation of old literature is a good thing in itself, but because, so it was argued, it showed democratic tendencies.

Some of the worst effects of political obscurantism were seen in the schools. From 1936 onwards nothing was taught in Mongol schools about the country's pre-revolutionary culture for about twenty years, as we have seen in chapter 6. The break with the old life was both symbolized and reinforced by the adoption, from 1941 onwards, of the Cyrillic script, which was accompanied by a spelling reform and the progressive abandonment, for all official purposes, of the old script. Children could not read old books even if they could get hold of them, and today it is still common to meet people around the age of thirty who cannot read their own traditional alphabet. This was part of a deliberate process on the part of the Party to subordinate feelings of Mongolianness to the wider 'loyalties' of proletarian internationalism. Between 1936 and 1956, as we have seen, no reprints of old books were issued: although the printing programme included such books, they were invariably dropped from it, according to Damdinsuren by 'comrades who were doing responsible work in the cultural field'.[22] Publishing capacity was turned over in these years to communist literature, translations from Russian, and to new creative writing which fulfilled the narrow demands of socialist realism.

Actual economic and social reconstruction, though noticeable, took second place during the 'thirties to the political ideal of creating a *tabula rasa* for socialism. In fact a great deal was done, but progress was hampered by several factors, apart from the disastrous setbacks at the start of the decade. One factor was the necessity to devote up to half the state budget, year after year, to building up the armed forces to face a possible attack from Japan. There was probably no alternative to this, though Gendung maintained, as late as 1936, that Mongolia's rearmament served only the purposes of the USSR, not Mongolia's own. Given the existence of a number of influential men who would have been prepared to welcome the alternative of autonomous government under Japanese protection, with a chastened and purified lamaist church allowed to exist, as was happening under Te Wang in Inner Mongolia, there was some logic in Gendung's objection. But equally, given the political realities of the time, Mongolia could not hope to do anything but go along with the USSR and pay her share of rearmament. Military expenditure reached a maximum of over 50 per cent of budget outlay in 1938.

Secondly, the USSR was unable or unwilling to devote much of her own overstretched resources to help Mongolia except in the field of rearmament. Some help was given: one or two factories were built, the industrial combine in Ulan Bator and the wool washing plant at Khatgal, medical workers were sent, machinery supplied for the new haymaking stations, lorries, telegraph and radio equipment and so on sent in. But on the whole, Mongolia had to rely on her own resources for her slow development. Imports from the USSR were to be reduced drastically in the war years too, and until foreign aid started to pour in in the mid-'fifties, Mongolia's modernization went on at a painfully slow rate. After 1932 industry was relegated once more to a subordinate position, ancillary to the herding economy. The grandiose factory schemes of the leftists had wrecked what little industry there had been: plans had hardly been realized at all in some sectors, and discouraged workers had abandoned their workshops and gone home to the countryside. For military reasons expenditure had to be devoted to projects not essential to Mongolia's development. A prime example of this is the fact that her first international railway was built in the east to serve the army's build up against Japan. It was only in 1949 that a line linked Ulan Bator, the main centre of population and industrial production, with the Trans-Siberian line. A third factor inhibiting progress was the subordination of the growth of material wealth to the demands of revolutionary change. This ordering of priorities was deliberate, and a significant criticism made of Gendung is that he considered the *nökhörlöl* or informal, seasonal labour-pooling arrangements which Mongol herdsmen began to make during the 'thirties, not as a means towards the ultimate socialization of the economy, but as a way for the people to build up their own private prosperity. The failures of the first collectivization had left behind them a sort of traumatic hangover. Not only had the Party had to admit its failure, and devote its attention to building up the private herding economy again to save the country, but collectivization got such a bad name that even those groups which were working reasonably well and which should have been retained, were disbanded along with the others. In 1935 some small beginnings were attempted again, but the collectivization movement had received such a setback that it was only in the mid-'fifties that it once again became declared policy.

In less tangible ways too, the forced march of the 'thirties involved losses which are now regretted. Much of the evidence of Mongolia's old material culture disappeared with her lamaseries, and learning, teaching and intellectual initiative were frustrated by the strict control of the politicians over scholars and writers, and by the persecution and imprisonment of many of the country's best brains.

Nevertheless the foundations had been laid for future material progress, though the actual showing in 1940 and the rate of development over the next fifteen years were meagre enough. If the statistics are to be believed, all earlier losses of livestock had been made good, and the national stocks stood at nearly 27,500,000 head. This figure has subsequently been scaled down by a million or so, and as it represents a total never achieved, by several million either before or after 1940-41, it may well have been a euphoric exaggeration. Winter shelters for animals were being built, wells dug, hay cut and the ground tilled, though it must be remembered that all this was being done to some extent before the revolution, and the mere fact that it is worthy of mention at all shows how elementary was the technical progress so far made. Some veterinary work was being carried on, and Mongols were being trained for it, but the figures for losses of livestock remained high, and were attributable to the three traditional causes – lack of winter fodder, disease, and the ravages of wolves. In 1936, for example, over one million head perished from these causes. Herding was still being carried out under primitive nomadic conditions which practically excluded the breeding of new varieties. Lack of protection from the climate meant that animal types had above all to be resistant to cold, and lack of fencing made controlled breeding almost impossible.

The lamas were gradually being absorbed into civil life. A new industrial class was slowly emerging as factories expanded and new machinery – lorries and tractors, reapers, telephones and radio – required specialized technicians to look after them. Nevertheless, by 1940 only some thirteen thousand individuals were accounted as industrial workers out of a population of seven hundred thousand. Education showed a slow but steady growth. In 1934 there were fifty-nine state elementary schools, and in 1939 there were ninety-three. Alongside these there were over one hundred voluntary schools, supported by the parents. These were seasonal in activity, working only from April till September. The first two had been opened in 1934, and in 1939–40 all were taken over by the state system. But altogether in 1940 only 11 per cent of children were being educated in schools of any sort, and the literacy rate for that year is given as 127,000, or about one-fifth of the population of eight and over. Only some six to seven thousand persons were reckoned in that year to belong to the 'national intelligentsia'. Medical care was advancing, but was nowhere near adequate, though at least the spread of ideas of elementary cleanliness was helping to turn a net population loss into a gain. Statistically, Mongolia's medical services advanced enormously in the 'thirties, from one hospital recorded in 1930 to ten in 1940, and from twenty-seven doctors to 108. But much remained untouched. The legacy of venereal disease persisted, and special venereal hospitals, of which there are now twenty, did not begin to appear till 1947.

Some attention had also been given to information and entertainment services. By 1940 there were for example five newspapers, though with a total circulation of only sixty-two thousand, a number of cinemas which showed Soviet films and the few films made by Mongolia's own new studio, a theatre in Ulan Bator, and a radio service. All aimaks were linked to the capital by telegraph, though only five had a telephone connection. Real modernization was to be a phenomenon of the post-war years, and in particular of the late 'fifties.

CHAPTER 9

POST-WAR MONGOLIA: ACHIEVEMENTS AND PROSPECTS

The war and Mongolia's position in the world

The year 1940 was a critical one in Mongolia's evolution, marked by the adoption of a new constitution and a new programme of socialist development. The war which followed did not touch Mongolia directly till August 1945, but nevertheless it slowed down the tempo of her development, and 1948 is the most convenient starting point for the review of her recent progress. It was only then, the first year of the first five-year plan, that a real beginning was made in the programme of modernization which had brought about such a decisive change in Mongol society as compared with the pre-war years. And even so, it was not till the mid-'fifties, when foreign aid programmes, stimulated by China's intention to regain something of her lost position in Mongolia at Russia's expense, began to compete with each other to finance reconstruction, that any significant progress became apparent. Without wishing to belittle in any way the effort put into their country's modernization by the Mongols themselves, it is safe to assert that by 1966 more than ever before the Mongol economy was being carried by the more developed countries of the communist world. The USSR shoulders the major part of the burden, but the other countries of eastern Europe, East Germany, Poland, Czechoslovakia and Hungary in particular, do their share as well. It is east Europeans and Russians who are, for example, responsible for financing and building the industrial complex being laid out at the new town of Darkhan, between Ulan Bator and the Russian frontier. Russian, Chinese and east European money, expertise, equipment and labour, supplied free or at low charges often remitted, have alone made possible the changes in Mongolian society which we shall look at in this chapter.

The war years were lost years for Mongolia's economy and social progress. True, something was accomplished. The most striking affirmation of faith in the future was the founding of a small university in 1942, a year or two after Mongolia's first pupils to finish a full ten years' course of schooling had left school. However, the demands of Soviet wartime consumption fell heavily on Mongolia. She supplied Russia with huge numbers of horses, with wool and furs. Some of these deliveries were in the form of ordinary exports, but a lot was given free, and Mongolia financed the equipment of certain Red Army units. Deliveries of animals, together with an exceptionally dry summer and hard winter in 1945, were responsible for a sharp fall in the total number of livestock which has never been made good. Food rationing lasted till 1950. The German invasion meant that Russia could not keep up her exports of capital and consumer goods to Mongolia, and the infant Mongol industry had to do its best to tide the country over the shortage of goods. By 1943 imports had almost entirely dried up. Where, in 1940, clothing to the value of 13,500,000 roubles had come in, less than 2,000,000 roubles worth was bought in 1943. The value of communications equipment dropped from 795,000 roubles in 1941 to nil in 1942 and was only 29,000 roubles in 1943.

In one way Mongolia's position at the end of the war was fundamentally different from what it had been. Under terms agreed at Yalta, a plebiscite had been held, and China, still under Chiang Kai-shek, had formally, if grudgingly, accepted the Mongolian people's unanimous vote for national independence. Diplomatic representatives were, however, never exchanged because of a border incident at the Baitag Bodgo mountains on the borders of Sinkiang, which China used as a pretext for delay. But when the communists took over in China, this existing formal recognition of Mongolia's independence was of great significance. The new régime honoured the obligation entered into by the nationalists, and now for the first time in history China and Mongolia exchanged ambassadors. The sovietization of eastern Europe at the end of the 'forties gave Mongolia a chance to extend her contacts in another, and unexpected, direction, while the emergence of new and independent countries in Asia and Africa provided her with yet a third field in which to assert her independent existence. To gain admittance to the United Nations took longer. While other emerging nations gained their independence in a clearly recognizable act of decolonization, there was nothing which in 1945 marked any real change in Mongolia's satellite relationship to the USSR. She was still sealed off from the outside world: the brief visit of Henry Wallace to Ulan Bator in 1944 was a unique event. Thus those countries which maintained that not enough was known about Mongolia to judge whether she had the capacity for independent foreign relations had a great deal of reason on their side. It took a long time for Mongolia to live down her equivocal past, and it was not till 1961, after some hard campaigning, that she was finally invited to become a member of the United Nations. Since then she has still further consolidated her world status by exchanging diplomatic recognition with a number of western countries, in the first place in 1963 with the United Kingdom, which maintains an embassy in Ulan Bator. The United States, embarrassed by its obligations towards nationalist China, which now regrets its not wholly voluntary generosity of 1945, has not recognized Mongolia. These widening contacts have not only meant a constantly growing diplomatic corps in Ulan Bator, now no longer exclusively a communist one, and a considerable number of Mongolian missions abroad, but have involved Mongolia with an ever larger circle of trade partners, and with diversified cultural contacts. In 1964, for the first time in history, Mongol students studied at an English university, when a group of eight senior students spent six months at the University of Leeds under the auspices of UNESCO. For Mongolia, one of the most important developments of the past twenty years has been the definitive confirmation of her independent statehood.

In other respects the war meant a standstill for Mongolia's development. It had proved impossible to plan on more than a year to year basis. In absolute terms industrial output was minute, less than a tenth, in 1940, of what it was to be in 1964. Between 1940 and 1945 this output had barely doubled. The number of schools had grown slightly, and the number of pupils had increased, but cultural life had little to show for nearly twenty-five years of socialism. In 1945 there was only one man with a scientific degree. Between 1940 and 1947 the number of doctors had climbed slowly from 108 to 134, and by 1952 had still reached only 180. The number of pharmacists, thirty-four in 1940, was thirty-six in 1947. Figures for other categories of skilled persons and of institutions were a little, but not much, better. One very good reason for this slow rate of progress, apart from Mongolia's inability to pull herself up by her own bootlaces at a time when her one trading partner, Russia, was fully occupied with the war, was the fact that, though not actually involved in the German war, she had for years been devoting a major share of her budget to rearmament. Only in August 1945, the day after the USSR moved against Japan, did Mongolia also enter the war and, in a week-long campaign, do something to justify the years of preparation. Victory in Manchuria and North China had already been assured by hard years of British and American campaigning against the Japanese, and fell easily into Russian and Mongol hands in the last week of the war, especially after the dropping of the atomic bombs had demoralized and confused the Japanese government. But the war brought Mongolia little material gain to compensate for her huge expenditure. Her armies, which had advanced across Inner Mongolia to the sea, were soon withdrawn, and the ultimate communization of Inner Mongolia was carried out under Chinese auspices. No incorporation of Inner Mongols into the People's Republic took place. What Mongolia did draw from her participation in the war was her share of the large number of Japanese troops captured, and these she put to use, not making good non-existent war damage, but as labourers in the building of the nucleus of post-war Ulan Bator. Expenditure on defence continued to run at a high level. In 1947 it formed 36 per cent of total expenditure, and only as China came under communist control did this proportion begin to decline, dropping to 19 per cent in 1952.

With the one exception made of the gap torn in the traditional picture by the physical destruction of the Church, there was, in 1945, little to distinguish Mongolia from what she had been twenty years before. Hers was still essentially a 'one crop' economy. In spite of the existence of a few small co-operatives, almost all animals were still in the hands of private owners, and were pastured in the age-old nomad way. Little hay was cut and stored, few animals had winter shelters, few wells were dug, and often they were not maintained. Motor transport was only beginning to play an important role. Only in 1949 was it possible to dispense with the onerous public obligation to perform relay service. Ulan Bator was still nearer old Urga than a modern town. The first big new buildings which survive today were those put up after 1945 by captured Japanese.

General lines of post-war development

The years since the war have seen changes of an extent and a quality which would have been unimaginable to anyone who had judged Mongolia's capacity to evolve solely on the basis of what she had been able to do for herself in the decades between the revolution and the end of the war, when foreign help was very niggardly. That the material, financial and technical basis for what is now taking place is to a major extent supplied from abroad, and that Mongolia's present-day diversified economy would collapse without regular transfusions of aid is irrelevant, since the same is true of a good many other previously backward countries. What is significant is, not so much that Mongolia relies on foreign aid, a little of it channelled through the United Nations but nearly all of it provided through Comecon, as that these injections of capital and technical skill are being used in a way, and according to theoretical preconceptions, which have set her upon a course of development which will one day completely change her way of life.

As the Mongols have realized, a modern civilization, with industry, schools and universities, radio and television and all the other stigmata of the complex culture of the 'developed country', is incompatible with a shifting, nomadic population existing almost entirely on the surplus production of extensively herded animals. If these amenities are wanted, and especially if they are wanted within the framework of a socialist society of wage-earners, a substitute has to be found for nomadism. It is perfectly true that the Mongols evolved one of the more advanced cultures known amongst nomadic peoples, in spite of the inherent drawbacks of nomadism, a way of life which excludes the collection of very much surplus wealth except in the form of livestock which can move around on its own feet and does not have to be carried. But this superiority was in fact only a relative one and the Mongols soon reached the limits of their possibilities. What true native literature they had was an oral one and comparatively primitive: literary entertainment for the Mongols in the nineteenth century was where it was for Europe at the time of the *chansons de geste*. Art and sculpture were almost non-existent. There was some depiction of scenes of nomadic life, executed in a rather stylized manner, but most artists were employed in the lamaseries producing religious wall paintings, temple banners, pieces of iconography and the mystic representations of deities and their attributes. Such art was repetitive, not creative, since it was directed to a ritual end, and the efficacy of a magic design in conjuring up the deity it referred to lay in its absolutely correct rendering. Mongols were skilled casters of images, at least in the early days of Buddhism. The first Jebtsundamba Khutuktu was especially famous for his talents. There were also many skilled and ingenious silversmiths, needle-men, saddle-makers and others, but their specialities were those of the craftsman rather than the artist, and the objects they produced were for use in daily life or in ritual. Sculpture in stone was a rarity, as was decorative painting. Mongolia's written culture was largely a monkish one and was centred on the lamaseries, which with time became too cumbrous to follow the nomadic pattern of life and settled down in fixed buildings. Printing in Mongolia was, in the nature of things, carried out in lamaseries which had the space to work with, and then store, the numerous wooden blocks required. But by far the largest centre of book production was not in Mongolia at all, but in Peking.

Above a minimum level of sophistication, cultural development is bound to depend on a certain stability in life. To take a single concrete example, a proper theatre cannot develop amongst wandering nomads. The Mongols were never averse to the theatre, but amongst the herdsmen themselves dramatic performances never seem to have grown much beyond the size of what they themselves call the 'conversation song', a sort of ballad opera performed in a sitting position by one or more artists playing a stringed instrument and singing to its accompaniment. Sometimes the various roles, always few in number, of the simple folk tales adapted to this form, would be allotted each to a different performer, though some singers would be skilled at bending their voices to sing all the parts alternately. There were no costumes, no make-up, and no action beyond the movement of the head and eyes. On the other hand, the lamaseries would stage temple dances at various seasons, and would also put on elaborate performances of Buddhist morality plays. There are still plenty of people alive today who took part in performances of the play 'Moon-cuckoo', composed by the nineteenth-century reincarnated lama Rabjai, and enacted at his lamasery in the Gobi. This play was very like a medieval morality: a well-known scriptural story was presented, with its scenes enlivened by comic or grotesque interludes. An important prince might be a literary Maecenas too. From the seventeenth century we know of Tsogtu taiji who built lamaseries and schools around his palace, and in the nineteenth century there were princes, like To-wang, who fostered learning and music. Especially in the western regions there were princes who befriended and patronized bards. But all this was done at times and in places where increased material wealth and civilization had made inroads on pure nomadism, and a permanent centre of fixed buildings could be maintained from the production of the surrounding herdsmen. Mongol nomadism has in fact always shown a tendency to compromise with the sedentary mode of life, and this has become sharper in recent years. If nowadays the Mongols are to integrate themselves in a world whose increasingly uniform culture demands factories, farms and cities, then nomadism will have to disappear. If the Mongols were to stand aside from this process they would finish up as curiosities, survivals in a reservation.

Mongolia has declared her intentions unequivocally. By 1960 her leaders were terming her an 'agricultural-industrial' state, and her new character was symbolized by the incorporation of sheaves of wheat and a cog-wheel into her national emblem. Eventually the order of priorities is to be reversed, and Mongolia, the former nomad society, is to be an 'industrial-agricultural' communist community. Naturally, this prospect has given rise to the doubt, expressed by some Mongols as well as by foreigners, as to whether it does not signify the onset of the gradual disappearance of the Mongols as an identifiable entity. In the sense that nomadism is bound to be whittled away, and that much of what goes with nomadism – the self-sufficient group of herders, the lore of the camel-puller, the dung fire in the felt tent, the nightly repetition of the old folk-tales – will disappear with it, there is a quantum of truth in this prognosis, but on the whole the problem is ill-conceived and badly posed. Nomadism is what first springs to mind when one thinks of the Mongol, but there is more to him than that. Perhaps the two most vital qualities which distinguish him from his neighbours, especially the Russians and the Chinese, are the sense of a long national history, and the possession and cherishing of a national language which has shown itself flexible and adaptable enough to encompass the terminology of both Buddhist philosophy and Marxism, as well as the demands of modern science. The Mongol language, even today, is remarkably free from borrowings, and prefers to coin neologisms from Mongol roots rather than import ready made terms. It is a paradox of modern Mongolian life that the present régime, professing as it does a Marx-Leninism imbued with the principle of 'proletarian internationalism' is at constant loggerheads with the virile and irrepressible patriotism of the Mongols which regularly effervesces in what is officially disapproved of as 'excessive manifestations of nationalism'. Prophecies of the disappearance of the Mongols may have had some justification before there was an independent Mongolia, but her generally accepted statehood both guarantees her continued existence and serves as the focus for her people's sentiments and enthusiasms.

In any case, the 'old life' was not at all calculated to preserve the Mongol race. What foreign travellers saw in Mongolia half a century ago, and much later in Inner Mongolia, was the last stage in the decadence of a fascinating, unique, but doomed way of life. To put it at its bluntest, the Mongol race was dying of inanition and syphilis. Every traveller noted the apathy of the people, their enslavement to a church which at the top level may have produced some fine scholars, but which, where it impinged on daily life, held the people at large in ignorant dependence on itself and on its outdated and corrupt ideals. Filth, disease and ignorance marked the Mongol. It is all too easy to dismiss these as accompaniments of a romantic survival, and not to see that they were not incidentals at all, but rather the outward expression of the essential rot within. The sores on so many a Mongol body were true symbols of the decay and corruption of the society where they were so common as to be the norm. Of course the unique features of central Asian society are threatened with extinction, but so are the unique features of all survivals of the past, and always have been whenever a more dynamic civilization touches them. But to suggest that modernization means the suppression of all that is individually Mongol begs the question: it implies that the Mongols are uniquely incapable of adaptation to new circumstances. The same might have been said of the Mongols at the time of the conversion to Buddhism, only what was being 'threatened' then was a different form of Mongolianness, the brutish evening of petty, squabbling feudalism and the shamanism which was the acme then of spiritual aspirations. It is far more realistic to note what has in fact been done since the revolution of 1921 to assure the actual physical survival of the Mongols as a people, to acknowledge the spread of ideas of hygiene, the development of a medical service, the universal education of the young and their equipment to compete on less unequal terms with world at large, than to lament the disappearance of a way of life which would eventually have reduced the Mongols to the level of the bushmen of South Africa – mere interesting remnants of a lost civilization and otherwise of no account.

Mongolia has strong guarantees of her independent future in that her frontiers are agreed by treaty with her neighbours and that, with the exception of a small Kazakh minority in the west, she has a more or less homogeneous population, no longer over-disposed to regional separatism. The more distant provinces, especially in the west, do, it is true, sometimes put on a show of disregard for Ulan Bator in non-essentials. Central control is hard enough to exercise even with modern means of communication over such huge distances, in an extreme climate and with insufficient people. To take one example: when the Party newspaper *Unen* ran a campaign in 1964 to alert people to shortcomings in the handling of children and to persuade them to activity, it had to note, with regret, that enthusiasm tailed off outside the capital, and that the three westernmost aimaks had taken no interest in the campaign at all. But essentially Mongolia's population is united, and moreover is not open to dilution. Inside large multi-national communist states such as the USSR and China it is quite feasible to speed up development by moving large numbers of the more active race to the more retarded areas. From the point of view of the locals, this has the effect of swamping them racially, sometimes to the point where, as in Chinese Inner Mongolia, the immigrants outnumber the colonized to an overwhelming degree. Moreover, in such a situation, progress is a purely mechanical phenomenon: the original inhabitants do not necessarily draw the full benefit from it, as leading positions continue to be occupied by the outsiders simply because the factors which kept the indigenous race back still operate. The Chinese, further, look on the rapidity with which racial differences are eliminated, as a measure of the achievement of communism.

In Mongolia this racial dilution cannot, under present conditions, arise, since Soviet colonialism abroad, though operating with commercial and financial techniques of exploitation, does not involve the transfer of population outside the borders of the USSR as settlers. So Mongolia's situation is at present a very favourable one. International recognition assures her survival as a state, while the need for her level of development to be brought up to something more nearly approaching that of the other members of Comecon ensures that the USSR will go on underwriting her reconstruction.

Mongolia is still hopelessly underpopulated for the tasks she has set herself. Her population, too, is very unbalanced, due to a very high birth-rate in recent years. She has an excessive load of children to be carried by an insufficient number of people of working age, and for the time being the disproportion of these two categories continues to grow. This is a temporary situation which will right itself with time, but at present, faced with a crash programme of development, Mongolia lacks skill, experience, and sheer manpower, in every field. Her growing industries with their administrative tail, her double party and government apparatus, her expanding supervisory apparatus necessitated by the growing complexity of integrated, state-controlled production and sales, swallow up more and more herdsmen, so that until herding can be rationalized and mechanized, a significant increase in stocks is not to be looked for. Foreign technical help and even labour is desperately needed. The former has for many years been supplied by the USSR, the latter, until political differences sapped mutual esteem, by the Chinese, At the present (1966), the USSR is supplying thousands of soldiers to make good the gaps left on the building sites by the departed Chinese. This is not a programme of settlement: builders and technicians are periodically replaced and will be withdrawn when the Mongols can be left to carry on. Progress has been slower than it might have been if Mongolia were not so thoroughly dependent on the Russians. Political aberrations, especially in the 'thirties, set Mongolia back incalculably, and her continued working to Russian standards, for example in the building of flats, means that qualitatively she is permanently behind. But Russian involvement in Mongol affairs is essential to the continued existence of an undiluted Mongol race as masters in their own country: the alternative, to be swamped by colonizing Chinese, has been clearly demonstrated in Inner Mongolia.

Mongolia has certainly made great strides since 1945 and these have received some publicity abroad, but her efforts need to be got into proportion. Recently, Mongol writers have begun to show a euphoric tendency to compare her achievements in quantitative terms with the situation in highly developed capitalist countries. Such comparisons may serve to confuse her own people as to the realities of the situation: they certainly sap the foreigner's faith in Mongol objectivity. To take one example: the *History of the Mongol People's Republic*, published in 1966, observes that 'in cultural progress the MPR even heads advanced capitalist countries in some respects. In the number of students per head of the population Mongolia is ahead of West Germany, Italy, Japan, Turkey, Pakistan and Iran'. The current five-year plan, valid from 1966 to 1970, makes a similar comparison, to Mongolia's advantage, with France as well. That Mongolia has a decent network of schools and some institutes of higher education is a fact, but without definition of what a student is, what sort of institution he goes to, what standard of education he has already attained and what he aims at, and above all, what intellectual resources and drive are behind the system, such comparisons as this are totally absurd. At the lowest level, a 'student' can be a person of minimal capacity, ambitions and potentialities. In the countryside work is still going on to eradicate illiteracy in the age-group thirteen to forty-five. These figures are significant: the minimum period of schooling for Mongol children is four years, from eight to twelve. The group thirteen to forty-five, then, covers all persons born since the revolution of 1921 who are now above primary school age. Illiterates in this group are presumably counted as students for the purpose of statistical comparison.

While at the top Mongolia has a university and institutions for training doctors, vets, economists and teachers, at the bottom there are petty rural units, known as 'base-schools' which appear to be very primitive. A 'base' is the smallest working unit in a herding collective and consists of a group of people, usually a couple of households, actually out in the countryside doing the ordinary work of looking after the animals. A base-school seems to be a unit for elementary adult education. A typical one was described in a press article in mid-1966 written by the teacher concerned, a girl called Tserenbaljir. Her base consisted of fourteen persons looking after five hundred goats. There were six children from one to seven, four persons between nineteen and twenty-seven, two of forty-six to fifty one and two of fifty-four to fifty-eight. Excluding the children below school age and the two 'old people' as they were termed, the rest, six in all, were students at the base school. Three were reckoned to be at fourth year primary standard, two could read a little and manage to write short words, and one, the teacher's mother, was illiterate and quite ignorant. Teaching had to be fitted in around the work of goat-herding and had to be done in shifts, with the older people having to be taught in the day time because their eyesight was too poor for evening study. The teaching was elementary, as the teacher's report indicated:

The pupils of our school seem to have made some progress, however small, in writing and in sums in the 1965 to 1966 school year, that is, between 6 December 1965 and 31 March 1966. For example, Magsarjav and his wife Dashnyam, who finished primary school fourteen or fifteen years ago, had forgotten practically everything, and didn't know the rules any more, and couldn't manage more than elementary reading and writing, but still, at the end of the school year they could write properly and could do simple sums with several figures. My father and Doljmaa could write copies before, but now they can write by heart and read well. My mother, at the previous examination, could do no more than half read the thirty-five letters of the alphabet, but now she can read, put short words together in writing, and add or subtract up to a hundred.

It is not to detract from the enthusiasm and optimism of the young teacher and of the many like her whose experience she must typify, to say that her 'students' are not of a level that makes statistical comparison of them with part-time adult students in a western country very meaningful. Mongolia's progress since 1921 is real enough, but it is not startling. Indeed, one wonders that in some respects more has not been achieved after nearly half a century of socialism. And certainly, in comparison with the economies of industrialized western countries, with whom Mongolia is beginning to measure herself, both culturally and in matters of production, her showings are embarrassingly modest.

Many visitors to Mongolia, especially those prone to see in communism a promise for the future so bright that all present defects and failures can be confidently disregarded, are so infected with the beauty of the countryside, the clarity and crispness of its plateau air with its pervading scent of wild herbs, the cheerful competence of the Mongol herdsman on his pony, and above all the courteous and dignified welcome they receive, that they overvalue what they see, confuse pipe-dreams with reality, and ignore, or explain away as temporary shortcomings, what fails to come up to standard. Mongol propaganda in foreign languages suffers from a similar one-sidedness. It overplays a goodish hand so clumsily that credibility is lost, and the real achievements of Mongolia are obscured by the meretricious glossiness of the picture it offers. A suitable corrective would be to read the native Mongol press. With painful regularity, year after year, this exposes the chronic faults of apathy, fecklessness, carelessness with machinery, neglect of collectivized livestock, dishonesty in the management of public funds and property, and, above all, it deplores the lack of enough people of a proper standard of competence and reliability. From time to time special press campaigns are organized to air special social problems and suggest corrective action. The campaign to improve attitudes towards children mentioned above is typical. Visitors to Mongolia often remark on the happy appearance of the children, yet here, as elsewhere, there is a dark side to the picture. *Crèches* and kindergartens, of which the tourist will see the best, are far too few to go round. This is a serious matter in a society where it is understood that both parents will have to work, and it means that little children of one or two years of age may have to be left to fend for themselves all day. Some *crèches* have been publicly branded as filthy. The children's medical service is supposed to attend *crèches*, but it can be very perfunctory in the performance of its duties, and some *crèches* never get visited at all. Proper supplies of food can be difficult to get, and *crèches* have been known to have to go without milk or eggs for weeks on end. The red tape which forbids them to buy from anyone but their allotted suppliers – not even from a local farm with surplus produce – exacerbates the frustration. Another problem which continually exercises the Mongols is that of addiction to alcohol. This is recognized as a serious social evil. It is tempered to some extent by the high prices fixed by the state monopoly, but nevertheless in a sample year, 1959, over three-quarters of 'offences against public order' were said to be due to drunkenness, as were nearly half the cases of assault. Addiction drives individuals to more serious crime, theft of state property and murder. Cases are only rarely mentioned in detail in the press: one of which was that of the chief cashier of the railway restaurant in Ulan Bator who filched fifty thousand tugrigs to feed his own appetite and that of his friends. Similar, if not identical, social problems of course plague every country, and to point out their existence in Mongolia is not to denigrate her efforts at social improvement. But as defects of this kind are constantly being exposed in the Mongol press, and as some of them may perhaps be traced back to peculiarities of organization typical of a communist state, such as the obligation imposed on married women to go on working outside the home, it is essential to refer to them, not in a spirit of disparagement, but to correct the glossy picture offered by many tourists and by Mongol propaganda.

The achievement of socialism

From the point of view of the authorities, the manner in which modernization is being effected, and the irreversible social changes which have already been brought about, are probably more significant than the actual material achievements themselves. Though Mongolia is slowly becoming more affluent, and the range of consumer goods has widened to include motor-cars and motor-cycles as well as bicycles, sewing machines and radios, the amassing of public capital is looked upon mainly as the process of forming the necessary 'material and technical basis' for achieving the ultimate aim, the building of communism. The last decade has seen the final socialization of all aspects of the Mongol economy, followed by the tightening of the grip of central control. All means of production are now in public ownership. Private enterprise of all sorts has officially been eliminated and the right to employ is in the hands of the state or of collectives. Members of collectives are still allowed to retain a number of animals for their own use, but the number of herding families still uncollectivized can be ignored, having dropped from 62 per cent of the population in 1956 to 0·18 in 1963. The process of proletarianization of Mongol society is now, theoretically at least, complete.

As long as capital was scarce and expansion fettered by lack of a working class and of a market, small co-operative craft-shops played the major role in Mongolian industry. In recent years, however, huge investments of foreign as well as native capital, have quite altered the situation. The productivity of the craft-shops has been outstripped by that of new state-owned factories: in 1964 the value of state-owned production was over 726,000,000 tugrigs, while that of the co-operatives was less than 200,000,000. Mongolia's production, though rising steadily, is still minimal by world standards, and does not begin to satisfy local demand. Figures for 1964 shows that only 1,415,000 pairs of leather shoes were produced, or 1·3 pairs per head of the population. As it is openly confessed that styles are poor, and that owing to lack of market research and of liaison between factories and shops the most demanded sizes are underproduced and unpopular sizes are overproduced, so that the shops carry big stocks of unsaleable goods, the supply can be seen to be quite inadequate. In 1957 only 224,000 bars of toilet soap were produced: by 1964 this quantity had risen to nearly 2,397,000 tablets, or enough for two bars a year per person. Most of the population still lives in felt tents, even in Ulan Bator and other towns, including the unfinished Darkhan industrial complex, but annual production of wooden tent frames stands at only about 4,300 sets: the population is increasing annually by about thirty-six thousand persons. The remarkable things about Mongol industry are rather the fact that it is now to an overwhelming extent the province of wage-earning factory labourers, not of small co-operators, and secondly that production is no longer based exclusively on the produce of herding and hunting. Heavy industry is still not envisaged, and a project to build a steel works at Darkhan seems to have been dropped, but Mongolia's factories now produce a growing proportion of capital goods, especially building materials.

Agriculture proper, too, is run as a direct state venture. Most of the large state farms have been set up since the war. They are concerned primarily, though not exclusively, with tilling the land, and in implementing a 'virgin lands' programme in the last few years they have increased production to a remarkable extent. The massive cultivation of crops being to all intents and purposes a recent innovation, it was possible for the state to plan from the beginning and to take over large tracts of land without disturbing an existing pattern of production. A wage-earning proletariat now forms the basis of this new, nationalized agriculture.

In dealing with herding, however, the authorities had a different and more intractable problem to tackle. Traditionally there had always been a certain amount of labour-pooling and mutual aid amongst Mongol herders, but till long after the war ownership was almost exclusively private. Families could market their produce individually, though from 1941 onwards they were bound by compulsory state delivery quotas. From the mid-'thirties onwards a few elementary co-operatives came into existence, but these made little inroad on the pattern of private enterprise. The destruction of the herds of the nobility and the lamaseries, and the persecution in the early 'thirties of the so-called kulaks and middle herdsmen, ordinary herding families with more than a minimum of animals, meant that herds had become fragmented and were in the hands of most of the families of Mongolia. A certain evening out of wealth had taken place. In 1927 62·5 per cent of all families were classed as 'poor herdsmen', meaning that they owned from one to twenty *bod* or cattle-units. Families owning from twenty-one to one hundred *bod* formed 31 per cent of the total. By 1939 these figures were 40 and 55 per cent respectively, and while their relationship had changed, the percentage of rich owners too can be seen to have fallen: those owning over one hundred *bod* were now only 5 per cent of the total.

It was this extensive ownership of livestock which was, in conditions of scarcity of capital, technical skill, fodder growing and storage facilities, machinery, and veterinary help, put forward as the main reason for the failure of the Mongol herds to grow in numbers after the war, or to improve in quality. The Party exploited the situation as a pretext for initiating its collectivization programme during the 'fifties: only under collective ownership and management, it was said, could herding be modernized and numbers increased. However, the real reason for collectivization must have been a doctrinal rather than a practical one. Mongolia had to be brought into line with the rest of the Soviet bloc, where collectivization was being forced at the same time. The elimination of private enterprise in the most important sector of the country's economy had always been in the Party's mind, and in realizing their aim they acted in conscious imitation of, and reference to, the 'rich experiences of the USSR and other socialist countries'. The relative failure of the Soviet kolkhoz system, and the empirical dismantling of collectivization in Poland cast doubt on the true richness of this experience, and strengthen the opinion just expressed that theoretical considerations of Marxist social organization weighed more heavily with the Mongols than purely technical ones.

Whether in fact the Mongol collectives will prove more successful than the kolkhozes have been is a matter for the future. Statistics so far are not encouraging. In 1957 there was a total of 23,339,000 animals. The national plan for the next three years envisaged a 7·2 per cent increase to a total of 25,000,000 by 1960. In fact, stocks fell slightly to 23,000,500. By the end of 1961 a further sharp fall to 20,392,900 had occurred and the third five-year plan, which ran from 1961 to 1965 proposed what was described as an 'increase' of 11 per cent, to bring total stocks back to a figure of 22,900,000. This increase was of course calculated on the excessively low basic figure of 1961 and in absolute terms meant that in 1965 the herds were not expected to reach anything like their 1957, or pre-collectivization, total. The actual rate of growth has more or less kept pace with this revised plan. The figure given for 1964 is 22,847,000 head. But this is still a smaller number of animals than there had been ten years before – a very modest return indeed for all the upheaval and continuing expense of the collectivization campaign. Compared with the alleged successes of the New Turn, when private enterprise is supposed to have brought the country's stocks from disaster point to unique heights in 1940 and 1941, this is not much of an achievement, at least in quantitative terms.

The transition from private enterprise to collective ownership in the agricultural sector has nowhere come about spontaneously. In every socialist country it has had to be forced through by propaganda and compulsion, and at the worst, by violence and terror as in the USSR. Very little has been published about the actual process of collectivization in Mongolia, except in official, general terms. However, it is perfectly plain that here too the campaign was conceived from the centre and effected in the course of a concerted programme planned and run by the Central Committee, and was not the reflection of popular demand. There were certain manifestations of popular opposition which, though not described in detail, were important enough to find mention in official accounts of the campaign. The net result of collectivization has been to make wage-earners out of the previously independent cattle herders. Each family was allowed, at the moment of collectivization, to retain certain numbers of animals for its own use. However, once the collectives had been formed, this allowance was drastically cut, effectively on the average by about half, and by the early 1960s wages from the funds of the collectives, paid to begin with in kind, but then to an increasing degree in cash, and based on the number of labour-day units worked, began to outstrip the private herd as the main source of income for the ordinary herding family. It is worth noting that Mongol writers, describing this process, usually speak of the collectivization of the herders, not of the herds, thus emphasizing that what has been attempted is more of a social revolution than a mere transformation of farming methods.

The initiative in forming collectives came, then, from the Central Committee of the Party, and the subsequent tendency has been towards stricter internal organization and public supervision. This is inevitable, since the role of the herding collectives in the Mongol economy is different from that of the old domestic herds. They are for one thing subsidized by huge state loans and are being developed under a programme of big capital investment from central funds. Secondly, instead of merely supporting the family unit, the produce of the herds is primarily a cash crop, supplying the ever expanding urban population of industrial workers and officials – in 1963 over 46 per cent of the population – against repayment at prices fixed by the State. Collectives nowadays are very different from the old producers' associations. Model regulations for herding collectives first drawn up in 1942 provided for the introduction of labour brigades formed on a permanent basis, and for payment according to labour-day units. However, as long as the producers' associations remained primitive voluntary organizations, nothing was done in practice to implement these proposals. The number of producers' associations was small. From one in 1935 they had increased to ninety-one in 1940 and to 165 in 1952, but they were tiny units affecting only a minute proportion of the country's livestock. In 1940 the average size of an association was twenty-two households. In the same year only sixty-two thousand animals all told belonged to producers' associations, state farms and other state units such as haymaking stations. In 1952, a year for which the figures have been broken down, the producers' associations embraced only 280,000 animals out of a national total of 22,794,000. They were thus insignificant quantitatively, and, in addition, they were useless as a model for future progress. To a great extent they were co-operatives in name only, since the members lived off their own animals and did an absolute minimum of pooled labour, only when it suited them. There was no internal organization, no work-norms, no labour-day accounting, no regular system of distribution of income. It was not practicable to build on this foundation, and the whole problem had to be studied again. This time, in contrast to the Gadarene rush of 1929, considerable time and thought were given to the subject, and almost a decade of preparation preceded the implementation of the campaign. The Central Committee was first charged with the task of examining the situation in 1947. Between 1950 and 1952 certain preliminary work was done. Offices were set up in the provinces to run the campaign under a central office in the Ministry of Livestock. In 1953 the Central Committee took over the management of the collectivization apparatus. Concrete proposals were elaborated which included the setting up of permanent labour brigades within the new collectives, proper accounting based on the labour-day unit system, the allotment of fixed territories to each collective, the issuing of development loans, arrangements for the sale of produce to the state purchasing agency, and proposals for technical assistance. Party and Youth League cells were set up in the new collectives as they emerged, and training courses were run for future managers and accountants. Veterinary and other specialists were attached to the larger collectives.

Propaganda and economic compulsion were the chief weapons used to persuade people into the collectives. State loans were granted to the collectives on an ever growing scale. Differential rates of taxation were imposed on livestock so as to weigh most heavily on larger private owners and make it unprofitable to them to go on on their own. Thirdly, differential norms of compulsory deliveries of animal produce to the state were set, so that, for instance, private herders with over 260 head of cattle had to deliver twice as much meat for every ox owned, twice as much wool per sheep, and nearly twice as much milk per cow, as owners with less than thirty head. At the same time compulsory deliveries from collectives were set at a low figure, regardless of the size of the herds. The allotment of veterinary workers to collectives rather than to general service, and, more decisively, the allotment to them of specified pastures which were thus removed from common use, made it less and less possible for private herders to continue to stay outside the system.

In 1955 the first Co-operative congress was held in Ulan Bator with the aim of speeding up the process of collectivization. Tsedenbal, the premier, outlined the Party's aims, stressing the social role of collectivization: it was, he said, an essential prerequisite to the building of socialism in the country. With less practical justification he maintained also that only with public ownership of the means of production and with co-operative labour could the Mongol people attain an affluent and cultured standard of life. Collectives were to be formed and run along the lines proposed in 1953. The programme now went forward at speed, reaching its peak in 1958. By the end of 1957 about a third of the country's herders had joined collectives, by the end of 1958 three-quarters had joined, and, by April 1959 all but an insignificant few were members. Officially they were said to have joined enthusiastically, realizing that by relying on their own efforts they would never be able to reach the standard of living promised them by the collectives, and, somehow, inspired by the dubious example offered by the Soviet kolkhozes. Officials and workers who owned animals 'actively supported the Party's policy and voluntarily socialized their herds'. In many areas the movement to join was said to have been a mass one. Whole *sumuns* and *bags* (at that time a sub-unit of a *sumun*) joined up *en masse*. How closely this tale of enthusiastic herders suddenly handing over their animals to the collectives approximates to reality there is no way of judging. The campaign was carried through victoriously, so that it has been possible to play down the opposition to it in a way that was not possible after the fiasco of 1929. But certainly it did not go off as smoothly as one is led to accept. There were many richer households who joined the collectives only to escape the burden of discriminatory taxation and compulsory deliveries, and who saw themselves otherwise being squeezed out of existence. We are told in undefined terms of 'ill-disposed elements' who slaughtered their cattle, as was done in the first collectivization drive, or who joined only to try to sabotage the new organizations from within. Many people, in selecting the animals they were allowed to keep for their private use, did not keep as might have been expected, the best breeders, but sterile females and old males. Their reasoning, as revealed later by a responsible minister, was as follows: 'If we keep good animals, they'll be round a second time to confiscate these too. Much better keep the old and useless ones, and at least we'll be able to eat them'.[1] The number of cattle in the private possession of collective members dropped year by year between the peak year of 1959, when stocks of over six million were held, to 1961 when they stood at 3,600,000, and by 1964 they showed only a modest recovery to just about four million. The fall in this sector of ownership was responsible for the major part of the total losses of over three million head between 1959 and 1961. We read also, in the *History of the Mongol People's Republic*, that 'in some aimaks there were irregularities in the implementation of the Party's instructions about the socialization of livestock, but these were exposed and corrected in time'. The form these irregularities took is not mentioned. The official line today, as explained for instance in the Fourth Party Programme of 1966, is that the collectivization of livestock was carried out on a voluntary basis. It was found possible to complete the task without resorting to the confiscation of the property of 'exploiting elements' in the countryside. The word 'voluntary' is of course susceptible of such infinite gradations of meaning that it no longer has much meaning at all: we saw in the last chapter for example how the lamaseries were persuaded to volunteer to close down. It would also be of interest to know exactly who were the 'exploiting elements' left in the countryside thirty-five years after the revolution and how they were distinguished. Presumably they were herders who had more than a certain norm of animals and employed other persons to help them, but this point is not made clear.

The new form the collectives were to take after 1955 was symbolized by a change of name. The old producers' associations (*ardyn uildverleiin negdel*) were in future to be called *rural economy collectives* (*khödöö aj akhuin negdel*). The Mongol term *negdel* which is translated in two different ways here, first as 'association' and then as 'collective' means literally a 'union', but it is clear from what the Mongols say about the collectives that they represent a considerably more advanced stage of collectivization than the old voluntary associations, and the variant translation has been adopted to bring out this difference. The new *negdels* are much more than mere co-operatives which is the English term which has usually been used up to now to describe them, and are similar in structure to the Russian kolkhozes. The means of production, that is, the livestock, is owned jointly, and income is apportioned not according to a member's capital contribution, which has to be his total holding less his personal allowance, but according to the amount of work he is calculated to have performed. The collectives are of very considerable size compared with the old associations: in 1963 for example each consisted on the average of 502 households, and in 1966 of 477. Family members over the age of sixteen are accounted members of the collective. Collectives engage in a certain amount of ancillary agricultural work, as well as rearing livestock. Their sheer size and complexity, the largest of them having over one hundred thousand head of cattle, demand a standard type of organization and accounting procedure, and constant liaison with the state organs to whom they are responsible for delivery of produce and servicing of loans. More and more the collective is coming to coincide with its local *sumun* or county, so that it is customary nowadays to refer to a *sumun-negdel* in one word, and the *negdel* is developing into a distinct political unit as well as being an economic organization. Thus the new collectives are the antithesis of the old *nökhörlöl* of the 'thirties: informal labour-pooling agreements have been replaced by huge monopolistic organs, run by managers appointed from the centre and integrated in the state apparatus and planning system.

New regulations for the collectives were promulgated in 1955, and since then the tendency has been to tighten up control of the participating families and to increase their dependence on cash wages by reducing the number of private beasts. That is, the proletarianization of the herder is the ultimate aim. In 1959 the number of animals a herder was allowed to keep for his own use was reduced to ten, with a maximum of fifty per household, or fifteen and seventy-five respectively in the harder Gobi areas, and at the same time the norm of labour days to be worked during the year was doubled from 75 to 150. Women, who form half the rural labour force, had to work one hundred units. Disciplinary punishments were introduced, starting with a reprimand and increasing in severity through fines in terms of labour-day units to expulsion from the collective.

The organization and financing of this ambitious project involved the state in certain difficulties. It is one thing to decree a new structure for the livelihood of a whole people, and another to put it into effect, and at the end of 1959 the Central Committee was complaining that members of collectives 'were not sufficiently enrolled in collective labour', that productivity remained low, the minimum number of labour-day units was often not being worked, little attention was being paid to the principle of distribution according to labour, and that there was no adequate calculation or book-keeping. It even felt it necessary to state what should have been obvious – that it was essential to 'begin to introduce planning' in all branches of the economy of the collectives. The situation as disclosed in South Gobi aimak illustrates in concrete detail the sort of thing covered by these phrases. In the three years since collectivization, this province managed to lose three hundred thousand head of cattle. South Gobi had not been subject to blizzards, and the losses could not be attributed to natural causes but were due to mismanagement by local Party officials. These had been 'systematically discouraging' the people from looking after their private beasts, and at the same time allowing them to draw up to the limit from the common herds for consumption regardless of whether they worked or not. South Gobi had been extracting three times the national average income from social property, which naturally profited the herders to a very acceptable degree, but had been ruinous to the national plan. Mismanagement on the spot was exacerbated by Mongolia's heavy commitments in the early 1960s to supply meat to the USSR. Until the Russians agreed to cut their demands, exports had had to be made up by slaughtering productive females. At the same time waste in processing was noted, and continued to be noted year after year, the meat factory at Ulan Bator being littered with unused heads, shins and guts.

At the peak there were 728 collectives. This number was progressively reduced by mergers to the 1965 figure of 289. But even this modified addition to the country's over-extended administrative apparatus meant a demand for trained managers, accountants and inspectors which has by no means been met. In 1960 it was not even expected that deficiencies in personnel would be made up before 1967. The existence of these large production units demands strict control. In 1963 the rules were again revised. All members were to be issued with labour-books in which the amount of work done and pay received was to be recorded. New methods of payment were recommended, leading towards the ultimate goal of complete substitution of cash payments for recompense in kind. There is, of course, still a big gap between promise and performance, and especially in the Gobi areas, with their hard life and sparse population, it is still hard to persuade people to settle down and organize their labour on a wage-earning basis.

The financial backing for the collectives was furnished partly by state loans, partly by guaranteed prices for produce delivered, which have more than once been raised, and partly, especially in the early days, by voluntary contributions, amounting to millions of tugrigs, raised from other sectors of the population, who thus found themselves directly bearing the expense of part of the remoulding of the country's major industry. The USSR is also currently supplying a considerable amount of financial and technical aid, building laboratories and machine and repair stations, helping to expand veterinary work, and even helping to build cattle pens.

Along with the closer organization of the former nomads has gone their progressive settlement around the *negdel*-centres. These little villages, of tents and wood or brick buildings, provide the convenience of schools, clinics, veterinary stations, clubs, libraries, shops and post-offices: cinemas are mostly still itinerant. But sheer material poverty will mean that it will be a long time before extensive semi-nomadism yields to livestock farms equipped with warm winter shelters and an adequate fodder supply. Year after year Mongolia remains vulnerable to the disaster of the *dzud*, when spring snow freezes and deprives the animals of their grazing: for instance, only Soviet and Chinese intervention in the spring of 1964 saved losses from being much graver than they were. Nowadays mobile columns using lorries and helicopters can relieve a disaster to some extent if fodder is available, but losses can still be heavy, especially as beasts which have already weathered the severe winter are quickly weakened by spring hardships.

Factors limiting Mongolia's future progress

Mongolia's abrupt entry into modern life and her generous ambitions have some serious implications. Though her population has been increasing for a number of years, and is now probably twice what it was in 1921, it is both numerically insufficient for the tasks facing it and, as mentioned earlier, unbalanced as to age groups. If nineteenth century Mongolia suffered from hidden underemployment, in that thousands of men could be drawn off into an idle cloistered life, while those outside were sufficient to keep the herds going at the primitive level of efficiency then acceptable, nowadays there is just not enough labour to go round. There is a shortage of managers and specialists of all sorts, and of manual labourers also, which has to some extent been temporarily relieved by imported, but not immigrant, foreign labour. Mongolia's population explosion coincides with urbanization and industrialization. In general, her population is young. In 1963 nearly 45 per cent were aged eighteen or under, with over 40 per cent belonging to the age group up to fifteen. This youthful sector has been increasing both quantitatively and as a percentage of the whole: in 1956 only 32 per cent of the population was aged fifteen and under. The annual net rate of increase of the population rose in the same seven years from twenty-three to thirty-four per thousand. But at the same time there is underpopulation. There are a little over one million people in the country,[1a] giving an average density of two persons per square mile. The labour force, that is, the number of men from sixteen to fifty-nine and of women from sixteen to fifty-four, has decreased since 1956 in terms of percentage of the whole, and showed only a modest absolute rise of rather over eighteen thousand up to 1963 to cope with a rapidly expanding economy and a rising demand for educational and social services resulting from the high birthrate. With time, of course, the present imbalance between the number of children and the number of able-bodied adults will adjust itself, and the population explosion will turn into an asset. The working population is expected to increase by fifteen to twenty thousand a year between 1965 and 1970. But families are large, with over forty thousand mothers enjoying in 1963 the grants awarded to mothers of five or more children. Yet women are badly needed in the labour force, of which they form nearly half, and are more or less forced to take jobs.

Acute social problems are bound to arise from this situation. Broken homes, juvenile delinquency and so on are only partly relieved by the considerable, but quite insufficient attention which is being devoted to the provision of medical services, children's clinics, *crèches* and schools, and to the after-care of delinquents.

There are human and organizational failings, to which the press periodically draws attention. Thus, in spite of the existence of a law regulating marriage and aimed at the protection of the home, an amazing number of couples do not bother to register their marriages. Figures given for one locality showed that out of 712 unions only 166 had been properly registered. Schools are criticized for expelling recalcitrant pupils and then taking no further interest in them, so that they drift into crime. Parents are taken to task for all sorts of neglect: one curious practice which is condemned is that of giving children ridiculous propitiatory names, such as 'Bad Dog' to avert the attentions of evil spirits.

It is also evident that many parents are too hard pressed to give their children proper care. The state, ultimately the only employer, makes careful regulations regarding the employment of women, but often fails to observe them. These regulations are not always over generous in any case. The 1964 Labour Code prescribes for instance that pregnant women, nursing mothers and mothers of children up to one year old, with no one at home to look after these children, may not be employed on night work or overtime. Mothers with children under three are allowed to opt for a shortened working day of six hours, payment to be *pro rata*. But even these provisions can be ignored, so the Press wrote in 1964, and the state was criticized for evading its obligation to put pregnant women on to light work and allow them proper rest periods. An article published in the newspaper *Unen* that year sums up pathetically what parents in a state-monopoly system have to put up with, and illustrates the reverse side of the often admirable social system as advertised in propaganda. Under the heading: 'The working hours of mothers with many children should be cut down' the writer said that he had five children aged between one and eight years. One of these was in a *crèche*, but the others had to stay at home by themselves all day because there was no *crèche* or kindergarten for them to go to. Even when there was a *crèche* it was a great loss of time going there and back every day. If you fetched the children late you had to pay extra and if you were persistently late they would get expelled. The only alternative was to leave work early. The writer suggested a working day of seven hours for mothers with several children and proposed with unconscious irony that one or other parent might be excused 'evening cultural work' so as to get on with the task of bringing up their own children.

The socialization of production in Mongolia has ended the era of exploitation as defined in communist terms, that is, the employment of one man by another for profit. Whether the elimination of private enterprise and the elevation of the State into being the sole employer does anything but create a new exploiter where previously the producer was on his own, or to change one form of exploitation for another, is a fundamental argument which goes far beyond the limits of Mongolian circumstances. It seems, however, that the expansion of the public sector of ownership has opened the way to a novel type of exploitation of society as a whole, through offences against 'socialist property'. At one end of the scale this shows itself in an indifference towards machinery or collectivized livestock, and in a tendency on the part of trained persons, doctors and medical technicians for example, to abandon their posts in the undeveloped provinces and drift back, either to their native districts or to the bright lights of Ulan Bator. Since 1964 increasing attention has been paid to checking and control in the country's public life, and publicity is given to the multifarious instances of back-sliding on the part of workers which are brought to light. Machinery is found to be abandoned in the fields as soon as it is finished with, to lie about and rust till it is wanted again the next year, publicly-owned cars are used for private hunting trips and travel, or disappear altogether, and, something which can hardly ever have occurred in the days of private enterprise, collectivized horses and other animals have been found neglected by those deputed to look after them, who did not bother to water them for days on end. At the other end of the scale slackness and irresponsibility shade off into positive dishonesty and criminality in the management of public property, and from time to time widespread rackets are found to be operating inside official organizations. A typical example was the discovery in early 1966 that for years officials in the Ulan Bator Retailing Directorate and the shops and stores it controlled had been lining their own pockets from the proceeds of theft and dishonesty. They had stolen tons of meat for private sale, made personal profits by such primitive ruses as loading the scales inside with stones or by buying meat at third grade prices and selling at first grade, and so on. Defects such as this in society may well be only marginal to the general economic life of the country, but as the socialist sector now embraces all production, and the economy is being increasingly complex and dependent on responsible executives, the problem of instituting, and paying for, effective control at all levels will more and more exercise the minds of Party and state officials.

Another double-edged feature in Mongol life in the 'sixties is rapid urbanization. Ulan Bator accounts for close on a quarter of the total population, and the aimak centres, though none of them is itself a large town, contain another fifth. Thus something like 40 per cent of Mongolia's people have given up the rural life, though they continue to live in tents as the construction of urban flats nowhere keeps pace with urban drift. One result of this drift to the capital and to other towns is the starving of the countryside of workers. The shortage of labour in Mongolia is not at a uniform level throughout the country. Some areas, especially the relatively fertile *khangai* areas of pasture and wooded hills in the centre and west, have a surplus of labour, resulting in seasonal unemployment, while Gobi areas have a shortage. Ulan Bator has a labour surplus, Darkhan is undermanned. What is wanted is to get people out of the capital into the countryside, and from rural centres out into the actual brigades and bases where the work is done. In 1961 some ten thousand unnecessary officials were said to have been purged from public offices and put to more useful work, and regularly people's passports are checked and those found to have moved to the capital without authorization or sufficient reason are sent back to their original domicile or put to work. In twelve months from 1965 to 1966, alone, some 1,500 families, consisting of five thousand individuals, were expelled from Ulan Bator. But this action does not provide a sufficient braking effect to reduce the rate of growth of Ulan Bator. From 164,000 in 1960 the population has continued to grow so as to reach nearly a quarter of a million by 1965 and the trend continues.

Prospects for development

Outwardly the direction of Mongolia's development is now assured, provided aid continues to come from the Soviet bloc and the Chinese do not make trouble. Her slow evolution towards the ideal of a mixed industrial and agrarian economy will continue, with herding becoming progressively less dominant in the economy and employing a decreasing proportion of the people. This tendency is already apparent. In 1959 two-thirds of the population were members of collectives, while by 1963 the proportion was only just over half. In 1956 only a quarter were officials and workers, including those employed on state farms: by 1963 over 46 per cent were so employed. Factory building and industrial expansion will continue. An earnest of this is the building of the Darkhan complex, associated with large near-by coal deposits. Again, provided the money for capital investment and current spending continues to come in from abroad, the little luxuries of life which have begun to ease the life of Mongolia's steppe-dwellers in the last decade or so will continue to trickle over the shop-counters. A television service was opened in 1967. Education, already universal, will ultimately become the privilege of all children for a minimum of eight years, instead of the four which have been all that could be achieved up to now in country districts. The school programme elaborated in 1965 for what are rather grandiosely-termed 'Eight-year general education and labour-polytechnic schools' envisages a comprehensive course of education both academic and manual, with one foreign language, presumably Russian, for all pupils from the third school year onwards. The avowed aim of the new programme is to instil into all pupils a *communist* education. This ideological slant is naturally most clearly expressed in the history programme, which is taught from the fifth class onwards. This prescribes that children shall be taught the 'inevitable victory of communism' and that they shall be brought up to reject all manifestations of old-fashioned habits and bourgeois views. They are to be trained to understand history on what is termed a scientific basis. The function of history teaching, then, is seen as exemplifying dogma and producing believers, and not as provoking free inquiry. Education will evidently continue in Mongolia to be prejudiced and sectarian.

In production and distribution the tendency to pay more attention to the needs of the consumer, and less to the mechanical fulfilment of the plan, already dimly observable, may persist and techniques of management, advertising and market research, previously associated with western, 'capitalist' economics, may gradually extend the tentative foothold they have recently planted.

A significant hint of this is the discussion, in the last few years, of the concept of cybernetics, hitherto tabooed in the communist world. Already by mid-1966 a Mongol neologism had been coined for this term, and this will presumably find its way into the vocabulary as the technique itself begins to affect doctrinaire rigidity in planning.

Nevertheless, it must be remembered that all material progress in Mongolia depends ultimately on the willingness of her allies to go on carrying much of the cost of her development: As a corollary, Mongolia will doubtless remain inside the Soviet section of the divided communist world. Soviet influence in Mongolia today is of a different type from the brutal police dictatorship of the 1930s. In the 1950s it was found advisable to give the Mongols tangible inducements to keep away from too close a *rapprochement* with China: the excesses of the great cultural revolution of 1966 probably removed any leanings the Mongols may have still had towards China, however. But the necessity of demonstrating to other underdeveloped countries that communist development can proceed in an orderly way, free from the turmoil characteristic of Chinese communism, together with the perennial care of securing her southern Siberian flank, will together ensure that the USSR goes on subsidizing the Mongol economy, and this underwriting will probably grow more, rather than less, expensive, as the complexity of life in Mongolia demands more money and more expertise to keep it buoyant.

Cultural life

What of artistic and intellectual life over the last twenty years? A measure of the relaxation of official control and artificial tension is that it is now possible to give some sort of answer to this question. Anyone taking up the study of the Mongol language and culture in western countries even as late as about 1950 was forced to plan his studies as if they related to a dead civilization. No books had been available from Mongolia for decades, no paper or journal could be subscribed to, even if one knew what was being published. Nothing at all was to be found in the new cyrillic script. There was no possibility of contact with Mongolian scholars. It was an event of some significance when in 1954 Soviet scholars for the first time attended the triennial International Congress of

Orientalists in Cambridge: at a time when they were so wary of corresponding with their colleagues abroad it was too much to expect that the Mongols, who had never had a tradition of international co-operation, should show themselves more forthcoming. In this respect the situation has changed enormously for the better, and the climax of Mongolia's intellectual liberation was probably the holding of the First International Congress of Mongolists in Ulan Bator in 1959, which was attended by scholars from all parts of the world.

But before this the isolation in which Mongolia had been kept had taken its toll not only of individual scholars who had suffered death or imprisonment, but of academic values. These were distorted and thought was compressed into the narrow channels of Marx-Leninism, stunting progress for decades. A corrupting influence on thought and learning is especially serious when it coincides with the emergence for the first time of an academic profession. Echoes of the falsification of history practised in the past can still be caught in current publications. The doctoring of official documents has already been illustrated in an earlier chapter. Equally instructive is the occasional hangover of communist dogmatism and perversion of fact which comes to light because it has been allowed to creep into a foreign language publication where its absurdity stands out with particular clarity and illustrates the pernicious influence exercised on scholarship by political necessity. An extreme example of this is to be found in a booklet published in English and in French in 1966 under the title *The Mongolian People's Struggle for National Independence and the Building of a New Life*. This booklet appeared under the distinguished patronage of the Academy of Science, the country's highest academic authority. Amongst other questionable statements it makes the following: '. . . the notorious Munich agreement of 1938, when the United States, Britain and France gave Hitler Czechoslovakia as payment for a commitment to start a war against the USSR'. The shock of reading such a preposterous piece of historical nonsense forces us to examine critically the quality and basic assumptions of all Mongolian historical writing. That such a statement can be printed for circulation in the English speaking world does not necessarily imply ignorance of facts on the part of leading academicians and politicians in Mongolia who are perfectly well informed about world affairs, but betrays rather a willingness to falsify facts for temporary advantage. Such a statement appearing in the Mongol language would presumably be accepted at face value by its readers, few or none of whom would have the knowledge to challenge it, or even realize that it was vulnerable to challenge. The ordinary Mongol is still almost totally isolated from the world: few people know any foreign language except Russian and fewer still have access to any foreign books or any opportunity to travel abroad or meet foreigners. The appearance in a western language of such an assertion as this puts the reader on the alert as to the basic principles which guide Mongolian writing even today and imposes the realization that, in spite of a regulated relaxation of official control, scholarship and by implication writing of all sorts, are still regarded primarily as weapons in the class war, not as a vehicle for the free investigation of events for its own sake.

The principles which guide creative literature are certainly of this sort, and were well expressed in a resolution passed by the Political Bureau of the Central Committee in 1953. This stated:

> The central duty of our writers consists in writing, on the basis of socialist realism, of the tenacious and selfless labour of our herdsmen and popular intelligentsia, who are building socialism in their own land, of the role of the Mongol People's Revolutionary Party in encouraging and organizing all the victories of our people in this great struggle, of the great and truly inexhaustible significance of the friendship established between our people, the great Soviet people, and the peoples of the popular democracies, and of the struggle being waged by the whole of progressive mankind, headed by the USSR, for the establishment of peace throughout the whole world.[2]

Literature is thus defined solely in terms of its political utility, and it is against this background that we have to look at some of the disputes which have enlivened Mongol life over the past decade or so. It will become clear that the efforts of many Mongol intellectuals to secure a relaxation of official control do not in fact go beyond this limited objective. There is no sign that the struggle has been taken out of the arena of communist dogmatics: it is by and large a struggle over the degree of political direction, not the rightness of political direction itself.

In circumstances where literature is at the mercy of political control, the reputation of a writer depends less on his talents as an artist than on the degree to which his work is acceptable to political ideology, and as the demands of ideology vary at different times, so reputations are made and unmade arbitrarily with sole reference to political expediency, and are susceptible also to retrospective adjustment. The disowning and suppression of men of letters and their work has been one of the less acceptable features of public life in revolutionary Mongolia as in the USSR. The case of the poet Buyannemekh, whose name has already been mentioned in connection with the Danzan affair of 1924, is a typical instance of this process of manipulation. Buyannemekh had an exemplary revolutionary career. He was born in 1902, the son of an impoverished *taiji*, was as a child given away in adoption, made his way to Urga and managed to get an education. In 1920 he was in Irkutsk, working on the first revolutionary newspaper, *Mongolyn Unen* or 'Mongol Truth'. In 1921 he was in Moscow for the Congress of the Peoples of the East and met Lenin. He was a founder member of the first Literary Circle set up in Ulan Bator in 1929 as a result of a resolution of the Central Committee of the Party. Other members of this circle, which came to grief in 1937, were writers like Ayush and Yadamsuren, both 'unmasked' as enemies of the people, Rintchen and Damdinsuren, who both suffered imprisonment on false charges in the late 'thirties but who fortunately survived to become two of the foremost contemporary Mongolian scholars, Natsagdorj, one of the young people who studied in Germany in the 'twenties and who has been built up since his death in 1937 into the founder of modern Mongolian literature, and one or two others. In 1937 Buyannemekh was executed as a traitor on a framed charge. From then on, for twenty years, he was an un-person. His work was never reprinted. In 1955 the young communist critic Ch. Chimid, in a preface to the collected works of Natsagdorj, referred to Buyannemekh as one of a number of enemies of the people who had wormed their way into certain literary organizations and who, as representatives of feudal and capitalist interests 'attempted to divorce our revolutionary literature from life and from the representation of the revolutionary struggle and creative labour of our people'. He 'wrought havoc in literary work, fought to destroy the party nature of literature and to divorce literature from the life of society'. By 1962 with the disowning of the cult of personality, fashions had changed, and the literary newspaper *Soyol* or 'Culture' published a brief biography of Buyannemekh with a portrait, referring to him as 'one of the first representatives of our new literature, a famous writer and public worker'. A few of his poems were reprinted at the same time. These contortions had all taken place without any detailed reference to what the subject had been or had actually written, his works remaining all the time inaccessible. His rehabilitation was a grudging one. Speaking at an ideological congress in early 1963 a party spokesman warned that the rehabilitation of the personal level of men like Buyannemekh did not mean that on the ideological level their work was free from important faults, particularly in its leaning towards nationalism. However, the restoration of names like that of Buyannemekh to the history of Mongolia's cultural life indicates a considerable concession to reason. Though he is still to be approached warily, his work, and the work of others like him who disappeared during the 'thirties is at least being partially disinterred and examined, though necessarily within the limits imposed by communist dogmatics.

How the limitations imposed by political control curb the freedom of discussion was briefly mentioned in the previous chapter. The fight put up by Damdinsuren to halt the denigration and destruction for ideological reasons of Mongolia's old literature was, whatever its basic motivation and ultimate purpose, carried on in terms acceptable to communist argumentation. His quarrel with authority, if it may be so termed, while one in which basic values were at stake, was formulated in terms common to both sides. We are faced with the significant fact that in one of his earliest articles on the theme, written in 1955, Damdinsuren found it appropriate to separate and to point up the 'democratic tendencies' which existed in ancient Mongol literature alongside its 'feudal tendencies'. The implication was that for the sake of these democratic features the old literature ought not to be discarded as a whole. Damdinsuren was also careful to attack both those who derided the old culture and those who displayed an excessive nationalism, steering a middle course between two extremes. Both of these attitudes he found equally dangerous, and remarked:

> In building up our new popular literature we ought to examine our old cultural heritage, and exploit whatever is useful and good. There are many useful and good items in our seven hundred year old literature. It is a holy duty for us to study these and exploit them in building our new culture.[3]

In itself this was at the time a courageous new departure in literary and political criticism, for up to 1955 it had been fashionable to deny that pre-1921 Mongolia had any culture at all. This perversion of the truth was still being repeated later than 1955 by younger scholars who had grown up in the difficult years, and in 1957 Damdinsuren took one of them to task for denying his country's past. In conclusion he wrote:

Since the 1921 revolution the Mongol people have flourished and have produced many specialists, and have brought their culture to a level never reached before. But in praising these fine achievements we must not deny the earlier ones. If Mishig thinks to make today's achievements stand out the more by decrying earlier achievements, he is in error. It is desirable that the previous state of culture and present developments should be described on a basis of truth.[4]

Damdinsuren followed up his early blow for reason and truthfulness with other essays. By 1959 the Committee of Sciences was in a position to begin an imaginative programme of reprinting of old literature. Besides what was published in Mongolia, several volumes of folklore gathered by Academician Rintchen in earlier years began to be published in West Germany. None of this happened without incurring the displeasure of official circles, but a measure of the return of a certain amount of academic autonomy is the fact that the party theorists were able only to complain of the publishing plan, but not to obstruct the plan itself to any significant extent, as they had been able to do before 1955. Inside the Academy of Sciences, as it became in 1961, the appearance in Germany of Rintchen's volumes was quietly hailed as an academic distinction, though in 1963 it was the subject of disapproval out of all proportion to its public impact by the same party spokesman who had referred to Buyannemekh. These volumes, published in a limited and learned edition and at a high price, in Mongol without translation, and likely to come to the notice of only a handful of scholars, were condemned as doing nothing but 'bring comfort to reactionary imperialist propaganda'. Even Damdinsuren's own reprints of old literature which were being sold in all bookshops and street stalls in 1959 were the subject of similar disapproval in 1963. The rigid attitudes of the Choibalsang period had not entirely thawed. But though the Party condemned Damdinsuren for issuing old texts which it found 'completely without interest even from the artistic point of view', instead of following the party line strictly, it was fortunately not able to interfere at all decisively any more with the Academy's work.[5]

The basis of the conflict between some intellectuals and the Party is expressed with some clarity in an article which appeared in 1959 in the Press criticizing some of the work of the poet and scholar Rintchen. Rintchen, now a man of rather over sixty, has had a long life of creative work, as journalist, academician, novelist, script writer and translator. He is a man of wide culture, at home in several European and oriental languages. On various occasions in the past his outspoken nationalism has brought him into conflict with authority. In the late 'thirties he was imprisoned for several years as an 'enemy of the people'. In the 'forties he made, with Soviet collaboration, a film on the theme of Tsogtu Taiji, playing him up as a patriot who took up the anti-Manchu struggle led by the Chahar emperor Ligdan Khan. For this work he received a Choibalsang prize. A few years later, when excessive nationalism was found to be flourishing in Mongolia, this film was severely taken to task by the critic Chimid. It was discovered to have been produced in a spirit of *bourgeois* nationalism. Rintchen had idealized feudal society, drawing a picture of harmony in class interests between the people and the feudal nobility, depicting Tsogtu Taiji as a champion of freedom and independence, a leader and teacher of the people. The article which now concerns us was entitled, significantly: 'Struggling positively against manifestations of nationalistic opinions' and while directed specifically against Rintchen it uttered certain dogmatic principles of general application which make it worth quoting:

> The great Lenin said that bourgeois nationalism and proletarian internationalism are outlooks which express the interests of two opposting classes. In the ideological struggle either the socialist view mus-prevail or the capitalist – *there is no middle course*. The attempt to reconcile the ideologies of two antagonistic classes results in the retreat of the socialist ideology before the bourgeois, in the blunting of class interests. Now the ideological attacks of the imperialists, directed towards the furtherance of the revival of the old, sow distrust and enmity among the peoples of the socialist countries. It is necessary to note that manifestations of nationalism are to be observed amongst us, preparing the ground for bourgeois intrigues. One of the spokesmen for nationalism is Professor Rintchen.[6]

POST-WAR MONGOLIA: ACHIEVEMENTS AND PROSPECTS

It is not the personal fate of an individual scholar which is under consideration here, but a formulation of principles which is of general validity in modern Mongol intellectual life and which merits attention beyond its specific application to a single case. It brings out the ultimate dependence of artists and scholars upon the requirements of dogma, and defines the role they have to play, which is primarily a political one, and only in second place an artistic or intellectual one. This being so, the partial relaxation of party control in recent years has admitted a number of paradoxical situations, of which perhaps the most interesting, since the central figure is the one Mongol whose name is familiar to the whole world, was the strange fate of the celebration arranged in 1962 for the eight hundredth anniversary of the birth of Genghis Khan. For the Chinese, Genghis counts as the founder of the Yüan or Mongol dynasty, for the Russians he was a destructive invader, but for the Mongols he has always been the centre and origin of their national history, the founder of their independent statehood. He is more even than this. Until the 'thirties he had been the object of a special religious cult, observed all over Mongolia but centred on the Ordos region of west China where a sanctuary existed, supposedly containing relics of the great conqueror. These were of great mystical significance, so great that the Japanese had planned a massive mausoleum in their part of Inner Mongolia, to which they proposed to move the relics, if they could get hold of them, to serve as the talismanic rallying point of a revivified, and, they hoped, pro-Japanese Mongol nationalism. This plan never materialized, as the relics were moved far to the west. In the Mongolian People's Republic the Genghis Khan cult was suppressed and the shrines destroyed, but in Inner Mongolia the worship of the deified emperor survived. The hereditary family custodians of the shrines lived on there, guarding the ancient manuscripts of the ritual texts, written partly in an unintelligible gibberish known as the 'language of the Gods'. After the communist victory in China, the Chinese authorities, with an eye to rallying Mongol nationalism in Inner Mongolia to themselves, had a large mausoleum built in Ordos, closely resembling in its execution the Japanese sketch. They gathered the old sanctuary-tents there, confirmed the guardians of the cult in office, and subsidized the annual sacrifices.

The eight hundredth anniversary of the birth of Genghis Khan seemed a suitable opportunity to reassess his historical role as well as to organize a celebration. A large stone monument was erected at his putative birth-place in north Mongolia, and a special meeting of the Academy of Sciences was devoted to Genghis Khan. Professor Natsagdorj, the head of the Historical Committee, gave a lecture entitled 'Genghis as the founder of the Mongol state' which was reprinted in summary form in Unen. In this he assessed Genghis's role fairly objectively, stressing the positive benefits he had brought to Mongolia – unification, national organization, codification of laws, literacy – against which he balanced his destructive military campaigns which eventually impoverished Mongolia. He covered himself politically by identifying those who wished to misinterpret Genghis's role with those denied Mongolia's statehood, that is, the Chinese Nationalists. The Academy announced a special volume of papers to be published in 1962 on the joint occasion of this anniversary and the fiftieth anniversary of the national revolution against the Manchus. It is uncertain whether this volume ever appeared or not, but certainly a special set of commemorative stamps was printed and issued, showing a portrait of Genghis, his war banner, and other historical relics.

However, what might elsewhere have been no more than a piece of harmless historical reminiscence soon turned into a manifestation of sharp ideological cleavage. In September 1962 a secretary of the Central Committee, Tömör-ochir, was suddenly dismissed from office for a variety of reasons, including the accusation that he had inflamed nationalist feelings amongst the people, especially through his connection with the Genghis Khan anniversary. The special stamps were withdrawn, and intermittently throughout the rest of the year the Press sniped at those intellectuals who had identified themselves too closely with nationalistic sentiment. The whole matter was aired thoroughly in early 1963 at the ideological congress already mentioned, which was attended by a strong Soviet delegation under the party theoretician Ilichev. In the course of this meeting Mongolia's continued adherence to the current Soviet view of the nature and role of communism was affirmed. Probably what brought the Genghis Khan celebrations to such an abrupt end was their entanglement with the unrelated Sino-Soviet dispute, since the Chinese, viewing Genghis as an important Chinese emperor, had organized big celebrations of their own. But basically the disowning of the anniversary celebrations was a minor victory for rigidity and party solidarity in the chronic contradiction between the claims of communism and of Mongol nationalism.

Conclusion

All experience shows Mongolia's state system to be totalitarian, and not democratic in the sense that this term is understood in western society. Power, initiative and control are in the hands of the Party, and, to be explicit, those of the Central Committee. Elections take place regularly, with the expected result that the powers that be obtain a unanimous vote of approval, and people are constantly taking part in meetings and other demonstrations of solidarity. As a corollary to this, all decisions of any importance emanate from the Central Committee, whether what is involved is the liquidation of a social class, as in 1929, or the partial denunciation of the excesses of the period of the cult of personality, as in 1956 and again in 1962. Central control of all aspects of life involves the authorities in artificially created problems which would not exist in a more flexible society, and also in the burden of considering, at the highest level, questions which ought to be the province of those at subordinate levels who are directly concerned with them. For example, the Academy of Sciences is subject to the direction of the Central Committee, which also has to bend its attention to the vagaries of individual scholars and writers who may swerve from the narrow path of socialist realism. For the Party this means a considerable deflection of energy: for those affected it means that the essential role of the creative writer as an intellectual pathfinder, from whose imagination a new and productive synthesis of ideas might emerge, is devalued so that he becomes, or should become, a mere mouth-piece of a political party. On the other hand the Party finds itself dealing at the highest level with details of planning. It concerns itself for instance with book production – and with amazement one notes that in 1957, after thirty-five years of socialism it was thinking of arranging for a translation of *Das Kapital* to be made and issued.[7] At the very lowest level of detail we find the Central Committee devoting its attention to matters of shop-window display and publicity for the retail trade, which it discussed at its second plenary meeting in 1958: whether or not to permit advertising was presumably a matter for theoretical argument.[8]

In the political sphere, rigidity of thinking and the inadmissability of an organized opposition excludes effective public discussion and democratic participation in the shaping of events, and results in intra-party disagreements continuing to escalate to the most bitter denunciations and denigration of the losing group by the winners. The Party is still subject to sudden and publicly unprepared purges, during which leading members, who up to the moment of expulsion have continued, at least in the public eye, to be esteemed colleagues, are suddenly dismissed and held up to sustained obloquy. Naturally, the normal demotions and reshuffles of officials take place continually and without excessive publicity, but the indignant unmasking of anti-party groups and other hostile elements within the party leadership has been one of the unique features of public life in Mongolia in the 'sixties. Successive groups were expelled from their posts and subjected to vilification, more or less intense, and more or less sustained, in 1959, 1962, 1963 and 1964. It is difficult to decide what may have been the effective reason for these purges, whether the individuals concerned were really as hopelessly inept, unco-operative, dishonest, greedy and generally base as their denouncers insisted, or whether their evaluation of problems and policies was so at variance with the officially agreed one as to constitute a threat to the leadership which could survive only by destroying the reputations and careers of the challengers. What on the surface is intriguing is the apparent lack of concern with which the Party can admit that, as in the case of L. Tsend, a secretary of the Central Committee who was dismissed in 1963, it has for years on end been led by dishonest and self-seeking intriguers, who were at the same time incompetents. Of course, this may or may not be literally true: what is probably of greater significance is the evidence these purges and the bitterness of the tone in which they are carried out, afford of the tense and brittle quality of intra-party life in Mongolia.

In purely material terms the years since the revolution have brought considerable change and undeniable advance to Mongolia, the rate having accelerated enormously in the decade since 1955. Her basic food supplies are assured from her own production to an extent unique in Asia, and if present conditions of international co-operation persist, it seems that the only limitation to be placed on Mongolia's material progress will be her capacity to digest and exploit what she is given from abroad and what she creates for herself. This is an important qualification, as we have seen: underpopulation, shortage of technical experience and skilled workers coupled with an inflated party and state bureaucracy, and that social immaturity which is covered by the contemporary phrase 'evidence of the survivals of past ideology' together constitute an effective drag on Mongol progress. Of more interest than the fact itself is the manner and spirit in which Mongolia is intended to develop. These are summarized in the closing words of the Fourth Party Programme of 1966: 'We shall finish building socialism under the leadership of the Mongol People's Revolutionary Party and gradually create the conditions for the transition to a communist society, which is the mighty summit of our aims'.[9] The Mongol Party is thus running on a course parallel to, but rather behind, that of the USSR, and this spiritual dependence on Moscow in political matters is perhaps the most relevant thing about Mongolia's present condition and future prospects. In the political sphere, initiative generally waits upon the USSR. We have seen, for instance, how the dismantling of the cult of personality could only follow, and not anticipate, the Russian example. The same imitative tendencies are to be seen in the handling of all delicate themes. Mongolia's attitude to the Yugoslav question varies in accordance with Soviet convenience, and even her alternate protests and silences in the Sino-Soviet dispute are correlated in time and in tone with Russian outbursts of activity. A case in point is the reaction to a statement made in July 1965 to some Japanese visitors by Mao Tse-tung, in which the Chinese leader appeared to deny Mongolia's statehood: only after *Pravda* had taken issue with this statement on 2 September did *Unen* also condemn it on 6 September with a Mongol translation of *Pravda*'s article.

There are various possible reasons for Mongolia's ideological subordination. Geographically her situation means that she cannot stand aloof from disagreements between Russia and China, and as distances contract she can less and less afford to be noncommittal. In practical terms this means that both her recent history and present Chinese intransigence dispose her to the continuance of the existing Russian connection. But beyond this, Mongolia's whole contemporary ethos is something new and originating from abroad. Ideologically, at the official level, she is a Soviet creation. Her old culture, while not obliterated, has been emasculated, and new modes of thought have been imposed with which she has to operate in the absence of any alternative. The break with the past has been far more complete than it has been for the countries of eastern Europe. For them sovietization meant indeed a thorough re-ordering of society, but it has been, one hopes, only a temporary aberration in their association in the main stream of European civilization. Mongolia has suffered a complete alienation from her past. Until 1921 her spiritual roots were in Tibet, her religious solidarity with the Buddhist world. For commercial contacts and material culture she looked to China. After the revolution she was isolated from her past, slowly at first, and ruthlessly from 1929 onwards, and was reorientated towards Russia which monopolized her politically, financially and culturally. The price of Mongol statehood, one might say, was the sealing off of the new state from Mongols elsewhere and from the world at large. Whatever the private feelings of the individual Mongol may be, the attitude towards the USSR officially fostered continues to be that of pupil to teacher, or, at the most, a 'brotherly' relationship in which the USSR is the elder brother and Mongolia the younger brother. 'Learning from Soviet experience' is still the commonest theme in the Press after nearly half a century of independence. This relationship is perhaps symbolized by the abolition of Mongolia's own alphabet, which for over seven hundred years was perfectly adequate to her needs, and its replacement by the Russian script. Arguments of utility were, and still are, put forward for this change. But that the overriding consideration in such operations as this is a political and not a practical one is made apparent by the fate of alphabet reform in Inner Mongolia a few years later. In 1956 the Chinese replaced the old Mongol script there by the same form of the Russian script which was in use in the People's Republic, moved by considerations of utility and in particular by the advantages for Mongols on both sides of the frontier to have a common vehicle of communication. Two years later the growing rift between China and Russia had so reduced the aptness of this reasoning that the change was reversed, and the Inner Mongols had to abandon the newly introduced alphabet and revert to their old script once more.

Mongolia is, to sum up, in the early stages of a fundamental transformation of her whole way of life. On the material and organizational plane, if all goes well, the Mongols hope to evolve a balanced industrial and agrarian economy in which nomadism will have disappeared and even the felt tent will have yielded to the fixed dwelling. What outwardly distinguishes the Mongol from his Russian and Chinese neighbours will be eroded to the point where the average Mongol will be a city dweller working in factory or office, or a rural farm labourer tilling the soil with the help of agricultural machinery, or looking after animals on farms equipped with proper accommodation, fodder supplies and veterinary care. Spiritually the Party plans a much more difficult transformation of society. It promises:

to pay constant attention to the determined struggle against anti-socialist views and behaviour, against the remnants in people's minds and lives of past times, against the remnants of ideas of private ownership and the expression of out of date habits and shameless views such as the exploiting of the labour of others, greediness, selfishness, personal ambition and humbug.[10]

Evidently Mongolia is set on a course intended to lead to complete communization. The stages of the journey remain to be observed as they are traversed.

AFTERWORD

When the Fourth Programme of the Mongolian People's Revolutionary Party (MPRP) was adopted by the party's 15th Congress in June 1966, its architect, Yumjaagiyn Tsedenbal, little dreamt that within the span of the few Five-Year Plans he had estimated were needed to finish 'building socialism' in Mongolia, he would have left the political scene and his grand edifice would be crumbling. Moreover, he hardly imagined that the time could come when he and his creation would be the target of harsh, even bitter words spoken not by those he perceived as Mongolia's foreign enemies but by Mongolians, testing the limits of a newly proclaimed era of *il tod*, the Mongolian equivalent of Soviet leader Mikhail Gorbachev's *glasnost'* or 'openness'.

Notwithstanding the setbacks, shortages and underfulfilled plans and the country's continuing relative backwardness, in the past twenty years Mongolia has undoubtedly experienced real economic and social advance. Yet perhaps its greatest steps ever towards the promise of real freedom, democracy and prosperity are only now about to be taken. The measure of these steps will be the degree to which Mongolian society as a whole and its members individually can face up to the realities of their own past and present and those of the outside world.

Sooner or later, such a self-revaluation was inevitable. The disparity between word and deed, promise and fulfilment, as the demands of political and economic life increasingly outstripped the capabilities of Tsedenbal's leadership, was obvious to all, but for many years incompetence and failure were concealed by lies, silence and fear.

In 1965, Mongolia had diplomatic relations with 35 countries; by January 1987, when Mongolia was finally recognised by the United States of America, the total exceeded 100. Yet the intervening period had been one of growing Mongolian dependence on Soviet economic and military power. A new twenty-year treaty with the USSR was signed by Tsedenbal and Brezhnev in 1966, and Soviet troops returned to Mongolia in 1969 as part of the response to the perceived threat from China. China's relations with the Soviet Union and Mongolia had deteriorated in the late 1960s, and they remained bad throughout the 1970s, with Mongolian charges of Chinese 'annexationism' towards Mongolia, and Chinese charges of Soviet 'colonialism' towards Mongolia. There were border violations by Chinese troops, and disturbances in Ulan Bator by Chinese residents stirred by the passions of China's Maoist 'cultural revolution'.

Anti-Chinese sentiments in Mongolia, with their firm roots in Mongolia's modern history, continued to be expressed for some time after Moscow and Peking had begun to mend their fences, and most of Mongolia's Chinese community was expelled in the early 1980s. However, relations between Mongolia and China eventually took a turn for the better, a new protocol to their border treaty was signed and inter-governmental contacts and trade were restored, albeit at a modest level. On the other hand, there was no restoration of inter-party contacts. The withdrawal of some of the Soviet troops stationed in Mongolia in 1987 was seen to be a measure of the increasing confidence in Sino-Soviet relations.

Soviet control of Mongolia had tightened considerably in the 1970s through party, government and economic as well as military links. Whereas in 1973 there had been direct links between eight Soviet and Mongolian ministries (construction, fuel, water supply, agriculture, transport, education, health and defence), by 1978 over 50 ministries and government departments and 100 research organisations had direct links with their Soviet counterparts. A permanent representative of the Soviet Ministry of Finance was placed in the Mongolian Ministry of Finance in 1977. The 1970s and 1980s were a period of great legislative initiative in Mongolia, the many new laws and codes which went onto the statute books – on the family, labour, public health, people's control, corrective labour, forestry, military service, education, etc – being based on their Soviet counterparts.

Soviet aid financed the building of whole new towns like the industrial processing centre of Darhan and the copper-mining town of Erdenet, which were built in the empty steppe and linked by branch lines to the trans-Mongolian railway. Between 1976 and 1983, Soviet aid almost doubled (from an estimated US$330 million to 620 million). The number of Soviet workers in

Mongolia reached about 32,000, with almost the same number of dependants.

Mongolia's political and economic dependence on the Soviet Union had obliged it in most things to follow the Kremlin's example, even to the point where the idiosyncrasies of Brezhnev's regime were reflected in the actions of Tsedenbal, his Mongolian counterpart. Thus, following the example set by Brezhnev in 1967, while remaining First Secretary of the MPRP Tsedenbal gave up the post of Premier (Chairman of the Council of Ministers) in 1974 to become President (Chairman of the Presidium of the People's Great Hural – the post had been held vacant since the death of Jamsrangiyn Sambuu in 1972). Two years later, Tsedenbal celebrated his 60th birthday with a fifth Order of Sühbaatar, Mongolia's highest decoration, and the unveiling of his bust at Ulaangom, the centre of his home province. Brezhnev celebrated his own 70th birthday in the same year with a fifth Order of Lenin.

Tsedenbal was publicly named Chairman of the Mongolian Defence Council in 1979 and awarded the military rank of Marshal of the MPR, previously awarded to Mongolia's Stalin-like dictator Horloogiyn Choybalsan, who died in 1952. Photographs were published of Tsedenbal in his new dress uniform with 11 rows of medal ribbons and his new Marshal's star, with diamonds. Brezhnev had been promoted to the rank of Marshal in May 1976.

During the official celebrations in 1980 of the 40th anniversary of his leadership of the MPRP, Tsedenbal modestly denied having made any 'contributions to Marxist-Leninist theory' and disclaimed any pretensions to being 'head of the Politburo' – an epithet currently in wide use. Supposedly at the request of 'a number of comrades', however, he also ordered the publication of a secret letter he had sent to the Politburo in 1949 criticising the establishment of a 'personality cult' around him and calling for the revision of Mongolian history books. A new revision of Mongolian history books was ordered. Meanwhile, five of a set of seven postage stamps issued to mark the 60th anniversary of the Mongolian revolution in 1981 featured portraits of Tsedenbal.

At the 18th Congress of the MPRP in 1981, following Brezhnev's earlier example, Tsedenbal changed his title – without evident change of function – from First Secretary to General Secretary, which it had been before, from 1940 to 1954. Policy decisions were increasingly being circulated in the early 1980s in the form not of openly published MPRP Central Committee resolutions and *Hural* and government decrees, but of confidential numbered instructions from the *darga*, Tsedenbal himself. Tsedenbal began to be addressed – almost in the style of the North Korean dictator Kim Il-sung – as the 'dear leader Comrade Marshal Tsedenbal'.

Tsedenbal next initiated a series of purges, which he called 'uprooting weeds' in the party. The President of the Academy of Sciences, Badzaryn Shirendev, a historian, was removed from his post in January 1982. The Minister of State Farms, Hayangiyn Bandzragch, was sacked for inefficiency in February 1982 and posted as ambassador to Afghanistan; the ministry was disbanded. The Chairman of the Trade Union Council, Gombojavyn Ochirbat, was dismissed in May 1982.

Sampilyn Jalan-Aajav, member of the Politburo and Secretary of the MPRP Central Commitee and also Deputy Chairman of the Presidium of the People's Great Hural – effectively Tsedenbal's No 2 man – was removed from power in July 1983. Six months later, it was disclosed in the MPRP monthly journal *Namyn Am'dral* that he was an 'anti-party element' who had supposedly been engaged for 20 years in 'vile intrigues' to overthrow Tsedenbal. New Ministers of Public Security and Defence were also appointed.

Tsedenbal's Russian wife, Anastasya Ivanovna Tsedenbal-Filatova, was playing a prominent public role as Chairman of the Central Commission of the Mongolian Children's Foundation, a quasi-charitable organisation superintending the building of mother and child care facilities. Awarded Mongolia's highest decoration, the Order of Sühbaatar, on her 60th birthday in February 1980, 'comrade' Tsedenbal-Filatova was variously described as a 'Honoured Cultural Worker', winner of MPR State Prizes and prizes of the Mongolian Revolutionary Youth League, and 'mentor of children and young people'. By early 1984, Tsedenbal-Filatova had been elected to two other bodies: President of the Association of Children's Literature and Art Workers, part of the Children's Foundation; and Deputy Chairman of the Central Council for Pioneer Camps, under the MPRP Central Commitee. The prominence afforded her in the Mongolian media seemed not to be in keeping with her low official status, which usually precluded her from participation in her husband's official duties.

AFTERWORD

As was his habit, Tsedenbal went to the Soviet Union on holiday at the end of July 1984. On 23 August, an extraordinary plenum of the MPRP Central Committee relieved him of his duties as General Secretary and member of the Politburo 'on account of his state of health, and with his agreement'. An extraordinary session of the People's Great Hural held the same day was told that Tsedenbal was also stepping down from the post of Chairman of the Presidium and of the Defence Council.

Tsedenbal had suffered several bouts of ill-health, especially in 1974–5, spending long periods out of the public eye in the Soviet Union. However, despite the fulsome praise from his erstwhile colleagues for Tsedenbal's 'outstanding services' to the party and the people, which accompanied his departure from the political scene, the long period of absolute silence about him which followed was a clear enough indication that political considerations had been uppermost in the mind of his successor, Jambyn Batmönh.

The removal of Tsedenbal from power in August 1984 was a cathartic moment in Mongolia's modern history whose significance is only gradually becoming clear. It marked not merely the end of a political era spanning some forty years from Stalin to stagnation, but, far more important, the opening up of a new period of real opportunities for meaningful change. In Mongolia, however, with its oriental traditions and nomadic background, change comes slowly and unspontaneously. History has taught the need for caution and calculation, and left a legacy of secretiveness.

Jambyn Batmönh, who became General Secretary at the age of 58, had been Rector of the Mongolian State University for many years before taking over the running of the MPRP's science and education department in 1973. After only 34 days in the post of Deputy Chairman, he was appointed Chairman of the Council of Ministers (Premier) when Tsedenbal gave up the premiership for the presidency in June 1974. The Premier is *ex officio* a member of the Politburo. Batmönh was elected to the presidency in December 1984, and chose Dumaagiyn Sodnom, 51, an economist who had been Chairman of the State Planning Commission, to replace him as premier.

Batmönh's immediate task was to prepare the Central Committee's report to the 19th MPRP Congress in May 1986 and complete the draft of the party's basic guidelines for the new Five-Year Plan

1986-90. These contained appeals to the people to achieve a 'basic breakthrough in the acceleration of socio-economic development' and the 'perfecting of national economic management'. The Mongolian leaders claimed that their policy of 'renewal' (*öörchlön shinechlel*) was not exactly the same as Soviet 'perestroika' or 'restructuring' (*öörchlön bayguulalt*), but it was 'in harmony' with it 'despite differences in size and scale'.

The Fourth Party Programme adopted in 1966 under Tsedenbal had declared that the Mongolian people would 'achieve the completion of building socialism and create the conditions for the gradual transition in the future to the building of a communist society'. Ten years later, Tsedenbal developed this theme further at the 17th MPRP Congress. Mongolia, he said, 'ought to develop at an accelerated pace and, despite its relative backwardness, set out on the path of building communism more or less simultaneously with the fraternal socialist countries, depending on aid'. It seemed that Tsedenbal wanted Mongolia, having 'bypassed capitalism', to 'bypass socialism', too.

The statistics for Mongolia's industrial growth in the 1960s and 1970s looked very impressive. Soviet money, equipment and manpower had poured in. Coal extraction had increased from 989,500 tonnes in 1965 to 4.3 million tonnes in 1980; electricity generation rose from 267.5 million kW to 1.63 billion kW over the same period; production of sawn timber trebled, output of woollen cloth nearly doubled, and footwear manufacture rose by 50%.

In agriculture, however, the country's basic economic branch, grain production in 1979 and 1980 was about the same as it had been in 1965, with larger sown areas but declining yields. The number of livestock, 23.8 million head in 1965, exceeded 24 million in 1978–9, then slipped back to 23.7 million in 1980.

Whereas gross industrial production rose nearly fivefold between 1960 and 1980, gross agricultural production rose by only 22%. Exports of foodstuffs and raw materials of animal and plant origin in 1980 still constituted over 63% of Mongolia's exports, which had increased around fourfold since 1960. Over the same period the country's population grew from 936,900 to 1.64 million, and the urban population roughly doubled.

The result was the gradual stagnation of the economic situation, with the population suffering increasing difficulties with supplies of foodstuffs and consumer goods from an inadequate industrial production and distribution system. The rural population began to drift into the towns in search of better wages and working conditions, exacerbating the labour shortage in the countryside, further overloading the towns' already stretched housing and community services and creating small-scale unemployment.

Batmönh's first step in the reform of economic management was to amalgamate all building industry and construction departments under a new State Construction Commitee in December 1986 (thereby reversing a decision taken by Tsedenbal in 1968) with the aim of developing modern building methods and increasing housing construction.

At a meeting in Moscow in June 1987, Batmönh and Gorbachev had what was described as a 'friendly but frank' discussion about Soviet aid to Mongolia. In 1986, the deficit in trade with the USSR – 80% of all Mongolia's foreign trade – reached 727.6 million roubles which, if non-refundable, amounted to Soviet aid worth £383 per head of the Mongolian population. Gorbachev said that the living standards of the Mongolian people could be improved if the Mongolian party implemented a policy of reaching out for new frontiers in economic and social development. Batmönh assured Gorbachev that the Mongolians were inspired by the Soviet policy of 'restructuring', whose ideas and spirit were 'clear and close' to them. Batmönh denied that the Mongolian party was 'shutting its eyes to the difficulties and existing shortcomings'.

The two leaders agreed to improve the quality and efficiency of Mongolian-Soviet economic co-operation. Meanwhile, Soviet preoccupation with the shortcomings of Soviet economic aid projects in Vietnam and Cuba as well as Mongolia led to an efficiency drive in the USSR Foreign Economic Commission and, later, to new pledges by European members of the Council for Mutual Economic Aid (CMEA or Comecon) to help achieve the 'gradual equalisation of their levels of development'.

A plenary meeting of the MPRP Central Committee in June 1987 was told by Dumaagiyn Sodnom, the Chairman of the Council of Ministers, that the 'basic shortcoming' of Mongolia's system of economic management was 'overcentralisation'. In future, the State Planning Commission would limit itself to general capital investment policy; ministries and state committees would be left to decide on purchases of machinery and equipment; and local administrations and factory managers would have greater autonomy in production and construction matters but would be financially accountable, their performance being judged by the fulfilment of sales contracts and export orders.

The end of 1987 and the beginning of 1988 were marked by a further restructing of ministries and state committees:

A Deputy Chairman of the Council of Ministers was appointed Minister of Light and Food Industry concurrently, and the Minister of Agriculture was appointed a Deputy Chairman of the Council of Ministers, also concurrently. Two of the most important ministries thus passed under the direct control of the Presidium of the Council of Ministers, joining the State Construction Committee, State Planning Commission and CMEA Affairs Commission, already represented at that level. Shortly afterwards, the ministries were redesignated the Ministry of Light Industry and the Ministry of Agiculture and Food Industry, in keeping with a more realistic appraisal of ways to manage development of food production and light engineering. (The Ministries of Food Industry and of Light Industry had been amalgamated by Tsedenbal in 1968).

A new Ministry of Foreign Economic Relations and Supply was formed by amalgamation of the old Ministry of Foreign Trade, the State Committee for Foreign Economic Relations and the State Committee for Material and Technical Supply. There was clearly no need to continue differentiating organisationally between trade and aid or delivery and distribution when most of the imported equipment and materials for Mongolian and Soviet projects in Mongolia came from one country – the Soviet Union.

A new Ministry of the Protection of Nature and the Environment was established, absorbing the forestry and hunting department of the Ministry of Forestry and Woodworking Industry, which was abolished. The protection of the environment had become a national issue following public pressure for action to prevent pollution of Mongolia's lakes and rivers and reduce industrial smog in the large towns. In another rationalisation move, the Ministry of the Fuel and Power Industry and the Ministry of Geology and Mining Industry (split by Tsedenbal in 1976) were amalgamated.

Completing this series of steps to restructure economic

management, in January 1988 the Mongolian government abolished the State Planning Commission, the State Committee for Prices and Standards and the State Committee for Labour and Social Security and replaced them with a new State Committee for Planning and the Economy chaired by a Deputy Chairman of the Council of Ministers.

In many instances, however, the same people were still responsible for running the economy, even if their posts were now differently designated, and it remained to be seen how much impact this reorganisation would have on the country's industrial and economic development.

Unlike previous annual plans, которая had set detailed production targets down to the lowest levels of economic activity, the annual plan for 1988 set state tasks and economic targets for only a limited range of indices. Factories and other enterprises drew up their own plans, based on production contracts and orders received.

The changes introduced at the lower levels seemed likely to prove more effective in the longer term. Previously, the *aymag* and town *hurals* or assemblies of deputies had been unwilling to interfere in the affairs of centrally controlled enterprises and mostly concerned themselves with land use and labour protection. Under new regulations brought in with the restructuring of economic management, the *hurals* co-ordinated the activity of all enterprises on their territory and used part of these enterprises' funds for public building projects. This was said to be helping restore the balance between production infrastructure and the 'social sphere' – provision of housing and shops.

Meanwhile, so as to employ ablebodied people of working age 'who for one reason or another cannot participate in socially useful activity', to increase the production of consumer goods and widen the range of services available to the population, every support was to be given to the setting up of voluntary public co-operatives and the broadening of 'individual labour activity'.

People living in towns and larger rural settlements were permitted an increase in the size of their private livestock holdings. In the countryside, members of agricultural production associations or *negdels* were allowed to own a hundred head of stock per family in the Gobi zone and seventy-five head per family in the Hangay (forest-steppe) zone, compared with the previously permitted seventy-five and fifty head respectively. However, the *negdels*' practice of buying privately produced milk and meat at state prices continued.

The economic reforms begun in Mongolia in 1986-7 were accompanied by the gradual growth of *il tod*, the Mongolian equivalent of Gorbachev's *glasnost* or 'openness'. The need for this was explained in some detail by Batmönh at the June 1987 plenum: 'In my view it is worth emphasising especially here that it would be a serious delusion to believe thoughtlessly that the measures we are planning for raising quality and efficiency by perfecting planning and introducing financial autonomy will be carried out without much bother. . . . We shall not only have to overcome the difficulties connected with the transition to new economic methods. A great deal of work will also have to be done to restructure people's old way of thinking.'

Initially 'openness' was perceived by the country's leaders as a means for the mobilisation of the populace by the party-controlled mass media whose duty it was to influence public opinion, bringing about a creative atmosphere in society and 'an active approach to life in the individual' in 'relentless struggle' against bureaucracy, stagnation, passivity, conservatism, formalism, red tape, etc. Openness was particularly manifested in the Mongolian newspapers, which introduced regular columns of readers' letters on essentially non-controversial issues. Later on, readers found a common cause in criticising the bureaucracy over such issues as nature protection and pollution.

However, it was not until the spring of 1988 that more obviously political topics began to crop up. The party journal *Namyn Am'dral* serialised a discussion held by Mongolian historians and sociologists which went to the roots of 'stagnation' in Mongolia – the final years of Tsedenbal's rule, although no one yet mentioned Tsedenbal by name. One of the chief spokesmen for Mongolian 'restructuring' and 'openness' was Kinayatyn Dzardyhan, head of a department of the MPRP Institute of Social Sciences and a former Secretary of the Mongolian Trade Union Council. Dzardyhan – judging by his name, one of Mongolia's Kazakh minority – was very outspoken about 'stagnation', saying that the 'braking mechanism' at work in the Mongolian economy and the country's social problems were the consequence of a 'dogmatic interpretation of socialism based on oversimplification'.

According to Dzardyhan, in the period from the 1950s to the

1970s — when Tsedenbal was running the country — the government was gradually taken over by 'bureaucratic centralism', a multi-layer administration which had no time for the views and needs of ordinary people. Old habits of secrecy about economic information led to 'voluntarism' in the 1970s and 1980s. Managers kept their heads down because they were afraid of the 'negative consequences' of criticism, and this led to lack of motivation and inertia in the work force.

It had been incorrectly concluded (i.e. by Tsedenbal) that, from the beginning of the 1960s, the social differences between workers and herdsmen and between state and co-operative property would merge and that commodity-money relations, the market and private property would disappear, Dzardyhan said. Everything was to have been based on state ownership. Even the theory of Mongolia's 'non-capitalist road of development' — hallowed down the years as an example of Lenin's testimony to the Third World in action — had never been properly evaluated, he added.

Citing Tsedenbal's report to the 15th MPRP Congress in 1966 as saying that about 15 years would be required to complete Mongolia's transition from being an agrarian-industrial country to being an industrial-agrarian one (in which industry rather than agriculture predominated), Dzardyhan pointed out that the transition should therefore have been completed by the end of the 1970s, but the 'material and technical base' for this was still lacking.

Dzardyhan's views were supported by MPRP Central Committee Secretary Balhaajav, who said in the Soviet *Pravda* not long afterwards: 'In Mongolia the 1960s and 1970s should have been a period of consolidation . . . . but they (i.e. Tsedenbal) put the cart before the horse. They rushed to the conclusion that the completion of the building of socialism had already begun.' Balhaajav also said that Mongolia had still to 'complete the creation of the material and technical base of socialism and turn the country into an industrial-agrarian one'. Dr Minis of the Institute of Social Sciences declared: 'Today we have almost no idea which stage of building socialism Mongolia has reached.'

Mongolia's philosophers and historians began to speak out on other matters in the new spirit of *il tod*, although Dzardyhan admitted that there was still 'quite a big gulf between talk of openness and reality'. Turning to the subject of Mongolia's cultural heritage, he asked why Mongolian studies were more developed in the USSR, USA, Japan and China than in Mongolia itself. The 'stagnation' of the 1960s was to blame, Dzardyhan said, 'political and mental dogmatism'. His colleague Dashdavaa expressed dissatisfaction with Mongolian election practices, saying that the law on the election of *hurals* or assemblies of people's deputies still essentially retained its 1949 form: 'All the voter has to do is to raise his hand for the only candidate.' It was time to 'experiment with a system of nominating several candidates'. 'The nation itself must propose and elect its leaders,' he added.

Academician Shirendev, the historian sacked from the post of President of the Academy in 1982, declared that there was still no *il tod* in the Institute of History. Historical research was 'stagnant' because the archives were closed. Dr Minis said that the modern history of the party (the period dominated by Tsedenbal) had been curtailed without justification and limited to the activities of a few individuals while party documents had been published in abbreviated or re-edited form. 'This is distortion of history,' Minis declared. 'The party documents must be republished in full in their original form. The spread of secretiveness with regard to historical documents and the growth of closed archives and documents has a negative effect on research. The super-secrecy of documents has obliged historians to pass over many events in silence.'

Thus the Mongolia of 1988 was on the face of it a very different place from the Mongolia of 1968. A new mood was abroad, and new things were happening, although no one knew how long they would last or how far they would go. The stilted official language of Montsame despatches and party documents was beginning to give way to a livelier and more natural style. The teaching of classical Mongolian in the old script was being revived. Buddhism was enjoying something of a revival, too, but it had become more an instrument of foreign policy in relations with other Buddhist countries than a source of spiritual enrichment for the faithful. Television had begun to show the people of Mongolia what life was like in other countries, and contacts with foreigners from the West as well as the East were on the increase.

Post-Tsedenbal Mongolia could expect in the foreseeable future a modest development of its relations with the West, including some measure of cultural and economic exchange. As a member of the CMEA, however, Mongolia pledged itself to continue its economic integration with other members. At the levels of inter-party co-operation and inter-governmental collaboration, Mongolia had committed itself to co-ordination of policy, including foreign policy, with Moscow and its other allies. Although perhaps resigned to being prisoners of geopolitics, the Mongolians still hoped to turn their position to their own advantage and, sharing the hopes and fears of Gorbachev's 'restructuring' and *glasnost*, re-evaluate the legacy of Tsedenbal and his predecessor Choybalsan and build a more prosperous, equal and democratic society on their own terms.

ALAN J. K. SANDERS

Caversham, June 1988

NOTES

CHAPTER 1: AN INTRODUCTION TO MONGOLIA

1 Text in the Chinese chronicle *Huang-Ch'ing K'ai-kuo Fang-lüeh*. Best consulted in the German translation of Erich Hauer, *Huang-Ts'ing K'ai-kuo Fang-lüeh, Die Gründung des mandschurischen Kaiserreiches*, Berlin and Leipzig, 1926, p. 125.

2 From the Mongol text published in W. Heissig and Charles R. Bawden, *Mongγol Borjigid Oboγ-un Teuke von Lomi (1732)*, Wiesbaden, Otto Harrassowitz, 1957.

3 N. M. Prshewalski, *In das Land der wilden Kamele*, Leipzig, 1954, p. 26. Przhevalskii can also be consulted in English in, *Mongolia, The Tangut Country and the Solitudes of Northern Tibet*, 2 vols., London, 1876.

4 Hsiao Ta-heng is best consulted in the French translation by Henry Serruys, *Pei-lou foung-sou, Les Coutumes des Esclaves Septentrionaux*, in *Monumenta Serica*, 10 (1945).

5 op. cit., p. 36.

6 op. cit., p. 39.

7 G. Nawaannamjil, *Övgön Bicheechiin Ügüülel* (Tales of an old Secretary), Ulan Bator, 1956, pp. 43–4 (in Mongol).

8 From an eighteenth-century blockprint in the British Museum.

9 I. J. Schmidt, *Geschichte der Ost-Mongolen und Ihres Fürstenhauses*, St Petersburg and Leipzig, 1829. Repr. The Hague, 1961, p. 225.

CHAPTER 2: THE LOSS OF MONGOL INDEPENDENCE

1 N. P. Shastina, *Shara Tudji, Mongol'skaya Letopis' xvii veka*, Moscow and Leningrad, 1957, p. 150.

2 Hauer, op. cit., p. 99, and Sh. Natsagdorj, *Khalkhyn Tüükh* (History of Khalkha), Ulan Bator, 1963, p. 22 (in Mongol).

3 Schmidt, op. cit., p. 203.

3a The name Abhai has recently been shown to be a baseless invention; the correct name was Hung Taiji.

4 Galdan, *Erdeni-yin Erike*, ed. Ts. Nasanbaljir, Ulan Bator, 1960 (Monumenta Historica, Vol. III, Fasc. 1) p. 91a (in Mongol). The Russian edition by A. M. Pozdneev, *Mongol'skaya Letopis' 'Erdeniin Erikhe'*, St Petersburg, 1883, is a bibliographical rarity.

5 *Khalkhyn Tüükh*, p. 22, and I. Ya. Zlatkin, *Ocherki Novoi i Noveishei Istorii Mongolii*, Moscow, 1957, pp. 29–30.

6 *Khalkhyn Tüükh*, p. 36.
7 I. Ya. Zlatkin, *Istoriya Dzhungarskovo Khanstva*, Moscow, 1964, p. 241.
8 op. cit., p. 95a.
9 *Khalkhyn Tüükh*, p. 43, and Zlatkin, *Istoriya*, p. 269.
10 *Khalkhyn Tüükh*, pp. 44-5.

CHAPTER 3: KHALKHA IN THE EIGHTEENTH CENTURY

1 *Khalkhyn Tüükh*, p. 86.
2 *Khalkhyn Tüükh*, p. 132.
3 Zhamtsarano and Dylykov, *Khalkha Dzhirum*, Moscow, 1965, p. 81, item 9. See also Zamcarano, *Qalq-a Jirum*, Ulan Bator, 1959 (Studia Mongolica, Vol. I, Fasc. 1), p. 45 (in Russian), and V. A. Riasanovsky, *Fundamental Principles of Mongol Law*, Tientsin, 1937. Repr. Indiana University, Bloomington and Mouton and Co., The Hague, 1965, p. 116.
4 *Khalkhyn Tüükh*, p. 136.
5 For the case of Sonom and Yondon, see *Khalkhyn Tüükh*, pp. 134-5.
6 For the case of Ombokh see *Manjiin Türemgiilegchdiin Üe dekh Mongolyn Emegteichüüdiin Darlaglal* (The Oppression of Mongol Women in the Period of Manchu Domination), Ulan Bator, 1958, pp. 8-29 (in Mongol).
7 For the case of Ölziit and that of the threatened suicide see M. Sanjdorj, *Khalkhad Khyatadyn Möngö Khüülegch Khudaldaa Nevterch Khöljsön N' (xviii zuun)* (The Penetration and Expansion of Chinese Usury-trading in Khalkha (18th century)), Ulan Bator, 1963, p. 57 and p. 58 (in Mongol). (Studia Historica, Vol. III, Fasc. 5.)
8 Ts. Damdinsüren, *Övgön Jambalyn Yaria* (Old Jambal's Tales), Ulan Bator, 1959, pp. 15-16 (in Mongol). This little book of reminiscences of an old lama is a mine of curious stories and legends.
9 *Mongol Ardyn Juramt Tsergiin Durdatgaluud* (Reminiscences of Soldiers of the Mongol People's Volunteers), Ulan Bator, 1961, p. 594 (in Mongol). (Subsequently: *Volunteers*.)
10 G. N. Potanin, *Ocherki Severo-Zapadnoi Mongolii*, St Petersburg, 1881-3, Vol. 3, p. 48.
11 N. Ishjamts, *Mongolyn Ard Tümnii 1755-1758 Ony Tusgaar Togtnolyn Zevsegt Temtsel* (The Armed Struggle of the Mongol People for Independence, 1755-1758), Ulan Bator, 1962. (Studia Historica, Vol. III, Fasc. 3), p. 51 (in Mongol).
12 *Khalkhyn Tüükh*, p. 65.
13 For Choijav see *Khalkhyn Tüükh*, p. 67 (footnote).
14 Ö. Chimid: *Chingünjavaar Udirduulsan Ar Mongol dakh' Tusgaar Togtnolyn Temtsel* (The Independence Struggle in North Mongolia Led by Chin-

NOTES

gunjav), Ulan Bator, 1963, p. 27 (in Mongol). This book is a collection of sixty-six contemporary documents.

15 Ishjamts, op. cit., p. 54.
16 For Yakobi's activities see Zlatkin, *Ocherki*, p. 104.
17 Chimid, op. cit., p. 52.
18 Zlatkin, *Ocherki*, p. 105.
19 Chimid, op. cit., p. 78.
20 Chimid, op. cit., p. 45.
21 Chimid, op. cit., p. 110.
22 Chimid, op. cit., p. 94.
23 Chimid, op. cit., pp. 98–9.
24 N. Ishjamts, *Manjiin Darlalyg Esergüütssen Mongolyn Ard Tümen 1755–57 Ony Zevsegt Boslogo* (The Armed Uprising of 1755–57 of the Mongol People in Opposition to Manchu Oppression), Ulan Bator, 1955, p. 17 (in Mongol).
25 D. Tsedev, *Ikh Shav'* (The Shabi Estate), Ulan Bator, 1964. (Studia Historica Vol. VI, Fasc. 2) p. 11 (in Mongol).

CHAPTER 4: SOCIAL AND ECONOMIC DEVELOPMENTS IN THE NINETEENTH CENTURY

1 For this case see *Manjiin Türemgiilegchdiin* . . ., pp. 4–7.
2 For this case see *Manjiin Türemgiilegchdiin* . . ., pp. 30–57. The institution of slavery is dealt with by B. Vladimirtsov, *Le Régime Social des Mongols*, Paris, 1948, and also by Sh. Natsagdorj, *Geriin Khüvüüdiin Uchir* (On Tent-slaves), Ulan Bator, 1965. (Reports of the Mongolian Academy of Sciences, 1965, 2, pp. 83–8) (in Mongol).
3 Quoted by I. J. Slatkin (same as I. Ya. Zlatkin, above), *Die Mongolische Volksrepublik*, Berlin, 1954, p. 51, from the unpublished third volume of Pozdneev's *Mongoliya i Mongoly*.
4 For this case see *Manjiin Türemgiilegchdiin* . . ., pp. 58–64.
5 For this and the following autobiographical accounts see *Volunteers* under the respective names.
6 J. Sambuu, *Am'dralyn Zamnalaas* (From My Life's Path), Ulan Bator, 1965 (in Mongol).
7 This episode is described in the author's essay 'An Event in the Life of the Eighth Jebtsundamba Khutuktu' in *Collectanea Mongolica*, Wiesbaden, Otto Harrassowitz, 1966.
8 *Khalkhyn Tüükh*, p. 185.
9 S. Pürevjav, *Khuv'sgalyn Ömnökh Ikh Khüree* (Urga Before the Revolution), Ulan Bator, 1961, pp. 106–7 (in Mongol).
10 Sh. Natsagdorj, *Ar Mongold Garsan Ardyn Khödölgöön* (Popular Movements in North Mongolia), Ulan Bator, 1956, p. 109 (in Mongol). A Russian

version of this book appeared in Moscow in 1958 under the title of *Iz Istorii Aratskovo Dvizheniya vo Vneshnei Mongolii*. See p. 94. This monograph deals fully with the cases of To wang and of Ayushi, both of which are also taken up in *Khalkhyn Tüükh*.

11 M. W. Pewzow, *Wo man mit Ziegeltee Bezahlt*, Leipzig, 1953, pp. 238–40.
12 Pozdneev, *Mongoliya i Mongoly*, St Petersburg, 1896–8, Vol. I, p. 277.
13 Pewzow, op. cit., p. 36.
13a op. cit., p. 327.
14 Pürevjav, op. cit., p. 134.
15 Nawaannamjil, op. cit., p. 142.
16 *Khalkhyn Tüükh*, p. 115.
17. *Khalkhyn Tüükh*, pp. 116–17.
18. D. Tsedev, op. cit., p. 53.
19. Pürevjav, op. cit., p. 124.
20 For these two cases of indiscipline see Pürevjav, op. cit., p. 145.
21 Pürevjav, op. cit., p. 125.
22 Pürevjav, op. cit., pp. 140–1.
23 Rintchen, *Üüriin Tuyaa* (Ray of Dawn), Ulan Bator, 1951, Vol. I, p. 134.
24 For the case of Tudeng see *1921 Ony Ardyn Khuw'sgalyn Tüükhend Kholbogdokh Barimt Bichgüüd* (Documents concerned with the People's Revolution of 1921), Ulan Bator, 1957, pp. 36–43 (in Mongol). (Subsequently: *Documents I*.)
25 Ts. Damdinsüren, *Günjiin Süm* (The Princess's Temple), Ulan Bator, 1961. (Studia Ethnographica Vol. II, Fasc. 3), p. 4 (in Mongol).
26 *Khalkhyn Tüükh*, p. 225.
27 I. J. Slatkin, op. cit., p. 28.
28 *Khalkhyn Tüükh*, p. 225.

CHAPTER 5: FROM AUTONOMY TO REVOLUTION, 1911–21

1 *Khalkhyn Tüükh*, p. 274.
2 Pozdneev, op. cit., Vol. I, p. 46.
3 *Shagdar Soliyatu*, Köke qota, 1959, p. 54 (in Mongol). See also W. Heissig, *Helden-, Höllenfahrts- und Schelmengeschichten der Mongolen*, Manesse Verlag, 1962.
4 Puntsagnorov, *Mongolyn Avtononmit Üeiin Tüükh (1911–1919)* (History of the Autonomous Period in Mongolia), Ulan Bator, 1955, p. 36 (in Mongol).
5 *Mongol Ulsyn Avtonomi Gedeg öörtöö ezerkhen zasakh erkht zasgiin üeiin ünenkhüü yavdal chukham baidal, chukhal uchryg temdeglesen tovch ögüülel gedeg tüükh bichig* (History known as the Summary Account Describing the True Course, Actual Situation and Real Nature of the Administration of

NOTES

Mongolia with the Right of Self-government, known as Autonomy), Ulan Bator, 1960. (Studia Historica Vol. I, Fasc. 4) p. 14 (in Mongol).

6 *Mongol Ulsyn . . . bichig*, p. 15.
7 Choibalsang, *Meng-ku ko-ming chien-shih* (Brief History of the Mongol Revolution), Peking, 1951, p. 16 (in Chinese).
8 *Documents, I*, p. 80.
9 *Documents, I*, p. 88. See also B. Shirendyv, *Mongoliya na Rubezhe xix-xx Vekov*, Ulan Bator, 1963, p. 326 (in Russian) and R. A. Rupen, *Mongols of the Twentieth Century*, Part I, p. 137, Indiana University, Bloomington and Mouton and Co., The Hague, 1964.
10 Shirendyv, op. cit., p. 201.
11 Shirendyv, op. cit., p. 205.
12 D. *Sükhbaataryn Tukhai Durdatgaluud* (Reminiscences of D. Sukebator), Ulan Bator, 1965, p. 83 (in Mongol). (Subsequently: *Reminiscences*.)
13 *Reminiscences*, pp. 83–4.
14 Zagd's story is told in *Volunteers*, pp. 370–86.
15 For Laasag's account see *Reminiscences*, pp. 193–4.
16 Slatkin, op. cit., p. 161.
17 Slatkin, op. cit., p. 157.
18 *Reminiscences*, preface, pp. 9–10.
19 *Documents, I*, p. 93, and *Reminiscences*, p. 86.
20. D. *Sükhbaataryn Namtar* (Biography of Sukebator), Ulan Bator, 1965, p. 67 (in Mongol).
21 For the preamble and the platform see *Documents*, I, pp. 95–102, Shirendyv, op. cit., pp. 248 et seq., and Rupen, op. cit., pp. 142–3.
22 See respectively *Ardyn zasgaas 1921–1924 onuudad avsan khuv'sgalt arga khemjeenüüd* (Revolutionary Measures taken by the People's Government from 1921 to 1924), Ulan Bator, 1954, p. 6; *Documents, I*, p. 103 and Shirendyv, p. 268.
23 References as in previous footnote, to pp. 7, 104 and 269 respectively. The text of 1956 is to be found in *MAKhN Ikh Baga Khural, Töv Khoroony Bügd Khurluudyn Togtool Shiidver* (Decisions of the Great and Small Khurals and the Plenary Meetings of the MPRP) I, Ulan Bator, 1956, pp. 24 et seq. (in Mongol). (Subsequently: *Decisions, I*.)
24 *Mongol Ardyn Namyn Guravdugaar Ikh Khural* (The Third Great Congress of the Mongol People's Party), Ulan Bator, 1966, p. 50 (in Mongol). Comparison of this selection of documents with the now rare booklet in English entitled: *Mongolia: Yesterday and Today*, published by the Tientsin Press (no date) and according to G. M. Friters, *Outer Mongolia and its International Position*, London, 1951, p. 315, purporting to be a verbatim report of the Congress, shows the latter to be substantially accurate, and at times fuller than the Mongol documents. (Subsequently: *Third Congress*.)
25 *Documents, I*, p. 113.

CHAPTER 6: FIRST STEPS IN REVOLUTION, 1921-8

1 *Decisions*, I, p. 476.
2 Slatkin, op. cit., p. 209.
3 Kh. Choibalsang: *Iledkel ba Ögülelüd* (Reports and Speeches), Ulan Bator, 1951, Vol. II, p. 262 (in Mongol).
4 *Third Congress*, p. 63.
5 Ts. Damdinsüren, *Soyolyn Öviig Khamgaal'ya* (Let us Protect our Cultural Heritage), Ulan Bator, 1959, p. 29 (in Mongol).
6 ibid. pp. 20-21.
7 Rintchen, *Folklore Mongol*, Vol. 4, Wiesbaden, Otto Harrassowitz, 1965, p. viii.
8 *Soyolyn Öviig Khamgaal'ya*, p. 30.
9 *Reminiscences*, p. 330. This is a personal reminiscence and not accurately dated. There exists a document abolishing the use of torture and cruel punishments, notably that of shutting people up in coffins, in Zasagtu Khan aimak dated September 1921: text in *Ardyn Zasgaas . . . khemjeenüüd*, pp. 131-2.
10 *Reminiscences*, p. 381.
11 Quoted by Rupen, op. cit., p. 200.
12 *Third Congress*, p. 54.
13 *Decisions*, I, p. 168.
14 Text in *Bügd Nairamdakh Mongol Ard Ulsyn Ikh Baga Khurlyn Togtool. Ündsen Khuul'. Tunkhguud*. (Decisions of the Great and Small Khurals of the Mongolian People's Republic. Constitution. Proclamations), Ulan Bator, 1956, p. 57 (in Mongol).
15 S. Pürevjav and D. Dashjamts, *BNMAU-D Süm Khiid, Lam Naryn Asuudlyg Shiidverlesen N' 1921-1940 On* (The Solution to the Problem of the Lamaseries and the Lamas in the Mongolian People's Republic, 1921-1940), Ulan Bator, 1965, p. 61 (in Mongol). (Subsequently: *Lamaseries*.)
16 *Lamaseries*, p. 67.
17 *Lamaseries*, p. 69.
18 *Lamaseries*, p. 93.
19 *Khalkhyn Tüükh*, pp. 18-19.
20 This point of view is concisely expressed by Tch. Jougder, 'La Dure Lutte contre le Poison du Lamaisme', in *La Seconde Épopée Mongole*, a special number of Démocratie Nouvelle, Paris, October 1965.
21 For Darva see *Lamaseries*, p. 97.
22 *Lamaseries*, p. 110.
23 Slatkin, op. cit., p. 160.
24 For this expression of opinion see Slatkin, p. 196.

25 *Third Congress*, p. 24.
26 ibid., p. 10.
27 ibid, pp. 52–3.
28 ibid, p. 64.
29 ibid, pp. 59–60.
30 ibid, p. 186.
31 ibid, p. 156, et seq.
32 *Reminiscences*, p. 384.
33 *Third Congress*, p. 172.
34 ibid, p. 212.
35 *Lamaseries*, p. 111.
36 ibid. p. 112.
37 ibid, p. 113.
38 *Decisions*, I, p. 314. Text also in *Mongol Ardyn Khuv'sgalt Namyn Tüükhend Kholbogdokh Barimt Bichgüüd* (Documents concerning the History of the Mongol People's Revolutionary Party), I, Ulan Bator, 1966, p. 249 (in Mongol).

CHAPTER 7: THE SOCIALIST FIASCO, 1929–32

1 Choibalsang, *Reports and Speeches*, I, p. 61.
2 Sambuu, op. cit., p. 149.
3 J. Sambuu, *Shashin ba Lam Naryn Asuudald* (On the Question of Religion and the Lamas), Ulan Bator, 1961, p. 151 (in Mongol).
4 *Am'dralyn Zamnalaas*, p. 128.
5 *Démocratie Nouvelle*, October 1965, p. 49.
6 *Decisions*, I, p. 273. Quoted from a commentary to the report of the Eighth Party Congress.
7 R. Nansal, *MAKh Namaas Namyn Shine Ergeltiin Bodlogyg Bielüülekhiin Tölöö Temtsen N' (1932–1934 on)* (The Struggle of the MPRP to Implement the Party's New Turn Policy, 1932–1934), Ulan Bator, 1958, pp. 21–2 (in Mongol).
8 Slatkin, op. cit., p. 201.
9 *Am'dralyn Zamnalaas*, pp. 143–4.
10 L. Dügersüren, 'Mongol Ardyn Khuv'sgalt Namaas Yavuulsan Shine Ergeltiin Bodlogo ba Tüünii Ekhnii Ür Düng' (The New Turn Policy Effected by the Mongol People's Revolutionary Party and its First Results), an essay in a collection entitled *Mongol Ardyn Khuv'sgalt Nam ba Ardyn Khuv'sgalyn Döchin Jil* (Forty Years of the Mongol People's Revolutionary Party and the People's Revolution), Ulan Bator, 1961, p. 110 (in Mongol).
11 *Am'dralyn Zamnalaas*, p. 130, et seq.
12 Nansal, op. cit., p. 15.

13 Slatkin, op. cit., p. 209.
14 *Lamaseries*, pp. 135–6.
15 Slatkin, op. cit., p. 204.
16 *Decisions*, I, p. 484.
17 V. Maslennikov, *Mongol'skaya Narodnaya Respublika*, Moscow, 1955, p. 25.
18 *Decisions*, I, pp. 273–4.
19 *Lamaseries*, pp. 138–9.
20 ibid., p. 139. For the inability to correct errors see also L. Dügersüren, op. cit., pp. 111–12, and *Lamaseries*, pp. 146 and 149.

CHAPTER 8: THE DESTRUCTION OF THE OLD ORDER, 1932–40

1 *Decisions*, I, p. 597.
2 *Mongol'skaya Narodnaya Respublika, Sbornik Statei*, Moscow, 1952, pp. 321–2.
3 Introduction by I. Maiskii to Slatkin, op. cit., p. 10, and *Mongol'skaya Narodnaya Respublika*, p. 12.
4 Choibalsang, *Reports and Speeches*, II, p. 270.
5 *Decisions*, I, p. 578.
6 For Choibalsang's denunciation of these officers see his *Reports and Speeches*, I, pp. 477–519. For the trial see *BNMA Uls Khöröngötnii Bish Khögjliin Tölöö Temtseld* (The MPR in the Struggle for the Non-capitalist Path), Ulan Bator, 1956, pp. 168–75 (in Mongol).
7 *Decisions*, I, p. 597.
8 Choibalsang, op. cit., p. 497.
9 *MAKhN-yn Ikh Khural, Töv Khoroony Bügd Khurluudyn Togtool Shiidver, III kheseg* (Decisions of the Great Khural and the Plenary Meetings of the Central Committee of the MPRP, III), Ulan Bator, 1963, p. 221 (in Mongol). (Subsequently: *Decisions*, III).
10 *Reports and Speeches*, Vol. II, p. 14. See also Rupen, op. cit., p. 229.
11 D. Dorjsüren, 'Ezerkheg Türemgii Feodalyg Esergüütssen Ardchilsan Khuv'sgalyg Tögsgökhiin Tölöö MAKhN-yn Temtsliin Zarim Asuudald' (On Some Questions of the MPRP's Struggle to Complete the Anti-Imperialist, Anti-feudalist Democratic Revolution), an essay in the collection *Mongol . . . Döchin Jil*, p. 160 (in Mongol).
12 *Lamaseries*, p. 242.
13 *Mongolia Today*, Vol. VIII, No. 7–8, July–August 1966, New Delhi, p. 13.
14 Nansal, op. cit., p. 22.
15 Choibalsang, *Reports and Speeches*, Vol. I, p. 351.
16 L. Dügersüren, op. cit., p. 136.
17 Slatkin, op. cit., p. 248.

18 *Lamaseries*, pp. 224-5.
19 *Lamaseries*, pp. 181-2.
20 *Lamaseries*, pp. 190-1.
21 *Mongol Ardyn Khuv'sgalt Namyn Programm* (Programme of the Mongol People's Revolutionary Party), Ulan Bator, 1966, p. 11 (in Mongol).
22 *Soyolyn Öviig Khamgaal'ya*, p. 27.

CHAPTER 9: POST-WAR MONGOLIA: ACHIEVEMENTS AND PROSPECTS

1 Press report of the report by Jagvaral, Vice-chairman of the Council of Ministers, to the Central Committee of the Party, 7 February 1963.
1a In 1988, two million, of whom probably about 600,000 live in Ulan Bator.
2 D. Tsend, *Mongolyn Uran Zokhiol* (Mongol Literature), Ulan Bator, 1959, p. 7 (in Mongol).
3 *Soyolyn Öviig Khamgaal'ya*, p. 21.
4 ibid, pp. 36-7.
5 Quotations from Mongol Press reports of a speech by Lkhamsüren, secretary of the Central Committee of the Party, to the Congress on Ideology held in Ulan Bator in January 1963.
6 Sovremennaya Mongoliya, No. 10, October 1959 (in Russian). This is an abbreviated version of an article which appeared in the Mongol Party daily *Ünen* (Truth) on 18 August 1959.
7 *Decisions*, III, p. 13.
8 ibid, p. 105.
9 op. cit., p. 43.
10 ibid, p. 34.

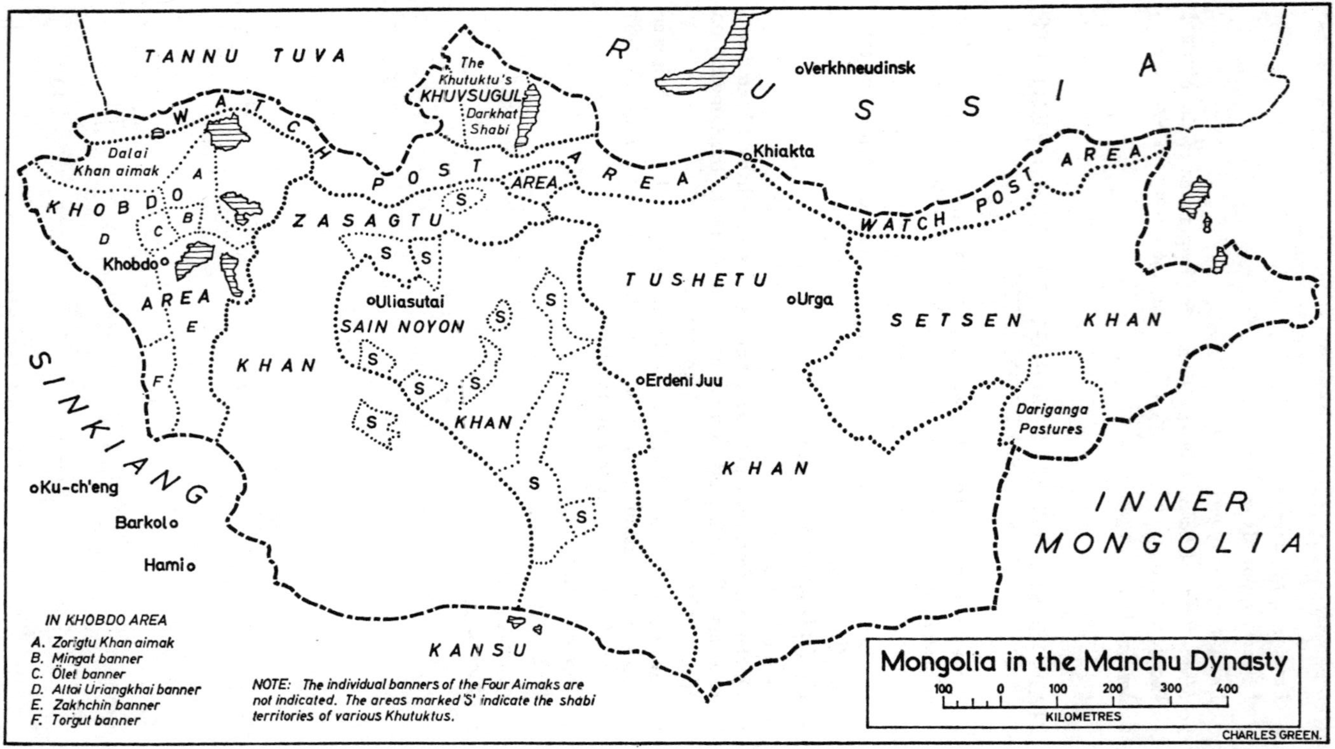

Mongolia in the Manchu Dynasty
100 0 100 200 300 400
KILOMETRES
CHARLES GREEN.
TANNU TUVA
RUSSIA
oVerkhneudinsk
The Khutuktu's KHUVSUGUL
Darkhat Shabi
WATCH POST AREA
oKhiakta
Dalai Khan aimak
KHOBDO
Khobdo
AREA
ZASAGTU
TUSHETU
oUrga
SETSEN KHAN
oUliasutai
SAIN NOYON
KHAN
KHAN
KHAN
oErdeni Juu
Dariganga Pastures
INNER MONGOLIA
SINKIANG
oKu-ch'eng
Barkol
Hami
KANSU
IN KHOBDO AREA
A. Zorigtu Khan aimak
B. Mingat banner
C. Ölet banner
D. Altai Uriangkhai banner
E. Zakhchin banner
F. Torgut banner
NOTE: The individual banners of the Four Aimaks are not indicated. The areas marked 'S' indicate the shabi territories of various Khutuktus.

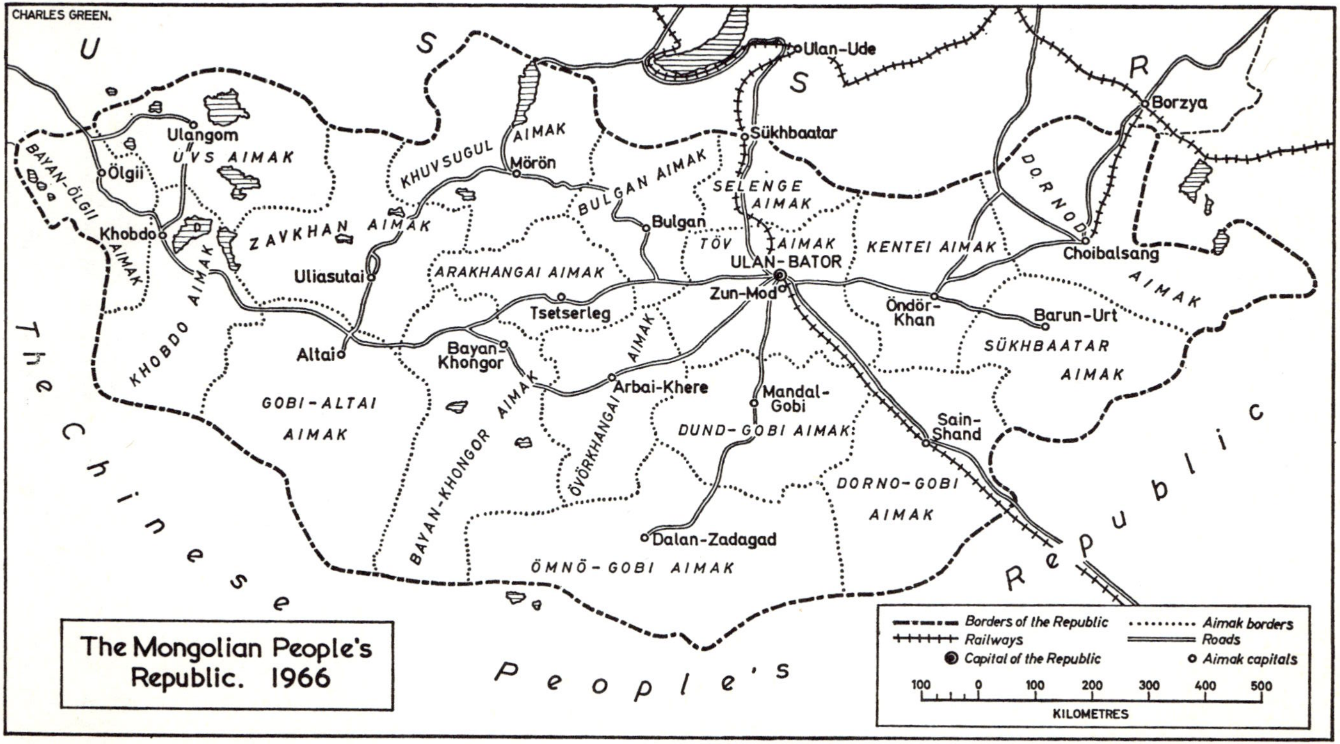

The Mongolian People's Republic. 1966

BIBLIOGRAPHICAL NOTE

Comprehensive bibliographies of works on Mongolia can be found in the following books: Robert A. Rupen, *Mongols of the Twentieth Century*, Uralic and Altaic Series, volume 37. Indiana University, Bloomington and Mouton and Co., The Hague, 1964. (Part II of this work, obtainable separately, consists entirely of a bibliography containing over 2,800 entries.) Gerard M. Friters, *Outer Mongolia and its International Position*, George Allen and Unwin, London, 1951. Peter S. H. Tang, *Russian and Soviet Policy in Manchuria and Outer Mongolia, 1911–1931*, Durham, North Carolina, 1959. Erich Thiel, *Die Mongolei*, Munich, 1958. E. M. Murzaev, *Die Mongolische Volksrepublik*, Gotha, 1954. (Lists mainly Russian works and concentrates on geography.)

All five books are important in their own right. The first is an encyclopaedic compilation of facts, the second and third political and historical studies of recent times, the fourth a general handbook, and the fifth a detailed geography with a useful general introduction.

One of the most prolific writers in English on Mongolian affairs is Owen Lattimore, and a bibliography of his work can be found in his *Studies in Frontier History*, Oxford University Press, 1962.

Bibliographical information about the majority of the works used in writing this book has been given in the Notes and is not repeated in the following suggestions for further reading in European languages.

Chapter 1

A useful general survey of the Mongolian People's Republic from the official point of view is given in the handbook *The Mongolian People's Republic*, Ulan Bator, 1956. For travel before the revolution Mrs Beatrix Bulstrode's book, *A Tour in Mongolia*, Methuen, London, 1920, may still be read with profit. An author who knew Mongolia intimately, and whose books better than any others catch the atmosphere, is Henning Haslund. All his work is of interest, in particular *Tents in Mongolia*, London, 1935 (also Puffin Story Books, 1943) and *Mongolian Journey*, Routledge and Kegan Paul, London, 1949. Ivor Montagu's book *Land of Blue Sky*, Dennis Dobson, London, 1956, presents the views of the first British traveller to spend any time in Mongolia since the revolution. Owen Lattimore, *Nomads and Commissars*, Oxford University Press, New York and London, 1962, sketches the history of post-revolutionary Mongolia. Interesting discussions of many historical and literary themes are to be found in W. Heissig, *A Lost Civilization, The Mongols Rediscovered*, Thames and Hudson, London, 1966. (The German original, *Ein Volk sucht seine Geschichte*, Düsseldorf-Wien, 1964, contains a number of plates not reproduced in the English version.) The same author's travel book *Ostmongolische Reise*, Darmstadt, 1955, describing his wartime experiences in Inner Mongolia, is relevant in many respects to our theme. His monograph, *Die Familien – und Kirchengeschichtsschreibung der Mongolen*, I, Wiesbaden, Otto Harrassowitz, 1959, discusses Mongol traditional historical writing in general and touches on topics mentioned in this and the following chapter, especially those of the 'Two Principles', the standpoint of Lomi, and the career of Ligdan Khan. His article, 'A Mongolian Source to the Lamaist Suppression of Shamanism in the 17th Century', published in *Anthropos*, 48, 1952, is a valuable study of Mongol history in the early seventeenth century.

Chapter 2

The most comprehensive discussion of Oirat affairs, apart from Zlatkin's book, is still M. Courant, *L'Asie Centrale aux xviie et xviiie Siècles: Empire Kalmouk ou Empire Mantchou?* Lyon, 1912. For relations between the Mongols and the Russians see also N. P. Shastina, *Russko-mongol'skie Posol'skie Otnosheniya xvii Veka*, Moscow, 1958.

Chapter 3

The rebellion of 1756 is mentioned briefly in Michel Pavlovsky, *Chinese-Russian Relations*, New York, 1949. Much of the information about the Jebtsundamba Khutuktus given in Pozdneev's book, *Mongoliya i Mongoly*, St Petersburg, 1896–8 can be consulted more easily in I. J. Korostovets, *Von Chinggis Khan zur Sowjetrepublik*, Berlin and Leipzig, 1926. (This book is, however, of particular use for the events of 1911 and after.)

For questions of Mongol law see also C. Alinge, *Mongolische Gesetze*, Leipzig, 1934.

Chapter 4

For a detailed survey of life at the end of this period see H. H. Vreeland, *Mongol Community and Kinship Structure*, New Haven, 1957. On urbanization see especially R. A. Rupen, 'The City of Urga in the Manchu Period', in *Studia Altaica*, Wiesbaden, Otto Harrassowitz, 1957. A useful book on lamasery life, though referring specifically to Inner Mongolia, is R. J. Miller, *Monasteries and Culture Change in Inner Mongolia*, Wiesbaden, Otto Harrassowitz, 1959.

Chapter 5

H. Consten, *Weideplätze der Mongolen*, Berlin, 1919 and 1920, is an account by a traveller who was in Mongolia soon after the events of 1911. O. Lattimore, *Nationalism and Revolution in Mongolia*, E. J. Brill, Leiden, 1955, offers an English translation of the official life of Sukebator, preceded by a long introduction. I. M. Maiskii, *Mongoliya nakanune Revolutsii*, Moscow, 1960, is a reissue of a book originally published in Irkutsk in 1921 under the title *Sovremennaya Mongoliya*.

Chapter 6

Invaluable for the history of the 'twenties is John de Francis, *Chinese Agent in Mongolia*, Baltimore, 1949. J. Geleta: *The New Mongolia*, London, 1936, offers a contemporary's account of events in the early 'twenties. Sven Hedin, *Von Peking nach Moskau*, Leipzig, 1924, also has most useful contemporary comment. S. M. Wolff, 'Mongol Delegations in Western Europe, 1925–9', in *Royal Central Asian Journal*, 32 (1945) and 33 (1946) describes a little-known episode in recent Mongol history.

Chapter 7

There is little material in western European languages for the period covered by this chapter. On Tannu Tuva see O. Maenchen-Helfen, *Reise ins Asiatische Tuva*, Berlin, 1931.

Chapter 8

As for chapter 7, little or nothing is available in English for this period.

Chapter 9

Contemporary Mongolia still awaits a comprehensive description in book form. A useful short survey is R. A. Rupen, *The Mongolian People's Republic*, Hoover Institution Studies, 12, Stanford University, California, 1966. Among short articles in journals and newspapers the following may be mentioned: C. R. Bawden, 'Economic Advance in Mongolia', in *The World Today*, June 1960 (Royal Institute of International Affairs); 'Mongolian People's Republic', Nos. 1, 2 and 3 in *China News Analysis*, Hong Kong, 1962-3 (Nos. 445, 468 and 493); 'Mongolian Review', in *Royal Central Asian Journal*, October 1965. Harrison E. Salisbury published a series of full articles in the *New York Times* during the week of 3 August 1959. Harry Hamm wrote in the *Frankfurter Allgemeine Zeitung* on 6, 11, 14 and 15 October 1962, and Klaus Arnsperger published useful reports in the *Süddeutsche Zeitung* in September 1962. On contemporary literature see L. K. Gerasimovich, *Literatura Mongol'skoi Narodnoi Respubliki, 1921-64 godov*, Leningrad, 1965.

SUPPLEMENTARY BIBLIOGRAPHY

Useful books in English which have been published since the first edition of this book include:

A. J. K. Sanders: The People's Republic of Mongolia, a general reference guide, London, Oxford University Press 1968

A. J. K. Sanders: Mongolia: politics, economics and society, London, Frances Pinter 1987

Thomas E. Ewing: Between the hammer and the anvil: Chinese and Russian policies in Outer Mongolia 1911–1921, Bloomington, Indiana University Uralic and Altaic Series, vol. 138, 1980

Owen Lattimore and Fujiko Isono: The Diluv Khutagt: memoirs and autobiography of a Mongol Buddhist reincarnation in religion and revolution, Wiesbaden, Otto Harrassowitz, Asiatische Forschungen Band 74 1982

Urgunge Onon (tr.): Manchu Chinese colonial rule in northern Mongolia, London, C. Hurst 1980 (This is a translation from the Mongolian original of M. Sanjdorj)

Urgunge Onon (tr.): Mongolian heroes of the 20th century, New York, AMS Press 1976

William A. Brown and Urgunge Onon (trs.) History of the Mongolian People's Republic, Cambridge, Mass., Harvard University Press 1976 (This is a translation of the third volume of the three-volume history of the MPR which appeared in 1969)

INDEX

INDEX

Abahai, 41, 44, 46, 47, 54, 58, 59, 60, 61
Abdai Khan, 12, 26, 31, 32, 35, 37, 52
Ablin, Seitkul, 64
Abunai, 66
Academy of Sciences (*also* Committee of Sciences), 11, 214, 411, 415, 416, 418, 419
Achitu beise banner, debt of, 203
Achitu gelung, 70, 71
administration, Manchu, 56, 82, 92, 100, 101, 103, 107, 141, 202, 256
Afghanistan, 2
agriculture (*see also* farms, farming, fields) 7, 15, 21, 22, 52, 83, 94, 109, 142, 155, 156, 164, 180, 190, 202, 387, 395
aimak (khanate), 13, 14, 55, 69, 81, 90, 93, 106, 107, 108, 149, 150, 196, 203, 224, 253
aimak (in Urga), 12, 57, 161, 165
    cattle of, herded, 149
aimak (province), 8, 261, 316, 401
aimak general, 108
airag, 15
Alashan, (p.n.), 187
alba (see also corvée), 106, 137
albatu, 137
alms, 85, 165
    distribution of, 155, 165, 272
Altai mountains (p.n.), 6, 7, 78, 114
Altai district, (p.n.), 312
Altan Bulak (Mongol Khiakta), (p.n.), 217, 230, 231, 233, 248, 375
    dramatic group at, 376
    tannery at, 246
Altan Gerel, 36
Altangerel, 254
Altan Khan (of N.W. Mongolia), 45, 49, 50, 62
Altan Khan (Tumet), 24, 25, 27, 28, 29, 30, 31, 32, 34, 36, 49, 54
Altan Ölgii (p.n.), 10
Amagaev, 297
Amarbayasgalangt lamasery, 35, 57, 85, 167
amban, 56, 82, 83, 107, 114, 201

Amdonar (p.n. district of Urga), 255
Amindoo, 140
Amor, 330, 334-5, 339
Amur river, (p.n.), 48, 72
Amursana, 66, 112, 115-19, 122, 129, 131, 192, 199
Anderson Meyer, 164
An-fu clique, 208, 215
Angara river (p.n.), 72
angju, 167
Ania, 145
Anti-Buddhist League, 313, 352
Anti-religious campaign, 206, 245, 259, 270, 273, 304-5, 350
Aoba, 32, 44
Arani, 71, 74, 75, 79
Aravdan, 127
architecture, 11, 366
arkhi, 15
army, Chinese, 153, 217
    Manchu, 101, 103, 125
    Mongol, 82, 144, 175, 190, 191, 194, 201, 204, 218, 220, 225, 231, 264, 280, 285, 320, 323, 328-9, 338, 341, 343, 345, 349, 360
    alleged treason of high command of, 329, 336-7, 342-4, 346, 358
    demobilized, 1920, 205
    intelligence, 233, 254, 264, 280
    and liquidation of Church, 365-6
    Russian aid to, 200, 201
    Partisan, 144, 202, 216, 220, 224, 227, 230
    character of, 220
    engagement at Orkhon, 220
    engagement with Chinese foragers, 219
    Soviet, 10, 188, 213, 220, 225, 229, 233, 235, 237, 243, 254, 264, 315, 320, 331, 349, 357, 359
    Mongol support of, 382
art, 22, 385-6
Artased, 158
artels, 310
artillery, (*see* guns)

INDEX

Ashikhai, 49
Astrakhan, (p.n.), 161
atlas, first Mongolian, 291
Autonomous Government, 13, 177, 197, 199
Autonomy, 3, 91, 136, 137, 160, 188, 189, 190, 200, 201, 204, 214
   loss of, 159, 188, 204–5, 235–6
Avalokiteshvara, 29
Ayush (partisan), 144
Ayush, (writer), 413
Ayushi, 152, 183–6, 204
Ayushi-statues, 147

Baasanjav, 330
Baarin, 36, 41, 61, 192
badarchin, 265
Badarchin, 249
Badmadorji, 159
Badmagarav, 168
Badmayoga, college, 163
Badrakh, 296, 306
bag, 400
Baikal, Lake, (p.n.), 1, 9, 62
Baitag Bogdo (p.n.), 382
Bakunaev, 253
Baljir, 369
Bandi, 112, 117
bandi, 166
Bandid Gegen lamasery, 318–19
banditry, 6, 125, 126, 143, 174
banishment, 93, 127, 141
Banjur, 126
Bank, Mongol, 264, 274, 288
banking, 98, 142
banner, 5, 12, 49, 55, 62, 81, 88, 90, 91, 92, 97, 99, 100, 103, 104, 105, 107, 108, 109, 114, 140, 141, 145, 151, 157, 177, 185, 186, 203, 224, 256
   desertions from, 243
   boundaries, 90, 109
   and private debts, 100, 143
banner prince (*see also zasag*), 81, 88, 89, 91, 97, 103, 107, 126, 143, 144
Baran, 119
bards, 387
Barga (p.n.), 161, 187, 195, 275
   revolt of, 1912, 199
Barguts, 197
Barun örgöö, 12
base-schools, 391–2
bastardy, 249
Batsukh, 368–9

Battömör, 330, 344
Batur, jinong, 66
Bavaasan, 282
Bavuujav, 204
Bayan Khongor aimak, (p.n.), 134
Bayan Ölgii aimak, (p.n.), 8
Bayantumen, (p.n.), 266
Bayar (ambassador to Tushetu Khan), 74
Bayar, (slave), 139
Bayar, (herdsman), 143
Bayart, 117
beggars and beggary, 43, 127, 143, 155
Beggars' Hill (p.n.), 155
beile, 5, 119
beise, 5
Bilegsaikhan, 227, 228, 248
Black Faith, 178
Blue Faith, 178
bod, 311, 396
Bodhicaryavātarā, 26
Bodo, 207, 210, 214, 228, 229, 234, 237, 251, 254, 257, 271, 295
Bogdo Uul mountain, (p.n.), 103
Bolsheviks, 206, 207
Bolur Toli, 60, 64
'Book known as the people's pure principle', 270
books, 23, 36, 84, 87, 367
   destruction of, 87, 247
Bor, 295, 329
Borisov, 208, 210
Borjigid, clan, 3, 5
Boshugtu Khan, 66, 67
Boxer rebellion, 172
bride-price, 138, 139, 140
Buddha, Buddha Shakyamuni, 28, 58, 268, 285, 286
Buddhism, (*see also* Lamaism), 4, 9, 12, 25–8, 31, 32, 33, 35–8, 41, 46, 50, 53, 75, 86, 113, 167, 269, 270, 286, 287, 314, 369, 388
Buddhism, reformed, 161, 261, 268, 269, 287
Buddhist Church, (*see also* Lamaist Church), 29, 30, 34, 35
Buddhist Faith, 30, 36, 46, 54, 194, 209, 222, 233, 237, 260, 265, 268, 285, 286, 287
Bujig, 166
Bukharin, 240, 273, 355
Bulgan aimak (p.n.), 266, 365
Bulstrode, Mrs B., 16, 354
Bumtsend, 375

460

INDEX

Buntar, 61, 63
bureaucracy, (*see also* administration), 91, 108
Buriat Autonomous Republic, 9
Buriat Mongolia, 23, 275
Buriats, 1, 8, 28, 62, 73, 136, 161, 168, 202, 236, 244, 263, 275, 281, 285, 332, 338
Burni, 66
Buura, (p.n.), 192
Buyannemekh, 274, 343–4, 376, 413–15

capitalism, 273, 274, 278, 353
caravans, 86, 163
Carruthers, D, 101, 168, 169
cattle, 89, 163, 311, 312, 353, 379, 397–9, 401–3
    transferred from Church to commoners, 303
Central Committee of the Party, 206, 225, 227, 228, 234, 242, 261, 262, 263, 269, 270, 275, 277, 282, 284, 291, 292, 293, 296, 297, 298, 304–9, 311, 320–23, 325, 326, 332, 334, 336, 337–42, 344, 355, 357, 369, 373, 374, 376, 397, 398, 399, 403, 412, 413, 418, 419, 420
    and Buddhism, 269
    condemns own policy, 322
    and culture, 376, 412
    Declaration on Religion, 270
    and cult of personality, 345
    penetrated by Japanese intelligence, 325, 328
Central Crafts Bureau, 371
Chagan Suburga (p.n.), 36
Chagdarjav, 142, 210, 214, 228, 229, 231, 254
Chahar, Chahars, 3, 4, 13, 25, 39, 40, 43, 44, 45, 46, 59, 60, 116, 122, 137
Chahar emperor, 25, 40, 42, 45, 46, 59, 60, 416
Chakhundorji, 34, 47, 62, 63, 68, 72, 74, 75, 76, 78, 80
Chang Tso-lin, 254
chavgants, 361
chekists, 243, 332
Ch'en I, 204, 215, 231
Chiang Kai-shek, 239, 382
Chicherin, 215
Ch'ien Ch'ing Gate (p.n.), 102
Ch'ien Lung, 33, 48, 57, 69, 101, 115, 117, 118, 119, 120, 122, 123, 129, 130, 132, 149

children, selling of, 93
Chimid, Ch., 413, 416
Ch'in dynasty, 81
Chin Sujigt Nomun Khan, 134
China and Chinese, passim
Chinese language, 86, 159
Ch'ing dynasty (*see also* Manchu dynasty), 47, 58, 76
Ch'ing Shih-lu, 111
Chingunjav, 6, 57, 101, 111, 112, 116, 118–31, 138, 192
ch'in wang, 83
Choibalsang, 10, 159, 202, 205–7, 210–15, 223, 226–8, 231, 235, 237, 242, 243, 246, 249–51, 255, 280, 282, 291–4, 296, 301, 306, 325, 328–42, 345, 347, 348, 355, 356, 359, 360, 364, 371, 375, 415
Choibalsang aimak, (p.n.), 19
Choibalsang Combine, 336, 354, 378
Choibalsang prize, 416
Choijav, 114
Choijin, 320
Choinzon, 286
Choivsuren, 162
Chökhur, 65, 66
chorji, 71
Choros, 65
chronicles, 5, 27, 30, 37, 41, 42, 43, 53, 87, 111
Chultem-ochir, 314
Church and State, 29, 34, 260–73, 283, 284–8
    separated by law, 260, 263, 319, 363
Church Boneman, 156
class differences, 138, 310, 396
    and violence in Urga, 272
class discrimination, 311
    in Church, 313, 361–2
class struggle, 157, 158, 244
climate, 18
coal mining, 190, 202, 243, 246
Code of 1640, 55
coffins, 255
collectives, 13, 302, 307, 310–12, 314, 351–2, 391, 394, 397–404, 409
collectivization, 242, 273, 301, 303, 304, 307, 310, 311, 314, 327, 347, 360, 379, 396–404
    in USSR, 240, 242
colonialism, Soviet, 239, 273, 390
COMECON, 385, 390

INDEX

Comintern, 188, 191, 208, 209, 210, 215, 216, 222, 224, 225, 227, 237, 239, 240, 241, 244, 259, 260, 264, 271, 288, 292, 296, 297, 298, 301, 306, 316, 322, 323, 334, 335, 364
    directive of 1932, 241, 306, 307, 322, 324, 325, 326
Committee of Sciences, 207, 248, 288, 376, 415
commoners, 82, 88, 90, 91, 105, 138, 142, 149, 150, 151, 161, 176, 183, 203
communes, 309, 310, 311
communications, 380
communism, 15, 18, 136, 206, 209, 265, 268, 269, 286, 394, 418
communist literature, 206
Communist Manifesto, 206
Communist University of the Toilers of the East, 300
complaints, 143, 167, 175–86
concentration camps, 301, 322
Concise History of the Mongol Revolution, 206, 215, 226,
confiscation of property, 290, 293, 296, 301, 308, 309, 314, 396
Congress of the Peoples of the East, 413
Consten, H, 16
Constitution of 1924, 240, 291
    of 1940, 373, 381
Control Commission, 242, 306, 321
'Conversation between a Sheep, a Goat and an Ox', 170
conversation song, 386
cooperation, low-level (*see also* labour-pooling), 307, 396
Cooperative Congress, First, 400
corvée (*see also alba*), 88, 93, 98, 101–6, 137, 141, 148–51, 178, 182
    nobility loses right to, 258
    substitution, 142, 143, 150
Council of Ministers, 242
Country Opposition, 288, 291, 292
Courant, M, 111
craft cooperatives, 350, 360, 371–3, 394–5
crèches, 393, 405, 406
crime, 394, 407
criminal cases, reports of, 176
Cult of personality, 212, 214, 222, 292, 333, 345, 419, 421
culture, pre-revolutionary, 23, 86–7, 246–8, 375, 379, 385–6, 415, 421
    revolutionary, 375, 410–19

currency units, 149
Czechoslovakia, 381

Da Lama, 158
Dagvadorji, 85
Dalai Lama, 11, 25, 29, 30, 31, 34, 35, 46, 49, 50, 52, 53, 54, 63, 64, 65, 66, 67, 68, 69, 70, 71, 74, 79, 262–3, 333
    Third, 25, 27, 29, 30, 31, 32, 34, 36, 54
    Fourth, 33
    Fifth, 52, 54
    Eighth, 133
Damba (lama), 255
Damba (revolutionary), 335
Dambadarjaa lamasery, 85
Dambadorj, 223, 227, 231, 239, 260, 273, 276, 279, 280, 281, 282, 284, 285, 287, 288, 292, 323
Dambajav, 119
Dambijantsan, 192, 197, 198, 199, 251–4, 254
Damchaa, 126
Damdin (high lama), 249
Damdin (father of Sukhebator), 14
Damdinbazar, *see* Jalkhantsa Khutuktu
Damdinsuren (general), 159, 197, 198, 214, 236
Damdinsuren (lama), 166
Damdinsuren, Ts., 179, 246–7, 377, 413–15
Damdinsuren (*zangi* and revolutionary), 219
Damiran, 126
Dampil, 127
Dandar, 171–2
dangjaad, 97
Danzan, 207, 210, 213, 214, 215, 223, 224, 225, 229, 230, 231, 234, 254, 274, 276–82 297, 413
Danzan ('Japan'), 260
Daraisun, Daraisun Küdeng, 25, 34
Dariganga, (p.n.), 7, 84, 89, 187
Darigangas, 8
Darijav, 218, 223, 330, 342
Darkhan (p.n.), 381, 395, 408, 409
Darkhan gung banner, debt of, 203
Darkhat, 69, 124, 142
Darva Bandida, 269–71
Dashjid, 139–41
Dashzeveg, 146
datsang, 161
Dauria, 204

462

INDEX

Dawachi, 116
day-labourers, 153
Dayan Khan, 3, 24, 25, 48
deel, 16
debts, 93, 97–101, 132, 142, 143, 150, 162, 167, 169, 183, 184, 203
Delger, 167
delivery quotas, 396, 399, 400
Demberel, 224
Demid, 215, 330, 332, 336–42, 346
Demo Khutuktu, 133
democracy, 374
Dendev, 145
Derbets, 22, 50, 197, 199, 211, 244, 318
destitution, (*see also* poverty), 185, 203
deviation, leftist, 158, 241, 245, 250, 252, 273, 294–8, 301–3, 305, 320, 321, 324–7, 351, 374
deviation, rightist, 228, 241, 272, 273, 287, 305, 324–6
Dilowa Khutuktu, 149, 158, 317–19
diplomatic recognition, 382, 383
divination and magic, 77, 146, 250–51
doctors, 146, 380, 383
documentation, criticism of, 221–3, 226, 227–8
Dogsom, 210, 213, 214, 223, 330
Dolonnor, 96, 114, 134
  Convention of, 79, 80, 81, 110
  prison at, 141
  services at, 102
Dondubdorji, 58, 117
Doolin, 127
Dorji, 126
Dorjijab, 74, 75
Dovchin, 207, 293, 321, 330, 334–5
dramatic groups, 375
drunkenness, 393–4
Duchingalabyn temple, 12
Dugar, 75
Dugartsembel, 102
  banner of, 177
duguilang, 176, 177, 184, 185
dui, 234
dulduichin, 155
Dungans, 153, 154, 174, 175
dzud, 19, 404

earthquakes, 19
education (*see also* schools), 190, 250, 271, 327, 380, 389, 391, 409

Eenden, 151, 152
Eldev-ochir, 306, 312, 364, 370
elections, 256, 419
electoral rights, 352
emigration, 257, 307, 312, 317, 352
Emil river (p.n.), 50
encyclical letters (*see also* lungdeng), 164, 172, 194–5, 365, 370
Enggeder, 37
English language, 17
Erdene Batur Khungtaiji, 50
Erdene Khoshuuch, 66
Erdene Toyin, 61
Erdeni Batu Khan, 283
Erdeni Juu lamasery, 7, 31, 53, 75, 84, 85, 96, 100, 112, 114, 115, 237, 349, 366, 367
Erdeni-yin tobchi, 30
Erdeni-yin erike, 31, 59, 67, 111
Erinchindorji, 82, 117, 118, 119, 123
Erkhe Chökhur, 61
Esen, 24
Exalted by All, 195, 196
exorcisms, 147
  to repel the Red Army, 234

factories, 288, 372, 378, 379
farms, farming (*see also* agriculture and fields), 13, 21, 22, 93, 108, 149, 150, 154, 303
Fascism, 294
Far Eastern Commission, 345
feudalism, feudal organization, 82, 87, 88, 89, 91, 92, 105, 202, 299, 389
feudal ranks abolished, 256
fields, army (*see also* agriculture and farms), 103, 109, 154, 156
firms, Chinese, *see* shops
First International Congress of Mongolists, 411
fishing, 142, 180
'five', 167
Five-year Plan, First, 304, 327
  First, of 1948, 387
  Fourth, 391
floods, 19
foreign aid, 378, 381, 385, 390, 394, 404, 408
foreign specialists, 291, 341, 355
France, Mongol relations with, 283
fugitives, 64, 70, 72, 119
Furdeng, 113
Fumintai, 275

463

INDEX

Galdan, 3, 5, 51, 52, 55, 63–70, 72, 74–8, 80, 95, 113
Galdan Shiretu, 71, 74
Galdandorji, 75
Galdantseren, 113, 114
Galsang, 166
Galsangjamts, 145
Galsangnamjil, 198
Ganbolod, 157
Gandang escarpment, (p.n.), 11
Gandang lamasery, 10, 154, 173, 249, 255, 362, 367, 368, 370, 371
Gapon, 211, 213
Garvi, 139
Gelegbalsang, 159
Gembarzhevskii, 206
Genden, 198
Gendenjamts, 145
Gendung, 242, 296, 297, 306, 309, 330, 332, 336–42, 351, 354–7, 359, 363, 364, 377, 378
Gendung-Demid conspiracy, 335–42
Genghis Khan, 1, 2, 3, 7, 22, 24, 26, 31, 33, 40, 43, 47, 55, 58, 66, 88, 113, 114, 115, 116, 123, 130, 170, 171, 192, 195, 196, 320
    anniversary celebrations, 417–18
    relics, 45, 46, 47, 417
    sanctuary and cult, 175, 417
    title, 37, 43
ger, 12, 96
Geresenje, 48, 49
Germany, Germans, 288, 291, 361, 376, 381, 413, 415
    Mongol relations with, 21, 239, 283
Geser Khan, 376
    temple of, 154
Gilmour, James, 160
Ginggun Elhe, 117
Girl Khutuktu, 57, 131
Girl Prince, 57
Gobi (p.n.), 7, 8, 47, 48, 387, 402, 404, 408
Gobi Altai aimak (p.n.), 266
Golovin, F. A., 52, 72, 73, 75, 77
Gombo, 126
Gombodoo, 371
Gombodorji, 33, 53, 54, 55, 58, 61, 62, 68, 69
Gombojav (delegate to Third Party Congress), 231
Gombojav (*gabj*), 370
Gombojav, (student), 280

Gombojav (lama), 368
Gonjoon, 280
Government, at Urga, 1921, 220, 227, 229, 230, 231, 234, 236
Government, independent of 1911, 159
Government, of July 1921, 234–5
Green Banner army, 153
Gumbe Ildeng, 63
gung, 5
Gunggataya, 168
guns, 49, 59, 66, 80, 128
Gushri Khan, 50, 54, 65

Hadaha, 118
Hailar, 199, 337
Hanamand, 263
handicrafts, 94, 142
Haslund, H, 17, 291
hay, 91, 307, 379, 384
Hedin, Sven, 264
Heissig, W., 36
herding and herdsmen, 13, 15, 16, 88, 94, 104, 142, 148, 180–81, 244, 298, 302, 305, 309, 310, 311, 322, 324, 327, 351, 371, 379, 384, 396–404, 409, 412
herds, 1, 88, 95, 101, 259, 302, 314
herds, official, 84, 93, 103, 109
historical writing, 23
history, falsification of, 336, 346, 411
History of Khalkha, 190
History of the Mongolian People's Republic,
    1955, 324, 337, 339
    1966, 337, 339, 391, 401
History of the Mongol-Borjigid Clan, 3
horses, 15, 25, 95, 101, 170
hou, 5
Hsi-mergen, 208
Hsi-ning, (p.n.), 1, 27
Hsiao Ta-heng, 15, 27, 29, 35
Hsü Shu-tseng, 204, 205, 208, 211, 215, 233
human sacrifice, 29, 33, 197, 320
Hungary, 381
hunting, 15, 142, 180
    as military training, 82
Huturinga, 126

ideological congress, 414, 418
Ilagugsan Khutuktu, 54
Iledkel Shastir, 52, 64, 111
Ili (p.n.), 139
Ilichev, 418

INDEX

illiteracy, 86, 249, 391
immigration, Chinese, 191
imperial subjects, 105, 106, 137, 139, 143, 144, 148, 151, 159, 169, 175, 185
imperial temples, 85, 164
imperialism, Japanese, 294, 356
  red, 239, 273, 292, 341, 356
incarnations, 35, 58, 68, 69, 132–3, 137, 157, 158, 261
  forbidden, 263
  Party and discovery of, 261, 263
  traditions concerning, 263
India, 23, 51, 57, 86, 196
industrial working class, 380
industry, 9, 93, 245–6, 323, 327, 360, 371, 378, 382, 383, 397, 380, 394, 405, 409
Injanashi, 5, 86, 170
insurrection of 1932, 285, 293, 315, 316, 321, 322
'Instructions' of To-wang, 180–81
intermarriage
  of Chinese traders, 96, 98
  of nobility with Manchus, 47, 77, 81, 82
Internal Affairs, Ministry of, 331, 332, 341, 342, 364
International, Third, 225
International Congress of Orientalists, 410
Irkutsk, (p.n.), 9, 52, 72, 215, 216, 218, 257, 413
  Mongol children study at, 202, 205, 246, 255
  Mongolyn Unen appears at, 206
  Revolutionaries at, 212
  Sukhebator and Choibalsang at, 214
Irtysh river, (p.n.), 114
irugel, 159
Ishidanzangwangjil, 172, 268
Ismail Khan, 65

Jajibulag, (p.n.), 60, 62
Jalkhantsa Khutuktu, 145, 197, 205, 207, 208, 236–7, 271
Jambal, (lama), 369–70
Jambal (partisan), 144
Jambaljav, 145
Jamtsarano, 190, 191, 202, 210, 212, 223, 225, 235, 246, 271, 282, 285, 287, 288, 294
Jamyang, 207, 211, 214, 248
Jamyangdanzan, *see* Saji lama

Jangjia Khutuktu, 121, 317
Japan, Japanese, 2, 46, 187, 192, 199, 200, 204, 208, 210, 223, 224, 243, 262, 263, 266, 267, 316–18, 323, 325, 328–9, 335, 337–43, 345, 356, 357, 359, 370, 377, 378, 384, 417
  prisoners, 10, 384–5
  and search for the ninth Khutuktu, 263–4
Jarbunai, 70, 71
jas, 85, 98, 100, 156, 161, 163, 164, 185, 261, 269, 284, 312, 315, 352, 358, 362
Jas-campaign, 302, 303, 314–15
jasaa, 93, 108
Jasagtu, Tumen Jasagtu (emperor), 28, 30
Jaya Pandita (Khalkha), 34, 367
Jaya Pandita, (Oirat), 32, 34, 37, 51, 68
jayig, 365
Jebtsundamba Khutuktu, (*see also* Living Buddha), 11, 12, 14, 33, 35, 37, 55, 56, 57, 58, 84, 85, 86, 94, 102, 106, 107, 132, 134, 136, 149, 160, 161, 162, 163, 164, 165, 173, 286, 317
  First, 33, 34, 48, 52, 53, 55, 56, 57, 68–80, 133, 386
  Second, 58, 82, 111, 112, 114, 117–22, 124, 125, 128, 133
  Third, 33, 133, 134, 163
  Fourth, 133, 134, 162
  Fifth, 134, 171
  Sixth, 133, 134, 263
  Seventh, 158, 165, 171
  Eighth, 56, 58, 107, 133, 134, 147, 158, 165–8, 178, 187, 188, 193, 194, 195, 196, 198, 199, 200, 204, 205, 208, 210–16, 225, 229, 232–5, 237, 238, 251–4, 257, 258, 260–62, 274, 370
  Ninth, 134, 261–4, 284
Jerim League, 13
Jesuits, 70
Jews, 232
Jigjid, 344
jinong, 24
Jobo Atisha, 286
joint companies, 313
Jungaria, (p.n.), 1, 25, 52, 55, 63, 64, 74, 81, 112, 113, 115, 116, 118, 131
Jungars, 37, 39, 48, 50, 51, 55, 56, 57, 59, 63–8, 74–8, 80, 83, 85, 93, 94, 100, 101, 107, 110, 111, 113–19, 128, 129, 132, 138
justice, 92, 93, 141, 255

465

INDEX

Kachanov, 73
Kalgan, (p.n.), 44, 61, 78, 96, 139, 254
Kalmucks, 1, 51, 136, 233–4, 264, 332
Kalmuck Autonomous Republic, 1
Kamenev, 215
K'ang Hsi, 3, 5, 6, 47, 48, 52, 58, 67, 71–5, 77–81, 117, 156
Kanjur, 23, 35, 36, 42
Kansu province, (p.n.), 2, 66
Kapital, Das, 419
Karakorum, (p.n.), 7, 24, 26, 29, 31, 94
Kashgar, (p.n.), 65
Kazakhs, 8, 118, 389
Kemchik river, (p.n.), 63
Kentei aimak, (p.n.), 353, 362
Kentei mountains, (p.n.), 7
Kerulen river, (p.n.), 23, 49, 75, 76, 80, 102
khadag, as currency, 149
khailang, 147
Khaisan, 194, 197
Khalkha, Kalkha Mongols, 4, 5, 8, 22, 25, 31, 33, 35, 37, Chs, 2, 3, 4, passim, 144, 150, 156, 161, 170, 174, 177, 187, 192, 199, 200, 211
Khalkha Code, (*Khalkha Jirum*), 90, 167
Khalkha Mongol language, 8
Khalkha river, (Khalkhyn gol), (p.n.), 79, battle of, 323, 329
khamba, 160
khamjilga, 105, 106, 136, 137, 138, 139, 141, 143, 145, 148, 151, 159, 202, 203, 258
khan, khanate, 5, 25, 31, 34, 35, 37, 39, 41, 45, 47, 49, 52, 55, 58, 59, 62, 71, 77, 78, 79, 80, 81, 92, 95, 102, 107
Khan Khatan, river, (p.n.), 117
Khandadorji, 147, 194, 200
Khandajamtso, 55
khandma, 31
Khangai mountains, (p.n.), 7, 49, 75, 76
khangai, 408
Khara Baishing, (p.n.), 26
Kharakhula, 50, 51, 64, 66
Kharchins, 3, 4, 44, 109
Khasbator, 219, 231
Khatgal, (p.n.), 378
Khiakta, (p.n.), 13, 22, 56, 94, 97, 103, 107, 124, 125, 126, 149, 154, 188, 201, 202, 205, 209, 210, 212, 216, 217, 218, 220, 221, 224, 227, 246
    Capture of, 230–31

Three-power conference at, 201, 235
Treaty of, 1727, 112
Treaty of, 1915, 188, 201, 211, 226, 233
Watch posts, 104
Khingan mountains, (p.n.), 25
Khitan, 26
Khobdo, (p.n.), 13, 22, 33, 51, 80, 85, 86, 94, 103, 107, 109, 130, 132, 149, 150, 153, 154, 159, 175, 184, 185, 187, 196, 197, 198, 199, 201, 203, 231, 236, 244, 266, 267, 312, 320
Khobdo, amban of, 196, 197, 211
Khoits, 132
Khorchin, 4, 32, 40, 44, 84, 117
Khorloo, (mother of Ayush), 144
Khorloo, (mother of Choibalsan), 248
Khoshut, 34, 50, 65, 257
Khotogoit, 58, 111, 116, 118, 119, 123, 124
Khrushchev, 331–3
Khubilai, Khan, 26, 29, 30, 34
Khuder, (p.n.), 219
Khui, (p.n.), 126
Khujirbulang, (p.n.), military school at, 201, 218
Khural, Little, 333, 342, 375
Khural, National, 10, 229, 252, 263, 342, 375
    First, 371
    Sixth, 344
Khuren Belchir, (p.n.), 71, 74
Khutuktu, *see* Jebtsundamba Khutuktu
khutuktu, 157, 160
Khutuktu Setsen Khungtaiji, 29, 30
khuv, 311, 351
Khuvsugul, aimak, (p.n.), 294, 315, 318, 320
Khuvsugul, Lake, (p.n.), 156
Khyaraan, watchpost, (p.n.), 219
kindergartens, 393, 406
Kirei-Kirghis, 168
Kirov, 330
Ko, General, 230
Kodama, episode, 201
Köke qota, (p.n.), 25, 27, 31, 36, 41, 60, 71, 78, 96, 123, 185
Köke sudur, 170
Kolesnikov, 214
kolkhoz, 396, 397, 400, 402
kontaisha, 64
Koreans, 37

466

INDEX

Korostovets, 194, 200
Korovin, 73
koumis, 15
Kozin, 201
Krasnoyarsk, (p.n.), 49
Ku-ch'eng, (p.n.), 184
Kucherenko, 206, 209
Kukunor, (p.n.), 2, 6, 25, 46, 47, 55, 65, 66, 75, 78, 113, 114
Kukunor, (in east Mongolia), (p.n.), 6
kung, 5
Kupon, (*see* Gapon).

Laasag, 219–20
labour brigades, 399
Labour Code, 1964, 406
labour-day unit system, 399, 402
labour-pooling, (*see also* cooperation), 310, 352, 378, 396, 402
Laikhur, 49
lamaism, (*see also* Buddhism), 15, 25, 26, 76, 84, 264, 286
lamaist church, (*see also* Buddhist Church), 15, 37, 51, 52, 53, 54, 55, 76, 84, 86, 88, 89, 106, 108, 111, 136, 146, 154, 156, 157, 159, 160, 161, 162, 164, 167, 168, 169, 170–73, 190, 244–5, 258, 259, 260–73, 290, 301, 313–15, 322, 347, 350, 359
    attacks on, 245, 304, 357
    career possibilities in, 159
    condition in 1921, 244
    desertions from, 168, 261, 313, 347
    destruction of, 326–7, 330, 348–9, 359–73, 374
    and disease, 146
    during autonomy, 190
    and extravagance, 147, 158
    moral decline of, 166–8
    Party's attitude toward, 245, 260–64
    and propaganda, 265
    reforms in, 258
    size, 160
    and surplus manpower, 168–9
    weakening of, 360–65
lamas, 4, 10, 15, 16, 17, 23, 28, 32, 33, 36, 44, 84, 91, 102, 106, 108, 121, 134, 137, 138, 140, 141, 147, 152, 154, 157, 158, 159, 160, 161, 162, 165, 167, 168, 169, 172, 173, 175, 179, 182, 183, 185, 193, 199, 202, 203, 244, 249, 252, 253, 260, 262, 268, 270, 271, 272, 287, 302, 313–15, 316, 322, 324, 335, 336, 337, 348–9, 350, 351, 358, 359–73, 375
    after closure of lamaseries, 367, 370–73, 379
    alleged conspiracy of, 336
    attacks on property of, 315, 362
    class divisions, 137, 157, 168, 259, 268, 305, 313, 360–62, 368
    critical of degeneracy in Church, 166–7
    desecularization of, 352
    desert Church, 261, 303, 347, 360
    discrimination against, 303, 361
    education of, 360, 368
    as envoys, 4, 44, 70
    expelled from lamaseries, 314, 319
    form proletariate, 155
    illegal actions of, 363
    and insurrection of 1932, 316, 319
    as members of cooperatives, 371–3
    and military service, 261, 303, 350, 361
    as missionaries, 32
    as money lenders, 164
    as Party members, 260, 276, 290
    poor lamas, 165
    as rebels, 128, 267
    tales about, 57
Lamas' Journal, 369, 371
lamaseries, 12, 15, 16, 27, 83, 85, 89, 100, 130, 137, 152, 159, 160, 164, 168, 169, 182, 253, 258, 261, 273, 287, 313–15, 318, 319, 358, 363, 364
    and agriculture, trade and transport, 164, 261
    and Chinese traders, 83, 98
    Choibalsang and, 347
    closure, 158, 245, 348–9, 359, 365–7, 370
    discipline in, 167–8
    and herding out of animals, 148, 163, 303
    internal administration, 363, 365
    sources of income, 85–6, 163, 261
    and trade, 142
    uprisings organized by, 266, 318
land, control of, 88, 89
land, personal rights in, 91
land transfer, 89, 91, 164
Langdarma, 265
Lasran, 128
Latin alphabet, 250
Lattimore, Owen, 330–31

INDEX

Law, (*see also* complaints), 86, 167
   law suits, legal cases, 90, 91, 92, 100, 107, 167, 168
   legal codes, 55, 64, 92, 255
   legal procedure, 139–41
   legal reforms, 255, 264
League, 55, 99, 107, 108, 140, 141, 150, 183
   League assemblies, 107, 121, 149
   Complaints brought to, 175, 121, 149
   League chief, 92, 93, 106, 107, 177
League of Militant Godless, 313
League of Revolutionary Youth, 231, 239, 265, 274, 277, 280, 286, 287, 306, 307, 313, 314, 316, 322, 358, 399
Leeds, University of, 383
Left Wing, 24, 48, 63
Legtseg, 166
Lenin, 9, 136, 214, 215, 265, 270, 273, 286, 292, 313, 413, 416
Lhagva, 196, 198
Lhamjav, 113, 114
Lhasa, (p.n.), 34, 35, 50, 52, 54, 64, 65, 69, 132, 163, 367
Lhunbo, 336, 338, 339, 342
Li Fan Yüan, 92, 96, 107, 109, 140
   Regulations of, 150
Liao-tung, (p.n.), 25, 37
Liao-yang, (p.n.), 37
Ligdan Khan, 3, 5, 23, 33–6, 40–47, 53, 54, 58, 59, 60, 66, 416
Limbeldorji, 122, 125
Lin-hsi hsien, (p.n.), 192
Litang, (p.n.), 133
literacy, 22, 35, 246, 247, 380
literacy circles for lamas, 368
literature, 23, 171, 247, 250, 343, 367, 376, 385, 412–14, 415
Literary Circle in Ulan Bator, 413
Little Hsü, *see* Hsü Shu-tseng
Living Buddha of Urga (*see also* Jebtsundamba Khutuktu), 11, 33, 53, 58, 333
loans and loan trading, 95, 99
Lobsang taiji, 62, 70
Lobsanggomborabdan, 74
local government, 231, 238, 255
local particularism, 244
Lomi, 3, 4, 24
Losol, 159, 207, 210, 214, 215, 223, 228, 282, 294, 330
Luvsan, 'Fiddler', 376

Luvsanjambaa, 371
Luvsanjamts, 177
Luvsansharav, 330
Luvsantseren, 310
lungden, (*see also* encyclical letter), 172

Maajinshan mountains, (p.n.), 253
Macdonald, 297
Maenchen-Helfen, O., 300
magic, 77, 250–51
magicians, 146
Magsar, 234–5
Magsarjav, 196, 197, 198, 207, 214, 216, 231, 236, 237, 253
Mahakala, 33
Maidari temple, 11, 12
maikhan, 96
Maimai khota, (p.n.), 154
Makata, 47
Makstinyak, 209, 210, 212, 216, 217
Malji, 330
Manchukuo, 76
Manchus chs. 1–4 passim
   Manchu conquest, 40, 56
   Manchu dynasty, 47, 81, 82, collapse of, 6, 82, 135, 193, 194
   Manchu emperor, 4, 31, 33, 35, 36, 37, 43, 54, 58, 59, 61, 62, 63, 65, 66, 67, 70, 74, 88, 89, 102, 106, 112, 113, 114, 117–20, 128, 131, 133, 137, 173, 188
   Manchu empire, 1, 3, 50, 81
   Manchu expansion, 44, 58
   Manchu language, 76, 86
   expulsion from Mongolia, 56, 184, 194, 196, 418
   and Jungar conflict, 110–34
Manchuli, (p.n.), 342
Manchuria, 317, 318, 323, 384
Manggus, 44
Manibadar, 155, 165
Manibazar, 183–5
Manjita lama, 70
manuscripts, 248
Mao Tse-t'ung, 10, 421
markets, 13, 25, 29, 94, 108
Marx, Karl, 270, 286
Marx-Leninism, 9, 10, 129, 130, 136, 158, 207, 232, 250, 262, 269, 270, 284, 285, 334, 349, 357, 388, 411
Marxism and Buddhism, 259, 268, 269, 284–7
meadows, 91

INDEX

medicine, medical services, 146, 201, 202, 257, 264, 288, 327, 352, 380, 389, 405
mendicant lamas, 260, 265
Mergen Bandida Khutuktu, 14
Mergen Gegen, 84
Mergen Sume, 84
mkha-hgro-ma, 31
military camps, Manchu, 94, 96, 100
military expenditure, 378
military service, 101
military system, Manchu, 105
Ming dynasty, 25, 27, 39, 40, 41, 43, 44, 59, 94, 95
Mingat, 130
Mishig, 415
monarchy, 136, 168, 187, 188, 234, 288
money, 149, 163
Mongolia, Mongols, passim
  Mongolia, Inner, 2, 8, 13, 17, 22, 27, 39–47, 48, 53, 58, 66, 68, 72, 77, 78, 79, 95, 96, 109, 113, 156, 161, 170, 176, 187, 191, 192, 195, 197, 200, 241, 275, 318, 323, 378, 384, 388, 389, 391, 417
  Inner Mongolian Autonomous Region, 2
  Mongolia, Outer, 2, 6, 13, 25, 27, 28, 39, 48, 113, 191
  alphabet and alphabet reform, 17, 344, 377, 422
  Mongol Central Cooperative, 274, 279, 290
  Mongol Code, 141
  Mongol currency, 264, 274, 288, 312
  Mongol dynasty, (*see also* Yüan), 4, 23
  Mongol emperor and empire, 1, 24, 25, 26, 28, 30, 31, 34, 40, 66
  Mongol independence, 3, 5, 6, 13, 40, 47, 56, 121, 124, 128, 129, 131, 134, 135, 147, 180, 187, 191, 229, 328, 332, 382
  King of Mongolia, 14, 107, 134, 166
  Mongol language and script, 1, 22, 26, 76, 86, 87, 272, 344, 365, 387–8
  Mongol nationalism, 6, 416–18
  Mongol League of Revolutionary Youth and Religion, 286
  Mongolian People's Government, 49, 58, 107, 134, 136, 151, 158, 160, 167, 168, 179, 228, 258, 267, 271, 288, 290, 302, 316, 318, 320, 324, 342, 348, 349, 350
  Mongolian People's Republic, 1, 2, 3, 8, 10, 14, 17, 155, 188, 205, 233, 238, 274, 319, 384, 391, 417
  Mongolian People's (Revolutionary) Party, 10, 87, 134, 190, 209, 213–14, 217, 220, 223, 224, 225, 227, 232–5, 237, chs., 6, 7, 8, passim, 396, 399, 400, 412, 415, 416, 419, 420, 421, 423
  Mongol reunification, 41, 45
  Mongol submission to Manchus, 52, 59, 61, 63, 76–7
  Mongoltrans, 313
  Mongols, West, 8, 28, 37, 39, 48, 49, 50, 65, 116, 244, 257
Mongolyn Unen, 206, 412
Monguors, 2
Moon Cuckoo, 386
Moscow, (p.n.), 48, 50, 52, 62, 65, 70, 72, 73, 159, 214, 215, 216, 317, 341, 413
mountains, worship of, 102
Mukden, (p.n.), 54, 66, 67
music, 22
Murzaev, 18
mutinies, 144, 174, 189, 192, 204

Nagarjuna, 286
Nagwangkhaidav, 170–71
Naidan, 335
Naidan taiji, 105
Naidansuren, 255
Nalaikha, (p.n.), 202, 246, 329
names, propitiatory, 406
Namjil, 370
Namnan Uul lamasery, 267
Namsrai, 146
Namsrai, (head of security), 331, 338, 339, 341
Nanzad, 253
Narabanchen Khutuktu, 158
Narabanchen lamasery, 109, 149
National Assembly, *see* Khural, National
Natsagdorj, D., 321, 413
Natsagdorj, Sh., 105, 149, 169, 181, 182, 190, 269, 418
Nawaangnamjil, 21, 155, 198
Nawangneren, 205
Nawangtseren, 20, 198
negdel, 401, 402

INDEX

Neichi toyin, 32, 33
Nerchinsk, (p.n.), 52
New Economic Policy, 273, 274
New Turn Policy, 241, 293, 296, 303, 310, 326, 327, 330, 341, 344, 346, 351, 353, 355, 357, 358, 397
Niislel Khureenii Medee, 202
'nine', 141, 167
Nine Whites, 59, 61, 62, 102
niru, 105
NKVD, 331, 332, 342, 359
nobles and nobility, 4, 5, 6, 23, 30, 32, 33, 34, 36, 40, 45, 47, 56, 61, 63, 69, 71, 73, 76, 77, 78, 79, 81, 82, 83, 87, 88, 89, 91, 105, 107, 111–14, 116–18, 120, 124, 125, 128–35, 137, 141, 148–50, 158, 160, 189, 192, 193, 208, 253, 256, 258, 264, 276, 284, 290, 309, 315, 316, 319
  extermination of, 301–2
nökhörlöl, 378, 402
nomadism, 1, 7, 11, 12, 13, 14, 50, 82, 93, 107, 108, 110, 354, 379, 385, 387
Nomon, 139
Noonokh, 49
Norovjantsan, 125
North Khangai aimak, (p.n.), 294, 296, 308, 318, 319, 320
nuns, 170
Nurhachi, (T'ai-tsu), 5, 37, 41, 43, 44, 76
nurses, Swedish, 246
Nuvsh, 126
Nyingmapa, 31

Oath-taking Treaty, 213, 260
Ob, river, (p.n.), 117
obo, 22, 84, 103, 109, 179

Ochirbat's Yamen, 319
Ochirtu Setsen Khan, 65, 66, 74
official correspondence, 108, 110
Ogedei, 26
Ögöömör, (p.n.), 75
Oirats, 3, 23, 24, 29, 32, 35, 39, 41, 48, 50, 58, 67, 75, 77, 116, 138, 139,
  Oirat script, 32, 51
Olgoi Nor, (p.n.), 76
Olon sume, (p.n.), 41
Ölziit, 100
Ombo Erdene, 45, 49, 62
Ombokh, 92
Öndör Gegen, (*see also* First Jebtsundamba Khutuktu), 58

Ongin river, (p.n.), 75
Ongnigut, 32
ongons, 32, 33
Opium Wars, 83
oracle, 166
Oracle Lama, 158, 319
Oracle temple, 11, 158, 367
Ordos, (p.n.), 31, 44, 45, 47, 175, 176, 177, 417
Orjin, 139, 140
Orkhon river (p.n.), 7, 51, 75, 100, 220
otog, 105, 139, 151, 152, 162, 167, 224
otor, 13

Padma Sambhava, 31
Pagspa Lama, 29, 30
Palta, Prince, 197
pan-Mongolism, 194, 195, 199, 200, 204, 211, 226, 275, 287, 342
Panchen Lama, 11, 46, 53, 54, 64, 263, 266, 316, 317, 318, 319
panzchin, 154
partisans, memoirs of, 144
Party Congress,
  First, 217, 220–27
  Second, 225, 275, 277, 371
  Third, 207, 231, 241, 244, 258, 260, 273–82, 290, 291
  Fifth, 262, 285, 290
  Seventh, 238, 263, 284, 287, 288, 290–303, 307, 308, 375
  Eighth, 268, 287, 293, 299, 303, 305, 309, 310, 311, 315, 327
  Ninth, 246, 323, 326, 333, 359
  Tenth, 250, 326, 373
  Fifteenth, 374
party line, 215, 237, 241, 242, 243, 274, 298, 299, 306, 326, 341, 347
Party Oath, 209
Party Platform, First, 225–7, 236
Party Programme,
  Third, 373
  First and Second, 374
  Fourth, 374, 401, 421
pastures and pasturing, 88, 89, 90, 91, 94, 104, 156
pastures, imperial, 84, 89
Pavlovsky, M., 111
Peking (p.n.), 6, 8, 11, 23, 26, 29, 36, 48, 54, 56, 57, 61, 62, 66, 70–73, 75, 79, 84, 86, 87, 92, 95, 96, 97, 102, 114, 117, 118, 122, 123, 126, 141, 149, 159, 173, 194, 205, 210, 266, 317, 386

INDEX

Peking, North (p.n.), 131
Pelliot, P., 248
People's Assemblies, 242
Perfiryev, 72, 73
Petrov letter, 323
Pevtsov, 21, 152, 153, 154
piao, see trade licences
plots, counterrevolutionary, 243, 253, 260, 266-7, 285
po, 5
Pokhabov, 62
Poland, 147, 381
police, 264, 285, 323, 332
political consciousness, lack of, 252
Pope, 70
population, 6, 8, 169, 389, 404, 409
population figures, 142, 405
    losses, 345-6
    problems, 390, 405, 408, 422
    shifts, 134
Potanin, 110
poverty (*see also* destitution), 142, 144, 151, 161
Pozdneev, 41, 110, 111, 141, 153, 191
Preamble to the Mongol People's Party's Proclamation to the Masses, 225
press campaigns, 393-4
printing, 23, 26, 36, 84, 86, 202, 246, 265, 386
proctors, 167-8
producers' associations, 398, 401, 402
proletariat, 93, 143, 155, 245, 246, 402
propaganda, 369, 393
propaganda, atheistic, 260, 268, 287, 399
    anti-communist, 260, 265, 327
    party, 268, 272
    anti-Soviet, 265, 370
prostitutes, 153
Protocol of 1912, 200
Provisional Government of 1911, 194, 195
Provisional Government of 1921, 188, 217, 220, 227-34, 236, 256
Przhevalskii, 11, 18, 19, 110
P'u Yi, 76
publishing, 377
Puntsag (partisan), 212, 218, 220
Puntsag (*shabi* official), 167
Puntsagdorji, 207, 208, 210, 234, 236, 254
Purevdagva, 144
purges, political, 210, 234, 249, 323, 326, 330, 338, 346

    of officials, 408
    party, 252, 273, 299, 300, 316, 353, 359, 420
Puzorin, 213

Rabdan, 76
Rabjai, 171, 386
railways, 191, 327, 378
rain-making, 251
Rakhuli, 61
Ramstedt, 190
Rashaant, (p.n.), 318, 320
rationing, 346, 382
Ravdan, 126
Ray of Dawn, 172
rebellion, in T'o wang's banner, 182-3
Rebellion of 1756, 83, 95, 101, 110-34, 138
Red Sect, 27, 30, 31, 46
Red Star, 219
rehabilitation, 332, 335, 340
relay stations, 16, 83, 89, 93, 99, 101, 103, 108, 109, 112, 113, 123, 163, 258
religious commission, 352, 364
religious freedom, 352, 357
Religious Museum, 158, 367
retail cooperatives, 311, 355
Renewal movement, 287
rent, 88, 91
requisitioning, 130
revenants, 130
revolution, 1911, 130, 147, 184, 189, 190, 193-5
revolution, 1921, 87, 93, 136, 143, 151, 157, 168, 188, 189, 190, 205-9, 216-17, 252, 271, 311
revolutionaries, 229
    characterization of, 207, 222
    liquidation, 207
    rehabilitation, 207
    standpoint in 1921, 222
revolutionary clubs, 205, 206, 208, 209
revolutionary delegation to Russia, 1920, 210-15
revolutionary placard, 208
Right Wing, 24, 25, 48, 63, 74
Rinchino, 210, 212, 231, 239, 276-82, 294
Rintchen, 172, 248, 375-6, 413, 415, 416
riots, 144, 173-4, 189, 285, 316, 370
robbery, 155
Romanization Bureau, 344
round robins, 176

rural economy collectives, 401
Russia and Russians, passim
Russian language and alphabet, 17, 327, 344, 377, 410, 412
Russians, White, 188, 215, 224, 228, 229, 230, 233, 234, 236, 238

sabotage, 336, 354
Sagang Setsen, 30
sain er, 143, 174
Sain Noyon Khan, 31, 47, 49, 200, 201
Sain Noyon Khan aimak, 89, 107, 150, 203, 269
Sain Noyon Khan district, 253
St Petersburg, 200
Saji Lama, 234, 251, 253
salaries, 114
Sambuu, J., 145, 181, 214, 251, 296, 297, 305, 308–10, 314, 320, 322
Sambuu (deputy Premier), 330
Sambuu (lama), 167
Sambuu (rebel C. in C.), 320
Sampilon, 283
San-fan rebellion, 66, 67
Sando, 174, 193, 368
sang, 149, 158
Sangaa, 125
Sangs-rgyas-rgya-mts'o, 65
Sanjaidorji (general), 83, 120, 123, 134
Sanjaidorji (Setsen Khan), 177, 179
Saturday Meeting, 367
scholarship, nature of, 411–12
schools, 13, 17, 86, 181, 202, 216–17, 264, 268, 271, 283, 287, 288, 311, 364, 368–9, 377, 380, 382, 383, 391, 406
seal, granted to Galdan, 67
seal, government, 188, 266
seal, imperial, 47, 66
seal, party, 211
Secret History of the Mongols, 22, 376
secret police, 237, 264
secret treaties, 187, 199
Security, Office of Internal, 253, 264, 281, 282, 331, 338, 342
security services, 243, 323, 331, 332, 336
Selba (Selbe), river, (p.n.), 11, 19
Selenga river (p.n.), 9, 49, 51, 60, 62, 72, 79
Selenga aimak, (p.n.), 375
Selenginsk, (p.n.), 52, 72, 73, 74, 75, 77, 120
Semba Chembo Khutuktu, 71
Sengge, 63, 64, 65, 70

serfs, *see shabi*
Setsen Khan, 5, 26, 35, 41, 49, 55, 59, 60, 62, 75, 78, 80, 114, 158, 205, 235
Setsen Khan aimak, 90, 102, 107, 114, 115, 142, 149, 150, 151, 152, 174, 175, 178, 197, 248
settled life, (*see also* nomadism), 7, 50, 94, 108, 404
Sevdenbaljir, 117
Shaalov, 267
shabi, 14, 15, 37, 69, 84, 85, 90, 105, 106, 107, 125, 137, 138, 139, 148, 151, 152, 157, 161, 162, 203, 224, 253, 261
Shabi-yamen, 69, 159, 161, 162, 165, 167, 168, 174
Shadar chiang-chün, 111
Shagdar, Crazy, 192
shamanism, 27, 28, 32, 33, 50, 179, 269, 320, 389
shamans, 32, 33, 77, 178
Shambala, 262, 263, 264, 266, 318
Shangjodba, (shanzav), 72, 84, 106, 145, 155, 168
Shansi, (p.n.), 95
Shara, 74
Sharav, 125
Shara süme, (p.n.), 197
Sharin, 122
Shastin, P. N., 257
shelters, 351, 353, 379, 384, 404
Sherab, 84
Shidishiri, 52, 72, 74, 75
Shijee, (lama), 171
Shijee, (leftist revolutionary), 296, 320, 326
Shine Toli, 202
Shira Tuguji, 42
Shira Uighur, 28
Shirendyv, B., 214
Shishmarev, 111, 130
Shmeral, B., 297, 298, 325, 341, 359
Sholoi, 26, 41, 49, 54, 61, 62
Sholoi ubashi, 49
shops, Chinese, (*see also* firms), 83, 87, 95, 96, 97, 98, 99, 100, 124, 125, 143, 150, 151, 154, 173, 174, 184, 185, 189, 193, 197, 203, 290
shops, foreign, 164, 290
shuang ch'in wang, 117
shulengge, 167
Shumyatskii, B., 210, 212
Shun Chih, 67
Shun-i-wang, 28

Shuo-mo fang-lüeh, 64
silver, 98, 100, 102, 150, 151, 161, 167
Sinkiang, (p.n.), 13, 184, 197, 218, 228, 253, 267, 319
Sino-Russian Accord, 1913, 188, 200
Sino-Soviet dispute, 418, 421, 422
Six Tumen, 23, 42
Sixty-four point agreement, 204
slaves, 126, 127, 138, 139
social problems, 393–4, 405–6
socialism, 37, 241, 293, 299, 307, 310, 311, 347, 377, 394
socialist property, offences against, 407
soldiers, 100, 104, 106, 343, 358
Sonom, 146
Sonom (proctor), 167, 168
Sonom, (taiji), 91
Sorokovikov, 209, 212, 258, 280, 332
South Gobi aimak, (p.n.), 293, 295, 297, 307, 315, 317, 318, 319, 320, 322, 403
South Khangai aimak, (p.n.), 363
sovereignty, Chinese, 202
Soviet-Mongol Treaty, 1921, 252
Soviet revolution, 136, 188, 199
Soviet Union, Soviet Russia, 1, 11, 16, 159, 188, 189, 190, 191, 209, 210, 211, 214, 216, 217, 224, 226, 227, 228, 238–43, 267, 272, 273, 274, 276, 278, 282, 283, 284, 288, 289, 290–93, 298–301, 304, 307, 308, 313, 321, 323, 324, 326, 327, 328, 329–35, 340–44, 346–7, 355, 356, 374, 377, 378, 381–3, 389, 396, 397, 403, 404, 410, 412, 413, 421, 422
  Communist Party of, 209, 212, 229, 232, 237, 240, 260, 271, 273, 288, 296, 316, 322, 324, 326, 347, 351, 364, 421
  Party Congress, Twentieth, 332
Soyol, 413
Spafarii, 70
special commissioners, 256
Stalin, 18, 136, 226, 240, 242, 243, 284, 291, 292, 298, 300, 301, 304, 308, 323, 324, 325, 326, 331, 333, 334, 335, 336, 342
Stalinism, 246, 283, 288
starvation, 93, 142, 146, 203
state farms, 7, 312, 395, 409
'Stone Text', 267
Strong, Anna L., 260
Sukebator, 10, 14, 151, 159, 202, 206, 209–25, 227, 228, 230–34, 236, 237, 248, 251, 253, 255, 257, 258, 280, 281, 292, 332, 334
  Biography of, 222
  Memoirs concerning, 223
Sukebator Square, (p.n.), 10
Sumiya beise, 13, 218, 228
sumun (administrative division), 5, 13, 105, 108, 114, 152, 175, 310
sumun-negdel, 402
sumun-people, (*see also* imperial subjects), 105, 137
Sunit, 60, 75
superstition, 251
surgaal, 172, 268
Suvagadai, 49
suzerainty, Chinese, 188, 201, 233, 252
Swedes, 10, 146, 288, 291
Swiss, 10, 288

T'ai-tsu, (Nurhachi), 5
taiji, 5, 29, 69, 88–91, 104, 105, 126, 141, 142, 144, 145, 146, 152, 175, 176, 183, 185, 203, 413
Taikha, 62
tamga, 267
Tamir river, (p.n.), 132
tang-chia-ti, 97
T'ang T'ai-tsung, 34
Tanjur, 23, 35
Tannu Tuva, (p.n.), 45, 63, 201, 228–9, 239, 240, 273, 275, 279, 298, 300, 319, 339
Tannu Ula, (p.n.), 7
Taranata, 58
Tarbagatai, (p.n.), 50, 59
Tariyat, (p.n.), 369
Tariatyn lamasery, 318
Tashilhumpo, (p.n.), 64
taxes, taxation, 14, 88, 93, 98–103, 106, 107, 112, 141, 148–52, 158, 162, 169, 176, 178, 182, 183, 185, 203, 261, 271, 303, 361–3, 399
Te Wang, 378
tea, 94, 98
tea-units, 140, 149, 151, 152
temple territories, 109
Ten-fold Virtuous White Chronicle of the Faith, 30
Tenggidei, 60
Tengis, 60, 61
Tengri Nor, (p.n.), 50
tent, cloth, 96
tent, felt, 9, 10, 11, 12, 96, 395

INDEX

tent schools, 248
terror, 351
theatre, 356
three manly games, 16
Tibet, 17, 25, 28, 29, 33, 46, 50, 51, 53, 54, 57, 58, 64, 65, 69, 71, 76, 102, 106, 113, 132, 133, 134, 161, 163, 187, 195, 201, 262, 286, 422
    king of, 46, 50
    regent, 52, 65, 66, 69, 71, 79
    Tibetan school in Peking, 102
    treaty with Mongolia, 200
Tibetan language and script, 17, 23, 54, 87, 159, 248, 265, 272, 327, 365, 368
tiiz, 149
Tobolsk, (p.n.), 51, 62, 64
Togd, 127
Togon Temur, 5
Tögs, 127
Tögsbuyant lamasery, 318–19
Togtokh taiji, 193, 197, 198, 254
Togtokhtör, *see* To-wang
Tokyo, 266
Tömör, (p.n.), 75
Tömörjin, 196, 197, 198
Tömör-ochir, 418
Torguts, 1, 13, 34, 50, 51, 55, 128, 256
To-wang, 94, 151, 176–83, 387
towns, 87, 94, 108, 152, 154, 245, 408
trade, 49, 51, 56, 67, 68, 81, 83, 86, 94–100, 104, 142, 163, 164, 276, 283, 290, 312, 323, 353, 360, 371, 382
trade supervisors, 97, 107
traders, Chinese, 56, 83, 95–8, 103, 112, 124, 127, 132, 143, 152, 153, 159, 173, 178, 181, 184, 185, 186, 279, 290
trades unions, 246
trading licences, 56, 96, 97
Transbaikalia, (p.n.), 48, 51, 52, 72, 73, 77
translation of scriptures, 23, 32, 35, 42, 51, 86, 180
transport, 163, 164, 291, 312–13, 371, 384
treason trials, 218, 328, 336, 360
tribal system, 37
tribute, 47, 59, 60, 61, 62, 65, 71, 77, 95, 102
Troitskosavsk, (p.n.), 216
Trotsky, 240, 294
ts'ai-tzu, 97
Tsaidam, (p.n.), 2
Tsam, 173

Tsar, 45, 50, 62, 73, 120, 122, 128, 285
Tsedenbal, 325, 333, 375, 400
Tsedendorji, 150, 177
Tsembel, 168
Tsend, L., 420
Tsendjav, 261
Tsengun, 70, 74
Tsengunjav, 121, 123
Tserenchimid, 159, 194, 199
Tserenbaljir, 392
Tserendorji, (Manjushri Khutuktu), 266
Tserendorji, (Premier), 205, 235, 236, 277
Tserendorji, (proctor), 167
Tsereng, 47, 48, 112, 117
Tseringjab, 167
Tsetserlig, (p.n.), 26, 308, 309, 367
Tsetserlig Mandal aimak, (p.n.), 314
Tsevden, 119, 120
Tsevdenjav, 117
Tseveen, 140
Tsevegjav, 113
Tsewangrabdan, 51, 70, 78, 113
Tso mergen, 62
Tsogchen, 12
Tsogdos, Nor (p.n.), 75
Tsogtu taiji, 41, 45, 46, 50, 387
    film of, 416
Tsongkhapa, 286
Tsiu, General, 192
Tudeng, 177, 178, 254
Tugeemel Amarjuulagch lamasery, 85
Tugj, 320
Tukhashevskii, Marshal, 215, 332, 341
Tula river, (p.n.), 7, 11, 19, 41, 49, 76 80
tumen, 23, 24, 42, 43
Tumen Jasagtu Khan, *see* Jasagtu
Tumenkin, 31, 47
Tumet, 24, 25, 29, 31, 33, 36, 44, 45, 60, 109
t'ung-shih, 99
Tungus uprising, 131
tunsh, 99
Turfan, (p.n.), 25, 26
Turkestan, (p.n.), 48, 50, 65, 139
Turkhai, 62
Turks, 7
tusalagchi, 254
Tushetu Khan, 5, 26, 33, 34, 35, 47, 48, 49, 52, 53, 58–61, 63, 64, 65, 67, 68, 70–80, 106, 118, 120, 122, 134

474

INDEX

Tushetu Khan, (of Khorchin), 32
Tushetu Khan aimak, 88, 91, 100, 107, 142, 150, 156, 175, 224
    general of, 83, 101, 120, 122, 194
Tuvan People's Republic, 228
Two principles, 30, 42, 160, 189
typewriter, first Mongol, 290

ubashi, 361
Ubsa, (Uvs), nor (p.n.), 116
Udinsk, (p.n.), 72
Uighur script, 22
Ujumchin, (p.n.), 79
Ulaangom, (p.n.), 154, 231, 266, 318, 319
Ulan Bator, (p.n.), 6, 7, 9–12, 16, 18, 19, 26, 41, 58, 94, 111, 318, 322, 324, 331, 337, 340, 360, 365, 367–9, 378, 381, 383, 384, 389, 394, 395, 400, 403, 407, 408, 411, 413
Ulan Ude, (p.n.), 9
Ulanbudang, (p.n.), 79
Uliasutai, (p.n.), 13, 22, 56, 94, 101, 103, 107, 108, 116, 123, 141, 149, 152, 154, 185, 192–3, 196, 201, 231, 236, 253
    amban of, 107, 196, 211, 253
    general of, 98, 107, 108, 112, 117, 152, 153, 196
Unen, 268, 310, 340, 389, 406, 418, 421
UNESCO, 383
Ungern-Sternberg, 147, 188, 215, 216, 217, 224, 225, 229, 231–6, 246
United Kingdom, 16, 383
United Nations, 189, 382–3, 385
university, 16, 376, 382, 391
United States of America, 1, 211, 254, 283, 383
uprisings, 266–7, 316
urban drift, 407, 408
urbanization, 93, 108, 152, 153, 405, 408
Urga, (p.n.), 9, 11–14, 22, 23, 55, 56, 57, 73, 75, 83, 84, 93, 94, 96, 97, 102, 103, 108, 111, 112, 121, 122, 124, 125, 134, 141, 145, 146, 147, 149, 153, 154, 155, 157, 159, 160, 161, 163, 164, 165, 166, 169, 171, 172, 173, 183, 185, 188, 193, 194, 197, 201, 202, 204, 205, 206, 208–11, 213, 215, 216, 220, 224, 229, 232, 233, 234, 237, 243, 253, 264, 266, 267, 291, 334, 367, 413
    amban of, 56, 83, 91, 103, 106, 107, 108, 134, 149, 152, 158, 165, 174, 183, 184, 194, 211

Urga, East, 154
Urga before the Revolution, 174
Urga News, 202
Uriangkhai, 14, 117, 118, 119, 123, 124, 197
Urjinjav, 92, 93, 104, 139, 140
usury, 83, 85, 98, 100, 101, 142, 163, 258, 303
Uvs aimak, (p.n.), 294, 318

vagrancy, vagrants, 14, 93, 100, 143, 151, 152, 153, 245
    vagrancy offices, 93
Vasiliev, 275, 282, 297
venereal disease, 146, 380, 388
Venyukov, 72
Verkhneudinsk, (*see also* Ulan Ude), (p.n. 210, 212, 376
veterinary work, 202, 353, 379, 399
Volga river, (p.n.), 1, 50, 55

Wallace, Henry, 383
wang, 5
Wangbudorji, 124
Wangchig, (Zasagtu Khan), 62, 70
Wangchig, (of Setsen Khan aimak), 90
Wangdanov, 236
Wangjil, 139
War, of 1912–13, 200
    of 1921, 144
    Civil, of 1932, 293, 315–20, 321, 322, 357
    Second World, 7, 228, 288, 304, 323, 381–4
    declared on Japan, 384
war casualties, 345
watch-posts, 16, 82, 83, 89, 93, 99, 101, 103, 104, 108, 109, 112, 123, 149
    Altai posts, 103
    gold posts, 104
    internal posts, 82, 104
    Khalkha posts, 104
    sumun-posts, 104
    tent-posts, 104
wells, 307, 353, 379, 384
White Pagoda, (p.n.), 36, 41, 53
Wickersdorf, school at, 283
women, 402, 406
    bought and sold, 139–40
    in labour force, 402
working class, 93, 235, 245–6, 276
Wu-ch'ang uprising, 193
Wu San-kuei, 66

INDEX

Yadamsuren, 343, 376, 413
Yakobi, 120, 122
Yalta conference, 382
Yandag, 344
Yarkand, (p.n.), 65
Yeguuzer, lamasery, 267
Yellow Sect, (*also* Yellow Church, Yellow Faith), 25, 27, 30, 31, 34, 35, 46, 50, 52, 71, 178, 244, 285, 286
Yellow Temple, 85, 154, 174
Yondon, 145
Yondon, (commoner), 91
Young Pioneers, 12
Yüan dynasty, 30, 417
Yüan, Northern, 23
Yüan Shih-k'ai, 194, 200
Yundendorji, 83
Yugoslavia, 421

yurt, 12, 152, 153

Zabolotskii, Y., 62
Zagd, 218–19
zangi, 175, 178
zasag, 5, 62, 89, 92, 105, 114, 140, 141, 145, 148, 150, 151, 156, 175, 178, 184, 203, 204, 208, 256
Zasagtu Khan, 5, 26, 34, 47, 49, 60, 61, 63, 64, 68, 70, 74, 75, 78, 80, 113, 253
Zasagtu Khan aimak, 101, 119, 152, 183
Zavkhan aimak, (p.n.), 294
Zlatkin, I. Ya., 181, 222, 242, 274, 292, 294, 302, 312, 314, 338, 350, 365, 368
Zoogoo aimak, 163
Zuun Khuree, *see* Urga, East